BIOLOGY AND CULTURE IN MODERN PERSPECTIVE

Readings from

**SCIENTIFIC
AMERICAN**

BIOLOGY AND CULTURE
IN MODERN PERSPECTIVE

with introductions by
Joseph G. Jorgensen
The University of Michigan

W. H. Freeman and Company
San Francisco

Most of the SCIENTIFIC AMERICAN articles in
Biology and Culture in Modern Perspective are
available as separate Offprints. For a complete
list of more than 900 articles now available as
Offprints, write to W. H. Freeman and Company,
660 Market Street, San Francisco, California
94104.

Printed in the United States of America

Library of Congress Catalog Card Number: 72-4237

Standard Book Number: 0-7167-0862-0 (cloth)
0-7167-0861-2 (paper)

9 8 7 6 5 4 3 2 1

PREFACE

For more than a century anthropologists have pursued several interrelated but seemingly diverse topics in seeking explanations about the origin, biological variations, and social development of man. In the following collection we will explore the most current thinking on these topics by some eminent students of human biology (biological anthropologists), animal behavior (biological anthropologists, social anthropologists, ethologists, and others), human prehistory (archaeologists), and ethnology (cultural anthropologists, social anthropologists, demographers, cultural ecologists, and so forth).

I have not attempted to provide exhaustive coverage of every anthropological topic that has appeared in the pages of SCIENTIFIC AMERICAN during the past fifteen years. Rather, I have focused in Part I on evolutionary concerns in biological anthropology; I emphasize developmental concerns in human prehistory in Part II; and in Part III I stress the most contemporary concerns of ethnologists—including cultural ecology or neofunctionalism, but especially the dynamics of poverty as a negative effect of the dynamics of economic development.

It is hoped that this collection will enhance the reader's understanding of biological and cultural evolution and, in addition, give insight especially into human behavior, but also into the behavior of primates. The articles have been selected and arranged to provide supplementary reading in beginning anthropology and other social science courses that study man and his ancestors, both as individuals and as social animals.

Joseph G. Jorgensen
Ann Arbor, Michigan

May, 1972

CONTENTS

PART I: BIOLOGICAL ANTHROPOLOGY
Human Origins and the History of Life

Human Genetics and Evolution

Evolution of Animal Behavior

PART II: HUMAN PREHISTORY
Tools and the Development of Culture

The Rise of Civilization in the Old World

The Rise of Civilization in the New World

PART III: CULTURAL ANTHROPOLOGY
Traditional Concerns: Kinship, Polity, Economy, Society

A Variation on Traditional Concerns:
The Neofunctional Ecology of Hunters, Farmers, and Pastoralists

New Concerns: "Haves" and "Have-Nots"

Note on cross-references: References to articles included in this book are noted by the title of the article and the page on which it begins; references to articles that are available as Offprints, but are not included here, are noted by the article's title and Offprint number; references to articles published by SCIENTIFIC AMERICAN, but which are not available as Offprints, are noted by the title of the article and the month and year of its publication.

BIOLOGY AND CULTURE IN MODERN PERSPECTIVE

I

BIOLOGICAL ANTHROPOLOGY

Biological anthropology has three major and many minor components. We will look most closely at the major components, that is, fossil prehistory and the place of the genus Homo *within that record; genetics, with special emphasis on human genetics and the role played by the cultural factors in influencing the genetics of man; and comparative behavior in animals as diverse as fish and monkeys.*

Human Origins and the History of Life

HUMAN ORIGINS AND
THE HISTORY OF LIFE

Perhaps no puzzles have caught and maintained the interests of students of man longer than those about the origin and diversity of human beings. The five articles in this section outline the latest solutions to these puzzles.

Norman D. Newell sets the stage for our inquiry about man in "Crises in the History of Life." Newell shows how the history of life—both prehuman and human—has been filled with periods of mass extinctions of species, even families, of plants and animals, though major floral changes have not coincided with faunal changes. The most decimating of these changes occurred at the end of the Permian period when nearly half of all animal families throughout the world disappeared. Over the long haul that began perhaps 600 million years ago, the time at which the fossil record of the Cambrian period begins to become fairly rich, until about 11 thousand years ago, the time of the advent of modern man in the Quaternary period, in general the groups of plants and animals that survived each of the great extinctions were those that were the most conservative or the most generalized in their evoluton. But this was not always so. Some of the nongeneralized species were able to survive the times of crisis too. Newell observes that periods of extinction were often followed by upswings of evolutionary activity. Throughout the fossil record is evidence that animals long native to one habitat were replaced by immigrant (or newly evolved) animals, and that sometimes this replacement was completed within a few million years.

Since the late Quaternary, say 11 thousand years ago (a mere drop in the bucket in the duration of life) modern man has expanded his range over the earth, and in expanding, has compounded the processes that led to the extermination of the Pleistocene mammals and, more recently, the disappearance, in whole or nearly so, of more than 450 other species of animals. As a factor in all of these recent changes man, as a predator, has also destroyed habitats. Whereas Newell has no complete, foolproof explanation of the causes of periodic exterminations of life before the time of modern man, in describing their nature he provides perspective to our view of the kind of world in which man's generalized ancestors lived. Moreover, he gives us a brief, enlightening look at the part man has played in the crises that have led to faunal and floral extinctions since the late Pleistocene.

Modern man, in all his diversity, belongs to the most widely distributed single animal species. In the second essay, "The Distribution of Man," William W. Howells discusses both the past and the present distribution of *Homo sapiens*. Howells speculates that *Homo sapiens* evolved as a species sometime between 150,000 and 50,000 years ago and began to differentiate into races more than 35,000 years ago. The chief determinants of intragroup change are genetic, and Howells emphasizes natural selection and genetic drift as the most important factors of basic racial divergence. Natural selection favors the genetic complexions of naturally favored individuals in a population. Genetic drift emphasizes the consequence of an accidental change in the gene proportions of relatively isolated populations. The early populations of *Homo sapiens* were mobile, but relatively isolated, frequently moving into ecological niches in which genetic selection became an important factor in adaptation. More will be said about genetics and selection in the next section.

Howells concludes his essay by saying that though genetic processes have become overshadowed in their effect on the distribution of man by the development of technology and nation states, race (a cultural phenomenon rather than a subspecies phenomenon) has not by any means been overshadowed by such developments. Indeed, in many ways race has become a critical component in intra- and international political issues.

The third and fourth essays are addressed to the question of how man's primate family tree should be formulated. Elwyn L. Simons provides data from his recent excavations in Egypt for the trunk of such a tree, in "The Earliest Apes." Specifically, Simons discusses his recent discovery of *Aegyptopithecus zeuxis*, a primate of the late Oligocene (about 28 million years before present), which seems to be the anatomically ideal prototype for the *Dryopithecus* primate of the early Miocene (about 22 million years before present). It is significant to tie *Aegyptopithecus*, as a precursor, to *Dryopithecus* because, though *Dryopithecus* evolved into several species, three of which became the apparent forebears of gorillas, chimpanzees, and man, no apparent forebear of *Dryopithecus* was known until *Aegyptopithecus* was discovered; an unexplained gap lay between *Propliopithecus* (about 32 million years before present) and *Dryopithecus*, which is filled well by *Aegyptopithecus*. Just as *Aegyptopithecus* serves as the most probable direct descendant of the higher primates, *Propliopithecus*, from the middle Oligocene, represents the most probable direct descendant of *Aegyptopithecus*.

William Howells's second contribution to this volume, "Homo Erectus," discusses the more recent fossil history of man. Whereas Simons has pushed the fossil record back 32 million years or more, Howells deals with the most immediate known relative of modern man, *Homo erectus*. The evidence for the existence of *Homo erectus* goes back perhaps one million years, and the species probably existed until about 500,000 years ago. At least eight subspecies of *Homo erectus* are known from around the Old World. Nevertheless, their discovery still leaves many parts of the puzzle of man's origin unresolved, for relationships between *Homo erectus* and *Homo sapiens* have not been fully accounted for, nor have the relationships between the australopithecines and *Homo erectus* been worked out satisfactorily. It is evident that the desire to solve the most intricate details in the puzzles about man's past is very much alive, and that the solution is still an elusive prize.

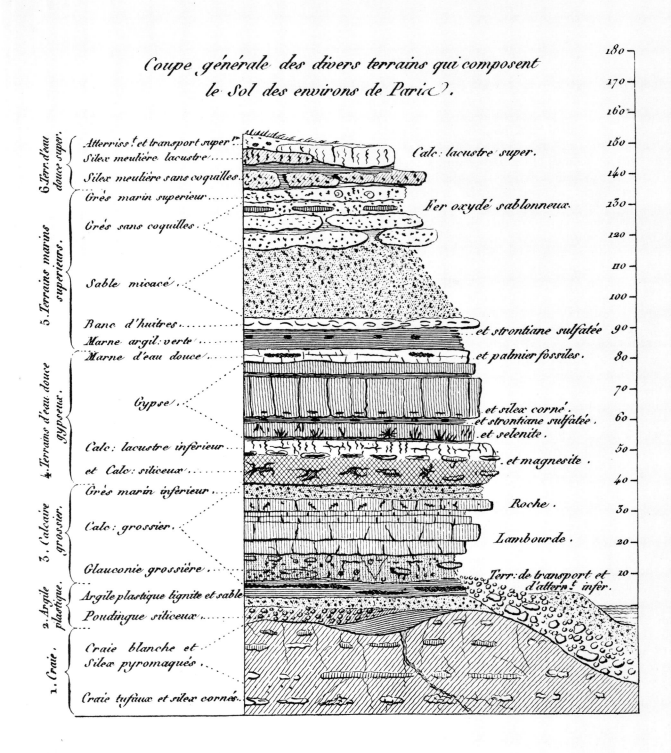

Coupe générale des divers terrains qui composent le Sol des environs de Paris.

"EVIDENCE" FOR CATASTROPHISM was adduced by the French naturalist Baron Georges Cuvier from his study of the Paris basin. He and Alexandre Brongniart published this diagram in 1822. Cuvier believed that the abrupt changes in the strata bespoke the occurrence of cataclysms. Although his observations were accurate, his conclusions are no longer generally accepted.

1

CRISES IN THE HISTORY OF LIFE

NORMAN D. NEWELL
February 1963

How is it that whole groups of animals have simultaneously died out? Paleontologists are returning to an earlier answer: natural catastrophe. The catastrophes they visualize, however, are not sudden but gradual

The stream of life on earth has been continuous since it originated some three or four billion years ago. Yet the fossil record of past life is not a simple chronology of uniformly evolving organisms. The record is prevailingly one of erratic, often abrupt changes in environment, varying rates of evolution, extermination and repopulation. Dissimilar biotas replace one another in a kind of relay. Mass extinction, rapid migration and consequent disruption of biological equilibrium on both a local and a world-wide scale have accompanied continual environmental changes.

The main books and chapters of earth history—the eras, periods and epochs—were dominated for tens or even hundreds of millions of years by characteristic groups of animals and plants. Then, after ages of orderly evolution and biological success, many of the groups suddenly died out. The cause of these mass extinctions is still very much in doubt and constitutes a major problem of evolutionary history.

The striking episodes of disappearance and replacement of successive biotas in the layered fossil record were termed revolutions by Baron Georges Cuvier, the great French naturalist of the late 18th and early 19th centuries. Noting that these episodes generally correspond to unconformities, that is, gaps in the strata due to erosion, Cuvier attributed them to sudden and violent catastrophes. This view grew out of his study of the sequence of strata in the region of Paris. The historic diagram on the opposite page was drawn by Cuvier nearly 150 years ago. It represents a simple alternation of fossil-bearing rocks of marine and nonmarine origin, with many erosional breaks and marked interruptions in the sequence of fossils.

The objection to Cuvier's catastrophism is not merely that he ascribed events in earth history to cataclysms; many normal geological processes are at times cataclysmic. The objection is that he dismissed known processes and appealed to fantasy to explain natural phenomena. He believed that "the march of nature is changed and not one of her present agents could have sufficed to have effected her ancient works." This hypothesis, like so many others about extinction, is not amenable to scientific test and is hence of limited value. In fairness to Cuvier, however, one must recall that in his day it was widely believed that the earth was only a few thousand years old. Cuvier correctly perceived that normal geological processes could not have produced the earth as we know it in such a short time.

Now that we have learned that the earth is at least five or six billion years old, the necessity for invoking Cuverian catastrophes to explain geological history would seem to have disappeared. Nevertheless, a few writers such as Immanuel Velikovsky, the author of *Worlds in Collision,* and Charles H. Hapgood, the author of *The Earth's Shifting Crust,* continue to propose imaginary catastrophes on the basis of little or no historical evidence. Although it is well established that the earth's crust has shifted and that climates have changed, these changes almost certainly were more gradual than Hapgood suggests. Most geologists, following the "uniformitarian" point of view expounded in the 18th century by James Hutton and in the 19th by Charles Lyell, are satisfied that observable natural processes are quite adequate to explain the history of the earth. They agree, however, that these processes must have varied greatly in rate.

Charles Darwin, siding with Hutton and Lyell, also rejected catastrophism as an explanation for the abrupt changes in the fossil record. He attributed such changes to migrations of living organisms, to alterations of the local environment during the deposition of strata and to unconformities caused by erosion. Other important factors that are now given more attention than they were in Darwin's day are the mass extinction of organisms, acceleration of the rate of evolution and the thinning of strata due to extremely slow deposition.

The Record of Mass Extinctions

If we may judge from the fossil record, eventual extinction seems to be the lot of all organisms. Roughly 2,500 families of animals with an average longevity of somewhat less than 75 million years have left a fossil record. Of these, about a third are still living. Although a few families became extinct by evolving into new families, a majority dropped out of sight without descendants.

In spite of the high incidence of extinction, there has been a persistent gain in the diversity of living forms: new forms have appeared more rapidly than old forms have died out. Evidently organisms have discovered an increasing number of ecological niches to fill, and by modifying the environment they have produced ecological systems of great complexity, thereby making available still more niches. In fact, as I shall develop later, the interdependence of living organisms, involving complex chains of food supply, may provide an important key to the understanding of how relatively small changes in the environment could have triggered mass extinctions.

The fossil record of animals tells more about extinction than the fossil record of plants does. It has long been known

6

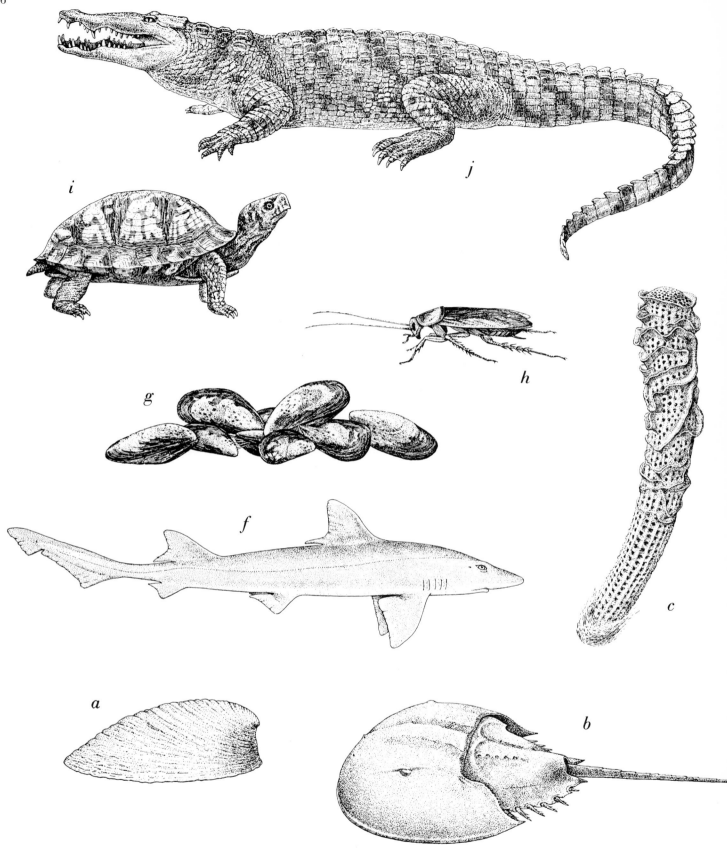

GALLERY OF HARDY ANIMALS contains living representatives of 11 groups that have weathered repeated crises in evolutionary history. Four of the groups can be traced back to the Cambrian period: the mollusk *Neopilina* (*a*), the horseshoe crab (*b*), the Venus's-flower-basket, *Euplectella* (*c*) and the brachiopod *Lingula* (*d*). One animal represents a group that goes back to the Ordovician period: the ostracode *Bairdia* (*e*). Two arose in the Devonian period: the shark (*f*) and the mussel (*g*). The cockroach

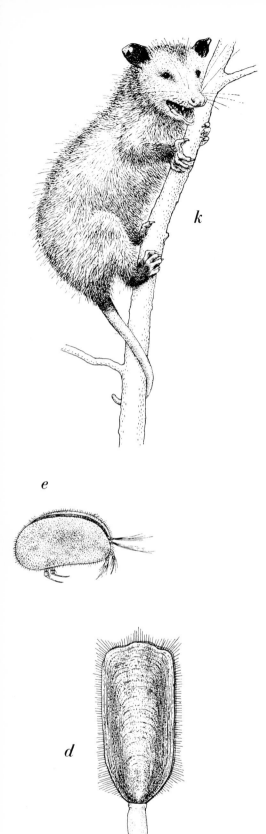

that the major floral changes have not coincided with the major faunal ones. Each of the three successive principal land floras—the ferns and mosses, the gymnosperms and angiosperms—were ushered in by a short episode of rapid evolution followed by a long period of stability. The illustration on page 9 shows that once a major group of plants became established it continued for millions of years. Many groups of higher plants are seemingly immortal. Since green plants are the primary producers in the over-all ecosystem and animals are the consumers, it can hardly be doubted that the great developments in the plant kingdom affected animal evolution, but the history of this relation is not yet understood.

Successive episodes of mass extinction among animals—particularly the marine invertebrates, which are among the most abundant fossils—provide world-wide stratigraphic reference points that the paleontologist calls datums. Many of the datums have come to be adopted as boundaries of the main divisions of geologic time, but there remains some uncertainty whether the epochs of extinction constitute moments in geologic time or intervals of significant duration. In other words, did extinction occur over hundreds, thousands or millions of years? The question has been answered in many ways, but it still remains an outstanding problem.

A good example of mass extinction is provided by the abrupt disappearance of nearly two-thirds of the existing families of trilobites at the close of the Cambrian period. Before the mass extinction of these marine arthropods, which are distantly related to modern crustaceans, there were some 60 families of them. The abrupt disappearance of so many major groups of trilobites at one time has served as a convenient marker for defining the upper, or most recent, limit of the Cambrian period [see illustration on page 10].

Similar episodes of extinction characterize the history of every major group and most minor groups of animals that have left a good fossil record. It is striking that times of widespread extinction generally affected many quite unrelated groups in separate habitats. The parallelism of extinction between some of the aquatic and terrestrial groups is particularly remarkable [see illustration on page 12].

One cannot doubt that there were critical times in the history of animals. Widespread extinctions and consequent revolutionary changes in the course of

animal life occurred roughly at the end of the Cambrian; Ordovician, Devonian, Permian, Triassic and Cretaceous periods. Hundreds of minor episodes of extinction occurred on a more limited scale at the level of species and genera throughout geologic time, but here we shall restrict our attention to a few of the more outstanding mass extinctions.

At or near the close of the Permian period nearly half of the known families of animals throughout the world disappeared. The German paleontologist Otto Schindewolf notes that 24 orders and superfamilies also dropped out at this point. At no other time in history, save possibly the close of the Cambrian, has the animal world been so decimated. Recovery to something like the normal variety was not achieved until late in the Triassic period, 15 or 20 million years later.

Extinctions were taking place throughout Permian time and a number of major groups dropped out well before the end of the period, but many more survived to go out together, climaxing one of the greatest of all episodes of mass extinction affecting both land and marine animals. It was in the sea, however, that the decimation of animals was particularly dramatic. One great group of animals that disappeared at this time was the fusulinids, complex protozoans that ranged from microscopic sizes to two or three inches in length. They had populated the shallow seas of the world for 80 million years; their shells, piling up on the ocean floor, had formed vast deposits of limestone. The spiny productid brachiopods, likewise plentiful in the late Paleozoic seas, also vanished without descendants. These and many other groups dropped suddenly from a state of dominance to one of oblivion.

By the close of the Permian period 75 per cent of amphibian families and more than 80 per cent of the reptile families had also disappeared. The main suborders of these animals nonetheless survived the Permian to carry over into the Triassic.

The mass extinction on land and sea at the close of the Triassic period was almost equally significant. Primitive reptiles and amphibians that had dominated the land dropped out and were replaced by the early dinosaurs that had appeared and become widespread before the close of the period. It is tempting to conclude that competition with the more successful dinosaurs was an important factor in the disappearance of these early land animals, but what bearing could this have had on the equally impressive and

(h) goes back to the Pennsylvanian period. Two arose in the late Triassic: the turtle (i) and the crocodile (j). The opossum (k) appeared during the Cretaceous period.

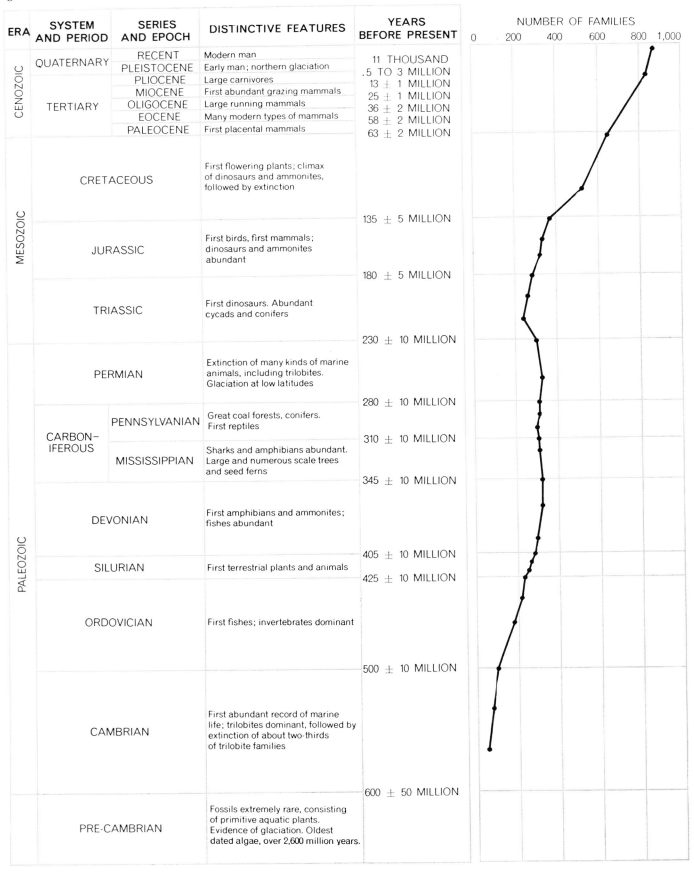

ERA	SYSTEM AND PERIOD	SERIES AND EPOCH	DISTINCTIVE FEATURES	YEARS BEFORE PRESENT
CENOZOIC	QUATERNARY	RECENT	Modern man	11 THOUSAND
		PLEISTOCENE	Early man; northern glaciation	.5 TO 3 MILLION
	TERTIARY	PLIOCENE	Large carnivores	13 ± 1 MILLION
		MIOCENE	First abundant grazing mammals	25 ± 1 MILLION
		OLIGOCENE	Large running mammals	36 ± 2 MILLION
		EOCENE	Many modern types of mammals	58 ± 2 MILLION
		PALEOCENE	First placental mammals	63 ± 2 MILLION
MESOZOIC	CRETACEOUS		First flowering plants; climax of dinosaurs and ammonites, followed by extinction	
	JURASSIC		First birds, first mammals; dinosaurs and ammonites abundant	135 ± 5 MILLION
	TRIASSIC		First dinosaurs. Abundant cycads and conifers	180 ± 5 MILLION
				230 ± 10 MILLION
PALEOZOIC	PERMIAN		Extinction of many kinds of marine animals, including trilobites. Glaciation at low latitudes	280 ± 10 MILLION
	CARBON-IFEROUS	PENNSYLVANIAN	Great coal forests, conifers. First reptiles	310 ± 10 MILLION
		MISSISSIPPIAN	Sharks and amphibians abundant. Large and numerous scale trees and seed ferns	345 ± 10 MILLION
	DEVONIAN		First amphibians and ammonites; fishes abundant	405 ± 10 MILLION
	SILURIAN		First terrestrial plants and animals	425 ± 10 MILLION
	ORDOVICIAN		First fishes; invertebrates dominant	500 ± 10 MILLION
	CAMBRIAN		First abundant record of marine life; trilobites dominant, followed by extinction of about two-thirds of trilobite families	600 ± 50 MILLION
	PRE-CAMBRIAN		Fossils extremely rare, consisting of primitive aquatic plants. Evidence of glaciation. Oldest dated algae, over 2,600 million years.	

NUMBER OF FAMILIES
0   200   400   600   800   1,000

GEOLOGICAL AGES can be dated by comparing relative amounts of radioactive elements remaining in samples of rock obtained from different stratigraphic levels. The expanding curve at the right indicates how the number of major families of fossil animals increased through geologic time. The sharp decline after the Permian reflects the most dramatic of several mass extinctions.

simultaneous decline in the sea of the ammonite mollusks? Late in the Triassic there were still 25 families of widely ranging ammonites. All but one became extinct at the end of the period and that one gave rise to the scores of families of Jurassic and Cretaceous time.

The late Cretaceous extinctions eliminated about a quarter of all the known families of animals, but as usual the plants were little affected. The beginning of a decline in several groups is discernible near the middle of the period, some 30 million years before the mass extinction at the close of the Cretaceous. The significant point is that many characteristic groups—dinosaurs, marine reptiles, flying reptiles, ammonites, bottom-dwelling aquatic mollusks and certain kinds of extinct marine plankton—were represented by several world-wide families until the close of the period. Schindewolf has cited 16 superfamilies and orders that now became extinct. Many world-wide genera of invertebrates and most of the known species of the youngest Cretaceous period drop out near or at the boundary between the Cretaceous and the overlying Paleocene rocks. On the other hand, many families of bottom-dwelling sea organisms, fishes and nautiloid cephalopods survived with only minor evolutionary modifications. This is also true of primitive mammals, turtles, crocodiles and most of the plants of the time.

In general the groups that survived each of the great episodes of mass extinction were conservative in their evolution. As a result they were probably able to withstand greater changes in environment than could those groups that disappeared, thus conforming to the well-known principle of "survival of the unspecialized," recognized by Darwin. But there were many exceptions and it does not follow that the groups that disappeared became extinct simply because they were highly specialized. Many were no more specialized than some groups that survived.

The Cretaceous period was remarkable for a uniform and world-wide distribution of many hundreds of distinctive groups of animals and plants, which was probably a direct result of low-lying lands, widespread seas, surprisingly uniform climate and an abundance of migration routes. Just at the top of the Cretaceous sequence the characteristic fauna is abruptly replaced by another, which is distinguished not so much by radically new kinds of animals as by the elimination of innumerable major groups that had characterized the late Cre-

taceous. The geological record is somewhat obscure at the close of the Cretaceous, but most investigators agree that there was a widespread break in sedimentation, indicating a brief but general withdrawal of shallow seas from the area of the continents.

Extinctions in the Human Epoch

At the close of the Tertiary period, which immediately preceded the Quaternary in which we live, new land connections were formed between North America and neighboring continents. The horse and camel, which had evolved in North America through Tertiary time, quickly crossed into Siberia and spread throughout Eurasia and Africa. Crossing the newly formed Isthmus of Panama at about the same time, many North American animals entered South America. From Asia the mammoth, bison, bear and large deer entered North America, while from the south came ground sloths and other mammals that had originated and evolved in South America. Widespread migration and concurrent episodes of mass extinction appear to mark the close of the Pliocene (some two or three million years ago) and the middle of the Pleistocene in both North America and

Eurasia. Another mass extinction, particularly notable in North America, occurred at the very close of the last extensive glaciation, but this time it apparently was not outstandingly marked by intercontinental migrations. Surprisingly, none of the extinctions coincided with glacial advances.

It is characteristic of the fossil record that immigrant faunas tend to replace the old native faunas. In some cases newly arrived or newly evolved families replaced old families quite rapidly, in less than a few million years. In other cases the replacement has been a protracted process, spreading over tens of millions or even hundreds of millions of years. We cannot, of course, know the exact nature of competition between bygone groups, but when they occupied the same habitat and were broadly overlapping in their ecological requirements, it can be assumed that they were in fact competitors for essential resources. The selective advantage of one competing stock over another may be so slight that a vast amount of time is required to decide the outcome.

At the time of the maximum extent of the continental glaciers some 11,000 years ago the ice-free land areas of the Northern Hemisphere supported a rich

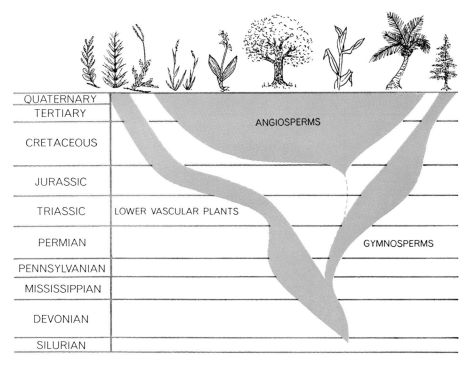

HISTORY OF LAND PLANTS shows the spectacular rise of angiosperms in the last 135 million years. The bands are roughly proportional to the number of genera of plants in each group. Angiosperms are flowering plants, a group that includes all the common trees (except conifers), grasses and vegetables. Lower vascular plants include club mosses, quillworts and horsetails. The most familiar gymnosperms (naked-seed plants) are the conifers, or evergreens. The diagram is based on one prepared by Erling Dorf of Princeton University.

and varied fauna of large mammals comparable to that which now occupies Africa south of the Sahara. Many of the species of bears, horses, elks, beavers and elephants were larger than any of their relatives living today. As recently as 8,000 years ago the horse, elephant and camel families roamed all the continents but Australia and Antarctica. Since that time these and many other families have retreated into small regions confined to one or two continents.

In North America a few species dropped out at the height of the last glaciation, but the tempo of extinction stepped up rapidly between about 12,000 and 6,000 years ago, with a maximum rate around 8,000 years ago, when the climate had become milder and the glaciers were shrinking [see illustration on page 16]. A comparable, but possibly more gradual, loss of large mammals occurred at about the same time in Asia and Australia, but not in Africa. Many of the large herbivores and carnivores had been virtually world-wide through a great range in climate, only to become extinct within a few hundred years. Other organisms were generally unaffected by this episode of extinction.

On the basis of a limited series of radiocarbon dates Paul S. Martin of the University of Arizona has concluded that now extinct large mammals of North America began to disappear first in Alaska and Mexico, followed by those in the Great Plains. Somewhat questionable datings suggest that the last survivors may have lived in Florida only 2,000 to 4,000 years ago. Quite recently, therefore, roughly three-quarters of the North American herbivores disappeared, and most of the ecological niches that were vacated have not been filled by other species.

Glaciation evidently was not a significant agent in these extinctions. In the first place, they were concentrated during the final melting and retreat of the continental glaciers after the entire biota had successfully weathered a number of glacial and interglacial cycles. Second, the glacial climate certainly did not reach low latitudes, except in mountainous areas, and it is probable that the climate over large parts of the tropics was not very different from that of today.

Studies of fossil pollen and spores in many parts of the world show that the melting of the continental glaciers was accompanied by a change from a rainy climate to a somewhat drier one with higher mean temperatures. As a result of these changes forests in many parts of the world retreated and were replaced by deserts and steppes. The changes, however, probably were not universal or severe enough to result in the elimination of any major habitat.

A number of investigators have proposed that the large mammals may have been hunted out of existence by prehistoric man, who may have used fire as a weapon. They point out that the mass extinctions coincided with the rapid growth of agriculture. Before this stage in human history a decrease in game supply would have been matched by a decrease in human populations, since man could not have destroyed a major food source without destroying himself.

In Africa and Eurasia, where man had lived in association with game animals throughout the Pleistocene, extinctions were not so conspicuously concentrated in the last part of the epoch. There was ample opportunity in the Old World for animals to become adapted to man through hundreds of thousands of years of coexistence. In the Americas and

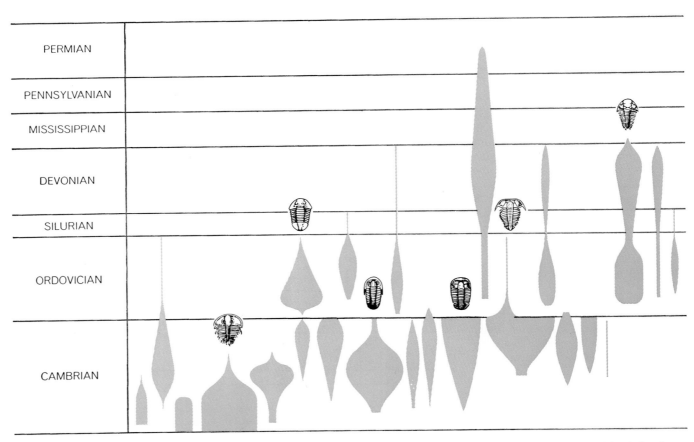

MASS EXTINCTION OF TRILOBITES, primitive arthropods, occurred at the close of the Cambrian period about 500 million years ago. During the Cambrian period hundreds of kinds of trilobites populated the shallow seas of the world. The chart depicts 15 superfamilies of Cambrian trilobites; the width of the shapes is roughly proportional to the number of members in each superfamily. Final extinction took place in the Permian. The chart is based on the work of H. B. Whittington of Harvard University.

Australia, where man was a comparative newcomer, the animals may have proved easy prey for the hunter.

We shall probably never know exactly what happened to the large mammals of the late Pleistocene, but their demise did coincide closely with the expansion of ancient man and with an abrupt change from a cool and moist to a warm and dry climate over much of the world. Possibly both of these factors contributed to this episode of mass extinction. We can only guess.

The Modern Crisis

Geological history cannot be observed but must be deduced from studies of stratigraphic sequences of rocks and fossils interpreted in the context of processes now operating on earth. It is helpful, therefore, to analyze some recent extinctions to find clues to the general causes of extinction.

We are now witnessing the disastrous effects on organic nature of the explosive spread of the human species and the concurrent development of an efficient technology of destruction. The human demand for space increases, hunting techniques are improved, new poisons are used and remote areas that had long served as havens for wildlife are now easily penetrated by hunter, fisherman, lumberman and farmer.

Studies of recent mammal extinctions show that man has been either directly or indirectly responsible for the disappearance, or near disappearance, of more than 450 species of animals. Without man's intervention there would have been few, if any, extinctions of birds or mammals within the past 2,000 years. The heaviest toll has been taken in the West Indies and the islands of the Pacific and Indian oceans, where about 70 species of birds have become extinct in the past few hundred years. On the continents the birds have fared somewhat better. In the same period five species of birds have disappeared from North America, three from Australia and one from Asia. Conservationists fear, however, that more North American birds will become extinct in the next 50 years than have in the past 5,000 years.

The savannas of Africa were remarkable until recently for a wealth of large mammals comparable only to the rich Tertiary and Pleistocene faunas of North America. In South Africa stock farming, road building, the fencing of grazing lands and indiscriminate hunting had wiped out the wild populations of large grazing mammals by the beginning of the 20th century. The depletion of ani-

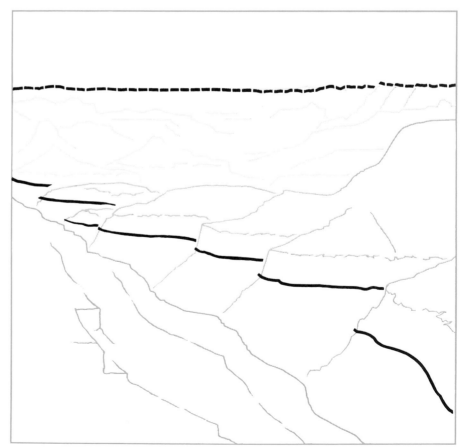

PALEONTOLOGICAL BOUNDARIES are clearly visible in this photograph of the Grand Canyon. The diagram below identifies the stratigraphic boundary between the Cambrian and Ordovician periods (*solid line*) and the top of the Permian rocks (*broken line*). These are world-wide paleontological division points, easily identified by marine fossils.

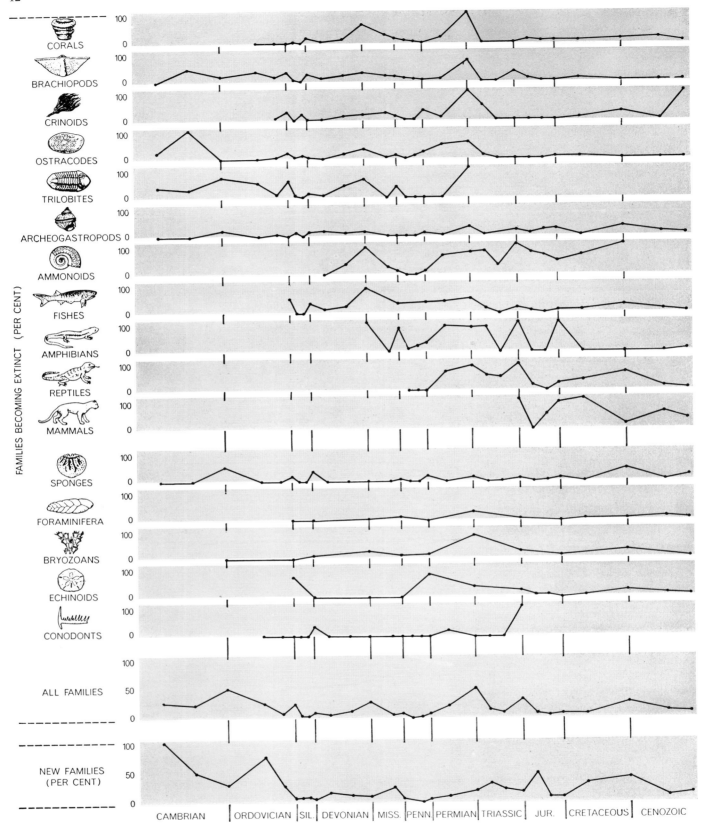

RECORD OF ANIMAL EXTINCTIONS makes it quite clear that the history of animals has been punctuated by repeated crises. The top panel of curves plots the ups and downs of 11 groups of animals from Cambrian times to the present. Massive extinctions took place at the close of the Ordovician, Devonian and Permian periods. The second panel shows the history of five other groups for which the evidence is less complete. (Curves are extrapolated between dots.) The next to bottom curve depicts the sum of extinctions for all the fossil groups plotted above (plus bivalves and caenogastropods). The bottom curve shows the per cent of new families in the main fossil groups. It indicates that periods of extinction were usually followed by an upsurge in evolutionary activity.

mals has now spread to Equatorial Africa as a result of poaching in and around the game reserves and the practice of eradicating game as a method of controlling human and animal epidemics. Within the past two decades it has become possible to travel for hundreds of miles across African grasslands without seeing any of the large mammals for which the continent is noted. To make matters worse, the great reserves that were set aside for the preservation of African wildlife are now threatened by political upheavals.

As a factor in extinction, man's predatory habits are supplemented by his destruction of habitats. Deforestation, cultivation, land drainage, water pollution, wholesale use of insecticides, the building of roads and fences—all are causing fragmentation and reduction in range of wild populations with resulting loss of environmental and genetic resources. These changes eventually are fatal to populations just able to maintain themselves under normal conditions. A few species have been able to take advantage of the new environments created by man, but for the most part the changes have been damaging.

Reduction of geographic range is prejudicial to a species in somewhat the same way as overpopulation. It places an increasing demand on diminishing environmental resources. Furthermore, the gene pool suffers loss of variability by reduction in the number of local breeding groups. These are deleterious changes, which can be disastrous to species that have narrow tolerances for one or more environmental factors. No organism is stronger than the weakest link in its ecological chain.

Man's direct attack on the organic world is reinforced by a host of competing and pathogenic organisms that he intentionally or unwittingly introduces to relatively defenseless native communities. Charles S. Elton of the University of Oxford has documented scores of examples of the catastrophic effects on established communities of man-sponsored invasions by pathogenic and other organisms. The scale of these ecological disturbances is world-wide; indeed, there are few unmodified faunas and floras now surviving.

The ill-advised introduction of predators such as foxes, cats, dogs, mongooses and rats into island communities has been particularly disastrous; many extinctions can be traced directly to this cause. Grazing and browsing domestic animals have destroyed or modified vegetation patterns. The introduction of

European mammals into Australia has been a primary factor in the rapid decimation of the native marsupials, which cannot compete successfully with placental mammals.

An illustration of invasion by a pathogenic organism is provided by an epidemic that in half a century has nearly wiped out the American sweet chestnut tree. The fungus infection responsible for this tragedy was accidentally introduced from China on nursery plants. The European chestnut, also susceptible to the fungus, is now suffering rapid decline, but the Chinese chestnut, which evolved in association with the blight, is comparatively immune.

Another example is provided by the marine eelgrass *Zostera*, which gives food and shelter to a host of invertebrates and fishes and forms a protective blanket over muddy bottoms. It is the

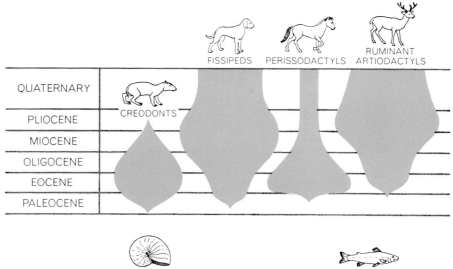

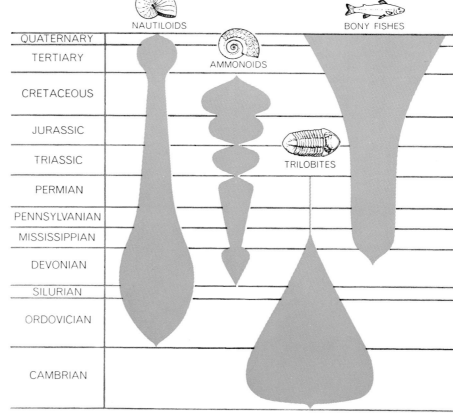

ECOLOGICAL REPLACEMENT appears to be a characteristic feature of evolution. The top diagram shows the breadth of family representation among four main groups of mammals over the last 60-odd million years. The bottom diagram shows a similar waxing and waning among four groups of marine swimmers, dating back to the earliest fossil records. The ammonoid group suffered near extinction twice before finally expiring. The diagrams are based on the work of George Gaylord Simpson of Harvard University and the author.

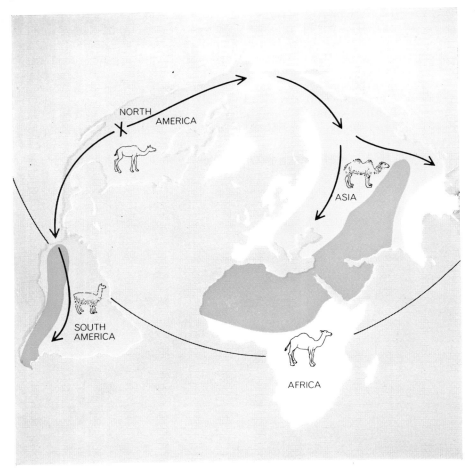

DISPERSAL OF CAMEL FAMILY from its origin (X) took place during Pleistocene times. Area in light color shows the maximum distribution of the family; dark color shows present distribution. This map is based on one in *Life: An Introduction to Biology*, by Simpson, C. S. Pittendrigh and L. H. Tiffany, published by Harcourt, Brace and Company.

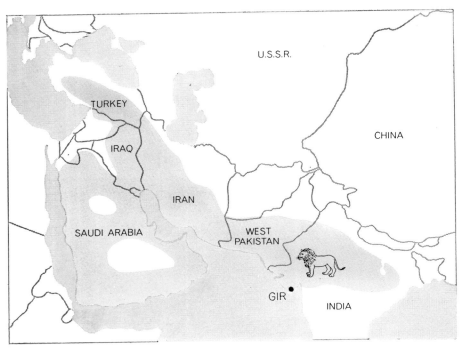

DISTRIBUTION OF ASIATIC LION has contracted dramatically just since 1800, when it roamed over large areas (*shown in color*) of the Middle East, Pakistan and India. Today the Asiatic lion is found wild only in Gir, a small game preserve in western India.

most characteristic member of a distinctive community that includes many plant and animal species. In the 1930's the eelgrass was attacked by a virus and was almost wiped out along the Atlantic shores of North America and Europe. Many animals and plants not directly attacked nevertheless disappeared for a time and the community was greatly altered. Resistant strains of *Zostera* fortunately escaped destruction and have slowly repopulated much of the former area. Eelgrass is a key member of a complex ecological community, and one can see that if it had not survived, many dependent organisms would have been placed in jeopardy and some might have been destroyed.

This cursory glance at recent extinctions indicates that excessive predation, destruction of habitat and invasion of established communities by man and his domestic animals have been primary causes of extinctions within historical time. The resulting disturbances of community equilibrium and shock waves of readjustment have produced ecological explosions with far-reaching effects.

The Causes of Mass Extinctions

It is now generally understood that organisms must be adapted to their environment in order to survive. As environmental changes gradually pass the limits of tolerance of a species, that species must evolve to cope with the new conditions or it will die. This is established by experiment and observation. Extinction, therefore, is not simply a result of environmental change but is also a consequence of failure of the evolutionary process to keep pace with changing conditions in the physical and biological environment. Extinction is an evolutionary as well as an ecological problem.

There has been much speculation about the causes of mass extinction; hypotheses have ranged from worldwide cataclysms to some kind of exhaustion of the germ plasm—a sort of evolutionary fatigue. Geology does not provide support for the postulated cataclysms and biology has failed to discover any compelling evidence that evolution is an effect of biological drive, or that extinction is a result of its failure. Hypotheses of extinction based on supposed racial old age or overspecialization, so popular among paleontologists a few generations ago and still echoed occasionally, have been generally abandoned for lack of evidence.

Of the many hypotheses advanced to explain mass extinctions, most are un-

LATE CRETACEOUS SEA covered large portions of Central and North America (*dark gray*). Fossil-bearing rocks laid down at that time, and now visible at the surface of the earth, are shown in dark color. The approximate outline of North America in the Cretaceous period is represented by the broken line. The map is based on the work of the late Charles Schuchert of Yale University.

16

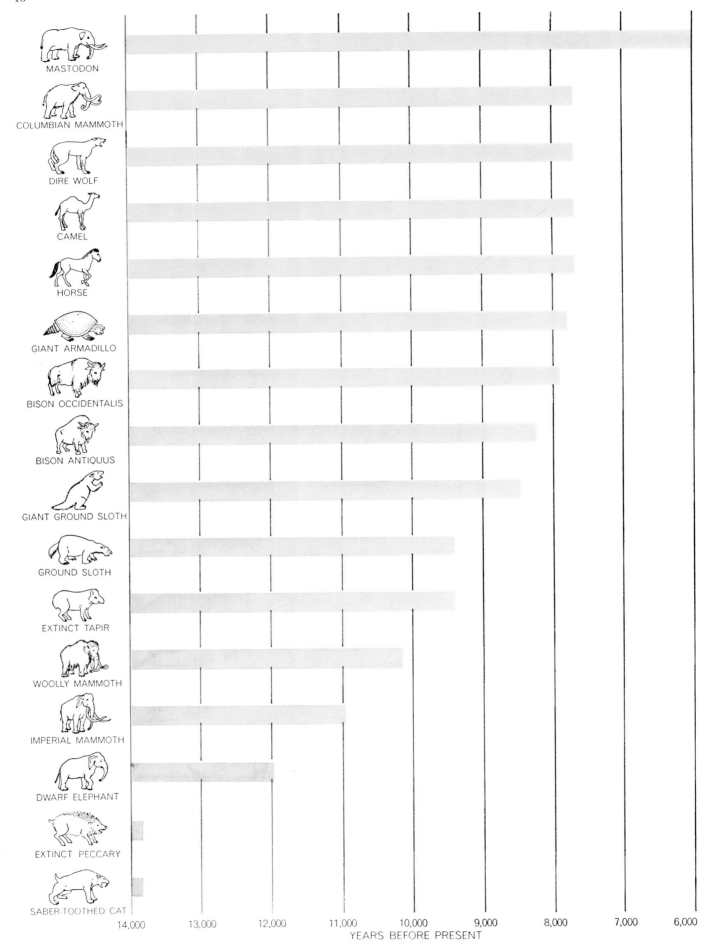

MASTODON

COLUMBIAN MAMMOTH

DIRE WOLF

CAMEL

HORSE

GIANT ARMADILLO

BISON OCCIDENTALIS

BISON ANTIQUUS

GIANT GROUND SLOTH

GROUND SLOTH

EXTINCT TAPIR

WOOLLY MAMMOTH

IMPERIAL MAMMOTH

DWARF ELEPHANT

EXTINCT PECCARY

SABER-TOOTHED CAT

14,000   13,000   12,000   11,000   10,000   9,000   8,000   7,000   6,000

YEARS BEFORE PRESENT

satisfactory because they lack testable corollaries and are designed to explain only one episode of extinction. For example, the extinction of the dinosaurs at the end of the Cretaceous period has been attributed to a great increase in atmospheric oxygen and alternatively to the explosive evolution of pathogenic fungi, both thought to be by-products of the dramatic spread of the flowering plants during late Cretaceous time.

The possibility that pathogenic fungi may have helped to destroy the dinosaurs was a recent suggestion of my own. I was aware, of course, that it would not be a very useful suggestion unless a way could be found to test it. I was also aware that disease is one of the most popular hypotheses for explaining mass extinctions. Unfortunately for such hypotheses, pathogenic organisms normally attack only one species or at most a few related species. This has been interpreted as an indication of a long antecedent history of coadaptation during which parasite and host have become mutually adjusted. According to this theory parasites that produce pathological reactions are not well adapted to the host. On first contact the pathogenic organism might destroy large numbers of the host species; it is even possible that extinction of a species might follow a pandemic, but there is no record that this has happened in historical times to any numerous and cosmopolitan group of species.

It is well to keep in mind that living populations studied by biologists generally are large, successful groups in which the normal range of variation provides tolerance for all the usual exigencies, and some unusual ones. It is for this reason that the eelgrass was not extinguished by the epidemic of the 1930's and that the human race was not eliminated by the influenza pandemic following World War I. Although a succession of closely spaced disasters of various kinds might have brought about extinction, the particular virus strains responsible for these diseases did not directly attack associated species.

Another suggestion, more ingenious

ICE-AGE MAMMALS provided North America with a fauna of large herbivores comparable to that existing in certain parts of Africa today. Most of them survived a series of glacial periods only to become extinct about 8,000 years ago, when the last glaciers were shrinking. The chart is based on a study by Jim J. Hester of the Museum of New Mexico in Santa Fe.

than most, is that mass extinctions were caused by bursts of high-energy radiation from a nearby supernova. Presumably the radiation could have had a dramatic impact on living organisms without altering the climate in a way that would show up in the geological record. This hypothesis, however, fails to account for the patterns of extinction actually observed. It would appear that radiation would affect terrestrial organisms more than aquatic organisms, yet there were times when most of the extinctions were in the sea. Land plants, which would be more exposed to the radiation and are more sensitive to it, were little affected by the changes that led to the animal extinctions at the close of the Permian and Cretaceous periods.

Another imaginative suggestion has been made recently by M. J. Salmi of the Geological Survey of Finland and Preston E. Cloud, Jr., of the University of Minnesota. They have pointed out that excessive amounts or deficiencies of certain metallic trace elements, such as copper and cobalt, are deleterious to organisms and may have caused past extinctions. This interesting hypothesis, as applied to marine organisms, depends on the questionable assumption that deficiencies of these substances have occurred in the ocean, or that a lethal concentration of metallic ions might have diffused throughout the oceans of the world more rapidly than the substances could be concentrated and removed from circulation by organisms and various common chemical sequestering agents. To account for the disappearance of land animals it is necessary to postulate further that the harmful elements were broadcast in quantity widely over the earth, perhaps as a result of a great volcanic eruption. This is not inconceivable; there have probably been significant variations of trace elements in time and place. But it seems unlikely that such variations sufficed to produce worldwide biological effects.

Perhaps the most popular of all hypotheses to explain mass extinctions is that they resulted from sharp changes in climate. There is no question that large-scale climatic changes have taken place many times in the past. During much of geologic time shallow seas covered large areas of the continents; climates were consequently milder and less differentiated than they are now. There were also several brief episodes of continental glaciation at low latitudes, but it appears that mass extinctions did not coincide with ice ages.

It is noteworthy that fossil plants,

which are good indicators of past climatic conditions, do not reveal catastrophic changes in climate at the close of the Permian, Triassic and Cretaceous periods, or at other times coincident with mass extinctions in the animal kingdom. On theoretical grounds it seems improbable that any major climatic zone of the past has disappeared from the earth. For example, climates not unlike those of the Cretaceous period probably have existed continuously at low latitudes until the present time. On the other hand, it is certain that there have been great changes in distribution of climatic zones. Severe shrinkage of a given climatic belt might adversely affect many of the contained species. Climatic changes almost certainly have contributed to animal extinctions by destruction of local habitats and by inducing wholesale migrations, but the times of greatest extinction commonly do not clearly correspond to times of great climatic stress.

Finally, we must consider the evidence that so greatly impressed Cuvier and many geologists. They were struck by the frequent association between the last occurrence of extinct animals and unconformities, or erosional breaks, in the geological record. Cuvier himself believed that the unconformities and the mass extinctions went hand in hand, that both were products of geologic revolutions, such as might be caused by paroxysms of mountain building. The idea still influences some modern thought on the subject.

It is evident that mountains do strongly influence the environment. They can alter the climate, soils, water supply and vegetation over adjacent areas, but it is doubtful that the mountains of past ages played dominant roles in the evolutionary history of marine and lowland organisms, which constitute most of the fossil record. Most damaging to the hypothesis that crustal upheavals played a major role in extinctions is the fact that the great crises in the history of life did not correspond closely in time with the origins of the great mountain systems. Actually the most dramatic episodes of mass extinction took place during times of general crustal quiet in the continental areas. Evidently other factors were involved.

Fluctuations of Sea Level

If mass extinctions were not brought about by changes in atmospheric oxygen, by disease, by cosmic radiation, by trace-element poisoning, by climatic changes or by violent upheavals of the earth's crust, where is one to look for a satisfactory—and testable—hypothesis?

The explanation I have come to favor, and which has found acceptance among many students of the paleontological record, rests on fluctuations of sea level. Evidence has been accumulating to show an intimate relation between many fossil zones and major advances and retreats of the seas across the continents. It is clear that diastrophism, or reshaping, of the ocean basins can produce universal changes in sea level. The evidence of long continued sinking of the sea floor under Pacific atolls and guyots (flat-topped submarine mountains) and the present high stand of the continents indicate that the Pacific basin has been subsiding differentially with respect to the land at least since Cretaceous time.

During much of Paleozoic and Mesozoic time, spanning some 540 million years, the land surfaces were much lower than they are today. An appreciable rise in sea level was sufficient to flood large areas; a drop of a few feet caused equally large areas to emerge, producing major environmental changes. At least 30 major and hundreds of minor oscillations of sea level have occurred in the past 600 million years of geologic time.

Repeated expansion and contraction of many habitats in response to alternate flooding and draining of vast areas of the continents unquestionably created profound ecological disturbances among offshore and lowland communities, and repercussions of these changes probably extended to communities deep inland and far out to sea. Intermittent draining of the continents, such as occurred at the close of many of the geologic epochs and periods, greatly reduced or eliminated the shallow inland seas that pro-

vided most of the fossil record of marine life. Many organisms adapted to the special estuarine conditions of these seas evidently could not survive along the more exposed ocean margins during times of emergence and they had disappeared when the seas returned to the continents. There is now considerable evidence that evolutionary diversification was greatest during times of maximum flooding of the continents, when the number of habitats was relatively large. Conversely, extinction and natural selection were most intense during major withdrawals of the sea.

It is well known that the sea-level oscillations of the Pleistocene epoch caused by waxing and waning of the continental glaciers did not produce numerous extinctions among shallow-water marine communities, but the situation was quite unlike that which prevailed during much of geological history. By Pleistocene times the continents stood high above sea level and the warm interior seas had long since disappeared. As a result the Pleistocene oscillations did not produce vast geographic and climatic changes. Furthermore, they were of short duration compared with major sea-level oscillations of earlier times.

Importance of Key Species

It might be argued that nothing less than the complete destruction of a habitat would be required to eliminate a world-wide community of organisms. This, however, may not be necessary. After thousands of years of mutual accommodation, the various organisms of a biological community acquire a high order of compatibility until a nearly steady state is achieved. Each species

plays its own role in the life of the community, supplying shelter, food, chemical conditioners or some other resource in kind and amount needed by its neighbors. Consequently any changes involving evolution or extinction of species, or the successful entrance of new elements into the community, will affect the associated organisms in varying degrees and result in a wave of adjustments.

The strength of the bonds of interdependence, of course, varies with species, but the health and welfare of a community commonly depend on a comparatively small number of key species low in the community pyramid; the extinction of any of these is sure to affect adversely many others. Reduction and fragmentation of some major habitats, accompanied by moderate changes in climate and resulting shrinkage of populations, may have resulted in extinction of key species not necessarily represented in the fossil record. Disappearance of any species low in the pyramid of community organization, as, for example, a primary food plant, could lead directly to the extinction of many ecologically dependent species higher in the scale. Because of this interdependence of organisms a wave of extinction originating in a shrinking coastal habitat might extend to more distant habitats of the continental interior and to the waters of the open sea.

This theory, in its essence long favored by geologists but still to be fully developed, provides an explanation of the common, although not invariable, parallelism between times of widespread emergence of the continents from the seas and episodes of mass extinction that closed many of the chapters of geological history.

2

THE DISTRIBUTION OF MAN

WILLIAM W. HOWELLS
September 1960

Homo sapiens *arose in the Old World, but has since become the most widely distributed of all animal species. In the process he has differentiated into three principal strains*

Men with chins, relatively small brow ridges and small facial skeletons, and with high, flat-sided skulls, probably appeared on earth in the period between the last two great continental glaciers, say from 150,000 to 50,000 years ago. If the time of their origin is blurred, the place is no less so. The new species doubtless emerged from a number of related populations distributed over a considerable part of the Old World. Thus *Homo sapiens* evolved as a species and began to differentiate into races at the same time.

In any case, our direct ancestor, like his older relatives, was at once product and master of the crude pebble tools that primitive human forms had learned to use hundreds of thousands of years earlier. His inheritance also included a social organization and some level of verbal communication.

Between these hazy beginnings and the agricultural revolution of about 10,-000 years ago *Homo sapiens* radiated over most of the earth, and differentiated into clearly distinguishable races. The processes were intimately related. Like the forces that had created man, they reflected both the workings of man's environment and of his own invention. So much can be said with reasonable confidence. The details are another matter. The when, where and how of the origin of races puzzle us not much less than they puzzled Charles Darwin.

A little over a century ago a pleasingly simple explanation of races enjoyed some popularity. The races were separate species, created by God as they are today. The Biblical account of Adam and Eve was meant to apply only to Caucasians. Heretical as the idea might be, it was argued that the Negroes appearing in Egyptian monuments, and the skulls of the ancient Indian mound-builders of Ohio, differed in no way from their living descendants, and so there could have been no important change in the only slightly longer time since the Creation itself, set by Archbishop Ussher at 4004 B.C.

With his *Origin of Species*, Darwin undid all this careful "science" at a stroke. Natural selection and the immense stretch of time provided by the geological time-scale made gradual evolution seem the obvious explanation of racial or species differences. But in his later book, *The Descent of Man*, Darwin turned his back on his own central notion of natural selection as the cause of races. He there preferred sexual selection, or the accentuation of racial features through long-established ideals of beauty in different segments of mankind. This proposition failed to impress anthropologists, and so Darwin's demolishing of the old views left something of a void that has never been satisfactorily filled.

Not for want of trying. Some students continued, until recent years, to insist that races are indeed separate species, or even separate genera, with Whites descended from chimpanzees, Negroes from gorillas and Mongoloids from orangutans. Darwin himself had already argued against such a possibility when a contemporary proposed that these same apes had in turn descended from three different monkey species. Darwin pointed out that so great a degree of convergence in evolution, producing thoroughgoing identities in detail (as opposed to, say, the superficial resemblance of whales and fishes) simply could not be expected. The same objection applies to a milder hypothesis, formulated by the late Franz Weidenreich during the 1940's. Races, he held, descended separately, not from such extremely divergent parents as the several great apes, but from the less-separated lines of fossil men. For example, Peking man led to the Mongoloids, and Rhodesian man to the "Africans." But again there are more marked distinctions between those fossil men than between living races.

Actually the most reasonable—I should say the only reasonable—pattern suggested by animal evolution in general is that of racial divergence within a stock already possessing distinctive features of *Homo sapiens*. As I have indicated, such a stock had appeared at the latest by the beginning of the last glacial advance and almost certainly much earlier, perhaps by the end of the preceding glaciation, which is dated at some 150,000 years ago.

Even if fossil remains were more plentiful than they are, they might not in themselves decide the questions of time and place much more accurately. By the time *Homo sapiens* was common enough to provide a chance of our finding some of his fossil remains, he was probably already sufficiently widespread as to give only a general idea of his "place of origin." Moreover, bones and artifacts may concentrate in misleading places. (Consider the parallel case of the australopithecine "man-apes" known so well from the Lower Pleistocene of South Africa. This area is thought of as their home. In fact the region actually was a geographical *cul-de-sac*, and merely a good fossil trap at that time. It is now clear that such prehumans were widespread not only in Africa but also in Asia. We have no real idea of their first center of dispersion, and we should assume that our earliest knowledge of them is not from the actual dawn of their existence.)

In attempting to fix the emergence

of modern races of man somewhat more precisely we can apply something like the chronological reasoning of the pre-Darwinians. The Upper Paleolithic invaders of Europe (*e.g.*, the Cro-Magnons) mark the definite entrance of *Homo sapiens,* and these men were already stamped with a "White" racial nature at about 35,000 B.C. But a recently discovered skull from Liukiang in China, probably of the same order of age, is definitely not Caucasian, whatever else it may be. And the earliest American fossil men, perhaps 20,000 years old, are recognizable as Indians. No other remains are certainly so old; we cannot now say anything about the first Negroes. Thus racial differences are definitely older than 35,000 years. And yet—this is sheer guess—the more successful *Homo sapiens* would probably have overcome the other human types, such as Neanderthal and Rhodesian men, much earlier if he had reached his full development long before. But these types survived well into the last 50,000 years. So we might assume that *Homo sapiens,* and his earliest racial distinctions, is a product of the period between the last two glaciations, coming into his own early during the last glaciation.

When we try to envisage the causes of racial development, we think today of four factors: natural selection, genetic drift, mutation and mixture (interbreeding). With regard to basic divergence at the level of races, the first two are undoubtedly the chief determinants. If forces of any kind favor individuals of one genetic complexion over others, in the sense that they live and reproduce more successfully, the favored individuals will necessarily increase their bequest of genes to the next generation relative to the rest of the population. That is selection; a force with direction.

Genetic drift is a force without direction, an accidental change in the gene proportions of a population. Other things being equal, some parents just have more offspring than others. If such variations can build up, an originally homogeneous population may split into two different ones by chance. It is somewhat as though there were a sack containing 50 red and 50 white billiard balls, each periodically reproducing itself, say by doubling. Suppose you start a new population, drawing out 50 balls without looking. The most likely single result would be 25 of each color, but it is more likely that you would end up with some other combination, perhaps as extreme as 20 reds and 30 whites. After this population divides, you make a new drawing, and so on. Of course at each

subsequent step the departure from the then-prevailing proportion is as likely to favor red as white. Nevertheless, once the first drawing has been made with the above result, red has the better chance of vanishing. So it is with genes for hereditary traits.

Both drift and selection should have stronger effects the smaller and more isolated the population. It is easy to imagine them in action among bands of ancient men, living close to nature. (It would be a great mistake, however, to imagine that selection is not also effective in modern populations.) Hence we can look upon racial beginnings as part accident, part design, design meaning any pattern of minor change obedient to natural selection.

Darwin was probably right the first time, then, and natural selection is more important in racial adaptation than he himself later came to think. Curiously, however, it is extremely difficult to find demonstrable, or even logically appealing, adaptive advantages in racial features. The two leading examples of adaptation in human physique are not usually considered racial at all. One is the tendency among warm-blooded animals of the same species to be larger in colder parts of their territory. As an animal of a given shape gets larger, its inner bulk increases faster than its outer surface,

DISTRIBUTION OF MAN and his races in three epochs is depicted in the maps on these and the following two pages. Key to the races appears in legend below. Solid blue areas in map at top represent glaciers. According to available evidence, it is believed that by 8000 B.C. (*map at top*) early Mongoloids had already spread from the Old World to the New World, while late Mongoloids inhabited a large part of northern Asia. Distribution in A.D. 1000 (*map at bottom*) has late Mongoloids dominating Asia, northern Canada and southern Greenland, and early Mongoloids dominating the Americas. The Pygmies and Bushmen of Africa began a decline that has continued up to the present (*see map on next two pages*).

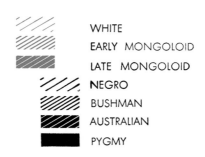

WHITE
EARLY MONGOLOID
LATE MONGOLOID
NEGRO
BUSHMAN
AUSTRALIAN
PYGMY

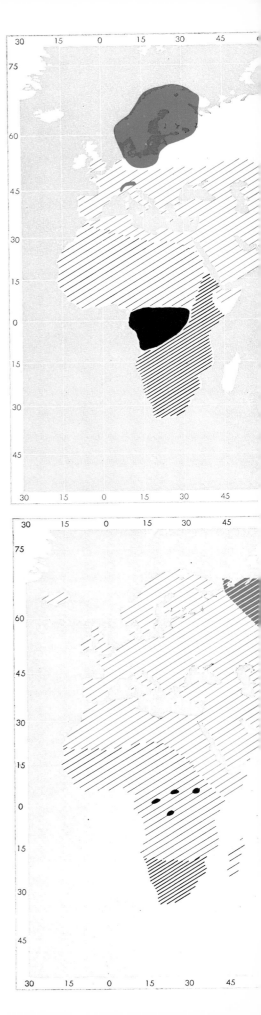

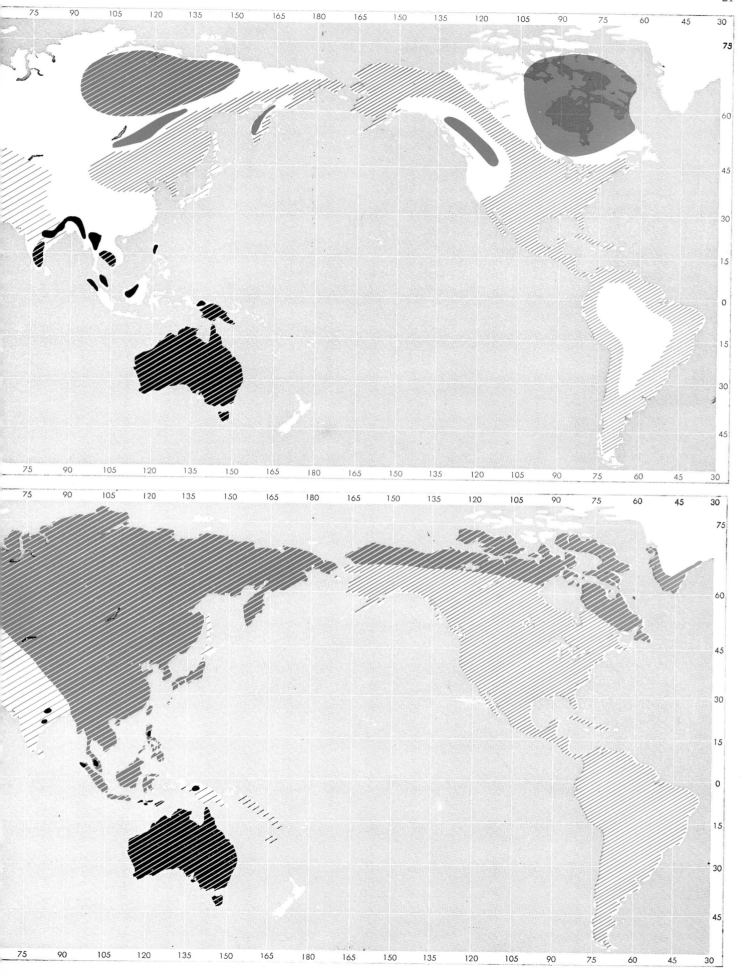

so the ratio of heat produced to heat dissipated is higher in larger individuals. It has, indeed, been shown that the average body weight of man goes up as annual mean temperature goes down, speaking very broadly, and considering those populations that have remained where they are a long time. The second example concerns the size of extremities (limbs, ears, muzzles). They are smaller in colder parts of the range and larger in warmer, for the same basic reason—heat conservation and dissipation. Man obeys this rule also, producing lanky, long-limbed populations in hot deserts and dumpy, short-limbed peoples in the Arctic.

This does not carry us far with the major, historic races as we know them. Perhaps the most striking of all racial features is the dark skin of Negroes. The color of Negro skin is due to a concentration of melanin, the universal human pigment that diffuses sunlight and screens out its damaging ultraviolet component. Does it not seem obvious that in the long course of time the Negroes, living astride the Equator in Africa and in the western Pacific, developed their dark skins as a direct response to a strong sun? It makes sense. It would be folly to deny that such an adaptation is present. But a great deal of the present Negro habitat is shade forest and not bright sun, which is in fact strongest in the deserts some distance north of the Equator. The Pygmies are decidedly forest dwellers, not only in Africa but in their several habitats in southeastern Asia as well.

At any rate there is enough doubt to have called forth other suggestions. One is that forest hunters needed protective coloration, both for stalking and for their protection from predators; dark skin would have lowest visibility in the patchy light and shade beneath the trees. Another is that densely pigmented skins may have other qualities—e.g., resistance to infection—of which we are unaware.

A more straightforward way out of the dilemma is to suppose that the Negroes are actually new to the Congo forest, and that they served their racial apprenticeship hunting and fishing in the sunny grasslands of the southern Sahara. If so, their Pygmy relatives might represent the first accommodation of the race to the forest, before agriculture but after dark skin had been acquired. Smaller size certainly makes a chase after game through the undergrowth less exhausting and faster. As for woolly hair, it is easy to see it (still without proof) as an excellent, nonmatting insulation against solar heat. Thick Negro lips? Every suggestion yet made has a zany sound. They may only be a side effect of some properties of heavily pigmented

WHITE
EARLY MONGOLOID
LATE MONGOLOID
NEGRO
BUSHMAN
AUSTRALIAN
PYGMY

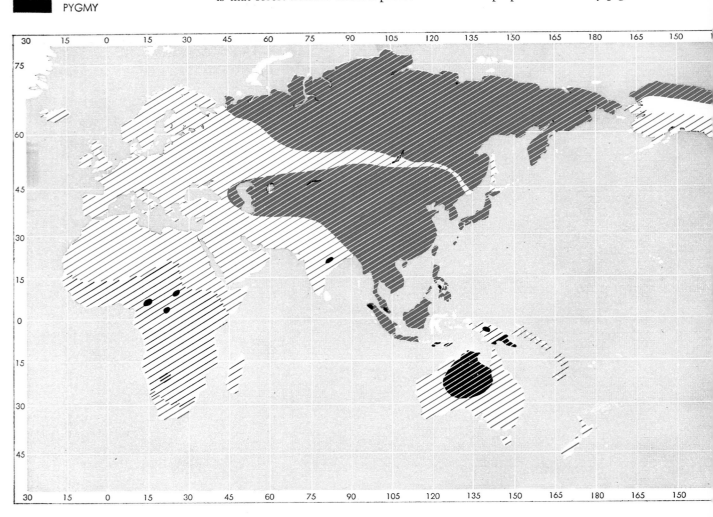

PRESENT DISTRIBUTION OF RACES OF MAN reflects dominance of White, late Mongoloid and Negro races. Diffusion of Whites has been attended by decline of early Mongoloids in America, Bushmen in Africa and indigenous population in Australia.

skin (ability to produce thick scar tissue, for example), even as blond hair is doubtless a side effect of the general depigmentation of men that has occurred in northern Europe.

At some remove racially from Negroes and Pygmies are the Bushmen and Hottentots of southern Africa. They are small, or at least lightly built, with distinctive wide, small, flat faces; they are rather infantile looking, and have a five-cornered skull outline that seems to be an ancient inheritance. Their skin is yellowish-brown, not dark. None of this has been clearly interpreted, although the small size is thought to be an accommodation to water and food economy in the arid environment. The light skin, in an open sunny country, contradicts the sun-pigment theory, and has in fact been used in favor of the protective-coloration hypothesis. Bushmen and background blend beautifully for color, at least as human beings see color.

Bushmen, and especially Hottentots, have another dramatic characteristic:

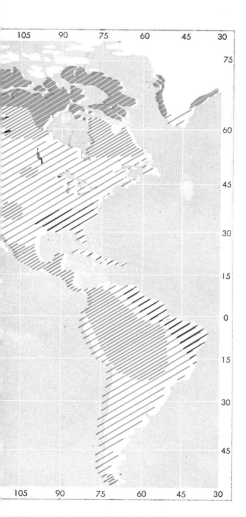

Narrow band of Whites in Asia represents Russian colonization of southern Siberia.

steatopygia. If they are well nourished, the adult women accumulate a surprising quantity of fat on their buttocks. This seems to be a simple storehouse mechanism reminiscent of the camel's hump; a storehouse that is not distributed like a blanket over the torso generally, where it would be disadvantageous in a hot climate. The characteristic nicely demonstrates adaptive selection working in a human racial population.

The Caucasians make the best argument for skin color as an ultraviolet screen. They extend from cloudy northern Europe, where the ultraviolet in the little available sunlight is not only acceptable but desirable, down to the fiercely sun-baked Sahara and peninsular India. All the way, the correspondence with skin color is good: blond around the Baltic, swarthy on the Mediterranean, brunet in Africa and Arabia, dark brown in India. Thus, given a long enough time of occupation, and doubtless some mixture to provide dark-skinned genes in the south, natural selection could well be held responsible.

On the other hand, the Caucasians' straight faces and often prominent noses lack any evident adaptive significance. It is the reverse with the Mongoloids, whose countenances form a coherent pattern that seems consistent with their racial history. From the standpoint of evolution it is Western man, not the Oriental, who is inscrutable. The "almond" eyes of the Mongoloid are deeply set in protective fat-lined lids, the nose and forehead are flattish and the cheeks are broad and fat-padded. In every way, it has been pointed out, this is an ideal mask to protect eyes, nose and sinuses against bitterly cold weather. Such a face is the pole toward which the peoples of eastern Asia point, and it reaches its most marked and uniform expression in the cold northeastern part of the continent, from Korea north.

Theoretically the Mongoloid face developed under intense natural selection some time during the last glacial advance among peoples trapped north of a ring of mountain glaciers and subjected to fierce cold, which would have weeded out the less adapted, in the most classic Darwinian fashion, through pneumonia and sinus infections. If the picture is accurate, this face type is the latest major human adaptation. It could not be very old. For one thing, the population would have had to reach a stage of advanced skill in hunting and living to survive at all in such cold, a stage probably not attained before the Upper Paleolithic (beginning about 35,000 B.C.). For an-

other, the adaptation must have occurred after the American Indians, who are Mongoloid but without the transformed face, migrated across the Bering Strait. (Only the Eskimos reflect the extension of full-fledged, recent Mongoloids into America.) All this suggests a process taking a relatively small number of generations (about 600) between 25,000 and 10,000 B. C.

The discussion so far has treated human beings as though they were any mammal under the influence of natural selection and the other forces of evolution. It says very little about why man invaded the various environments that have shaped him and how he got himself distributed in the way we find him now. For an understanding of these processes we must take into account man's own peculiar abilities. He has created culture, a milieu for action and development that must be added to the simplicities of sun, snow, forest or plain.

Let us go back to the beginning. Man started as an apelike creature, certainly vegetarian, certainly connected with wooded zones, limited like all other primates to tropical or near-tropical regions. In becoming a walker he had begun to extend his range. Tools, social rules and intelligence all progressed together; he learned to form efficient groups, armed with weapons not provided by nature. He started to eat meat, and later to cook it; the more concentrated diet widened his possibilities for using his time; the hunting of animals beckoned him still farther in various directions.

All this was probably accomplished during the small-brained australopithecine stage. It put man on a new plane, with the potential to reach all parts of the earth, and not only those in which he could find food ready to his hand, or be comfortable in his bare skin. He did not actually reach his limits until the end of the last glaciation, and in fact left large tracts empty for most of the period. By then he had become *Homo sapiens,* with a large brain. He had tools keen enough to give him clothes of animal skin. He had invented projectiles to widen the perimeter of his striking power: bolas, javelins with spear throwers, arrows with bows. He was using dogs to widen the perimeter of his senses in tracking. He had found what could be eaten from the sea and its shores. He could move only slowly, and was probably by no means adventurous. But hunting territory was precious, and the surplus of an expanding population had

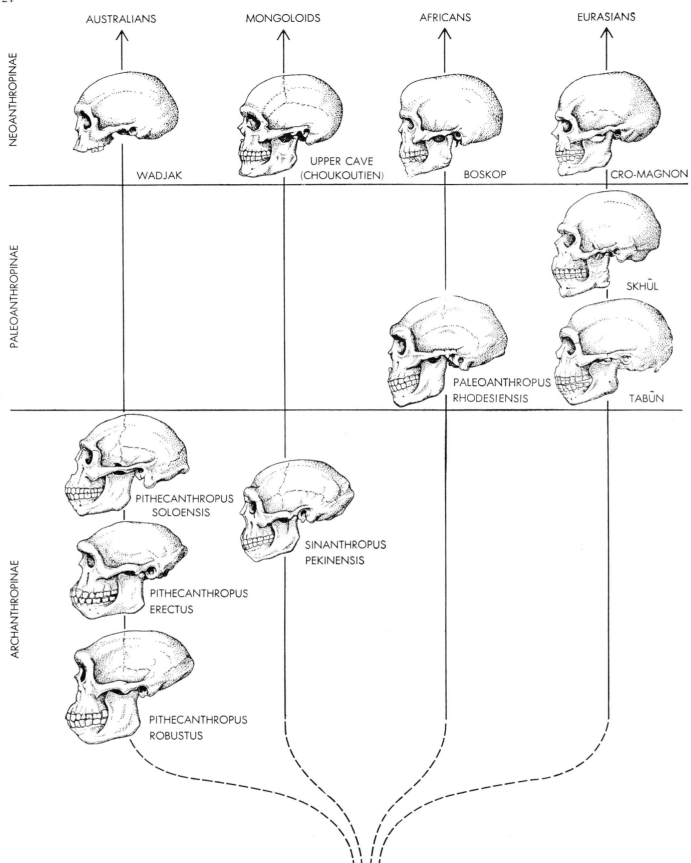

AUSTRALIANS   MONGOLOIDS   AFRICANS   EURASIANS

NEOANTHROPINAE

WADJAK   UPPER CAVE (CHOUKOUTIEN)   BOSKOP   CRO-MAGNON

PALEOANTHROPINAE

SKHŪL

PALEOANTHROPUS RHODESIENSIS   TABŪN

ARCHANTHROPINAE

PITHECANTHROPUS SOLOENSIS

SINANTHROPUS PEKINENSIS

PITHECANTHROPUS ERECTUS

PITHECANTHROPUS ROBUSTUS

POLYPHYLETIC SCHOOL of anthropology, chiefly identified with Franz Weidenreich, conceives modern races of man descending from four ancestral lines. According to this school, ancestors of Australians (*left*) include *Pithecanthropus soloensis* (Solo man) and *Pithecanthropus erectus* (Java man). Original ancestor of Mongoloids is *Sinanthropus pekinensis* (Peking man); of Africans, *Paleoanthropus rhodesiensis* (Rhodesian man). Four skulls at top are early *Homo sapiens*. Alternative theory is shown on next page.

to stake out new preserves wherever there was freedom ahead. So this pressure, and man's command of nature, primitive though it still was, sent the hunters of the end of the Ice Age throughout the Old World, out into Australia, up into the far north, over the Bering Strait and down the whole length of the Americas to Tierra del Fuego. At the beginning of this dispersion we have brutes barely able to shape a stone tool; at the end, the wily, self-reliant Eskimo, with his complicated traps, weapons and sledges and his clever hunting tricks.

The great racial radiation carried out by migratory hunters culminated in the world as it was about 10,000 years ago. The Whites occupied Europe, northern and eastern Africa and the Near East, and extended far to the east in Central Asia toward the Pacific shore. Negroes occupied the Sahara, better watered then, and Pygmies the African equatorial forest; south, in the open country, were Bushmen only. Other Pygmies, the Negritos, lived in the forests of much of India and southeastern Asia; while in the open country of these areas and in Australia were men like the present Australian aborigines: brown, beetle-browed and wavy-haired. Most of the Pacific was empty. People such as the American Indians stretched from China and Mongolia over Alaska to the Straits of Magellan; the more strongly Mongoloid peoples had not yet attained their domination of the Far East.

During the whole period the human population had depended on the supply of wild game for food, and the accent had been on relative isolation of peoples and groups. Still close to nature (as we think of nature), man was in a good position for rapid small-scale evolution, both through natural selection and through the operation of chance in causing differences among widely separated tribes even if selection was not strong.

Then opened the Neolithic period, the beginning of a great change. Agriculture was invented, at first inefficient and feeble, but in our day able to feed phenomenally large populations while freeing them from looking for food. The limit on local numbers of people was gradually removed, and with it the necessity for the isolation and spacing of groups and the careful observation of boundaries. Now, as there began to be surpluses available for trading, connections between communities became more useful. Later came a spreading of bonds from higher centers of trade and of authority. Isolation gave way to contact,

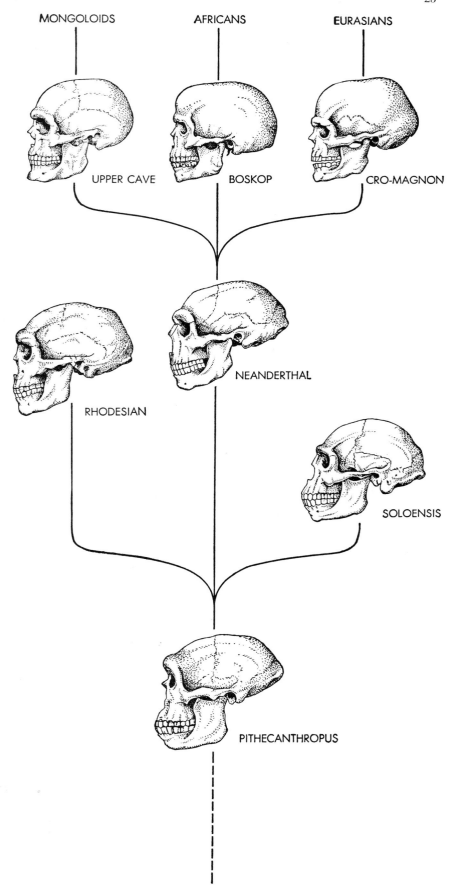

UNILINEAR OR "HAT-RACK" SCHOOL predicates three races descending from single ancestral line, as opposed to polyphyletic theory depicted at left. Rhodesian, Neanderthal and Solo man all descend from *Pithecanthropus*. Neanderthal is ancestor of early *Homo sapiens* (Upper Cave, Boskop and Cro-Magnon) from which modern races descended.

COLOR OF HUMAN SKIN is sometimes measured by physical anthropologists on the von Luschan scale. Reproduced here somewhat larger than natural size, the scale consists of numbered ceramic tiles which are compared visually to color of the underside of subject's forearm. Both sides of the scale are shown; colors range from almost pure white (*top right*) to black (*bottom left*).

even when contact meant war.

The change was not speedy by our standards, though in comparison with the pace of the Stone Age it seems like a headlong rush. The new economy planted people much more solidly, of course. Farmers have been uprooting and displacing hunters from the time of the first planters to our own day, when Bushman survivors are still losing reservation land to agriculturalists in southwestern Africa. These Bushmen, a scattering of Australian aborigines, the Eskimos and a few other groups are the only representatives of their age still in place. On the other hand, primitive representatives of the Neolithic level of farming still live in many places after the thousands of years since they first became established there.

Nevertheless mobility increased and has increased ever since. Early woodland farmers were partly nomadic, moving every generation following exhaustion of the soil, however solidly fixed they may have been during each sojourn. The Danubians of 6,000 years ago can be traced archeologically as they made the same kind of periodic removes as central Africans, Iroquois Indians and pioneer Yankee farmers. Another side of farming—animal husbandry—gave rise to pastoral nomadism. Herders were much lighter of foot, and historically have tended to be warlike and domineering. With irrigation, villages could settle forever and evolve into the urban centers of high civilizations. Far from immobilizing man, however, these centers served

as fixed bases from which contact (and conflict) worked outward.

The rest of the story is written more clearly. New crops or new agricultural methods opened new territories, such as equatorial Africa, and the great plains of the U. S., never successfully farmed by the Indians. New materials such as copper and tin made places once hopeless for habitation desirable as sources of raw material or as way stations for trade. Thus an island like Crete rose from nothing to dominate the eastern Mediterranean for centuries. Well before the earliest historians had made records, big population shifts were taking place. Our mental picture of the aboriginal world is actually a recent one. The Bantu Negroes moved into central and

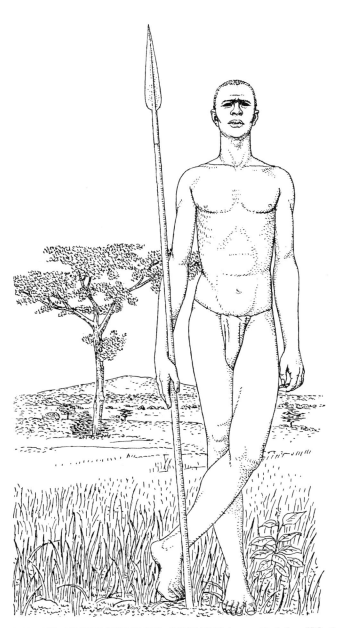

HUMAN ADAPTATION TO CLIMATE is typified by Nilotic Negro of the Sudan (*left*) and arctic Eskimo (*right*). Greater body surface of Negro facilitates dissipation of unneeded body heat; proportionately greater bulk of the Eskimo conserves body heat.

southern Africa, peoples of Mongoloid type went south through China and into Japan, and ancient folk of Negrito and Australoid racial nature were submerged by Caucasians in India. Various interesting but inconsequential trickles also ran hither and yon; for example, the migration of the Polynesians into the far Pacific.

The greatest movement came with the advent of ocean sailing in Europe. (The Polynesians had sailed the high seas earlier, of course, but they had no high culture, nor did Providence interpose a continent across their route at a feasible distance, as it did for Columbus.) The Europeans poured out on the world. From the 15th to the 19th centuries they compelled other civilized peoples to accept contact, and subjected or erased the uncivilized. So today, once again, we have a quite different distribution of mankind from that of 1492.

It seems obvious that we stand at the beginning of still another phase. Contact is immediate, borders are slamming shut and competition is fierce. Biological fitness in races is now hard to trace, and even reproduction is heavily controlled by medicine and by social values. The racial picture of the future will be determined less by natural selection and disease resistances than by success in government and in the adjustment of numbers. The end of direct European dominance in Africa and Asia seems to mean the end of any possibility of the infiltration and expansion of the European variety of man there, on the New World model. History as we know it has been largely the expansion of the European horizon and of European peoples. But the end in China of mere absorption of Occidental invention, and the passionate self-assertion of the African tribes, make it likely that racial lines and territories will again be more sharply drawn than they have been for centuries. What man will make of himself next is a question that lies in the province of prophets, not anthropologists.

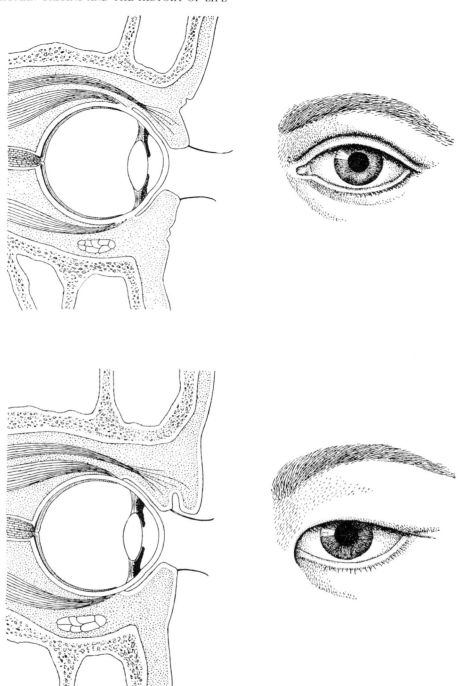

"ALMOND" EYE OF MONGOLOID RACES is among latest major human adaptations to environment. The Mongoloid fold, shown in lower drawings, protects the eye against the severe Asian winter. Drawings at top show the Caucasian eye with its single, fatty lid.

3

THE EARLIEST APES

ELWYN L. SIMONS
December 1967

What kind of animal gave rise to modern apes and man? The answer has been brought considerably closer by the unearthing in Egypt of the skull of an ancestral ape that dates back 28 million years

When it was that the early primates of the Old World first gave rise to the hominoid line from which the modern apes and man evolved is a question that has not had a satisfactory answer since it was first asked a century ago. Just where hominoid primates first evolved and why they evolved at all are rather more recent questions, but they too have lacked generally accepted answers. All three questions now appear to be answerable on the basis of evidence provided by fossil discoveries made during a recent series of Yale University expeditions to the Fayum region of Egypt. Our most exciting discovery, an almost complete primate cranium dating back between 26 and 28 million years, is the oldest ape skull ever found. It belongs to an individual of the newly established genus *Aegyptopithecus*. Studies of the skull, of abundant jawbones and teeth, of scarcer limb bones and of a few other skull fragments that represent this genus and five more genera of Fayum primates have added substance and precision to what was formerly a scant and hazy chapter in the record of primate evolution.

Only 60 miles southwest of Cairo, the Fayum is an area in which fertile fields gradually give way to desert badlands surrounding a large, brackish body of water called Lake Qârûn. (The name of the region is derived from the ancient Egyptian word for lake: *pa-yom*.) The desert buttes and escarpments have been a fossil-hunter's paradise since late in the 19th century, when a few commercial collectors and professional paleontologists first explored the area. The Mediterranean coast is 120 miles away, but during Oligocene times it cut across the Fayum. There large rivers entered the sea and gradually built up layers of sand and mud that reach a total thickness of more than 600 feet. What is desert today was then a well-watered landscape in which forest was interspersed with open glades. Many fossilized tree trunks have been found; some are nearly 100 feet long. In trying to reconstruct the appearance of the Fayum during the Oligocene

REMOVAL OF STONES that form a protective layer of "desert pavement" on the surface of a quarry lets the Fayum windstorms blow the loose grains of sand away, laying fossils bare.

FOSSIL JAWBONES exposed by the wind are those of a fish-eating crocodilian, the false gavial. Reptiles, fishes and mammals lived in the rivers of the Fayum in Oligocene times.

one gains the overall impression of a tropical forest along the banks of meandering rivers.

The fossil remains show that fishes, turtles, dugongs, crocodiles and their narrow-snouted cousins, false gavials, lived in the rivers. In the open areas there were carnivores the size of weasels, small and large cousins of the modern elephant and a four-horned herbivore as big as a modern rhinoceros. The forest was inhabited by bats, perhaps by tiny rodents and by several species of primates. The fossilized bones of the primates are found in the sands of the former riverbeds. Of the scores of primate jaws we have uncovered in these deposits, only one, judging by the eruption and wear of the teeth, belonged to an individual that had lived to a ripe old age. These fossils apparently originated with a young animal's misjudged leap through the trees beside the river or its carelessness while drinking.

Hunting for fossil primates in the Fayum is largely a matter of examining two specific sedimentary layers called the upper and lower fossil-wood zones. The upper zone lies some 300 feet above the lower, and the fossil-rich sites are found on slopes adjacent to an escarpment of volcanic rock above Lake Qârûn. The volcanic rock, which lies some 250 feet above the upper fossil-wood zone, has been dated by the potassium-argon method. Actually there have been two age determinations; one made at the University of California at Berkeley gives a figure of $24.7 \pm .4$ million years, and one made at Yale 27 ± 2 million years. Either date approximates the end of the Oligocene period, placing the upper fossil-wood zone in the later Oligocene. Comparisons with fossils in Europe suggest that the lower fossil-wood zone is perhaps six million years older and thus belongs to the early Oligocene.

The search for fossils is aided by the fact that in many places the desert winds have blown away the sand and soil and laid bare the upper surfaces of buried bones [see lower illustration on page 29]. The winds had plagued earlier Fayum fossil-hunters, but to us they have been a blessing in more ways than one. When we have quarried for fossils, our crews have been able simply to remove overlying rock or to sweep away the "desert pavement," or surface stones; the wind has then scoured tons of unconsolidated sediments out of the quarries, leaving the fragile fossils still in place. Once the wind has done its work it is still necessary to clear the fossils further and to protect and remove them. Apparently there has been little percolation

of groundwater through the Fayum sandstones, with the result that the bones have little or none of the mineral content characteristic of most vertebrate fossils. We have found, however, that modern synthetic resins make excellent "instant" fossilizers.

Until the Yale expeditions to the Fayum were inaugurated under my direction in 1961 the entire inventory of primate fossils from the area was seven fragments of bone and teeth. These fragments nonetheless played a major role in the development of modern theories about primate evolution. The greatest service the Fayum expeditions may have performed is that they have uncovered enough new fossils to correct several misconceptions arising from the fact that the original sample of fossils was so small.

The recent discoveries are seen most clearly against a background of the earlier interpretations that our findings have confirmed or modified. I shall begin my review of these earlier interpre-

tations with two Fayum primate genera that are *not* apes. They belong to the family Parapithecidae, a group that **may** be ancestral to the Old World monkeys.

One genus of this family accounts **for** more fossils than any other primate found in the Fayum beds. It is the genus *Apidium*, represented by two species: *Apidium phiomense* and *A. moustafai*. The first fossil of the genus—a lower jaw—was discovered early in this century by the German fossil-hunter Richard Markgraf, who was working for the American Museum of Natural History. The generic name, proposed in 1908, is derived from Apis, the sacred bull of Egypt. This odd choice was made because at first the specimen was not clearly recognized as belonging to a primate. Paleontologists have gradually come to agree, however, that *Apidium* may be related to the evolutionary line from which the Old World monkeys evolved or to *Oreopithecus*, an apelike fossil primate found in Italy. As a result of our six seasons of work, *Apidium* is now rep-

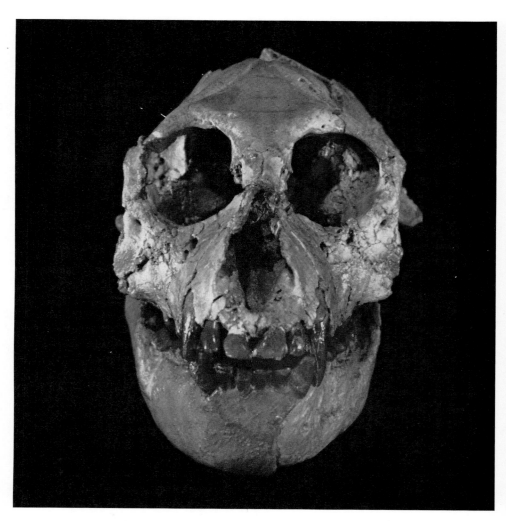

EARLIEST APE SKULL, found in the Fayum region of Egypt last year, comes from a stratum of later Oligocene age. The front and side photographs show it one-half larger than life size. The lower jaw is a restoration based on jaw fragments not found in association

resented by parts of more than 50 lower jaws and four upper jaws. *Apidium* had a short face and was evidently about the size of a squirrel monkey. Like this monkey of the New World, it had 36 teeth arranged according to the "dental formula" that is written in anatomical shorthand as 2 : 1 : 3 : 3. This is to say that on each side of the upper and lower jaw there were two incisors, one canine, three premolars and three molars [*see illustration on page 36*].

The other member of the family Parapithecidae found in the Fayum is the species that gave the family its name: *Parapithecus fraasi*. This fossil primate was also discovered by Markgraf; it was described and named in 1910 by the German paleontologist Max Schlosser, who had become acquainted with fossil primates while studying specimens from North America in a collection at Yale that had been assembled by Othniel Marsh. What Markgraf found was both sides of a lower jaw, cracked at the midline but otherwise apparently com-

plete except for one tooth. Counting the specimen's teeth, Schlosser concluded that the animal had the same dental formula—1 : 1 : 3 : 3—as certain living "prosimians" such as the tarsiers. He and most later students interpreted the crack at the midline of the jaw as further evidence supporting this view; among prosimians the suture between the two halves of the lower jaw rarely fuses as it does early in life among the higher primates. Together with the specimen's small size—about the same as the jaw of a tarsier or a squirrel monkey—these were clues enough for Schlosser. He concluded that *Parapithecus* represented a transition between the early prosimians and the higher primates. Later, counting the teeth in a different way, Schlosser and others decided that the animal had affinities with man.

With the advantage of hindsight and many more specimens to study, it is easy to see how Schlosser's findings were in error. In fact, his conclusions exemplify the difficulties inherent in reaching wide-

ranging evolutionary conclusions on the basis of a single fragmentary specimen. One can scarcely blame Schlosser for expressing his opinion before other specimens had been found, but if he had been able to wait, he would never have been deceived. For example, additional *Parapithecus* jaws we have found show that both sides of the jaws are solidly fused in front, even among the juvenile specimens, as they are in the higher primates. Moreover, the *Parapithecus* dental formula is like that of *Apidium*: 2 : 1 : 3 : 3. The jaw discovered by Markgraf had evidently broken apart at the front suture at the time of burial or of discovery. Somehow the two side incisors and their supporting bone were lost, leaving posterity with the false impression that the specimen had only one pair of front teeth.

The fact that both of these Oligocene primates have the same tooth count as New World monkeys should not be considered evidence of any particularly close relation with such monkeys. There

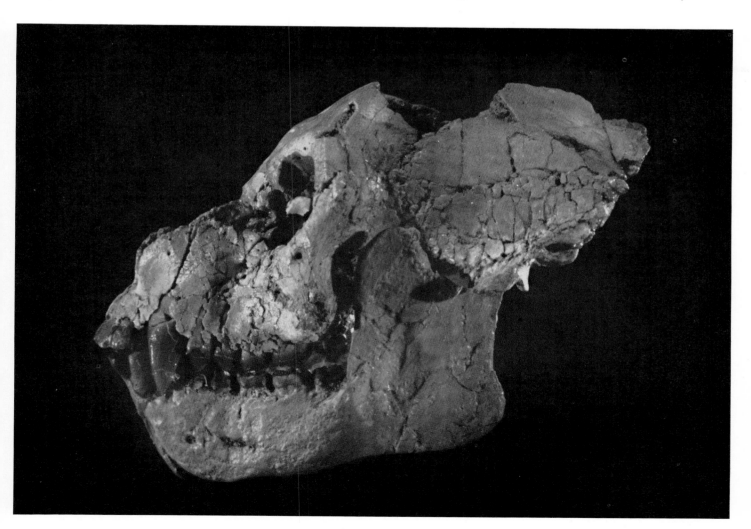

with the cranium; the four incisor teeth of the upper jaw are also restorations. Generally monkey-like, the skull belongs to a species of ape recently named *Aegyptopithecus zeuxis* by the author. The species was probably ancestral to the dryopithecine apes of the Miocene (*see illustration on page 33*). The latter, once abundant in Africa and Eurasia, apparently gave rise to modern apes and man.

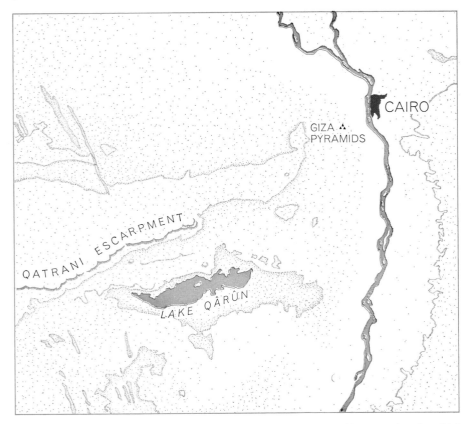

FAYUM REGION, 60 miles southwest of Cairo, is noted for its Oligocene fossils, which are found along the slope that rises from Lake Qârûn, 150 feet below sea level, to the top of the 1,000-foot-high Qatrani escarpment, which is capped with post-Oligocene volcanic rock.

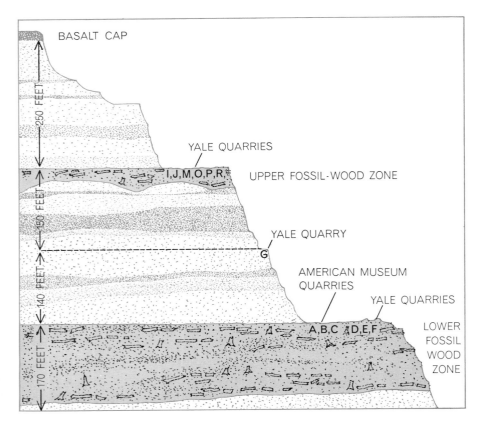

FOSSIL-RICH QUARRY SITES lie at various levels in thick Fayum deposits of unconsolidated sandstones and mudstones, seen here in a schematic cross section. Most of the animal remains have been found in two strata that also contain fossilized wood. The bones of primates are quite scarce; they have been found only in the four quarries E, G, I and M.

is no theoretical reason why the ancestors of Old World monkeys should not once have had an extra premolar all around. Indeed, it is the exception rather than the rule for all members of a mammalian suborder to have the same dental formula. Actually the formula of *Parapithecus* and *Apidium* is the same as that of an even earlier forebear of the Old World primates: *Amphipithecus,* found in an Eocene formation of Burma [see "The Early Relatives of Man," by Elwyn L. Simons; SCIENTIFIC AMERICAN Offprint 622].

Almost certainly the oldest of all the Fayum primates is *Oligopithecus savagei,* an animal that was unknown until our first season of work in 1961. *Oligopithecus* is represented by the left half of a lower jaw from which both incisors and the rear molar have been lost; the jaw was found in the lower fossil-wood zone. Unlike *Parapithecus* and *Apidium,* this animal apparently had the same advanced dental formula as the Old World monkeys, the apes and man (2 : 1 : 2 : 3). *Oligopithecus* appears to be the descendant of a primate that had arrived in the region in the Eocene period. Its molars, although they clearly can be classified as belonging to an advanced primate, are related in form to the molars of the primitive prosimian family Omomyidae, whose fossil remains are found in Eocene formations of Europe, Asia and North America. Such a generalized tooth structure agrees well with the antiquity of the strata that contain the remains of *Oligopithecus,* which were probably laid down more than 32 million years ago.

Perhaps the best-known Oligocene primate is *Propliopithecus haeckeli,* another of Markgraf's discoveries. In giving it this name Schlosser was expressing his belief that the animal, then represented by two nearly complete halves of a lower jaw, could have been ancestral to the fossil gibbon *Pliopithecus,* found in younger formations of the Miocene and Pliocene in France. Later workers agreed with this assessment, and *Propliopithecus* was generally accepted as an early ape, ancestral to the modern gibbons. As we shall see, this is a position it should probably not occupy.

As a result of our fossil collecting, the remains of *Propliopithecus* now include two more lower jaws and about a dozen teeth. The site of Markgraf's discovery cannot be located with certainty today. Some of our *Propliopithecus* specimens, however, come from the site we call Quarry G. In terms of stratigraphy Quarry G lies about halfway between the lower and the upper fossil-wood zone. The *Propliopithecus* fossils from this location must therefore be younger than *Oligopithecus* from the lower zone. The same may be true of Markgraf's find.

In any case, the teeth of the proposed ancestral gibbon show few exclusively apelike characteristics. Among the apes the front premolars are elongated and the canines are large. In the fossil apes of the Miocene, and in the modern gorilla and orangutan, the three molars at the rear of the jaw usually increase in size from front to back. None of these characteristics is evident in *Propliopithecus*. Moreover, to judge from the tooth sockets and the adjacent bone, the animal's incisors appear to be placed vertically rather than jutting forward as they usually do in apes and monkeys.

These and a few other details of *Propliopithecus'* dentition make the animal seem more closely related to man's family, the Hominidae, than to either of the two families of apes: the Hylobatidae (which include the gibbon and the siamang) and the Pongidae (which include the chimpanzee, the gorilla and the orangutan). Indeed, some students have taken this hominid trait in *Propliopithecus* to mean that apes ancestral to the human line had branched off the main line of ape evolution as early as Oligocene times. I would prefer an alternative interpretation, at least for the present.

Still another of Markgraf's discoveries was described by Schlosser; it was named *Moeripithecus markgrafi* in honor of the indefatigable fossil-hunter. The original specimen, preserved in the paleontological collection at Stuttgart, consists of a juvenile jaw fragment in which only the first and second molars are in place. In 1963 I visited Stuttgart to compare the original with several of the individual teeth attributable to *Propliopithecus* that we had found in Quarry G. This comparison and later study of other specimens convinces me that almost every consideration on which Schlosser based his designation of *Moeripithecus* as a genus is attributable to the fact that the original jaw fragment came from a young animal whose molars had not been much worn down. The jaw appears to belong to a species of the genus *Propliopithecus*, although not the species *P. haeckeli*. Consequently *Moeripithecus* should be dropped as a genus and the fossil assigned to the genus *Propliopithecus*.

During our third season in the Fayum, one of the best fossils to be collected from Quarry I in the upper fossil-wood zone was a full lower jaw, fused at the front suture and containing almost a full

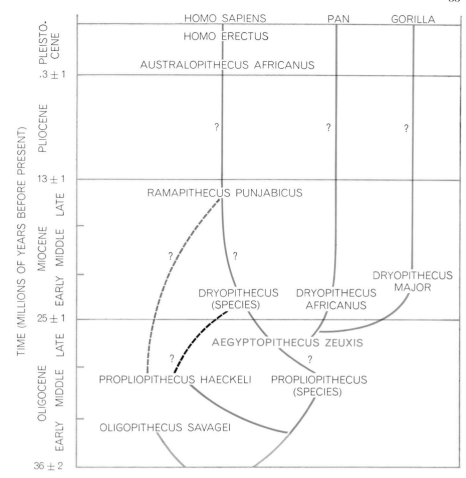

TENTATIVE FAMILY TREE prepared by the author shows alternate ways in which the Oligocene primates of the Fayum may be connected with the main lines of ape and human evolution. The ancestral position of *Oligopithecus*, the earliest in the group to have an advanced dental formula, is uncertain; the animal therefore is put to one side of the main line that leads to various species of *Propliopithecus* in the mid-Oligocene. These are shown to be most probably ancestral to *Aegyptopithecus* of the later Oligocene, the genus that in turn is proposed as the most probable forebear of the dryopithecine apes of the next geological epoch, the Miocene. Lesser probabilities are that one species of *Propliopithecus*, *P. haeckeli*, gave rise to those dryopithecines from which *Ramapithecus* and the hominid line arose (**broken black line**) or was directly ancestral to *Ramapithecus* (**broken gray line**). In either event, *Aegyptopithecus* remains ancestral to the two dryopithecine species, *D. africanus* and *D. major*, the apparent forebears of the chimpanzees and gorillas respectively.

complement of teeth. The incisors were gone, but fortunately the bony sockets that had held them were still intact. The jaw differs from the jaws of most of the other Fayum primates in having elongated first premolars and relatively massive canines with thick roots. These are apelike characteristics. Still other characteristics, including a quite small third molar and a decrease in the depth of the jaw from front to back, are reminiscent of the gibbons. I have named this species, which was about half the size of a modern gibbon, *Aeolopithecus chirobates*. It is possible that this animal, rather than *Propliopithecus*, was the Oligocene forebear of the full-fledged gibbons that are found as fossils in Miocene formations of East Africa and Europe dated eight to 10 million years later. Both *Aeolopithe-*

cus and *Propliopithecus*, however, may have been diminutive early apes that left no descendants.

The largest Fayum primate, to which I have given the name *Aegyptopithecus zeuxis*, was known until recently only from four incomplete lower jaws and half a dozen individual upper teeth that were also found at Quarry I in the upper fossil-wood zone. The size of the animal's lower jaw is about equal to that of a gibbon; it is nearly a third larger than the jaw of *Propliopithecus*. Several characteristics of the teeth make it clear that this new genus of upper Oligocene primate could have evolved from a species of *Propliopithecus* during the several million years or so separating it from the fossil remains of the earlier genus.

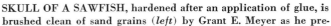

SKULL OF A SAWFISH, hardened after an application of glue, is brushed clean of sand grains (*left*) by Grant E. Meyer as he pre-

pares to remove the fossil from the rock that surrounds it. Next (*center*) Meyer pours water on the fossil as Thomas F. Walsh holds

The evolution had been in a direction that gives the younger animal a close resemblance to the still later apes of the genus *Dryopithecus*, which were a major element of the Old World primate population in Miocene times.

Students of primate evolution today generally agree that it was from the dryopithecine apes of the Miocene period that the lines of development arose leading on the one hand to the great apes and on the other, by way of *Ramapithecus* and *Australopithecus*, to modern man's immediate precursor *Homo erectus*. It is therefore of great interest to discover an ape with teeth particularly like those of the earliest species of *Dryopithecus* but that is something between eight and 12 million years older. The earliest dryopithecine is another fossil from Africa, *Dryopithecus africanus* ("Proconsul"), a skull of which was discovered in a Miocene formation of Kenya by Mary Leakey in 1948. Until recently this was the only known skull of a fossil ape.

Aegyptopithecus, although no larger than a gibbon, has teeth much like a gorilla's; the canines are large and the front premolars are elongated. From front to back the three lower molars increase markedly in size; the entire jaw is more apelike than the jaw of *Propliopithecus* and is much deeper under the canines. It quickly became apparent to

us that, however useful our other fossil discoveries might be in disposing of old misconceptions and clarifying the picture of Oligocene primate life in the Fayum, our discovery of *Aegyptopithecus* could provide a major contribution to the understanding of early primate evolution. Here was an animal of the right form and the right age to be ancestral to the dryopithecine apes of the following epoch. It could thus occupy an early position in man's lineage and even perhaps be the direct forebear of apes such as the modern gorilla as well.

Late in the 1966 season my research associate Grant E. Meyer was making a surface reconnaissance of Quarry M in the upper fossil-wood zone. He came on the frontal bone and both parietal bones of a skull—an exciting find because six seasons of work had yielded only a few fragments of cranial bone. Meyer at once soaked the bones and the surrounding matrix with glue so that a sizable chunk of quarry floor could be safely dug out, covered with plaster and burlap and shipped to our laboratory at Yale for the delicate job of cleaning. It would be hard to say whether our surprise or our delight was the greater when the cleaning process revealed that Meyer had found not just a few skull fragments but a nearly whole skull of *Aegyptopithecus* from which only portions of the

top and bottom of the skull and the four incisor teeth proved to be missing [*see illustrations on pages 30 and 31*].

With the world's oldest-known ape skull added to the rest of the fossils available for analysis, we return to the three questions raised at the beginning. As to when it was that the hominoid line leading to modern apes and man first evolved from a more generalized Old World primate, the almost inescapable answer today is during the Oligocene epoch. At least with respect to the great apes and man, the specific primate involved in the branching is *Aegyptopithecus*, although *Aeolopithecus* is perhaps a twig pointing toward the lesser apes. In turn, the primate stock from which the main branch grew could be the earlier fossil form *Propliopithecus*. An even earlier connecting link could be *Oligopithecus* of the early Oligocene, with its teeth that bear resemblances to Eocene primates as well as to most later monkeys and apes.

Obviously the second question, as to where these events took place, has already been answered. They certainly occurred in this one area of forest and glade where nameless rivers entered the sea. Presumably they were also taking place elsewhere to the west and south in Africa as boisterous populations

a basin for mixing plaster. Finally (*right*) layers of paper cover the damp specimen. They will keep the plaster, which protects the fossil during transit, from adhering to its surface.

of proto-monkeys and near-apes flourished and evolved over a span of some 12 million years. An accident of fossil preservation requires that, if we are asked, "Exactly where?" we must reply, "In the Fayum." Someday the answer may be much more wide-ranging.

It is well to remember in this connection that almost nothing is known of the Paleocene and Eocene animals of Africa, although together the two epochs comprise nearly half of the length of the Age of Mammals. Africa's fossil fauna in Oligocene and Miocene times, although better known, remain painfully scanty. The evolutionary scheme I have proposed here and the fossil genera on which it is founded represent a rationale based on chance fossil preservation and discovery. The evidence is still susceptible to a number of alternative interpretations. Many early African primates must have existed about which we now know nothing. No one can say if some of them were more directly related to living man and the apes than any we now know.

There remains the question of why it is that hominoid primates evolved. The answer, it seems to me, is that the Oligocene primates' arboreal way of life, involving feeding on leaf buds and fruits near the end of branches, gave survival value to certain kinds of dexterity. If this suggestion regarding the arboreal life is to be useful in assessing the Fayum fossils, it is necessary to digress briefly and examine some surprising parallels between the behavior of some modern apes and that of certain lower primates, specifically the large lemurs *Indri* and *Propithecus*.

These large lemurs, familiarly known as indris and sifakas, are specialized in various quite distinct ways for a life of arboreal foraging; the same is true of the lesser apes, in particular the gibbon and the siamang of Asia. The gibbon and the siamang are exclusively tree-dwellers and primarily eaters of insects and fruit. Their ability to move out among small branches in order to feed while in a suspended position, as well as their dexterity in swinging by their arms, is extraordinary. Among the apes of Africa the arboreal way of life is less extreme; the gorilla spends more time on the ground than in the trees, although in evolutionary terms this is a recent adaptation. The chimpanzee is mainly terrestrial in locomotion. Its dexterity when feeding in the branches of trees, however, is exceeded only by that of the Asian apes. Nor is large size an absolute barrier to arboreal life: the orangutan spends all its years as a tree-dwelling forager, although the male may weigh 160 pounds at maturity.

The dexterity of the large lemurs in tree-climbing, clinging and leaping is equal to that of their more advanced primate kin. These animals' snouts are somewhat flattened, and their eyes are far enough forward in the skull to add depth perception to their manual dexterity and locomotor versatility. Yet no one could anatomically confuse the indris and sifakas with the apes. Their dental formula is different, and so are many other details of skull, limb and hand. Moreover, one of them—the sifaka—has a long tail. The resemblances are in behavior and in locomotion, not in anatomy. Like the gibbons, the two large lemurs form small social groups and communicate with loud, hooting cries. Seeing them in the trees, clinging with their torsos erect, or on the ground moving on their hind limbs (the sifaka curls its tail neatly out of the way on such occasions), one is struck by the similarity between these prosimians and the fossil apes of the Fayum, whose pattern of life was apparently much like theirs. The large lemurs demonstrate that, even at the quite primitive prosimian level of primate evolution, striking behavioral advances and locomotor adaptations are possible. It seems evident that the apes first arose from one such adaptive shift; the Fayum apes are apparently not far from that point.

It should come as no surprise, then, to learn that among the fossil discoveries in Quarry I are a number of tailbones, almost certainly assignable to *Aegyptopithecus*. Speaking anatomically, it was to be expected that some ancestral primate would cross the threshold separating monkey from ape and still bring its monkey tail along. The successful tree life of the tailed lemur, however, helps us to realize that possession of a tail was not necessarily a handicap to *Aegyptopithecus*' adaptation as an arboreal ape.

The skull of *Aegyptopithecus,* and also three fragments of frontal bone we have found (belonging to at least two different species), show that the Fayum primates' eyes had shifted forward, with a consequent enhancement of depth perception. *Aegyptopithecus* has a narrow snout (still long by ape standards), some expansion of the forebrain and a related reduction in the dimensions of the brain's olfactory lobes [*see illustrations on pages 30 and 31*]. These are changes in form that are correlated with a greater predominance of the visual sense over the olfactory, and they are typical adaptations with survival value for arboreal life. The foot bones and many other limb bones we have found, which probably belong mainly to *Apidium,* are suggestive of adaptation to life in the trees. The few that appear to belong to *Aegyptopithecus* suggest the same habitat.

To me it seems probable that the selective pressures of millions of years in the trees forced a comparatively primitive population of the kind represented by the anatomically generalized early *Oligopithecus*—with its echoes of even more primitive Eocene forebears—along the road to apehood. That the pressures were effective is shown by the evolution en route of several anatomically intermediate species of *Propliopithecus.* When the pressures culminated near the end of the Oligocene, the evolutionary process had brought forth an anatomical-

ly ideal prototype for the dryopithecines in the form of *Aegyptopithecus.*

The primitiveness of such hand, foot and limb bones of dryopithecines as are now known has allowed scholars to characterize the dryopithecines somewhat flippantly as animals with the heads of apes attached to the bodies of monkeys. If I were to characterize *Aegyptopithecus* in the same fashion, I would have to speak of the skull of a monkey equipped with the teeth of an ape. Why not? If my analyses, both of the evolutionary sequence and of the skull's anatomy, are correct, this animal was an oversized tree-dweller, still carrying a tail in spite of anatomical advances such as suture-closing and hominoid teeth. The animal's braincase, in relation to its face, was

smaller than that of any subsequent hominoid. The bone behind the eyes formed a less complete closure than it does in hominoids or in Old World and New World monkeys. The auditory canals are not enclosed in an external tube, as they are in all the later Old World monkeys, the apes and man, and the tympanic ring is fused in a manner resembling the prosimian lorises and the New World monkeys. But what is more important than the primitive anatomical traits of *Aegyptopithecus* is the clear stamp of the higher primates to be seen in it. The animal was evidently pursuing an arboreal pattern of life directing it along the evolutionary path leading from lemur-like and monkey-like forms to apes and perhaps ultimately to man.

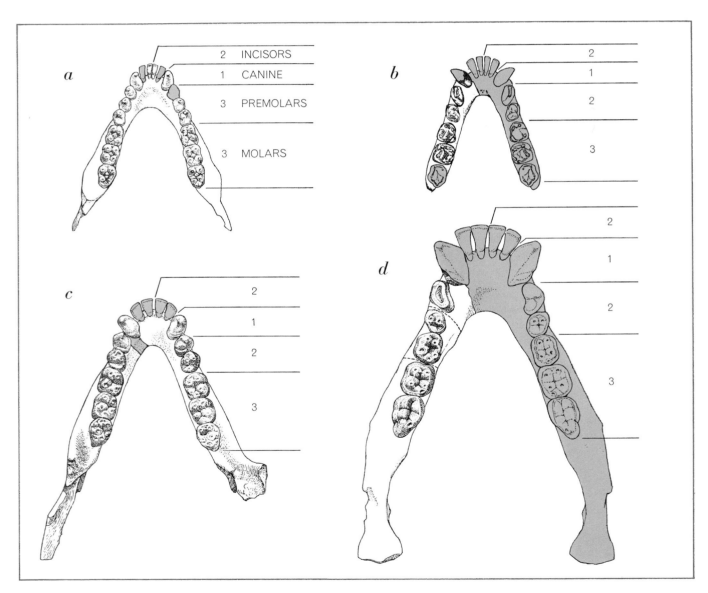

LOWER JAWS of four Fayum primates illustrate the relative size of the fossils and the difference between the New World and Old World "dental formula." *Apidium* (*a*) is a small parapithecid and the most abundant Fayum fossil primate; the number of its teeth is the same as that of New World monkeys. *Oligopithecus* (*b*) is probably the oldest Fayum primate. Like *Propliopithecus* (*c*) and the largest Fayum primate, *Aegyptopithecus* (*d*), its tooth count is the same as that of all Old World monkeys, the apes and man. The teeth and jawbones shown in detail are based on fossil specimens; where teeth or bones are in color they represent reconstructions.

4

HOMO ERECTUS

WILLIAM W. HOWELLS
November 1966

This species, until recently known by a multiplicity of other names, was probably the immediate predecessor of modern man. It now seems possible that the transition took place some 500,000 years ago

In 1891 Eugène Dubois, a young Dutch anatomist bent on discovering early man, was examining a fossil-rich layer of gravels beside the Solo River in Java. He found what he was after: an ancient human skull. The next year he discovered in the same formation a human thighbone. These two fossils, now known to be more than 700,000 years old, were the first remains to be found of the prehistoric human species known today as *Homo erectus.* It is appropriate on the 75th anniversary of Dubois's discovery to review how our understanding of this early man has been broadened and clarified by more recent discoveries of fossil men of similar antiquity and the same general characteristics, so that *Homo erectus* is now viewed as representing a major stage in the evolution of man. Also of interest, although of less consequence, is the way in which the name *Homo erectus,* now accepted by many scholars, has been chosen after a long period during which "scientific" names for human fossils were bestowed rather capriciously.

Man first received his formal name in 1758, when Carolus Linnaeus called him *Homo sapiens.* Linnaeus was trying simply to bring order to the world of living things by distinguishing each species of plant and animal from every other and by arranging them all in a hierarchical system. Considering living men, he recognized them quite correctly as one species in the system. The two centuries that followed Linnaeus saw first the establishment of evolutionary theory and then the realization of its genetic foundations; as a result ideas on the relations of species as units of plant and animal life have become considerably more complex. For example, a species can form two or more new species, which Linnaeus originally thought was impossible. By today's definition a spe-

cies typically consists of a series of local or regional populations that may exhibit minor differences of form or color but that otherwise share a common genetic structure and pool of genes and are thus able to interbreed across population lines. Only when two such populations have gradually undergone so many different changes in their genetic makeup that the likelihood of their interbreeding falls below a critical point are they genetically cut off from each other and do they become separate species. Alternatively, over a great many generations an equivalent amount of change will take place in the same population, so that its later form will be recognized as a species different from the earlier. This kind of difference, of course, cannot be put to the test of interbreeding and can only be judged by the physical form of the fossils involved.

In the case of living man there is no reason to revise Linnaeus' assignment: *Homo sapiens* is a good, typical species. Evolution, however, was not in Linnaeus' ken. He never saw a human fossil, much less conceived of men different from living men. Between his time and ours the use of the Linnaean system of classification as applied to man and his relatives past and present became almost a game. On grasping the concept of evolution, scholars saw that modern man must have had ancestors. They were prepared to anticipate the actual discovery of these ancestral forms, and perhaps the greatest anticipator was the German biologist Ernst Haeckel. Working on the basis of fragmentary information in 1889, when the only well-known fossil human remains were the comparatively recent bones discovered 25 years earlier in the Neander Valley of Germany, Haeckel drew up a theoretical ancestral line for man. The line began among some postu-

lated extinct apes of the Miocene epoch and reached *Homo sapiens* by way of an imagined group of "ape-men" (Pithecanthropi) and a group of more advanced but still speechless early men (Alali) whom he visualized as the worldwide stock from which modern men had evolved [*see illustration on page 39*]. A creature combining these various presapient attributes took form in the pooled imagination of Haeckel and his compatriots August Schleicher and Gabriel Max. Max produced a family portrait, and the still-to-be-discovered ancestor was given the respectable Linnaean name *Pithecanthropus alalus.*

Were he living today Haeckel would never do such a thing. It is now the requirement of the International Code of Zoological Nomenclature that the naming of any new genus or species be supported by publication of the specimen's particulars together with a description showing it to be recognizably different from any genus or species previously known. Haeckel was rescued from retroactive embarrassment, however, by Dubois, who gave Haeckel's genus name to Java man. The skull was too large to be an ape's and apparently too small to be a man's; the name *Pithecanthropus* seemed perfectly appropriate. On the other hand, the thighbone from the same formation was essentially modern; its possessor had evidently walked upright. Dubois therefore gave his discovery the species name *erectus.* Since Dubois's time the legitimacy of his finds has been confirmed by the discovery in Java (by G. H. R. von Koenigswald between 1936 and 1939 and by Indonesian workers within the past three years) of equally old and older fossils of the same population.

In the 50 years between Dubois's discovery and the beginning of World

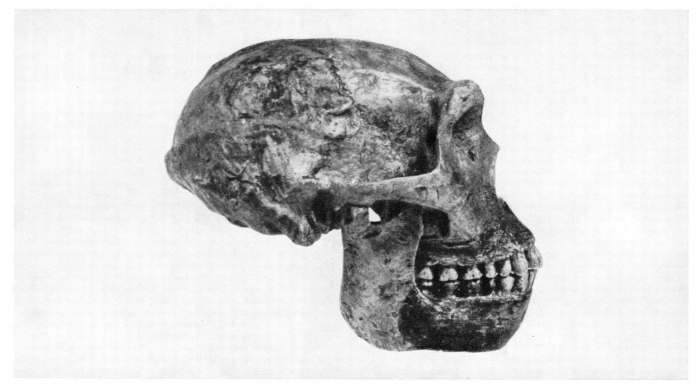

JAVA MAN, whose 700,000-year-old remains were unearthed in 1891 by Eugène Dubois, is representative of the earliest *Homo erectus* population so far discovered. This reconstruction was made recently by G. H. R. von Koenigswald and combines the features of the more primitive members of this species of man that he found in the lowest (Djetis) fossil strata at Sangiran in central Java during the 1930's. The characteristics that are typical of *Homo erectus* include the smallness and flatness of the cranium, the heavy brow-ridge and both the sharp bend and the ridge for muscle attachment at the rear of the skull. The robustness of the jaws adds to the species' primitive appearance. In most respects except size, however, the teeth of *Homo erectus* resemble those of modern man.

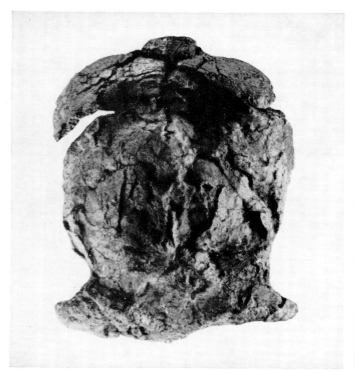

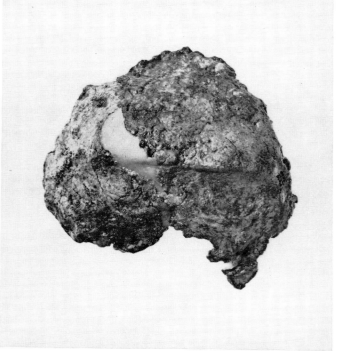

LANTIAN MAN is the most recently found *Homo erectus* fossil. The discovery consists of a jawbone and this skullcap (*top view, browridge at bottom*) from which the occipital bone (*top*) is partially detached. Woo Ju-kang of the Chinese Academy of Sciences in Peking provided the photograph; this fossil man from Shensi may be as old as the earliest specimens of *Homo erectus* from Java.

OCCIPITAL BONE found at Vértesszöllös in Hungary in 1965 is 500,000 or more years old. The only older human fossil in Europe is the Heidelberg jaw. The bone forms the rear of a skull; the ridge for muscle attachment (*horizontal line*) is readily apparent. In spite of this primitive feature and its great age, the skull fragment from Vértesszöllös has been assigned to the species *Homo sapiens*.

War II various other important new kinds of human fossil came into view. For our purposes the principal ones (with some of the Linnaean names thrust on them) were (1) the lower jaw found at Mauer in Germany in 1907 (*Homo heidelbergensis* or *Palaeanthropus*), (2) the nearly complete skull found at Broken Hill in Rhodesia in 1921 (*Homo rhodesiensis* or *Cyphanthropus*), (3) various remains uncovered near Peking in China, beginning with one tooth in 1923 and finally comprising a collection representing more than 40 men, women and children by the end of 1937 (*Sinanthropus pekinensis*), and (4) several skulls found in 1931 and 1932 near Ngandong on the Solo River not far from where Dubois had worked (*Homo soloensis* or *Javanthropus*). This is a fair number of fossils, but they were threatened with being outnumbered by the names assigned to them. The British student of early man Bernard G. Campbell has recorded the following variants in the case of the Mauer jawbone alone: *Palaeanthropus heidelbergensis, Pseudhomo heidelbergensis, Protanthropus heidelbergensis, Praehomo heidelbergensis, Praehomo europaeus, Anthropus heidelbergensis, Maueranthropus heidelbergensis, Europanthropus heidelbergensis* and *Euranthropus*.

Often the men responsible for these redundant christenings were guilty merely of innocent grandiloquence. They were not formally declaring their conviction that each fossil hominid belonged to a separate genus, distinct from *Homo*, which would imply an enormous diversity in the human stock. Nonetheless, the multiplicity of names has interfered with an understanding of the evolutionary significance of the fossils that bore them. Moreover, the human family trees drawn during this period showed a fundamental resemblance to Haeckel's original venture; the rather isolated specimens of early man were stuck on here and there like Christmas-tree ornaments. Although the arrangements evinced a vague consciousness of evolution, no scheme was presented that intelligibly interpreted the fossil record.

At last two questions came to the fore. First, to what degree did the fossils really differ? Second, what was the difference among them over a period of time? The fossil men of the most recent period—those who had lived between roughly 100,000 and 30,000 years ago—were Neanderthal man, Rhodesian man and Solo man. They have been known traditionally as *Homo neanderthalensis, Homo rhodesiensis* and *Homo soloensis*, names that declare each of the three to be a separate species, distinct from one another and from *Homo sapiens*. This in turn suggests that if Neanderthal and Rhodesian populations had come in contact, they would probably not have interbred. Such a conclusion is difficult to establish on the basis of fossils, particularly when they are few and tell very little about the geographical range of the species. Today's general view is a contrary one. These comparatively recent fossil men, it is now believed, did not constitute separate species. They were at most incipient species, that is, subspecies or variant populations that had developed in widely separated parts of the world but were still probably able to breed with one another or with *Homo sapiens*.

It was also soon recognized that the older Java and Peking fossils were not very different from one another. The suggestion followed that both populations be placed in a single genus (*Pithecanthropus*) and that the junior name (*Sinanthropus*) be dropped. Even this, however, was one genus too many for Ernst Mayr of Harvard University. Mayr, whose specialty is the evolutionary basis of biological classification, declared that ordinary zoological standards would not permit Java and Peking man to occupy

THE NAME "PITHECANTHROPUS," or ape-man, was coined by the German biologist Ernst Haeckel in 1889 for a postulated precursor of *Homo sapiens*. Haeckel placed the ape-man genus two steps below modern man on his "tree" of primate evolution, adding the species name *alalus*, or "speechless," because he deemed speech an exclusively human trait.

a genus separate from modern man. In his opinion the amount of evolutionary progress that separates *Pithecanthropus* from ourselves is a step that allows the recognition only of a different species. After all, Java and Peking man apparently had bodies just like our own; that is to say, they were attacking the problem of survival with exactly the same adaptations, although with smaller brains. On this view Java man is placed in the genus *Homo* but according to the rules retains his original species name and so becomes *Homo erectus*. Under the circumstances Peking man can be distinguished from him only as a subspecies: *Homo erectus pekinensis*.

The simplification is something more than sweeping out a clutter of old names to please the International Commission on Zoological Nomenclature. The reduction of fossil hominids to not more than two species and the recognition of *Homo erectus* has become increasingly useful as a way of looking at a stage of human evolution. This has been increasingly evident in recent years, as human fossils have continued to come to light and as new and improved methods of dating them have been developed. It is now possible to place both the old discoveries and the new ones much more precisely in time, and that is basic to establishing the entire pattern of human evolution in the past few million years.

To consider dating first, the period during which *Homo erectus* flourished occupies the early middle part of the Pleistocene epoch. The evidence that now enables us to subdivide the Pleistocene with some degree of confidence is of several kinds. For example, the fossil animals found in association with fossil men often indicate whether the climate of the time was cold or warm. The comparison of animal communities is also helpful in correlating intervals of time on one continent with intervals on another. The ability to determine absolute dates, which makes possible the correlation of the relative dates derived from sequences of strata in widely separated localities, is another significant development. Foremost among the methods of absolute dating at the moment is one based on the rate of decay of radioactive potassium into argon. A second method showing much promise is the analysis of deep-sea sediments; changes in the forms of planktonic life embedded in samples of the bottom reflect worldwide temperature changes. When the absolute ages of key points in sediment sequences are determined by physical or chemical methods,

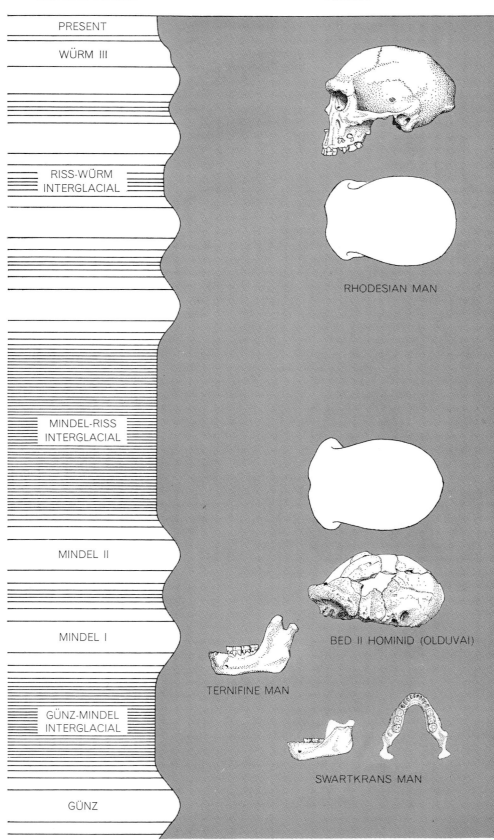

GLACIAL STAGES

AFRICA

PRESENT

WÜRM III

RISS-WÜRM
INTERGLACIAL

RHODESIAN MAN

MINDEL-RISS
INTERGLACIAL

MINDEL II

MINDEL I

BED II HOMINID (OLDUVAI)

TERNIFINE MAN

GÜNZ-MINDEL
INTERGLACIAL

SWARTKRANS MAN

GÜNZ

FOSSIL EVIDENCE for the existence of a single species of early man instead of several species and genera of forerunners of *Homo sapiens* is presented in this array of individual remains whose age places them in the interval of approximately 500,000 years that separates the first Pleistocene interglacial period from the end of the second glacial period (*see scale at left*). The earliest *Homo erectus* fossils known, from Java and China, belong to the first interglacial period; the earliest *Homo erectus* remains from South Africa may be equally

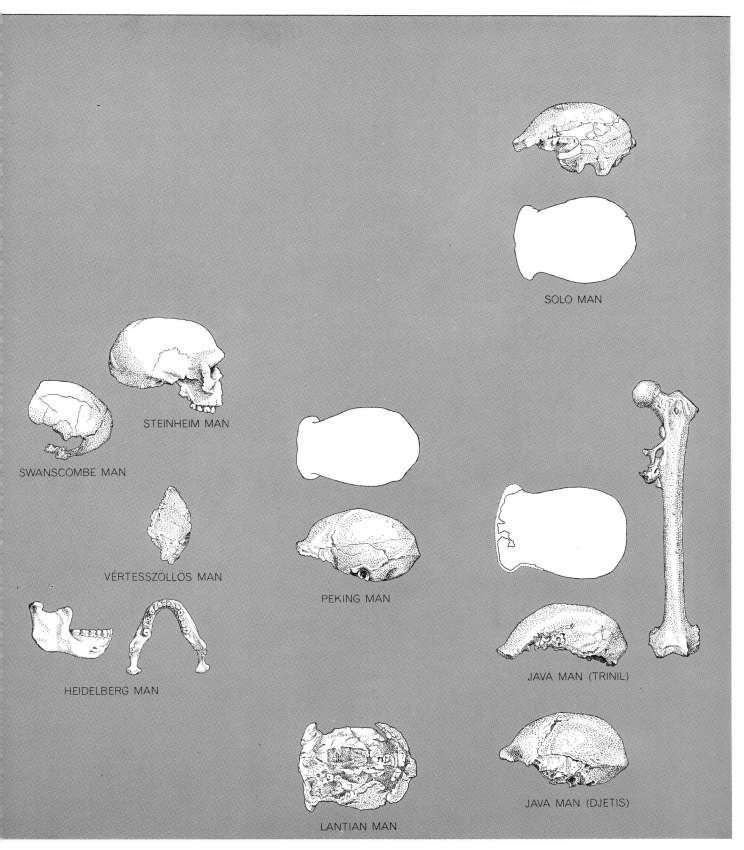

SOLO MAN

STEINHEIM MAN

SWANSCOMBE MAN

VÉRTESSZÖLLÖS MAN

PEKING MAN

JAVA MAN (TRINIL)

HEIDELBERG MAN

JAVA MAN (DJETIS)

LANTIAN MAN

old. Half a million years later *Homo erectus* continued to be represented in China by the remains of Peking man and in Africa by the skull from Olduvai Gorge. In the intervening period this small-brained precursor of modern man was not the only human species inhabiting the earth, nor did *Homo erectus* become extinct when the 500,000-year period ended. One kind of man who had apparent-ly reached the grade of *Homo sapiens* in Europe by the middle or later part of the second Pleistocene glacial period was unearthed recently at Vértesszöllös in Hungary. In the following inter-glacial period *Homo sapiens* is represented by the Steinheim and Swanscombe females. Solo man's remains indicate that *Homo erectus* survived for several hundred thousand years after that.

it ought to be possible to assign dates to all the major events of the Pleistocene. Such methods have already suggested that the epoch began more than three million years ago and that its first major cold phase (corresponding to the Günz glaciation of the Alps) may date back to as much as 1.5 million years ago. The period of time occupied by *Homo erectus* now appears to extend from about a million years ago to 500,000 years ago in terms of absolute dates, or from some time during the first interglacial period in the Northern Hemisphere to about the end of the second major cold phase (corresponding to the Mindel glaciation of the Alps).

On the basis of the fossils found before World War II, with the exception of the isolated and somewhat peculiar Heidelberg jaw, *Homo erectus* would have appeared to be a human population of the Far East. The Java skulls, particularly those that come from the lowest fossil strata (known as the Djetis

beds), are unsurpassed within the entire group in primitiveness. Even the skulls from the strata above them (the Trinil beds), in which Dubois made his original discovery, have very thick walls and room for only a small brain. Their cranial capacity probably averages less than 900 cubic centimeters, compared with an average of 500 c.c. for gorillas and about 1,400 c.c. for modern man. The later representatives of Java man must be more than 710,000 years old, because potassium-argon analysis has shown that tektites (glassy stones formed by or from meteorites) in higher strata of the same formation are of that age.

The Peking fossils are younger, probably dating to the middle of the second Pleistocene cold phase, and are physically somewhat less crude than the Java ones. The braincase is higher, the face shorter and the cranial capacity approaches 1,100 c.c., but the general construction of skull and jaw is similar. The teeth of both Java man and Peking man

are somewhat larger than modern man's and are distinguished by traces of an enamel collar, called a cingulum, around some of the crowns. The latter is an ancient and primitive trait in man and apes.

Discoveries of human fossils after World War II have added significantly to the picture of man's distribution at this period. The pertinent finds are the following:

1949: Swartkrans, South Africa. Jaw and facial fragments, originally given the name *Telanthropus capensis*. These were found among the copious remains at this site of the primitive subhumans known as australopithecines. The fossils were recognized at once by the late Robert Broom and his colleague John T. Robinson as more advanced than the australopithecines both in size and in traits of jaw and teeth. Robinson has now assigned *Telanthropus* to *Homo erectus*, since that is where he evidently

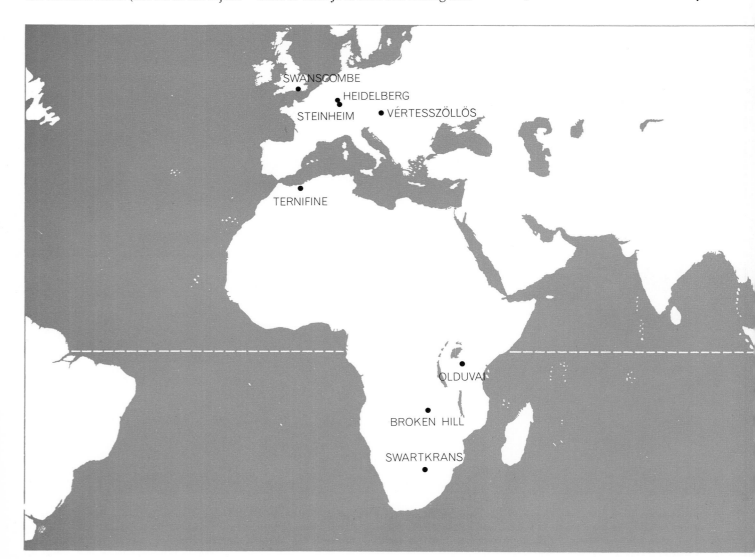

DISTRIBUTION of *Homo erectus* seemed to be confined mainly to the Far East and Southeast Asia on the basis of fossils unearthed before World War II; the sole exception was the Heidelberg jaw. Postwar findings in South, East and North Africa, as well as dis-

belongs.

1955: Ternifine, Algeria. Three jaws and a parietal bone, given the name *Atlanthropus mauritanicus*, were found under a deep covering of sand on the clay floor of an ancient pond by Camille Arambourg. The teeth and jaws show a strong likeness to the Peking remains.

1961: Olduvai Gorge, Tanzania. A skullcap, not formally named but identified as the Bed II Hominid, was discovered by L. S. B. Leakey. Found in a context with a provisional potassium-argon date of 500,000 years ago, the skull's estimated cranial capacity is 1,000 c.c. Although differing somewhat in detail, it has the general characteristics of the two Far Eastern subspecies of *Homo erectus*. At lower levels in this same important site were found the remains of a number of individuals with small skulls, now collectively referred to as "Homo habilis."

1963–1964: Lantian district, Shensi, China. A lower jaw and a skullcap were found by Chinese workers at two separate localities in the district and given the name *Sinanthropus lantianensis*. Animal fossils indicate that the Lantian sites are older than the one that yielded Peking man and roughly as old as the lowest formation in Java. The form of the skull and jaw accords well with this dating; both are distinctly more primitive than the Peking fossils. Both differ somewhat in detail from the Java subspecies of *Homo erectus*, but the estimated capacity of this otherwise large skull (780 c.c.) is small and close to that of the earliest fossil cranium unearthed in Java.

1965: Vértesszöllös, Hungary. An isolated occipital bone (in the back of the skull) was found by L. Vértes. This skull fragment is the first human fossil from the early middle Pleistocene to be unearthed in Europe since the Heidelberg jaw. It evidently dates to the middle or later part of the Mindel glaciation and thus falls clearly within the *Homo erectus* time zone as defined here. The bone is moderately thick and shows a well-defined ridge for the attachment of neck muscles such as is seen in all the *erectus* skulls. It is unlike *erectus* occipital bones, however, in that it is both large and definitely less angled; these features indicate a more advanced skull.

In addition to these five discoveries, something else of considerable importance happened during this period. The Piltdown fraud, perpetrated sometime before 1912, was finally exposed in 1953. The detective work of J. S. Weiner, Sir Wilfrid Le Gros Clark and Kenneth Oakley removed from the fossil record a supposed hominid with a fully apelike jaw and manlike skull that could scarcely be fitted into any sensible evolutionary scheme.

From this accumulation of finds, many of them made so recently, there emerges a picture of men with skeletons like ours but with brains much smaller, skulls much thicker and flatter and furnished with protruding brows in front and a marked angle in the rear, and with teeth somewhat larger and exhibiting a few slightly more primitive traits. This picture suggests an evolutionary level, or grade, occupying half a million years of human history and now seen to prevail all over the inhabited Old World. This is the meaning of *Homo erectus*. It gives us a new foundation for ideas as to the pace and the pattern of human evolution over a critical span of time.

Quite possibly this summary is too tidy; before the 100th anniversary of the resurrection of *Homo erectus* is celebrated complications may appear that we cannot perceive at present. Even today there are a number of fringe problems we cannot neglect. Here are some of them.

What was the amount of evolution taking place within the *erectus* grade? There is probably a good deal of accident of discovery involved in defining *Homo erectus*. Chance, in other words, may have isolated a segment of a continuum, since finds from the time immediately following this 500,000-year period are almost lacking. It seems likely, in fact practically certain, that real evolutionary progress was taking place, but the tools made by man during this period reveal little of it. As for the fossils themselves, the oldest skulls—from Java and Lantian—are the crudest and have the smallest brains. In Java, one region with some discernible stratigraphy, the later skulls show signs of evolutionary advance compared with the earlier ones. The Peking skulls, which are almost certainly later still, are even more progressive. Bernard Campbell, who has recently suggested that all the known forms of *Homo erectus* be formally recognized as named subspecies, has arranged the names in the order of their relative progressiveness. I have added some names to Campbell's list; they appear in parentheses in the illustration on page 44. As the illustration indicates, the advances in grade seem indeed to correspond fairly well with the passage of time.

What are the relations of *Homo erectus* to Rhodesian and Solo man? This is a point of particular importance, because both the African and the Javanese fossils are much younger than the date we have set as the general upward boundary for *Homo erectus*. Rhodesian man may have been alive as recently as 30,000 years ago and may have actually overlapped with modern man. Solo man probably existed during the last Pleistocene cold phase; this is still very recent compared with the time zone of the other *erectus* fossils described here. Carleton S. Coon of the University of Pennsylvania deems both late fossil men to be *Homo erectus* on the basis of tooth size and skull flatness. His placing of Rhodesian man is arguable, but Solo man is so primitive, so like Java man in many aspects of his skull form and so close to Peking man in brain size that his classification as *Homo erectus* seems almost inevitable. The meaning of his survival hundreds of thousands of years after the period I have suggested, and his relation to the modern men who

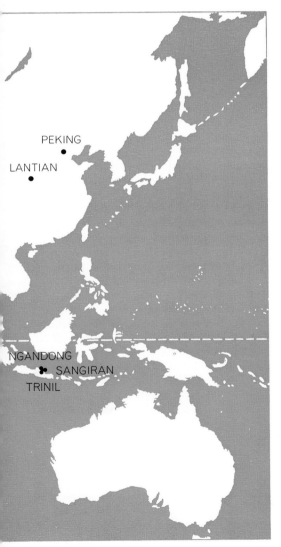

PEKING

LANTIAN

NGANDONG
SANGIRAN
TRINIL

covery of a new *Homo erectus* site in northern China, have extended the species' range.

GRADE	EUROPE	NORTH AFRICA	EAST AFRICA	SOUTH AFRICA	EAST ASIA	SOUTHEAST ASIA
(5)	HOMO SAPIENS (VÉRTESSZÖLLÖS)					
(4)						(HOMO ERECTUS SOLOENSIS)
3	HOMO ERECTUS HEIDELBERGENSIS	HOMO ERECTUS MAURITANICUS	HOMO ERECTUS LEAKEYI		HOMO ERECTUS PEKINENSIS	
2						HOMO ERECTUS ERECTUS
1			HOMO ERECTUS HABILIS	HOMO ERECTUS CAPENSIS	(HOMO ERECTUS LANTIANENSIS)	HOMO ERECTUS MODJOKERTENSIS

EIGHT SUBSPECIES of *Homo erectus* that are generally accepted today have been given appropriate names and ranked in order of evolutionary progress by the British scholar Bernard G. Campbell. The author has added Lantian man to Campbell's lowest *Homo erectus* grade and provided a fourth grade to accommodate Solo man, a late but primitive survival. The author has also added a fifth grade for the *Homo sapiens* fossil from Vértesszöllös (*color*). Colored area suggests that Heidelberg man is its possible forebear.

succeeded him in Southeast Asia in recent times, are unanswered questions of considerable importance.

Where did *Homo erectus* come from? The Swartkrans discovery makes it clear that he arose before the last representatives of the australopithecines had died out at that site. The best present evidence of his origin is also from Africa; it consists of the series of fossils unearthed at Olduvai Gorge by Leakey and his wife and called Homo habilis. These remains seem to reflect a transition from an australopithecine level to an *erectus* level about a million years ago. This date seems almost too late, however, when one considers the age of *Homo erectus* finds elsewhere in the world, particularly in Java.

Where did *Homo erectus* go? The paths are simply untraced, both those that presumably lead to the Swanscombe and Steinheim people of Europe during the Pleistocene's second interglacial period and those leading to the much later Rhodesian and Neanderthal men. This is a period lacking useful evidence. Above all, the nature of the line leading to living man—*Homo sapiens* in the Linnaean sense—remains a matter of pure theory.

We may, however, have a clue. Here it is necessary to face a final problem. What was the real variation in physical type during the time period of *Homo erectus?* On the whole, considering the time and space involved, it does not appear to be very large; the similarity of the North African jaws to those of Peking man, for example, is striking in spite of the thousands of miles that separated the two populations. The Heidelberg jaw, however, has always seemed to be somewhat different from all the others and a little closer to modern man in the nature of its teeth. The only other European fossil approaching the Heidelberg jaw in antiquity is the occipital bone recently found at Vértesszöllös. This piece of skull likewise appears to be progressive in form and may have belonged to the same general kind of man as the Heidelberg jaw, although it is somewhat more recent in date.

Andor Thoma of Hungary's Kossuth University at Debrecen in Hungary, who has kindly given me information concerning the Vértesszöllös fossil, will publish a formal description soon in the French journal *L'Anthropologie*. He estimates that the cranial capacity was about 1,400 c.c., close to the average for modern man and well above that of the known specimens of *Homo erectus*. Although the occipital bone is thick, it is larger and less sharply angled than the matching skull area of Rhodesian man. It is certainly more modern-looking than the Solo skulls. I see no reason at this point to dispute Thoma's estimate of brain volume. He concludes that Vértesszöllös man had in fact reached the *sapiens* grade in skull form and brain size and accordingly has named him a subspecies of *Homo sapiens*.

Thoma's finding therefore places a population of more progressive, *sapiens* humanity contemporary with the populations of *Homo erectus* 500,000 years ago or more. From the succeeding interglacial period in Europe have come the Swanscombe and Steinheim skulls, generally recognized as *sapiens* in grade. They are less heavy than the Hungarian fossil, more curved in occipital profile and smaller in size; they are also apparently both female, which would account for part of these differences.

The trail of evidence is of course faint, but there are no present signs of contradiction; what we may be seeing is a line that follows *Homo sapiens* back from Swanscombe and Steinheim to Vértesszöllös and finally to Heidelberg man at the root. This is something like the Solo case in reverse, a *Homo sapiens* population surprisingly early in time, in contrast to a possible *Homo erectus* population surprisingly late. In fact, we are seeing only the outlines of what we must still discover. It is easy to perceive how badly we need more fossils; for example, we cannot relate Heidelberg man to any later Europeans until we find some skull parts to add to his solitary jaw.

Human Genetics and Evolution

HUMAN GENETICS AND EVOLUTION

In the preceding section the reader was introduced to the role of genetics in human adaptation. Here, in more depth, several eminent geneticists explore the topic of genetics, the theory and mechanics of the very stuff of evolution.

Gregor Mendel spelled out the principal mechanism of heritability in 1866, but his work was not incorporated in the field of biology until 1900 when the principle of heritability was rediscovered independently by Hugo deVries, Carl Correns, and Erich Tschermak. Subsequent geneticists have concerned themselves with analyzing the unit of inheritance, which became called the gene, and the manner in which genes determine the development of the organism.

Norman H. Horowitz provides the first essay, simply and appropriately titled "The Gene." He describes the principles of Mendelian genetics, the concept of the gene, the relation of the gene to the chromosome in which it is located, and what, when he wrote in 1956, were then the most recently solved problems associated with gene function and replication, together with some that were to be solved subsequently by molecular geneticists.

The second paper, "The Genetic Code: III," is by one of these molecular geneticists, F. H. C. Crick, who, along with J. D. Watson, in 1954 discovered the structure of deoxyribonucleic acid (DNA), for which they were awarded a Nobel Prize in 1962. Their dramatic discovery led to most of the present knowledge about the chemical nature of the gene. Most importantly, the discovery of the structure of DNA allows geneticists to account for the way in which genes influence protein synthesis, which in turn, largely accounts for the nature and activities of cells.

In this paper Crick shows the relationship between specified molecules of nucleic acid (genes) and amino acids (components of proteins), explaining how deoxyribonucleic acid transcribes a genetic code into RNA (ribonucleic acid) and how the four nucleic acid bases of RNA, each identified by a letter, form various concatenations of letters (nucleic acid molecules) that are "read" three at a time to specify the twenty amino acids needed for protein formation. Each amino acid is specified by a three-letter codon transcribed from the genetic code of DNA.

If DNA does not replicate itself exactly, permutations are introduced that are transcribed as part of the genetic code. Until an organism dies or a second mutation replaces the first, such variabilities are permanent parts of organismic evolution. In "Ionizing Radiation and Evolution," James F. Crow introduces us to the role in evolution of heritable variability arising from such mutations. Focusing on mutation, which along with recombination provides variability in genetic systems, Crow analyzes spontaneous mutation rates (the rate of mutations for which a cause is not known) in both long-lived and short-lived organisms, comparing this with mutagenic ionizing radiation rates (where these can be known). He concludes that species with long life spans, such as man, are affected more by ionized radiation than are species of short-lived plants and animals, and that whereas mutagens can either be harmless or harmful in most plant and animal evolution, in the evolution of man probably all mutagens, including ionizing radiation, are harmful.

What kinds of harmful effects can a mutagen cause in humans? Ida Macalpine and Richard Hunter describe the typical symptoms of one heritable metabolic deficiency disease, porphyria, showing how in one fascinating case—that of King George III of England—this mutagenically-caused disease played an important role in influencing British history. By way of a relatively complete royal genealogy that begins with Mary, Queen of Scots and ends with Queen Victoria, Macalpine and Hunter show that three royal houses were afflicted with the disease. The personage most tragically affected was King George III, whose disease was misdiagnosed during his lifetime. Even though "Porphyria and King George III" does not contain an analysis of the biochemical sources of porphyria, it is an important contribution to our understanding of the deleterious effect of a single mutagen and a fascinating study of human genetics and history.

In the final paper, "The Present Evolution of Man," Theodosius Dobzhansky underscores the point made by James Crow that average genetic mutation has detrimental effects, and that an increase in mutation rates caused by radiation from man's technological enterprises, particularly military and industrial operations and medical X-rays, would be especially dangerous to man. But Dobzhansky also shows that on the other hand, in solving many symptoms of diseases associated with heredity, thereby saving the life in which the mutant gene for that disease is one constituent, man has not prevented people who suffer from hereditary problems from transmitting those genetic mutations to their offspring. Dobzhansky wonders whether technological development has outstripped biological evolution, and if so, what the effects of this phenomenon might be.

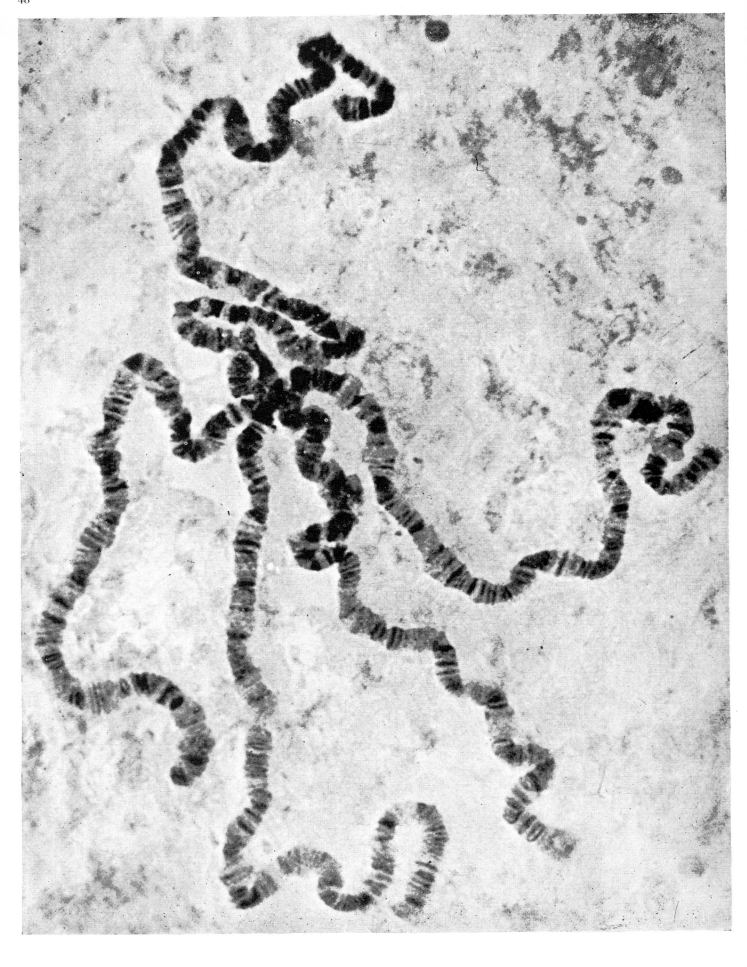

5

THE GENE

NORMAN H. HOROWITZ
October 1956

*Biologists have yet to see it or to find out exactly what
it is made of, but its role in determining the continuity
and the variation of living things grows steadily clearer*

The distinguished theoretical physicist Erwin Schrödinger has called the science of genetics "easily the most interesting of our days." No branch of science in the 20th century has contributed more to man's understanding of himself and the living world in general. Genetic discoveries have provided new insights into such fundamental problems as the origin of life, the structure of living matter and evolution; and they have yielded practical benefits over a broad range of human concerns, from plant and animal breeding to the investigation of disease. Genetics, in short, has become the theoretical backbone of biology.

The central concept of genetics is the

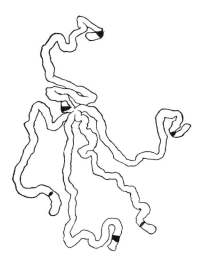

CHROMOSOMES in the cells of the salivary glands of *Drosophila*, sometimes called the vinegar fly (*opposite*), are useful to geneticists because they are large and easy to "read." On the diagram above are marked the loci of certain identifiable features in the chromosomes which are found in association with heritable characteristics, especially color, in the eye of the vinegar fly.

gene, the elementary unit of inheritance. This article presents an account of the development of the gene concept and of modern researches into the nature and mode of action of genes.

Almost everyone knows that the science of genetics was founded by a monk named Gregor Mendel, who carried on plant breeding experiments as a hobby in the garden of his monastery at Brünn in Moravia (now Brno, Czechoslovakia). The story of how Mendel's remarkable paper, published in 1866 in the proceedings of a provincial natural history society, was ignored by his contemporaries and was rescued from oblivion by three separate investigators in the year 1900, 16 years after Mendel's death, is one of the most dramatic incidents of modern science. Many historians of biology have speculated on why so far-reaching an advance was disregarded at the time it was made, only to be enthusiastically welcomed 35 years later. The interment of Mendel's paper is commonly attributed to the fact that he was an amateur and to the obscurity of the journal in which it was published. But Charles Darwin also was an amateur, and the standing of amateurs in science was still strong in the 19th century. As for the journal—the *Proceedings of the Brünn Society for the Study of Natural Science*—it was regularly received by the leading research centers of Europe, and Mendel is known to have called his paper to the attention of Carl K. von Nägeli, one of the leading botanists of the day. A more likely answer to the puzzle is that Mendel's contemporaries were incapable of appreciating the significance of his discoveries. His conclusions were essentially of an abstract nature, based on numerical data obtained by counting the various kinds of offspring produced by crosses of pea

plants. Because chromosomes and many other aspects of the biology of reproduction were unknown in Mendel's day, his paper must have seemed to his contemporaries arbitrary and formalistic—mere numerology.

It is curious to reflect that although Mendel is justly entitled to acclaim for his discovery, the development of genetics would have been the same even if he had never lived. His three rediscoverers—Carl Correns in Germany, Hugo de Vries in Holland, Erich Tschermak in Austria—were led to his paper only after they had independently arrived at the same conclusions. Some geneticists believe that Correns, Tschermak and de Vries were greatly aided in the interpretation of their experiments by Mendel's brilliant paper, but this cannot be proved by the historical record.

"The Elementary Game"

The essence of Mendel's discovery was that hereditary traits—or "characters"—are independent of one another and each is transmitted as a separate unit from a parent to the offspring: in other words, the organism is a mosaic of distinct and independent qualities. The units of inheritance are distributed in families and populations according to the laws of independent events—*i.e.*, the laws of chance. This view contrasts with the older idea that the characteristics of the parents are blended in the offspring, as one might blend two liquids by mixing them together (a misconception which still persists in the expressions "full-blooded," "half-blood" and the like). Mendel showed that there is no blending or dilution of individual characters in a hybrid. The expression of a given character may disappear, but the hybrid

GREGOR MENDEL published his first comprehensive report on his investigations in 1866. Copies of his paper were circulated to most of the university libraries of Europe and to many contemporary scientists, yet its significance went unrecognized until 1900.

carries the character as a "recessive" unit, and it may emerge in later generations. Mendelian inheritance is essentially atomistic, the heritable qualities of the organism behaving as if they were determined by irreducible particles (we now call them genes). Mendel was not concerned with the nature of the particles but with showing that inheritance can be understood in these terms and with working out the rules of transmission of traits.

An individual is composed of thousands of heritable characteristics. Each character may take one of several possible forms. For example, there are three principal forms, called A, B and O, of a gene for human blood type. Every person carries a pair of the genes, the possible combinations being AA, AO, BB, BO, AB and OO. A and B are "dominant" and O is "recessive" to them, so that the blood of a person with the combination AO, for instance, shows the properties of the blood group A.

Mendel's laws can be understood in terms of a game of chance in which the genes are represented by counters. There are two players (the parents) and each is provided with a pair of counters for each of the thousands of hereditary characters (e.g., AA or AO or the like for blood group). To play the game each player selects at random one counter from each of his pairs and puts it in a pile in the middle of the table. In the end the pile will contain just as many counters as were originally held by each player, half of them contributed by each player. The pile of counters represents the genetic endowment of an offspring of the two players. In principle this is all there is to the game of Mendelian inheritance. We shall call it the "elementary game."

Mendel's great achievement was to recognize that this simple game—that is, the random separation and reuniting of pairs of inheritance determiners in the germ cells—would provide an orderly explanation of the seemingly unsystematic results of his experiments. Mendel found the evidence for the separation of determiners in a statistical analysis of pea-plant offspring: the characters tended to occur in certain orderly proportions among the members of successive generations as the determiners were shuffled and reshuffled. Nowadays the separation of genes (technically called "segregation") can be demonstrated in a direct way by experiments with some of the lower plants, such as the red bread mold Neurospora [see "The Genes of Men and Molds," by George W. Beadle; SCIENTIFIC AMERICAN Offprint 1]. For example, the segregation of a certain gene pair results in exactly equal numbers of black and white spores in every mature set of eight spores produced by this fungus. The Lysenkoists in the U.S.S.R. used to attack Mendelian genetics on the ground that it was based on statistics, which, for reasons not explained, they aimed to eliminate from biology. It was a moment of some dramatic interest, therefore, when, at the International Botanical Congress in Stockholm in 1950, a Portuguese scientist rose to ask a Soviet speaker how he explained the nonstatistical demonstration of segregation in Neurospora and similar organisms. It appears from the official account of the meeting that the Soviet delegate was unaware of these demonstrations.

Enter the Chromosome

In the years following the rediscovery of Mendel's laws at the turn of the century, the new science of genetics advanced rapidly. Investigators soon showed that the Mendelian rules of inheritance applied to animals as well as plants. The most important advance came when T. H. Morgan and his group at Columbia University, working with the vinegar fly Drosophila, discovered that the genes are material particles carried in the chromosomes of the cell nucleus. They were led to this discovery by their finding that genes are not altogether independent, as Mendel had thought, but tend to be transmitted in groups. In terms of the elementary game, we would say that the choice of counters is not entirely free: when one counter is selected, there is a tendency for certain other counters to be selected also, as if they were linked by a weak physical bond. Morgan and his students A. H. Sturtevant, C. B. Bridges and H. J. Muller found that genes in the same chromosome (where they are arranged like beads on a string) are transmitted sometimes as an intact group, sometimes not. That is to say, a pair of chromosomes may exchange segments of their strings of genes, forming new chromosomes which consist in part of one and in part of the other—a process known as "crossing over." By grouping genes in chromosomes and yet allowing them some freedom to change their lodgings, nature reconciles two conflicting requirements of inheritance and evolution. On the one hand, total disorganization of the genes in a cell would make the reproduction of cells exceedingly difficult. The tiny vinegar fly has something of the order of 10,000 genes. If they were loose in the cell nucleus, like buckshot, the problem of passing them on in exactly equal number to every daughter cell would be formidable. The problem is reduced to manageable proportions by the fact that the genes are grouped in four pairs of chromosomes: thus the cell has only eight objects to cope with, instead of 10,000. On the other hand, if the genes were forever bound in the same chromosomes, the organism would lack the flexibility for recombination of genes which is essential for evolutionary development. The situation is saved by the fact that genes may cross over from one chromosome to its partner when the germ cells are formed.

The Mendelian theory led to a new understanding of the biological significance of sex. It showed that the sexual method of reproduction provides an elaborate lottery which serves the function of recombining genes in new ways, thus permitting living things to explore a practically limitless range of possible variations. If each of 10,000 genes determining the make-up of a species of organism existed in only two different forms, the number of different gene combinations possible would be $3^{10,000}$ As we have seen, some genes are known to occur in more than two forms. The practically infinite number of possible combinations provides a vast reservoir of potential variability upon which the species can draw for its evolutionary

BOTANIQUE. — Sur la loi de disjonction des hybrides. Note de M. Hugo DE VRIES, présentée par M. Gaston Bonnier.

« D'après les principes que j'ai énoncés ailleurs (Intracellulare Pangenesis, 1889), les caractères spécifiques des organismes sont composés d'unités bien distinctes. On peut étudier expérimentalement ces unités soit dans des phénomènes de variabilité et de mutabilité, soit par la production des hybrides. Dans le dernier cas, on choisit de préférence les hybrides dont les parents ne se distinguent entre eux que par un seul caractère (les monohybrides), ou par un petit nombre de caractères bien délimités, et pour lesquels on ne considère qu'une ou deux de ces unités en laissant les autres de côté.

» Ordinairement les hybrides sont décrits comme participant à la fois des caractères du père et de la mère. A mon avis, on doit admettre, pour comprendre ce fait, que les hybrides ont quelques-uns des caractères simples du père et d'autres caractères également simples de la mère. Mais quand le père et la mère ne se distinguent que sur un seul point, l'hybride ne saurait tenir le milieu entre eux; car le caractère simple doit être considéré comme une unité non divisible.

» D'autre part l'étude des caractères simples des hybrides peut fournir la preuve la plus directe du principe énoncé. L'hybride montre toujours le caractère d'un des deux parents, et cela dans toute sa force; jamais le

HUGO DE VRIES, in Holland, discovered Mendel's paper after he had performed the same experiments and come to the same conclusion. His first publication was in March, 1900.

19. C. Correns: G. Mendel's Regel über das Verhalten der Nachkommenschaft der Rassenbastarde.

Eingegangen am 24. April 1900.

Die neueste Veröffentlichung HUGO DE VRIES': „Sur la loi de disjonction des hybrides"[1]), in deren Besitz ich gestern durch die Liebenswürdigkeit des Verfassers gelangt bin, veranlasst mich zu der folgenden Mittheilung.

Auch ich war bei meinen Bastardirungsversuchen mit Mais- und Erbsenrassen zu demselben Resultat gelangt, wie DE VRIES, der mit Rassen sehr verschiedener Pflanzen, darunter auch mit zwei Mais rassen, experimentirte. Als ich das gesetzmässige Verhalten und die Erklärung dafür — auf die ich gleich zurückkomme — gefunden hatte, ist es mir gegangen, wie es DE VRIES offenbar jetzt geht: ich habe das alles für etwas Neues gehalten[2]). Dann habe ich mich aber überzeugen müssen, dass der Abt GREGOR MENDEL in Brünn in den sechziger Jahren durch langjährige und sehr ausgedehnte Versuche mit Erbsen nicht nur zu demselben Resultat gekommen ist, wie DE VRIES und ich, sondern dass er auch genau dieselbe Erklärung gegeben hat, soweit das

CARL CORRENS, in Germany, saw de Vries' paper and wrote in April, 1900: "The same thing happened to me." He thought he had something new but then found Mendel's work.

26. E. Tschermak: Ueber künstliche Kreuzung bei Pisum sativum[1]).

Eingegangen am 2. Juni 1900.

Angeregt durch die Versuche DARWIN's über die Wirkungen der Kreuz- und Selbstbefruchtung im Pflanzenreiche, begann ich im Jahre 1898 an Pisum sativum Kreuzungsversuche anzustellen, weil mich besonders die Ausnahmefälle von dem allgemein ausgesprochenen Satze über den Nutzeffect der Kreuzung verschiedener Individuen und verschiedener Varietäten gegenüber der Selbstbefruchtung interessirten, eine Gruppe, in welche auch Pisum sativum gehört. Während bei den meisten Species, mit welchen DARWIN operirte (57 gegen 26 bezw. 12), die Sämlinge aus einer Kreuzung zwischen Individuen ierselben Species beinahe immer die durch Selbstbefruchtung erzeugten Concurrenten an Höhe, Gewicht, Wuchs, häufig auch an Fruchtbarkeit übertrafen, verhielt sich bei der Erbse die Höhe der aus der Kreuzung stammenden Pflanzen zu jener der Erzeugnisse von Selbstbefruchtung wie 100:115. DARWIN erblickte den Grund dieses Verhaltens in der durch viele Generationen sich wiederholenden Selbstbefruchtung der Erbse in den nördlichen Ländern. In Anbetracht

ERICH TSCHERMAK, in Austria, was busy on "the second correction of my own paper" when he saw de Vries' and Correns' reports. His abstract was published in June, 1900.

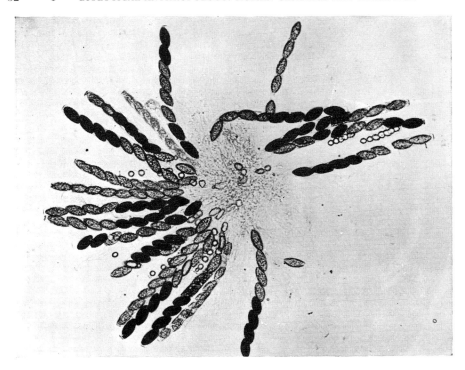

NEUROSPORA SPORES reflect crossing of dark- and light-colored strains. Spore groups have four light and four dark spores, just as pea plants bear peas in fixed ratios (*see opposite*).

progress. This is true of all species that reproduce sexually, from microbes to man.

Self-Duplication

Let us turn to the genes themselves. How are genes reproduced in the cell? How do they act in controlling heredity? What are they made of?

The genes are, of course, self-reproducing. In this they are like the cell or an organism as a whole, such as a bacterium. Bacteria, as we know, arise only from pre-existing bacteria. We can prepare a broth that contains all of the raw materials needed for the production of bacteria, and we can provide all the necessary environmental conditions—acidity, temperature, oxygen supply and so on—but if we fail to inoculate the broth with at least one bacterial cell, then no bacteria will ever be produced in it. The situation is the same with respect to gene production, the only difference being that we cannot prepare an artificial broth for growing genes: the only medium in which they are known to multiply is in the living cell itself. Indeed, it appears that the genes are the only self-replicating elements in a cell; all the other components of cells apparently are produced, directly or indirectly, by the activities of genes.

Just what is involved in the process of self-duplication as we have defined

it? One way to explore this question is to look into certain chemical reactions which seem to parallel reproduction by a living organism. An interesting case in point is pepsin, a gastric enzyme which is important for the digestion of proteins. As a catalyst, pepsin acts upon pepsinogen, a protein found in the wall of the stomach, and the product of its breakdown of pepsinogen is pepsin itself. Thus pepsin in the formal sense is self-duplicating: it acts upon the appropriate substance to produce a molecule exactly like itself. Moreover, its production of pepsin from pepsinogen over a period shows a curve of increase like the growth curve of a population of organisms. In other words, the equations for the production of pepsin and the production of cells are the same. The question now is: Does this formal similarity reflect a similarity in the mechanism of duplication?

A number of years ago Roger M. Herriott, Quentin R. Bartz and John H. Northrop at the Rockefeller Institute for Medical Research carried out the following interesting experiment. They added pepsin obtained from chickens to pepsinogen prepared from pigs, and *vice versa*. Their purpose was to learn whether the pepsin produced would depend on the species of pepsin or on the species of pepsinogen. If pepsin behaved like a living organism, the pepsin formed should be the same as the pepsin added, regardless of the source of the pepsino-

gen, just as the species of bacteria obtained from a culture depends on the species inoculated, not on the nutrients supplied. But the results were just the opposite. Swine pepsin reacting with chicken pepsinogen produced only chicken pepsin, and the mixture of chicken pepsin with swine pepsinogen yielded swine pepsin.

It follows that pepsin is not strictly self-duplicating. The product is determined not by the pepsin but by the material on which it acts. This is not the case with living organisms, as we have seen, and neither is it the case with genes. The reproduction of genes is a *copying* process: they copy themselves when they multiply, and if a gene happens to mutate to a new form, the new type reproduces itself in its mutant version. No such copying process has been found in simple chemical reactions.

Mutation

The mutation of genes has been investigated very extensively by experimental work with X-rays and other radiations. This exploration began in 1927, when Muller, working with Drosophila, and L. J. Stadler, working independently with barley, discovered that treatment of cells with X-rays speeded up the rate of mutation. The alteration of the genes undoubtedly is due to a chemical change, which is caused by the ionization of atoms (*i.e.*, removal of electrons) by the radiation. The main conclusion drawn from the many experiments with radiation is that a single ionization, in the right place, suffices to cause a gene mutation. This conclusion is particularly interesting because it suggests that the gene is a single molecule. Other ideas have strong champions—among them the theory that the only real unit is the chromosome, a kind of supermolecule—but there is little doubt that at the present time the gene-molecule theory provides the most satisfactory general account of the properties and behavior of genes.

From a practical point of view this

MENDELIAN LAWS are illustrated on the opposite page. At top, a plant bearing smooth yellow peas is mated with one bearing wrinkled green peas. In the first generation (*middle*) the plants bear only smooth yellow peas because smooth and yellow are dominant. In the next generation (*bottom*) the plants bear smooth yellow, wrinkled yellow, smooth green and wrinkled green in the approximate ratios 9:3:3:1.

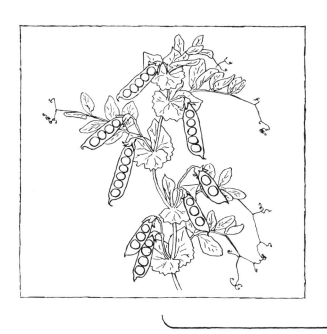
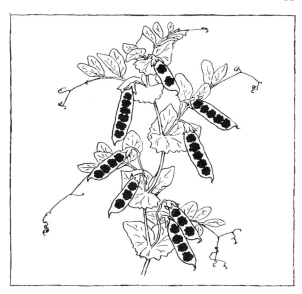

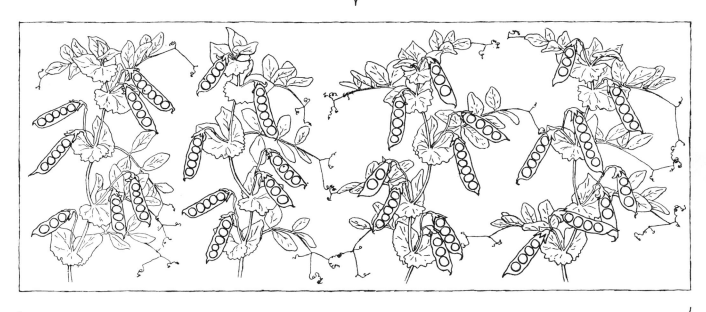

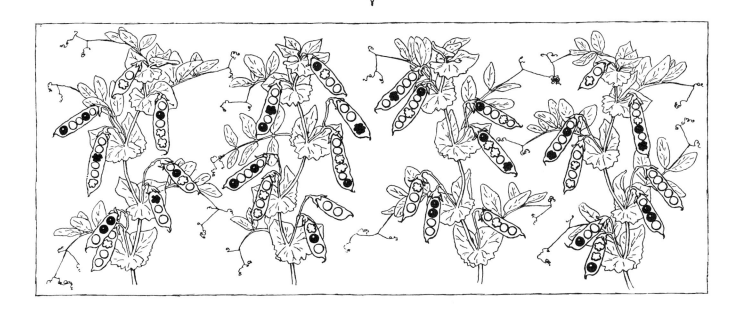

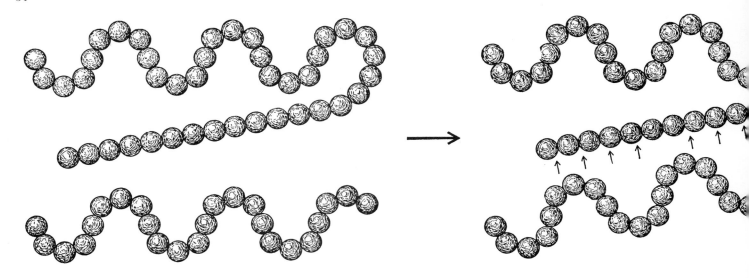

SELF-DUPLICATION OF PEPSIN, an example of autocatalytic reaction in the biosynthesis of proteins, is shown in three steps in this highly schematic diagram. In the first stage (*at left*) a molecule of pepsinogen, the precursor of pepsin, appears at top and a molecule of pepsin below. The beads represent the amino acid units out of which pepsins are made. As indicated, pepsinogen is

interpretation has an important bearing on the possible harmful effects of atomic and other man-made radiations. If the gene is a single molecule, mutable by a single quantum of radiation, then even the smallest exposure to radiation may produce a mutation: in other words, there is no "safe" dose. Experiments bear out this view. Over a wide range of X-ray dosages the frequency of mutation in Drosophila is directly proportional to the number of ionizations, with no indication of a threshold below which mutations are not induced. It is possible that a tolerance level might be found at doses lower than have yet been tested, but such a threshold would be very difficult to detect, because as the dose decreases, we approach the natural, spontaneous

rate of mutation, which acts as a background "noise" to obscure the small additional effect of the radiation. Clearly it would be rash to base one's hopes or the national policy on the chance that a threshold exists. The only reasonable course is to assume that no amount of ionizing radiation, however small, is without an effect on the genes. Knowing that gene mutations are irreparable and for the most part harmful, we must weigh this hazard as best we can against the expected benefits of X-rays and other uses of ionizing radiation.

Genes and Enzymes

The sensitivity of genes to radiation brings us to our second question: How

do genes act on the cell? A gene mutation can sterilize the cell or permanently alter all of its descendants. Considering that this profound effect is triggered by an almost infinitesimal change in the gene—a single ionization—we must conclude that the genes function in a far-reaching way. That is to say, they act not merely as enzymes (which themselves have profound effects in the cell, determining the rate and direction of its chemical activities) but as catalysts for the production of enzymes.

This idea occurred to the early workers in genetics, but techniques for exploring it have not been available until fairly recently. By now it has won strong support, as the result of the pioneer experiments of George W. Beadle and E.

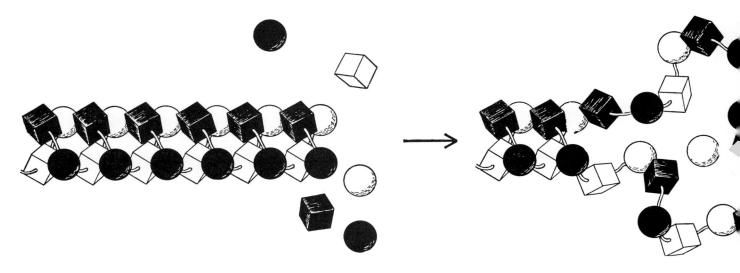

SELF-DUPLICATION OF NUCLEIC ACID, which is thought to be the ultimate genetic material, is shown in three stages in this diagram. In the first stage (*at left*) the nucleic acid is seen as a structure of two helices coiled about one another, with four different nucleotides (represented by cubes and spheres) arranged in complementary order. In the second stage (*center*) the structure

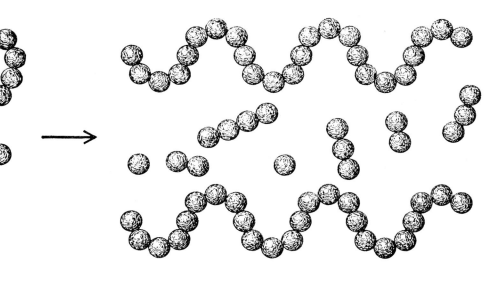

a more complex molecule, incorporating the structure of pepsin itself plus a "tail." In the second stage (*center*) the two molecules enter into reaction with one another. In the third stage the tail has been separated from pepsinogen and there appear two pepsin molecules.

L. Tatum on Neurospora and of many other studies of microorganisms, notably the colon bacillus, *Escherichia coli.* Hundreds of mutations have been produced in these organisms and in each case the effect of the mutation is to abolish the organism's ability to make some essential chemical, for example, a vitamin or an amino acid. The mutation usually blocks just one step in the series of reactions required to make the vitamin or amino acid. It evidently interferes with the production of a single specific enzyme: all the other enzymes involved in catalyzing the series of reactions are apparently unaffected.

In order to account for this selectivity, it is necessary to assume that the structure of the enzyme is related in some way to the structure of the gene. By a logical extension of this idea we arrive at the concept that the gene is a representation—a blueprint, so to speak—of the enzyme molecule, and that the function of the gene is to serve as a source of information regarding the structure of the enzyme. It seems evident that the synthesis of an enzyme—a giant protein molecule consisting of hundreds of amino acid units arranged end-to-end in a specific and unique order—requires a model or set of instructions of some kind. These instructions must be characteristic of the species; they must be automatically transmitted from generation to generation, and they must be constant yet capable of evolutionary change. The only known entity that could perform such a function is the gene. There are many reasons for believing that it transmits information by acting as a model, or template.

If the template theory is correct, a mutant gene may produce a mutant enzyme—an enzyme whose structure and properties are changed in some way. A systematic search for mutations of this sort has been started recently, and already several interesting examples have been found.

In our laboratory at the California Institute of Technology we have been studying an enzyme of Neurospora which converts the amino acid tyrosine into melanin—a black pigment widely distributed in nature (it is the black pigment of hair, skin and of the ink of the squid). We find that this enzyme, tyrosinase, may occur in either of two different forms in Neurospora. The forms differ only in their stability toward heat. At a temperature of 138 degrees Fahrenheit, for example, one form is reduced to half of its original activity in three minutes; the other in 70 minutes. Our experiments show that this difference in stability is inherited in a simple Mendelian way—*i.e.*, it is controlled by a single gene. One form of the gene causes the organism to produce tyrosinase which is comparatively stable to heat; the other yields unstable tyrosinase. It is interesting that the forms of the enzyme produced by the two strains of Neurospora are exactly alike in every detail, as far as we have tested them, except in stability to heat. This fact indicates that the genetic control of enzyme structure is exceedingly fine-grained, permitting the separate alteration, as in this case, of a single feature of that structure.

Another example of a gene which influences the structure of a protein is one affecting the hemoglobin of human blood. There is a mutant which is known as the sickle-cell gene, because it leads to production of a form of hemoglobin that causes the red blood cells to take a sickle shape. Linus Pauling and a group of his co-workers at the California Institute of Technology found that the sickle-cell hemoglobin molecule has a different electric charge from normal hemoglobin. A very interesting feature of the sickle-cell mutation, from the evolutionary point of view, is the fact that it apparently confers resistance to malaria [see "Sickle Cells and Evolution," by Anthony C. Allison; SCIENTIFIC AMERICAN Offprint 1065].

The discovery of structural mutations of proteins is gratifying but is only one step toward a proof of the template theory: to prove conclusively that genes do

uncoils, freeing the components of each helix for attachment to free nucleotide units diffused in the nearby environment. In the third stage (*right*) each helix has bound nucleotide units to itself, thus beginning the formation of two complete new nucleic acid molecules.

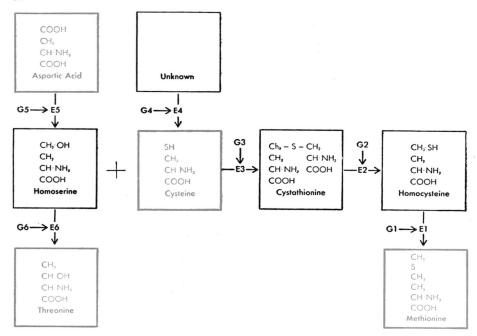

SYNTHESIS OF AMINO ACIDS may be mediated by many genes; absence of any one gene will stop the cycle. Each gene (G) catalyzes a specific enzyme (E) which in turn catalyzes one step in the reaction. Compounds boxed in red lines are stable end-product amino acids.

in fact act as templates, it would have to be demonstrated that every specific property of a protein can be modified by a gene mutation. Experiments along these lines are being pursued actively in several laboratories.

DNA and RNA

Final answers to our first two questions—how genes reproduce themselves and how they function—will not be obtained until we have found the answer to the third: What are they made of? It may seem strange, considering the great power of modern methods of chemical analysis, that the chemical composition of the genetic material in the chromosomes should still be something of a mystery. The explanation is quite simple: no one has ever isolated a gene from any animal or higher plant—at least so far as anyone is aware, for we have no way so far of recognizing a gene after it has been removed from the cell.

Nevertheless, we do have some definite ideas about the chemical nature of

FOUR-LETTER CODE suggests one way in which the four nucleotide components of nucleic acid, here designated as A, B, C, D, may control the synthesis of the 20 different amino acids of which proteins are made.

genes. There is very good evidence that the genetic material of some bacteria and viruses consists of nucleic acid, and there is some reason to believe that this is also true in higher organisms. It has been known for a long time that desoxyribonucleic acid (DNA) is a prominent constituent of the chromosomes; this fact marked it for special attention as possible genic material. A number of studies of bacteria and viruses confirm that it does indeed play a genetic role.

Some years ago a substance with gene-like properties was extracted from heat-killed cells of *Pneumococcus*, the pneumonia organism. Strains of Pneumococcus grown in the presence of this substance acquired hereditary characteristics of the particular strain from which it was derived; the characteristics included virulence, resistance to drugs, the ability to synthesize certain enzymes and so on. The transformations were permanent: they were passed on from generation to generation of the bacteria. Moreover, the substance appeared to be subject to mutation. Eventually Oswald T. Avery, Colin M. MacLeod and Maclyn McCarty of the Rockefeller Institute identified the transforming agent as DNA. More recently a new series of transforming agents, also varieties of DNA, has been found in another species of bacteria, *Hemophilus influenzae*.

In the realm of the viruses, there have been two definite identifications of nu-

cleic acid as genetic material. A. D. Hershey and Martha Chase at the Cold Spring Harbor Biological Laboratory have found that DNA plays a genetic role in a bacterial virus which attacks the bacterium *E. coli*. Heinz Fraenkel-Conrat at the University of California identified the genetic substance of the tobacco mosaic virus as ribonucleic acid (RNA).

All the available evidence thus points toward nucleic acid as the ultimate genetic material. Naturally its chemical structure has come in for a great deal of attention. F. H. C. Crick and J. D. Watson at the University of Cambridge have proposed a structure for DNA which not only accounts for many of its known physical and chemical properties but also seems capable of accounting for the properties of a gene [see "The Structure of the Hereditary Material," by F. H. C. Crick; SCIENTIFIC AMERICAN Offprint 5]. According to their scheme DNA is composed of two close-fitting, complementary chains, each chain consisting of a long series of nucleotides in linear order. There are only four kinds of nucleotides in DNA, but since the number of nucleotide molecules per chain is of the order of 10,000, the number of possible arrangements is very large indeed. Replication of the molecule is thought to involve separation of the two complementary chains, each of which then acts as a template for the synthesis of a new partner.

The idea of the two-stranded structure seems to have a firm basis. However, it is not easy to see how this model can account for template action by genes. The specificity of the Watson-Crick structure rests on the sequence of nucleotides in each chain, suggesting that the genetic information is coded on a linear tape in an alphabet of four symbols. Mutation would consist of the rearrangement, deletion or substitution of parts of this coded message. The difficulty is that whereas the nucleic acid alphabet contains only four symbols (corresponding to the four different nucleotides), the protein alphabet contains 20 or more (corresponding to the 20-odd kinds of amino acids). There is no known mechanism at the present time for translating instructions from the nucleotide code into the amino acid code. But this difficulty may not be insuperable [see "Information Transfer in the Living Cell," by George Gamow; SCIENTIFIC AMERICAN, October, 1955].

Thus for the first time we have a definite working hypothesis as to the structure of the gene. There is, however, a puzzling feature about the present situation. The experiments on the tobacco mosaic virus clearly show that RNA is capable of performing a genetic function. But RNA does not usually act in this way, as far as can be determined. It is found chiefly in the cytoplasm of cells (*i.e.*, outside the nucleus), and genetic experimentation with animals has failed to show any regular mechanism of inheritance in the cytoplasm. Hereditary mechanisms do exist in the cytoplasm of plant cells (for example, in connection with the production of chlorophyll) but they are of minor significance compared to the chromosomal mechanism.

Possibly the RNA that controls heredity in the tobacco mosaic virus (and other plant viruses) is of a different kind from that found in the cytoplasm of animal cells. Such a difference could explain why RNA acts like a gene in one situation and apparently not in the other. But this possibility cannot be tested at the present time, because the chemistry of RNA is still relatively unknown.

The Origin of Life

A general article on the gene ought to make at least some mention of what bearing all this may have on the problem of the origin of life. Probably no question in biology has a wider appeal than this one—especially among nonbiologists. Historically the basic difficulty has been to define "life." Up to the 17th century the most primitive forms of life known were worms, fleas, scorpions and the like, and there was a notion that these creatures originated spontaneously from decaying organic matter. This idea was demolished in 1668 by the Italian physician Francesco Redi, when he showed that no maggots developed in meat shielded from egg-laying insects. But it was reborn at another level when, a few years later, Anton van Leeuwenhoek discovered bacteria. They seemed so small and rudimentary that many people were convinced they must be on the dividing line between living and nonliving matter. Actually bacteria are just as complex as any cell of our own bodies, and their spontaneous origin from nonliving material is not much more likely than the spontaneous generation of scorpions.

Nowadays many biologists and biochemists tend to regard the question of how life started as essentially meaningless. They view living and nonliving matter as forming a continuum, and the drawing of a line between them as arbitrary. Life, on this view, is associated with the complex chemical paraphernalia of the cell—enzymes, membranes, metabolic cycles, etc.—and no one can say at what point it begins. Geneticists are apt to take a different view. If genes are required to produce enzymes, then life began only when they began.

We can imagine the spontaneous origin of some chemical substance capable of reproducing itself, of mutating and of directing the production of specific catalysts in its environment. It would not be long before this substance, trying out new molecular arrangements by blind mutation, began to evolve along lines favored by natural selection. In time all the complexity that is now associated with living matter might well develop.

It may be objected that an unstated assumption is hidden in this theory: namely, that the gene arose in an environment which was already prepared to supply all the materials needed for its multiplication and other chemical activi-

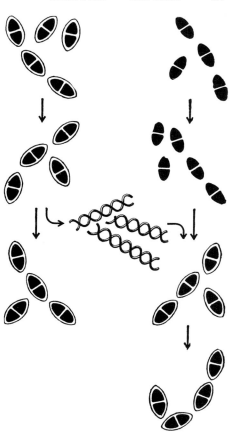

PNEUMOCOCCUS is genetically transformed by mixing cells of one strain with nucleic acid from another. The first strain (*right*) thereupon assumes the characteristics which mark the second strain (*left*).

ties. But if this is an objection, it holds for any theory which supposes that life began in some accidental combination of chemicals. The material of life as we know it could have come into being only in a complex chemical environment.

6

THE GENETIC CODE: III

F. H. C. CRICK
October 1966

The central theme of molecular biology is confirmed by detailed knowledge of how the four-letter language embodied in molecules of nucleic acid controls the 20-letter language of the proteins

The hypothesis that the genes of the living cell contain all the information needed for the cell to reproduce itself is now more than 50 years old. Implicit in the hypothesis is the idea that the genes bear in coded form the detailed specifications for the thousands of kinds of protein molecules the cell requires for its moment-to-moment existence: for extracting energy from molecules assimilated as food and for repairing itself as well as for replication. It is only within the past 15 years, however, that insight has been gained into the chemical nature of the genetic material and how its molecular structure can embody coded instructions that can be "read" by the machinery in the cell responsible for synthesizing protein molecules. As the result of intensive work by many investigators the story

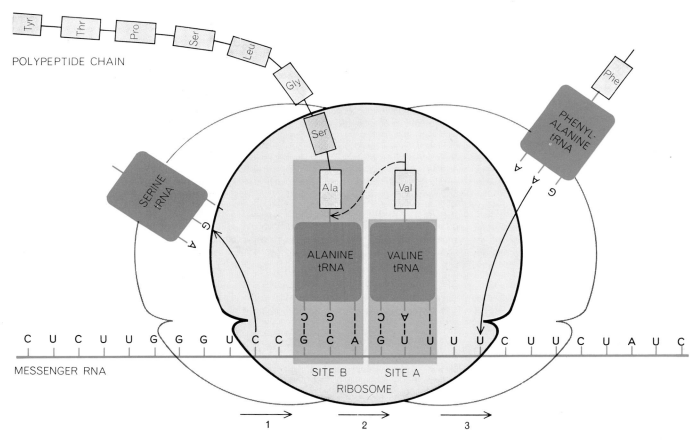

SYNTHESIS OF PROTEIN MOLECULES is accomplished by the intracellular particles called ribosomes. The coded instructions for making the protein molecule are carried to the ribosome by a form of ribonucleic acid (RNA) known as "messenger" RNA. The RNA code "letters" are four bases: uracil (U), cytosine (C), adenine (A) and guanine (G). A sequence of three bases, called a codon, is required to specify each of the 20 kinds of amino acid, identified here by their abbreviations. (A list of the 20 amino acids and their abbreviations appears on the next page.) When linked end to end, these amino acids form the polypeptide chains of which proteins are composed. Each type of amino acid is transported to the ribosome by a particular form of "transfer" RNA (tRNA), which carries an anticodon that can form a temporary bond with one of the codons in messenger RNA. Here the ribosome is shown moving along the chain of messenger RNA, "reading off" the codons in sequence. It appears that the ribosome has two binding sites for molecules of tRNA: one site (*A*) for positioning a newly arrived tRNA molecule and another (*B*) for holding the growing polypeptide chain.

AMINO ACID	ABBREVIATION
ALANINE	Ala
ARGININE	Arg
ASPARAGINE	AspN
ASPARTIC ACID	Asp
CYSTEINE	Cys
GLUTAMIC ACID	Glu
GLUTAMINE	GluN
GLYCINE	Gly
HISTIDINE	His
ISOLEUCINE	Ileu
LEUCINE	Leu
LYSINE	Lys
METHIONINE	Met
PHENYLALANINE	Phe
PROLINE	Pro
SERINE	Ser
THREONINE	Thr
TRYPTOPHAN	Tryp
TYROSINE	Tyr
VALINE	Val

TWENTY AMINO ACIDS constitute the standard set found in all proteins. A few other amino acids occur infrequently in proteins but it is suspected in each case that they originate as one of the standard set and become chemically modified after they have been incorporated into a polypeptide chain.

of the genetic code is now essentially complete. One can trace the transmission of the coded message from its original site in the genetic material to the finished protein molecule.

The genetic material of the living cell is the chainlike molecule of deoxyribonucleic acid (DNA). The cells of many bacteria have only a single chain; the cells of mammals have dozens clustered together in chromosomes. The DNA molecules have a very long backbone made up of repeating groups of phosphate and a five-carbon sugar. To this backbone the side groups called bases are attached at regular intervals. There are four standard bases: adenine (A), guanine (G), thymine (T) and cytosine (C). They are the four "letters" used to spell out the genetic message. The exact sequence of bases along a length of the DNA molecule determines the structure of a particular protein molecule.

Proteins are synthesized from a standard set of 20 amino acids, uniform throughout nature, that are joined end to end to form the long polypeptide chains of protein molecules [see illustration at left]. Each protein has its own characteristic sequence of amino acids. The number of amino acids in a polypeptide chain ranges typically from 100 to 300 or more.

The genetic code is not the message itself but the "dictionary" used by the cell to translate from the four-letter language of nucleic acid to the 20-letter language of protein. The machinery of the cell can translate in one direction only: from nucleic acid to protein but not from protein to nucleic acid. In making this translation the cell employs a variety of accessory molecules and mechanisms. The message contained in DNA is first transcribed into the similar molecule called "messenger" ribonucleic acid—messenger RNA. (In many viruses—the tobacco mosaic virus, for example—the genetic material is simply RNA.) RNA too has four kinds of bases as side groups; three are identical with those found in DNA (adenine, guanine and cytosine) but the fourth is uracil (U) instead of thymine. In this first transcription of the genetic message the code letters A, G, T and C in DNA give rise respectively to U, C, A and G. In other words, wherever A appears in DNA, U appears in the RNA transcription; wherever G appears in DNA, C appears in the transcription, and so on. As it is usually presented the dictionary of the genetic code employs the letters found in RNA (U, C, A, G) rather than those found in DNA (A, G, T, C).

The genetic code could be broken easily if one could determine both the amino acid sequence of a protein and the base sequence of the piece of nucleic acid that codes it. A simple comparison of the two sequences would yield the code. Unfortunately the determination of the base sequence of a long nucleic acid molecule is, for a variety of reasons, still extremely difficult. More indirect approaches must be used.

Most of the genetic code first became known early in 1965. Since then additional evidence has proved that almost all of it is correct, although a few features remain uncertain. This article describes how the code was discovered and some of the work that supports it.

Scientific American has already presented a number of articles on the genetic code. In one of them ["The Genetic Code," Offprint 123] I explained that the experimental evidence (mainly indirect) suggested that the code was a triplet code: that the bases on the messenger RNA were read three at a time and that each group corresponded to a particular amino acid. Such a group is called a codon. Using four symbols in groups of three, one can form 64 distinct triplets. The evidence indicated that most of these stood for one amino acid or another, implying that an amino acid was usually represented by several codons. Adjacent amino acids were coded by adjacent codons, which did not overlap.

In a sequel to that article ["The Genetic Code: II," Offprint 153] Marshall W. Nirenberg of the National Institutes of Health explained how the composition of many of the 64 triplets had been determined by actual experiment. The technique was to synthesize polypeptide chains in a cell-free system, which was made by breaking open cells of the colon bacillus (*Escherichia coli*) and extracting from them the machinery for protein synthesis. Then the system was provided with an energy supply, 20 amino acids and one or another of several types of synthetic RNA. Although the exact sequence of bases in each type was random, the proportion of bases was known. It was found that each type of synthetic messenger RNA directed the incorporation of certain amino acids only.

By means of this method, used in a quantitative way, the *composition* of many of the codons was obtained, but the *order* of bases in any triplet could not be determined. Codons rich in G were difficult to study, and in addition a few mistakes crept in. Of the 40 codon compositions listed by Nirenberg in his article we now know that 35 were correct.

The Triplet Code

The main outlines of the genetic code were elucidated by another technique invented by Nirenberg and Philip Leder. In this method no protein synthesis occurs. Instead one triplet at a time is used to bind together parts of the machinery of protein synthesis.

Protein synthesis takes place on the comparatively large intracellular structures known as ribosomes. These bodies travel along the chain of messenger RNA, reading off its triplets one after another and synthesizing the polypeptide chain of the protein, starting at the amino end (NH_2). The amino acids do not diffuse to the ribosomes by themselves. Each amino acid is joined chemically by a special enzyme to one of the codon-recognizing molecules known both as soluble RNA (sRNA) and transfer RNA (tRNA). (I prefer the latter designation.) Each tRNA molecule has its own triplet of bases, called an anticodon, that recognizes the relevant codon on the messenger RNA by pairing bases with it [*see illustration on page* 59].

Leder and Nirenberg studied which amino acid, joined to its tRNA molecules, was bound to the ribosomes in the presence of a particular triplet, that is, by a "message" with just three letters. They did so by the neat trick of passing the mixture over a nitrocellulose filter that retained the ribosomes. All the tRNA molecules passed through the filter except the ones specifically bound to the ribosomes by the triplet. Which they were could easily be decided by using mixtures of amino acids in which one kind of amino acid had been made artificially radioactive, and determining the amount of radioactivity absorbed by the filter.

For example, the triplet GUU retained the tRNA for the amino acid valine, whereas the triplets UGU and UUG did not. (Here GUU actually stands for the trinucleoside diphosphate GpUpU.) Further experiments showed that UGU coded for cysteine and UUG for leucine.

Nirenberg and his colleagues synthesized all 64 triplets and tested them for their coding properties. Similar results have been obtained by H. Gobind Khorana and his co-workers at the University of Wisconsin. Various other groups have checked a smaller number of codon assignments.

Close to 50 of the 64 triplets give a clearly unambiguous answer in the binding test. Of the remainder some evince only weak binding and some bind more than one kind of amino acid. Other results I shall describe later suggest that the multiple binding is often an artifact of the binding method. In short, the binding test gives the meaning of the majority of the triplets but it does not firmly establish all of them.

The genetic code obtained in this way, with a few additions secured by other methods, is shown in the table below. The 64 possible triplets are set out in a regular array, following a plan

SECOND LETTER

FIRST LETTER	U	C	A	G	THIRD LETTER
U	UUU, UUC: Phe UUA, UUG: Leu	UCU, UCC, UCA, UCG: Ser	UAU, UAC: Tyr UAA: OCHRE UAG: AMBER	UGU, UGC: Cys UGA: ? UGG: Tryp	U C A G
C	CUU, CUC, CUA, CUG: Leu	CCU, CCC, CCA, CCG: Pro	CAU, CAC: His CAA, CAG: GluN	CGU, CGC, CGA, CGG: Arg	U C A G
A	AUU, AUC, AUA: Ileu AUG: Met	ACU, ACC, ACA, ACG: Thr	AAU, AAC: AspN AAA, AAG: Lys	AGU, AGC: Ser AGA, AGG: Arg	U C A G
G	GUU, GUC, GUA, GUG: Val	GCU, GCC, GCA, GCG: Ala	GAU, GAC: Asp GAA, GAG: Glu	GGU, GGC, GGA, GGG: Gly	U C A G

GENETIC CODE, consisting of 64 triplet combinations and their corresponding amino acids, is shown in its most likely version. The importance of the first two letters in each triplet is readily apparent. Some of the allocations are still not completely certain, particularly for organisms other than the colon bacillus (*Escherichia coli*). "Amber" and "ochre" are terms that referred originally to certain mutant strains of bacteria. They designate two triplets, UAA and UAG, that may act as signals for terminating polypeptide chains.

that clarifies the relations between them.

Inspection of the table will show that the triplets coding for the same amino acid are often rather similar. For example, all four of the triplets starting with the doublet AC code for threonine. This pattern also holds for seven of the other amino acids. In every case the triplets XYU and XYC code for the same amino acid, and in many cases XYA and XYG are the same (methionine and tryptophan may be exceptions). Thus an amino acid is largely selected by the first two bases of the triplet. Given that a triplet codes for, say, valine, we know that the first two bases are GU, whatever the third may be. This pattern is true for all but three of the amino acids. Leucine can start with UU or CU, serine with UC or AG and arginine with CG or AG. In all other cases the amino acid is uniquely related to the first two bases of the triplet. Of course, the converse is often not true. Given that a triplet starts with, say, CA, it may code for either histidine or glutamine.

Synthetic Messenger RNA's

Probably the most direct way to confirm the genetic code is to synthesize a messenger RNA molecule with a strictly defined base sequence and then find the amino acid sequence of the polypeptide produced under its influence. The most extensive work of this nature has been done by Khorana and his colleagues. By a brilliant combination of ordinary chemical synthesis and synthesis catalyzed by enzymes, they have made long RNA molecules with various repeating sequences of bases. As an example, one RNA molecule they have synthesized has the sequence UGUG-UGUGUGUG.... When the biochemical machinery reads this as triplets the message is UGU–GUG–UGU–GUG.... Thus we expect that a polypeptide will be produced with an alternating sequence of two amino acids. In fact, it was found that the product is Cys–Val–Cys–Val.... This evidence alone would not tell us which triplet goes with which amino acid, but given the results of the binding test one has no hesitation in concluding that UGU codes for cysteine and GUG for valine.

In the same way Khorana has made chains with repeating sequences of the type XYZ... and also XXYZ.... The type XYZ... would be expected to give a "homopolypeptide" containing one amino acid corresponding to the triplet XYZ. Because the starting point is not clearly defined, however, the homopolypeptides corresponding to YZX... and ZXY... will also be produced. Thus

poly-AUC makes polyisoleucine, polyserine and polyhistidine. This confirms that AUC codes for isoleucine, UCA for serine and CAU for histidine. A repeating sequence of four bases will yield a single type of polypeptide with a repeating sequence of four amino acids. The general patterns to be expected in each case are set forth in the table on this page. The results to date have amply demonstrated by a direct biochemical method that the code is indeed a triplet code.

Khorana and his colleagues have so far confirmed about 25 triplets by this method, including several that were quite doubtful on the basis of the binding test. They plan to synthesize other sequences, so that eventually most of the triplets will be checked in this way.

The Use of Mutations

The two methods described so far are open to the objection that since they do not involve intact cells there may be some danger of false results. This objection can be met by two other methods of checking the code in which the act of protein synthesis takes place inside the cell. Both involve the effects of genetic mutations on the amino acid sequence of a protein.

It is now known that small mutations are normally of two types: "base substitution" mutants and "phase shift" mutants. In the first type one base is changed into another base but the total number of bases remains the same. In the second, one or a small number of bases are added to the message or subtracted from it.

There are now extensive data on base-substitution mutants, mainly from studies of three rather convenient proteins: human hemoglobin, the protein of tobacco mosaic virus and the A protein of the enzyme tryptophan synthetase obtained from the colon bacillus. At least 36 abnormal types of human hemoglobin have now been investigated by many different workers. More than 40 mutant forms of the protein of the tobacco mosaic virus have been examined by Hans Wittmann of the Max Planck Institute for Molecular Genetics in Tübingen and by Akita Tsugita and Heinz Fraenkel-Conrat of the University of California at Berkeley [see "The Genetic Code of a Virus," by Heinz Fraenkel-Conrat; SCIENTIFIC AMERICAN Offprint 193]. Charles Yanofsky and his group at Stanford University have characterized about 25 different mutations of the A protein of tryptophan synthetase.

RNA BASE SEQUENCE	READ AS	AMINO ACID SEQUENCE EXPECTED
(XY)ₙ . . .	X Y X Y X Y X Y X Y X Y . . .	αβαβ
(XYZ)ₙ . . .	X Y Z X Y Z X Y Z . . .	ααα
. . .	Y Z X Y Z X Y Z X . . .	βββ
. . .	Z X Y Z X Y Z X Y . . .	γγγ
(XXYZ)ₙ . . .	X X Y Z X X Y Z X X Y Z . . .	αβγδαβγδ
(XYXZ)ₙ . . .	X Y X Z X Y X Z X Y X Z . . .	αβγδαβγδ

VARIETY OF SYNTHETIC RNA's with repeating sequences of bases have been produced by H. Gobind Khorana and his colleagues at the University of Wisconsin. They contain two or three different bases (X, Y, Z) in groups of two, three or four. When introduced into cell-free systems containing the machinery for protein synthesis, the base sequences are read off as triplets (*middle*) and yield the amino acid sequences indicated at the right.

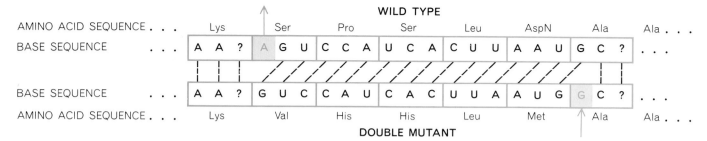

"PHASE SHIFT" MUTATIONS help to establish the actual codons used by organisms in the synthesis of protein. The two partial amino acid sequences shown here were determined by George Streisinger and his colleagues at the University of Oregon. The sequences are from a protein, a type of lysozyme, produced by the bacterial virus T4. A pair of phase-shift mutations evidently removed one base, A, and inserted another, G, about 15 bases farther on. The base sequence was deduced theoretically from the genetic code.

The remarkable fact has emerged that in every case but one the genetic code shows that the change of an amino acid in a polypeptide chain could have been caused by the alteration of a single base in the relevant nucleic acid. For example, the first observed change of an amino acid by mutation (in the hemoglobin of a person suffering from sickle-cell anemia) was from glutamic acid to valine. From the genetic code dictionary on page 61 we see that this could have resulted from a mutation that changed either GAA to GUA or GAG to GUG. In either case the change involved a single base in the several hundred needed to code for one of the two kinds of chain in hemoglobin.

The one exception so far to the rule that all amino acid changes could be caused by single base changes has been found by Yanofsky. In this one case glutamic acid was replaced by methionine. It can be seen from the genetic code dictionary that this can be accomplished only by a change of *two* bases, since glutamic acid is encoded by either GAA or GAG and methionine is encoded only by AUG. This mutation has occurred only once, however, and of all the mutations studied by Yanofsky it is the only one not to back-mutate, or revert to "wild type." It is thus almost certainly the rare case of a double change. All the other cases fit the hypothesis that base-substitution mutations are normally caused by a single base change. Examination of the code shows that only about 40 percent of all the possible amino acid interchanges can be brought about by single base substitutions, and it is only these changes that are found in experiments. Therefore the study of actual mutations has provided strong confirmation of many features of the genetic code.

Because in general several codons stand for one amino acid it is not possible, knowing the amino acid sequence, to write down the exact RNA base sequence that encoded it. This is unfortu-nate. If we know which amino acid is changed into another by mutation, however, we can often, given the code, work out what that base change must have been. As an example, glutamic acid can be encoded by GAA or GAG and valine by GUU, GUC, GUA or GUG. If a mutation substitutes valine for glutamic acid, one can assume that only a single base change was involved. The only such change that could lead to the desired result would be a change from A to U in the middle position, and this would be true whether GAA became GUA or GAG became GUG.

It is thus possible in many cases (not in all) to compare the nature of the base change with the chemical mutagen used to produce the change. If RNA is treated with nitrous acid, C is changed to U and A is effectively changed to G. On the other hand, if double-strand DNA is treated under the right conditions with hydroxylamine, the mutagen acts only on C. As a result some C's are changed to T's (the DNA equivalent of U's), and thus G's, which are normally paired with C's in double-strand DNA, are replaced by A's.

If 2-aminopurine, a "base analogue" mutagen, is added when double-strand DNA is undergoing replication, it produces only "transitions." These are the same changes as those produced by hydroxylamine—plus the reverse changes. In almost all these different cases (the exceptions are unimportant) the changes observed are those expected from our knowledge of the genetic code.

Note the remarkable fact that, although the code was deduced mainly from studies of the colon bacillus, it appears to apply equally to human beings and tobacco plants. This, together with more fragmentary evidence, suggests that the genetic code is either the same or very similar in most organisms.

The second method of checking the code using intact cells depends on phase-shift mutations such as the addi-tion of a single base to the message. Phase-shift mutations probably result from errors produced during genetic recombination or when the DNA molecule is being duplicated. Such errors have the effect of putting out of phase the reading of the message from that point on. This hypothesis leads to the prediction that the phase can be corrected if at some subsequent point a nucleotide is deleted. The pair of alterations would be expected not only to change two amino acids but also to alter all those encoded by bases lying between the two affected sites. The reason is that the intervening bases would be read out of phase and therefore grouped into triplets different from those contained in the normal message.

This expectation has recently been confirmed by George Streisinger and his colleagues at the University of Oregon. They have studied mutations in the protein lysozyme that were produced by the T4 virus, which infects the colon bacillus. One phase-shift mutation involved the amino acid sequence ...Lys—Ser—Pro—Ser—Leu—AspN—Ala—Ala—Lys.... They were then able to construct by genetic methods a double phase-shift mutant in which the corresponding sequence was ...Lys—Val—His—His—Leu—Met—Ala—Ala—Lys....

Given these two sequences, the reader should be able, using the genetic code dictionary on page 61, to decipher uniquely a short length of the nucleic acid message for both the original protein and the double mutant and thus deduce the changes produced by each of the phase-shift mutations. The correct result is presented in the illustration above. The result not only confirms several rather doubtful codons, such as UUA for leucine and AGU for serine, but also shows which codons are actually involved in a genetic message. Since the technique is difficult, however, it may not find wide application.

Streisinger's work also demonstrates what has so far been only tacitly as-

ANTICODON	CODON
U	A G
C	G
A	U
G	U C
I	U C A

"WOBBLE" HYPOTHESIS has been proposed by the author to provide rules for the pairing of codon and anticodon at the *third* position of the codon. There is evidence, for example, that the anticodon base I, which stands for inosine, may pair with as many as three different bases: U, C and A. Inosine closely resembles the base guanine (G) and so would ordinarily be expected to pair with cytosine (C). Structural diagrams for standard base pairings and wobble base pairings are illustrated at the bottom of this page.

sumed: that the two languages, both of which are written down in a certain direction according to convention, are in fact translated by the cell in the same direction and not in opposite directions. This fact had previously been established, with more direct chemical methods, by Severo Ochoa and his colleagues at the New York University School of Medicine. In the convention, which was adopted by chance, proteins are written with the amino (NH_2) end on the left. Nucleic acids are written with the end of the molecule containing a "5 prime" carbon atom at the left. (The "5 prime" refers to a particular carbon atom in the 5-carbon ring of ribose sugar or deoxyribose sugar.)

Finding the Anticodons

Still another method of checking the genetic code is to discover the three bases making up the anticodon in some particular variety of transfer RNA. The first tRNA to have its entire sequence worked out was alanine tRNA, a job done by Robert W. Holley and his collaborators at Cornell University [see "The Nucleotide Sequence of a Nucleic Acid," by Robert W. Holley; SCIENTIFIC AMERICAN Offprint 1033]. Alanine tRNA, obtained from yeast, contains 77 bases. A possible anticodon found near the middle of the molecule has the sequence IGC, where I stands for inosine, a base closely resembling guanine. Since then Hans Zachau and his colleagues at the University of Cologne have established the sequences of two closely related serine tRNA's from yeast, and James Madison and his group at the U.S. Plant, Soil and Nutrition Laboratory at Ithaca, N.Y., have worked out the sequence of a tyrosine tRNA, also from yeast.

A detailed comparison of these three sequences makes it almost certain that the anticodons are alanine–IGC, serine–IGA and tyrosine–GΨA. (Ψ stands for pseudo-uridylic acid, which can form the same base pairs as the base uracil.) In addition there is preliminary evidence from other workers that an anticodon for valine is IAC and an anticodon for phenylalanine is GAA.

All these results would fit the rule that the codon and anticodon pair in an antiparallel manner, and that the pairing in the first two positions of the codon is of the standard type, that is, A pairs with U and G pairs with C. The pairing in the third position of the codon is more complicated. There is now good experimental evidence from both Nirenberg and Khorana and their co-workers that one tRNA can recognize several codons, provided that they differ only in the last place in the codon. Thus Holley's alanine tRNA appears to recognize GCU, GCC and GCA. If it recognizes GCG, it does so only very weakly.

The "Wobble" Hypothesis

I have suggested that this is because of a "wobble" in the pairing in the third place and have shown that a reasonable theoretical model will explain many of the observed results. The suggested rules for the pairing in the third position of the anticodon are presented in the table at the top of this page, but this theory is still speculative. The rules for the first two places of the codon seem reasonably secure, however, and can be used as partial confirmation of the genetic code. The likely codon-anticodon pairings for valine, serine, tyrosine, alanine and phenylalanine satisfy the standard base pairings in the first two places and the wobble hypothesis in the third place [see *illustration on page 65*].

Several points about the genetic code remain to be cleared up. For example, the triplet UGA has still to be allocated.

STANDARD AND WOBBLE BASE PAIRINGS both involve the formation of hydrogen bonds when certain bases are brought into close proximity. In the standard guanine-cytosine pairing (*left*) it is believed three hydrogen bonds are formed. The bases are shown as they exist in the RNA molecule, where they are attached to 5-carbon rings of ribose sugar. In the proposed wobble pairing (*right*) guanine is linked to uracil by only two hydrogen bonds. The base inosine (I) has a single hydrogen atom where guanine has an amino (NH_2) group (*broken circle*). In the author's wobble hypothesis inosine can pair with U as well as with C and A (*not shown*).

The punctuation marks—the signals for "begin chain" and "end chain"—are only partly understood. It seems likely that both the triplet UAA (called "ochre") and UAG (called "amber") can terminate the polypeptide chain, but which triplet is normally found at the end of a gene is still uncertain.

The picturesque terms for these two triplets originated when it was discovered in studies of the colon bacillus some years ago that mutations in other genes (mutations that in fact cause errors in chain termination) could "suppress" the action of certain mutant codons, now identified as either UAA or UAG. The terms "ochre" and "amber" are simply invented designations and have no reference to color.

A mechanism for chain initiation was discovered fairly recently. In the colon bacillus it seems certain that formylmethionine, carried by a special tRNA, can initiate chains, although it is not clear if all chains have to start in this way, or what the mechanism is in mammals and other species. The formyl group (CHO) is not normally found on finished proteins, suggesting that it is probably removed by a special enzyme. It seems likely that sometimes the methionine is removed as well.

It is unfortunately possible that a few codons may be ambiguous, that is, may code for more than one amino acid. This is certainly not true of most codons. The present evidence for a small amount of ambiguity is suggestive but not conclusive. It will make the code more difficult to establish correctly if ambiguity can occur.

Problems for the Future

From what has been said it is clear that, although the entire genetic code

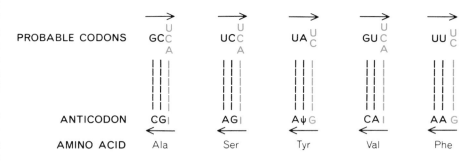

CODON-ANTICODON PAIRINGS take place in an antiparallel direction. Thus the anticodons are shown here written backward, as opposed to the way they appear in the text. The five anticodons are those tentatively identified in the transfer RNA's for alanine, serine, tyrosine, valine and phenylalanine. Color indicates where wobble pairings may occur.

is not known with complete certainty, it is highly likely that most of it is correct. Further work will surely clear up the doubtful codons, clarify the punctuation marks, delimit ambiguity and extend the code to many other species. Although the code lists the codons that *may* be used, we still have to determine if alternative codons are used equally. Some preliminary work suggests they may not be. There is also still much to be discovered about the machinery of protein synthesis. How many types of tRNA are there? What is the structure of the ribosome? How does it work, and why is it in two parts? In addition there are many questions concerning the control of the rate of protein synthesis that we are still a long way from answering.

When such questions have been answered, the major unsolved problem will be the structure of the genetic code. Is the present code merely the result of a series of evolutionary accidents, so that the allocations of triplets to amino acids is to some extent arbitrary? Or are there

profound structural reasons why phenylalanine has to be coded by UUU and UUC and by no other triplets? Such questions will be difficult to decide, since the genetic code originated at least three billion years ago, and it may be impossible to reconstruct the sequence of events that took place at such a remote period. The origin of the code is very close to the origin of life. Unless we are lucky it is likely that much of the evidence we should like to have has long since disappeared.

Nevertheless, the genetic code is a major milestone on the long road of molecular biology. In showing in detail how the four-letter language of nucleic acid controls the 20-letter language of protein it confirms the central theme of molecular biology that genetic information can be stored as a one-dimensional message on nucleic acid and be expressed as the one-dimensional amino acid sequence of a protein. Many problems remain, but this knowledge is now secure.

7

IONIZING RADIATION AND EVOLUTION

JAMES F. CROW

September 1959

Living things evolve as a result of random mutations in hereditary characteristics that survive when they make the organism more fit. What role does ionizing radiation play in the evolutionary process?

The mutant gene—a fundamental unit in the mechanism of heredity that has been altered by some cause, thereby changing some characteristic of its bearers—is the raw material of evolution. Ionizing radiation produces mutation. Ergo, ionizing radiation is an important cause of evolution.

At first this seems like a compelling argument. But is it really? To what extent is the natural rate at which mutations occur dependent upon radiation? Would evolution have been much the same without radiation? Is it possible that increased exposure to radiation, rising from human activities, has a significant effect upon the future course of human evolution?

Radiation has been of tremendous value for genetic research, and therefore for research in evolution. To clarify the issue at the outset, however, it is likely that ionizing radiation has played only a minor role in the recent evolutionary history of most organisms. As for the earliest stages of evolution, starting with the origin of life, it is problematical whether ionizing radiation played a significant role even then. Laboratory experiments show that organic compounds, including the amino acid units of the protein molecule, may be formed from simple nitrogen and carbon compounds upon exposure to ionizing radiation or an electric discharge. But ultraviolet radiation serves as well in these demonstrations, and was probably present in large amounts at the earliest ages of life. In the subsequent history of life the development of photosynthesis in plants and of vision in animals indicates the much greater importance of nonionizing radiation in the terrestrial environment.

Nonetheless, as will be seen, man presents an important special case in any discussion of the mutation-inducing effects of ionizing radiation. The mutation rate affects not only the evolution of the human species but also the life of the individual. Almost every mutation is harmful, and it is the individual who pays the price. Any human activity that tends to increase the mutation rate must therefore raise serious health and moral problems for man.

H. J. Muller's great discovery that radiation induces mutations in the fruit fly *Drosophila*, and its independent confirmation in plants by L. J. Stadler, was made more than 30 years ago. One of the first things to be noticed by the Drosophila workers was that most of the radiation-induced changes in the characteristics of their flies were familiar, the same changes having occurred repeatedly as a result of natural mutation. Not only were the external appearances of the mutant flies recognizable (white eyes, yellow body, forked bristles, missing wing-veins); it could also be shown that the mutant genes were located at the same sites on the chromosomes as their naturally occurring predecessors. Thus it seems that radiation-induced mutants are not unique; they are the same types that occur anyhow at a lower rate and that we call spontaneous because we do not know their causes.

The prevailing hypothesis is that the hereditary information is encoded in various permutations in the arrangement of subunits of the molecule of deoxyribonucleic acid (DNA) in the chromosomes. A mutation occurs when this molecule fails, for some reason, to replicate itself exactly. The mutated gene is thereafter reproduced until its bearer dies without reproducing, or until, by chance, the altered gene mutates again.

A variety of treatments other than radiation will induce mutation. Most agents, including radiation, seem to affect the genes indiscriminately, increasing the mutation rate for all genes in the same proportion. But some chemical mutagens are fairly selective in the genes they affect. It is even conceivable that investigators may find a chemical that will regularly mutate a particular gene and no other. This will probably be very difficult to achieve: A mutagen capable of affecting a specific gene would probably have to have the same order of informational complexity as the gene itself in order to recognize the gene and influence it.

Moreover, different mutant genes known to be at different locations on the chromosome frequently produce effects that mimic each other. Geneticists who work with fruit flies are familiar with several different genes that result in indistinguishable eye colors. This is not surprising when we consider the complexity of the relationship between the genes and the characteristics that they produce. There are many different paths by which any particular end-point may be reached; it is to be expected that many different gene changes can lead to the same result, though the chemical pathways by which this is accomplished may be greatly different.

To consider another kind of example, many insects have come to survive insecticides. They do so by such diverse means as behavior patterns that enable them to avoid the insecticide, mechanisms that interfere with the entrance of the insecticide into the body, enzymes that detoxify the insecticide, and by somehow becoming able to tolerate more of the insecticide. All these modes of survival develop by selection of mutant genes that are already present in low frequency in the population. This is one of the characteristic features of evolution: its opportunism. It makes use of the raw materials—that is, the mutant genes—that happen to be available.

As a first conclusion it appears that radiation-induced mutations do not play any unique role in evolution. The same gene mutations would probably occur anyhow. Even if they did not, the same end result could be achieved with other mutants.

One might still suspect that spontaneous mutations are caused by natural radiations. This was quickly ruled out as a possibility in Drosophila. For one thing, the spontaneous-mutation rate is strongly dependent upon temperature, which would be surprising if mutation were a simple and direct consequence of

radiation. But much more decisive evidence comes from the fact that the amount of natural radiation is entirely inadequate to account for the rate of spontaneous mutation. The natural-mutation rate in Drosophila, if it were caused solely by radiation, would require 50 or more r. Yet the amount of radiation received by a fly in the 12-day interval between egg and mature adult is about .004 r. Natural radiation would have to be increased more than 10,000 times to account for the natural Drosophila mutation rate! Thus, in Drosophila at least, radiation accounts for only a trivial part of the spontaneous rate. The same is true for mice. Although the fraction of spontaneous mutations that owe their origin to radiation is higher than that in Drosophila, it is still less than .1 per cent.

It is clear that natural-mutation rates, if they are measured in absolute time-units, cannot be the same in all organisms. One example will demonstrate this decisively. The spontaneous-mutation rate in Drosophila is such that about one embryo in 50 carries a lethal mutation (a mutation harmful enough to cause death) that occurred during the preceding generation. Most such mutations are recessive, that is, they have a lethal effect only when they are in a double dose, but this does not prevent the death; it only postpones it. The reproductive life-cycle in man is approximately 1,000 times as long as that of a fly: some 30 years as compared with 12 days. If the absolute mutation-rate in man were the same as that in Drosophila, each human embryo would bear an average of 20

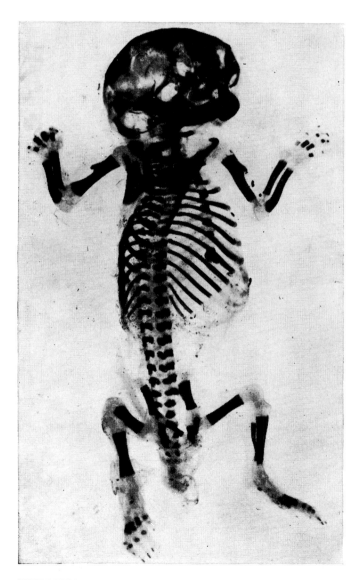
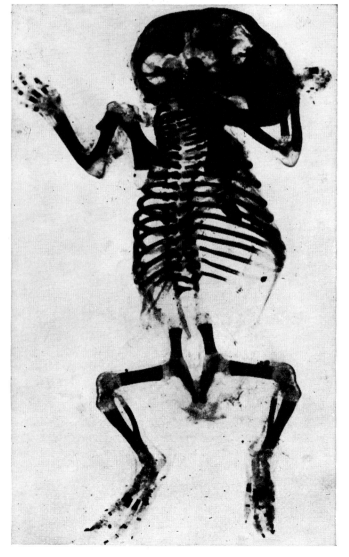

MUTATION of a single gene in a mouse results in offspring that have an unusually short tail (*skeleton at left*). A mouse that receives such a mutant gene from both of its parents has more serious defects, including the absence of the lower part of its spine (*skeleton at right*); it dies soon after birth. These specimens were prepared in the laboratory of L. C. Dunn of Columbia University. The soft tissues were treated with strong alkali and glycerin to make them transparent; the bones were stained with a red dye.

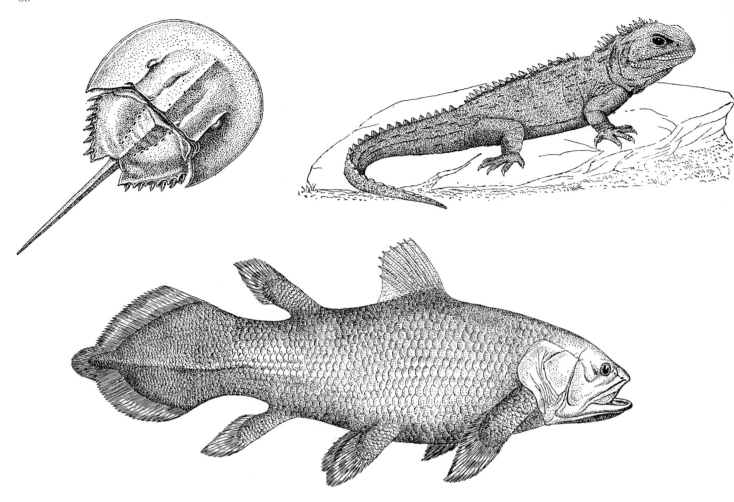

RATE OF EVOLUTION in certain organisms is extremely slow. Depicted in these drawings are four animals that have not changed appreciably over a period of millions or even hundreds of millions of years. At top left is the horseshoe crab; at top center, the tuatara;

new lethal mutations; man would quickly become extinct.

Actually, if the rate is measured in mutations per generation, the spontaneous-mutation rate of those few human genes whose mutation rates can be effectively measured is roughly the same as that of Drosophila genes. The rule seems to be that the absolute mutation-rate divided by the generation period is much more nearly constant from one species to another than the rate itself. The implication of this is exciting. It can only mean that the mutation rate itself is capable of modification; that it, too, is changed by natural selection. By being brought into adjustment with the life cycle, the underlying mechanism of evolution itself is undergoing evolution!

It appears, however, that the rates of radiation-induced mutations are not as readily modified. If these rates were being adjusted along with the rates of mutations from other causes, we would expect that mice would show a lesser response to radiation than do fruit flies be-cause their life cycle is longer. The facts are otherwise; mouse genes average some 15 times as many mutations per unit of radiation as Drosophila genes.

This strongly suggests that the process whereby mutations are produced by radiation is less capable of evolutionary adjustment than other mutation-producing processes. The implication is that organisms with a long life-cycle—Sequoia trees, elephants, men—have a larger fraction of mutations due to natural radiations. It may be that the majority of mutations in a very long-lived organism are due to radiations. Possibly this sets an upper limit on the length of the life cycle.

Unfortunately the rate of radiation-induced mutations is not known for any organism with a long life-cycle. If we assume that the susceptibility of human genes to mutation by radiation is the same as that of mouse genes, we would conclude that less than 10 per cent of human mutations are due to natural radiations. But the exact fraction is quite uncertain, because of inaccurate knowledge of the rate of spontaneous human mutations. So it cannot be ruled out that even a majority of human mutations owe their origin to radiation.

Thus the over-all mutation rate is not determined by radiation to any significant extent, except possibly in some very long-lived organisms. In general, radiation does not seem to play an important role in evolution, either by supplying qualitatively unique types of mutations or by supplying quantitatively significant numbers of mutations.

There is another question: To what extent is the rate of evolution dependent on the mutation rate? Will an organism with a high mutation-rate have a correspondingly higher rate of evolution? In general, the answer is probably no.

The measurement of evolutionary rates is fraught with difficulty and doubt. There is always some uncertainty about the time-scale, despite steady improvements in paleontology and new techniques of dating by means of the decay

at bottom center, the recently discovered coelacanth; at the far right, the opossum.

of radioactive isotopes. In addition there is the difficulty of determining what a comparable rate of advance in different species is. Is the difference between a leopard and a tiger more or less than that between a field mouse and a house mouse? Or has man changed more in developing his brain than the elephant has by growing a trunk? How is it possible for one to devise a suitable scale by which such different things can be compared?

Despite these difficulties, the differences in rates of evolution in various lines of descent are so enormous as to be clear by any standard. One criterion is size. Some animals have changed greatly. The horse has grown from a fox-sized ancestor to its present size while many other animals have not changed appreciably. (The British biologist J. B. S. Haldane has suggested that the word "darwin" be used as a unit for rate of size change. One darwin is taken to be an increase by a factor e per million years. By this criterion the rate of evolution of tooth size in the ancestors of the horse was about 40 millidarwins.)

More difficult to quantify, but more significant, are changes in structure. Some animals have changed very little in enormous lengths of time. There are several examples of "living fossils," some of which are depicted on the preceding two pages. During the time the coelacanth remained practically unchanged whole new classes appeared: the birds and mammals, with such innovations as feathers, hair, hoofs, beaks, mammary glands, internal temperature-regulation and the ability to think conceptually. What accounts for such differences in rate?

The general picture of how evolution works is now clear. The basic raw material is the mutant gene. Among these mutants most will be deleterious, but a minority will be beneficial. These few will be retained by what Muller has called the sieve of natural selection. As the British statistician R. A. Fisher has said, natural selection is a "mechanism for generating an exceedingly high level of improbability." It is Maxwell's famous demon superimposed on the random process of mutation.

Despite the clarity and simplicity of the general idea, the details are difficult and obscure. Selection operates at many levels—between cells, between individual organisms, between families, between species. What is advantageous in the short run may be ruinous in the long run. What may be good in one environment may be bad in another. What is good this year may be bad next year. What is good for an individual may be bad for the species.

A certain amount of variability is necessary for evolution to occur. But the comparison of fossils reveals no consistent correlation between the measured variability at any one time and the rate of evolutionary change. George Gaylord Simpson, now at Harvard University, has measured contemporary representatives of low-rate groups (crocodiles, tapirs, armadillos, opossums) and high-rate ones (lizards, horses, kangaroos) and has found no tendency for the latter to be more variable. Additional evidence comes from domesticated animals and plants. G. Ledyard Stebbins, Jr., of the University of California has noted that domesticated representatives of slowly evolving plant groups produce new horticultural varieties just as readily as those from more rapidly evolving groups. Finally, the rates of "evolutionary" change in domestic animals and plants under artificial selection by man are tremendous compared with even the more rapidly evolving natural forms—perhaps thousands of times as fast. This can only mean that the genetic variability available for selection to work on is available in much greater abundance than the variability actually utilized in nature. The reasons why evolution is so slow in some groups must lie elsewhere than in insufficient genetic variability.

Instances of rapid evolution are probably the result of the opening-up of a new, unfilled ecological niche or environmental opportunity. This may be because of a change in the organism itself, as when the birds developed the power of flight with all the new possibilities this offered. It may also be due to opening-up of a new area, as when a few fortunate colonists land on a new continent.

One of the best-known examples of rapid change is to be found in the finches of the Galápagos Islands that Charles Darwin noted during his voyage on the *Beagle*. Darwin's finches are all descendants of what must have been a small number of chance migrants. They are a particularly striking group, especially in their adaptations to different feeding habits. Some have sparrow-like beaks for seed feeding; others have slender beaks and eat insects; some resemble the woodpeckers and feed on insect larvae in wood; still others feed with parrot-like beaks on fruits. The woodpecker type is of special interest. Lacking the woodpecker's long tongue it has evolved the habit of using a cactus spine or a twig as a substitute—it is the only example of a tool-using bird. In the rest of the world the finches are a relatively homogeneous group. Their tremendous diversity on these islands must be due to their isolation and the availability of new, unexploited ecological opportunities. A similar example of multiple adaptations is found in the honey creepers of the Hawaiian Islands [*see illustration on page 71*].

When paleontologists look into the ancestry of present-day animals, they find that only a minute fraction of the species present 100 million years ago is represented by descendants now. It is estimated that 98 per cent of the living vertebrate families trace their ancestry to eight of the species present in the Mesozoic Era, and that only two dozen of the tens of thousands of vertebrate species that were then present have left any descendants at all. The overwhelmingly probable future of any species is extinction. The history of

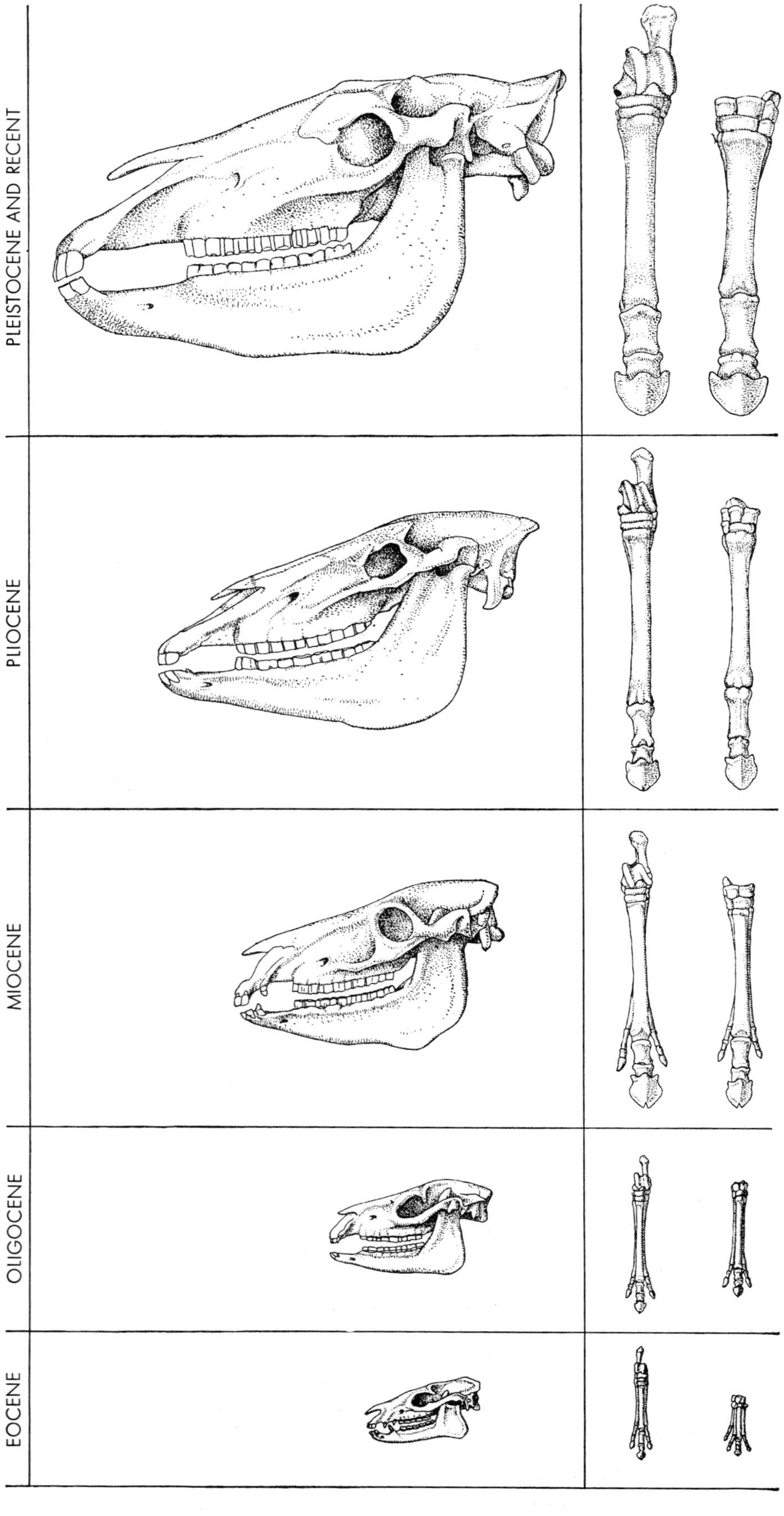

PLEISTOCENE AND RECENT

PLIOCENE

MIOCENE

OLIGOCENE

EOCENE

RAPID RATE OF EVOLUTION is illustrated by the horse. Comparisons of the skulls, hindfeet and forefeet of animals of successive periods indicate the changes which led from a fox-sized ancestor in the Eocene period, 60 million years ago, to the modern horse (top).

evolution is a succession of extinctions along with a tremendous expansion of a few fortunate types.

The causes of extinctions must be many. A change of environment—due to a flood, a volcanic eruption or a succession of less dramatic instances—may alter the ecological niche into which the species formerly fitted. Other animals and plants are probably the most important environmental variables: one species is part of the environment of another. There may be a more efficient predator, or a species that competes for shelter or food supply, or a new disease vector or parasite. As Theodosius Dobzhansky of Columbia University has said, "Extinction occurs either because the ecological niche disappears, or because it is wrested away by competitors."

Extinction may also arise from natural selection itself. Natural selection is a short-sighted, opportunistic process. All that matters is Darwinian fitness, that is, survival ability and reproductive capacity. A population is always in danger of becoming extinct through "criminal" genes—genes that perpetuate themselves at the expense of the rest of the population. An interesting example is the so-called SD gene, found in a wild Drosophila population near the University of Wisconsin by Yuichiro Hiraizumi. Ordinarily the segregation ratio—the ratio of two alternative genes in the progeny of any individual that carries these genes—is 1:1. In this strain the segregation is grossly distorted to something like 10:1 in favor of the SD gene; hence its name, SD, for segregation distorter. The SD gene somehow causes the chromosome opposite its own chromosome to break just prior to the formation of sperm cells. As a result the cells containing the broken chromosome usually fail to develop into functional sperm. The SD-bearing chromosome thus tends to increase itself rapidly in the population by effectively killing off its normal counterpart. Such a gene is obviously harmful to the population. But it cannot be eliminated except by the extinction of the population, or by the occurrence of a gene that is immune to the SD effect.

A similar gene exists in many mouse populations. Causing tail abnormalities, it is transmitted to much more than the usual fraction of the offspring, though in this case the detailed mechanism is not known. L. C. Dunn of Columbia University has found this gene in many wild-mouse populations. Most of these genes are highly deleterious to the mouse (a mouse needs a tail!), and some are lethal when they are borne in a double dose, so that the gene never completely takes over despite its segregational advantage. The result is an equilibrium frequency determined by the magnitude of the two opposing selective forces: the harmfulness of the gene and its segregational advantage. The population as a whole suffers, a striking illustration of the fact that natural selection does not necessarily improve the fitness of the species.

A gene causing extremely selfish, antisocial behavior—for example genes for cannibalism or social parasitism—could have similar effects in the human population. Any species must be in constant danger from the short-sightedness of the process of natural selection. Those that are still here are presumably the descendants of those that were able to avoid such pitfalls.

Aside from mutation itself, the most important evolutionary invention is sexual reproduction, which makes possible Mendelian heredity. The fact that such an elaborate mechanism exists throughout the whole living world—in viruses and bacteria, and in every major group of plants and animals—attests to its significance.

In a nonsexual population, if two potentially beneficial mutations arise in separate individuals, these individuals and their descendants can only compete with each other until one or the other type is eliminated, or until a second mutation occurs in one or the other

HONEY CREEPERS of Hawaii are a striking example of rapid evolution. Dozens of varieties, adapted to different diets, arose from a common ancestor. The long bills of *Hemignathus lucidus affinis* (1), *Hemignathus wilsoni* (4) and *Hemignathus o. obscurus* (7) are used to seek insects as woodpeckers do or to suck nectar. The beaks of *Psittirostra kona* (2), *Psittirostra cantans* (3), and *Psittirostra psittacea* (6) are adapted to a diet of berries and seeds. *Loxops v. virens* (5) sucks nectar and probes for insects with its sharp bill. *Pseudonestor xanthrophrys* (8) wrenches at hard wood to get at burrowing insects. Some of these species are presently extinct.

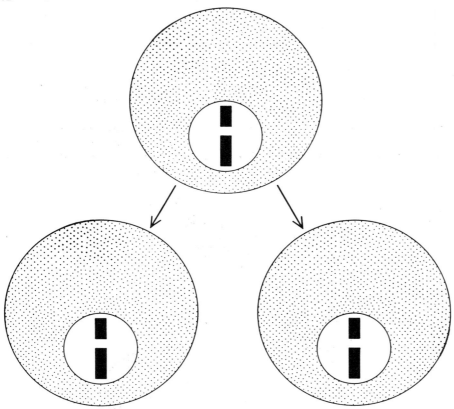

ASEXUAL REPRODUCTION permits little variability in a population; the evolution of asexual organisms depends entirely on mutation. At top is a schematic diagram of an asexual cell. Within its nucleus (*open circle*) are chromosomes (*rectangles*). When the cell divides (*bottom*), its two daughter cells have replicas of the original chromosomes and are exactly like the parent. To simplify the diagram only two of the chromosomes of a cell are shown.

group. A Mendelian species, with its biparental reproduction and consequent gene-scrambling, permits both mutants to be combined in the same individual. An asexual species must depend upon newly occurring mutations to provide it with variability. Sexual reproduction permits the combination and recombination of a whole series of mutants from the common pool of the species. Before they enter the pool the mutants have been to some extent pretested and the most harmful ones have already been eliminated.

Suppose that a population has 50 pairs of genes: Aa, Bb, Cc, etc. Suppose that each large-letter gene adds one unit of size. The difference between the smallest possible individual in this population (aa bb cc . . .) and the largest possible (AA BB CC . . .) is 100 units. Yet if all the genes are equally frequent, the size of 99.7 per cent of the population will be between 35 and 65 units. Only one individual in 2^{100} (roughly 1 followed by 30 zeros) would have 100 size units. Yet if the population is sexual, this type can be produced by selection utilizing only the genes already in the population.

This example illustrates the evolution-

ary power of a system that permits Mendelian gene-assortment. In an asexual system the organism would have to wait for new mutations. Most of the size-increasing mutations would probably have deleterious side effects. If the asexual organism had a mutation rate sufficient to give it the potential variability of a sexual population, it would probably become extinct from harmful mutations.

The very existence of sexual reproduction throughout the animal and plant kingdoms argues strongly for the necessity of an optimum genetic variability. This is plain, even though there is no consistent correlation between evolution rates as observed in the fossil record and the variability of the animals observed. It must be that a certain level of genetic variability is a necessary, but by no means sufficient, condition for progressive evolution.

Evolution is an exceedingly complex process, and it is obviously impossible, even in particular cases, to assign relative magnitudes to the various causal factors. Perhaps species have become extinct through mutation rates that are too high or too low, though there is no

direct observational evidence for this. Probably many asexual forms have become extinct because they were unable to adapt to changes. Other forms have become overspecialized, developing structures that fit them for only a particular habitat; when the habitat disappears, they are lost. The population size and structure are also important. To be successful in evolution, by the criterion of having left descendants many generations later, a species has the best chance if it has an optimum genetic system. But among a number of potentially successful candidates, only a few will succeed, and probably the main reason is simply the good luck of having been at the right place at the right time.

Of all the natural selection that occurs, only a small fraction leads to any progressive or directional change. Most selection is devoted to maintaining the status quo, to eliminating recurrent harmful mutations, or to adjusting to transitory changes in the environment. Thus much of the theory of natural selection must be a theory of statics rather than dynamics.

The processes that are necessary for evolution demand a certain price from the population in the form of reduced fitness. This might be said to be the price that a species pays for the privilege of evolving. The process of sexual reproduction, with its Mendelian gene-shuffling in each generation, produces a number of ill-adapted gene combinations, and therefore a reduction in average fitness. This can be avoided by a nonsexual system, but at the expense of genetic variability for evolutionary change in a changing environment.

The plant breeder knows that it is easy to maintain high-yielding varieties of the potato or sugar cane because they can be propagated asexually. But then his potential improvement is limited to the varieties that he has on hand. Only by combining various germ plasms sexually can he obtain varieties better than the existing best. But the potato and cane breeder can have his cake and eat it. He gets his new variants by sexual crosses; when he gets a superior combination of genes, he carries this strain on by an asexual process so that the combination is not broken up by Mendelian assortment.

Many species appear to have sacrificed long-term survival for immediate fitness. Some are highly successful. A familiar example is the dandelion; any lawn-keeper can testify to its survival value. In dandelion reproduction, although seeds are produced by what looks superficially like the usual method, the chromosome-assorting features of the sexual process are bypassed and the seed contains exactly the same combination of genes as the plant that produced it. In the long run the dandelion will probably become extinct, but in the present environment it is highly successful.

The process of mutation also produces ill-adapted types. The result is a lowering of the average fitness of the population, the price that asexual, as well as sexual, species pay for the privilege of evolution. Intuition tells us that the effect of mutation on fitness should be proportional to the mutation rate; Haldane has shown that the reduction in fitness is, in fact, exactly equal to the mutation rate.

The environment is never constant, so any species must find itself continually having to adjust to transitory or permanent changes in the environment. The most rapid environmental changes are usually brought about by the continuing evolution of other species. A simple example was given by Darwin himself. He noted that a certain number of rabbits in every generation are killed by wolves, and that in general these will be the rabbits that run the slowest. Thus by gradual selection the running speed of rabbits would increase. At the same time the slower wolves would starve, so that this species too has a selective premium on speed. As a result both improve, but the position of one with respect to the other does not change. It is like the treadmill situation in Lewis Carroll's famous story: "It takes all the running *you* can do, to keep in the same place."

A change in the environment will cause some genes that were previously favored to become harmful, and some that were harmful to become beneficial. At first it might seem that this does not make any net difference to the species. However, when the change occurs, the previously favored genes will be common as a result of natural selection in the past. The ones that were previously deleterious will be rare. The population will not return to its original fitness until the gene numbers are adjusted by natural selection, and this has its costs.

Just how much does it cost to exchange genes in this way? Let us ask the question for a single gene-pair. If we start with a rare dominant gene present in .01 per cent of the population, it requires the equivalent of about 10 selective "genetic deaths" (*i.e.*, failure to survive or reproduce) per surviving individual in the population to substitute this gene for its predecessor. This means

that if the population is to share an average of one gene substitution per generation, it must have a sufficient reproductive capacity to survive even though nine out of 10 individuals can die without offspring in each generation. The cost is considerably greater if the gene is recessive. The surprising part of this result is that the number does not depend on the selective value of the gene. As long as the difference between two alternative genes is small, the cost of replacing one by the other depends only on the initial

frequency and dominance of the gene and not at all on its fitness.

If the gene is less rare, the cost is lowered. Thus the species can lower the price of keeping up with the environment by having a higher frequency of deleterious genes that are potentially favorable. One way to accomplish this is to have a higher mutation rate, but this, too, has its price. Once again there is the conflict between the short-term objective of high fitness and the longer-term objective of ability to change with

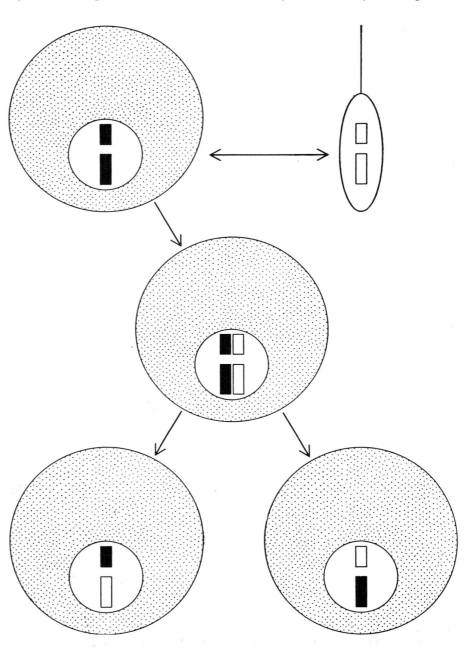

SEXUAL REPRODUCTION, also depicted in highly schematic form, depends on the union of two cells that may be from different lines of descent. At top left is an egg cell; at top right, a sperm cell. Each contains one set of chromosomes (*rectangles*). They join to form a new individual with two sets of chromosomes in its body cells (*center*). When this organism produces its own sperm or egg cells (*bottom*), each receives a full set of chromosomes. Some, however, may be from the father and some from the mother. Evolution in sexual organisms thus does not depend entirely on new mutations, because the genes already present in the population may be combined in different ways leading to improvements in the species.

the environment.

There are known to be genes that affect the mutation rate. Some of them are quite specific and affect only the mutation rate of a particular gene; others seem to enhance or depress the over-all rate. A gene whose effect is to lower the mutation rate certainly has selective advantage: it will cause an increase in fitness. This means that in most populations there should be a steady decrease in the mutation rate, possibly so far as to reduce the evolutionary adaptability of the organism. This is offset by selection for ability to cope with fluctuating environments.

How does man fare in this respect? From the standpoint of his biological evolution, is his mutation rate too high, is it too low or is it just right? It is not possible to say.

In general one would expect the evolutionary processes to work so that the mutation rate would usually be below the optimum from the standpoint of long-term evolutionary progress, because selection to reduce the mutation load has an immediate beneficial effect. Yet selection for a mutation-rate-adjusting gene is secondary to selection for whatever direct effects this gene has on the organism, such as an effect on size or metabolic rate. So we do not have much idea about how rapidly such selection would work.

Our early simian ancestors matured much more rapidly than we do now. This means that the mutation rate would have to be lowered in order to be brought into adjustment with the lengthening of our life cycle. To whatever extent the adjustment is behind the times, the mutation rate is too high. Furthermore, if it is true (as it appears to be) that radiation-induced mutation rates are less susceptible to evolutionary adjustment than those due to other causes, then an animal with a life cycle so long that it receives considerable radiation per generation may have too many from this cause.

I think it is impossible, however, to say whether man has a mutation rate that is too high or too low from the viewpoint of evolutionary advantage. It is worth noting that man, like any sexually reproducing organism, already has a tremendous store of genetic variability available for recombination. If all mutation were to stop, the possibilities for evolution would not be appreciably altered for a tremendous length of time —perhaps thousands of generations. Consider the immense range of human variability now found, for example the difference between Mozart, Newton, da Vinci and some of our best athletes, in contrast to a moron or the genetically impaired. Haldane once said: "A selector of sufficient knowledge and power might perhaps obtain from the genes at present available in the human species a race combining an average intellect equal to that of Shakespeare with the stature of Carnera." He goes on to say: "He could not produce a race of angels. For the moral character or for the wings he would have to await or produce suitable mutations." Surely the most hopefully naive eugenist would settle for considerably less!

I would argue that from any practical standpoint the question of whether

RECESSIVE MUTATION cannot be expressed in a sexual organism unless the corresponding gene of the paired chromosome has the same defect. Thus a harmful mutation can remain latent for generations. In this diagram the bars representing chromosomes are divided into squares, each symbolizing the gene for a different character. In row A the chromosomes of normal parents are paired (*arrows*). In row B a gene of their offspring mutates (*black*). In row C the mutant gene has been transmitted to the next generation but is still latent because the other parent has supplied a normal gene. This continues (*rows E and F*) until two individuals harboring the mutant gene mate (*row G*). The full effect of the mutation, harmful or otherwise, is expressed in offspring receiving a pair of mutant genes (*row H*).

man's mutation-rate is too high or too low for long-term evolution is irrelevant. From any other standpoint the present mutation rate is certainly too high. I suspect that man's expectations for future progress depend much more on what he does to his environment than on how he changes his genes. His practice has been to change the environment to suit his genes rather than vice versa. If he should someday decide on a program of conscious selection for genetic improvement, the store of genes already in the population will probably be adequate. If by some remote chance it is not, there will be plenty of ways to increase the number of mutations at that time.

There can be little doubt that man would be better off if he had a lower mutation-rate. I would argue, in our present ignorance, that the ideal rate for the foreseeable future would be zero. The effects produced by mutations are of all sorts, and are mostly harmful. Some cause embryonic death, some severe disease, some physical abnormalities, and probably many more cause minor impairments of body function that bring an increased susceptibility to the various vicissitudes of life. Some have an immediate effect; others lie hidden to cause their harm many generations later. All in all, mutations must be responsible for a substantial fraction of human premature death, illness and misery in general.

At the present time there is not much that can be done to lower the spontaneous-mutation rate. But at least we can do everything possible to keep the rate from getting any higher as the result of human activities. This is especially true for radiation-induced mutations; if anything they are probably more deleterious and less likely to be potentially useful than those from other causes. It is also important to remember that there are very possibly things in the environment other than radiation that increase the mutation rate. Among all the new compounds to which man is exposed as a result of our complex chemical technology there may well be a number of mutagenic substances. It is important that these be discovered and treated with caution.

The general conclusion, then, is that ionizing radiation is probably not an important factor in animal and plant evolution. If it is important anywhere it is probably in those species, such as man, that have a long life span, and at least for man it is a harmful rather than a potentially beneficial factor.

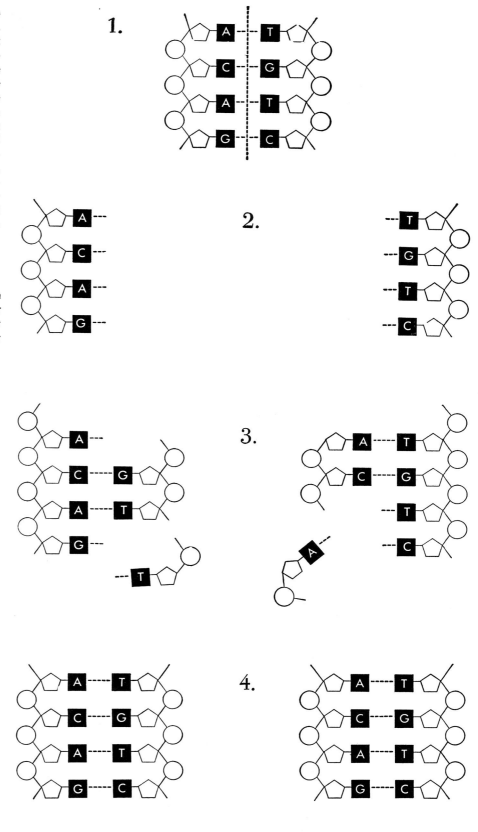

THE GENETIC MATERIAL, deoxyribonucleic acid (DNA), consists of a chain of sugar units (*pentagons*) and phosphate groups (*circles*) with side chains of bases: adenine (A), cytosine (C), thymine (T) and guanine (G). One possible mechanism for replication postulates that DNA normally contains two complementary strands, linked A—T and C—G (1). The chains then separate (2), and separate precursor units assemble along each chain (3). When they are completed, the double strands are identical to the original (4).

8

PORPHYRIA AND KING GEORGE III

IDA MACALPINE AND RICHARD HUNTER
July 1969

*The British monarch at the time of the American Revolution
is generally believed to have been insane. In the light of
modern knowledge it seems that he suffered from a
metabolic disease*

King George III, who is held in low regard on both sides of the Atlantic as the stubborn monarch whom the American colonies fought for their independence, was not a well man. His putative "madness" affected the course of Britain's history and, among other things, led to the establishment of psychiatry (then called the "mad-business") as a serious branch of medicine. Oddly enough, it has now become clear, a century and a half after his death, that George III was by no means psychotic. The much maligned king suffered spells of a painful and delirious metabolic disease that has only recently been recognized.

While working on a history of psychiatry, we learned with considerable interest how greatly its origins and development had been influenced by George III's alarming attacks, and we decided to find out what we could about the illness itself. Fortunately we were able to round up the notes and records of physicians who examined the king at the time; their manuscripts were preserved in Windsor Castle, the British Museum, the Lambeth Palace Library and in the hands of descendants. The recently published correspondence of George III also was helpful. The physicians' descriptions of the king's illness (not previously examined in recent times), together with the other available evidence, enabled us to arrive at a firm diagnosis of his disease in the light of present medical knowledge.

Let us begin with a review of his medical history as it was reported at the time. The first severe attack came in the fall of 1788, when the king was 50 years old. He had had a seizure of acute abdominal pain in June; his physician, Sir George Baker, diagnosed the cause as "biliary concretions in the gall duct" and sent him to Cheltenham Spa to drink the waters. The episode subsided, but in October the pains returned, accompanied by constipation, darkening of the urine, weakness of the limbs, hoarseness and a fast pulse. In the ensuing weeks the king was afflicted with insomnia, headache, visual disturbances and increasing restlessness. By the third week he became delirious, and over the weekend of November 8–9 he had convulsions, followed by prolonged stupor. His doctors feared that a fever had "settled on the brain" and that his life was in imminent danger. For a week he apparently hovered between life and death. Then his physical condition began to improve, but his mind was "deranged." There were periods of great excitement, interspersed with moments of lucidity and calm. "Wrong ideas" took hold of the king, and his physicians found him increasingly difficult to manage.

During all this time, although he was attended by coveys of physicians, the patient was not really examined in the present sense of the word. The doctors looked at the king's tongue, felt his pulse, inquired about his excretory functions, listened to his complaints and attempted to pronounce a diagnosis by "an estimate of symptoms and appearances." There were, indeed, no tools for examination to speak of in that era—no stethoscope, not even a reliable clinical thermometer to measure fever. The physicians often could not agree on the pulse rate, presumably because their timepieces differed. Doctors did not listen to the chest; even if they had, they would not have known what to make of what they heard. They were also handicapped by the fact that they did not dare to question the king about his symptoms unless he addressed them first. (After one session of fruitless silence the physi-cians plaintively reported: "His Majesty appears to be very quiet this morning, but not having been addressed we know nothing more of His Majesty's condition of mind or body than what is obvious in his external appearance.")

In contrast to the obscurity and vagueness of the physical symptoms, the king's mental symptoms spoke loudly and clearly. His physicians needed no modern aids to observe that his behavior was excited and irrational and his mind confused. Moreover, his mental state caused much concern about his fitness to rule and the dangers to the nation and the empire. The mental symptoms therefore overshadowed the physical complaints. Thus it came about that the king's physical sufferings were minimized (and later disregarded), whereas his mental derangement was magnified as if it were the whole illness. Physicians who specialized in "intellectual maladies" were called in, took up residence in the palace and took charge of the sickroom.

One of these practitioners was the Reverend Dr. Francis Willis, called "Doctor Duplicate" because he was a doctor of medicine as well as of theology. Dr. Willis, who managed a madhouse, arrived at Kew Palace with the aids and tools of his establishment, including attendants and a straitjacket. He applied to the king the usual treatment of the day for insane persons: coercion and restraint. The king was put in the straitjacket for infringements of discipline such as throwing off his necktie and wig when he had attacks of sweating, or refusing to eat when he had difficulty swallowing, or walking about the room when he became too restless to lie down. The king's unpredictable and obstreperous behavior was taken to be the ebullition of furious mania, and his fierce (and understandable) dislike of his doc-

GEORGE WILLIAM FREDERICK, the third Hanoverian king of England, is seen in an official portrait by Allan Ramsay, painted when the monarch was 30 years old. Born in 1738, George III ruled from 1760 to 1811, when the fourth in a series of misdiagnosed bouts of "madness," apparently a hereditary enzyme imbalance known today as porphyria, required the appointment of a regent.

WINE-COLORED URINE, shown in the middle test tube, was produced by a patient during an acute attack of porphyria. For comparison, normal urine is at left, port wine at right. James I, who also had porphyria, commented that his urine resembled port.

tors and keepers was attributed to delusions.

His illness precipitated a historic party struggle in Parliament known as the "Regency Crisis." The Whigs, led by Charles James Fox, Edmund Burke and Richard Brinsley Sheridan (who was a member of Parliament as well as a celebrated playwright), tried to oust the king's prime minister, William Pitt, and the other members of his cabinet. For four months Parliament gave its entire attention to the king's illness and the constitutional issues it raised. Members of Parliament interrogated the physicians exhaustively on the question of whether the king was suffering merely a prolonged delirium, from which he could be expected to recover with unimpaired mind, or was actually afflicted with "a lunacy" that would permanently cloud his judgment.

Then, just as Parliament was about to pass a bill setting up a regency, George's mind suddenly began to clear. At the end of February, 1789, his doctors announced "the entire cessation" of his illness. Although Willis claimed the credit for the cure, in retrospect it is clear that the king's recovery must have been spontaneous. He was soon well enough to leave his confinement in Kew Palace and return to Windsor Castle, his favorite residence. His recovery was celebrated with demonstrations of national rejoicing the like of which had never before been witnessed.

In 1801 and again in 1804 George III had recurrences of the same illness. Each time he was at first dangerously ill with identical physical symptoms and then deranged mentally for only a brief period. Eventually, in 1810, he fell into an illness that incapacitated him to the point where he was replaced by the Prince of Wales under the regency act of 1811. For at least a year there were hopes that he would again recover, and his son, as regent, refrained from dismissing George's ministers to avoid embarrassing him in case he became able to resume the throne. The king did experience periods of recovery, but each time he relapsed. He was then well past 70, blind and much reduced physically and mentally by the repeated onslaughts of his illness. Senility had set in. During his last years George was on the whole tranquil, played the harpsichord and had intervals of good humor and cheerfulness; however, he was often "sullen and lost in mind," tears and laughter would come in quick succession and from time to time he was stricken with the old, painful paroxysms. A month before his death,

PORPHIN

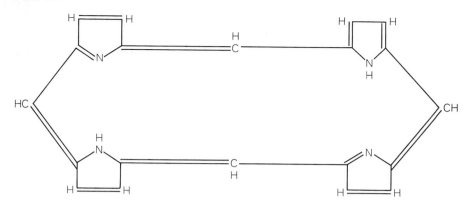

HEMIN

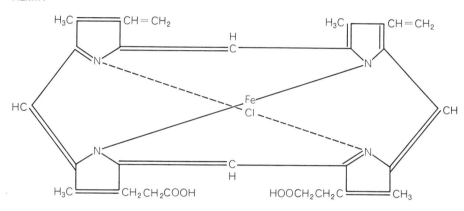

PORPHYRIN BUILDING BLOCK, the porphin molecule, is comprised of four pyrrole rings joined together by four methene bridges. The pigments that may be constructed from porphin molecules include three that are essential to animal and plant life: hemoglobin, chlorophyll and cytochrome. For comparison a hemin molecule is illustrated; it differs from porphin mainly in having an iron and a chlorine atom attached to the pyrrole rings.

in the last of these attacks, he spent 58 turbulent hours without sleep or rest and "gave other remarkable proof of the extraordinary energies of his constitution." He died quietly on January 29, 1820, at the age of 81.

After his death political bias and professional opinion developed an image of George III as a "mad king" who was more or less deranged throughout his life. A spell of sickness he had experienced in 1765, when he was 26, was taken to have been an early sign of his madness. There is not a shred of evidence that any mental disturbance accompanied that early illness, but it was popularly believed the king must have been insane to permit the 1765 enactment of the infamous Stamp Act that sowed the seeds of the American War of Independence. Furthermore, psychiatrists who later diagnosed George III's illnesses as primarily mental also adopted the lunacy interpretation of the king's 1765 illness to support their theory; it

would not make sense to suppose that the king, if mentally unstable, would have come through the first 28 stormy years of his reign without any sign of psychological distress.

The great prominence given to George III's supposed insanity aroused wide public and professional interest in mental illness and generated the first systematic attempts to deal with it as a medical problem. William Black, a contemporary teacher of medicine who was intrigued by the physicians' fumbling efforts to forecast the prospects for the king's recovery, looked into the question statistically and thus became the founder of psychiatric statistics. Studying the records of people who had been pronounced insane, he came to the conclusion, which may be called "Black's law," that a third of such patients could be expected to recover to full mental health, a third recovered somewhat but did not regain all their former mental capacities and a third did not improve at all or sank into deeper illness.

Richard Powell, another physician with a statistical bent, found that in the years immediately following the king's 1788 attack there was a big increase in the number of insane persons admitted to private asylums. He presented his findings graphically in a histogram, introducing this device into medical reporting for the first time. Dr. Powell attributed the apparent rise in mental illness to the mounting complexities of civilization, and his social interpretation is still widely put forward as an explanation of increases in the incidence of mental disorders.

Two of George III's sons, the dukes of Kent and Sussex, set up the first fund for research in psychiatry and initiated the first controlled trial of a treatment for insanity. The trial was conducted by two laymen who had developed a secret remedy they hoped would be used on the king. A London physician named Edward Sutleffe also offered a remedy; he called it a "herbaceous tranquillizer," thereby introducing the term that describes the dominant treatment of mental illness with drugs today.

Parliament, prodded by demands for better care of the mentally ill, particularly among the poor ("pauper lunatics"), set up a committee "to enquire into Madhouses." Under the chairmanship of George III's personal friend George Rose, the committee took evidence for two years and published reports that paved the way to the system of caring for mental patients in "asylums," which

lasted well into our century and whose memorials are still with us. This advance had some unfortunate consequences. It isolated patients from society, often in remote establishments, and it created an artificial separation between mental and physical disease, each with its own specialists. Thus psychiatry was unhappily set apart from the mainstream of medicine, and physicians and psychiatrists became two separate breeds.

In view of the historic importance of George III's illness, it is remarkable that so little inquiry has since been made, either by psychiatrists or by physicians, into what was really the matter with the king. Astonishingly, only two medical studies have ever been attempted. Both were made by individual U.S.

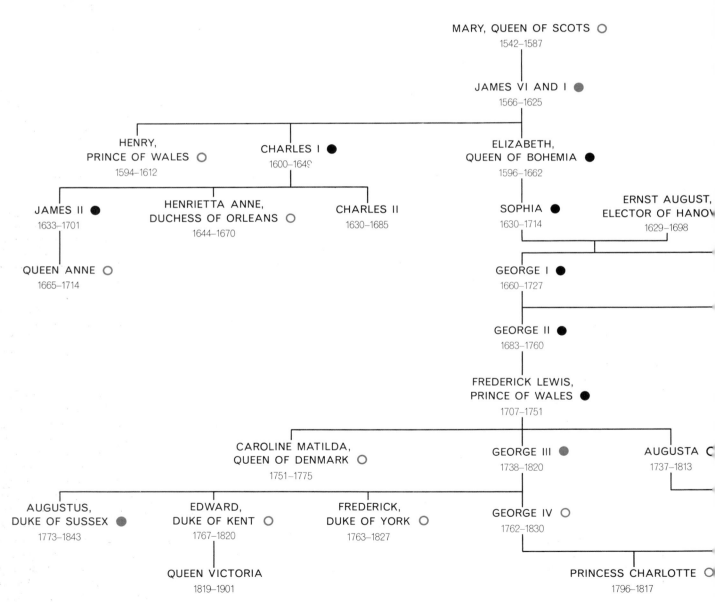

THREE ROYAL HOUSES suffered from porphyria. First to be afflicted was Mary, Queen of Scots, a Stuart. From her descendants the disorder spread to both the Hanoverian and the Prussian royal lines. Colored circles mark those who showed some signs of the

psychiatrists, almost a century apart, and both completely missed the medical complexities of the case.

In 1855 Isaac Ray, the distinguished president of the Association of Medical Superintendents of American Institutions for the Insane (since renamed the American Psychiatric Association), reviewed the then available information on George's sickness. He was surprised by the lack of background for the king's attacks of mental derangement. Dr. Ray wrote: "Few men would have seemed less likely to be visited by insanity. His general health had always been good; his powers were impaired by none of those indulgences almost inseparable from the kingly station; he was remarkably abstemious at the table, and took much exercise in the open air. Insanity had never appeared in his family, and he was quite free from those eccentricities and peculiarities which indicate an ill-balanced mind." Nevertheless, on the basis of the reports to which he had access Dr. Ray diagnosed George III's malady as "mania" (which is as unspecific for mental illness as "fever" is for a physical complaint). Ray's attempt at diagnosis was severely handicapped by the paucity of facts he had on the case and by the comparatively primitive state of medical knowledge in the 19th century.

In 1941 the eminent Baltimore psychiatrist Manfred S. Guttmacher reexamined George III's case from the angle of modern psychoanalysis. It is characteristic of the psychoanalytic point of view that, given a case of mental aberration, it attaches little weight to physical symptoms and causes. Guttmacher dismissed the king's physical complaints, attributing them in part to efforts by the court to cover up the king's madness and in part to neurotic imaginings by the king himself. Describing the illness in modern terms as manic-depressive psychosis, Guttmacher added: "Self-blame, indecision and frustration destroyed the sanity of George III.... A vulnerable individual, this unstable man ...could not tolerate his own timorous uncertainty [and] broke under the strain. [Had the king] been a country squire, he would in all probability not have been psychotic." (Actually the king was known to his subjects as Farmer George because of his interest in agriculture.)

When we came to our detailed study of George III's career and illnesses, we found no grounds for support of this psychoanalytic interpretation of his case. George's contemporaries and early biographers described him as one of Britain's most devoted and best-informed rulers; he was a musician, a book collector (whose collection forms an important part of the British Museum), a patron of the arts and sciences, fond of country life and his family. If he had been emotionally and mentally unbalanced, how could he have lived through the disastrous period of his reign—the loss of the American colonies and the 18-year struggle leading up to it—without a suspicion of breakdown? In view of the political troubles that beset him, not to mention his large and unruly family, one should be surprised that he was ever sane at all, if the psychoanalytic diagnosis of his personality were correct.

The fact is that, before physical illness and senility finally incapacitated him, George had only three attacks of mental derangement, and all together these periods did not add up to more than six months. In each instance the nervous disorder was ushered in by serious physical symptoms that perplexed his physicians and brought him to the brink of death. "It is not merely the delirium of fever, nor is it any common form of insanity," said one of his doctors, William Heberden, Jr. "The whole frame has been more or less disordered, both body and mind... [due to] a peculiarity of constitution of which I can give no distinct account." Sir Henry Halford, another eminent physician of the time, remarked: "The King's case appears to have no exact precedent in the records of insanity."

There were clues to the root of George's illness, if the physicians had

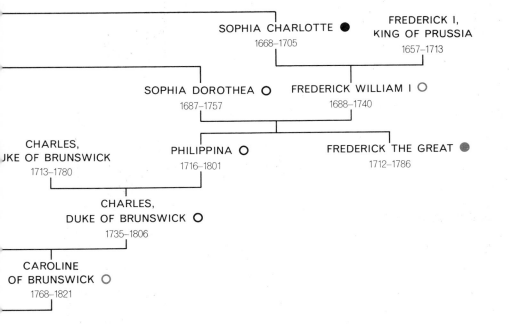

SOPHIA CHARLOTTE ●
1668–1705

FREDERICK I,
KING OF PRUSSIA
1657–1713

SOPHIA DOROTHEA ○
1687–1757

FREDERICK WILLIAM I ○
1688–1740

CHARLES,
DUKE OF BRUNSWICK
1713–1780

PHILIPPINA ○
1716–1801

FREDERICK THE GREAT ●
1712–1786

CHARLES,
DUKE OF BRUNSWICK ○
1735–1806

CAROLINE
OF BRUNSWICK ○
1768–1821

disorder, colored dots those whose urine was also abnormal. Black dots mark transmitters who did not suffer from the disorder; black circles, those who may have been transmitters.

"DOCTOR DUPLICATE" WILLIS, the chief physician during George III's first porphyria attack, maintained a private asylum, shown here in a cartoon by Thomas Rowlandson. Willis' nickname derived from his being both a physician and a doctor of divinity.

His method of treatment emphasized restraint and discipline for any disorderly patient; two here are in "winding sheets." Use of his method, including straitjacketing when his delirious royal patient failed to follow his orders, earned all doctors the king's enmity.

SAVAGE CARICATURE of the royal family was published in the year preceding the king's first seizure. The work, by James Gillray and titled "Monstrous Craws at a New Coalition Feast," was inspired by popular belief that "foreign" Hanoverians squandered

the nation's funds for their own benefit. The queen (*left*), the Prince of Wales (*center*) and the king (*right*) are shown seated outside the Treasury, gorging themselves on gold. The king was in fact frugal, but the Prince of Wales (later his regent) was a notorious spender.

only known how to interpret them. The doctors reported, for instance, that his attacks appeared to be caused by "the force of a humour" that first showed itself in the legs, then drove "into the bowels" and finally was projected "upon the brain." Quaint as this description now sounds, it was a significant account of the course of the king's attacks, involving a progression of symptoms from the limbs to the abdomen to the brain. Of all the king's symptoms, the most revealing one, which has led us now to the discovery of the true nature of his illness, is the color of his urine. At least half a dozen times the doctors who examined him noted that the king's urine was "dark," red or discolored.

Considered in connection with the king's other symptoms and the character of his attacks, it is quite clear today that this discoloration of his urine must have been due to the presence of porphyrins. Porphyrin is a pigment, contained in the hemoglobin of the blood, that normally is metabolized in the body cells. Hence its presence in the urine is a signal of faulty metabolism: namely, inability of the cells to convert porphyrin, presumably because of the absence of a necessary enzyme. The clinical seriousness of such defects was first called to the attention of the medical world in 1908 by the London physician Sir Archibald Garrod, who discovered that "inborn errors of metabolism" could cause profound disorders [see "The Chemistry of Hereditary Disease," by A. G. Bearn; SCIENTIFIC AMERICAN, December, 1956]. It has since been found that the inability to metabolize porphyrin produces a disease, called porphyria, that attacks the nervous system [see "Pursuit of a Disease," by Geoffrey Dean; SCIENTIFIC AMERICAN, March, 1957]. The attack usually begins in the autonomic system, then advances to the peripheral nerves, the cranial nerves and finally the brain itself. At the height of the attack the patient is paralyzed, delirious and in agonizing pain.

George III's symptoms, the sequence of their development and the climaxes of his illness read like a textbook case of porphyria. His attacks started with colic, constipation and nausea; there followed a painful weakness of the limbs, so that he could not walk or stand, a speedup of his pulse, attacks of sweating, hoarseness, visual disturbances, difficulty in swallowing, intractable insomnia, mounting excitement, nonstop rambling, dizziness, headache, tremors, stupor and convulsions. The physicians described his climactic mental state thus: "Delirious

LIKENESS OF WILLIS appeared on one side and a patriotic injunction on the other of a medal that "Doctor Duplicate" distributed to the public when the king, in February, 1789, spontaneously recovered four months after the onset of his chief porphyria attack.

PHYSICIANS' JOURNAL, a chronological record of the king's illness, notes events of December 23 and 24, 1788, as follows: "The waistcoat was taken off at nine--& blisters drefs'd—discharg'd well—very sore—Pulse 96—perspir'd through the night profusely—but little sleep—& very quiet & in good humour for the most part—Tongue white. Copy of the letter to the Prince of Wales—not sign'd by Dr. Willis—The straight waistcoat was taken off from his Majesty at noon yesterday, but was put on again soon after two oClock & was not taken off till nine this morning. His Majesty has not had more than an hours sleep in the night, is good humour'd but as incoherent as ever. Mr. Keate is of opinion that the blisters on his legs are in a healing state—Bulletin—His Majesty pafs'd the night quietly but with little sleep—& is quiet this morning—Sometime betwixt 10 & 11—fell fast a sleep upon a Sophy—nearly an hour—awak'd & lay very compos'd. Before He fell asleep He had a very pertinent conversation with my Father [Dr. Willis] concerning Mr. Smelt & religion—his sense [struck out] & worthinefs but too much refinement—&c. [conclusion of page]."

all day...impressed by false images... continually addressed people dead or alive as if they were present...engrossed in visionary scenery...his conversation like the details of a dream in its extravagant confusion."

These mental symptoms are the hallmarks of a state in which the brain is disordered by toxin. Other aspects of the king's attacks also were characteristic of porphyria: they were usually precipitated by mild infections; his condition fluctuated rapidly, and each attack was followed by a protracted convalescence. Porphyria is usually accompanied by high blood pressure; there were of course no measurements of the king's blood pressure, but the repeated crises that made his doctors fear "a paralytic stroke" may well have been hypertensive. As for the illness of 1765, that was probably a mild attack of porphyria that did not go on to involve the brain.

Since porphyria is a hereditary disease, we looked into the medical histories of George III's blood relatives. The available records showed that signs of porphyria in his family went as far back as his 16th-century ancestor Mary, Queen of Scots. Her son, King James, suffered from colics (which he told his physician he had inherited from his mother) and described his urine as the color of his favorite Alicante wine. George III's sister, Queen Caroline Matilda of Norway and Denmark (who is the subject of many novels and of a Verdi opera), died at 23 of a mysterious illness that was featured by rapidly progressive paralysis. Some of George's children were afflicted with his disorder. The son who succeeded him on the throne, George IV, had a disease that his physicians called "unformed gout" but that must certainly have been porphyria. George IV's daughter, Princess Charlotte, showed characteristic symptoms of the disease and died in childbirth, apparently during an acute attack. George III's son Augustus, the Duke of Sussex, had severe attacks of illness accompanied by discoloration of his urine. Another son, the Duke of Kent (who was the father of Queen Victoria), suffered severely from colics and died of an attack a week before the death of George III. Porphyria, introduced into the House of Brandenburg-Prussia by George I's sister, also claimed Frederick the Great as a victim. The disease has persisted in descendants of George III up to the present day. We examined some of them and found the characteristic signs, including the discoloration of the urine. Our laboratory tests showed that the family had a form of porphyria that makes the skin sensitive to the sun and to injury.

We see, then, from the perspective of 20th-century medical knowledge, that George III's image, like his pain-racked body, has been the victim of a cruel misunderstanding. His episodes of derangement were merely the mutterings of a delirious mind temporarily disordered by an intoxicated brain. The royal malady was not "insanity" or "mania" or "manic-depressive psychosis"—whatever meaning these nebulous terms may retain in the modern era of diagnostic and investigative medicine. Partly because of the backwardness of medical knowledge at the time and partly because of the king's position, the bodily disorder he suffered was pushed into the shadows. With a good diet, avoidance of medication with drugs and generally rational treatment his attacks of delirium might have been curtailed.

PORCELAIN PLAQUE, made by Josiah Wedgwood in commemoration of the king's recovery, shows George III crowned with laurels. It bears the inscription "Health restored."

9

THE PRESENT EVOLUTION OF MAN

THEODOSIUS DOBZHANSKY
September 1960

*Man still evolves by natural selection for his environment,
but it is now an environment largely of his own making.
Moreover, he may be changing the environment faster than
he can change biologically*

In tracing man's evolution, several contributors to this volume have dealt with a natural process that has transcended itself. Only once before, when life originated out of inorganic matter, has a comparable transcendence occurred.

After that first momentous step, living forms evolved by adapting to their environments. Adaptation—the maintenance or advancement of conformity between an organism and its surroundings—takes place through natural selection. The raw materials with which natural selection works are supplied by mutation and sexual recombination of hereditary units: the genes.

Mutation, sexual recombination and natural selection led to the emergence of *Homo sapiens*. The creatures that preceded him had already developed the rudiments of tool-using, toolmaking and cultural transmission. But the next evolutionary step was so great as to constitute a difference in kind from those before it. There now appeared an organism whose mastery of technology and of symbolic communication enabled it to create a supraorganic culture. Other organisms adapt to their environments by changing their genes in accordance with the demands of the surroundings. Man and man alone can also adapt by changing his environments to fit his genes. His genes enable him to invent new tools, to alter his opinions, his aims and his conduct, to acquire new knowledge and new wisdom.

Other SCIENTIFIC AMERICAN authors have shown how the possession of these faculties brought the human species to its present biological eminence. Man has spread to every section of the earth, bringing high culture to much of it. He is now the most numerous of the mammals. By these or any other reasonable standards, he is by far the most successful product of biological evolution.

For better or worse, biological evolution did not stop when culture appeared. In this final article we address ourselves to the question of where evolution is now taking man. The literature of this subject has not lacked for prophets who wish to divine man's eventual fate. In our age of anxiety, prediction of final extinction has become the fashionable view, replacing the hopes for emergence of a race of demigods that more optimistic authorities used to foresee. Our purpose is less ambitious. What biological evolutionary processes are now at work is a problem both serious and complex enough to occupy us here.

The impact of human works on the environment is so strong that it has become very hard to make out the forces to which the human species is now adjusting. It has even been argued that *Homo sapiens* has already emancipated himself from the operation of natural selection. At the other extreme are those who still assume that man is nothing but an animal. The second fallacy is the more pernicious, leading as it does to theories of biological racism and the justification of race and class prejudice which are bringing suffering to millions of people from South Africa to Arkansas. Assuming that man's genetic endowment can be ignored is the converse falsehood, perhaps less disastrous in its immediate effects, but more insidious in the long run.

Like all other animals, man remains the product of his biological inheritance. The first, and basic, feature of his present evolution is that his genes continue to mutate, as they have since he first appeared. Every one of the tens of thousands of genes inherited by an individual has a tiny probability of changing in some way during his generation. Among the small, and probably atypical,

sample of human genes for which very rough estimates of the mutation frequencies are available, the rates of mutation vary from one in 10,000 to one in about 250,000. For example, it has been calculated that approximately one sex cell in every 50,000 produced by a normal person carries a new mutant gene causing retinoblastoma, a cancer of the eye affecting children.

These figures are "spontaneous" frequencies in people not exposed to any special agents that can induce mutation. As is now widely known, the existence of such agents, including ionizing radiation and certain chemicals, has been demonstrated with organisms other than man. New mutagens are constantly being discovered. It can hardly be doubted that at least some of them affect human genes. As a consequence the members of an industrial civilization have increased genetic variability through rising mutation rates.

There is no question that many mutations produce hereditary diseases, malformations and constitutional weaknesses of various kinds. Some few must also be useful, at least in certain environments; otherwise there would be no evolution. (Useful mutants have actually been observed in experiments on lower organisms.) But what about minor variations that produce a little more or a little less hair, a slightly longer or a slightly shorter nose, blood of type O or type A? These traits seem neither useful nor harmful. Here, however, we must proceed with the greatest caution. Beneficial or damaging effects of ostensibly neutral traits may eventually be discovered. For example, recent evidence indicates that people with blood of type O have a slightly higher rate of duodenal ulcer than does the general population. Does it follow that O blood is bad? Not necessarily; it is the most frequent type in many populations, and it may conceivably confer some advantages yet undiscovered.

Still other mutants that are detrimental when present in double dose (the so-called homozygous condition, where the same type of gene has been inherited from both parents) lead to hybrid vigor in single dose (the heterozygous condition). How frequently this happens is uncertain. The effect surely operates in the breeding of domestic animals and plants, and it has been detected among X-ray-induced mutations in fruit flies. Only one case is thus far known in man. Anthony C. Allison of the University of Oxford has found that the gene causing sickle-cell anemia in the homozygous condition makes its heterozygous carriers relatively resistant to certain forms of malaria. This gene is very frequent in the native population of the central African lowlands, where malaria has long been endemic, and relatively rare in the inhabitants of the more salubrious highlands. Certainly there are other such adaptively ambivalent genes in human populations, but we do not know how many.

Despite these uncertainties, which cannot be glossed over, it is generally agreed among geneticists that the effects of mutation are on the average detrimental. Any increase of mutation rate, no matter how small, can only augment the mass of human misery due to defective heredity. The matter has rightly attracted wide attention in connection with ionizing radiation from military and industrial operations and medical X-rays. Yet these form only a part of a larger and more portentous issue.

Of the almost countless mutant genes that have arisen since life on earth began, only a minute fraction were preserved. They were preserved because they were useful, or at least not very harmful, to their possessors. A great majority of gene changes were eliminated. The agency that preserved useful mutants and eliminated injurious ones was natural selection. Is natural selection still operating in mankind, and can it be trusted to keep man fit to live in environments created by his civilization?

One must beware of words taken from everyday language to construct scientific terminology. "Natural" in "natural selection" does not mean the state of affairs preceding or excluding man-made changes. Artificially or not, man's environment has altered. Would it now be natural to try to make your living as a Stone Age hunter?

Then there are phrases like "the struggle for life" and "survival of the fittest." Now "struggle" was to Darwin a metaphor. Animals struggle against cold by growing warm fur, and plants against dryness by reducing the evaporating leaf surface. It was the school of so-called social Darwinists (to which Darwin did not belong) who equated "struggle" with violence, warfare and competition

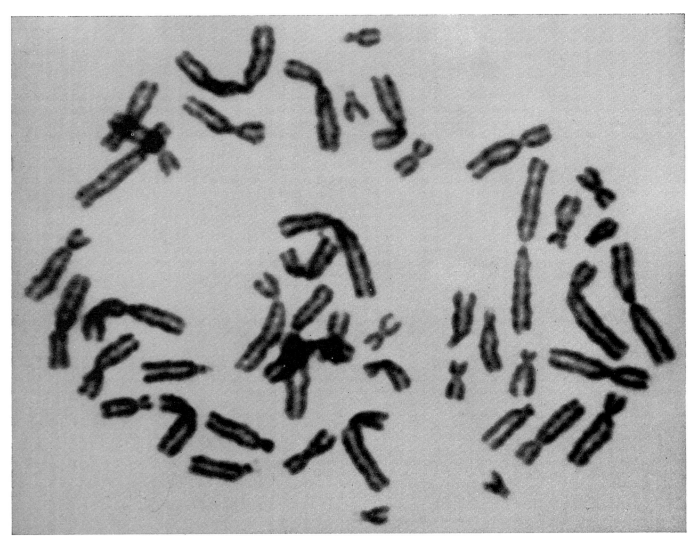

HUMAN CHROMOSOMES are enlarged some 5,000 times in this photomicrograph made by J. H. Tjio and Theodore T. Puck at the University of Colorado Medical Center. The photomicrograph shows all of the 46 pairs of chromosomes in a dividing body cell.

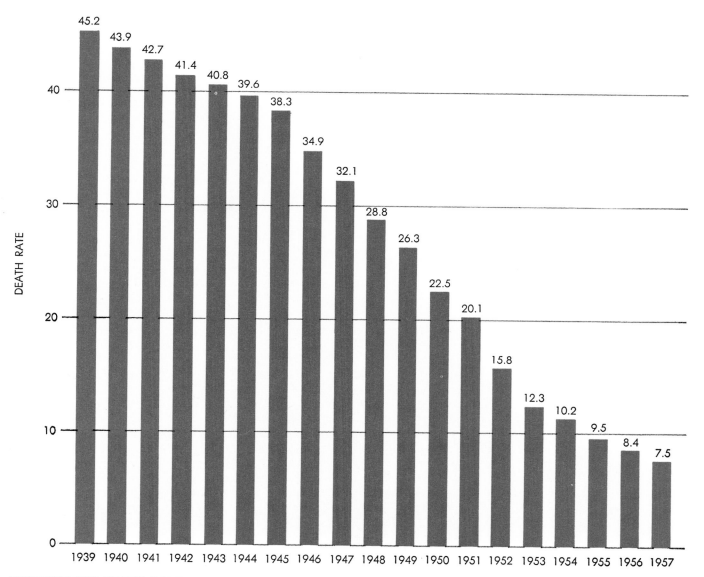

GENERAL DISTRIBUTION OF PENICILLIN | GENERAL DISTRIBUTION OF STREPTOMYCIN
INTRODUCTION OF STREPTOMYCIN IN HOSPITALS |
INTRODUCTION OF PENICILLIN IN HOSPITALS | INTRODUCTION OF ISONIAZID

TUBERCULOSIS DEATH RATE per 100,000 people showed a dramatic decline with the introduction of antibiotics and later of the antituberculosis drug isoniazid. As tuberculosis becomes less prevalent, so does its threat to genetically susceptible individuals, who are enabled to survive and reproduce. The chart is based upon information from the U. S. National Office of Vital Statistics.

without quarter. The idea has long been discredited.

We do not deny the reality of competition and combat in nature, but suggest that they do not tell the whole story. Struggle for existence may be won not only by strife but also by mutual help. The surviving fit in human societies may in some circumstances be those with the strongest fists and the greatest readiness to use them. In others they may be those who live in peace with their neighbors and assist them in hour of need. Indeed, co-operation has a long and honorable record. The first human societies, the hunters of the Old Stone Age, depended on co-operation to kill big game.

Moreover, modern genetics shows that "fitness" has a quite special meaning in connection with evolution. Biologists now speak of Darwinian fitness, or adaptive value, or selective value in a reproductive sense. Consider the condition known as achondroplastic dwarfism, caused by a gene mutation that produces people with normal heads and trunks, but short arms and legs. As adults they may enjoy good health. Nevertheless, E. T. Mørch in Denmark has discovered that achondroplastic dwarfs produce, on the average, only some 20 surviving children for every 100 children produced by their normal brothers and sisters. In technical terms we say that the Darwinian fitness of achondroplasts is .2 or, alternatively that achondroplastic dwarfism is opposed by a selection-coefficient of .8.

This is a very strong selection, and the reasons for it are only partly understood. What matters from an evolutionary point of view is that achondroplasts are much less efficient in transmitting their genes to the following generations than are nondwarfs. Darwinian fitness is reproductive fitness. Genetically the surviving fittest is neither superman nor conquering hero; he is merely the parent of the largest surviving progeny.

With these definitions in mind, we can answer the question whether natural selection is still active in mankind by considering how such selection might be set aside. If all adults married, and each couple produced exactly the same number of children, all of whom survived to get married in turn and so on, there would be no selection at all. Alternatively, the number of children, if any, that each person produced might be determined by himself or some outside authority on the basis of the desirability of his hereditary endowment. This would be replacing natural selection by artificial selection. Some day it may come to pass. Meantime natural selection is going on.

It goes on, however, always within the context of environment. As that changes, the Darwinian fitness of various traits changes with it. Thus by his own efforts man is continually altering the selective pressure for or against certain genes.

The most obvious example, and one with disturbing overtones, is to be found in the advance of medicine and public health. Retinoblastoma, the eye cancer of children, is almost always fatal if it is not treated. Here is "natural" selection at its most rigorous, weeding out virtually all of the harmful mutant genes

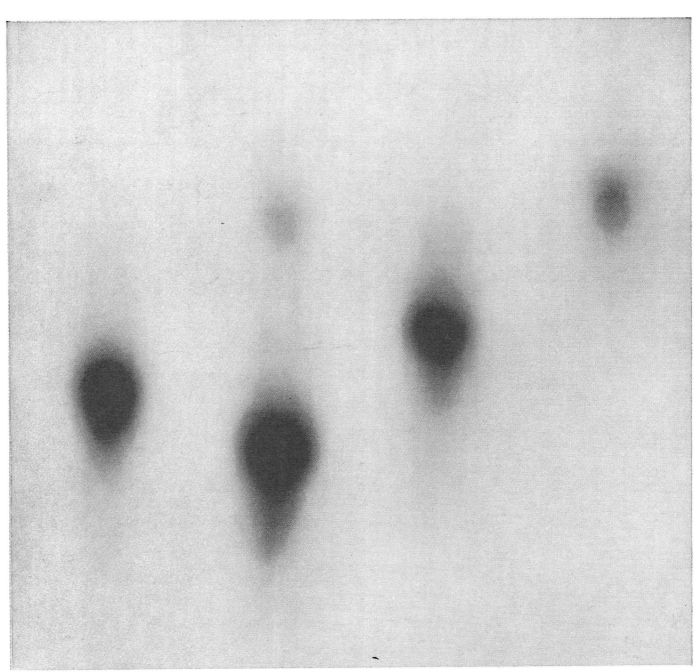

CHEMICAL STRUCTURE OF HEMOGLOBIN in an individual's blood is determined by his genes. Normal and abnormal hemoglobins move at different speeds in an electric field. This photograph, made by Henry G. Kunkel of the Rockefeller Institute, shows surface of a slab of moist starch on which samples of four kinds of human hemoglobin were lined up at top, between a negative electrode at top and a positive electrode at bottom (electrodes are not shown). When current was turned on, the samples migrated toward positive electrode. At right hemoglobin C, the cause of a rare hereditary anemia, has moved down only a short way. Second from right is hemoglobin S, the cause of sickle-cell anemia, which has moved farther in same length of time. Normal hemoglobin, third from right, has separated into its A and A_2 constituents. At left is normal fetal hemoglobin F, obtained from an umbilical cord.

before they can be passed on even once. With proper treatment, however, almost 70 per cent of the carriers of the gene for retinoblastoma survive, become able to reproduce and therefore to transmit the defect to half their children.

More dramatic, if genetically less clear-cut, instances are afforded by advances in the control of tuberculosis and malaria. A century ago the annual death rate from tuberculosis in industrially advanced countries was close to 500 per 100,000. Improvement in living conditions and, more recently, the advent of antibiotic drugs have reduced the death rate to 7.5 per 100,000 in the U. S. today. A similarly steep decline is under way in the mortality from malaria, which used to afflict a seventh of the earth's population.

Being infectious, tuberculosis and malaria are hazards of the environment. There is good evidence, however, that individual susceptibility, both as to contracting the infection and as to the severity of the disease, is genetically conditioned. (We have already mentioned the protective effect of the gene for sickle-cell anemia. This is probably only one of several forms of genetic resistance to malaria.) As the prevalence of these diseases decreases, so does the threat to susceptible individuals. In other words, the Darwinian fitness of such individuals has increased.

It was pointed out earlier that one effect of civilization is to increase mutation rates and hence the supply of harmful genes. A second effect is to decrease the rate of discrimination against such genes, and consequently the rate of their elimination from human populations by natural selection. In thus disturbing the former genetic equilibrium of inflow and outflow, is man not frustrating natural selection and polluting his genetic pool?

The danger exists and cannot be ignored. But in the present state of knowledge the problem is tremendously complex. If our culture has an ideal, it is the sacredness of human life. A society that refused, on eugenic grounds, to cure children of retinoblastoma would, in our eyes, lose more by moral degradation than it gained genetically. Not so easy, however, is the question whether a person who knows he carries the gene for retinoblastoma, or a similarly deleterious gene, has a right to have children.

Even here the genetic issue is clear, although the moral issue may not be. This is no longer true when we come to genes that are harmful in double dose,

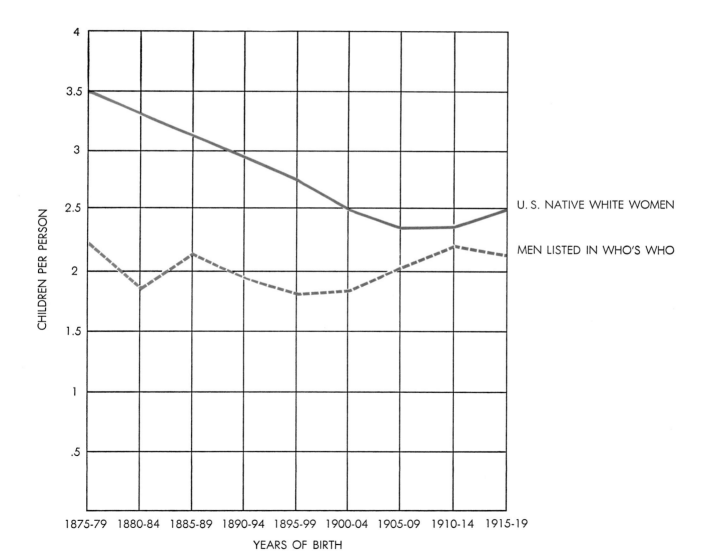

FERTILITY RATE among relatively intelligent people, as represented by a random sample of men listed in *Who's Who in America* for 1956 and 1957, is lower than fertility rate of the U. S. population as a whole, as represented by all native white women. The two fertility rates have recently been moving toward each other. Vertical scale shows average number of children per person; horizontal scale shows approximate birth date of parents. Chart is based upon information collected by Dudley Kirk of the Population Council.

but beneficial in single. If the central African peoples had decided some time ago to breed out the sickle-cell gene, they might have succumbed in much larger numbers to malaria. Fortunately this particular dilemma has been resolved by successful methods of mosquito control. How many other hereditary diseases and malformations are maintained by the advantages their genes confer in heterozygous carriers, we simply do not know.

Conversely, we cannot yet predict the genetic effect of relaxing selection pressure. If, for example, susceptibility to tuberculosis is maintained by recurrent mutations, then the conquest of the disease should increase the concentration of mutant genes as time goes on. On the other hand, if resistance arises from a single dose of genes that make for susceptibility in the double dose, the effects of eradication become much less clear. Other selective forces might then determine the fate of these genes in the population.

In any case, although we cannot see all the consequences, we can be sure that ancient genetic patterns will continue to shift under the shelter of modern medicine. We would not wish it otherwise. It may well be, however, that the social cost of maintaining some genetic variants will be so great that artificial selection against them is ethically, as well as economically, the most acceptable and wisest solution.

If the evolutionary impact of such biological tools as antibiotics and vaccines is still unclear, then computers and rockets, to say nothing of social organizations as a whole, present an even deeper puzzle. There is no doubt that human survival will continue to depend more and more on human intellect and technology. It is idle to argue whether this is good or bad. The point of no return was passed long ago, before anyone knew it was happening.

But to grant that the situation is inevitable is not to ignore the problems it raises. Selection in modern societies does not always encourage characteristics that we regard as desirable. Let us consider one example. Much has been written about the differential fertility that in advanced human societies favors less intelligent over more intelligent people. Studies in several countries have shown that school children from large families tend to score lower on so-called intelligence tests than their classmates with few or no brothers and sisters. Moreover, parents who score lower on these tests have more children on the average

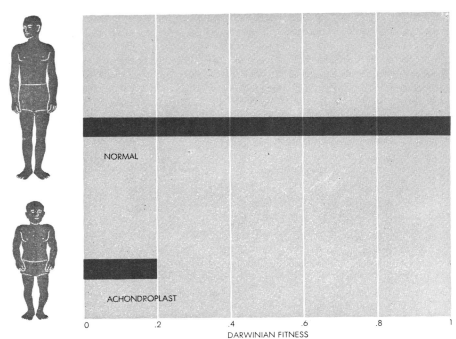

DARWINIAN FITNESS of achondroplastic dwarfs is low. Dwarfs may be healthy, but they have only 20 surviving children to every 100 surviving children of normal parents.

than those who get higher marks.

We cannot put our finger on the forces responsible for this presumed selection against intelligence. As a matter of fact, there is some evidence that matters are changing, in the U. S. at least. People included in *Who's Who in America* (assuming that people listed in this directory are on the average more intelligent than people not listed there) had fewer children than the general population during the period from 1875 to 1904. In the next two decades, however, the difference seemed to be disappearing. L. S. Penrose of University College London, one of the outstanding human geneticists, has pointed out that a negative correlation between intelligence and family size may in part be corrected by the relative infertility of low-grade mental defectives. He suggests that selection may thus be working toward maintaining a constant level of genetic conditioning for intelligence in human populations. The evidence presently available is insufficient either to prove or to contradict this hypothesis.

It must also be recognized that in man and other social animals qualities making for successful individuals are not necessarily those most useful to the society as a whole. If there were a gene for altruism, natural selection might well discriminate against it on the individual level, but favor it on the population level. In that case the fate of the gene would be hard to predict.

If this article has asked many more questions than it has answered, the purpose is to suggest that answers be sought with all possible speed. Natural selection is a very remarkable phenomenon. But it does not even guarantee the survival of a species. Most living forms have become extinct without the "softening" influence of civilization, simply by becoming too narrowly specialized. Natural selection is opportunistic; in shaping an organism to fit its surroundings it may leave the organism unable to cope with a change in environment. In this light, man's explosive ability to change his environment may offer as much threat as promise. Technological evolution may have outstripped biological evolution.

Yet man is the only product of biological evolution who knows that he has evolved and is evolving further. He should be able to replace the blind force of natural selection by conscious direction, based on his knowledge of nature and on his values. It is as certain that such direction will be needed as it is questionable whether man is ready to provide it. He is unready because his knowledge of his own nature and its evolution is insufficient; because a vast majority of people are unaware of the necessity of facing the problem; and because there is so wide a gap between the way people actually live and the values and ideals to which they pay lip service.

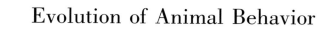

Evolution of Animal Behavior

EVOLUTION OF ANIMAL BEHAVIOR

In recent decades anthropologists have become concerned with the effect of genetics and evolutionary processes on learning, animal behavior, and social organization as they attempt to distinguish behavior that is learned from behavior that is genetically controlled. In this section several leading students of the evolution of animal behavior, intelligence, and social organization give the reader insight into their specialties.

The first of these, the noted ethologist Konrad Z. Lorenz, argues that not only animal structure, but also animal behavior has evolved. Ultimately, then, Lorenz's explanation of animal behavioral evolution must in some way be explainable with the basic genetic material DNA, just as structural evolution is so explained. In the present article, "The Evolution of Behavior," Lorenz compares the behavior patterns of several species of birds in order to establish a control group for studying individual variation within species, at the same time comparing similarities and differences between hybrid species. The influence of population genetics and the concept of variation within populations is unmistakable in his article, the outcome of which is the conclusion that because innate motor pattern differences could be duplicated by hybridization among the species being studied, behavior must be genetically related.

M. E. Bitterman, in "The Evolution of Intelligence," directs our attention away from genetically related behavior to the origins of learning. By comparing the learning behavior of five different animals—fish, turtle, pigeon, rat, and monkey—in tasks requiring habit reversal and probability learning, Bitterman concludes that the evolution of animal intelligence has not been a constant development in all species. Indeed, pigeons, rats, and monkeys can all perform the complex tasks in which Bitterman tested their intelligence, whereas turtles performed but one such task and fishes performed none. Bitterman concludes that in higher animals brain structures must be able to mediate new modes of intellectual adjustment as well as replicate old functions. The differences that distinguish "fishlike" learning (in which no improvement is observed in habit reversal and probability learning) from "ratlike" learning (in which progressive improvement is observed) might well be due to different development in the size and complexity of the cerebral cortexes in those animals that are fishlike and others that are ratlike.

Moving from comparative evolutionary studies to an analysis of single species, we see that even the social behavior of turkeys is most convincingly described when it is compared with the behavior of other species, including man. The third essay, "The Social Order of Turkeys," by C. Robert Watts and Allen W. Stokes, focuses on the behavior of a single wild species of turkey. Watts and Stokes suggest that much of the social behavior of the turkeys they have observed might be determined by the nature of their habitat—a sort of "turkey ecology" explanation. When species inhabit plentiful, open grasslands they organize themselves into large flocks and establish a male dominated hierarchy that is rigorously maintained, in which only dominant males mate with hens.

Next, two anthropologists—S. L. Washburn, a specialist in biology, and I. DeVore, a specialist in social anthropology—team up to describe sociableness, grooming, cohesion, and self-preservation among a baboon troop on an African game preserve. In this now famous article, "The Social Life of Baboons," the authors show how the dominant members of the troop distribute themselves in such a fashion as to be able to protect their more vulnerable troop members from predators while the troop travels. Washburn and DeVore also describe how baboons, with their keen eyesight, and impalas, with their keen sense of smell, have developed a symbiotic relationship that contributes to the security of both.

The final essay in the section is Sheo Dan Singh's "Urban Monkeys," in which we are treated to an analysis of adaptation of monkeys to cities rather than game preserves. Singh points out that there are differences in temperament and behavior between monkeys that dwell in cities and their forest congeners. For instance, whereas urban monkeys are less aggressive than their country cousins at the feeding place, they are more aggressive in their interactions among themselves and with strangers. As a matter of fact, the urban monkey exhibits many of the behaviors that are closely associated with stereotypes of human urban life. That is to say, the urban monkey is nastier than his bumpkin relatives, but of the same intelligence.

10

THE EVOLUTION OF BEHAVIOR

KONRAD Z. LORENZ
December 1958

Beneath the varying behavior which animals learn lie unvarying motor patterns which they inherit. These behavior traits are as much a characteristic of a species as bodily structure and form

A whale's flipper, a bat's wing and a man's arm are as different from one another in outward appearance as they are in the functions they serve. But the bones of these structures reveal an essential similarity of design. The zoologist concludes that whale, bat and man evolved from a common ancestor. Even if there were no other evidence, the comparison of the skeletons of these creatures would suffice to establish that conclusion. The similarity of skeletons shows that a basic structure may persist over geologic periods in spite of a wide divergence of function.

Following the example of zoologists, who have long exploited the comparative method, students of animal behavior have now begun to ask a penetrating question. We all know how greatly the behavior of animals can vary, especially under the influence of the learning process. Psychologists have mostly observed and experimented with the behavior of individual animals; few have considered the behavior of species. But is it not possible that beneath all the variations of individual behavior there lies an inner structure of inherited behavior which characterizes all the members of a given

species, genus or larger taxonomic group —just as the skeleton of a primordial ancestor characterizes the form and structure of all mammals today?

Yes, it is possible! Let me give an example which, while seemingly trivial, has a bearing on this question. Anyone who has watched a dog scratch its jaw or a bird preen its head feathers can attest to the fact that they do so in the same way. The dog props itself on the tripod formed by its haunches and two forelegs and reaches a hindleg forward in front of its shoulder. Now the odd fact is that most birds (as well as virtu-

SCRATCHING BEHAVIOR of a dog and a European bullfinch is part of their genetic heritage and is not changed by training. The widespread habit of scratching with a hindlimb crossed over a forelimb is common to most Amniota (birds, reptiles and mammals).

DISPLAY BEHAVIOR of seagulls shows how behavior traits inherent in all gulls have adapted to the needs of an aberrant species. At top is a typical gull, the herring gull, which breeds on the shore. It is shown in the "choking" posture which advertises its nest site. In middle the herring gull is shown in the "oblique" and "long call" postures, used to defend its territory. At bottom is the aberrant kittiwake, which unlike other gulls breeds on narrow ledges and has no territory other than its nest site. The kittiwake does not use the "oblique" or "long call" postures, but employs the "choking" stance for both advertisement and defense.

ally all mammals and reptiles) scratch with precisely the same motion! A bird also scratches with a hindlimb (that is, its claw), and in doing so it lowers its wing and reaches its claw forward in front of its shoulder. One might think that it would be simpler for the bird to move its claw directly to its head without moving its wing, which lies folded out of the way on its back. I do not see how to explain this clumsy action unless we admit that it is inborn. Before the bird can scratch, it must reconstruct the old spatial relationship of the limbs of the four-legged common ancestor which it shares with mammals.

In retrospect it seems peculiar that psychologists have been so slow to pursue such clues to hereditary behavior. It is nearly 100 years since T. H. Huxley, upon making his first acquaintance with Charles Darwin's concept of natural selection, exclaimed: "How stupid of me, not to have thought of that!" Darwinian evolution quickly fired the imagination of biologists. Indeed, it swept through the scientific world with the speed characteristic of all long-overdue ideas. But somehow the new approach stopped short at the borders of psychology. The psychologists did not draw on Darwin's comparative method, or on his sense of the species as the protagonist of the evolutionary process.

Perhaps, with their heritage from philosophy, they were too engrossed in purely doctrinal dissension. For exactly opposite reasons the "behaviorists" and the "purposivists" were convinced that behavior was much too variable to permit its reduction to a set of traits characteristic of a species. The purposivist school of psychology argued for the existence of instincts; the behaviorists argued against them. The purposivists believed that instincts set the goals of animal behavior, but left to the individual animal a boundless variety of means to reach these goals. The behaviorists held that the capacity to learn endowed the individual with unlimited plasticity of behavior. The debate over instinct versus learning kept both schools from perceiving consistent, inherited patterns in behavior, and led each to preoccupation with external influences on behavior.

If any psychologist stood apart from the sterile contention of the two schools, it was Jakob von Uexküll. He sought tirelessly for the causes of animal behavior, and was not blind to structure. But he too was caught in a philosophical trap. Uexküll was a vitalist, and he denounced Darwinism as gross materialism. He believed that the regularities he observed in the behavior of species were manifestations of nature's unchanging and unchangeable "ground plan," a notion akin to the mystical "idea" of Plato.

The Phylogeny of Behavior

But even as the psychologists debated, evolutionary thought was entering the realm of behavior studies by two back doors. At Woods Hole, Mass., Charles Otis Whitman, a founder of the Marine Biological Laboratory, was working out the family tree of pigeons, which he had bred as a hobby since early childhood. Simultaneously, but unknown to Whitman, Oskar Heinroth of the Berlin Aquarium was studying the phylogeny of waterfowl. Heinroth, too, was an amateur aviculturist who had spent a lifetime observing his own pet ducks. What a queer misnomer is the word "amateur"! How unjust that a term which means the "lover" of a subject should come to connote a superficial dabbler! As a result of their "dabbling," Whitman and Heinroth acquired an incomparably detailed knowledge of pigeon and duck behavior.

As phylogenists, Whitman and Heinroth both sought to develop in detail the relationship between families and species of birds. To define a given group they had to find its "homologous" traits: the resemblances between species which bespeak a common origin. The success or failure of their detective work hinged on the number of homologous traits they could find. As practical bird-fanciers, Whitman and Heinroth came to know bird behavior as well as bird morphology, and each independently reached an important discovery: Behavior, as well as body form and structure, displays homologous traits. As Whitman phrased it just 60 years ago: "Instincts and organs are to be studied from the common viewpoint of phyletic descent."

Sometimes these traits of behavior are common to groups larger than ducks or pigeons. The scratching habit, which I have already mentioned, is an example of a behavior pattern that is shared by a very large taxonomic group, in this case the Amniota: the reptiles, birds and mammals (all of whose embryos grow within the thin membrane of the amniotic sac). This widespread motor pattern was discovered by Heinroth, who described it in a brief essay in 1930. It is noteworthy that Heinroth observed the extreme resistance of such inborn habits to changes wrought by learning. He noticed that while most bird species maintain their incongruous over-the-shoulder

"HEAD-FLAGGING" is another form of display in which the kittiwake has adapted its behavioral birthright to meet unusual needs. Most gulls—like this pair of black-faced gulls— use this stance in courtship (by averting its menacing facial and bill coloration, the bird "appeases" the aggressive instinct of its mate). Kittiwakes alone evince this posture not only in mating adults but in ledge-bound nestlings, which use it to "appease" invaders.

scratching technique, some have lost this behavior trait. Among these are the larger parrots, which feed with their claws and use the same motion—under the wing—for scratching. Parakeets, however, scratch in the unreconstructed style, reaching around the lowered wing, and do not pick up food in their claws. There are a few exceptions to this rule. The Australian broadtailed parakeet has learned to eat with its claw. When eating, it raises its claw directly to its bill. But when scratching, it still reaches its claw around its lowered wing! This oddity is evidence in itself of the obstinacy of the old scratching habit. So far no one has been able to teach a parakeet to scratch without lowering its wing or to train a parrot to scratch around a lowered wing.

Today a growing school of investigators is working in the field opened up by Whitman and Heinroth. They have set themselves the task of discovering inherited patterns of behavior and tracing them from species to species. Many of these patterns have proved to be reliable clues to the origin and relationship of large groups of animals. There is no longer any doubt that animals in general do inherit certain deep-seated behavioral traits. In the higher animals such traits tend to be masked by learned behavior, but in such creatures as fishes and birds they reveal themselves with great clarity. These patterns of behavior must somehow be rooted in the common phys-

iological inheritance of the species that display them. Whatever their physiological cause, they undoubtedly form a natural unit of heredity. The majority of them change but slowly with evolution in the species and stubbornly resist learning in the individual; they have a peculiar spontaneity and a considerable independence of immediate sensory stimuli. Because of their stability, they rank with the more slowly evolving skeletal structure of animals as ideal subjects for the comparative studies which aim to unravel the history of species.

I am quite aware that biologists today (especially young ones) tend to think of the comparative method as stuffy and old-fashioned—at best a branch of research that has already yielded its treasures, and like a spent gold mine no longer pays the working. I believe that this is untrue, and so I shall pause to say a few words in behalf of comparative morphology as such. Every time a biologist seeks to know *why* an organism looks and acts as it does, he must resort to the comparative method. Why does the ear have its peculiar conformation? Why is it mounted behind the jaw? To know the answer the investigator must compare the mammalian frame with that of other vertebrates. Then he will discover that the ear was once a gill slit. When the first air-breathing, four-legged vertebrates came out of the sea, they lost all but one pair of gill slits, each of which happened to lie conveniently near the

"INCITING" is a threatening movement used by the female duck to signal her mate to attack invaders of their territory. At left a female of the European sheldrake (*with head lowered*) incites her mate against an enemy that she sees directly before her. The female at right (*with head turned*) has seen an enemy to one side. Each female watches her enemy regardless of her own body orientation.

labyrinth of the inner ear. The water canal which opened into it became filled with air and adapted itself to conducting sound waves. Thus was born the ear.

This kind of thinking is 100 years old in zoology, but in the study of behavior it is only now coming into its own. The first studies leading to a true morphology of behavior have concentrated largely on those innate motor patterns that have the function of expression or communication within a species. It is easy to see why this should be so. Whether the mode of communication is aural, as in the case of bird songs, or visual, as in the "dis-play" movements of courtship, many of these motor patterns have evolved under the pressure of natural selection to serve as sharply defined stimuli influencing the social behavior of fellow-members of a species. The patterns are usually striking and unambiguous. These qualities, so essential to the natural function of the behavior patterns, also catch the eye of the human observer.

Gulls, Terns and Kittiwakes

For some years N. Tinbergen of the University of Oxford has intensively studied the innate behavior of gulls and terns: the genus *Laridae*. He has organized an international group of his students and co-workers to conduct a world-wide study of the behavior traits of gulls and terns. They are careful to observe the behavior of their subjects in the larger context of their diverse life histories and in relationship to their different environments. It is gratifying that this ambitious project has begun to meet with the success which the enthusiasm of its participants so richly deserves.

Esther Cullen, one of Tinbergen's students, has been studying an eccentric

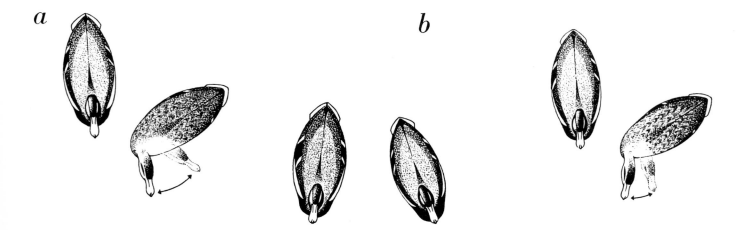

a   *b*

"RITUALIZED" INCITING is exhibited by mallards. In this species turning the head—as a female sheldrake does when inciting against an enemy to one side—has become an innate motor pattern. In situation *a* the female mallard turns her head toward the enemy. In *b*, with the enemy in front of her, she still turns her head even though this results in her turning it away from the enemy.

among the seagulls—the kittiwake. Most gulls are beachcombers and nest on the ground, and it is safe to assume that this was the original mode of life of the gull family. The kittiwake, however, is different. Except when it is breeding, it lives over the open sea. Its breeding ground is not a flat shore but the steepest of cliffs, where it nests on tiny ledges.

Mrs. Cullen has listed 33 points, both behavioral and anatomical, in which the kittiwake has come to differ from its sister species as a result of its atypical style of life. Just as the whale's flipper is a recognizable mammalian forelimb, so many of the kittiwake's habits are recognizably gull-like. But the kittiwake, like the whale, is a specialist; it has given its own twist to many of the behavior patterns that are the heritage of the *Laridae*.

For example, the male of most gull species stakes its claim to nesting territory by uttering the "long call" and striking the "oblique posture," its tail up and head down. To advertise its actual nesting site, it performs the "choking" movement. In the kittiwake the inherited patterns of behavior have been modified in accord with the habitat. On the kittiwake's tiny ledge, territory and nest sites are identical. So the kittiwake has lost the oblique posture and long call, and uses choking alone for display purposes.

Another example is the kittiwake gesture which Tinbergen calls "head-flagging." In other gull species a young gull which is not fully able to fly will run for cover when it is frightened by an adult bird. But its cliffside perch provides no cover for the young kittiwake. When it is frightened, the little kittiwake averts its head as a sign of appeasement. Such head-flagging does not occur in the young of other gulls, although it appears in the behavior of many adult gulls as the appeasement posture in a fight and in the rite of courtship. The kittiwake species has thus met an environmental demand by accelerating, in its young, the development of a standard motor habit of adult gulls.

Recently Wolfgang Wickler, one of my associates at the Max Planck Institute for Comparative Ethology, has found a similar case of adaptation by acceleration among the river-dwelling cichlid fishes. Most cichlids dig into the river bottom only at spawning time, when they excavate their nest pits. But there is an eccentric species (*Steatocranus*), a resident of the rapids of the Congo River, which lives from infancy in river-bottom burrows. In this cichlid the maturation of the digging urge of the mating fish is accelerated, appearing in

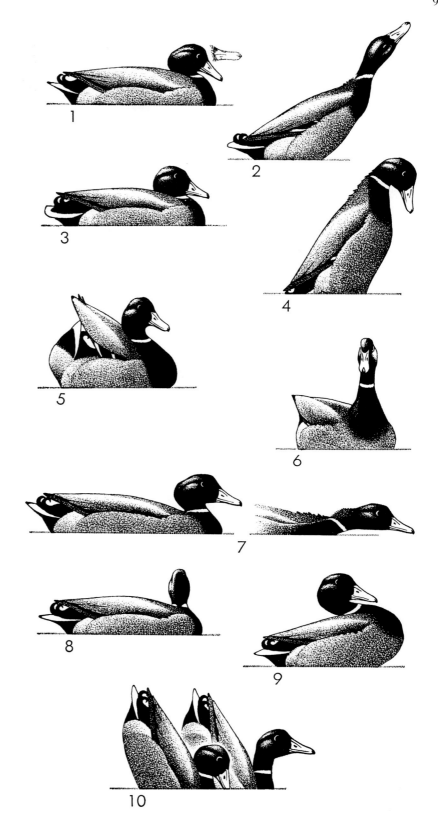

TEN COURTSHIP POSES which belong to the common genetic heritage of surface-feeding ducks are here shown as exemplified in the mallard: (1) initial bill-shake, (2) head-flick, (3) tail-shake, (4) grunt-whistle, (5) head-up—tail-up, (6) turn toward the female, (7) nod-swimming, (8) turning the back of the head, (9) bridling, (10) down-up. How the mallard and two other species form sequences of these poses is illustrated on pages 100 through 103.

the infant of the species. It is not hard to conceive how selection pressure could have led to this result.

The work of the Tinbergen school has had the important result of placing innate motor habits in their proper setting. He and his co-workers have shown that these traits are highly resistant to evolutionary change, and that they often retain their original form even when their function has diverged considerably. These findings amply justify the metaphor that describes innate patterns as the skeleton of behavior. More work of the Tinbergen kind is badly needed. There

is great value in his synthetic approach, uniting the study of the physical nature and environment of animals with study of their behavior. Any such project is of course a tall order. It requires concerted field work by investigators at widely separated points on the globe.

Behavior in the Laboratory

Fortunately it is quite feasible to approach the innate motor patterns as an isolated topic for examination in the laboratory. Thanks to their stability they are not masked in the behavior of the

captive animal. If only we do not forget the existence of the many other physiological mechanisms that affect behavior, including that of learning, it is legitimate for us to begin with these innate behavior traits. The least variable part of a system is always the best one to examine first; in the complex interaction of all parts, it must appear most frequently as a cause and least frequently as an effect.

Comparative study of innate motor patterns represents an important part of the research program at the Max Planck Institute for Comparative Ethology. Our

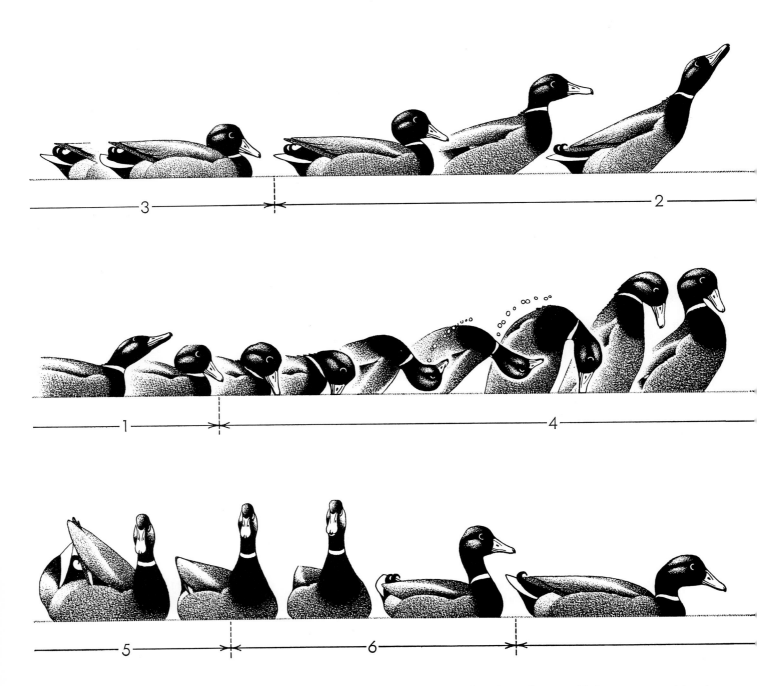

COURTSHIP SEQUENCES OF MALLARD are shown in this series of drawings, based on motion pictures made by the author at

his laboratory in Seewiesen, Germany. Each sequence combines in fixed order several of the 10 innate courtship poses illustrated on

subjects are the various species of dabbling, or surface-feeding, ducks. By observing minute variations of behavior traits between species on the one hand and their hybrids on the other we hope to arrive at a phylogenetics of behavior.

Our comparative studies have developed sufficient information about the behavior traits of existing species to permit us to observe the transmission, suppression and combination of these traits in hybrid offspring. Ordinarily it is difficult to find species which differ markedly with respect to a particular characteristic and which yet will produce fertile hybrids. This is true especially with respect to behavioral traits, because these tend to be highly conservative. Species which differ sufficiently in behavior seldom produce offspring of unlimited fertility. However, closely related species which differ markedly in their patterns of sexual display are often capable of producing fertile hybrids. These motor patterns serve not only to bring about mating within a species but to prevent mating between closely allied species. Selection pressure sets in to make these patterns as different as possible as quickly as possible. As a result species will diverge markedly in sexual display behavior and yet retain the capacity to interbreed. This has turned out to be the case with dabbling ducks.

The first thing we wanted to know was how the courtship patterns of ducks become fixed. Credit is due to Sir Julian Huxley, who as long ago as 1914 had observed this process, which he called "ritualization." We see it clearly in the so-called "inciting" movement of female dabbling ducks, diving ducks, perching ducks and sheldrakes.

To see "inciting" in its original unritualized form, let us watch the female

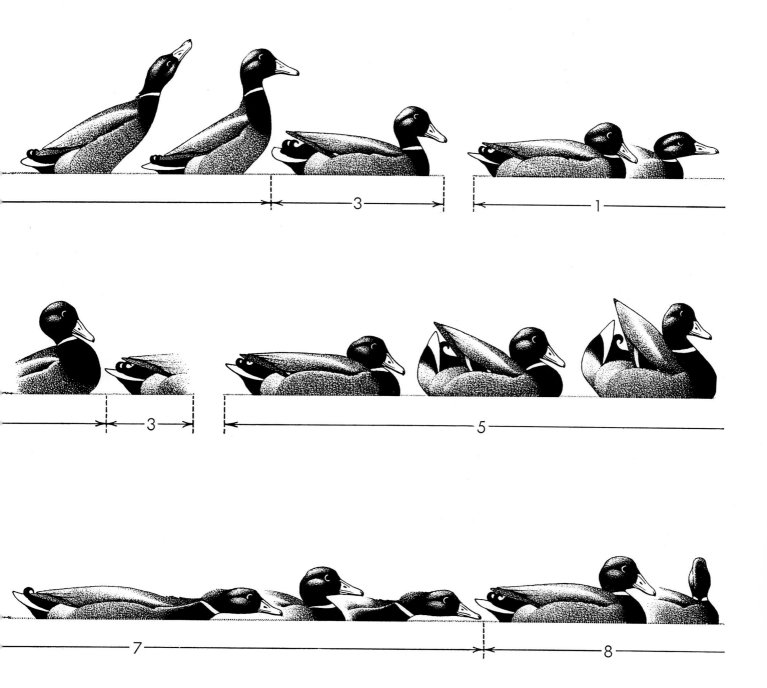

page 99. The numbers under the ducks refer to these poses. Shown here are the following obligatory sequences: tail-shake, head flick, tail-shake; bill-shake, grunt-whistle, tail-shake; head-up tail-up, turn toward female, nod-swimming, turning back of the head.

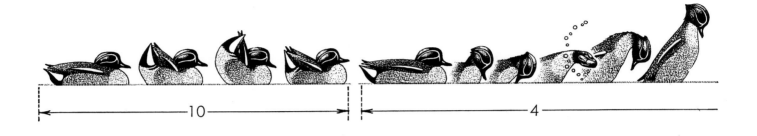

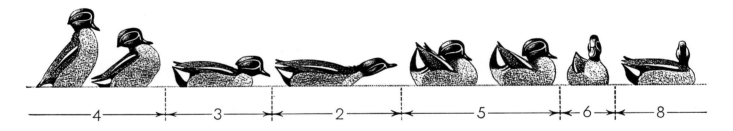

COURTSHIP OF EUROPEAN TEAL—another species of surface-feeding duck—includes tail-shake, head-flick, tail-shake (as in the mallard); down-up; grunt-whistle, tail-shake, head-flick, head-up–tail-up, turned toward the female, turning back of the head.

of the common sheldrake as she and her mate encounter another pair of sheldrakes at close quarters. Being far more excitable than her placid companion, the female attacks the "enemy" couple, that is, she adopts a threatening attitude and runs toward them at full tilt. It happens, however, that her escape reaction is quite as strong as her aggressive one. She has only to come within a certain distance of the enemy for the escape stimulus to overpower her, whereupon she turns tail and flees to the protection of her mate. When she has run a safe distance, she experiences a renewal of the aggressive impulse. Perhaps by this time she has retreated behind her mate. In that case she struts up beside him, and, as they both face the enemy, she makes threatening gestures toward them. But more likely she has not yet reached her mate when the aggressive impulse re-

turns. In that case she may stop in her tracks. With her body still oriented toward her mate, she will turn her head and threaten the enemy over her shoulder. In this stance she is said to "incite" an aggressive attitude in her partner.

Now the incitement posture of the female sheldrake does not constitute an innate behavior trait. It is the entirely plastic resultant of the pressure of two independent variables: her impulse to attack and her impulse to flee. The orientation of her head and body reflects the geometry of her position with respect to her mate and the enemy.

The same incitement posture in mallards, on the other hand, is distinctly ritualized. In striking her pose the female mallard is governed by an inherited motor pattern. She cannot help thrusting her head backward over her shoulder. She does this even if it means she must

point her bill away from the enemy! In the sheldrake this posture is the resultant of the creature's display of two conflicting impulses. In the mallard it has become a fixed motor pattern.

No doubt this motor pattern evolved fairly recently. It is interesting to note that while the female mallard is impelled to look over her shoulder when inciting, the older urge to look at the enemy is still there. Her head travels much farther backward when the enemy is behind her. If you observe closely, it is plain that her eyes are fixed on the enemy, no matter which way her head is turned.

Occasionally a female, impelled by the awkwardness of watching the enemy from the ritualized posture, will swing about and face them directly. In that case one may say that her old and new motor patterns are simultaneously active. Like the sheldrake, the mallard must once have faced the enemy during incitement. Overlying this instinct is a new one—to move her head backward over her shoulder regardless of the location of the enemy. The old orienting response survives in part. It usually displays itself at low levels of excitement. Especially at the beginning of a response, the female mallard may stretch her neck straight forward. As her excitement mounts, however, the new motor pattern irresistibly draws her head around. This is one of many instances in which the mounting intensity of a stimulus increases the fixity of the motor coordination.

What has happened is that two independent movements have been welded together to form a new and fixed motor pattern. It is possible that all new patterns are formed by such a welding process. Sometimes two patterns remain rigidly welded. Sometimes they weld only under great excitement.

Recently we have been studying be-

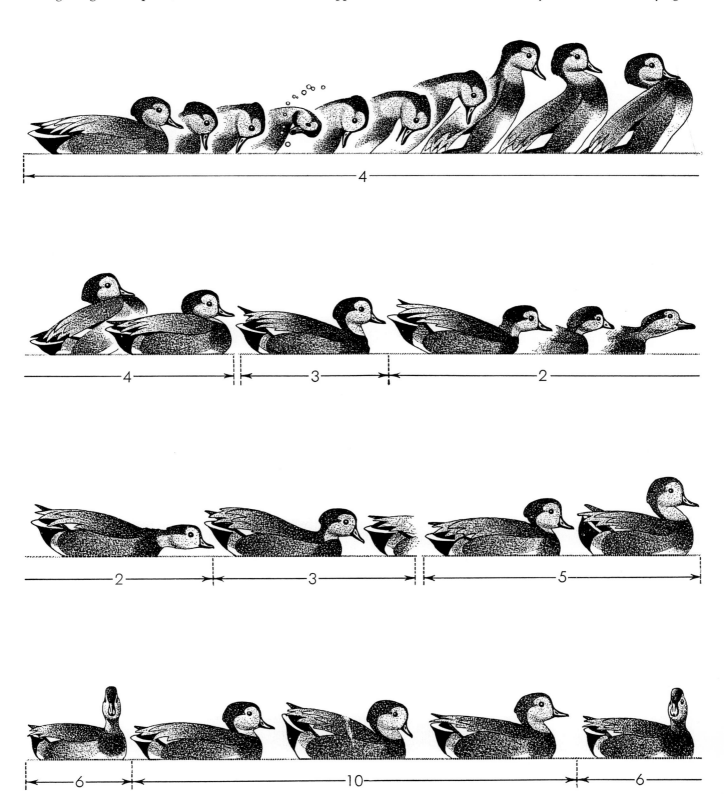

GADWALL COURTSHIP includes the grunt-whistle, always followed by the tail-shake, head-flick, tail-shake sequence also found in the other species illustrated. The head-up–tail-up (5) and the down-up (10) are always followed by a turn toward the female (6). During the most intense excitement of the courtship display, these pairs themselves become welded into the invariable sequence 5-6-10-6.

havior complexes in which more than two patterns are welded. In their courtship behavior our surface-feeding ducks display some 20 elementary innate motor patterns. We have made a special study of three species which have 10 motor patterns in common but display them welded into different combinations. As shown in the illustration on page 99, these patterns are (1) initial bill-shake, (2) head-flick, (3) tail-shake, (4) grunt-whistle, (5) head-up—tail-up, (6) turn toward the female, (7) nod-swimming, (8) turning the back of the head, (9) bridling, (10) down-up movement. Some of the combinations in which these motor patterns are displayed are shown on pages 100 through 103. In some species certain of the patterns occur independently (*e.g.*, 1 and 10 in the mallard). Some simple combinations have wide distribution in other species as well (*e.g.*,

4, 3 and 5, 6 in all the species). Many combinations are more complicated, as the illustrations show.

What happens when these ducks are crossbred? By deliberate breeding we have produced new combinations of motor patterns, often combining traits of both parents, sometimes suppressing the traits of one or the other parent and sometimes exhibiting traits not apparent in either. We have even reproduced some of the behavior-pattern combinations which occur in natural species other than the parents of the hybrid. Study of our first-generation hybrids indicates that many differences in courtship patterns among our duck species may also be due to secondary loss, that is, to suppression of an inherited trait. Crosses between the Chiloe teal and the Bahama pintail regularly perform the head-up—tail-up, although neither parent is ca-

pable of this. The only possible conclusion is that one parent species is latently in possession of this behavioral trait, and that its expression in a given species is prevented by some inhibiting factor. So far our only second-generation hybrids are crosses between the Chiloe pintail and the Bahama pintail. The results look promising. The drakes of this generation differ greatly from each other and display hitherto unheard-of combinations of courtship patterns. One has even fused the down-up movement with the grunt-whistle!

Thus we have shown that the differences in innate motor patterns which distinguish species from one another can be duplicated by hybridization. This suggests that motor patterns are dependent on comparatively simple constellations of genetic factors.

11

THE EVOLUTION OF INTELLIGENCE

M. E. BITTERMAN
January 1965

It has been assumed that the intelligence of animals on various rungs of the evolutionary ladder differs only in degree. New experiments on animals from fish to monkey show that the differences are qualitative

Suppose an animal is given a choice between two alternative courses of action, one of which is rewarded consistently and the other never. If the alternatives are readily discriminable, the animal will, after a number of trials, develop the habit of choosing the rewarded one. By plotting trials against errors, the experimental psychologist constructs a curve called a learning function that summarizes the course of the animal's mastery of the problem.

It has been known for some time that learning functions based on such simple problems do not differ significantly among diverse animals; the curves for a monkey and a fish, for example, have a similar shape. This fact, implying some intellectual continuity throughout the evolutionary hierarchy of animals, tended to corroborate a theory of animal intelligence that prevailed during the first half of the 20th century.

According to this theory, an animal is born with tendencies to react in certain ways to certain stimuli—tendencies based on inherited neural connections between sensory and motor systems. The animal's ability to learn is simply its ability to modify these connections (to break some and to form others) as needs and circumstances dictate. Differences in intelligence from species to species are differences only of degree. The higher animals can form more connections than the lower animals because of better sensory and motor development and because their nervous systems afford more elements for this purpose. Hence the evolution of intelligence merely entails refining old processes and replicating old neural equipment.

Since learning was thought to involve qualitatively similar processes throughout the evolutionary hierarchy it seemed that there was nothing to be gained from studying many different species, and that there was much to be lost in terms of experimental efficiency. Attention became concentrated on a few mammals—primarily the rat—selected for reasons of laboratory custom or convenience and treated as being representative of animals in general. The number of animals under study narrowed, and so did the likelihood of discovering any differences that might in fact exist.

The investigations I have been conducting for several years with my associates at Bryn Mawr College were inspired by the conviction that the traditional theory called for more critical scrutiny than it had received. We began with the knowledge that the simplest problems would not serve to reveal distinct modes of intelligence and different neural mechanisms at work in various animals. Hoping that experiments based on more complex problems would point to such differences, we complicated matters for our test animals by introducing certain inconsistencies in reward. Thus we developed several kinds of experiment on which our diverse subjects (monkey, rat, pigeon, turtle and fish) gave diverse performances. The two I shall describe in this article are habit-reversal and probability-learning experiments.

In habit-reversal experiments animals are rewarded for choosing alternative A rather than B until a preference for A has been established, then B rather than A is rewarded. When a preference for B has been established, A is again rewarded, and so forth. Trained in this way, a rat or monkey shows a steady improvement in performance. It may make many errors in mastering early reversals, persisting in the choice of previously rewarded alternatives, but as training continues it shifts its preference more and more readily. A fish, in contrast, shows no improvement at all; later reversals are accomplished no more readily than earlier ones.

Although the various sensory, motor and motivational characteristics of the five species we have been studying call for different experimental environments, we have been able to keep certain elements of the test apparatus analogous. In each case the animal is confronted with a pair of translucent Plexiglas panels on which various colors and patterns are projected from behind, and it makes a choice by pressing against one or the other of the panels in its own way: the fish strikes or bites, the pigeon pecks, the monkey pushes with its hand, the turtle or the rat presses with its head or forefoot or both. A correct choice is rewarded with food (a *Tubifex* worm for the fish, a bit of fish for the turtle, some grain for the pigeon, a pellet of sucrose for the rat, a peanut for the monkey), after which there is a brief interval of darkness and then the next choice is offered. If the animal makes an incorrect choice, there is a six-second interval of darkness (called a "time-out"), after which the correct panel alone is illuminated (a procedure called "guidance") and the animal is rewarded for responding to it. Guidance after error guarantees that the animal will not stop responding altogether in the course of a reversal before it has had a chance to learn that the previously unrewarded alternative now is rewarded. The time-out between error and guidance delays access to the reward and thus penalizes precipitous, undiscriminating choice. Without the time-out it would not matter much to the animal whether its choices were correct or not.

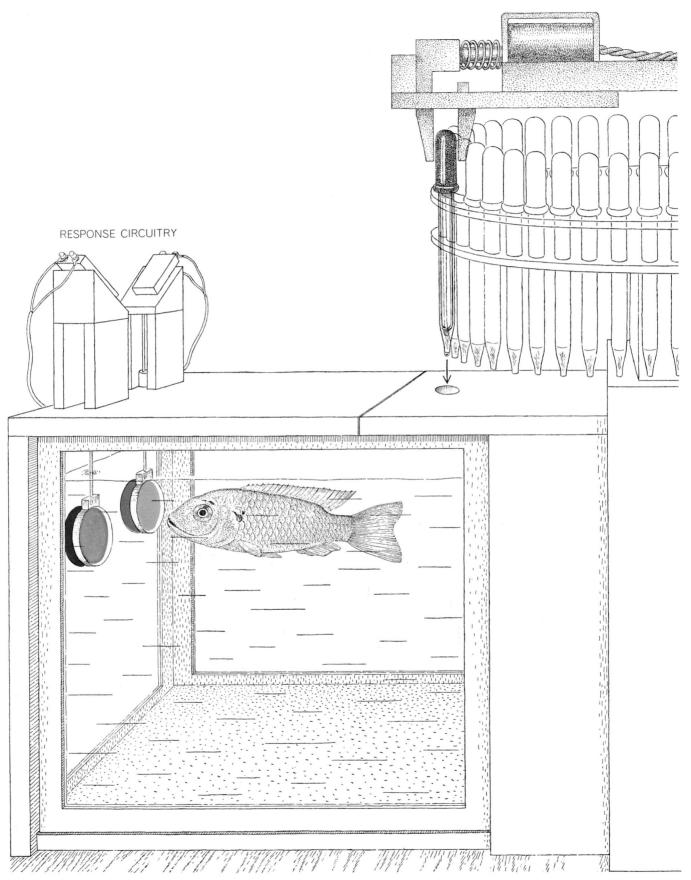

AUTOMATIC REWARD DEVICE

RESPONSE CIRCUITRY

FISH IN A DISCRIMINATION TANK is presented with a visual problem in which the lights projected on two stimulus disks are differently colored. By pressing its head against the proper disk the fish triggers an automatic reward device: the pincers above the eyedropper (*top right*) close, squirting a *Tubifex* worm into the tank. The experimental apparatus was designed by the author.

The entire experimental sequence is programmed by some simple relay circuitry and the responses are graphically recorded. With this introduction of automatic control and the removal of the experimenter there is a gain in objectivity: the animals can no longer be influenced by features of the experimenter's behavior. The task of data collection also becomes less arduous and can be entrusted to a co-worker of limited training, who can take data from several subjects concurrently.

In our experiments we employ both spatial and visual problems. A spatial problem is one in which the alternatives are identical to the eye (that is, the stimuli projected on the two Plexiglas panels are the same) and reward is correlated with the position of the panel. A visual problem is one in which the alternatives look different—blue light and green light, for example, or a triangle and a circle—and reward is correlated with appearance, regardless of position. The results of experiments based on spatial and visual problems can be plotted in comparable fashion, as the two graphs on page 109 indicate.

The experiment that provided the data plotted in the top graph was conducted with rats. Each animal was given 40 trials per day and was reversed whenever it made no more than six errors on any given day. The curve traces the average number of errors made in accomplishing each reversal by the group of rats tested. It reveals that the original problem (Reversal 0) was mastered with few errors, that the first reversal was mastered with difficulty and that adjustment to succeeding reversals was progressively less difficult. The bottom graph shows a similar progressive improvement in habit reversal made by pigeons as they were confronted with a visual problem. The plot of average errors per reversal points to a stage of increasing difficulty followed by a stage of steady improvement. Both for the pigeon and for the rat the first reversal is usually the point of maximum difficulty in spatial problems; the point of maximum difficulty tends to occur later in visual problems.

The fish follows a markedly different pattern. Neither of the two types of fish used in our experiments has shown progressive improvement in habit reversal. In two representative experiments fish were tested on spatial and visual problems, and each animal was reversed whenever it made six or fewer errors on a given 40-trial day. When

PIGEON MAKING A CHOICE is offered two visually distinct stimuli. (The center light is used in another type of test.) If the correct choice is made, some grain is presented in the rectangular opening. The experimental sequence is programmed by relay circuitry.

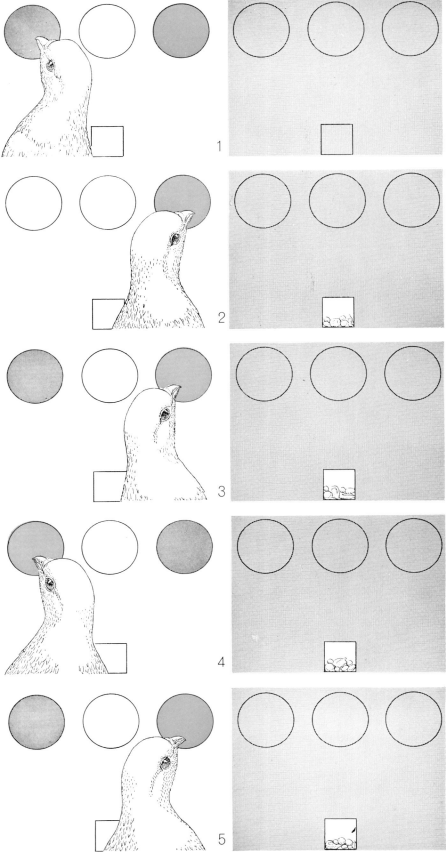

GUIDANCE is offered an animal after it makes an incorrect choice, as the pigeon has done on its first trial (*top left*). No reward is given and the lights go out in the box for six seconds (*top right*). Then the correct panel alone is lighted and the pigeon is rewarded for pecking at it (2). Thereafter the pigeon is shown selecting the proper panel even when faced with the wrong alternative (3) or a change in the position of the correct panel (4 and 5).

we plot the results in terms of average errors per reversal, both curves rise from the original problem to the first reversal but then fail to decline with continued training [*see upper illustrations on page 110*].

Before we can conclude that the fish is incapable of improvement in habit reversal, two other possibilities must be considered. The first is that the fish is in fact capable of progressive improvement, but only after more reversals than higher animals require. This possibility seems unlikely; in experiments with fish as many as 150 reversals have failed to yield evidence of improvement. Another possibility is that the conditions under which the fish has been tested are to blame for its poor showing, that the difference in performance is to be traced not to a difference in capability but to an inequality in some contextual variable such as sensory demand, motor demand, degree of hunger or attractiveness of reward.

Although the environments we construct for the various animals are roughly analogous, there is no way of equating them exactly with respect to such variables. Do a fish and a pigeon distinguish between a pair of red and green lamps with equal ease? Probably not. Does a *Tubifex* worm have the same reward value for a fish that a sucrose pellet has for a rat? Probably not. We do not know how to select stimuli that will be equally discriminable or rewards that will be equally attractive. Can we ever, then, rule out the possibility that a difference in performance of two different animals in such an experiment stems from a difference in some confounded contextual variable?

Fortunately, yes, thanks to a technique known as systematic variation. Consider, for example, the hypothesis that a fish fails to show progressive improvement in a given experiment because it is far less hungry (or far more hungry) than a rat that does show improvement. This hypothesis implies that at some level of hunger the fish will show progressive improvement. Thus we can test it—although we cannot produce in the fish the precise degree of hunger in a given rat—by repeating the experiment with subjects of widely different degrees of hunger. Hypotheses about other contextual variables have been tested by similar systematic variation. Progressive improvement in habit reversal has been sought without success in the fish under a wide variety of conditions, whereas the rat and the pigeon do progress under an equally wide range of conditions. Indeed, it is difficult to find a set of conditions under which the pigeon and the rat fail to show improvement.

The results of experiments on habit reversal in the painted turtle are in a sense intermediate between those for the fish on the one hand and those for the pigeon and the rat on the other. In spatial problems the turtle shows progressive improvement; in visual problems it does not. The data from two recent experiments with turtles, one group trained in a spatial problem and the other trained in a visual problem, are plotted at the bottom of page 110. Both curves give the average number of errors made per reversal. The curves rise from the initial presentation of the problem to the first reversal; then the spatial curve declines but the visual curve does not. We conclude simply that experiments on habit reversal tap an intellectual capability of higher animals that is not at all developed in the fish and is manifested by the turtle only in a restricted class of problems.

Other intellectual differences between our test animals appear when the rewarded alternative is changed within a given trial session (not from session to session). Experiments involving this technique are called probability-learning experiments. In a typical probability-learning experiment alternative A would be rewarded on, say, a random 70 percent of the trials and B would be rewarded the other 30 percent. As in experiments on habit reversal, we confront the animal with either a visual task or a spatial one. We can employ either the guidance method (in which an incorrect choice is followed by a time-out, presentation of only the correct alternative and finally a reward) or the noncorrection method (in which the trial ends whether the rewarded or the unrewarded alternative is chosen). Trained without guidance, subjects of all species tend to "maximize," choosing the 70 percent alternative on all the trials. (An occasional subject comes to the situation with a preference for the 30 percent alternative and persists in choosing it.) If guidance is used, however, striking differences appear among the various species.

Some representative results for the rat and the fish are presented in the two graphs on page 111. During the first stage of the experiments reflected in the graphs the animals were trained on a visual problem—horizontal

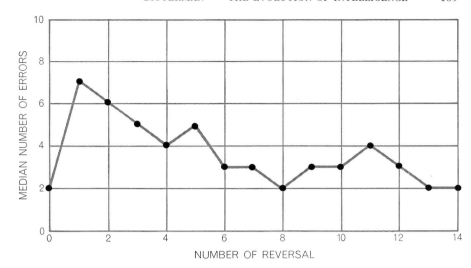

PROGRESSIVE IMPROVEMENT of a group of rats tested on spatial problems that required habit changes is plotted. In solving the original problem (*Reversal 0*) the group made a median number of two errors. When the rewarded alternative was switched (*Reversal 1*), many errors were made before the rats mastered the problem and the rewarded alternative could be switched again. The rats then made fewer errors in achieving reversals.

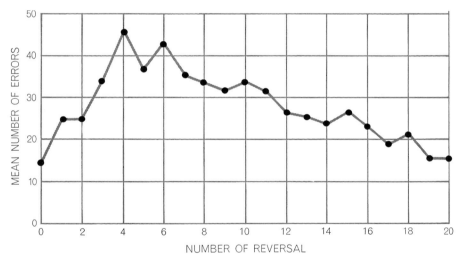

HABIT-REVERSAL EXPERIMENT involving a group of pigeons trained on visual problems yielded the results summarized in this graph. The birds were given 40 trials per day. They made a mean number of 15 errors in mastering the original problem. Difficulty in coping with reversals continued past the first one, reaching a maximum on the fourth reversal, when most animals had to be trained for six days before achieving reversal.

v. vertical stripes—by the guidance method. The choice of horizontal stripes was rewarded in 70 percent of the trials for the first 30 days and in 100 percent of the trials for the next 10 days. The rat tended to maximize under these conditions: after several days it began to choose the 70 percent alternative much more than 70 percent of the time; with the shift in the reward ratio to 100 percent the trend toward absolute preference continued as it might have even without the shift. In contrast, the fish showed a choice pattern we characterize as "matching." It began to choose the 70 percent alternative about 70 percent of the time after a few days of training,

and when the reward ratio was shifted to 100 percent, it rapidly began choosing the rewarded alternative in every instance. In other words, the fish produced a choice ratio that tended to match the reward ratio. We found that in spatial problems too the rat maximizes and the fish matches as long as guidance is used (although without guidance both species tend to maximize).

Whereas the rat and the monkey usually maximize in experiments on probability learning even when guidance is used, they sometimes show a correspondence between choice ratio and reward ratio of a rather different kind from that revealed by the fish. The mammals produce a pattern of systematic matching. Occasionally, for example, a group of rats will choose the rewarded alternative of the preceding trial. This tendency toward reward-following produces a 70 percent choice of the 70 percent alternative when the reward ratio is 70 to 30, and a 50 percent choice of each alternative in a problem in which the ratio is 50 to 50. An opposite strategy—to avoid the rewarded alternative of the preceding trial—sometimes has been used by the monkey. No such systematic tendencies are reflected in the matching of the fish, which can be characterized as random.

A pattern of random matching is also produced by the pigeon when it is tested on a visual problem. Since the rat either maximizes in such cases or begins

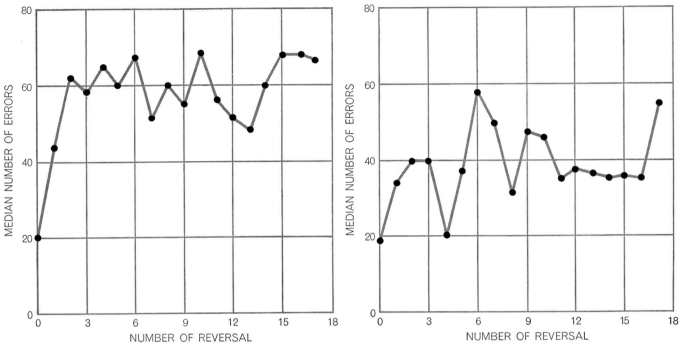

FISH TESTED ON SPATIAL PROBLEM yielded data for this graph, which reveals no progressive improvement in habit reversal. The curve remains approximately level after the first reversal.

FISH TESTED ON A VISUAL PROBLEM show no progressive improvement in habit-reversal experiments. Even graphs of experiments involving 150 reversals do not reveal any downward slope.

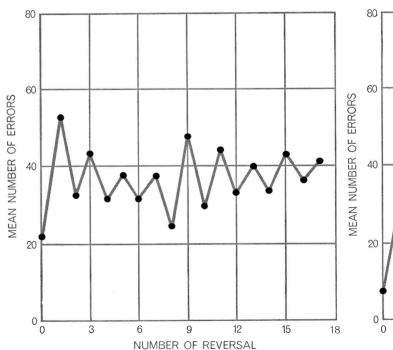

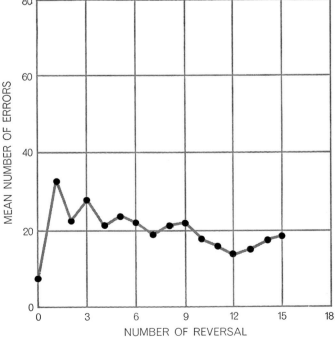

TURTLES TESTED VISUALLY failed to show any progressive improvement in habit reversal. Occasional drops between reversals have no significant statistical effect on the slope of the curve.

TURTLES SOLVING SPATIAL PROBLEMS do show progressive improvement when the results of a habit-reversal experiment are plotted. In this graph improvement follows the initial reversal.

reward-following, the experiments on probability learning have provided us with a clear functional difference between the rat and the pigeon.

Experiments on probability learning yield results for the turtle that are reminiscent of the result of experiments on habit reversal. The efforts of the turtle can be described as random matching in visual problems but maximizing or reward-following in spatial problems. In both kinds of experiment, then, its behavior is ratlike in spatial problems but fishlike in visual problems.

We can use such categories of intellectual behavior (ratlike or fishlike) to tabulate the results of our experiments on habit reversal and probability learning. Such a table [*see bottom illustration on page 112*] suggests the following generalizations: As we ascend the evolutionary scale we do not find a pattern of intellectual continuity but one of discontinuity. Moreover, the modes of adjustment evolved by the higher animals appear earlier in spatial than in visual contexts.

The monkey and the rat are not differentiated by the criteria used to construct our table. The two mammals do, however, show differences in their styles of probability learning, with the reward-following of the rat giving way in the monkey to the opposite strategy (avoiding the rewarded alternative of the preceding trial). It is notable that this strategy of the monkey has been observed so far only in spatial problems, providing support for the generalization that as we go up the evolutionary scale new modes of adjustment appear earlier in spatial than in visual settings.

The idea of advance has long been implicit in the idea of evolution. We are thus led to ask if the ratlike modes of adjustment are really effective in the sense that they help the animal to cope with its environment. Do they actually represent a higher intelligence? In general the answer is yes. Progressive improvement in habit reversal represents a flexibility that cannot help but be of value in an animal's adaptation to changing circumstances. As for probability learning, the ability to maximize produces a higher percentage of correct choices than does matching. In a problem where the reward ratio is 70 to 30, for example, the probability of correct choice is 70 percent if the subject is maximizing but only 58 percent—(.70 × .70) + (.30 × .30)—for an animal that is matching. Systematic matching is no more successful than random matching

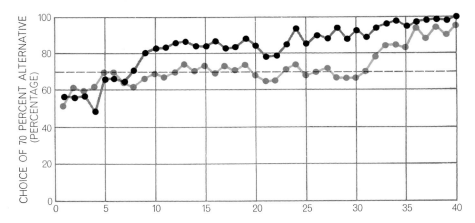

PROBABILITY LEARNING is the subject of experiments such as the one summarized in this graph. The graph compares results for a group of rats (*black curve*) and fish (*colored curve*) tested on visual problems. One alternative was rewarded on 70 percent of the trials for 30 days and on 100 percent of the trials thereafter. Almost from the outset the rat "maximized," tending to make the advantageous choice on 100 percent of the trials. The fish "matched," keeping its choice ratio equal to the reward ratio throughout the experiment.

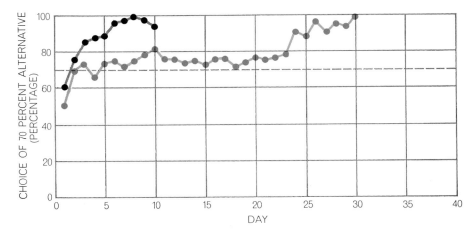

MAXIMIZING is illustrated for rats (*black curve*) and fish (*colored curve*). The animals were trained on spatial problems in which one alternative was rewarded on 70 percent of the trials. The rat, after 10 days, chose the advantageous alternative almost invariably. The fish matched its choice ratio with the reward ratio for 20 days, at which time guidance was discontinued and it tended to choose the advantageous alternative on almost every trial.

by this criterion, and yet we know that human subjects employ systematic matching in trying to find a principle that will enable them to make the correct choice 100 percent of the time. If the use of systematic matching by lower animals is based on some crude, strategic capability, it represents a considerable functional advance over random matching.

Having found behavioral differences among the various types of animal, we are now trying to trace them to physiological differences. My colleague R. C. Gonzales has lately been conducting experiments on habit reversal and probability learning with adult rats lacking extensive portions of the cerebral cortex, a prominent feature of the

mammalian brain that is absent from the brain of the fish and first appears in the reptilian brain. The decorticated rats showed progressive improvement in habit reversal on spatial but not on visual problems. In experiments on probability learning they maximized on spatial problems but took to random matching on visual problems. The intellectual behavior of these decorticated rats was exactly like that of the turtle, an animal with little cortex.

Summarizing the meaning of these experiments calls for sketching the origins of the study of animal intelligence. A century ago, as Charles Darwin developed his theory of evolution, he denied not only the physical uniqueness of man but also the intellectual uniqueness. In doing so he used the only evidence available to him: episodes described by naturalists, hunters, pet-owners and zoo-keepers. It was not until the start of the 20th century that the study of animal intelligence was brought from the realm of the anecdote into the laboratory by Edward L. Thorndike, who was then working at Harvard University. Thorndike's experiments led him to deny the existence of intellectual uniqueness anywhere in the evolutionary hierarchy of animals. It was he who set forth the theory that differences from species to species are only differences of degree, and that the evolution of intelligence involves only the improvement of old processes and the development of more neural elements.

Our studies of habit reversal and probability learning in the lower animals suggest that brain structures evolved by higher animals do not serve merely to replicate old functions and modes of intellectual adjustment but to mediate new ones (a contradiction of the Thorndike hypothesis). Work with decorticated rats points to the same conclusion. Yet it should be observed that these recent studies represent a new turn in the investigative path founded by Thorndike himself. Clearly bringing the study into the laboratory was the real first step toward replacing guesses with facts about the evolution of intelligence and its relation to the evolution of the brain.

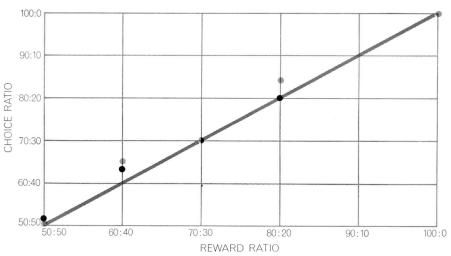

MATCHING of choice ratio (*vertical axis*) with reward ratio (*horizontal axis*) approaches a linear relation for both the pigeon (*colored dots*) and the fish (*black dots*). The graph is based on studies of fish given visual and spatial problems and pigeons given visual ones.

TEST ANIMAL	SPATIAL PROBLEMS		VISUAL PROBLEMS	
	REVERSAL	PROBABILITY	REVERSAL	PROBABILITY
MONKEY	RAT	RAT	RAT	RAT
RAT	RAT	RAT	RAT	RAT
PIGEON	RAT	RAT	RAT	FISH
TURTLE	RAT	RAT	FISH	FISH
FISH	FISH	FISH	FISH	FISH

DIFFERENCE IN INTELLIGENCE of the five animals studied by the author (*column at left*) are tabulated according to the subject's response to spatial and visual problems in experiments on habit reversal and probability learning. The behavior of each animal in each test situation is characterized as ratlike (progressive improvement in habit reversal and maximizing or nonrandom matching on probability-learning tests) or fishlike (no such improvement in habit reversal and random matching on probability-learning tests).

12

THE SOCIAL ORDER OF TURKEYS

C. ROBERT WATTS AND ALLEN W. STOKES
June 1971

The society of the wild turkeys that live in the semiarid grasslands of southeastern Texas is so rigidly stratified that most of the males never have an opportunity to mate

Social hierarchies existed in the animal world long before man crowned his first king. Investigating the structure and behavior of animal societies, one is increasingly impressed by how frequently their communities fall into a stratified pattern, with the members divided inexorably into dominant leaders and subordinates. Apparently this form of organization has high survival value, contributing in one way or another to the stability of a population or a species.

We made a detailed study of a population of wild turkeys living in and around the Welder Wildlife Refuge in Texas and found it to be characterized by an astonishing degree of social stratification, greater than had previously been seen in any society of vertebrates short of man. The status of each individual in this turkey society is determined during the first year of life, and it usually remains fixed for the animal's lifetime. One of the consequences is that most of the males never have an opportunity to mate! Presumably this phenomenon carries some benefits for the society, which presents an interesting subject for speculation.

The Welder Refuge is an area of 8,000 acres near Corpus Christi, Tex. Among its denizens are several hundred wild turkeys (*Meleagris gallopavo*) of the subspecies known as the Rio Grande turkey. By banding young turkeys in the Welder population with distinctive identification tags we were able to follow their subsequent career and behavior. We observed the social interactions of the tagged individuals and groups over a period of two years. As background for our findings let us first outline the yearly cycle of events in the life of the Welder turkeys as we observed it.

In March or sometimes as early as February, depending on the weather, the hens nest and begin to lay eggs, generally producing a clutch of 14 over a period of 15 or 16 days. The eggs hatch in 28 days. The resulting family of poults is subject to a high rate of attrition, owing to predators, vagaries of the weather and desertion. During the first six weeks it is not uncommon for a poult to leave its mother and join another family, particularly if it is the only survivor in the clutch. The mother of the switching offspring may also join the other family if she is compatible with the new mother. During the spring and summer the families combine in brood flocks; those hens that have lost their clutch of eggs or their poults and are left alone form broodless flocks.

The brood flock remains together until late fall, when the youngsters are six to seven months old. The young males of each family then break away as a sibling group. This group continues to be an inseparable unit for life. Even if it has been reduced to a single member, the survivor does not try to join another sibling group or form a group with other loners; he maintains an independent sibling identity.

After the male sibling unit breaks off from the brood flock it flocks with other males for the winter. Usually it attempts to join an established flock of adult males; the adult flocks, however, generally reject juveniles, so that the juvenile groups are relegated to joining together in flocks of their own.

It is at this stage in the life of the young male that his status is decided. In the exclusively male winter flock he is forced into two contests: one to establish his position within his own group of siblings, the other to determine the status of his sibling group with respect to other groups. Each sibling engages in physical combat with his brothers. The battle consists in wrestling, spurring in the fighting-cock style, striking with the wings and pecking at the head and neck. The fight often lasts more than two hours and ends when one or both of the contestants are too exhausted to continue. The strongest fighter in the group becomes the dominant bird, and the order of rank established among the siblings is seldom challenged thereafter as long as the dominant bird lives.

Meanwhile the sibling groups are testing one another and determining their relative ranking as units. Generally in a juvenile male flock the sibling group with the largest number of members wins the dominant status. When one flock encounters another, they also fight each other as units, again to determine which will be dominant. As in the case of individual contests, the group battles end in clear-cut decisions that create a remarkably stable society. The vanquished contestants accept their subordinate rank and rarely seek to renegotiate the result unless there is an important change in circumstances such as the death of a leader.

The society's stability is fortified by similar contests among the females, although in their case individual status appears to be less important than it is for the males when it comes to mating, as we shall see. While the juvenile males are still with the hens in the brood flocks, fighting occurs only between flocks, with victory generally going to the flock containing more males. After the males have left to form their own flocks for the winter the hens combine into large, all-female aggregations, and they then proceed to battle for individual rank among themselves. Each hen is on her own; there are no contests between sibling groups or families. In these fights adult hens usually prevail over juvenile females. Significantly, however, females that have been members of winning brood flocks often win over older hens that have not been thus "conditioned" to winning. This kind of conditioning was demonstrated in chickens during the 1930's by the Chinese biologist Z. Y. Kuo. He "trained" birds to win by never allowing them to lose.

We found that the turkey hens in and around the Welder Refuge congregated for the winter in two roosts within the refuge. The male flocks also had two winter roosts in the refuge, and in the

area around the refuge there were six additional male roosts, spaced about a mile to a mile and a half apart. This tended to minimize encounters between flocks, as the males rarely ventured more than six-tenths of a mile from their roost during the winter.

By the end of February the wintering flocks, both male and female, left their roosts to visit mating grounds. The signal for the breakup of winter roosting came when the hens set out at daybreak for certain display grounds. As the males left their winter quarters their tendency to flock together waned and their flocks gradually disintegrated. The sib-

ling groups, however, remained tightly knit.

At each display ground a band of females numbering 50 or more hens became available for courting. This group would receive the attention of 10 to 15 sibling groups totaling about 30 males in all. The sibling group that had gained dominance over all the others moved about within the ranks of the females, and the subordinate groups followed along at the periphery, taking what opportunities they could to display to females there. The display consisted in strutting before the hens. The members of each sibling group usually strut-

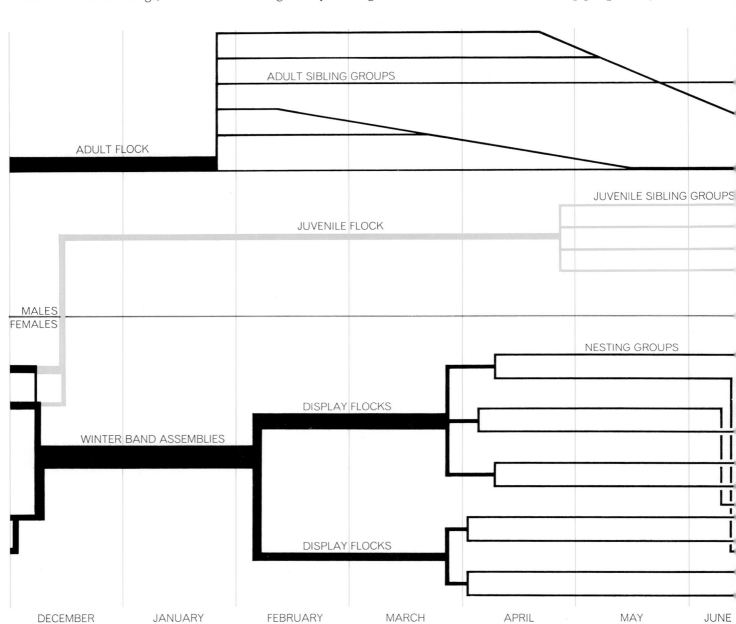

MALE AND FEMALE TURKEYS gather in flocks, divide into smaller units and flock together again in the course of a year. An idealized sequence appears in this chart. Two flocks of males (*top*) exist in late December. One (*color*) is made up of juvenile sibling groups newly departed from the summertime brood flocks. The other (*black*) is made up of adult sibling groups and remains aloof

from the juveniles. At this time the females (*bottom*) are gathered in a single large winter band. By February the adult male flock has divided into its component sibling groups. The juvenile males, however, continue to flock until near the end of the breeding season. The female band divides in February; smaller groups, numbering about 50 birds, appear on the display grounds. By April

ted in unison, more or less synchronously and close together. Occasionally more than one sibling group would strut to the same hen.

Notwithstanding the general participation in strutting, only the dominant male of the dominant group actually had the privilege of mating with hens at the height of the breeding season. We had tagged all the 170 males that used the four display grounds in the refuge and hence were able to identify them individually. In close observation of three of the display grounds we found that at two grounds just one male in each did

all the mating, and at the third ground only two males were involved in mating. At the fourth ground, which was lightly used by the turkeys that year, we were not able to keep a close watch, but it could reasonably be assumed that only one or two males dominated the mating there. Overall, then, of the 170 males using the four grounds no more than six males accounted for all the mating with the hens. We observed 59 copulations during this period.

The dominant leader's ability to monopolize the mating prerogative is aided by the circumstance that a complete copulation generally takes four minutes or

longer. A subordinate male presuming to couple with a hen does not have time to fulfill the mating attempt before the dominant male detects it. The dominant one, after driving off the presumptuous subordinate, proceeds to mate the prepared hen. Only once in two mating seasons did we see a member of a subordinate sibling group (the dominant member) succeed in achieving a mating on the display grounds; in that case two widely separated females in the area were ready to mate at the same time, and the leader of the subordinate group mated one while the flock leader was occupied with the other. There were also

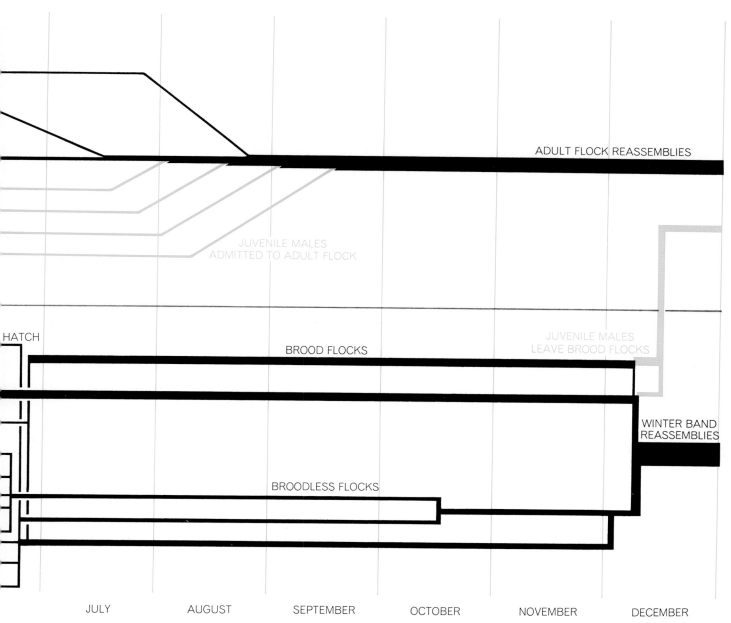

most breeding is over; the females have further divided into groups of two to five and are nesting. Some adult male sibling groups begin to recombine. Now the juvenile male flock splits into its sibling groups; these court any unattended females. By mid-June the year's hatch reaches a peak. Soon thereafter females with young collect in small brood flocks, and those without young form in broodless flocks. Meanwhile juvenile males are gradually allowed to enter the recombining flock of adult males, filling out ranks that have been thinned by the high mortality rate among adults. Finally, by December, the next generation of young males leaves the brood flock and forms a new juvenile flock. Adult and young females then join broodless females to reestablish winter band.

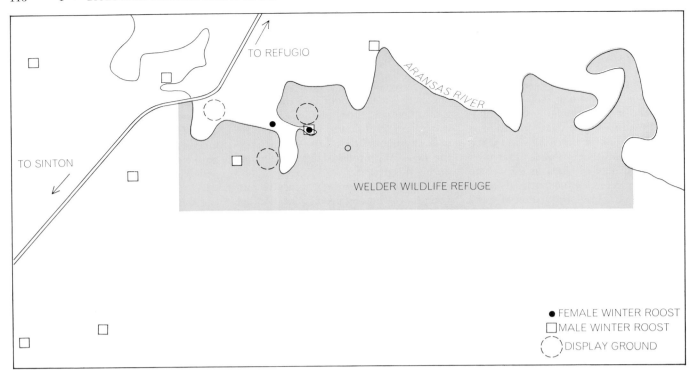

WELDER WILDLIFE REFUGE occupies a 12-square-mile strip of land (*colored area*) along the Aransas River near Corpus Christi. In winter the female turkeys in the area, gathered into two large seasonal flocks, occupy roosts less than a mile apart inside the refuge (*black*). The small winter flocks of males occupy roosts that are well separated; only two of the eight overlap female ranges.

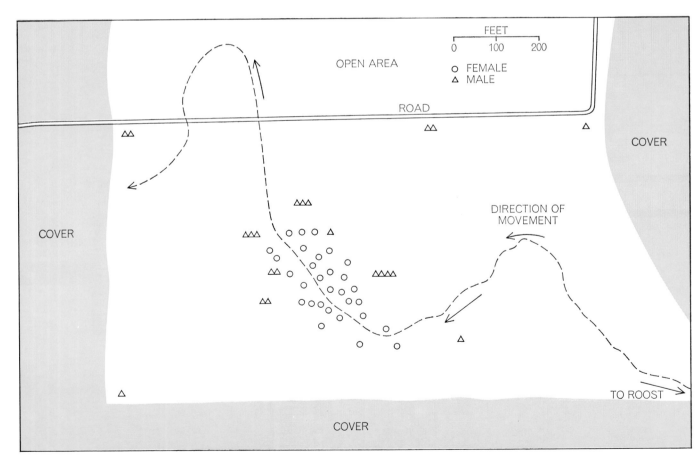

DISPLAY-GROUND ACTIVITY during a morning in mid-March, before the female flock breaks into nesting groups, is presented diagrammatically. Shortly after daylight 30 females began a slow passage across a display area, starting at lower right (*arrows*). A senior male sibling group, numbering three birds, soon moved into the midst of the females (*color*). Six junior male sibling groups, including a solitary male, have followed closely along the periphery of the band, displaying when they can but seldom managing to mate.

two instances in which a previously subordinate male of the dominant sibling group was able to mate after the dominant member of the group died during the display-ground period.

Although subordinate males had no chance to mate with hens at the display grounds, they did perform mock matings, often just before or after a mating by the dominant male. Mounting a pile of dry cow manure or a log or simply squatting on the ground, they would go through the stereotype of mating actions: treading the object, fluttering their wings, lowering their tail and even in some cases ejaculating. Some males that were not allowed to mate with hens at the display grounds did have opportunities to mate later. The hens left the display grounds within four weeks and went in groups of two to five (not as sibling groups) to a common nesting ground. During the nesting period male sibling groups roved about from one nesting area to another seeking receptive hens. Thus a sibling group that had had only subordinate status at the display grounds might have an uncontested meeting with a nesting group of hens. In that event the dominant member of the male group could mate with the hens unless he was interrupted by the arrival of a dominant sibling group. Our observations indicated, however, that the few dominant males that were engaged in all the mating at the display grounds probably accounted also for 75 percent of the later matings achieved during the hens' nesting period.

By May or June the adult males cease courting the females and go off in their own flocks, to which they now admit most of the year-old males that hang about the flock. Late in the season some sibling groups composed of year-old males, left alone either with females that are late nesters or with females nesting for a second time, can be seen strutting to the hens and performing other courtship acts, but they do not consummate mating. In this respect the behavior of the Rio Grande turkeys parallels that of other bird species such as the Canada goose and jungle fowl; the year-old males of those species also go through the courting ritual without actually breeding.

Such is the life style of the Welder turkeys. How are we to explain its unique features? Nowhere else in the world of birds has any investigator observed so rigidly structured a society: the permanent division of its members into dominant and subordinate classes, the lifelong cohesion of male sibling groups,

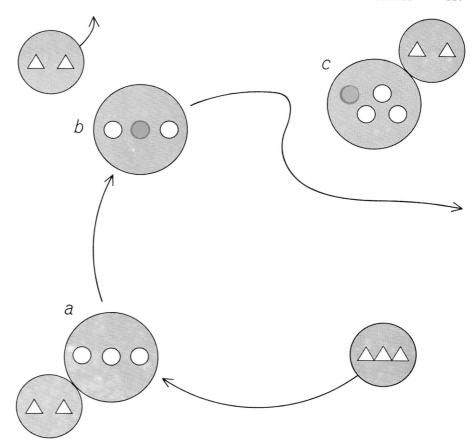

ROLE OF DOMINANCE in breeding activity is evident in this diagram of the encounters between three roaming males of a sibling group and female turkeys in various nesting groups. Each nesting group is attended by a group of males that is dominant over or subordinate to the roaming group. In the initial encounter (a) the roamers outranked the attendants but the females did not respond to their display and the roamers moved on. In the second encounter (b) the roamers were also senior to the attendants, and one of the nesting group (color) was responsive. The dominant male among the three roamers mated with the responsive female. In the final encounter (c), although a responsive female was present, the attendants outranked the roamers. The three therefore moved on to another nesting area.

the monopolization of mating by a few dominant males. The Welder turkeys' social pattern is not duplicated even by their close relative of the same species, the Eastern wild turkey inhabiting the Atlantic coastal states.

In seeking an explanation one factor to consider is the extent to which the Welder turkeys' life style may be dictated by the nature of their habitat. The Welder Refuge and its environs is an area of grassland and brush. Studies of the social weaverbirds in Africa by the British investigator John Crook have shown that weavers living in woodlands tend to form small social units; in contrast, those inhabiting open grasslands are inclined to form large flocks. In explanation Crook pointed out that the widely dispersed, year-round supply of food in a tropical forest can be exploited most efficiently by small groups of roving birds, whereas in a grassland, with a seasonally abundant, concentrated food supply and relatively few available nesting sites, the birds can make the most of the environment by flocking together in large social units. This interpretation is borne out by the habits of game birds in North America: woodland species such as the ruffed grouse and the spruce grouse typically are widely dispersed and tend to be loners except during the mating season; on the other hand, species with a habitat of grassland and brush such as the prairie chicken, the sharp-tailed grouse and the sage grouse live in large flocks. The Welder turkeys exhibit the same influence of habitat. They follow the grassland pattern of social organization, whereas the Eastern wild turkey, living in woodlands, favors small social units.

The nature of the habitat and food supply also influences the mating sys-

WRESTLING MATCH between juvenile wild turkeys, members of the same sibling group, is one of several forms of combat that eventually determine which male will dominate the other members of the group. The birds usually fight until exhausted. Dominant males at the Welder Wildlife Refuge in Texas act as sires in the great majority of annual matings among the turkeys resident there.

PRELUDE TO MATING on the display grounds at the Welder Refuge is stereotyped male strutting, with tail fanned and wings drooping. Two sibling pairs are shown strutting; the movements of each pair are almost perfectly synchronized. The female (left), the object of the males' display, stands in the characteristic pre-mating posture, awaiting the dominant male of the senior pair.

tems of birds. Where food is not easy to find and the young need parental help, the birds favor monogamy. This is particularly well illustrated by the quail and the partridge. Polygamy, on the other hand, tends to be the rule when food is readily available and the rearing of the young does not require help from the male parent. In some cases the polygamy system takes the form of the creation of harems; a male acquires several hens that stay with him until they are bred. The Eastern wild turkey uses this system. In contrast, the Welder turkeys have adopted the "lek" mode of polygamy, in which most of the mating is done in a common arena (called the lek). A number of ground-dwelling birds (including the prairie chicken, the sharp-tailed grouse and the sage grouse) practice the lek system; the Welder turkeys, however, have developed their own unique version. On a prairie-chicken or grouse lek each male forms a small territory and stays within it, waiting for a sexually ready female to seek him out. The hens in those societies do show a definite preference for relatively dominant males. However, the Welder modification of the system, with the males pursuing the females on the courting ground, applies a more positive control; there the males determine rigorously which of them will mate.

How can we account for the fact that the Texas wild turkeys use the lek mating system rather than the harem system favored by their Eastern relatives of the same species? The Texas climate suggests an answer. In the Welder Refuge area rainfall is comparatively infrequent, and when it occurs, it brings on a quick but short-lived growth of vegetation and insects. In order to take advantage of this ephemeral food supply it is important that the females be brought quickly into readiness for breeding. The displays and courtship by groups of males on a lek presumably have that effect. (It is interesting to note that in a part of Oklahoma that is less drought-ridden than the Welder Refuge region the turkeys of the Rio Grande subspecies display on leks but do not usually mate until afterward, when they go off to form harems. Their combination of the two systems apparently adds a string to their bow, enabling them to cope with whatever weather conditions may befall during the breeding season.) In addition to the rapid preparation of the females for breeding there is another obvious advantage in the lek system: it guards the birds against surprise attacks by predators, to which the turkeys are particularly vulnerable in the grasslands.

We are still left with a most puzzling question: How does one explain the remarkable restriction of mating to just a few males and the close lifelong bond that holds a sibling group together? We suggest a hypothesis that relates the two phenomena. A hen may be stimulated more strongly by the compact, synchronized strutting of a male sibling group than she would be by the display of an individual suitor. Hence the probability of eventual mating may be enhanced even for the subordinate members of the group in the event that the dominant bird dies. (The average annual mortality of adult male turkeys at Welder is 40 percent.) Sibling unity also provides protection for the member that does the mating: during the four minutes or more that he is coupled with the female his brothers stand by to fight off intruders or predators.

Perhaps most significant, the collaboration of the sibling members in assisting mating by one of their group helps to ensure the propagation of the family genes, since on the average between brothers 50 percent of the genes are exact duplicates. The dominant member thus acts as a representative of his brothers in passing on their genes; the British geneticist W. D. Hamilton calls natural selection of this kind "kin selection."

Such an arrangement may seem less than ideal with respect to those deprived of the opportunity to mate. In genetic and evolutionary terms, however, it may be advantageous to the community as a whole. Perhaps the Welder turkeys offer a moral for human conduct, suggesting that people might often benefit, even as individuals, by giving less attention to self-gratification and more to group effectiveness.

OUTRANKED MALES (*left*), interrupted in mid-display by four members of a senior sibling group (*center and right*), have begun to abandon the courtship effort directed at the five females in the foreground. One of the outranked males is starting to fold his tail.

13

THE SOCIAL LIFE OF BABOONS

S. L. WASHBURN AND IRVEN DEVORE
June 1961

A study of "troops" of baboons in their natural environment in East Africa has revealed patterns of interdependence that may shed light on the early evolution of the human species

The behavior of monkeys and apes has always held great fascination for men. In recent years plain curiosity about their behavior has been reinforced by the desire to understand human behavior. Anthropologists have come to understand that the evolution of man's behavior, particularly his social behavior, has played an integral role in his biological evolution. In the attempt to reconstruct the life of man as it was shaped through the ages, many studies of primate behavior are now under way in the laboratory and in the field. As the contrasts and similarities between the behavior of primates and man—especially preagricultural, primitive man—become clearer, they should give useful insights into the kind of social behavior that characterized the ancestors of man a million years ago.

With these objectives in mind we decided to undertake a study of the baboon. We chose this animal because it is a ground-living primate and as such is confronted with the same kind of problem that faced our ancestors when they left the trees. Our observations of some 30 troops of baboons, ranging in average membership from 40 to 80 individuals, in their natural setting in Africa show that the social behavior of the baboon is one of the species' principal adaptations for survival. Most of a baboon's life is spent within a few feet of other baboons. The troop affords protection from predators and an intimate group knowledge of the territory it occupies. Viewed from the inside, the troop is composed not of neutral creatures but of strongly emotional, highly motivated members. Our data offer little support for the theory that sexuality provides the primary bond of the primate troop. It is the intensely social nature of the baboon, expressed in a diversity of inter-individual relationships, that keeps the troop together. This conclusion calls for further observation and experimental investigation of the different social bonds. It is clear, however, that these bonds are essential to compact group living and that for a baboon life in the troop is the only way of life that is feasible.

Many game reserves in Africa support baboon populations but not all were suited to our purpose. We had to be able to locate and recognize particular troops and their individual members

GROOMING to remove dirt and parasites from the hair is a major social activity among baboons. Here one adult female grooms another while the second suckles a year-old infant.

and to follow them in their peregrinations day after day. In some reserves the brush is so thick that such systematic observation is impossible. A small park near Nairobi, in Kenya, offered most of the conditions we needed. Here 12 troops of baboons, consisting of more than 450 members, ranged the open savanna. The animals were quite tame; they clambered onto our car and even allowed us to walk beside them. In only 10 months of study, one of us (DeVore) was able to recognize most of the members of four troops and to become moderately familiar with many more. The Nairobi park, however, is small and so close to the city that the pattern of baboon life is somewhat altered. To carry on our work in an area less disturbed by humans and large enough to contain elephants, rhinoceroses, buffaloes and other ungulates as well as larger and less tame troops of baboons, we went to the Amboseli game reserve and spent two months camped at the foot of Mount Kilimanjaro. In the small part of Am-

boseli that we studied intensively there were 15 troops with a total of 1,200 members, the troops ranging in size from 13 to 185 members. The fact that the average size of the troops in Amboseli (80) is twice that of the troops in Nairobi shows the need to study the animals in several localities before generalizing.

A baboon troop may range an area of three to six square miles but it utilizes only parts of its range intensively. When water and food are widely distributed, troops rarely come within sight of each other. The ranges of neighboring troops overlap nonetheless, often extensively. This could be seen best in Amboseli at the end of the dry season. Water was concentrated in certain areas, and several troops often came to the same water hole, both to drink and to eat the lush vegetation near the water. We spent many days near these water holes, watching the baboons and the numerous other animals that came there.

On one occasion we counted more

than 400 baboons around a single water hole at one time. To the casual observer they would have appeared to be one troop, but actually three large troops were feeding side by side. The troops came and went without mixing, even though members of different troops sat or foraged within a few feet of each other. Once we saw a juvenile baboon cross over to the next troop, play briefly and return to his own troop. But such behavior is rare, even in troops that come together at the same water hole day after day. At the water hole we saw no fighting between troops, but small troops slowly gave way before large ones. Troops that did not see each other frequently showed great interest in each other.

When one first sees a troop of baboons, it appears to have little order, but this is a superficial impression. The basic structure of the troop is most apparent when a large troop moves away from the safety of trees and out onto open plains. As the troop moves the less dominant

MARCHING baboon troop has a definite structure, with females and their young protected by dominant males in the center of the formation. This group in the Amboseli reserve in Kenya includes a female (*left*), followed by two males and a female with juvenile.

BABOON EATS A POTATO tossed to him by a member of the authors' party. Baboons are primarily herbivores but occasionally they will eat birds' eggs and even other animals.

INFANT BABOON rides on its mother's back through a park outside Nairobi. A newborn infant first travels by clinging to its mother's chest, but soon learns to ride pickaback.

adult males and perhaps a large juvenile or two occupy the van. Females and more of the older juveniles follow, and in the center of the troop are the females with infants, the young juveniles and the most dominant males. The back of the troop is a mirror image of its front, with less dominant males at the rear. Thus, without any fixed or formal order, the arrangement of the troop is such that the females and young are protected at the center. No matter from what direction a predator approaches the troop, it must first encounter the adult males.

When a predator is sighted, the adult males play an even more active role in defense of the troop. One day we saw two dogs run barking at a troop. The females and juveniles hurried, but the males continued to walk slowly. In a moment an irregular group of some 20 adult males was interposed between the dogs and the rest of the troop. When a male turned on the dogs, they ran off. We saw baboons close to hyenas, cheetahs and jackals, and usually the baboons seemed unconcerned—the other animals kept their distance. Lions were the only animals we saw putting a troop of baboons to flight. Twice we saw lions near baboons, whereupon the baboons climbed trees. From the safety of the trees the baboons barked and threatened the lions, but they offered no resistance to them on the ground.

With nonpredators the baboons' relations are largely neutral. It is common to see baboons walking among topi, eland, sable and roan antelopes, gazelles, zebras, hartebeests, gnus, giraffes and buffaloes, depending on which ungulates are common locally. When elephants or rhinoceroses walk through an area where the baboons are feeding, the baboons move out of the way at the last moment. We have seen wart hogs chasing each other, and a running rhinoceros go right through a troop, with the baboons merely stepping out of the way. We have seen male impalas fighting while baboons fed beside them. Once we saw a baboon chase a giraffe, but it seemed to be more in play than aggression.

Only rarely did we see baboons engage in hostilities against other species. On one occasion, however, we saw a baboon kill a small vervet monkey and eat it. The vervets frequented the same water holes as the baboons and usually they moved near them or even among them without incident. But one troop of baboons we observed at Victoria Falls pursued vervets on sight and attempted, without success, to keep

LIONESS LEAPS AT A THORN TREE into which a group of baboons has fled for safety. Lions appear to be among the few animals that successfully prey on baboons. The car in the background drove up as the authors' party was observing the scene.

them out of certain fruit trees. The vervets easily escaped in the small branches of the trees.

The baboons' food is almost entirely vegetable, although they do eat meat on rare occasions. We saw dominant males kill and eat two newborn Thomson's gazelles. Baboons are said to be fond of fledglings and birds' eggs and have even been reported digging up crocodile eggs. They also eat insects. But their diet consists principally of grass, fruit, buds and plant shoots of many kinds; in the Nairobi area alone they consume more than 50 species of plant.

For baboons, as for many herbivores, association with other species on the range often provides mutual protection. In open country their closest relations are with impalas, while in forest areas the bushbucks play a similar role. The ungulates have a keen sense of smell, and baboons have keen eyesight. Baboons are visually alert, constantly looking in all directions as they feed. If they see predators, they utter warning barks

that alert not only the other baboons but also any other animals that may be in the vicinity. Similarly, a warning bark by a bushbuck or an impala will put a baboon troop to flight. A mixed herd of impalas and baboons is almost impossible to take by surprise.

Impalas are a favorite prey of cheetahs. Yet once we saw impalas, grazing in the company of baboons, make no effort to escape from a trio of approaching cheetahs. The impalas just watched as an adult male baboon stepped toward the cheetahs, uttered a cry of defiance and sent them trotting away.

The interdependence of the different species is plainly evident at a water hole, particularly where the bush is thick and visibility poor. If giraffes are drinking, zebras will run to the water. But the first animals to arrive at the water hole approach with extreme caution. In the Wankie reserve, where we also observed baboons, there are large water holes surrounded by wide areas of open sand

between the water and the bushes. The baboons approached the water with great care, often resting and playing for some time in the bushes before making a hurried trip for a drink. Clearly, many animals know each other's behavior and alarm signals.

A baboon troop finds its ultimate safety, however, in the trees. It is no exaggeration to say that trees limit the distribution of baboons as much as the availability of food and water. We observed an area by a marsh in Amboseli where there was water and plenty of food. But there were lions and no trees and so there were no baboons. Only a quarter of a mile away, where lions were seen even more frequently, there were trees. Here baboons were numerous; three large troops frequented the area.

At night, when the carnivores and snakes are most active, baboons sleep high up in big trees. This is one of the baboon's primary behavioral adaptations. Diurnal living, together with an

BABOONS AND THREE OTHER SPECIES gather near a water hole (*out of picture to right*). Water holes and the relatively lush vegetation that surrounds them are common meeting places for a wide variety of herbivores. In this scene of the open savanna of

arboreal refuge at night, is an extremely effective way for them to avoid danger. The callused areas on a baboon's haunches allow it to sleep sitting up, even on small branches; a large troop can thus find sleeping places in a few trees. It is known that Colobus monkeys have a cycle of sleeping and waking throughout the night; baboons probably have a similar pattern. In any case, baboons are terrified of the dark. They arrive at the trees before night falls and stay in the branches until it is fully light. Fear of the dark, fear of falling and fear of snakes seem to be basic parts of the primate heritage.

Whether by day or night, individual baboons do not wander away from the troop, even for a few hours. The importance of the troop in ensuring the survival of its members is dramatized by the fate of those that are badly injured or too sick to keep up with their fellows. Each day the troop travels on a circuit of two to four miles; it moves from the sleeping trees to a feeding area, feeds, rests and moves again. The pace is not rapid, but the troop does not wait for sick or injured members. A baby baboon rides its mother, but all other members of the troop must keep up on their own. Once an animal is separated from the troop the chances of death are high. Sickness and injuries severe enough to

be easily seen are frequent. For example, we saw a baboon with a broken forearm. The hand swung uselessly, and blood showed that the injury was recent. This baboon was gone the next morning and was not seen again. A sickness was widespread in the Amboseli troops, and we saw individuals dragging themselves along, making tremendous efforts to stay with the troop but falling behind. Some of these may have rejoined their troops; we are sure that at least five did not. One sick little juvenile lagged for four days and then apparently recovered. In the somewhat less natural setting of Nairobi park we saw some baboons that had lost a leg. So even severe injury does

the Amboseli reserve there are baboons in the foreground and middle distance. An impala moves across the foreground just left of center. A number of zebras are present; groups of gnus graze together at right center and move off toward the water hole (right).

not mean inevitable death. Nonetheless, it must greatly decrease the chance of survival.

Thus, viewed from the outside, the troop is seen to be an effective way of life and one that is essential to the survival of its individual members. What do the internal events of troop life reveal about the drives and motivations that cause individual baboons to "seek safety in numbers"? One of the best ways to approach an understanding of the behavior patterns within the troop is to watch the baboons when they are resting and feeding quietly.

Most of the troop will be gathered in small groups, grooming each other's fur or simply sitting. A typical group will contain two females with their young offspring, or an adult male with one or more females and juveniles grooming him. Many of these groups tend to persist, with the same animals that have been grooming each other walking together when the troop moves. The nucleus of such a "grooming cluster" is most often a dominant male or a mother with a very young infant. The most powerful males are highly attractive to the other troop members and are actively sought by them. In marked contrast, the males in many ungulate species, such as impalas, must constantly herd the members of their group together. But baboon males have no need to force the other troop members to stay with them. On the contrary, their presence alone ensures that the troop will stay with them at all times.

Young infants are equally important in the formation of grooming clusters. The newborn infant is the center of social attraction. The most dominant adult males sit by the mother and walk close beside her. When the troop is resting, adult females and juveniles come to the mother, groom her and attempt to groom the infant. Other members of the troop are drawn toward the center thus formed, both by the presence of the pro-

BABOONS AND IMPALAS cluster together around a water hole. The two species form a mutual alarm system. The baboons have keen eyesight and the impalas a good sense of smell. Between them they quickly sense the presence of predators and take flight.

tective adult males and by their intense interest in the young infants.

In addition, many baboons, especially adult females, form preference pairs, and juvenile baboons come together in play groups that persist for several years. The general desire to stay in the troop is strengthened by these "friendships," which express themselves in the daily pattern of troop activity.

Our field observations, which so strongly suggest a high social motivation, are backed up by controlled experiment in the laboratory. Robert A. Butler of Walter Reed Army Hospital has shown that an isolated monkey will work hard when the only reward for his labor is the sight of another monkey [see "Curiosity in Monkeys," by Robert A. Butler; SCIENTIFIC AMERICAN Offprint 426]. In the troop this social drive is expressed in strong individual prefer-

ences, by "friendship," by interest in the infant members of the troop and by the attraction of the dominant males. Field studies show the adaptive value of these social ties. Solitary animals are far more likely to be killed, and over the generations natural selection must have favored all those factors which make learning to be sociable easy.

The learning that brings the individual baboon into full identity and participation in the baboon social system begins with the mother-child relationship. The newborn baboon rides by clinging to the hair on its mother's chest. The mother may scoop the infant on with her hand, but the infant must cling to its mother, even when she runs, from the day it is born. There is no time for this behavior to be learned. Harry F. Harlow of the University of Wisconsin has shown that an infant monkey will auto-

matically cling to an object and much prefers objects with texture more like that of a real mother [see "Love in Infant Monkeys," by Harry F. Harlow; SCIENTIFIC AMERICAN Offprint 429]. Experimental studies demonstrate this clinging reflex; field observations show why it is so important.

In the beginning the baboon mother and infant are in contact 24 hours a day. The attractiveness of the young infant, moreover, assures that he and his mother will always be surrounded by attentive troop members. Experiments show that an isolated infant brought up in a laboratory does not develop normal social patterns. Beyond the first reflexive clinging, the development of social behavior requires learning. Behavior characteristic of the species depends therefore both on the baboon's biology and on the social situations that are present in the troop.

BABOONS AND ELEPHANTS have a relationship that is neutral rather than co-operative, as in the case of baboons and impalas. If an elephant or another large herbivore such as a rhinoceros moves through a troop, the baboons merely step out of the way.

As the infant matures it learns to ride on its mother's back, first clinging and then sitting upright. It begins to eat solid foods and to leave the mother for longer and longer periods to play with other infants. Eventually it plays with the other juveniles many hours a day, and its orientation shifts from the mother to this play group. It is in these play groups that the skills and behavior patterns of adult life are learned and practiced. Adult gestures, such as mounting, are frequent, but most play is a mixture of chasing, tail-pulling and mock fighting. If a juvenile is hurt and cries out, adults come running and stop the play. The presence of an adult male prevents small juveniles from being hurt. In the protected atmosphere of the play group the social bonds of the infant are widely extended.

Grooming, a significant biological function in itself, helps greatly to establish social bonds. The mother begins grooming her infant the day it is born, and the infant will be occupied with grooming for several hours a day for the rest of its life. All the older baboons do a certain amount of grooming, but it is the adult females who do most. They groom the infants, juveniles, adult males and other females. The baboons go to each other and "present" themselves for grooming. The grooming animal picks through the hair, parting it with its hands, removing dirt and parasites, usually by nibbling. Grooming is most often reciprocal, with one animal doing it for a while and then presenting itself for grooming. The animal being groomed relaxes, closes its eyes and gives every indication of complete pleasure. In addition to being pleasurable, grooming serves the important function

of keeping the fur clean. Ticks are common in this area and can be seen on many animals such as dogs and lions; a baboon's skin, however, is free of them. Seen in this light, the enormous amount of time baboons spend in grooming each other is understandable. Grooming is pleasurable to the individual, it is the most important expression of close social bonds and it is biologically adaptive.

The adults in a troop are arranged in a dominance hierarchy, explicitly revealed in their relations with other members of the troop. The most dominant males will be more frequently groomed and they occupy feeding and resting positions of their choice. When a dominant animal approaches a subordinate one, the lesser animal moves out of the way. The observer can determine the order of dominance simply by watching the reactions of the baboons as they move past each other. In the tamer troops these observations can be tested by feeding. If food is tossed between two baboons, the more dominant one will take it, whereas the other may not even look at it directly.

The status of a baboon male in the dominance hierarchy depends not only on his physical condition and fighting ability but also on his relationships with other males. Some adult males in every large troop stay together much of the time, and if one of them is threatened, the others are likely to back him up. A group of such males outranks any individual, even though another male outside the group might be able to defeat any member of it separately. The hierarchy has considerable stability and this is due in large part to its dependence on clusters of males rather than the fighting ability of individuals. In troops where the rank order is clearly defined, fighting is rare. We observed frequent bickering or severe fighting in only about 15 per cent of the troops. The usual effect of the hierarchy, once relations among the males are settled, is to decrease disruptions in the troop. The dominant animals, the males in particular, will not let others fight. When bickering breaks out, they usually run to the scene and stop it. Dominant males thus protect the weaker animals against harm from inside as well as outside. Females

and juveniles come to the males to groom them or just to sit beside them. So although dominance depends ultimately on force, it leads to peace, order and popularity.

Much has been written about the importance of sex in uniting the troop, it has been said, for example, that "the powerful social magnet of sex was the major impetus to subhuman primate sociability" [see "The Origin of Society," by Marshall D. Sahlins; SCIENTIFIC AMERICAN Offprint 602]. Our observations lead us to assign to sexuality a much lesser, and even at times a contrary, role. The sexual behavior of baboons depends on the biological cycle of the female. She is receptive for approximately one week out of every month, when she is in estrus. When first receptive, she leaves her infant and her friendship group and goes to the males, mating first with the subordinate males and older juveniles. Later in the period of receptivity she goes to the dominant males and "presents." If a male is not interested, the female is likely to groom him and then present again. Near the end of estrus the dominant males become very interested, and the female and a male form a consort pair. They may stay together for as little as an hour or for as long as several days. Estrus disrupts all other social relationships, and consort pairs usually move to the edge of

the troop. It is at this time that fighting may take place, if the dominance order is not clearly established among the males. Normally there is no fighting over females, and a male, no matter how dominant, does not monopolize a female for long. No male is ever associated with more than one estrus female; there is nothing resembling a family or a harem among baboons.

Much the same seems to be true of other species of monkey. Sexual behavior appears to contribute little to the cohesion of the troop. Some monkeys have breeding seasons, with all mating taking place within less than half the year. But even in these species the troop continues its normal existence during the months when there is no mating. It must be remembered that among baboons a female is not sexually receptive for most of her life. She is juvenile, pregnant or lactating; estrus is a rare event in her life. Yet she does not leave the troop even for a few minutes. In baboon troops, particularly small ones, many months may pass when no female member comes into estrus; yet no animals leave the troop, and the highly structured relationships within it continue without disorganization.

The sociableness of baboons is expressed in a wide variety of behavior patterns that reinforce each other and give the troop cohesion. As the infant matures the nature of the social bonds

	ECOLOGY			ECONOMIC SYSTEM	
	GROUP SIZE, DENSITY AND RANGE	HOME BASE	POPULATION STRUCTURE	FOOD HABITS	ECONOMIC DEPENDENCE
	GROUPS OF 50–60 COMMON BUT VARY WIDELY. ONE INDIVIDUAL PER 5–10 SQUARE MILES. RANGE 200–600 SQUARE MILES. TERRITORIAL RIGHTS; DEFEND BOUNDARIES AGAINST STRANGERS.	OCCUPY IMPROVED SITES FOR VARIABLE TIMES WHERE SICK ARE CARED FOR AND STORES KEPT.	TRIBAL ORGANIZATION OF LOCAL, EXOGAMOUS GROUPS.	OMNIVOROUS. FOOD SHARING. MEN SPECIALIZE IN HUNTING, WOMEN AND CHILDREN IN GATHERING.	INFANTS ARE DEPENDENT ON ADULTS FOR MANY YEARS. MATURITY OF MALE DELAYED BIOLOGICALLY AND CULTURALLY. HUNTING, STORAGE AND SHARING OF FOOD.
	10–200 IN GROUP. 10 INDIVIDUALS PER SQUARE MILE. RANGE 3–6 SQUARE MILES; NO TERRITORIAL DEFENSE.	NONE: SICK AND INJURED MUST KEEP UP WITH TROOP.	SMALL, INBREEDING GROUPS.	ALMOST ENTIRELY VEGETARIAN. NO FOOD SHARING, NO DIVISION OF LABOR.	INFANT ECONOMICALLY INDEPENDENT AFTER WEANING. FULL MATURITY BIOLOGICALLY DELAYED. NO HUNTING, STORAGE OR SHARING OF FOOD.

APES AND MEN are contrasted in this chart, which indicates that although apes often seem remarkably "human," there are fundamental differences in behavior. Baboon characteristics, which may be taken as representative of ape and monkey behavior in

changes continually, but the bonds are always strong. The ties between mother and infant, between a juvenile and its peers in a play group, and between a mother and an adult male are quite different from one another. Similarly, the bond between two females in a friendship group, between the male and female in a consort pair or among the members of a cluster of males in the dominance hierarchy is based on diverse biological and behavioral factors, which offer a rich field for experimental investigation.

In addition, the troop shares a considerable social tradition. Each troop has its own range and a secure familiarity with the food and water sources, escape routes, safe refuges and sleeping places inside it. The counterpart of the intensely social life within the troop is the co-ordination of the activities of all the troop's members throughout their lives. Seen against the background of evolution, it is clear that in the long run only the social baboons have survived.

When comparing the social behavior of baboons with that of man, there is little to be gained from laboring the obvious differences between modern civilization and the society of baboons. The comparison must be drawn against the fundamental social behavior patterns that lie behind the vast variety of human ways of life. For this purpose we have charted the salient features of baboon life in a native habitat alongside those of human life in preagricultural society [see chart below]. Cursory inspection shows that the differences are more numerous and significant than are the similarities.

The size of the local group is the only category in which there is not a major contrast. The degree to which these contrasts are helpful in understanding the evolution of human behavior depends, of course, on the degree to which baboon behavior is characteristic of monkeys and apes in general and therefore probably characteristic of the apes that evolved into men. Different kinds of monkey do behave differently, and many more field studies will have to be made before the precise degree of difference can be understood.

For example, many arboreal monkeys have a much smaller geographical range than baboons do. In fact, there are important differences between the size and type of range for many monkey species. But there is no suggestion that a troop of any species of monkey or ape occupies the hundreds of square miles ordinarily occupied by preagricultural human societies. Some kinds of monkey may resent intruders in their range more than baboons do, but there is no evidence that any species fights for complete control of a territory. Baboons are certainly less vocal than some other monkeys, but no nonhuman primate has even the most rudimentary language. We believe that the fundamental contrasts in our chart would hold for the vast majority of monkeys and apes as compared with the ancestors of man. Further study of primate behavior will sharpen these contrasts and define more clearly the gap that had to be traversed from ape to human behavior. But already we can see that man is as unique in his sharing, co-operation and play patterns as he is in his locomotion, brain and language.

The basis for most of these differences may lie in hunting. Certainly the hunting of large animals must have involved co-operation among the hunters and sharing of the food within the tribe. Similarly, hunting requires an enormous extension of range and the protection of a hunting territory. If this speculation proves to be correct, much of the evolution of human behavior can be reconstructed, because the men of 500,000 years ago were skilled hunters. In locations such as Choukoutien in China and Olduvai Gorge in Africa there is evidence of both the hunters and their campsites [see "Olduvai Gorge," by L. S. B. Leakey; Scientific American, January, 1954]. We are confident that the study of the living primates, together with the archaeological record, will eventually make possible a much richer understanding of the evolution of human behavior.

SOCIAL SYSTEM					COMMUNICATION
ORGANIZATION	SOCIAL CONTROL	SEXUAL BEHAVIOR	MOTHER-CHILD RELATIONSHIP	PLAY	
BANDS ARE DEPENDENT ON AND AFFILIATED WITH ONE ANOTHER IN A SEMIOPEN SYSTEM. SUBGROUPS BASED ON KINSHIP.	BASED ON CUSTOM.	FEMALE CONTINUOUSLY RECEPTIVE. FAMILY BASED ON PROLONGED MALE-FEMALE RELATIONSHIP AND INCEST TABOOS.	PROLONGED; INFANT HELPLESS AND ENTIRELY DEPENDENT ON ADULTS.	INTERPERSONAL BUT ALSO CONSIDERABLE USE OF INANIMATE OBJECTS.	LINGUISTIC COMMUNITY. LANGUAGE CRUCIAL IN THE EVOLUTION OF RELIGION, ART, TECHNOLOGY AND THE CO-OPERATION OF MANY INDIVIDUALS.
TROOP SELF-SUFFICIENT, CLOSED TO OUTSIDERS. TEMPORARY SUBGROUPS ARE FORMED BASED ON AGE AND INDIVIDUAL PREFERENCES.	BASED ON PHYSICAL DOMINANCE.	FEMALE ESTRUS. MULTIPLE MATES. NO PROLONGED MALE-FEMALE RELATIONSHIP.	INTENSE BUT BRIEF; INFANT WELL DEVELOPED AND IN PARTIAL CONTROL.	MAINLY INTERPERSONAL AND EXPLORATORY.	SPECIES-SPECIFIC, LARGELY GESTURAL AND CONCERNED WITH IMMEDIATE SITUATIONS.

general, are based on laboratory and field studies; human characteristics are what is known of preagricultural Homo sapiens. The chart suggests that there was a considerable gap between primate behavior and the behavior of the most primitive men known.

14

URBAN MONKEYS

SHEO DAN SINGH
July 1969

*In India rhesus monkeys have shared cities with man
for centuries. Has this urban way of life affected
their behavior and their ability to solve problems?*

The rhesus monkeys of India mainly comprise two different societies: forest and urban. The urban monkeys inhabit housetops, abandoned buildings and other city niches where they can spend their nights undisturbed by man. They are a common sight in villages, towns and cities in a number of regions in India. Many Hindus regard the monkey, like the cow, as being sacred; it is said that in ancient times a monkey named Hanuman came to the aid of the Hindu god Rama in battles with Ravana, the demon-king of Ceylon. As a result monkeys are still worshiped in many parts of India and freely share the urban habitat with man.

The urban monkeys differ noticeably from their forest-dwelling cousins in temperament and behavior. It occurred to me that from a study of these city-dwelling primates one might learn something about the elementary effects of the urban mode of life on man. My decision to undertake such a study was inspired by a meeting with Harry F. Harlow of the University of Wisconsin, whose investigations of monkey behavior in the laboratory have raised so many suggestive questions about human behavior [see "Love in Infant Monkeys," by Harry F. Harlow, SCIENTIFIC AMERICAN Offprint 429, and "Social Deprivation in Monkeys," by Harry F. and Margaret Kuenne Harlow, Offprint 473]. The following is an account of what my colleagues and I have been able to ascertain about the effects of city living on monkeys in India from observation and laboratory tests.

One clear effect has to do with the monkeys' food preferences. Forest-dwelling rhesus monkeys generally live principally on the leaves and fruits of trees such as the banyan, the fig, the mango, the tamarind and the jambos (often known as the rose apple). In con-

trast, the monkeys that have taken up life in villages and cities have developed a taste not only for fruits and vegetables but also for cooked human food such as *chapatis* (Indian bread), roasted grains, peanuts and even spiced items. In tests in which we offered the urban monkeys

choices among various foods the monkeys showed a distinct preference for things that had been cooked, whereas the forest monkeys passed over cooked or roasted items and were distinctly partial to fruits and raw vegetables.

The foraging habits of the urban mon-

MONKEYS OF JAIPUR, a city in the Indian state of Rajasthan, gather on the rooftops at twilight as the heat of a summer day abates. City-dwelling monkeys in India live in groups

keys are of course quite different from those of monkeys in the forest. People occasionally feed urban monkeys willingly (I myself used to do so during my school days), but in the main the monkeys live by pilfering. They raid food shops, kitchens in houses and the stands in open markets, and sometimes they even snatch food from people, particularly children, often injuring the person in the process. As a result monkeys are constantly warring with shopkeepers and are occasionally beaten. In spite of this measure of insecurity the urban monkeys have adjusted to the situation so thoroughly that they greatly prefer life in the city to life in the forest. When they are seized and taken out to the forest, they generally hurry back to town after they are released.

The city monkeys are characterized by comparatively settled housing and sleeping habits. The forest monkeys generally roost for the night in some convenient tree in the area where they have spent the day hunting for food and water; they rarely choose the same tree from one night to the next. The urban monkeys, on the other hand, invariably return to a particular lodging night after night; they move only when they are chased away. Since the places where they can enjoy undisturbed sleep in the city are limited, once they have found such a place they do not readily change their home.

The city monkeys, like their forest cousins and primates in general, live in groups united by strong emotional ties and a sense of mutual dependence. What holds nonhuman primate societies together? Many psychologists and anthropologists believe the primary bond is sexual [see "The Origin of Society," by Marshall D. Sahlins; SCIENTIFIC AMERICAN Offprint 602]. Our observations of the rhesus monkeys in India suggest, however, that sex is not the whole story. The monkeys, both the urban and the forest ones, maintain their group life not only in the breeding season but during the rest of the year as well. Indeed, we have observed that aggressive behavior tending to disrupt the group increases during the breeding season. Further, we can cite a significant and probably characteristic illustration of group concern and involvement that would be very difficult to explain strictly on the basis of sexual motivation. A baby monkey fell into a well; very quickly most of the members of the large group to which it belonged ran to the well in great distress, and they appeared about to jump into it when we arrived and pulled the infant out.

The monkey groups, both urban and nonurban, vary considerably in size; one we came across consisted of about 70 individuals. Among the adult members of a group females greatly outnumber males, probably because the dominant males limit the number of rivals. Charles H. Southwick of Johns Hopkins University found that in the average group of urban monkeys about 20 percent were adult males, 42 percent adult females, 26

of as few as two up to as many as 70 individuals. Not only is their environment completely unlike the forest habitat of their ancestors but also they are unlike their forest kin in group composition, in diet, in group leaders' behavior and in psychological complexity.

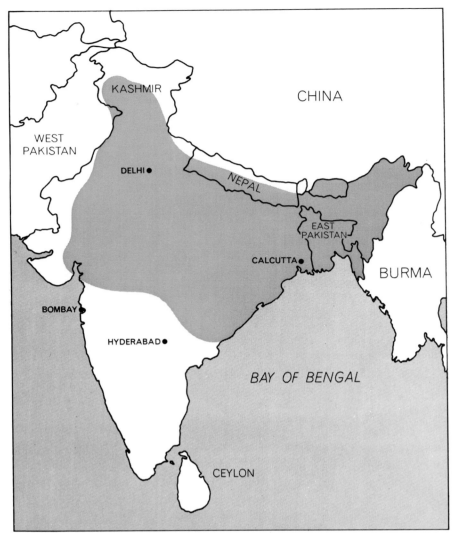

RANGE OF RHESUS MONKEYS in India extends generally from the northern barrier of the Himalayas south to between 20 and 17 degrees north longitude on the Deccan plateau.

percent infants and 12 percent juveniles. In forest groups the corresponding proportions were 11 percent adult males, 39 percent adult females, 23 percent infants and 27 percent juveniles. Southwick's censuses indicated that the average urban group consisted of 22 members; the average forest group, about 50 members. Our own count of certain forest groups showed an average membership of about 21 individuals. We have been unable to discern in these counts any significant pattern that would indicate a marked effect of city living per se on the size or composition of the monkey groups. The monkey population does, however, reflect the attitude of the people in the city in which it happens to live; in towns that are devoutly Hindu, and therefore permissive, the size of the monkey groups and the total monkey population are generally larger than elsewhere.

It is well known that societies of primate animals are generally marked by vigorous competition among the males and the establishment of a hierarchy of dominance, which is reflected in priorities in feeding and in sexual and other privileges. All the rhesus monkey groups we observed, in the city as well as in the forest, clearly followed this pattern. To identify the leader of a group one did not need to conduct an opinion poll; all we had to do was watch the group at a feeding place. The leader invariably presided over the food with the other monkeys hovering around him. In forest groups the leader usually monopolized the food. In a test in which we set out a food offering of 10 pounds of grain for the group, the dominant male would take charge; during the nonbreeding season he would not let any other member of the group eat with him, and even in the breeding season (the three fall months) he allowed only one adult female and her infant to share the food with him.

When the same experiment was conducted with an urban group of monkeys, a difference emerged. The dominant male in such a group would allow a number of adult females, infants and juveniles (as many as a fourth of all the group members) to partake of the food with him, regardless of the season. Moreover, there was much less aggressive behavior at the feeding place among the members of the urban group than was displayed by a forest group in the same situation. Presumably the urban monkeys become accustomed to sharing food because the supply available to them is limited.

The relatively unaggressive behavior of the urban monkeys at the feeding place does not mean that they are on the whole less aggressive than forest monkeys. On the contrary, laboratory experiments we conducted showed that they are basically much more aggressive. The experiments consisted in bringing together pairs or groups of previously unacquainted monkeys for the purpose of observing their social interactions. For the tests of pairs we used a six-foot cubic chamber and observed various pairings: two urban monkeys, two forest monkeys or an urban monkey with a forest monkey. Similarly, using a large room (18 by 18 by 18 feet), we put together groups of monkeys (each consisting of four to six members) that were strangers to one another, and these also were tried in various combinations: urban with urban, forest with forest, urban with forest.

When forest monkeys were placed together, they were relatively relaxed and uncombative. Urban monkeys, however, generally fell to fighting, regardless of whether the strangers to which they were introduced were urban monkeys or forest monkeys. Their battles were violent, usually resulting in severe injuries, and two of the combatants were actually killed. In experiments in which the monkeys competed for food we found that the forest monkeys generally yielded to the urban monkeys. Indeed, although male monkeys are usually dominant over females, in the urban versus forest matchings forest males often gave in to urban females.

Why are the urban monkeys so much more aggressive than the forest dwellers? Various explanations might be offered; I suggest that probably the principal reason is the restrictive urban environment, particularly the limited availability of food, which forces the monkeys to compete among themselves and with human beings for survival. The urban monkeys are highly aggressive toward people as well as toward members of

MOTHERS AND INFANTS cluster around a stone basin in the courtyard of a Jaipur house while two of the adults have a drink. Humans and rural monkeys seldom meet, but urban monkeys pilfer food, and they are often chased and even beaten by shopkeepers.

AT EASE IN THE MARKET, an adult Jaipur monkey munches on a peanut. The author's study shows that urban monkeys are more aggressive than rural monkeys and highly responsive and manipulative in dealing with novel or complex environmental features.

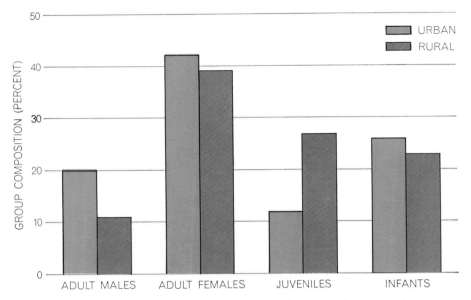

FEMALES OUTNUMBER MALES among adults in both urban and rural monkey groups. Urban groups contain more males because their leaders are less hostile to potential rivals.

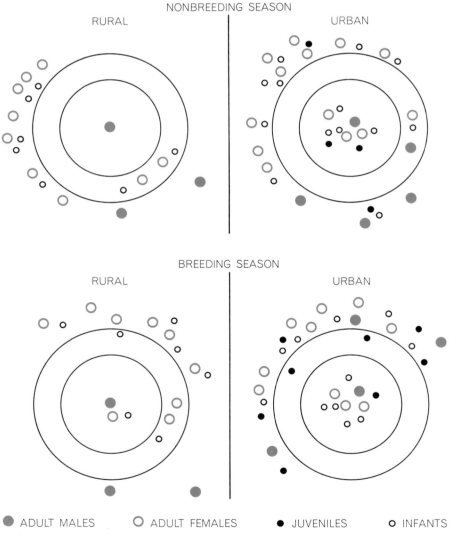

EXTENT OF DOMINANCE by group leaders is not the same for urban and rural monkeys. Observation of behavior at a forest feeding place (*left*) showed that the dominant male let no other monkeys feed with him in nonbreeding season and let only one adult female and her infant feed with him in breeding season. The urban leader (*right*) was far less strict.

their own species. Cases have been reported of people having been fatally bitten by monkeys in Indian cities. A member of our investigating team suffered a serious attack. An infant monkey he had accidentally touched set up a wail, whereupon several adult males and females jumped on him and bit him so badly that he was hospitalized.

Forest monkeys are shy and afraid of human beings: in the field they flee when approached by a person hundreds of yards away, and even after two years of acclimation in a laboratory they are agitated by the presence of a visitor. In contrast, urban monkeys are not at all afraid of human beings. They will come up close to a person and, as I have mentioned, even snatch food from his hands. In the laboratory they get out of their cages when they can (as a forest monkey will not, even when the door is left open) and boldly explore the surroundings. We have tested the urban monkeys with full-sized human skeletons, stuffed cobras and other novel objects that might be expected to evoke fear; the monkeys show no sign of fright and manipulate these objects with curiosity.

One can conjecture that, because of their experiences with the complexities of city life, the urban monkeys have acquired a well-developed capacity to respond to highly novel or complex situations. In the Regional Primate Research Center at the University of Wisconsin, Robert A. Butler found that monkeys have a rather sophisticated curiosity: they would press a lever to open a window for hours on end if the view outside was sufficiently interesting [see "Curiosity in Monkeys," by Robert A. Butler; SCIENTIFIC AMERICAN Offprint 426]. In current studies in the same laboratory Gene P. Sackett has shown that the level of a primate's curiosity, or exploratory behavior, depends on the extent of the animal's perceptual and motor experiences. Taking a cue from these experiments, we decided to investigate how the exploratory behavior of urban monkeys compares with that of forest monkeys.

Butler's apparatus, a closed box with windows that could be opened by pressing a lever, proved to be unworkable for the forest monkeys: we could not train them to press the lever to open the windows. We therefore used a box with windows that did not need to be opened; there were three windows, each in a different wall, and each showed a different view. One gave a view of a simple setup of some gray blocks; the second showed a battery group of empty rat cages; the third showed a toy train, bearing colored toys, that ran around a circular track. We put each monkey in this box for several days, and through a one-way screen in the fourth wall of the box we watched the animal for an hour and a half each day to observe which window view it favored.

None of the monkeys spent a great deal of time looking through the window at the wooden blocks. All of them, urban and forest, showed more interest in the view of rat cages, with the urban monkeys tending to spend a little more time at this window than the forest monkeys. The view of the moving toy train brought forth a really significant difference between the urban and the forest monkeys:

the urban monkeys were highly responsive to this complex display, whereas the forest monkeys showed no more interest in it than they did in the wooden blocks.

Could this difference be taken as an indication of greater intelligence in the urban monkeys? There were reasons to suppose that the city monkeys might indeed develop higher intellectual abilities. For one thing, the urban environment in which they grew up provided them with a richer variety of experiences than was available to monkeys in the forest. Furthermore, the hunters who caught monkeys for our laboratory experiments were convinced that the urban monkeys were more intelligent than those in the forest; although we offered the equivalent of $7 for each urban monkey, as

against only $2 for a forest monkey, the catchers preferred to hunt in the forest, believing the city monkeys were too smart to be trapped easily.

We conducted a series of elaborate tests to probe the relative intelligence of the urban and forest monkeys. Some of the problems presented to them were at a rather high level of difficulty—so taxing that they were not easy even for human youngsters. For example, in one case we used as test objects pieces of wood that varied in size (being either 10 square centimeters or 22 square centimeters in surface area), in shape (a square or a triangle) and in color (red or green). In each case three objects were set out before the monkey and it was required to select the one that differed from the

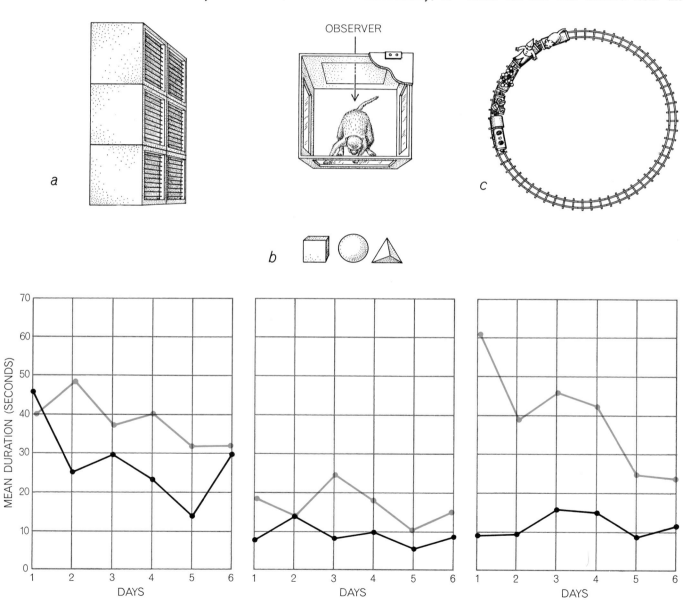

COMPARATIVE CURIOSITY of urban and rural monkeys was assessed by confining members of each group to a box with windows that offered a view of a battery of cages (a), of wooden blocks (b) and of a toy train, bearing colored toys, that ran on a circular track (c). The blocks held little interest for either group; more time was spent by both looking at the empty cages. The urban monkeys, however, were far more interested in the train than were the rural monkeys, who spent much more time looking at empty cages.

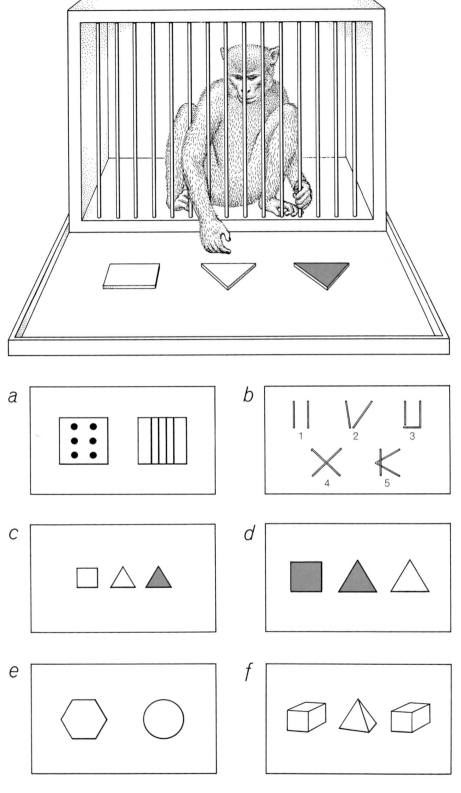

other two in a particular respect, depending on the context. For instance, the three objects might be a green square, a green triangle and a red triangle. If the three were of the small size, the monkey was rewarded for picking up the object that was odd in color (the red triangle); if, on the other hand, these objects were presented in the larger versions, the correct choice was the object that was odd in form (the green square). In order to solve such a problem the monkey had to learn that the shape or color of the object was important only in relation to another factor, in this case the size of the three objects. We complicated the problems for the monkeys by presenting the possible groupings of objects in random order from trial to trial.

To our surprise we found that the forest monkeys did about as well as the urban monkeys on these difficult problems. They performed poorly in an initial test calling for discrimination among various visual patterns, but that result can reasonably be attributed to the forest monkeys' shyness or fearfulness. Once they became used to the test situation they learned the solutions to all the test problems, simple or complex, as efficiently as the urban monkeys.

It appears that, whatever other effects urban living may produce in monkeys, it does not significantly promote their intelligence. This finding is in accord with what Harlow has learned from laboratory studies of monkeys; in experimental situations of quite a different kind he has also found that intellectual capability is not much affected by the environmental conditions. Monkeys that he raised in social isolation (that is, kept out of contact with other monkeys from birth) showed no significant impairment of their intelligence in later tests, although there were profound effects on their social, emotional and perceptual behavior.

To sum up our findings, we have observed that the urban way of life causes monkeys to change their feeding and sleeping habits, alters their behavior toward one another, increases their aggressiveness, makes them highly responsive and manipulative in their approach to novel or complex features of the environment and in general enhances their psychological complexity, but it does not advance their intelligence, although their behavior may appear to exhibit a high degree of shrewdness. I leave it to the reader to speculate on what implications these findings may have for understanding the impact of urban life on the behavior of man.

BATTERY OF TESTS was used to determine whether urban monkeys, raised in an enriched environment, had developed higher intellectual abilities than their forest-dwelling cousins. Members of each group could choose among various objects presented to them. The monkeys were rewarded if their choice was correct. The first test (a) required distinguishing among various visual patterns (only two are shown). The next (b) required the monkeys to pull the correct one of two strings in each pair. A third rewarded selection of the object "odd" in color when all three objects were small (c) and the object "odd" in shape when the three were larger (d). Other tests rewarded discrimination between two shapes (e) and selection of "odd" object among three (f). Scores are given on opposite page.

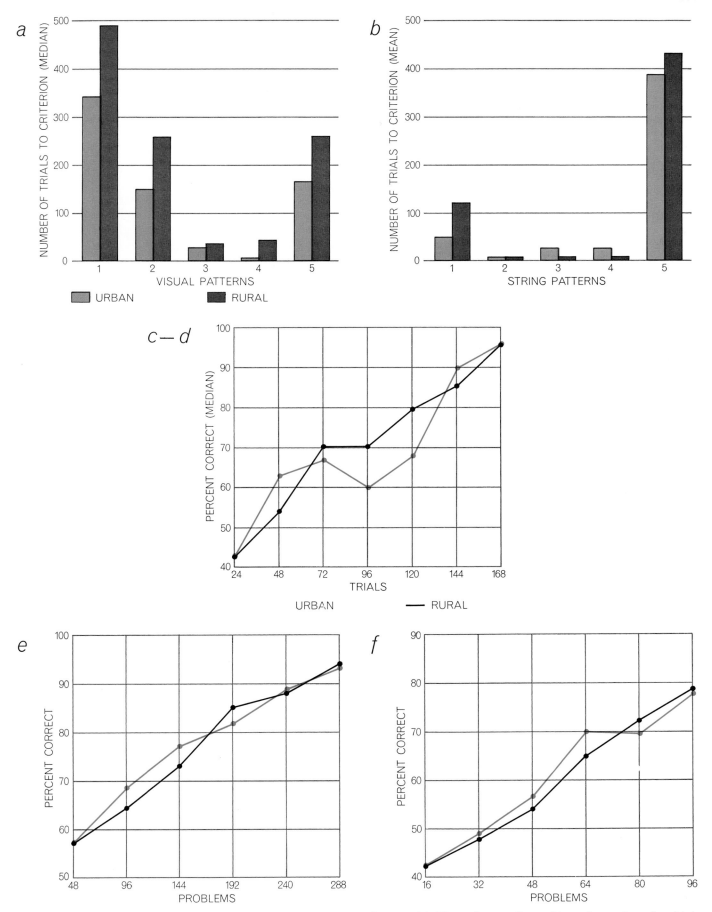

ESSENTIAL EQUALITY in the intelligence of rural and urban monkeys was demonstrated in all six tests, with the exception of poorer performance by rural monkeys on some problems in the first test (*a*). The author attributes this to the rural monkeys' initial fear of the test situation. He concludes that the urban monkeys' shrewdness reflects psychological complexity rather than intellect.

II

HUMAN PREHISTORY

In the following three sections we will assess the most current thinking about man's rise to civilization in the Old World and the New World. First we focus on the changes wrought in human evolution by the invention and sustained use of tools by prehuman hunters and gatherers. Then we turn our attention to the independent evolution of civilizations in the eastern and western hemispheres.

Tools and the Development of Culture

In S. L. Washburn's second essay in this collection, "Tools and Human Evolution," he picks up the discussion of the influence of man's technology on the course of human evolution, particularly on what he describes as the way in which "tools changed the pressures of natural selection and so changed the structure of man." We see the important multiple interrelated changes that occurred in the structure of pelvises, teeth, brow ridges, and brains as ape-men developed into man, the hunter, fully bipedal and capable of out-walking and outwitting his prey.

In "Stone Tools and Human Behavior" Sally and Lewis Binford present us with several new hypotheses about analyzing human prehistory and with a formally explicit method to evaluate those hypotheses—a taxonomy devised by French archaeologist Francois Bordes for artifact classification and factor analysis. Then the Binfords test their hypotheses on assemblages of implements from middle Paleolithic, or Mousterian, cultural complexes from Europe and the Middle East, sites dating from 100,000 to 35,000 years ago. The statistical results based on five factors of tool design are provocative inasmuch as they suggest that Mousterian sites in the same general locale were used for different, interrelated purposes: some were used as base or residential sites, some as sites for general hunting and butchering, and some as sites for more specialized preparation of food.

Whereas the Binfords focused on middle Paleolithic hunters and gatherers of the northern hemisphere, D. J. Mulvaney lays out the case for early hunters in the southern hemisphere. In "The Prehistory of the Australian Aborigine" Mulvaney describes his findings at a site in eastern Australia that indicate hunters first reached Australia at least 16,000 years ago. The late Paleolithic remains in this area suggest that the migrants possessed a very meager tool kit upon arrival. But how did Old World hunters get to Australia? Mulvaney's discoveries have opened the door to renewed speculation about the route they may have taken, and the nature of the cultural adaptations that occurred in the various environments of that huge land mass once they had settled there.

The final essay in this section, "Ishango" by Jean de Heinzelin, explicates the sophisticated hunting and fishing adaptation that took place on the shore of Lake Edward in the Congo about 9000 years ago. De Heinzelin alleges that a technique of harpoon manufacture invented first at Ishango, where the points were made of bone, diffused later to the east, north, and west throughout Africa. The discovery of a bone tool handle with a series of incised notches suggests that the inhabitants of the Ishango site had developed a number system and understood the concept of prime numbers. The Ishango site is particularly interesting because it demonstrates that a stable, sophisticated hunting, fishing, and gathering society was established in sub-Saharan Africa at about the time relatively sedentary settlements were being established elsewhere in the Old World.

TOOLS AND THE DEVELOPMENT OF CULTURE

15

TOOLS AND HUMAN EVOLUTION

SHERWOOD L. WASHBURN
September 1960

It is now clear that tools antedate man, and that their use by prehuman primates gave rise to Homo sapiens

A series of recent discoveries has linked prehuman primates of half a million years ago with stone tools. For some years investigators had been uncovering tools of the simplest kind from ancient deposits in Africa. At first they assumed that these tools constituted evidence of the existence of large-brained, fully bipedal men. Now the tools have been found in association with much more primitive creatures, the not-fully bipedal, small-brained near-men, or man-apes. Prior to these finds the prevailing view held that man evolved nearly to his present structural state and then discovered tools and the new ways of life that they made possible. Now it appears that man-apes—creatures able to run but not yet walk on two legs, and with brains no larger than those of apes now living—had already learned to make and to use tools. It follows that the structure of modern man must be the result of the change in the terms of natural selection that came with the tool-using way of life.

The earliest stone tools are chips or simple pebbles, usually from river

STENCILED HANDS in the cave of Gargas in the Pyrenees date back to the Upper Paleolithic of perhaps 30,000 years ago. Aurignacian man made the images by placing hand against wall and spattering it with paint. Hands stenciled in black (*top*) are more distinct and apparently more recent than those done in other colors (*center*).

gravels. Many of them have not been shaped at all, and they can be identified as tools only because they appear in concentrations, along with a few worked pieces, in caves or other locations where no such stones naturally occur. The huge advantage that a stone tool gives to its user must be tried to be appreciated. Held in the hand, it can be used for pounding, digging or scraping. Flesh and bone can be cut with a flaked chip, and what would be a mild blow with the fist becomes lethal with a rock in the hand. Stone tools can be employed, moreover, to make tools of other materials. Naturally occurring sticks are nearly all rotten, too large, or of inconvenient shape; some tool for fabrication is essential for the efficient use of wood. The utility of a mere pebble seems so limited to the user of modern tools that it is not easy to comprehend the vast difference that separates the tool-user from the ape which relies on hands and teeth alone. Ground-living monkeys dig out roots for food, and if they could use a stone or a stick, they might easily double their food supply. It was the success of the simplest tools that started the whole trend of human evolution and led to the civilizations of today.

From the short-term point of view, human structure makes human behavior possible. From the evolutionary point of view, behavior and structure form an interacting complex, with each change in one affecting the other. Man began when populations of apes, about a mil-

lion years ago, started the bipedal, tool-using way of life that gave rise to the man-apes of the genus *Australopithecus*. Most of the obvious differences that distinguish man from ape came after the use of tools.

The primary evidence for the new view of human evolution is teeth, bones and tools. But our ancestors were not fossils; they were striving creatures, full of rage, dominance and the will to live. What evolved was the pattern of life of intelligent, exploratory, playful, vigorous primates; the evolving reality was a succession of social systems based upon the motor abilities, emotions and intelligence of their members. Selection produced new systems of child care, maturation and sex, just as it did alterations in the skull and the teeth. Tools, hunting, fire, complex social life, speech, the human way and the brain evolved together to produce ancient man of the genus *Homo* about half a million years ago. Then the brain evolved under the pressures of more complex social life until the species *Homo sapiens* appeared perhaps as recently as 50,000 years ago.

With the advent of *Homo sapiens* the tempo of technical-social evolution quickened. Some of the early types of tool had lasted for hundreds of thousands of years and were essentially the same throughout vast areas of the African and Eurasian land masses. Now the tool forms multiplied and became regionally diversified. Man invented the

OLDUVAI GORGE in Tanganyika is the site where the skull of the largest known man-ape was discovered in 1959 by L. S. B. Leakey and his wife Mary. Stratigraphic evidence indicates that skull dates back to Lower Pleistocene, more than 500,000 years ago.

bow, boats, clothing; conquered the Arctic; invaded the New World; domesticated plants and animals; discovered
metals, writing and civilization. Today,
in the midst of the latest tool-making
revolution, man has achieved the capacity to adapt his environment to his need
and impulse, and his numbers have begun to crowd the planet.

The later events in the evolution of
the human species are subjects treated
by the authors of other essays in this
section of the book. This essay is concerned with the beginnings of the process by which, as Theodosius Dobzhansky says in his essay "The Present Evolution of Man," biological evolution has
transcended itself. From the rapidly accumulating evidence it is now possible
to speculate with some confidence on the
manner in which the way of life made
possible by tools changed the pressures
of natural selection and so changed the
structure of man.

Tools have been found, along with
the bones of their makers, at Sterkfontein, Swartkrans and Kromdraai in South
Africa and at Olduvai in Tanganyika.
Many of the tools from Sterkfontein are
merely unworked river pebbles, but
someone had to carry them from the
gravels some miles away and bring them
to the deposit in which they are found.
Nothing like them occurs naturally in
the local limestone caves. Of course the
association of the stone tools with man-
ape bones in one or two localities does
not prove that these animals made the
tools. It has been argued that a more
advanced form of man, already present,
was the toolmaker. This argument has
a familiar ring to students of human
evolution. Peking man was thought too
primitive to be a toolmaker; when the
first manlike pelvis was found with man-
ape bones, some argued that it must
have fallen into the deposit because it
was too human to be associated with the
skull. In every case, however, the repeated discovery of the same unantici-
pated association has ultimately settled
the controversy.

This is why the discovery by L. S. B.
and Mary Leakey in the summer of
1959 is so important. In Olduvai Gorge
in Tanganyika they came upon traces
of an old living site, and found stone
tools in clear association with the largest man-ape skull known. With the
stone tools were a hammer stone and
waste flakes from the manufacture of
the tools. The deposit also contained the
bones of rats, mice, frogs and some bones
of juvenile pig and antelope, showing
that even the largest and latest of the

SKULL IS EXAMINED *in situ* by Mary Leakey, who first noticed fragments of it protruding from the cliff face at left. Pebble tools were found at the same level as the skull.

SKULL IS EXCAVATED from surrounding rock with dental picks. Although skull was
badly fragmented, almost all of it was recovered. Fragment visible here is part of upper jaw.

146

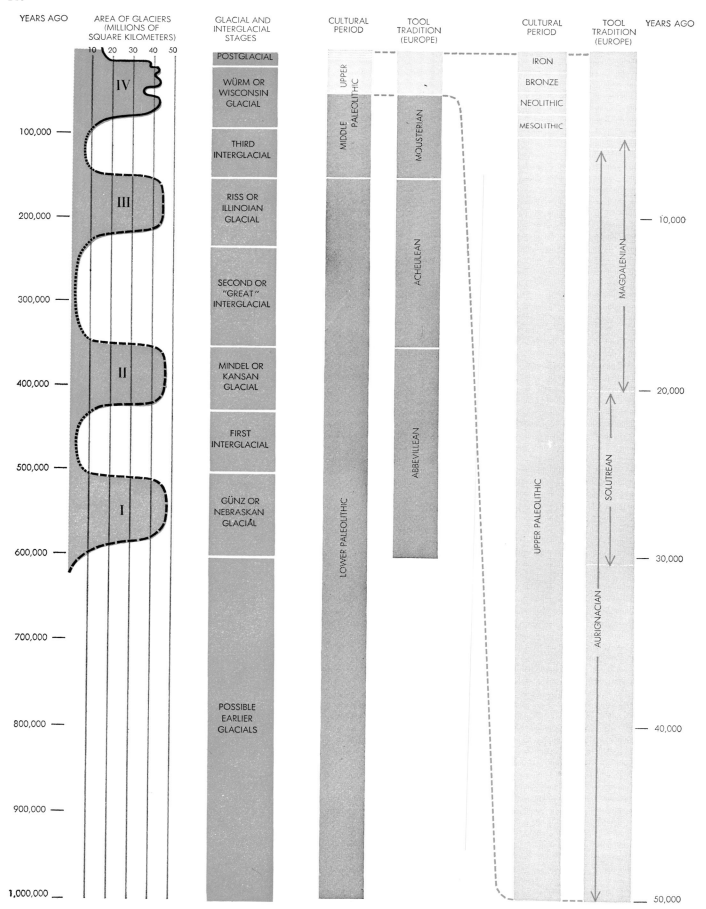

| YEARS AGO | AREA OF GLACIERS (MILLIONS OF SQUARE KILOMETERS) | GLACIAL AND INTERGLACIAL STAGES | CULTURAL PERIOD | TOOL TRADITION (EUROPE) | CULTURAL PERIOD | TOOL TRADITION (EUROPE) | YEARS AGO |

TIME-SCALE correlates cultural periods and tool traditions with the four great glaciations of the Pleistocene epoch. Glacial advances and retreats shown by solid black curve are accurately known; those shown by broken curve are less certain; those shown by dotted curve are uncertain. Light gray bars at far right show an expanded view of last 50,000 years on two darker bars at center. Scale was prepared with the assistance of William R. Farrand of the Lamont Geological Observatory of Columbia University.

man-apes could kill only the smallest animals and must have been largely vegetarian. The Leakeys' discovery confirms the association of the man-ape with pebble tools, and adds the evidence of manufacture to that of mere association. Moreover, the stratigraphic evidence at Olduvai now for the first time securely dates the man-apes, placing them in the lower Pleistocene, earlier than 500,000 years ago and earlier than the first skeletal and cultural evidence for the existence of the genus *Homo* [*see illustration on next two pages*]. Before the discovery at Olduvai these points had been in doubt.

The man-apes themselves are known from several skulls and a large number of teeth and jaws, but only fragments of the rest of the skeleton have been preserved. There were two kinds of man-ape, a small early one that may have weighed 50 or 60 pounds and a later and larger one that weighed at least twice as much. The differences in size and form between the two types are quite comparable to the differences between the contemporary pygmy chimpanzee and the common chimpanzee.

Pelvic remains from both forms of man-ape show that these animals were bipedal. From a comparison of the pelvis of ape, man-ape and man it can be seen that the upper part of the pelvis is much wider and shorter in man than in the ape, and that the pelvis of the man-ape corresponds closely, though not precisely, to that of modern man [*see top illustration on page 151*]. The long upper pelvis of the ape is characteristic of most mammals, and it is the highly specialized, short, wide bone in man that makes possible the human kind of bipedal locomotion. Although the man-ape pelvis is apelike in its lower part, it approaches that of man in just those features that distinguish man from all other animals. More work must be done before this combination of features is fully understood. My belief is that bipedal running, made possible by the changes in the upper pelvis, came before efficient bipedal walking, made possible by the changes in the lower pelvis. In the man-ape, therefore, the adaptation to bipedal locomotion is not yet complete. Here, then, is a phase of human evolution characterized by forms that are mostly bipedal, small-brained, plains-living, tool-making hunters of small animals.

The capacity for bipedal walking is primarily an adaptation for covering long distances. Even the arboreal chimpanzee can run faster than a man, and any monkey can easily outdistance him.

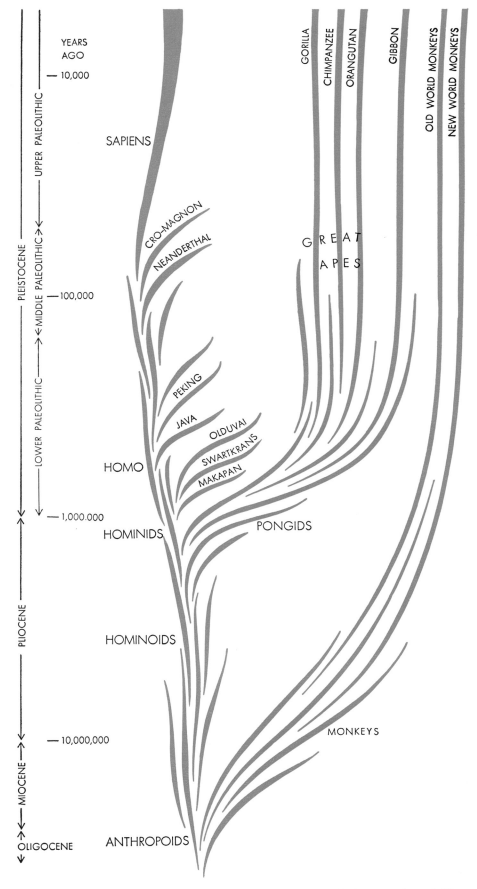

LINES OF DESCENT that lead to man and his closer living relatives are charted. The hominoid superfamily diverged from the anthropoid line in the Miocene period some 20 million years ago. From the hominoid line came the tool-using hominids at the beginning of the Pleistocene. The genus *Homo* appeared in the hominid line during the first interglacial (*see chart on opposite page*); the species *Homo sapiens*, around 50,000 years ago.

148

FOSSIL SKULLS of Pleistocene epoch reflect transition from man-apes (*below black line*) to *Homo sapiens* (top). Relative age of intermediate specimens is indicated schematically by their posi-

tion on page. Java man (*middle left*) and Solo man (*upper center*) are members of the genus *Pithecanthropus*, and are related to Peking man (*middle right*). The Shanidar skull (*upper left*) be-

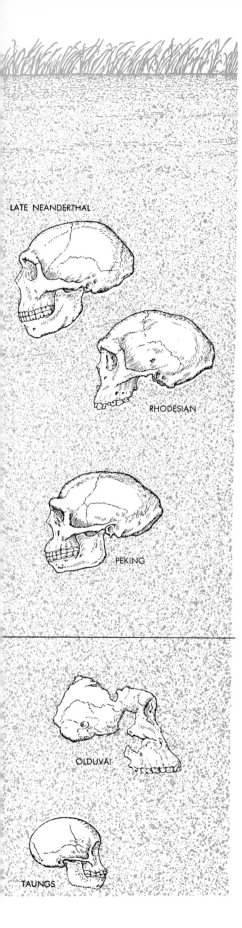

LATE NEANDERTHAL

RHODESIAN

PEKING

OLDUVAI

TAUNGS

longs to the Neanderthal family, while
Mount Carmel skull shows characteristics of Neanderthal and modern man.

A man, on the other hand, can walk for many miles, and this is essential for efficient hunting. According to skeletal evidence, fully developed walkers first appeared in the ancient men who inhabited the Old World from 500,000 years ago to the middle of the last glaciation. These men were competent hunters, as is shown by the bones of the large animals they killed. But they also used fire and made complicated tools according to clearly defined traditions. Along with the change in the structure of the pelvis, the brain had doubled in size since the time of the man-apes.

The fossil record thus substantiates the suggestion, first made by Charles Darwin, that tool use is both the cause and the effect of bipedal locomotion. Some very limited bipedalism left the hands sufficiently free from locomotor functions so that stones or sticks could be carried, played with and used. The advantage that these objects gave to their users led both to more bipedalism and to more efficient tool use. English lacks any neat expression for this sort of situation, forcing us to speak of cause and effect as if they were separated, whereas in natural selection cause and effect are interrelated. Selection is based on successful behavior, and in the man-apes the beginnings of the human way of life depended on both inherited locomotor capacity and on the learned skills of tool-using. The success of the new way of life based on the use of tools changed the selection pressures on many parts of the body, notably the teeth, hands and brain, as well as on the pelvis. But it must be remembered that selection was for the whole way of life.

In all the apes and monkeys the males have large canine teeth. The long upper canine cuts against the first lower premolar, and the lower canine passes in front of the upper canine. This is an efficient fighting mechanism, backed by very large jaw muscles. I have seen male baboons drive off cheetahs and dogs, and according to reliable reports male baboons have even put leopards to flight. The females have small canines, and they hurry away with the young under the very conditions in which the males turn to fight. All the evidence from living monkeys and apes suggests that the male's large canines are of the greatest importance to the survival of the group, and that they are particularly important in ground-living forms that may not be able to climb to safety in the trees. The small, early man-apes lived in open plains country, and yet none of them had large canine teeth. It would appear that the protection of the group must have shifted from teeth to tools early in the evolution of the man-apes, and long before the appearance of the forms that have been found in association with stone tools. The tools of Sterkfontein and Olduvai represent not the beginnings of tool use, but a choice of material and knowledge in manufacture which, as is shown by the small canines of the man-apes that deposited them there, derived from a long history of tool use.

Reduction in the canine teeth is not a simple matter, but involves changes in the muscles, face, jaws and other parts of the skull. Selection builds powerful neck muscles in animals that fight with their canines, and adapts the skull to the action of these muscles. Fighting is not a matter of teeth alone, but also of seizing, shaking and hurling an enemy's body with the jaws, head and neck. Reduction in the canines is therefore accompanied by a shortening in the jaws, reduction in the ridges of bone over the eyes and a decrease in the shelf of bone in the neck area [see illustration on page 152]. The reason that the skulls of the females and young of the apes look more like man-apes than those of adult males is that, along with small canines, they have smaller muscles and all the numerous structural features that go along with them. The skull of the man-ape is that of an ape that has lost the structure for effective fighting with its teeth. Moreover, the man-ape has transferred to its hands the functions of seizing and pulling, and this has been attended by reduction of its incisors. Small canines and incisors are biological symbols of a changed way of life; their primitive functions are replaced by hand and tool.

The history of the grinding teeth—the molars—is different from that of the seizing and fighting teeth. Large size in any anatomical structure must be maintained by positive selection; the selection pressure changed first on the canine teeth and, much later, on the molars. In the man-apes the molars were very large, larger than in either ape or man. They were heavily worn, possibly because food dug from the ground with the aid of tools was very abrasive. With the men of the Middle Pleistocene, molars of human size appear along with complicated tools, hunting and fire.

The disappearance of brow ridges and the refinement of the human face may involve still another factor. One of the essential conditions for the organi-

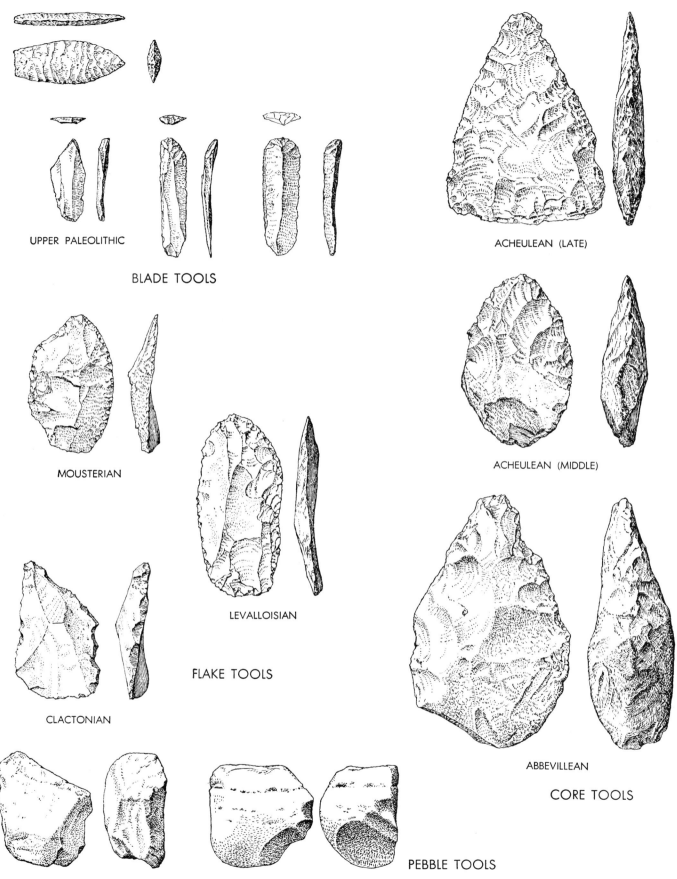

UPPER PALEOLITHIC

BLADE TOOLS

ACHEULEAN (LATE)

MOUSTERIAN

LEVALLOISIAN

FLAKE TOOLS

ACHEULEAN (MIDDLE)

CLACTONIAN

ABBEVILLEAN

CORE TOOLS

PEBBLE TOOLS

TOOL TRADITIONS of Europe are the main basis for classifying Paleolithic cultures. The earliest tools are shown at bottom of page; later ones, at top. The tools are shown from both the side and the edge, except for blade tools, which are shown in three views. Tools consisting of a piece of stone from which a few flakes have been chipped are called core tools (*right*). Other types of tool were made from flakes (*center and left*); blade tools were made from flakes with almost parallel sides. Tool traditions are named for site where tools of a given type were discovered; Acheulean tools, for example, are named for St. Acheul in France.

zation of men in co-operative societies was the suppression of rage and of the uncontrolled drive to first place in the hierarchy of dominance. Curt P. Richter of Johns Hopkins University has shown that domestic animals, chosen over the generations for willingness to adjust and for lack of rage, have relatively small adrenal glands. But the breeders who selected for this hormonal, physiological, temperamental type also picked, without realizing it, animals with small brow ridges and small faces. The skull structure of the wild rat bears the same relation to that of the tame rat as does the skull of Neanderthal man to that of *Homo sapiens*. The same is true for the cat, dog, pig, horse and cow; in each case the wild form has the larger face and muscular ridges. In the later stages of human evolution, it appears, the self-domestication of man has been exerting the same effects upon temperament, glands and skull that are seen in the domestic animals.

Of course from man-ape to man the brain-containing part of the skull has also increased greatly in size. This change is directly due to the increase in the size of the brain: as the brain grows, so grow the bones that cover it. Since there is this close correlation between brain size and bony brain-case, the brain size of the fossils can be estimated. On the scale of brain size the man-apes are scarcely distinguishable from the living apes, although their brains may have been larger with respect to body size. The brain seems to have evolved rapidly, doubling in size between man-ape and man. It then appears to have increased much more slowly; there is no substantial change in gross size during the last 100,000 years. One must remember, however, that size alone is a very crude indicator, and that brains of equal size may vary greatly in function. My belief is that although the brain of *Homo sapiens* is no larger than that of Neanderthal man, the indirect evidence strongly suggests that the first *Homo sapiens* was a much more intelligent creature.

The great increase in brain size is important because many functions of the brain seem to depend on the number of cells, and the number increases with volume. But certain parts of the brain have increased in size much more than others. As functional maps of the cortex of the brain show, the human sensory-motor cortex is not just an enlargement of that of an ape [*see illustrations on last three pages of this article*]. The areas

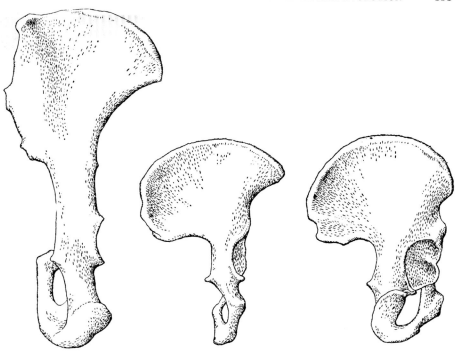

HIP BONES of ape (*left*), man-ape (*center*) and man (*right*) reflect differences between quadruped and biped. Upper part of human pelvis is wider and shorter than that of apes. Lower part of man-ape pelvis resembles that of ape; upper part resembles that of man.

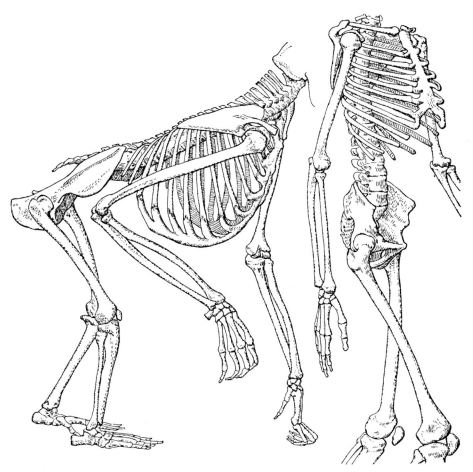

POSTURE of gorilla (*left*) and man (*right*) is related to size, shape and orientation of pelvis. Long, straight pelvis of ape provides support for quadrupedal locomotion; short, broad pelvis of man curves backward, carrying spine and torso in bipedal position.

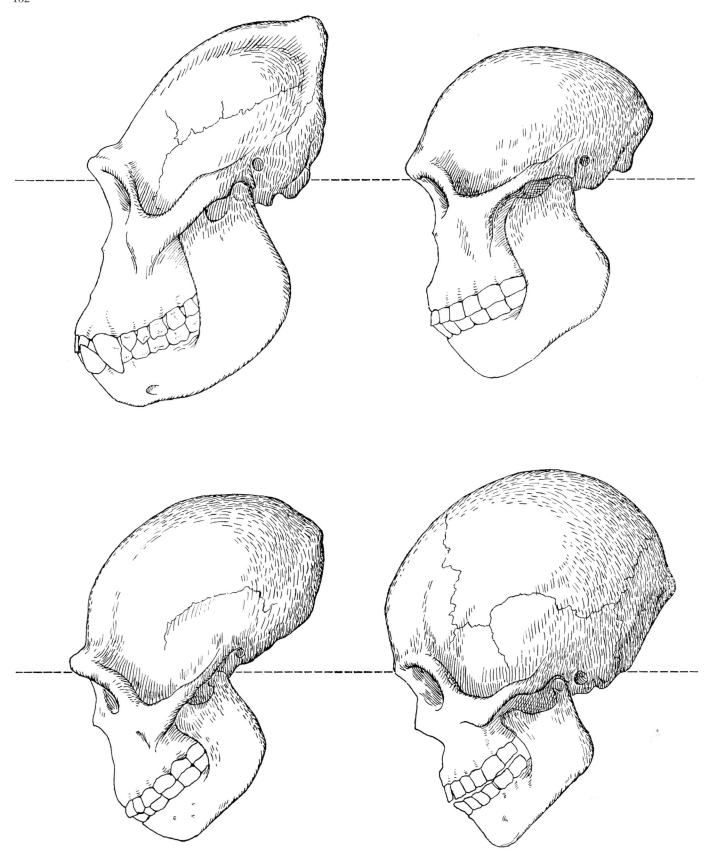

EVOLUTION OF SKULL from ape (*upper left*) to man-ape (*upper right*) to ancient man (*lower left*) to modern man (*lower right*) involves an increase in size of brain case (*part of skull above broken lines*) and a corresponding decrease in size of face (*part of skull below broken lines*). Apes also possess canine teeth that are much larger than those found in either man-apes or man.

for the hand, especially the thumb, in man are tremendously enlarged, and this is an integral part of the structural base that makes the skillful use of the hand possible. The selection pressures that favored a large thumb also favored a large cortical area to receive sensations from the thumb and to control its motor activity. Evolution favored the development of a sensitive, powerful, skillful thumb, and in all these ways —as well as in structure—a human thumb differs from that of an ape.

The same is true for other cortical areas. Much of the cortex in a monkey is still engaged in the motor and sensory functions. In man it is the areas adjacent to the primary centers that are most expanded. These areas are concerned with skills, memory, foresight and language; that is, with the mental faculties that make human social life possible. This is easiest to illustrate in the field of language. Many apes and monkeys can make a wide variety of sounds. These sounds do not, however, develop into language [see "The Origin of Speech," by Charles F. Hockett, Offprint 603]. Some workers have devoted great efforts, with minimum results, to trying to teach chimpanzees to talk. The reason is that there is little in the brain to teach. A human child learns to speak with the greatest ease, but the storage of thousands of words takes a great deal of cortex. Even the simplest language must have given great advantage to those first men who had it. One is tempted to think that language may have appeared together with the fine tools, fire and complex hunting of the large-brained men of the Middle Pleistocene, but there is no direct proof of this.

The main point is that the kind of animal that can learn to adjust to complex, human, technical society is a very different creature from a tree-living ape, and the differences between the two are rooted in the evolutionary process. The reason that the human brain makes the human way of life possible is that it is the result of that way of life. Great masses of the tissue in the human brain are devoted to memory, planning, language and skills, because these are the abilities favored by the human way of life.

The emergence of man's large brain occasioned a profound change in the plan of human reproduction. The human mother-child relationship is unique among the primates as is the use of tools. In all the apes and monkeys the baby clings to the mother; to be able to do so,

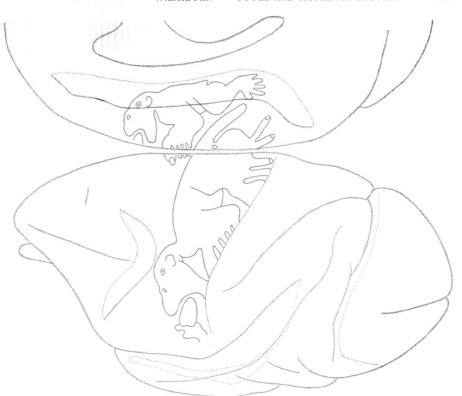

MOTOR CORTEX OF MONKEY controls the movements of the body parts outlined by the superimposed drawing of the animal (*color*). Gray lines trace the surface features of the left half of the brain (*bottom*) and part of the right half (*top*). Colored drawing is distorted in proportion to amount of cortex associated with functions of various parts of the body. Smaller animal in right half of brain indicates location of secondary motor cortex.

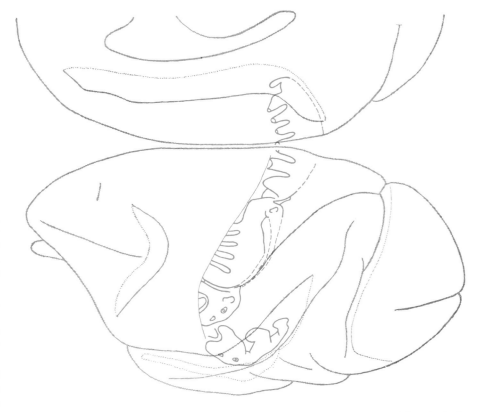

SENSORY CORTEX OF MONKEY is mapped in same way as motor cortex (*above*). As in motor cortex, a large area is associated with hands and feet. Smaller animal at bottom of left half of brain indicates location of secondary sensory cortex. Drawings are based on work of Clinton N. Woolsey and his colleagues at the University of Wisconsin Medical School.

the baby must be born with its central nervous system in an advanced state of development. But the brain of the fetus must be small enough so that birth may take place. In man adaptation to bipedal locomotion decreased the size of the bony birth-canal at the same time that the exigencies of tool use selected for larger brains. This obstetrical dilemma was solved by delivery of the fetus at a much earlier stage of development. But this was possible only because the mother, already bipedal and with hands free of locomotor necessities, could hold the helpless, immature in-fant. The small-brained man-ape probably developed in the uterus as much as the ape does; the human type of mother-child relation must have evolved by the time of the large-brained, fully bipedal humans of the Middle Pleistocene. Bipedalism, tool use and selection for large brains thus slowed human development and invoked far greater maternal responsibility. The slow-moving mother, carrying the baby, could not hunt, and the combination of the woman's obligation to care for slow-developing babies and the man's occupation of hunting imposed a fundamental pat-tern on the social organization of the human species.

As Marshall D. Sahlins suggests ["The Origin of Society," SCIENTIFIC AMERICAN Offprint 602], human society was heavily conditioned at the outset by still other significant aspects of man's sexual adaptation. In the monkeys and apes year-round sexual activity supplies the social bond that unites the primate horde. But sex in these species is still subject to physiological—especially glandular—controls. In man these controls are gone, and are replaced by a bewildering variety of social customs. In no

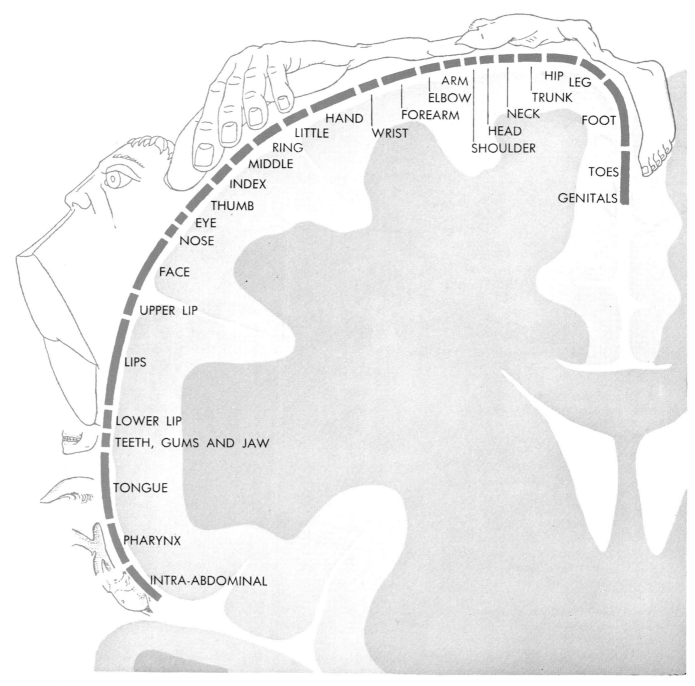

SENSORY HOMUNCULUS is a functional map of the sensory cortex of the human brain worked out by Wilder Penfield and his associates at the Montreal Neurological Institute. As in the map of the sensory cortex of the monkey that appears on the preceding page, the distorted anatomical drawing (*color*) indicates the areas of the sensory cortex associated with the various parts of the body.

other primate does a family exist that controls sexual activity by custom, that takes care of slow-growing young, and in which—as in the case of primitive human societies—the male and female provide different foods for the family members.

All these family functions are ultimately related to tools, hunting and the enlargement of the brain. Complex and technical society evolved from the sporadic tool-using of an ape, through the simple pebble tools of the man-ape and the complex toolmaking traditions of ancient men to the hugely complicated culture of modern man. Each behavioral

stage was both cause and effect of biological change in bones and brain. These concomitant changes can be seen in the scanty fossil record and can be inferred from the study of the living forms.

Surely as more fossils are found these ideas will be tested. New techniques of investigation, from planned experiments in the behavior of lower primates to more refined methods of dating, will extract wholly new information from the past. It is my belief that, as these events come to pass, tool use will be found to have been a major factor, beginning with

the initial differentiation of man and ape. In ourselves we see a structure, physiology and behavior that is the result of the fact that some populations of apes started to use tools a million years ago. The pebble tools constituted man's principal technical adaptation for a period at least 50 times as long as recorded history. As we contemplate man's present eminence, it is well to remember that, from the point of view of evolution, the events of the last 50,000 years occupy but a moment in time. Ancient man endured at least 10 times as long and the man-apes for an even longer time.

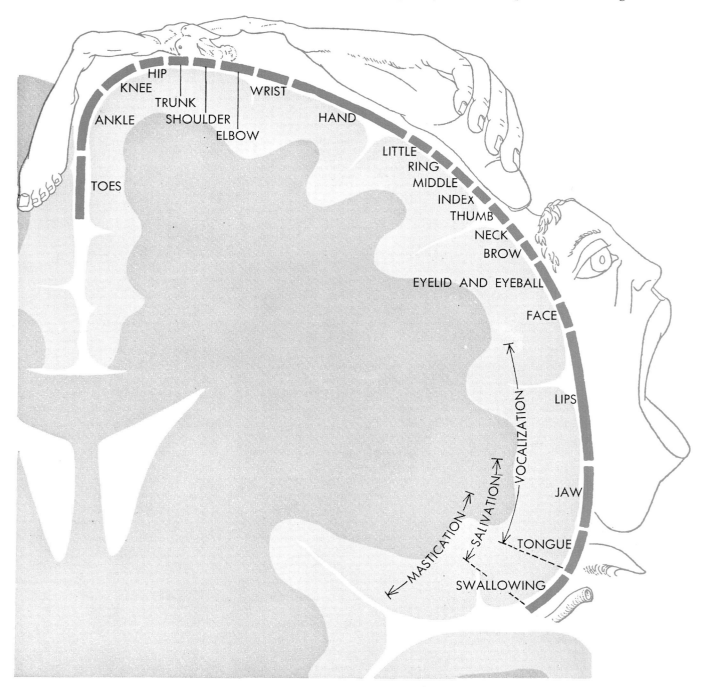

MOTOR HOMUNCULUS depicts parts of body and areas of motor cortex that control their functions. Human brain is shown here in coronal (ear-to-ear) cross section. Speech and hand areas of both motor and sensory cortex in man are proportionately much larger than corresponding areas in apes and monkeys, as can be seen by comparing homunculi with diagram of monkey cortex.

16

STONE TOOLS AND HUMAN BEHAVIOR

SALLY R. BINFORD AND LEWIS R. BINFORD
April 1969

Statistical analysis of the implements found at Paleolithic sites can identify the groups of tools that were used for various kinds of jobs. These groupings suggest how early man's life was organized

The main evidence for almost the entire span of human prehistory consists of stone tools. Over the more than three million years of the Pleistocene epoch hunting and gathering peoples left behind them millions of such tools, ranging from crudely fractured pebbles to delicately flaked pieces of flint. Modern students of these objects are attempting to understand their various functions, and much of current prehistoric research is concerned with developing methods for achieving this understanding.

For many years prehistorians devoted almost all their efforts to establishing cultural sequences in order to determine what happened when. Chronologies have been established for many parts of the Old World, both on the basis of stratigraphy and with the aid of more modern techniques such as radioisotope dating and pollen analysis. Although many details of cultural sequences remain to be worked out, the broad outlines are known well enough for prehistoric archaeologists to address themselves to a different range of questions, not so much what happened when as what differences in stone tools made at the same time mean.

Traditionally differences in assemblages of stone tools from the same general period were thought to signify different cultures. Whereas the term "culture" was never very clearly defined, it most often meant distinct groups of people with characteristic ways of doing things, and frequently it was also taken to mean different ethnic affiliations for the men responsible for the tools. Such formulations cannot readily be tested and so are scientifically unsatisfactory. If we were to examine the debris left behind by people living today, we would find that differences in such material could most often be explained by differences in human activities. For example, the kinds of archaeological remains that would be left by a modern kitchen would differ markedly from those left by miners. This variation in archaeological remains is to be understood in terms of function—what activities were carried out at functionally different locations—and not in terms of "kitchen cultures" or "mining cultures."

The example is extreme, but it serves to illustrate a basic difference between the assumptions underlying our research and those on which the more traditional prehistory is based. The obvious fact that human beings can put different locations to different uses leads us to the concept of settlement type and settlement system, the framework that seems most appropriate for interpreting prehistoric stone-tool assemblages. In what follows we are restating, and in some respects slightly modifying, some useful formulations put forward by Philip L. Wagner of Simon Fraser University in British Columbia.

All known groups of hunter-gatherers live in societies composed of local groups that can be internally organized in various ways; invariably the local group is partitioned into subgroups that function to carry out different tasks. Sex and age are the characteristics that most frequently apply in the formation of subgroups: the subgroups are generally composed of individuals of the same age or sex who cooperate in a work force. For example, young male adults often cooperate in hunting, and women work together in collecting plant material and preparing food. At times a larger local group breaks up along different lines to form reproductive-residence units, and these family subgroups tend to be more permanent and self-sustaining than the work groups.

Although we have no idea how prehistoric human groups were socially partitioned, it seems reasonable to assume that these societies were organized flexibly and included both family and work groups. If the assumption is correct, we would expect this organization to be reflected in differences both between stone-tool assemblages at a given site and between assemblages at different sites.

Geographical variations would arise because not all the activities of a given society are conducted in one place. The ways that game, useful plants, appropriate living sites and the raw materials for tool manufacture are distributed in the environment will directly affect where subgroups of a society perform different activities. One site might be a favorable place for young male hunters to kill and partly butcher animals; another might be a more appropriate place for women and children to gather and process plants. Both work locations might be some distance from the group's main living site. One would expect the composition of the tool assemblages at various locations to be determined by the kinds of tasks performed and by the size and composition of the group performing them.

Temporal variations can also be expected between assemblages of stone tools, for several reasons. The availability of plants and animals in the course of the year is a primary factor; it varies as a result of the reproductive cycles of the plants and animals. The society itself varies in an annual cycle; the ways the members of a society are organized and how they cooperate at different times of the year change with their activities at different seasons. Moreover, any society must solve integrative problems as a result of the maturation of the young, the death of some members, relations with other groups and so on. The behavioral modifications prompted by such considerations will be reflected in the society's use of a territory.

In addition to these factors that can affect the archaeological material left behind by a society, there are other determinants that profoundly modify site utilization. It is the kinds of site used for different activities and the way these specialized locations are related that are respectively termed settlement type and settlement system.

In technologically simple societies we can distinguish two broad classes of activities: extraction and maintenance. Extraction involves the direct procurement of foods, fuels and raw materials for tools. Maintenance activities consist in the preparation and distribution of foods and fuels already on hand and in the processing of raw materials into tools. Since the distribution of resources in the environment is not necessarily related to the distribution of sites providing adequate living space and safety, we would not expect extraction and maintenance activities to be conducted in the same places.

Base camps are chosen primarily for living space, protection from the elements and central location with respect to resources. We would expect the archaeological assemblages of base camps to reflect maintenance activities: the preparation and consumption of food and the manufacture of tools for use in other less permanent sites.

Another settlement type would be a work camp, a site occupied while smaller social units were carrying out extractive tasks. Archaeologically these would appear as kill sites, collecting stations and quarries for extracting flint to be used in toolmaking. The archaeological assemblages from these sites should be dominated by the tools used in the specific extractive tasks. If a work camp were occupied for a rather long period and by a fairly large subgroup, we would anticipate that some maintenance activities would also be reflected in the archaeological remains.

It is the way these two general classes of camps are used by any society that defines the settlement system. If a hunting-gathering society were relatively sedentary, we would expect the tools at the base camp to exhibit little seasonal variation because the base camp would have been occupied for most of the year. Under some conditions, however, we would expect to find more than one kind of base camp for a society. If the organization of

TYPICAL BORER

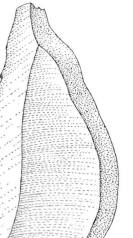

NATURALLY BACKED KNIFE

BEC

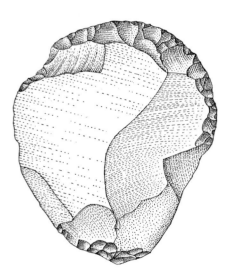

TYPICAL END SCRAPER

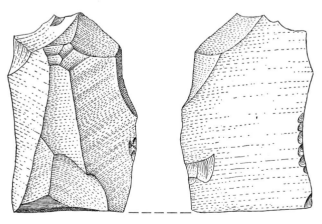

ATYPICAL BURIN

FIVE CLASSES OF STONE TOOLS predominate in the largest of the five groups, or factors, revealed by the authors' analyses. Of the 40 classes of tools subjected to multivariate analysis, 16 appear in this cluster, named Factor I. Few of the classes seem suited to hunting or heavy work; they were probably base-camp items for making other tools of wood or bone.

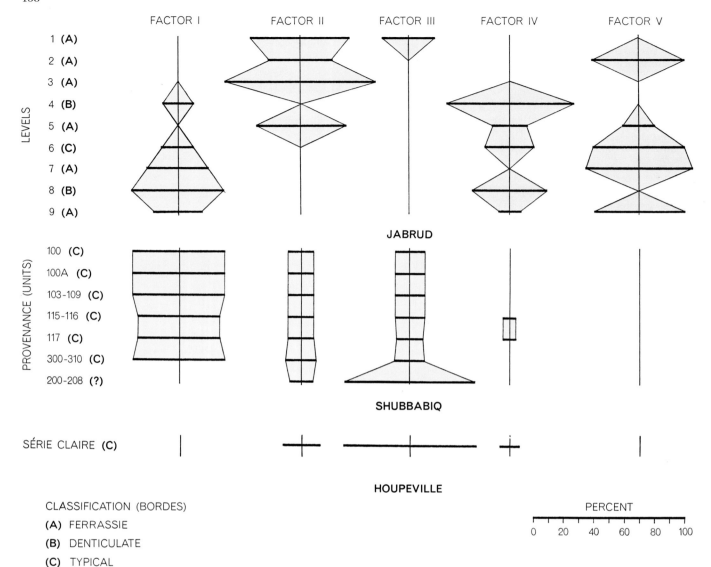

	FACTOR I	FACTOR II	FACTOR III	FACTOR IV	FACTOR V

LEVELS

1 (A)
2 (A)
3 (A)
4 (B)
5 (A)
6 (C)
7 (A)
8 (B)
9 (A)

JABRUD

PROVENANCE (UNITS)

100 (C)
100A (C)
103-109 (C)
115-116 (C)
117 (C)
300-310 (C)
200-208 (?)

SHUBBABIQ

SÉRIE CLAIRE (C)

HOUPEVILLE

CLASSIFICATION (BORDES)

(A) FERRASSIE
(B) DENTICULATE
(C) TYPICAL

PERCENT

0   20   40   60   80   100

RELATIVE SIGNIFICANCE of the five factors identified in the tool assemblages from three Mousterian sites is indicated by the percentage of total variation attributable to each factor in each sample analyzed. Every sample but one bears the name (*key, bottom left*) by which the French archaeologist François Bordes characterizes the entire assemblage. The homogeneity of the samples from the Mugharet es-Shubbabiq cave site in Israel (*center*) is in sharp contrast to the heterogeneity of the samples from the Jabrud rock-shelter in Syria (*top*). The authors suggest that the cave was a base camp but that the rock-shelter was only a work camp, occupied at different times by work parties with different objectives. The Houpeville assemblage (*bottom*) is not like either of the others.

the society changes during the year, perhaps consisting of larger groups during the summer months and dispersing into smaller family units during the lean winter months, there would be more than one kind of base camp, and each would have its distinct seasonal characteristics.

The work camps would display even greater variation; each camp would be occupied for a shorter time, and the activities conducted there would be more specifically related to the resources being exploited. One must also consider how easy or how difficult it was to transport the exploited resource. If a party of hunters killed some big animals or a large number of smaller animals, the entire group might assemble at the kill site

not only to eat but also to process the large quantities of game for future consumption. In such a work camp we would expect to find many of the kinds of tools used for food processing, even though the tasks undertaken would be less diverse than those at a base camp.

The extent to which maintenance tasks are undertaken at work camps will also be directly related to the distance between work camp and base camp. If the two are close together, we would not find much evidence of maintenance activities at the work camp. As the distance between work camp and base camp increases, however, the work-camp assemblage of tools would reflect an increase in maintenance activities. This leads us to

suggest a third type of settlement: the transient camp. At such a location we would find only the most minimal evidence of maintenance activities, such as might be undertaken by a traveling group in the course of an overnight stay.

We have outlined here the settlement system of technologically simple huntergatherers. Although the system is not taken directly from any one specific living group, it does describe the generalized kind of settlement system that ethnographers have documented for people at this level of sociocultural complexity. In order to assess the relevance of such a settlement system for huntergatherers in the Paleolithic period it was necessary first to relate stone tools to human activities and then to determine how these tools were distributed at different types of site.

The kind of analysis we carried out might well have been impossible without the basic work on the classification of stone tools done by François Bordes of the University of Bordeaux. The archaeological taxonomy devised by Bordes for the Middle Paleolithic has become a widely accepted standard, so that it is now possible for prehistorians working with Middle Paleolithic materials from different parts of the world to describe the stone tools they excavate in identical and repeatable terms.

In addition to compiling a type list of Mousterian, or Middle Paleolithic, tools, Bordes has offered convincing arguments against the "index fossil" approach to the analysis of stone tools. This approach, borrowed from paleontology, assigns a high diagnostic value to the disappearance of an old tool form or the appearance of a new one; such changes are assumed to indicate key cultural events. Bordes has insisted on describing assemblages of tools in their entirety without any a priori assumption that some tools have greater cultural significance than others. This radical departure in classification, combined with highly refined excavation techniques, provides a sound scientific basis on which much current prehistoric research rests.

According to what has become known as *la méthode Bordes,* stone artifacts are classified according to explicitly stated attributes of morphology and technique of manufacture. The population of stone tools from a site (the assemblage) is then described graphically, and the relative frequencies of different kinds of stone tools from various sites can be compared. Such a statistical technique, which deals with a single class of variables, is quite appropriate for the description of assemblages of stone tools. The explanation of multiple similarities and differences, however, requires different statistical techniques.

The factors determining the range and form of activities conducted by any group at any site may vary in terms of many possible "causes" in various combinations. The more obvious among these might be seasonally regulated phenomena affecting the distribution of game, environmental conditions, the ethnic composition of the group, the size and structure of the group regardless of ethnic affiliation and so on. Other determinants of activities might be the particular situation of the group with respect to

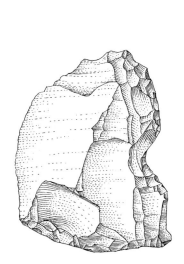

NOTCHED PIECE

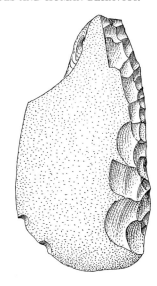

SIDE SCRAPER WITH ABRUPT RETOUCH

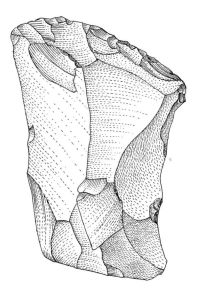

TRUNCATED FLAKE

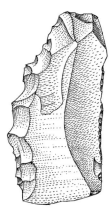

DENTICULATE

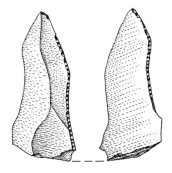

RACLETTE

UNIDENTIFIED TOOL KIT, with five predominant classes of artifacts, comprises Factor IV. The tasks for which it was intended are not known. Bordes has suggested, however, that denticulates (*bottom left*) may have been utilized for the processing of plant materials.

food, shelter, the supply of tools or the availability of raw materials. In short, the "causes" of assemblage variation are separate activities, each of which is related to the physical and social environment and to the others.

Given this frame of reference, the summary description of frequencies of tool types in an assemblage, which is the end product of Bordes's method, represents a blending of activity units and their determinants. We needed to partition assemblages into groups of tools that reflect activities. To use a chemical analogy, the end product of Bordes's method of describing the entire assemblage is a compound; we hoped to isolate smaller units, analogous to the constituent elements of a compound, that would represent activities. In our view variation in assemblage composition is directly related to the form, nature and spatial arrangement of the activities in which the tools were used.

Since the settlement-system model we had in mind is based on ethnographic examples, we wanted to ensure that the archaeological materials we analyzed were made by men whose psychological capacities were not radically different from our own. The Mousterian, a culture complex named after the site of Le Moustier in the Dordogne, dates from about 100,000 to 35,000 B.C. Mousterian tools are known from western Europe, the Near East, North Africa and even central China. Where human remains have been discovered in association with Mousterian tools they are the remains of Neanderthal man. Once considered to be a species separate from ourselves, Neanderthal man is generally accepted today as a historical subspecies of fully modern man. A great deal of archaeological evidence collected in recent years strongly suggests that the behavioral capacities of Neanderthal man were not markedly different from our own.

The Mousterian assemblages we chose for our analysis came from two sites in the Near East and one in northern France. One of us had excavated a cave site in Israel (Mugharet es-Shubbabiq, near Lake Tiberias) and had analyzed the stone tools found there in Bordes's laboratory and under his supervision. We also used assemblages that had been excavated in the 1930's by Alfred Rust at Jabrud, a rock-shelter near Damascus in Syria; this material had been studied and reclassified by Bordes. The French material came from the open-air site of Houpeville and had been excavated and analyzed by Bordes. We chose these samples because they represented three kinds of site, but more important because they had all been classified by Bordes. This meant that extraneous variation due to the vagaries of classification was eliminated.

To describe the two Near Eastern sites briefly, Shubbabiq is a large cave located in a narrow, deep valley that is dry for most of the year. The cave mouth faces east and its floor covers nearly 350 square meters, with slightly less than 300 meters well exposed to natural light. Un-

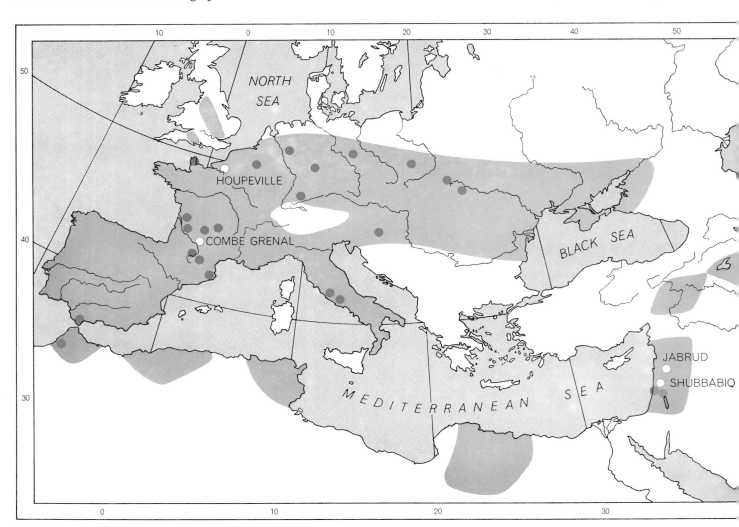

STONE TOOLS of the Mousterian tradition are found throughout Europe and also in the Near East. They were made from 100,000 to 35,000 years ago and are associated in many instances with the remains of Neanderthal man (*colored dots*). The authors' statistical

fortunately the Mousterian deposits in the main part of the cave had been destroyed by more recent inhabitants. Five of the samples from Shubbabiq used in our study came from deposits in the rear of the cave. The sixth, Unit 200–208, was a small deposit outside the cave entrance. The Syrian site, Jabrud Shelter I, is long and narrow. Like Shubbabiq, it faces east, and because it is more open it is much more exposed to the elements. Located on the edge of the Anti-Lebanon range, it looks down on the floor of a valley. At the time of the occupations that interested us the shelter had about 178 square meters of floor space. Rust excavated a trench some 23 meters long and three meters wide along the shelter's back wall. The shelter yielded many layers of Mousterian tools, but only the upper nine strata contained assemblages that could be compared with those from Shubbabiq.

Our study sought to answer three questions. First, does the composition of the total assemblage from any occupa-

analyses utilized tools from two sites in the Near East and two in Europe (*open circles*).

tion level correspond to any single human activity, or does information summarized in a single class of variables obscure the fact that each assemblage represents an assortment of activities? Second, is there any regularity in the composition of assemblages at a single location that can be interpreted in terms of regular patterns of human behavior? Third, is there some kind of directional change over a period of time in assemblages from a single location that suggests evolutionary changes in human behavior?

The statistical analysis of a single class of variables is termed univariate analysis. Multivariate statistical analysis allows one to calculate the measure of dependence among many classes of variables in several ways. Because we needed to determine the measure of dependence relating every one of some 40 classes of tools found in varying percentages in 17 different assemblages from three sites to every one of the remaining 39 classes, we faced a staggering burden of calculations. Such a job could not have been undertaken before the advent of high-speed computers. Factor analysis, which has been applied in areas as unrelated as geology and sociology, seemed the most appropriate method. Our analysis was run at the University of Chicago's Institute for Computer Research, with the aid of a modification of a University of California program for factor analysis (Mesa 83) and an IBM 7090 computer.

The factor analysis showed that in our samples the different classes of Mousterian artifacts formed five distinct clusters. The most inclusive of the five—Factor I—consists of 16 types of tools. Within this grouping the tools showing the highest measure of mutual dependence are, to use Bordes's taxonomic terminology, the "typical borer," the "typical end scraper," the "bec" (a small, beaked flake), the "atypical burin" (an incising tool) and the "naturally backed knife" [*see illustration on page 157*]. None of these tools is well suited to hunting or to heavy-duty butchering, but most are well designed for cutting and incising wood or bone. (The end scraper seems best adapted to working hides.) On these grounds we interpret Factor I as representing activities conducted at a base camp.

The next grouping produced by the factor analysis we interpret as a kit of related tools for hunting and butchering. The tools in this group—Factor II—are of 12 types. Three varieties of spear point are dominant; in Bordes's terminology they are the "plain Levallois point," the

"retouched Levallois point" and the "Mousterian point." Side scrapers of four classes are the other tools that show the highest measure of mutual dependence: the "simple straight," the "simple convex," the "convergent" and the "double" side scraper [*see illustration on next page*].

In Factor III the main diagnostic tools are cutting implements. They include the "typical backed knife," the "naturally backed knife" (also found in Factor I), "typical" and "atypical" Levallois flakes, "unretouched blades" and "end-notched pieces" [*see illustration on page 163*]. With the exception of the end-notched pieces all these tools appear to be implements for fine cutting. Their stratigraphic association with evidence of fire suggests that Factor III is a tool kit for the preparation of food.

Factor IV is distinctive. Its characteristic tools are "denticulates" (flakes with at least one toothed edge), "notched pieces," "side scrapers with abrupt retouch," "raclettes" (small flakes with at least one delicately retouched edge) and "truncated flakes." We find it difficult even to guess at the function of this factor. Bordes has suggested that some of these tools were employed in the processing of plant materials.

The tools with the highest measure of mutual dependence in Factor V are "elongated Mousterian points," "disks," "scrapers made on the ventral surfaces of flakes," "typical burins" (as opposed to the atypical burin in Factor I) and "unretouched blades" (which are also found in Factor III). The fact that there is only one kind of point and one kind of scraper among the diagnostic implements suggests that Factor V is a hunting and butchering tool kit that is more specialized than the one represented by Factor II.

What answers does the existence of five groups of statistically interdependent artifacts among Mousterian assemblages give to the three questions we raised? In response to the first question we can show that neither at Shubbabiq nor at Jabrud does the total assemblage correspond to any single human activity. The degree to which individual factors account for the variation between assemblages can be expressed in percentages [*see illustration on page 158*]. To consider the Shubbabiq findings first, the percentages make it plain that, with the exception of a group of tools in Unit 200–208, the assemblages as a whole are internally quite consistent. The major part of the variation is accounted for by

162

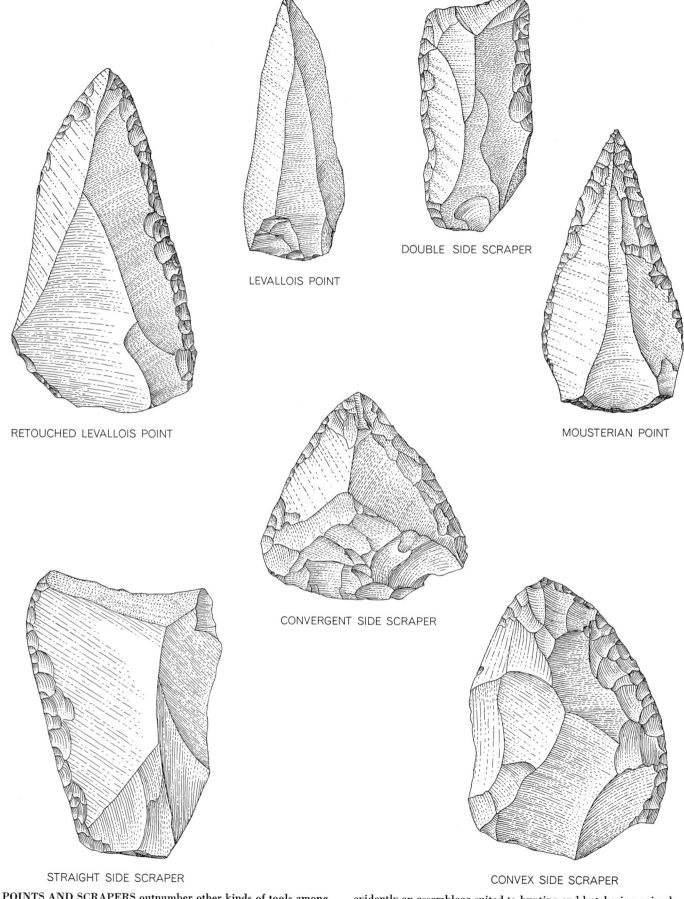

RETOUCHED LEVALLOIS POINT

LEVALLOIS POINT

DOUBLE SIDE SCRAPER

MOUSTERIAN POINT

CONVERGENT SIDE SCRAPER

STRAIGHT SIDE SCRAPER

CONVEX SIDE SCRAPER

POINTS AND SCRAPERS outnumber other kinds of tools among the 12 classes comprising the second-largest factor. The seven predominant classes in the assemblage are illustrated. Factor II is evidently an assemblage suited to hunting and butchering animals. This illustration and the others of Mousterian tools are based on original drawings by Pierre Laurent of the University of Bordeaux.

Factor I, the base-camp grouping; the remainder is shared between Factor II, the all-purpose hunting and butchering tool kit, and Factor III, the food-preparation cluster. The distinctive denticulate factor—Factor IV—appears in only two samples and represents less than 10 percent of the variability in each.

As we have mentioned, Unit 200–208 consists of tools from the deposit outside the cave mouth. Three small accumulations of ash—evidence of fires—were also found in the deposits. It seems more than coincidence that the tool grouping dominating this unit is the one associated with food preparation. In any event, the consistent homogeneity of the other excavation units at Shubbabiq suggests that the cave served the same purpose throughout its occupancy, a finding that also answers our second question. Although the occupation of the cave may have spanned a considerable period of time, the regularity of the factors suggests a similar regularity in the behavior of the occupants.

The percentages of variability accounted for at the Jabrud rock-shelter suggest in turn that Jabrud served repeatedly as a work camp where hunting was the principal activity. Evidently the valley the shelter overlooks was rich in game. The animal bones collected during the original excavation of the site have been lost, but recent work at the same site by Ralph S. Solecki of Columbia University indicates that the valley once abounded in horses—herd animals that were frequently killed by Paleolithic hunters.

The Jabrud findings also provide an answer to our third question. The decreasing importance of Factor V—the specialized hunting tool kit—and its replacement by the more generalized hunting equipment of Factor II suggests directional changes in the behavior of Jabrud's inhabitants. The same is true of the steady decline and eventual disappearance of the base-camp maintenance tools represented by Factor I.

Some of the data from Jabrud even provide a hint of a division of labor by sex in the Middle Paleolithic. The tools characteristic of Factor IV are quite consistently made of kinds of flint that are available in the immediate vicinity of the site, whereas the hunting tools tend to be made of flint from sources farther away. If, in accordance with Bordes's suggestion, the denticulates were used primarily to process plant materials, the expedient fashioning of denticulates out of raw materials on the spot coincides nicely with the fact that

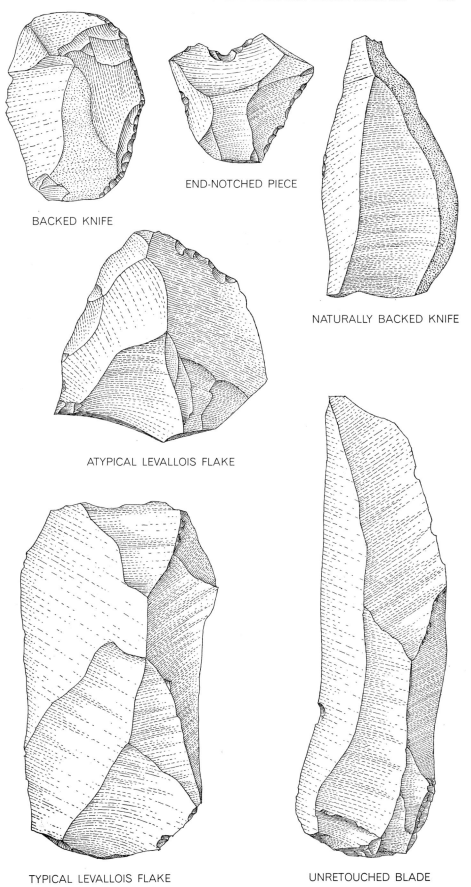

BACKED KNIFE

END-NOTCHED PIECE

NATURALLY BACKED KNIFE

ATYPICAL LEVALLOIS FLAKE

TYPICAL LEVALLOIS FLAKE

UNRETOUCHED BLADE

TOOLS FOR FINE CUTTING are the predominant implements of Factor III. An exception (*top middle*) belongs to the class of end-notched pieces. Their association with hearths suggests that the knives, blades and flakes of Factor III were used for food preparation.

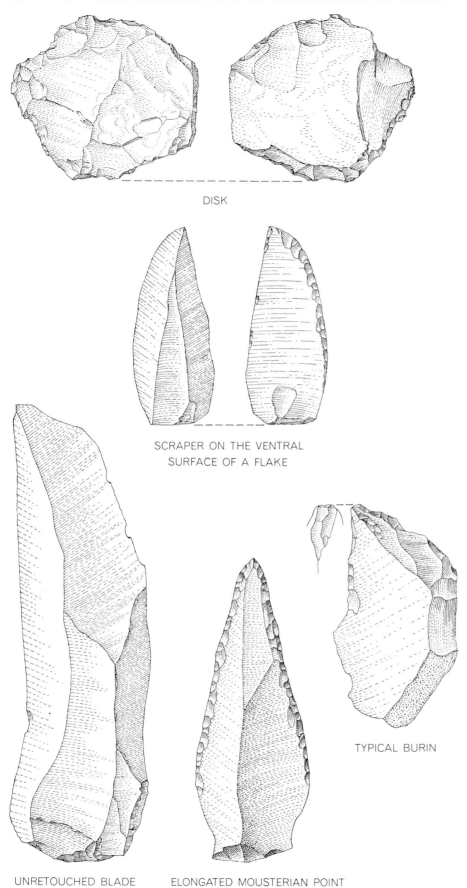

DISK

SCRAPER ON THE VENTRAL
SURFACE OF A FLAKE

TYPICAL BURIN

UNRETOUCHED BLADE   ELONGATED MOUSTERIAN POINT

MORE HUNTING TOOLS are found in Factor V; the five predominant classes are illustrated. The presence of only one class of points and one of scrapers suggests, however, that Factor V reflects specialized hunting rather than the general hunting implied by Factor II.

among living hunter-gatherers women are responsible for the collecting and processing of plant materials.

Recent advances in understanding of the minimum number of persons needed to maintain a self-sustaining human social unit provides additional evidence in favor of our view that Jabrud served as a work camp and that Shubbabiq was a base camp. William W. Howells of Harvard University has suggested that a self-sustaining group must number between 20 and 24 individuals. (He does not imply that the group would necessarily remain together during the entire year.) Taking Howells' estimate as a starting point, we can propose that any base camp where a group could live at full strength must include enough space for the daily activities of 20 to 24 people over a period of several months. Raoul Naroll of the State University of New York at Buffalo suggests that the minimum amount of sheltered space required by an individual is some 10 square meters. On this basis the 178 square meters of floor space in the Jabrud shelter could not have accommodated more than 18 individuals. Shubbabiq cave has enough sheltered floor space for 25 to 30 individuals. Taken together with the differences in the composition of the tool assemblages at the two sites, this leads us to conclude that the sites are basically different types of settlement within a differentiated settlement system.

The tools from Houpeville, called the *Série Claire*, has a totally different geographical context. Since Houpeville is an open-air site and the only one in the study, we feel that an attempt to draw conclusions about its function would be almost meaningless. The *Série Claire* sample nonetheless offers a further demonstration of the power of multivariate analysis. When calculated by univariate statistics, the total configuration of the Houpeville assemblage strongly resembles that of Shubbabiq, that is, the summarized statistics of frequencies of tool types are very similar. When subjected to factor analysis, however, the assemblages from the two sites look quite different. Factors I and V are missing altogether at Houpeville; Factor III, the cluster of food-preparation implements that constitutes a minor percentage of the variability at Shubbabiq, is the major component of the *Série Claire*.

Although we found the results of this factor analysis provocative, it was quite clear that many of our specific interpretations of the factors could not be tested on the basis of such limited data. We felt it essential to add other classes of information to the analysis: animal bones, pollen counts (as checks on climatic inferences) and the distribution of other traces of man (such as hearths) within each occupation level. Such data were available from the site of Combe Grenal, a deeply stratified rock-shelter in the Dordogne region of France excavated by Bordes. They are undoubtedly the finest and most complete Mousterian data in the world. Soil analysis has been done of all the deposits; animal bones are well preserved; pollen profiles have been made for all the 55 Mousterian occupation levels. The sophisticated excavation techniques used at Combe Grenal make it possible to reconstruct the relation of each tool at the site to other tools, to hearths and to clusters of animal bones. We were thus delighted when Bordes graciously volunteered to allow us to analyze his findings.

Our analysis of the Combe Grenal data has occupied the past eight months. (It has been made possible by a grant from the National Science Foundation.) While the work is far from complete, results of a preliminary factor analysis can be summarized here. First, the larger and more complete sample has shown a far wider range of variability than the smaller samples from the Near East have. The tool assemblages in all the Mousterian levels thus far analyzed—41 in number—consist of two or more factors. The factor analysis produced a total of 14 distinct tool groupings, in contrast to the five factors in the Near Eastern sites. In comparing the Combe Grenal analysis with that of the material from the Near East we note some gratifying consistencies. Such a replication of results with independent data from another region suggests that we have managed to isolate tool groupings that have genuine behavioral significance.

In attempting to relate clusters of tool types to environmental variables such as climate (measured by pollen and sediment studies) and game (as shown by animal bones) we have found no simple, direct form of correlation. There is, however, a nonrandom distribution of the frequency with which a given factor appears in levels that are representative of different environments. It appears that major shifts in climate, sufficient to cause shifts in the distribution of plants and animals, did precipitate a series of adaptive readjustments among the inhabitants of Combe Grenal.

Our present work on the material from Combe Grenal has led us to propose a series of refinements in interpretation. It is clear, for example, that the portability of game played a significant role in determining whether an animal was butchered where it was killed or after it was carried back to the site. We are now reclassifying the bones from that site by categories based on size, as well as by anatomical parts represented, and this should provide information that is not currently discernible. Whether an animal is an upland or a valley form and whether it occurs as one of a herd or as an individual is also evidently significant. We suggest that the behavior of the animals hunted had a profound effect on the degree of preparation for the hunt and on the size and composition of the hunting groups.

It should be stressed that the findings presented here are our own and not Bordes's. As a matter of fact, discussions of our interpretations with Bordes are usually lively and sometimes heated, although they are always useful. We all agree that Combe Grenal contains so much information in terms of so many different and independent classes of data that many kinds of hypothesis can be tested. Indeed, a procedure that requires the testing and retesting of every interpretation against independent classes of data could be the most significant outcome of our work.

If one goal of prehistory is the accurate description of past patterns of life, certainly it is the job of the archaeologist to explain the variability he observes. Explanation, however, involves the formulation and testing of hypotheses rather than the mere assertion of the meaning of differences and similarities. Many traditionalists speak of "reading the archaeological record," asserting that facts speak for themselves and expressing a deep mistrust of theory. Facts never speak for themselves, and archaeological facts are no more articulate than those of physics or chemistry. It is time for prehistory to deal with the data according to sound scientific procedure. Migrations and invasions, man's innate desire to improve himself, the relation of leisure time to fine arts and philosophy—these and other unilluminating clichés continue to appear in the literature of prehistory with appalling frequency. Prehistory will surely prove a more fruitful field of study when man is considered as one component of an ecosystem—a culture-bearing component, to be sure, but one whose behavior is rationally determined.

17

THE PREHISTORY OF THE AUSTRALIAN ABORIGINE

D. J. MULVANEY
March 1966

The native inhabitants of Australia were long thought to be relatively recent immigrants. In the past decade archaeologists have discovered that man first reached the remote continent at least 16,000 years ago

The prehistory of Australia ended in 1788, when the British landed at the site of modern Sydney. How many millenniums before that the continent's aboriginal inhabitants arrived has not been precisely established. Only a decade ago their prehistoric period was widely believed to have been no more than a brief prelude to the European colonization. Today it seems certain that the initial migration took place in Pleistocene times—no less than 16,000 years ago and probably much earlier. Here I shall review the archaeological findings that shed some light on the prehistory of the aborigines and then describe recent field studies that, in my opinion, quite drastically alter earlier views.

Sundered from Asia before *Homo sapiens* evolved, Australia is a land mass almost the size of the U.S. It has 12,000 miles of coastline and extends from 43 degrees South latitude to within 11 degrees of the Equator. A third of its area lies north of the Tropic of Capricorn. An equally extensive area annually receives less than 10 inches of rainfall. Only 7 percent of the land mass rises above 2,000 feet; indeed, the continent can be traversed from the Gulf of Carpentaria in the northeast to the southern coast without climbing higher than 600 feet. Australia's major mountain and river systems are restricted to its eastern and southeastern parts. These topographic realities must be reckoned with in considering prehistoric patterns of human settlement. Of equal significance are the usually dry watercourses and salt pans of the arid "outback," which testify to a more congenial climate in late Pleistocene or early postglacial times.

In 1788 Australia was inhabited by perhaps 500 aboriginal tribes; they probably mustered a total population of some 300,000. In coastal or river-valley environments, where the population density was comparatively high, there were one or two individuals per square mile. Elsewhere immense tracts supported no more than one person every 30 or 40 square miles. In so large an area one might expect considerable variety in the inhabitants' ecological and technological adaptations, and reports by early European observers and the scantier evidence of archaeology document such differences. For all its variety, however, the prehistoric period had an underlying unity. Over the entire continent the aborigines habitually hunted, fished and gathered wild plants; they had not learned agriculture. The extent of nomadism in each tribal area was largely determined by the local availability of food.

Regional variations in the Australian environment are actually more apparent than real. In other lands differences in topography, rainfall or latitude give

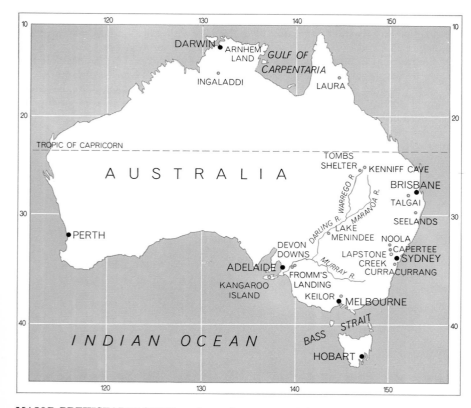

MAJOR PREHISTORIC SITES are located on a map of Australia. Devon Downs, in the Murray River valley, was the first stratified site to be found on the continent. Excavated in 1929, its lower levels are 4,500 years old. Kenniff Cave, a site the author found 1,000 miles north of Devon Downs in 1960, contains strata that span some 16,000 years of prehistory.

rise to diversity in plant and animal species; in Australia these factors may result merely in the substitution of one member of the same plant or animal family for another. The eucalyptus and the kangaroo are ubiquitous. Another phenomenon, universal in Australia and unique to it, is the absence in prehistoric times of formidable predatory animals competing with man for the same game. Such factors must have encouraged a degree of human standardization, both in the character of weapons and in the techniques of hunting and foraging. At the same time it can be postulated that these factors discouraged a dynamic experimental attitude within prehistoric Australian societies.

In terms of material culture few Paleolithic peoples were more impoverished than the aboriginal Australians. There were no horned, antlered or tusked species of animals to provide the raw material for the artifacts so valued in hunting societies elsewhere. Flint and similar fine-grained rocks were rare; instead the aborigines made most of their implements out of quartz or quartzite, materials from which even the most skilled knapper has difficulty producing elegant objects. As for the elements of culture beloved of so many writers on archaeology—dwellings, tombs, grave goods, ceramics, metals, precious stones, cultivated crops and domesticated animals (with the exception of the dog)—the aborigines had none.

Accordingly under the best of circumstances the investigator of Australian prehistory is faced with a paucity of archaeological evidence and a limited range of diagnostic cultural traits. To make matters worse, where bone artifacts might have survived, the high acidity of the soil has often eaten them away, and where desert dryness might have preserved wooden artifacts the voracious termite has destroyed them. These disadvantages are partly offset by the rich store of information on living aborigines, beginning with the first European descriptions and extending to the fieldwork of contemporary ethnographers. The prehistorian must guard against an anachronistic fallacy, however; he must not assume that customs and technologies recorded during the past 100 years constitute unambiguous evidence when it comes to interpreting prehistoric remains.

In 1929 a landmark in Pacific archaeology was established. In the valley of the Murray River east of Adelaide, Her-

BASE OF THE CLIFFS bordering the Murray River in South Australia was a popular prehistoric camping ground. Here, at Fromm's Landing rock-shelter No. 2, the excavation of a deep stratified deposit threw new light on earlier discoveries at nearby Devon Downs.

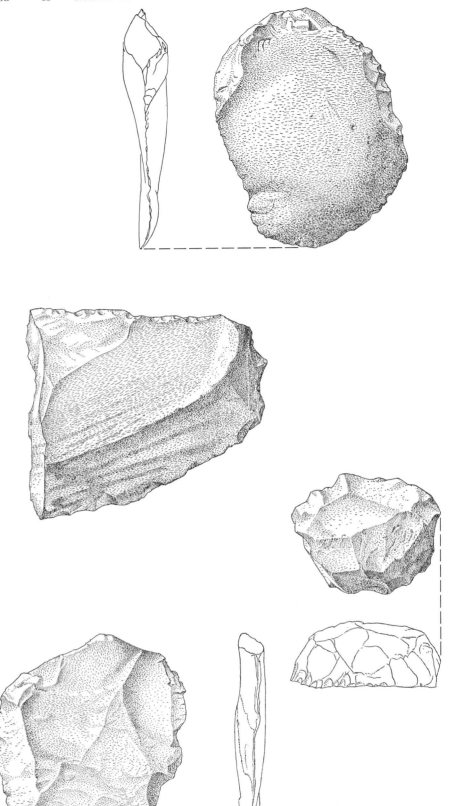

EARLIEST TOOLS found at Kenniff Cave were scrapers such as these, shown actual size. Made by trimming the edges of stone flakes, they were hand-held rather than hafted. They are (*top to bottom*) a quartzite side scraper, trimmed along its right edge; a scraper made from a broken quartzite flake, finely trimmed along its top edge; a round scraper, made from chert, that was trimmed very steeply (*see profile*), and a quartzite flake with trimmed projections and concavities on its bottom edge that suggest use in the manner of a spoke-shave to work wood. Eleven thousand years passed before more elaborate tools were made.

bert M. Hale and Norman B. Tindale of the South Australian Museum excavated a rock-shelter site, known as Devon Downs, that contained 20 feet of stratified deposits of human occupation. Hale and Tindale divided the occupation layers into three successive cultural stages on the basis of the presence or absence of stone or bone implements they believed possessed diagnostic significance. They called the earliest culture Pirrian, because the *pirri,* a symmetrical stone projectile point flaked only on one side, was restricted to the lower layers of the site. Pirris are aesthetically perhaps the most pleasing of all the prehistoric aboriginal artifacts [*"c-1" to "c-3" in illustration on opposite page*]. Many of them are found on the surface at sites in the interior of Australia, but it was at Devon Downs that they were first discovered in a stratigraphic context.

The excavators called the second culture Mudukian; *muduk* is the word used by the Murray River aborigines for a short length of bone, pointed at both ends, that resembles the simple kind of fishhook called a gorge [*"f" in illustration on opposite page*]. At Devon Downs muduks were found in the occupation strata above those that contained pirris. Hale and Tindale gave the uppermost occupation layers the label Murundian; this was derived from the subtribal name of the local aborigines. The Murundian layers contain no distinctive objects of either stone or bone; in effect the archaeological definition of the culture is negative. Carbon-14 dating techniques were not available in those days, but charcoal from a sample of earth preserved in the South Australian Museum since 1929 was recently analyzed and yielded a date for one of the Pirrian strata of about the middle of the third millennium B.C.

Within the past decade I have excavated two rock-shelters at Fromm's Landing, a point only 10 miles downstream from Devon Downs. Carbon-14 dating indicates that the lowest levels in these deposits were occupied early in the third millennium B.C. Fromm's Landing and Devon Downs are thus very close, both geographically and temporally. The sequence of three cultures identified by Hale and Tindale at Devon Downs, however, was not evident at Fromm's Landing. This is a matter of more than casual importance because Tindale has asserted—and the assertion has received wide acceptance—that the three cultures are distributed

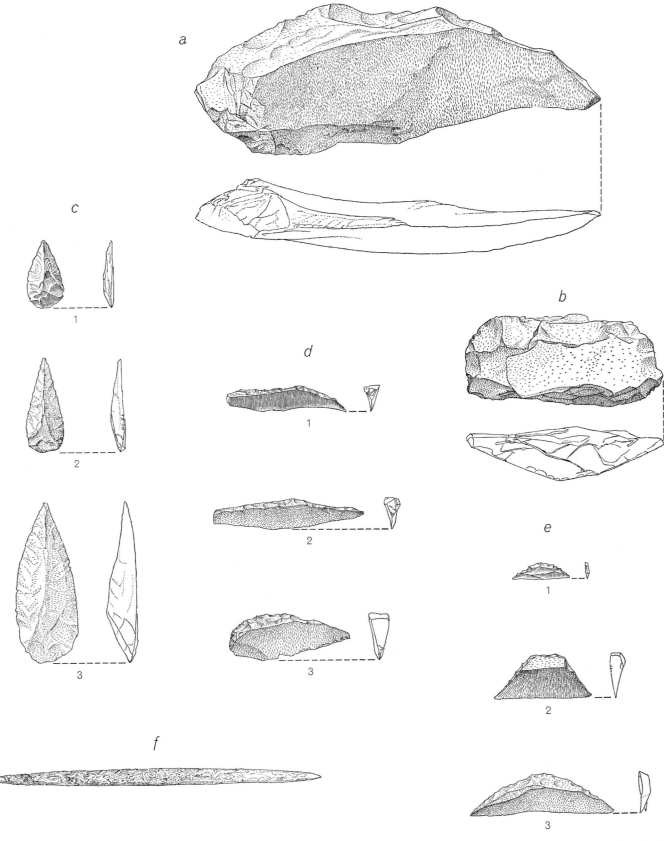

ARTIFACTS FOR HAFTING show a wide variety of forms. All are shown actual size. The knife *a* is from the topmost stratum at Kenniff Cave; stone blades like this, with resin or skin handgrips, were still used by Queensland aborigines early in the 19th century. The step-trimmed adze flake *b* was mounted on the end of a stick and served as a chisel or gouge. The neatly trimmed *pirri* points (*c-1 to c-3*) probably were projectile tips; *c-1* was excavated near Kenniff Cave and is 3,500 years old. The other two are surface finds from South Australia. The three blades (*d-1 to d-3*) are called Bondi points; their backs have been blunted by steep but delicate trimming. The three microliths (*e-1 to e-3*) show similar fine trimming on their backs. All presumably formed the working edges of various composite tools. The pointed bone (*f*) is a 400-year-old *muduk*; it may have served as a fishhook, a spear tip or even a nose ornament.

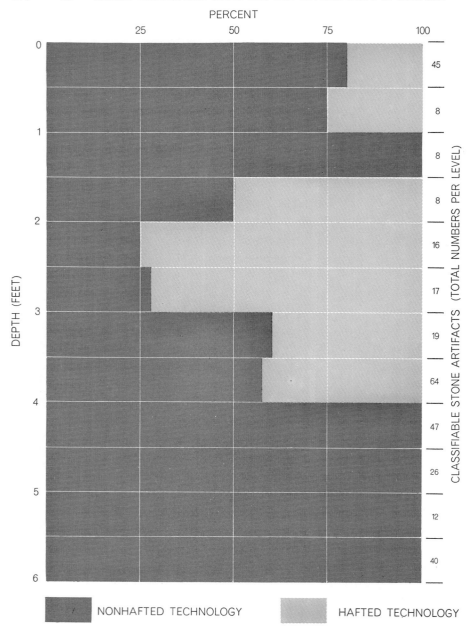

ADVANCE IN TECHNOLOGY at Kenniff Cave took place about 3000 B.C., when the concept of hafting was introduced. At four feet and deeper only hand-held scrapers (*gray*) were found; above that, entirely new kinds of stone artifact (*color*) appear among the scrapers (*see illustration on preceding page*). These artifacts are evidently parts of composite tools.

sources. Such an interpretation eliminates any need to imagine the successive arrival of separate culture groups, and all the elements of discontinuity that such a succession implies.

By the standards of archaeology in the Old World neither the Devon Downs nor the Fromm's Landing site is particularly ancient. Between 1960 and 1964, however, my associates and I excavated a rock-shelter in southern Queensland that contained 11 feet of stratified deposits; carbon-14 dating showed that the lowest levels at this site—Kenniff Cave on the Mount Moffatt cattle station—are at least 16,000 years old. Troweling and sieving 85 cubic yards of sand and ash, we recovered more than 21,000 stone flakes and waste fragments, most of them quartzite. Among them were some 850 deliberately shaped and retouched artifacts. About 60 percent of the artifacts were either broken or only lightly worked. As a result the total number of artifacts available for rigorous classification and measurement was little more than 350.

The sequence of stone artifacts at Kenniff Cave constitutes the point of departure for any current discussion of Australian prehistory. Two facts give the Kenniff Cave collection its special significance. First, it includes examples of most of the prehistoric implement types known in Australia, arranged in stratigraphic order. Second, the age of the collection ranges from the immediate past back to the late Pleistocene.

For those accustomed to the richness of Old World Paleolithic sites the Kenniff Cave assemblage will seem a small sample, but it is one of the largest Australian collections to be analyzed. Recent work in the vicinity of Sydney and in the Northern Territory (where one excavation has uncovered more than 2,000 worked projectile points) has been more productive, but the results have not yet been published. My experience elsewhere has often been daunting. An excavation in Victoria yielded 2,300 waste pieces and only eight artifacts; the strata of a South Australian site yielded an average of three artifacts per 1,000 years of occupation.

The Kenniff Cave assemblage includes 261 specimens of the generalized tool termed a scraper. Their distribution fluctuated with depth [*see illustration on this page*]. In the uppermost four feet of the deposit scrapers were

across the entire continent. I found the pirris at Fromm's Landing in association with microliths, tiny stone blades of the kind that in Old World cultures are sometimes set in a haft of bone or wood to form a composite tool. The association contradicts Tindale's belief that such microliths are artifacts typical not of the Pirrian but of the later Mudukian culture.

This finding and others at Fromm's Landing led me to question the basis of Tindale's cultural diagnosis at Devon Downs. It seemed more useful to consider the elements the three

Devon Downs assemblages had in common than to isolate discrete traits as Tindale did. Flakes of stone used as adzes, for example, were found in all three Devon Downs culture levels; there was no apparent break in the tradition of stoneworking from the earliest time to the latest. In reporting my findings at Fromm's Landing I suggested that the differences in the inventory of various Devon Downs strata might be attributable to changes in artifact preference on the part of an aboriginal population that was becoming increasingly adapted to life beside a river, with its varied and rich organic re-

relatively rare compared with other types of implement. Throughout the lower layers, however, they constituted 100 percent of all classifiable stone artifacts.

An implicit assumption underlies the use of a descriptive label such as "scraper." In this case the assumption is that scrapers were normally held in the user's hand. Scrapers are thus members of the family of nonhafted stone tools. They are technologically distinct from hafted, composite tools of the kind that presumably made use of the microliths unearthed at the Murray River sites in South Australia. Such tools possess handles or other extensions, together with fixatives such as resin or gum or lashings such as hair, vegetable fiber or sinew.

The sandy soil of Kenniff Cave is so acid that, if any such organic constituents of composite tools had once been present, no evidence of them now remains. The distinction between nonhafted and hafted artifacts at Kenniff Cave is therefore a subjective one. Nonetheless, the difference between the percentage of scrapers in the upper strata and in the lower led me to make a basic assumption about the place of nonhafted and hafted tools in Australian prehistory. I postulated that the apparent ignorance of hafting techniques on the part of the early inhabitants of Kenniff Cave was genuine ignorance, and that an extensive phase in the prehistory of the site occupied a period during which this advanced technology was literally unknown. Carbon-14 estimates indicate that this prehafting phase lasted for at least 11,000 years, or from about 14,000 to about 3000 B.C.

When the Kenniff Cave scrapers were set in their stratigraphic sequence and subjected to careful measurement and analysis, the results of the study confirmed that, as postulated, a continuity of tradition had existed during this period of 11 millenniums; the scrapers showed no significant change either in production technique or in size. Such technological stability—or lack of invention—may be relevant when one considers the social dynamics of a prehistoric culture.

In contrast to the long period of stability attested by the lower levels at Kenniff Cave, the upper levels told a sharply different story. Scrapers appear in diminishing percentages, and accompanying them are various types of small, delicately worked stone arti-

fact. Both the size and the shape of these objects—one specimen measuring only 1.7 centimeters by .5 by .1 centimeter is shown at *e-1* on page 5—imply their diverse functions as components of hafted implements. Such is certainly the case with the long stone knives and with the artifacts identifiable as adze flakes ["*a*" and "*b*" in illustration on page 169]. The latter objects, which have a characteristic stepped appearance, were the stone working edges of gouges or chisels, composite tools that are widely represented in Australian ethnographic collections. It is probably the case with the pirri points (which may have been mounted on projectile shafts) and geometric microliths (a type of artifact whose purpose is debated on other continents but that is everywhere assumed to be part of a hafted tool).

To judge from the level at which these tool types are first found in the stratigraphic sequence at Kenniff Cave, the technology of hafting materialized there about 5,000 years ago. The impact of the new technology was fundamental. During the 2,000 years that followed—until about 1000 B.C.—most of the characteristic types of stone implement that have been unearthed or collected on the surface by prehistorians in southern Australia were deposited in the upper strata of Kenniff Cave. It is of course conjectural that the acquired knowledge of hafting techniques was the factor that enabled the aboriginal populations of this period to develop greater flexibility in the design of tools, but it is unmistakable in the stratigraphic record at Kenniff Cave that the rate of technological advance accelerated during

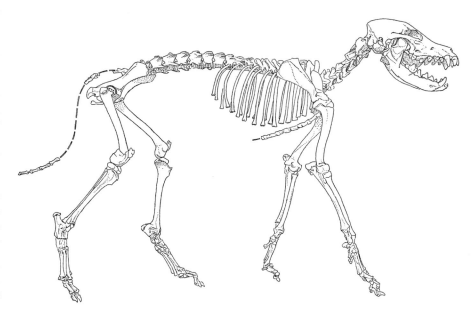

OLDEST KNOWN DINGO, the Australian dog, was unearthed at a depth of six feet at Fromm's Landing rock-shelter No. 6. Dating from 1000 B.C., the animal shows no morphological differences from the dingos of today. Man and the dingo were virtually the only predators in prehistoric Australia; they apparently killed off some species of marsupials.

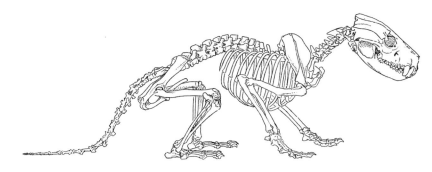

TASMANIAN DEVIL is one of two species of marsupials whose bones are found only in the lower strata at Fromm's Landing. Because no major climatic changes occurred during the 5,000 years the site was occupied, the disappearance of this animal and the Tasmanian wolf from the area in the second millennium B.C. may be attributable to man and the dingo.

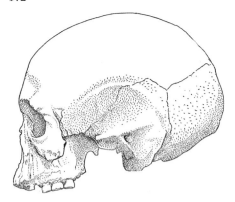
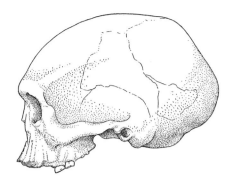
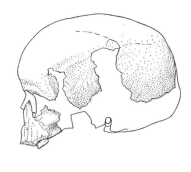

FOSSIL MAN in Australia may be most authentically represented by the skull unearthed at Keilor, near Melbourne, in 1940 (*left*); recent additional findings at Keilor suggest that the skull is as much as 18,000 years old. From the time of its discovery the Keilor skull has been considered nearly a twin of a fossil skull from Wad- jak in Java (*center*), discovered in 1890 and of unknown age. The discovery of an adolescent skull, possibly 40,000 years old (*right*), in the Niah Caves of Sarawak in 1959 has added another possible precursor to the aboriginal family tree. The scarcity of Australian fossil evidence, however, renders all these conclusions tentative.

the period from 3000 B.C. to 1000 B.C.

Bearing in mind the postulate that a long period of nonhafted-tool technology was followed by a briefer period of the more variable hafted-tool technology, it seems appropriate to review the findings of other archaeologists at a number of sites across the continent. Let us begin with the sites that seem, on the basis of established or assumed chronology, to belong to the nonhafted-tool phase. At the Tombs Shelter in Queensland, near Kenniff Cave, a few artifacts have been found that appear to date back to the eighth millennium B.C. They belong to the nonhafted tradition, and worked stones suitable for hafting are found in the strata above them. At Ingaladdi in the Northern Territory a stone-tool industry that consists of scrapers (and "cores" that were reworked as nonhafted scraping or chopping tools after flakes had been struck from them) yields a date in the fifth millennium B.C. Three sites in New South Wales—Seelands, Curracurrang and Capertee—cover a period from the sixth millennium to early in the second millennium B.C. All three evince non-hafted phases and all are overlain by layers containing artifacts suitable for hafting. These lower-level tool kits contain other nonhafted implements in addition to the ubiquitous scrapers; at least that is how I interpret saw-edged flakes at Capertee and core tools common to all three sites. The cores, flaked on one or both faces, suggest that they were held in the fist for some battering or chopping function. Specimens from Seelands have been measured by the prehistorian J. M. Matthews; he finds them comparable to the Southeast Asian pebble industry named Hoabhinian, after a Vietnamese site.

R. V. S. Wright of the University of Sydney has recently undertaken an important excavation at Laura, on Cape York in northeastern Queensland. The technological sequence he has uncovered may be comparable to that at Kenniff Cave. The same may be true of a ninth-millennium-B.C. occupation site Tindale has found at Noola, near Capertee in New South Wales. The Noola material has not yet been formally described, but Tindale's brief published note allows the relevant finds to be attributed to a nonhafted phase. Some years ago Tindale isolated a stone-tool industry on Kangaroo Island, off the coast of South Australia. No varieties of artifact associated with hafted implements were found there, but flaked pebbles, scrapers and massive core tools were numerous. Tindale postulated a Pleistocene date for the occupation; so far neither excavation nor carbon dating has been attempted. This is an intriguing field for further investigation.

Still another early date is proposed by Tindale and Richard Tedford of the University of California at Riverside for "nondescript" stone flakes found at a surface site at Lake Menindee in New South Wales. Charcoal samples at the site have yielded carbon-14 dates of 17,000 and 22,000 B.C., but detailed evidence for a direct association between the charcoal and the artifacts has not yet been published.

The reconstruction of the most recent 5,000 years of Australian prehistory is further along than the work on the earlier phases, although there is no better agreement on how the evidence from these five millenniums should be interpreted. It is nonetheless possible to relate my hypothesis concerning a significant technological change involv-

ing hafting techniques during this period to the culturally oriented descriptions of findings by other workers. Much of this work is in progress, and since it would be improper to anticipate the results here the survey that follows— like those that have preceded it—draws primarily on published reports and my own experience.

The Kenniff Cave site in Queensland is more than 1,000 miles from the Devon Downs and Fromm's Landing sites in the Murray River valley of South Australia. In comparing the equivalent upper and later levels of the three sites, however, it is worth noting that Kenniff Cave lies in the same system of river valleys as Devon Downs and Fromm's Landing. The upper levels at Kenniff Cave, like those at the South Australian sites, contain pirri points, microliths, adze flakes and other stone artifacts representative of the hafted-tool tradition. There are no bone muduks at Kenniff Cave, but the acid sands of the site would have destroyed any that had been buried. Significantly there is considerable contrast between the size and finish of similar artifacts from the Queensland and the South Australian sites. This tends to confirm my view that artifacts of the same general type were subject to a process of differentiation.

Although many more excavations are needed to bridge existing gaps in knowledge and lay the foundation for valid generalizations, some hint of the rate at which the concept of hafting diffused among the aboriginal populations is provided by the following carbon-14 results. As I have noted, the Fromm's Landing site and the upper strata at Kenniff Cave belong to the early third millennium B.C., and a layer containing pirri points at Devon Downs dates from later in the same millennium. This parallels the age of the oldest hafted types of stone artifact found in New South Wales, those unearthed at Seelands. The Ingaladdi site in the Northern Territory has yielded pirris and other points, some finished on one side and some on both. These points appear with relative suddenness in a layer that has not been dated. A stratum a few inches below the points, however, contains an assemblage of nonhafted artifacts that has been dated to the latter part of the fifth millennium B.C. It begins to look as if the period centered on the fourth millennium B.C. will prove to be a crucial one in the reconstruction of Australian prehistory.

For many years a key figure in the documentation of the prehistory of New South Wales has been Frederick D. McCarthy, principal of the Australian Institute of Aboriginal Studies; his excavations at Lapstone Creek and Capertee have provided a working basis for systematizing evidence from elsewhere in the state. Recent investigations in the Sydney and New England areas of New South Wales have served to test and elaborate McCarthy's pioneering studies. Under the sponsorship of the institute Wright and J. V. S. Megaw of the University of Sydney have carried out important excavations, and Isabel McBryde of the University of New England has undertaken an all-inclusive field survey.

McCarthy believed he had isolated two cultures at Lapstone Creek. The earlier of these he called Bondaian; its characteristic tool is a small, asymmetric, pointed blade reminiscent of a penknife, with a sharp cutting edge and a blunt back edge ["d" in illustration on page 169]. The later culture he named Eloueran; the characteristic tool is a flake shaped like a segment of an orange, with its back heavily blunted and its cutting edge often polished by use. Also found in the Bondaian levels are geometric microliths. This is scarcely surprising when one considers that the skills needed to make microliths and small blades are essentially the same. Both require as their raw material thin blades, one edge of which is then artificially blunted.

Carbon-14 dates from Curracurrang, Capertee and Seelands place the characteristic artifacts of the Bondaian and the Eloueran cultures in the second and first millenniums B.C. Both could be assigned to my hafted phase. This emphasis on technology rather than on any cultural context accords with McCarthy's own observation that, in spite of fluctuations in the fortunes of specific traits, there is an underlying similarity in the stoneworking techniques of the two cultures.

The present rub in classifying Australian artifacts is how to decide where to draw boundaries and what degree of emphasis to give single culture traits. Within each group of artifacts there are variations in size, shape and trimming. What criteria, for example, distinguish a thin Eloueran flake from a large, crescent-shaped microlith? It is unsatisfactory to lump all the pirris together, and there is diversity even among the bone muduks. The truth is that early workers, myself included, selected an ideal type and then blurred the edges of distinction by treating deviations from this ideal as atypical, even though the deviations possessed inherent definable characteristics. Today, in common with the trend in archaeology around the world, the analysis of artifacts in Australia has shifted away from the subjective methods of the past toward laborious quantitative definition. Most assemblages that have been excavated recently are undergoing rigorous statistical investigation. The Bondaian-Eloueran problem should benefit from this objective approach.

I have presented evidence in support of the view that Australian prehistory can be divided into two phases, distinguishable by a change in technology from the exclusive use of nonhafted, hand-held stone artifacts to the employment of many specialized stone artifacts that were hafted to form composite implements. What of the people who used these nonhafted and hafted tools? Some of the most interesting evidence for the antiquity of man in Australia comes from gravel quarries at Keilor on the outskirts of Melbourne, where a creek has cut a series of terraces. A human skull was unearthed there in 1940, but its exact origin became a matter of dispute. In attempting to resolve the controversy, Edmund D. Gill of the National Museum of Victoria has obtained a series of carbon-14 dates for the Keilor quarries; his earliest date, centered around 16,000 B.C., is for charcoal taken from a point some feet below the 1940 level of the quarry floor. The crucial issue is whether this charcoal is from an aboriginal campfire or from some natural conflagration. The fact that a number of stone artifacts have been found in the creek bed and embedded in the banks of the terraces does not automatically mean that the charcoal is also the work of men. These objects lack the authority of artifacts excavated from undisturbed stratified de-

EXCAVATION AT KENNIFF CAVE revealed evidence of human occupation from about the 14th millennium B.C. until the present. The paler strata along the walls of the 11-foot pit represent periods when the shelter was virtually deserted by prehistoric hunters; the darker strata are rich in organic material. The outline paintings of human hands on the overhanging rock were made by aboriginal tribesmen who have used the shelter during recent years.

posits under well-controlled conditions.

In 1965 the evidence favoring the authentic antiquity of the Keilor skull suddenly multiplied. Two miles from the scene of the 1940 discovery earth-moving equipment exposed a human skeleton that was in a fair state of preservation. Preliminary indications are that the skeleton belongs to the same level of terrace as that proposed for the Keilor skull. Charcoal is plentiful at the site, although some of it—tree roots that were burned where they had grown—is clearly the work not of man but of nature. Artifacts are also present. Obviously men lived here during the period of terrace formation, and carbon-14 determinations should establish the age of the site. The National Museum of Victoria is coordinating the investigations now under way at Keilor.

Man may have arrived in Australia at the time of the continent's climatic climax, when inland rivers flowed, lakes brimmed and the giant herbivorous marsupials flourished. In any case he almost certainly played a role in altering the ecological character of the continent (and, less directly, the soil) through selective hunting activities and frequent burning of vegetation. One ecological effect resulted from man's introduction of the dog. Man and the dingo together represented a scourge to the prehistoric fauna; the two were virtually the sole predatory carnivores on the continent. What caused the extermination of numerous marsupial species: man and dog or climatic change? The findings at Fromm's Landing indicate that the two carnivores played their part. There is nothing in the evidence to imply that, during the 5,000 years spanned by the deposits at the site,

there were important fluctuations in climate that might have exerted an ecological influence. Mammal bones identified at Fromm's Landing represent 685 individuals of 31 species. In two cases—*Sarcophilus,* the Tasmanian devil, and *Thylacinus,* the Tasmanian wolf—there are indications that the species became extinct there during the second millennium B.C. It is relevant that a 3,000-year-old stratum at the site has yielded the skeleton of a dingo; this is the earliest authenticated occurrence of the dingo in Australia.

What were the racial origins of the prehistoric Australians? This question has been much debated, but the debate is conducted virtually in a vacuum because of the scarcity of early human fossils in Australia. Until the discovery of the Keilor skeleton there was not one such fossil whose authenticity was unchallengeable. Now the Keilor skull found in 1940—and perhaps a badly crushed skull from Talgai in Queensland—may gain a more respectable status. Still, two or three specimens make a small sample for determining the origin of a race. Two fossil skulls found at Wadjak in Java, to the northwest of Australia, have been proposed as a link in aboriginal evolution; these fossils, however, remain undated. A skull from the Niah Caves in Sarawak, to the north of Java, is possibly 40,000 years old and has also been compared with prehistoric Australian remains. Caution must be the keynote when there are such wide spatial gaps in the fieldwork and so few fossils.

The origin of the prehistoric inhabitants of Tasmania, the large island to the south of Australia, also remains

an open subject. The last Tasmanians (none survived the 19th century) were an ethnographic rarity: a society using stone tools without hafts of any kind. Studies of changes in the sea level during Pleistocene times have made it a tenable theory that the Tasmanians walked to Tasmania from Australia when the intervening strait was dry land; carbon-14 estimates have established their presence in Tasmania 8,000 years ago. During the past two years Rhys Jones of the University of Sydney has achieved striking success in fieldwork in northern Tasmania. When his carbon samples are dated and his human skeletal material is analyzed, Tasmanian archaeology will have entered an objective era.

Now that it seems certain that Australia was colonized in Pleistocene times, the inadequacy of evidence on this period not only in Australia but also in its northern neighbors such as New Guinea is painfully apparent. If we are to retrace the steps of Australia's first colonists, detailed studies of changes in the sea level are required. If we are to seek out their early patterns of settlement, we need far more precise dating of environmental changes in the continent's interior. With much of Australia archaeologically unexplored, with increasing numbers of investigators undertaking fieldwork and with carbon-14 chronologies providing new perspectives, these are exciting times for the study of the continent's prehistory. It is certain that during the next few years the nearly blank outline map of that prehistory will come to be filled with detail.

18

ISHANGO

JEAN DE HEINZELIN
June 1962

*The men who lived at this site in Africa more than
8,500 years ago appear to have been inspired
inventors. They independently devised the harpoon,
and may even have created a number system*

About 30 years ago explorers in central Africa came across a number of bone harpoon points scattered along the bottom of the steep cliffs bordering Lake Edward at Ishango in the Congo. The pieces seemed to date from a prehistoric era. In 1935 the Belgian biologist H. Damas sank a test pit into the cliffs and sent back the material collected to the University of Brussels. Examining the samples, François Twiesselmann found a most peculiar fossil fragment. It was part of the jaw of a man-like individual, but a jaw that seemed to belong to one of man's more primitive ancestors rather than to a member of the species *Homo sapiens*. Yet no one believed that pre-sapiens creatures could have fashioned a tool as advanced as a harpoon. Moreover, the geological evidence indicated that the age of the site was less than 10,000 years, a time when the prehuman hominids had given way to man.

There matters rested until 1950, when Victor van Straelen, head of the Institute of National Parks of the Belgian Congo, put me in charge of a full-scale archaeological expedition to investigate the remains at Ishango. The mystery of the jawbone soon evaporated: additional fossil fragments showed that Ishango man, although he is no longer extant, was undoubtedly a true *Homo sapiens* of the Mesolithic era, the stage of culture between the Paleolithic and Neolithic eras. But the artifacts have proved far more interesting than we could have hoped. In fact, the complete picture

EXCAVATION SITE AT ISHANGO lay along the shore of Lake Edward in the Congo. Ishango was occupied between 9000 and 6500 B.C. The remains of its culture include tools, weapons and bones, found in the top layers of the 40-foot cliffs bordering the lake.

suggests that the site was an important way station in the road to "civilization."

Lake Edward, about 50 miles long and 30 miles wide, is fed from the east by the rivers of Uganda and from the south by the rivers born on the Virunga volcanoes; its outlet is the Semliki River, which flows northward into Lake Albert, the headwater of the Nile. Not far from the lake is a mountain range with peaks that have been active volcanoes for many thousands of years. Their eruptions have greatly increased the content of carbon 12 (the abundant nonradioactive isotope of carbon) in the lake, thereby upsetting the usual ratio of the carbon isotopes there and rendering old shells unfit for accurate dating by the carbon 14 method. Moreover, no charcoal was found at Ishango, so that there were no nonaquatic samples to which the method could be applied. The best archaeological and geological evidence date the site from some time between 9000 B.C. and 6500 B.C. It appears to have existed as a stable settlement for perhaps as long as a few hundred years before a volcanic eruption buried the entire countryside.

Fortunately a good record of the Ishango culture remains. Three distinct layers of sediment were deposited on the floor of Lake Edward during the period of the occupation, when the lake water was at a high level. Now the waters have receded and these layers are exposed near the top of the 40-foot cliffs that border the lake.

Time has not preserved any of the wood or leather articles that the Ishango people undoubtedly made and used, and the site does not contain any plant remains at all. Since we found not a single potsherd, it is obvious that Ishango represents a prepottery culture. Nevertheless, the length of the occupation itself, and the articles that actually were manufactured, bespeak a comparatively high level of culture. The people of Ishango were not nomads but members of a settled or semisettled community. It seems reasonable to assume that they had many more possessions than those that have been preserved, probably including rafts, ropes, cords and various other things made of leather and wood. On the whole their cultural habits seem comparable to those of their contemporaries in Europe.

There is, however, a rather remarkable exception to this general statement. It consists of the hundreds of quartz tools of various shapes and sizes that we found at Ishango. Consisting both of "cores" of larger pieces of quartz and of flakes chipped from such pieces, they are extremely crude and completely unlike any unearthed at other African sites dating from the same period or even earlier. Their style shows no variation from one layer of sediment to another and all of them resemble tools of the Paleolithic far more than those of the Mesolithic.

These primitive implements are in sharp contrast to the grinding and pounding stones found in large numbers at the Ishango site. The latter argue for a relatively advanced stage of culture: man only began to use them when he had learned to grind pigments for decorative purposes and to pound seeds and grain for food.

Although plant foods in all probability formed part of Ishango man's diet, he apparently ate much more meat and fish. We found thousands of fishbones and hundreds of animal bones scattered through the strata of the cliffs. Most of the animal bones—from such mammals as the hippopotamus, antelope, buffalo and pig—were broken, probably to extract the marrow.

The weapons used in hunting and fishing also indicate a fairly advanced technology. Moreover, a study of their development at Ishango and a comparison with weapons found in other parts of Africa suggest that this site may have been the fount from which one technique of manufacture spread over a considerable area.

The Ishango hunters relied chiefly on two types of weapon: the spear and the harpoon. The harpoon must have been thrown at the prey with the point embedding itself and the shaft then coming loose. One end of a line, presumably made of a vine, was tied to the harpoon point and the other was held by the thrower. All that now remains of the spears and harpoons are the barbed bone points. The shafts, which were probably made of wood, and the lines have rotted away. But from the distinctive workmanship of the bone pieces found in each of the three layers at the site we were able to trace the evolution of the weapons.

The lowest of the three layers, exposed

BLOCK DIAGRAM represents a 10½-mile section of the northern shore of Lake Edward. The elevation is exaggerated 20 times. The cross in center foreground represents the excavation site. To its left is the Semliki River, which flows northward to Lake Albert.

by our excavations, contains the earliest examples. Here we found points of both spears and harpoons. Although the two look much alike—both have barbs along each side—they are distinguishable from each other by differences in the shape of the base [*see two points at bottom of colored area in illustration on pages 180 and 181*]. The base of the spear point was so formed as to enable it to be fixed firmly in its shaft; the base of a harpoon point fitted loosely into its shaft. In addition, notches in the base of the harpoon head provided a point at which to attach the line.

The harpoon would have been far more useful than the spear for many purposes. Examining the weapons found in the lowest layer, one can almost see the idea developing among the men of Ishango. In addition to points that are obviously either spear points or harpoon points, we found a large number intermediate between the two. The intermediates give the distinct impression that the technique of making weapons with detachable points was not imported to Ishango from elsewhere in Africa but developed there as an independent invention, just as it developed independently in many other places throughout the world.

In the second layer were many harpoon points but no spear points at all. By this time the designers had become more sophisticated and were using a wide variety of styles. All the harpoon points retained the double row of barbs and all had notches for fixing the line.

The third layer from the bottom showed a further advance in technology. Now both spear points (which reappear in this layer) and harpoon points had a single row of barbs instead of two. This represents a considerable advance. The points are easier to make and equally effective in use. Although the earlier versions of these points were too long and poorly balanced, the makers soon evolved a better technique. In time they turned out a standard, rugged and well-balanced point that compares favorably with those made by Mesolithic peoples in Europe.

The process of manufacture of all the bone implements found at Ishango—chisels and other tools as well as harpoon and spear points—did not change through the entire span of the occupation. This fact lends further weight to the belief that the weapon points were invented on the spot. They were all made of the long bones of antelopes, split lengthwise and then chipped and trimmed along the edges. Next they were ground and polished—probably with

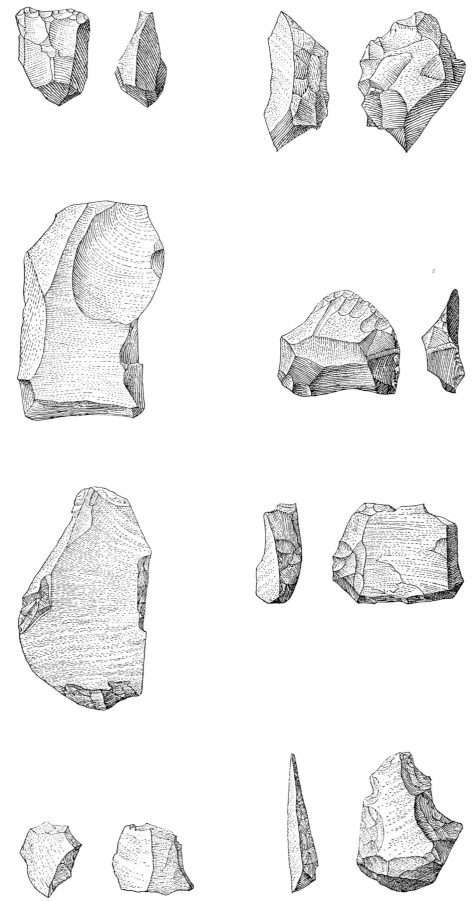

STONE TOOLS at Ishango were made of crudely chipped quartz. They are seen here one and a quarter times actual size. All but the two largest ones are seen in both front and side views.

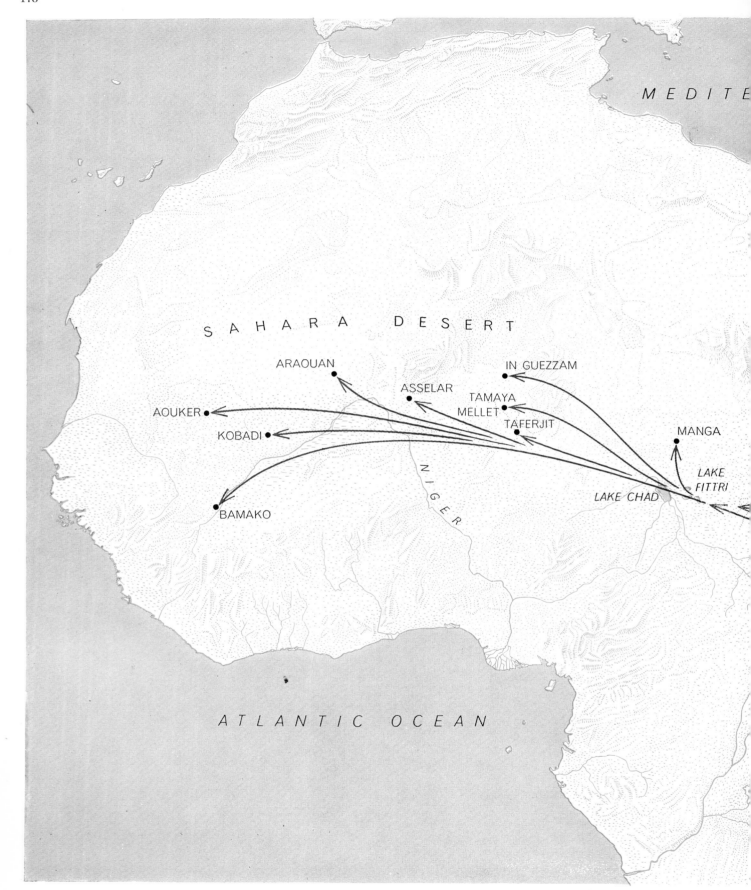

MAP OF NORTH AND CENTRAL AFRICA shows the excavation sites at which harpoon points have been found. The arrows suggest possible routes by which the Ishango technique of manufacture may have spread from its place of origin, at bottom right, to more northerly places on the Nile and more westerly ones on the southern border of the Sahara Desert. The Ishango harpoons date from the

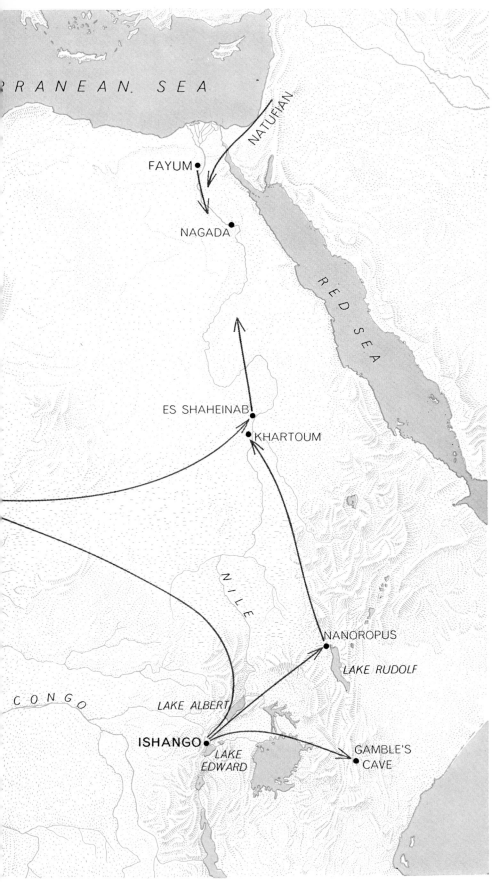

sandstone—until surface irregularities were evened out. As a final step the barbs were cut into the points with quartz tools.

Just as one can follow the technological sequence at Ishango itself, it is also possible to trace the influence of the Ishango technique on other African peoples by examining harpoon points at other sites [*see illustration on next two pages*]. The nearest ones are at Gamble's Cave in Kenya and at Nanoropus on Lake Rudolf. At both locations harpoon fragments have been found that in all likelihood are of more recent manufacture than any at Ishango. These points were clearly inspired by the later ones made at Ishango.

From central Africa the style seems to have spread northward. At Khartoum near the upper Nile there is a site that was occupied considerably later than Ishango. The harpoon points found there show a diversity of styles. Some have no special device for attaching the line. Others have a hole that must have served this purpose. But still others have the notches that seem to have been invented first at Ishango. Near Khartoum, at Es Shaheinab, is a Neolithic site that contains harpoon points bearing the imprint of Ishango ancestry; from here the Ishango technique moved westward, along the southern border of the Sahara. The points found in this section seem to have been used primarily for fishing. (Although the area where they were found is now arid, it was dotted with lakes during Neolithic times.) In addition to the characteristic Ishango notches, some of them have a hole at the base of the point.

The technology also seems to have followed a secondary branch northward from Khartoum along the Nile Valley to Nagada in Egypt. This site has both bone and copper harpoons. Made in the Neolithic period before the Egyptian dynasties began, many of them are notched at the head. Others show the influence of the Near Eastern Natufian technique and the Fayum technique, which is closely related to it.

The most fascinating and most suggestive of all the artifacts at Ishango is not a harpoon point but a bone tool handle with a small fragment of quartz still fixed in a narrow cavity at its head. In the first place, its shape and the sharp stone in its head suggest that it may have been used for engraving or tattooing, or even for writing of some kind. Even more interesting, however, are its markings: groups of notches arranged in three dis-

Mesolithic era; the others were made later. At Egyptian sites some harpoons show the influence of traditions from the Near East. At all others the harpoons derive primarily from those at Ishango. Illustration on next two pages shows harpoons found at all the sites.

tinct columns [*see illustration on page 182*]. The pattern of these notches leads me to suspect that they represent more than pure decoration. When one counts them, a series of number sequences emerges. In one of the columns they are arranged in four groups composed of 11, 13, 17 and 19 individual notches. In the

next they are arranged in eight groups containing 3, 6, 4, 8, 10, 5, 5 and 7 notches. In the third they are arranged in four groups of 11, 21, 19 and 9.

I find it difficult to believe that these sequences are nothing more than a random selection of numbers. The groupings in each column are quite different

from one another and each column contains internal relationships unlike those found in either of the others. Take the first column, for example: 11, 13, 17 and 19 are all prime numbers (divisible only by themselves and by one) in ascending order, and they are the only prime numbers between 10 and 20. Or consider

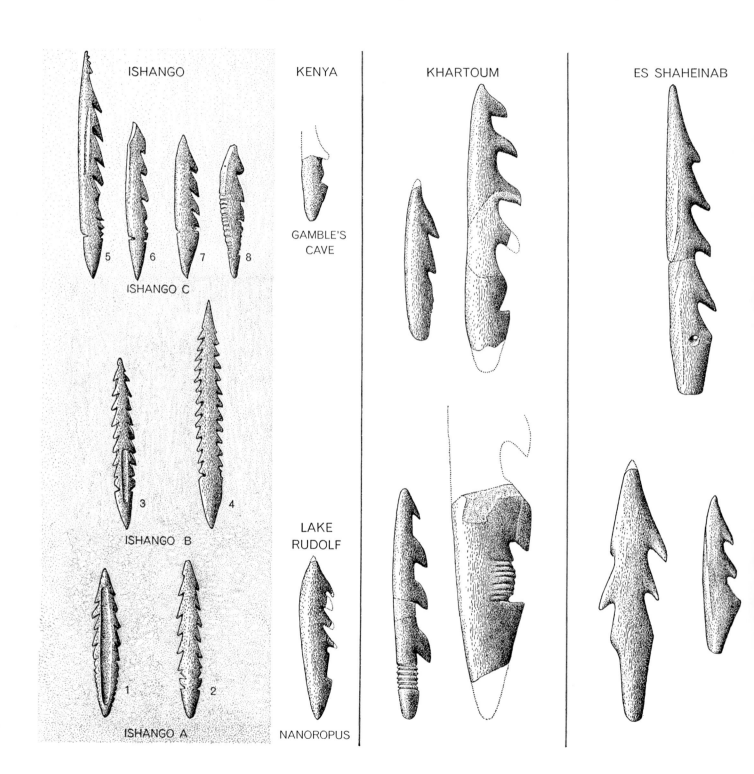

HARPOON AND SPEAR POINTS from various African sites are classified. At *1* is a spear point from the lowest level of the Ishango excavation; at *2* is a harpoon point from the same level. The difference between the two can be seen in the notches at the base of the harpoon point, to which a line could be attached. At *3* and *4* are harpoon points from the middle Ishango level. At *5, 6, 7* and

the third: 11, 21, 19 and 9 represent the digits 10 plus one, 20 plus one, 20 minus one and 10 minus one. The middle column shows a less cohesive set of relations. Nevertheless, it too follows a pattern of a sort. The groups of three and six notches are fairly close together. Then there is a space, after which the

four and eight appear—also close together. Then, again after a space, comes the 10, after which are the two fives, quite close. This arrangement strongly suggests appreciation of the concept of duplication, or multiplying by two.

It is of course possible that all the patterns are fortuitous. But it seems

probable that they were deliberately planned. If so, they may represent an arithmetical game of some sort, devised by a people who had a number system based on 10 as well as a knowledge of duplication and of prime numbers.

What did Ishango man look like? The 70-odd bits of human bone we found at

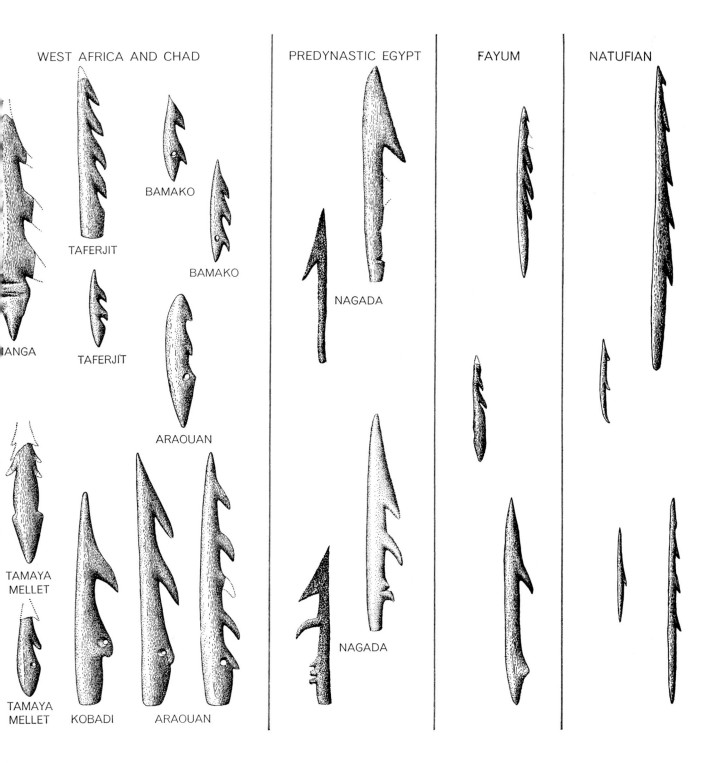

WEST AFRICA AND CHAD   PREDYNASTIC EGYPT   FAYUM   NATUFIAN

TAFERJIT

BAMAKO

BAMAKO

TAFERJIT

ARAOUAN

IANGA

TAMAYA MELLET

TAMAYA MELLET

KOBADI   ARAOUAN

NAGADA

NAGADA

8 are harpoon and spear points from the third level, where all the weapons had one row of barbs. Many of the points shown in the other drawings were inspired by those made at Ishango. Those from

Egypt also show the influence of the Natufian and Fayum traditions. Most of the points are made of bone. The lightest one is ivory; the darker ones are copper. All points are drawn one-half of actual size.

the site all seemed to come from a homogeneous group of people. These people may have been the harpoon makers, but it is not certain. The fact that the bones are part of the kitchen midden, and that many of them, like the animal bones, were broken as if to extract the marrow, suggests that they are the remains of another tribe or group that was captured and eaten by the toolmakers. On the other hand, some of the toolmakers may simply have eaten others; cannibalism was not uncommon among Mesolithic peoples. In any case, the remains do provide a picture of one type of early Mesolithic man in central Africa.

Most of the bone fragments come from some part of the head, but there are not enough of them to enable us to reconstruct Ishango man's skull in its entirety. We do know, however, that his jawbone was very large and heavy—a characteristic of Heidelberg man and of many other species that preceded *Homo*

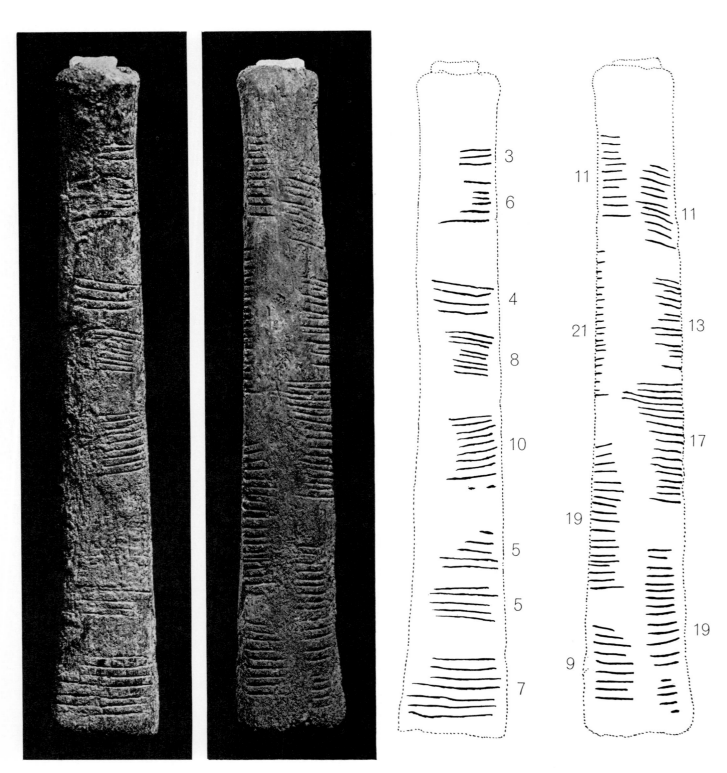

NOTCHED BONE TOOL HANDLE found at Ishango is seen in two views. It is the earliest artifact to suggest knowledge of a number system. The drawings at right of the photographs indicate how the notches were arranged. Column seen in drawing at left is notched to suggest a knowledge of multiplication by two. Columns seen in drawings at right are notched to suggest that 10 was the base of the number system and that the concept of prime numbers was understood. The tool handle is photographed actual size.

sapiens but not of modern man. This is one of the reasons that Twiesselmann and his colleagues at first assumed that Ishango man was probably prehuman. The size of the teeth would have given added weight to this assumption: some of the molars we found were as large as those of *Australopithecus*, the prehuman "man-ape." Moreover, the skull bones were thick—as much as three-eighths of an inch thick in many of the adults. This is approximately the thickness of Neanderthal skulls. All these features pointed to a pre-sapiens species.

On the other hand, Ishango man did not have the overhanging brow of Neanderthal and the other earlier forms. By the time he emerged, the supraorbital ridge had disappeared from the frontal bone of the skull. In addition his chin was shaped much like the chin of modern man, as was his ramus: the bone that rises from the lower jaw to join with the skull. Finally, the long bones of his body were quite slender.

All this adds up to a unique picture. No other fossil man shows such a combination of characteristics. Primitive and even Neanderthaloid in part, Ishango man was nevertheless a true *Homo sapiens*, possibly Negroid, who represented the emergence in Africa of an indigenous Negro population from an older Paleolithic stock. This interpretation of his place in history fits quite well with contemporary views of human evolution. Most students now believe that modern man did not descend from any single stock but from a mingling of many stocks that arose independently in a number of Paleolithic communities.

Some of the fossils we discovered at Ishango showed clearly that a second human population lived at the site hundreds of years after the volcanic eruption drove the first away. Although these later inhabitants were of the same physical type as Ishango man, the archaeological evidence indicates that they possessed few of his techniques. They had, for example, forgotten the use of the harpoon, but since this knowledge diffused through Africa by the paths already traced, this was a loss only to them and not to other peoples.

There is no evidence that they retained any knowledge of the numerical system that may have been invented at Ishango. Yet this knowledge too may have spread northward. The first example of a well-worked-out mathematical table dates from the dynastic period in Egypt. There are some clues, however, that suggest the existence of cruder systems in predynastic times. Because the Egyptian number system was a basis and a prerequisite for the scientific achievements of classical Greece, and thus for many of the developments in science that followed, it is even possible that the modern world owes one of its greatest debts to the people who lived at Ishango. Whether or not this is the case, it is remarkable that the oldest clue to the use of a number system by man dates back to the central Africa of the Mesolithic period. No excavations in Europe have turned up such a hint.

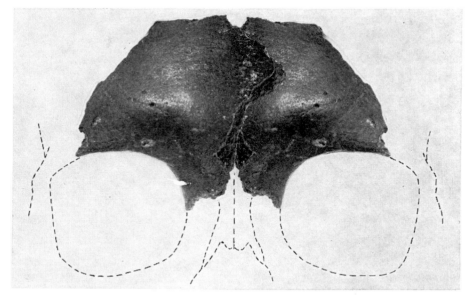

FRONTAL BONES of Ishango man were reconstructed from fragments of the right half found at the excavation site. The left half was duplicated by symmetry. Broken lines indicate the shape of the eye sockets and the nasal bone. The bones are shown here actual size.

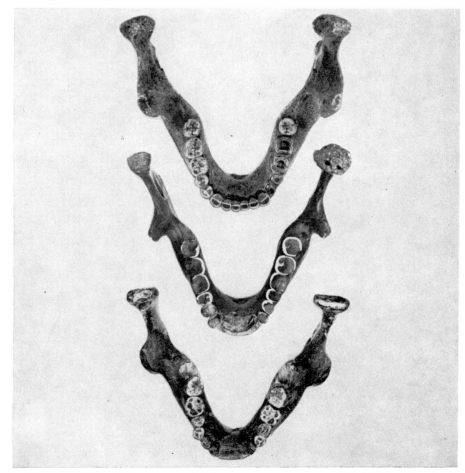

JAWBONES of Heidelberg man and Ishango man are compared. Heidelberg jaw (*top*) dates from Middle Pleistocene. Ishango jaws (*middle and bottom*) date from Mesolithic. Bottom jaw is from second population to live at Ishango. All bones are two-thirds actual size.

The Rise of Civilization
in the Old World

Archaeological interpretations can be both stable and volatile, as the articles in this section demonstrate. In the first essay, Robert J. Braidwood generalizes boldly about the end of nomad existence and about the topic he names in the title of his article, "The Agricultural Revolution," an occurrence that began about 8000 B.C. in the Old World first among relatively sedentary gathering and hunting groups. Slightly later, cultures in China, southeastern Asia, Central America, and perhaps in South America also reached corresponding levels of development. The gathering and hunting of food within limited regions gave rise, in turn, to the domestication of animals and plants. The new cultural complex of domesticated animals and crops, which led to sedentary village life, was adaptable, Braidwood maintains, beyond the habitats where specialized gathering of undomesticated food had been practiced, spreading beyond the Fertile Crescent of the Near East, for example, to encompass Europe. Braidwood, writing in 1960 about an exciting season of excavation in southwestern Asia, closes his article with a statement that he would not be surprised if his overview needed revision "by the time this article has appeared in print."

In 1970 Braidwood, jointly with Halet Çambel, revised the generalizations made ten years earlier, and wrote "An Early Farming Village in Turkey," the second article in this section. To read both articles is to see how far our understanding of the development of Old World civilization progressed in just a decade through archaeological discoveries, new analytical techniques, and new explanatory frameworks. For example, in 1960 Braidwood thought food gathering origins could be precisely located in a limited area of the Fertile Crescent, but subsequent discoveries have shown that at several locations beyond the Fertile Crescent sedentary groups gathered food rather than produced it. (One food-nonproducing culture had developed techniques of copper metallurgy!) It is probable that these more recent generalizations by Braidwood and Çambel, too, will be modified in the next decade, but as the picture fills in, the revisions will be more and more narrow in scope and consequence.

Robert M. Adams continues the discussion of the agricultural revolution by showing how, within 3000 to 4000 years, the new technology that produced predictable food supplies produced a revolutionary social process—a process that altered the relations among humans. This was the rise of cities, which, like the development of agriculture, took place in Mesopotamia, or the Fertile Crescent. Adams draws a distinction between civilizations and cities, though he points out that all highly developed civilizations, save perhaps the Maya in the New World, produced cities. (Although the Mayan civilization produced large temple complexes, these appear not to have served as cities where large numbers of food nonproducers resided.) The key to the origin of cities, as Adams sees it, is not only in the predictability of food surpluses but in basic political and economic innovations that allow people—particularly food nonproducers—to live together while depending on the products of farmers and pastoralists. Adams speculates about the origins of craft specialization as well as social stratification, which can be traced in the first cities, but he emphasizes that the first clear-cut trend in the archaeological record is the rise of temples. The concentration of new patterns of thought and power in these temples may have provided the framework for the social organization of cities.

C. C. and Martha Lamberg-Karlovsky, in "An Early City in Iran," writing eleven years after Adams about excavations at Tepe Yahyā, fill in a piece of the larger puzzle that Adams defined so well. The Lamberg-Karlovskys demonstrate that early cities east of Mesopotamia were not all alike, but varied in special functions and in size. At Tepe Yahyā, an example of a typical trade city in what is now Iran, numerous tablets with proto-Elamite writing were found, writing that is, along with that of the Sumerians, the oldest that have been found. But Tepe Yahyā also appears to have been the source of soapstone objects that were traded with cities in Mesopotamia in the west as well as to the Indus Valley in the east, and therefore, this center is perhaps only one of many in the Mesopotamian-Indian continuum that arose in the fourth millennium B.C. and, through trade to the east, contributed to the considerable achievements made in the Indus Valley in the third millennium B.C.

Colin Renfrew's essay, "Carbon 14 and the Prehistory of Europe," is another evidence of the foresight expressed by Braidwood in concluding "The Agricultural Revolution." Braidwood cautioned us about "the vagaries of establishing a reliable chronology, . . . the whimsical degree to which 'geobiochemical' contamination seems to have affected our radioactive-carbon age determinations." Carbon dates are based on the measure, in remains of organic material, of the amounts of isotopes of carbon 12 and carbon 14, which are taken up in equal amounts while an organism lives. Carbon 12 is non-radioactive, but carbon 14 diminishes with time at a regular rate. Renfrew, a decade after Braidwood's caveat, shows that even though contamination is not as serious a problem as had been thought, concentrations of carbon 14 in the atmosphere may have fluctuated during the past, throwing many estimated carbon-14 dates far off the dates subsequently established by the more precise dating technique based on tree-rings of the California bristlecone pine, which has been found to grow as old as 4600 years. By referring to a dendrochronology, or tree-ring dating sequence that spans more than 8000 years, Renfrew has been able to supply new dates for European prehistory. In turn, he challenges the interpretation of the rise of European civilization as a product of diffusion from Mesopotamia and the Aegean. Indeed, as an example, he argues that many European resemblances to Aegean culture actually preceded the Aegean forms, so diffusion from the Aegean culture, in Renfrew's view, is out of the question. In place of the theory of westward diffusion, Renfrew suggests independent invention of relatively complex technologies in, for instance, Mesopotamia and Europe, attributing these inventions to innovative originality and creativity among the inhabitants of both areas. The reader can surely anticipate that Renfrew will be challenged, soon moreover, inasmuch as his argument is applicable to all carbon-14 dates older than 1500 B.C. throughout the world, and few researchers will be able to amass the conclusive evidence that is needed to support his assertion that the same inventions occurred time after time without cross-diffusion in closely spaced locales, regardless of the doubt Renfrew has raised about the validity of carbon-14 dating.

JARMO IN IRAQI KURDISTAN is the site of the earliest village-farming community yet discovered. This photograph of an upper level of excavation shows foundation and paving stones. Site was occupied for perhaps 300 years somewhere around 6750 B.C.

EXCAVATION AT KARIM SHAHIR contained confused scatter of rocks brought there by ancient men and disturbed by modern plowing. This prefarming site had no clear evidence of permanent houses, but did have skillfully chipped flints and other artifacts.

19

THE AGRICULTURAL REVOLUTION

ROBERT J. BRAIDWOOD
September 1960

Until some 10,000 years ago all men lived by hunting, gathering and scavenging. Then the inhabitants of hills in the Middle East domesticated plants and animals and founded the first villages

Tool-making was initiated by pre-*sapiens* man. The first comparable achievement of our species was the agricultural revolution. No doubt a small human population could have persisted on the sustenance secured by the hunting and food-gathering technology that had been handed down and slowly improved upon over the 500 to 1,000 millennia of pre-human and pre-*sapiens* experience. With the domestication of plants and animals, however, vast new dimensions for cultural evolution suddenly became possible. The achievement of an effective food-producing technology did not, perhaps, predetermine subsequent developments, but they followed swiftly: the first urban societies in a few thousand years and contemporary industrial civilization in less than 10,000 years.

The first successful experiment in food production took place in southwestern Asia, on the hilly flanks of the "fertile crescent." Later experiments in agriculture occurred (possibly independently) in China and (certainly independently) in the New World. The multiple occurrence of the agricultural revolution suggests that it was a highly probable outcome of the prior cultural evolution of mankind and a peculiar combination of environmental circumstances. It is in the record of culture, therefore, that the origin of agriculture must be sought.

About 250,000 years ago wide-wandering bands of ancient men began to make remarkably standardized stone hand-axes and flake tools which archeologists have found throughout a vast area of the African and western Eurasian continents, from London to Capetown to Madras. Cultures producing somewhat different tools spread over all of eastern Asia. Apparently the creators of these artifacts employed general, non-specialized techniques in gathering and preparing food. As time went on, the record shows, specialization set in within these major traditions, or "genera," of tools, giving rise to roughly regional "species" of tool types. By about 75,000 years ago the tools became sufficiently specialized to suggest that they corresponded to the conditions of food-getting in broad regional environments. As technological competence increased, it became possible to extract more food from a given environment; or, to put the matter the other way around, increased "living into" a given environment stimulated technological adaptation to it.

Perhaps 50,000 years ago the mod-

AIR VIEW OF JARMO shows 3.2-acre site and surroundings. About one third of original area has eroded away. Archeologists dug the square holes in effort to trace village plan.

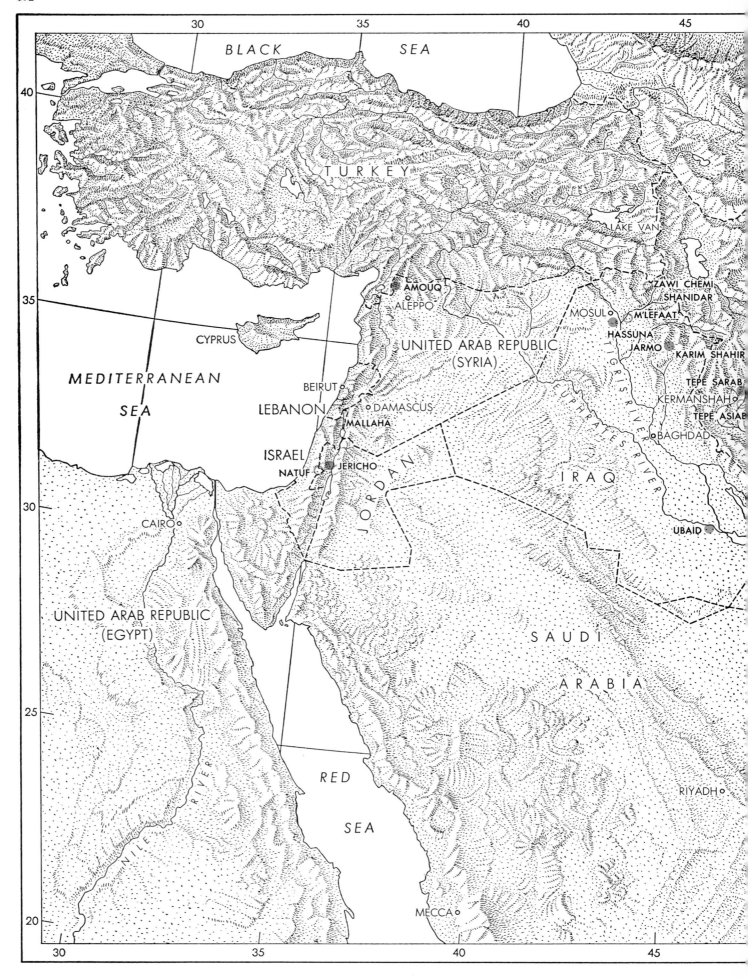

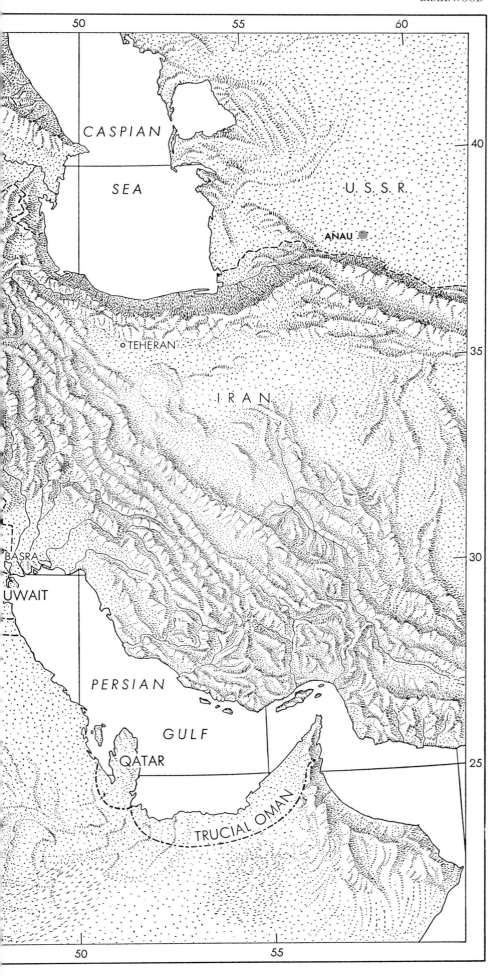

ern physical type of man appeared. The record shows concurrently the first appearance of a new genera of tools: the blade tools which incorporate a qualitatively higher degree of usefulness and skill in fabrication. The new type of man using the new tools substituted more systematic food-collection and organized hunting of large beasts for the simple gathering and scavenging of his predecessors. As time passed, the human population increased and men were able to adjust themselves to environmental niches as diverse as the tropical jungle and the arctic tundra. By perhaps 30,000 years ago they spread to the New World. The successful adaptation of human communities to their different environments brought on still greater cultural complexity and differentiation. Finally, between 11,000 and 9,000 years ago some of these communities arrived at the threshold of food production.

In certain regions scattered throughout the world this period (the Mesolithic in northwestern Europe and the Archaic in North America) was characterized by intensified food-collection: the archeological record of the era is the first that abounds in the remains of small, fleet animals, of water birds and fish, of snails and mussels. In a few places signs of plant foods have been preserved, or at least we archeologists have learned to pay attention to them. All of these remains show that human groups had learned to live into their environment to a high degree, achieving an intimate familiarity with every element in it. Most of the peoples of this era of intensified food-collecting changed just enough so that they did not need to change. There are today still a few relict groups of intensified food-collectors—the Eskimos, for example—and there were many more only a century or two ago. But on the grassy and forested uplands bordering the fertile crescent a real change was under way. Here in a climate that provided generous winter and spring rainfall, the intensified food-collectors had been accumulating a rich lore of experience with wild wheat, barley and other food plants, as well as with wild dogs,

HILLS FLANKING fertile crescent, where agricultural revolution occurred, are indicated in color. Hatched areas are probably parts of this "nuclear" zone of food-producing revolution. Sites discussed in this article are indicated by large circles. Open circles are prefarming sites; solid circles indicate that food production was known there.

goats, sheep, pigs, cattle and horses. It was here that man first began to control the production of his food.

Not long ago the proponents of environmental determinism argued that the agricultural revolution was a response to the great changes in climate which accompanied the retreat of the last glaciation about 10,000 years ago. However, the climate had altered in equally dramatic fashion on other occasions in the past 75,000 years, and the potentially domesticable plants and animals were surely available to the bands of food-gatherers who lived in southwestern Asia and similar habitats in various parts of the globe. Moreover, recent studies have revealed that the climate did not change radically where farming began in the hills that flank the fertile crescent. Environmental determinists have also argued from the "theory of propinquity" that the isolation of men along with appropriate plants and animals in desert oases started the process of domestication. Kathleen M. Kenyon of the University of London, for example, advances the lowland oasis of Jericho as a primary site of the agricultural revolution [see "Ancient Jericho," by Kathleen M. Kenyon; SCIENTIFIC AMERICAN, April, 1954].

In my opinion there is no need to complicate the story with extraneous "causes." The food-producing revolution seems to have occurred as the culmination of the ever increasing cultural differentiation and specialization of human communities. Around 8000 B.C. the inhabitants of the hills around the fertile crescent had come to know their habitat so well that they were beginning to domesticate the plants and animals they had been collecting and hunting. At slightly later times human cultures reached the corresponding level in Central America and perhaps in the Andes, in southeastern Asia and in China. From these "nuclear" zones cultural diffusion spread the new way of life to the rest of the world.

In order to study the agricultural revolution in southwestern Asia I have since 1948 led several expeditions, sponsored by the Oriental Institute of the University of Chicago, to the hills of Kurdistan north of the fertile crescent in Iraq and Iran. The work of these expeditions has been enriched by the collaboration of botanists, zoologists and geologists, who have alerted the archeologists among us to entirely new kinds of evidence. So much remains to be done, however, that we can describe in only a tentative and quite incomplete fashion how food production began. In part, I must freely admit, my reconstruction depends upon extrapolation backward from what I know had been achieved soon after 9,000 years ago in southwestern Asia.

The earliest clues come from sites of the so-called Natufian culture in Palestine, from the Kurdistan site of Zawi Chemi Shanidar, recently excavated by Ralph S. Solecki of the Smithsonian Institution, from our older excavations at Karim Shahir and M'lefaat in Iraq, and from our current excavations at Tepe Asiab in Iran [see map on preceding two pages]. In these places men appear to have moved out of caves, although perhaps not for the first time, to live in at least semipermanent communities. Flint sickle-blades occur in such Natufian locations as Mallaha, and both the Palestine and Kurdistan sites have yielded milling and pounding stones—strong indications that the people reaped and ground wild cereals and other plant foods. The artifacts do not necessarily establish the existence of anything more than intensified or specialized food-collecting. But these people were at home in a landscape in which the grains grew wild, and they may have begun to cultivate them in open meadows. Excavations of later village-farming communities, which have definitely been identified as such, reveal versions of the same artifacts that are only slightly more developed than those from Karim Shahir and other earlier sites. We are constantly finding additional evidence that will eventually make the picture clearer. For example, just this spring at Tepe Asiab we found many coprolites (fossilized excrement) that appear to be of human origin. They contain abundant impressions of plant and animal foods, and when analyzed in the laboratory they promise to be a gold mine of clues to the diet of the Tepe

SICKLE BLADES FROM JARMO are made of chipped flint. They are shown here approximately actual size. When used for harvest-ing grain, several were mounted in a haft of wood or bone. Other Jarmo flint tools show little advance over those found at earlier sites.

Asiab people. The nature of these "antiquities" suggests how the study of the agricultural revolution differs from the archeology of ancient cities and tombs.

The two earliest indisputable village-farming communities we have so far excavated were apparently inhabited between 7000 and 6500 B.C. They are on the inward slopes of the Zagros mountain crescent in Kurdistan. We have been digging at Jarmo in Iraq since 1948 [see "From Cave to Village," by Robert J. Braidwood; SCIENTIFIC AMERICAN, October, 1952], and we started our investigations at Tepe Sarab in Iran only last spring. We think there are many sites of the same age in the hilly-flanks zone, but these two are the only ones we have so far been able to excavate. Work should also be done in this zone in southern Turkey, but the present interpretation of the Turkish antiquities law discourages our type of "problem-oriented" research, in which the investigator must take most of the ancient materials back to his laboratory. I believe that these northern parts of the basins of the Tigris and Euphrates rivers and the Cilician area of Turkey will one day yield valuable information.

Although Jarmo and Tepe Sarab are 120 miles apart and in different drainage systems, they contain artifacts that are remarkably alike. Tepe Sarab may have been occupied only seasonally, but Jarmo was a permanent, year-round settlement with about two dozen mud-walled houses that were repaired and rebuilt frequently, creating about a dozen distinct levels of occupancy. We have identified there the remains of two-row barley (cultivated barley today has six rows of grains on a spike) and two forms of domesticated wheat. Goats and dogs, and possibly sheep, were domesticated. The bones of wild animals, quantities of snail shells and acorns and pistachio nuts indicate that the people still hunted and collected a substantial amount of food. They enjoyed a varied, adequate and well-balanced diet which was possibly superior to that of the people living in the same area today. The teeth of the Jarmo people show even milling and no marginal enamel fractures. Thanks apparently to the use of querns and rubbing stones and stone mortars and pestles, there were no coarse particles in the diet that would cause excessive dental erosion. We have calculated that approximately 150 people lived in Jarmo. The archeological evidence from the area indicates a population density of 27 people per square mile, about the same as today. Deforestation, soil deteriora-

JARMO WHEAT made imprint upon clay. Cast of imprint (*left*) resembles spikelet of present-day wild wheat *Triticum dicoccoides* (*right*). Specimens are enlarged seven times.

tion and erosion, the results of 10,000 years of human habitation, tend to offset whatever advantages of modern tools and techniques are available to the present population.

Stone vessels of fine craftsmanship appear throughout all levels at Jarmo, but portable, locally made pottery vessels occur only in the uppermost levels. A few impressions on dried mud indicate that the people possessed woven baskets or rugs. The chipped flint tools of Jarmo and Tepe Sarab, in both normal and microlithic sizes, are direct and not very distant descendants of those at Karim Shahir and the earlier communities. But the two farming villages exhibit a geo-

metric increase in the variety of materials of other types in the archeological catalogue. Great numbers of little clay figurines of animals and pregnant women (the "fertility goddesses") hint at the growing nonutilitarian dimensions of life. In both communities the people for the first time had tools of obsidian, a volcanic glass with a cutting edge much sharper and harder than stone. The obsidian suggests commerce, because the nearest source is at Lake Van in Turkey, some 200 miles from Jarmo. The sites have also yielded decorative shells that could have come only from the Persian Gulf.

For an explanation of how plants and animals might have been domesticated

KERNELS OF JARMO WHEAT were carbonized in fires of ancient village. They resemble kernels of wild wheat growing in area today. They are enlarged approximately four times.

between the time of Karim Shahir and of Jarmo, we have turned to our colleagues in the biological sciences. As the first botanist on our archeological team, Hans Helbaek of the Danish National Museum has studied the carbonized remains of plants and the imprints of grains, seeds and other plant parts on baked clay and adobe at Jarmo and other sites. He believes that the first farmers, who grew both wheat and barley, could

only have lived in the highlands around the fertile crescent, because that is the only place where both plants grew wild. The region is the endemic home of wild wheat. Wild barley, on the other hand, is widely scattered from central Asia to the Atlantic, but no early agriculture was based upon barley alone.

Helbaek surmises that from the beginning man was unintentionally breeding the kind of crop plants he needed.

Wild grasses have to scatter their seeds over a large area, and consequently the seed-holding spike of wild wheat and barley becomes brittle when the plant ripens. The grains thus drop off easily. A few wild plants, however, exhibit a recessive gene that produces tough spikes that do not become brittle. The grains hang on, and these plants do not reproduce well in nature. A man harvesting wild wheat and barley would necessarily reap plants with tough spikes and intact heads. When he finally did sow seeds, he would naturally have on hand a large proportion of grains from tough-spike plants—exactly the kind he needed for farming. Helbaek points out that early farmers must soon have found it advantageous to move the wheat down from the mountain slopes, from 2,000 to 4,300 feet above sea level (where it occurs in nature), to more level ground near a reliable water supply and other accommodations for human habitation. Still, the plant had to be kept in an area with adequate winter and spring rainfall. The piedmont of the fertile crescent provides even today precisely these conditions. Since the environment there differs from the native one, wheat plants with mutations and recessive characteristics, as well as hybrids and other freaks, that were ill adapted to the uplands would have had a chance to survive. Those that increased the adaptation of wheat to the new environment would have made valuable contributions to the gene pool. Domesticated wheat, having lost the ability to disperse its seeds, became totally dependent upon man. In turn, as Helbaek emphasizes, man became the servant of his plants, since much of his routine of life now depended upon the steady and ample supply of vegetable food from his fields.

The traces and impressions of the grains at Jarmo indicate that the process of domestication was already advanced at that place and time, even though human selection of the best seed had not yet been carried far. Carbonized field peas, lentils and vetchling have also been found at Jarmo, but it is not certain that these plants were under cultivation.

Apparently farming and a settled community life were cultural prerequisites for the domestication of animals. Charles A. Reed, zoologist from the University of Illinois, has participated in the Oriental Institute expeditions to Iraq and Iran and has studied animal skeletons we have excavated. He believes that animal domestication first occurred in this area, because wild goats, sheep, cattle, pigs, horses, asses and dogs were all present

CARBONIZED BARLEY KERNELS from Jarmo, enlarged four times, are from two-row grain. The internodes attached to kernels at right indicate tough spikes of cultivated barley.

there, and settled agricultural communities had already been established. The wild goat (*Capra hircus aegagrus*, or pasang) and sheep (*Ovis orientalis*), as well as the wild ass (onager) still persist in the highlands of southwestern Asia. Whether the dog was the offspring of a hypothetical wild dog, of the pariah dog or of the wolf is still uncertain, but it was undoubtedly the first animal to be domesticated. Reed has not been able to identify any dog remains at Jarmo, but doglike figurines, with tails upcurled, show almost certainly that dogs were established in the domestic scene. The first food animal to be domesticated was the goat; the shape of goat horns found at Jarmo departs sufficiently from that of the wild animal to certify generations of domestic breeding. On the other hand, the scarcity of remains of cattle at Jarmo indicates that these animals had not yet been domesticated; the wild cattle in the vicinity were probably too fierce to submit to captivity.

No one who has seriously considered the question believes that food needs motivated the first steps in the domestication of animals. The human proclivity for keeping pets suggests itself as a much simpler and more plausible explanation. Very young animals living in the environment may have attached themselves to people as a result of "imprinting," which is the tendency of the animal to follow the first living thing it sees and hears during a critically impressionable period in its infancy [see " 'Imprinting' in Animals," by Eckhard H. Hess; SCIENTIFIC AMERICAN Offprint 416].

Young animals were undoubtedly also captured for use as decoys on the hunt. Some young animals may have had human wet nurses—a practice in some primitive tribes even today. After goats were domesticated, their milk would have been available for orphaned wild calves, colts and other creatures. Adult wild animals, particularly goats and sheep, which sometimes approach human beings in search of food, might also have been tamed.

Reed defines the domesticated animal as one whose reproduction is controlled by man. In his view the animals that were domesticated were already physiologically and psychologically preadapted to being tamed without loss of their ability to reproduce. The individual animals that bred well in captivity would have contributed heavily to the gene pool of each succeeding generation. When the nucleus of a herd was established, man would have automatically selected against the aggressive and un-

CLAY FIGURES from Sarab, shown half size, include boar's head (*top*), what seems to be lion (*upper left*), two-headed beast (*upper right*), sheep (*bottom left*) and boar.

"FERTILITY GODDESS" or "Venus" from Tepe Sarab is clay figure shown actual size. Artist emphasized parts of body suggesting fertility. Grooves in leg indicate musculature.

STONE PALETTES from Jarmo show that the men who lived there were highly skilled in working stone. The site has also yielded many beautifully shaped stone bowls and mortars.

POTTERY MADE AT JARMO, in contrast to the stonework, is simple. It is handmade, vegetable-tempered, buff or orange-buff in color. It shows considerable technical competence.

manageable individuals, eventually producing a race of submissive creatures. This type of unplanned breeding no doubt long preceded the purposeful artificial selection that created different breeds within domesticated species. It is apparent that goats, sheep and cattle were first husbanded as producers of meat and hides; wild cattle give little milk, and wild sheep are not woolly but hairy. Only much later did the milk- and wool-producing strains emerge.

As the agricultural revolution began to spread, the trend toward ever increasing specialization of the intensified food-collecting way of life began to reverse itself. The new techniques were capable of wide application, given suitable adaptation, in diverse environments. Archeological remains at Hassuna, a site near the Tigris River somewhat later than Jarmo, show that the people were exchanging ideas on the manufacture of pottery and of flint and obsidian projectile points with people in the region of the Amouq in Syro-Cilicia. The basic elements of the food-producing complex —wheat, barley, sheep, goats and probably cattle—in this period moved west beyond the bounds of their native habitat to occupy the whole eastern end of the Mediterranean. They also traveled as far east as Anau, east of the Caspian Sea. Localized cultural differences still existed, but people were adopting and adapting more and more cultural traits from other areas. Eventually the new way of life traveled to the Aegean and beyond into Europe, moving slowly up such great river valley systems as the Dnieper, the Danube and the Rhone, as well as along the coasts. The intensified food-gatherers of Europe accepted the new way of life, but, as V. Gordon Childe has pointed out, they "were not slavish imitators: they adapted the gifts from the East . . . into a new and organic whole capable of developing on its own original lines." Among other things, the Europeans appear to have domesticated rye and oats that were first imported to the European continent as weed plants contaminating the seed of wheat and barley. In the comparable diffusion of agriculture from Central America, some of the peoples to the north appear to have rejected the new ways, at least temporarily.

By about 5000 B.C. the village-farming way of life seems to have been fingering down the valleys toward the alluvial bottom lands of the Tigris and Euphrates. Robert M. Adams believes that there may have been people living in the lowlands who were expert in collecting food from the rivers. They would have taken up the idea of farming from people who came down from the higher areas. In the bottom lands a very different climate, seasonal flooding of the land and small-scale irrigation led agriculture through a significant new technological transformation. By about 4000 B.C. the people of southern Mesopotamia had achieved such increases in productivity that their farms were beginning to support an urban civilization. The ancient site at Ubaid is typical of this period [see "The Origin of Cities," by Robert M. Adams, page 207].

Thus in 3,000 or 4,000 years the life of man had changed more radically than in all of the preceding 250,000 years. Before the agricultural revolution most men must have spent their waking moments seeking their next meal, except when they could gorge following a great kill. As man learned to produce food, instead of gathering, hunting or collecting it, and to store it in the grain bin and on the hoof, he was compelled as well as enabled to settle in larger communities. With human energy released for a whole spectrum of new activities, there came the development of specialized nonagricultural crafts. It is no accident that such innovations as the discovery of the basic mechanical principles, weaving, the plow, the wheel and metallurgy soon appeared.

No prehistorian worth his salt may end or begin such a discussion without acknowledging the present incompleteness of the archeological record. There is the disintegration of the perishable materials that were primary substances of technology at every stage. There is the factor of chance in archeological discovery, of vast areas of the world still incompletely explored archeologically, and of inadequate field techniques and interpretations by excavators. There are the vagaries of establishing a reliable chronology, of the whimsical degree to which "geobiochemical" contamination seems to have affected our radioactive-carbon age determinations. There is the fact that studies of human paleo-environments by qualified natural historians are only now becoming available. Writing in the field, in the midst of an exciting season of excavation, I would not be surprised if the picture I have presented here needs to be altered somewhat by the time that this article has appeared in print.

20

AN EARLY FARMING VILLAGE IN TURKEY

HALET ÇAMBEL AND ROBERT J. BRAIDWOOD
March 1970

Çayönü Tepesi, a site in a little-studied part of Asia Minor, adds to the growing record of man's agricultural origins. Also revealed there is the earliest evidence of man's use of metal

When and where did men first turn to farming and animal husbandry as a way of life? This question has increasingly come to occupy the attention of archaeologists in recent years. The first direct attempt to discover just when in human prehistory farming villages appeared was made in the Near East a little more than 20 years ago when a party from the Oriental Institute of the University of Chicago began digging at Jarmo in the foothills of the Zagros Mountains in northeastern Iraq. Today scores of such investigations are in progress in several parts of the Old World and the New World. In the Near East alone the area of interest has grown until it stretches from Turkestan and the Indus valley on the east to the Aegean and the Balkans on the west. This article concerns one Near Eastern investigation that has opened up a new area and has by chance brought to light the earliest evidence of man's use of metal.

Field results in the years since Jarmo allow a few broad generalizations about the dawn of cultivation and animal husbandry. We now know that somewhat earlier than 7500 B.C. people in some parts of the Near East had reached a level of cultural development marked by the production, as opposed to the mere collection, of plant and animal foodstuffs and by a pattern of residence in farming villages. It is not clear, however, when this level of development became characteristic of the region as a whole. Nor do we yet have a good understanding of conditions in the period immediately preceding. The reason is largely that few sites of this earlier period have yet been excavated, and that during the earliest phases of their manipulation the wild plants and animals would not yet possess features indicat-

ing that they were on the way to domestication. Moreover, even the most painstaking excavation may fail to turn up materials that constitute *primary* evidence for domestication, that is, the physical remains of the plants and animals in question. Fragments of plant material and bone—the objects that could tell us exactly which of a number of possible organisms were then in the process of domestication—are often completely missing from village sites.

What should be said of villages that yield plant and animal material that we cannot positively identify as being the remains of domesticated forms? Until recently we tended to believe that if such sites had every appearance of being permanently settled, and if their inventory of artifacts included flint "sickle" blades, querns (milling stones), storage pits and similar features, then they probably represented the next-earliest level of cultural development; we called it the level of incipient cultivation and animal husbandry. Over the years, however, it has become increasingly probable that early village-like communities of a somewhat different kind may also have existed in the Near East. At these sites the food supply tends at first to include plant and animal forms that were not subsequently domesticated. In other words, even though such items as flint sickles,

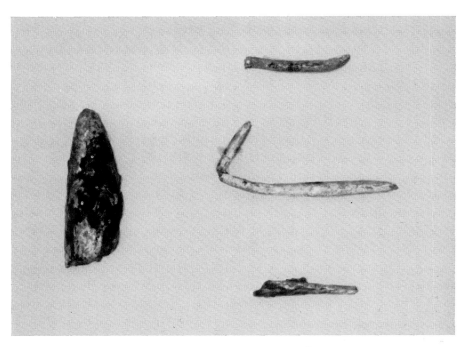

EVIDENCE OF METALWORKING at Çayönü Tepesi includes four objects, shown here twice actual size. At left is the point of a reamer, formed from a lump of native copper by hammering. Beside it are two copper pin fragments and a whole pin that has been bent. The pinpoints have been formed by abrasion. A source of native copper lies quite near the site.

querns and the like appear in their inventories, and the architectural traces of their settlement suggest some degree of permanence, it looks as if we are dealing here with villagers living on a level of intensive collection of wild foods alone. Our older notion that villages had to mean farmers has gone by the board.

A prime example of such a non-food-producing community is the village-like site of Mallaha, in northern Israel. The excavator of Mallaha, Jean Perrot of the French Archaeological Mission in Israel, was the first to suggest that when other sites of a similar nature were unearthed, they too might lack any evidence of food production. Mallaha was inhabited about 9000 B.C. The village site of Mureybet, on the middle reaches of the Euphrates in Syria, is somewhat later, say about 8250 B.C. Mureybet, which was excavated by Maurits N. van Loon for the Oriental Institute in 1964 and 1965, also shows no trace of food production. An even later example is the "hunters' village" of Suberde in Turkey, excavated by Jacques Bordaz of the University of Montreal in 1964 and 1965 [see "A Hunters' Village in Neolithic Turkey," by Dexter Perkins, Jr., and Patricia Daly; SCIENTIFIC AMERICAN, November, 1968]. As late as 6500 B.C. the people of Suberde fed themselves mainly by killing large numbers of wild sheep and wild cattle.

In very rough outline the available evidence now suggests that both the level of incipient cultivation and animal domestication and the level of intensified food-collecting were reached in the

Near East about 9000 B.C. In contrast to the moderately intensive food-collecting characteristic of the preceding level of development (the level of the late Upper Paleolithic period), what allowed this second kind of community to flourish was collecting of a most intensive kind. We believe such communities can be regarded as being incipiently food-producing, in the sense that their inhabitants were doubtless already manipulating both plants and animals to some extent. It seems to us that in much of the Near East this interval of incipient food production was just before or at the same time as what in Europe is called the Mesolithic period: a phase of cultural readaption, still on a food-collecting level, to the sequence of postglacial forested environments that formed in Europe about 11,000 years ago. (Food production proper did not reach most of Europe until sometime after 5000 B.C.)

The inventory of artifacts known as the Natufian assemblage, after the valley in Palestine where it was first discovered, provides examples, found both in caves and in village-like sites, of communities without food production. The artifacts uncovered at Mallaha, for instance, fit the Natufian classification. A different but contemporary inventory,

found east of the Euphrates and Tigris rivers, is named the Karim Shahirian assemblage, after Karim Shahir, a site on the flanks of the Zagros Mountains. The artifacts from Zawi Chemi, another early site in Iraq, are of this second kind, and Zawi Chemi appears to have the earliest evidence for domesticated sheep (about 9000 B.C.). A somewhat later site in neighboring Iran—Ganj Dareh, near Kermanshah—contains an assemblage that, although it is similar, is somewhat more developed than the basic Karim Shahirian. It is not yet clear, however, either along the Mediterranean littoral or in the regions east of the Euphrates, through how many successive phases the incipient food producer—hunters' village level may have passed before the next developmental step took place.

The early phase of that next step—the level of effective village-farming communities—is now known from sites throughout the Near East. Representative early-phase villages have been unearthed in most of the region's grassy uplands, in some middle reaches of its major river valleys, along the Mediterranean and even beyond the Near East in Cyprus, Crete and Greece. Originally one of us (Braidwood) believed the most ancient evidence of this early phase

● SITES WITH ESTABLISHED
  FOOD PRODUCTION.

○ SITES WITH SEVERAL PERIODS OF
  OCCUPATION, SOME FOOD-PRODUCING.

◆ SITES WITH EVIDENCE OF
  "INCIPIENT" FOOD PRODUCTION.

◇ SITES WITH INSUFFICIENT EVIDENCE
  OR NO EVIDENCE OF FOOD PRODUCTION.

  SITES KNOWN FROM BRIEF TESTS OR
? SURFACE COLLECTIONS; NO EVIDENCE
  OF FOOD PRODUCTION.

SOUTHWESTERN ASIA, from beyond the Caspian (right) to the Mediterranean shore (left), contains many of mankind's earliest farming settlements, most of them in or near the hilly regions flanking the Fertile Crescent of Mesopotamia. The region also contains a number of village-like sites whose inhabitants were only incipient food producers or won a living by means of intensified hunting and gathering (see key above).

would be found only within a geographically restricted area, which was defined as the hilly flanks of the Fertile Crescent [*see illustration below*]. Moreover, even within this area the expectation was that the evidence would be confined to the zone naturally occupied today by certain wild but potentially domesticable plants and animals. One consequence of this view was that for a time the search for early sites was restricted to the "hilly flank" area, with the result that a large proportion of the early village sites now known are either in that area or immediately adjacent to it.

Recently it has become apparent that in past millenniums the natural range of the potentially domesticable forms of what may be called the "wheat-barley/sheep-goat-cattle-pig complex" extended well beyond the hilly flanks of the Fertile Crescent. For example, while extending earlier investigations by the Oriental Institute in Iran, Herbert E. Wright, Jr., of the University of Minnesota and Willem van Zeist of the University of Groningen have collected samples from the beds of lakes and ponds for analysis of their pollen content. Wright and van Zeist find that since about 17,000 years ago the vegetation and climate along the flanks of the Zagros Mountains have

changed much more than had been supposed. At the same time test excavations by an Oriental Institute group at Koum, in the dry steppe country west of the Euphrates in Syria, have added another site to the growing list of early non-food-producing settlements. Koum, like Mureybet, lies well south of the hilly-flanks zone, just as Suberde in Asia Minor lies well north of it. We have yet to learn precisely how wide the natural range of the domesticable plants and animals constituting this Near Eastern complex was in early times. The question will be answered only with the continued help of our colleagues in the natural sciences.

In the 1950's there was a substantial increase of archaeological activity in the Near East, but not until the 1960's did it become possible to investigate one untouched area that formed a virtual keystone in the arch. This was the southern slopes and the piedmont of the Taurus Mountains in southeastern Turkey, an area that includes the entire northern watershed in the upper reaches of the Tigris and the Euphrates. We reasoned that, however extensive the ancient range of domesticable plants and animals may have been, the upper basin of the Tigris and the Euphrates must have been

somewhere near the center of the zone.

Much of this unexplored territory lay within three Turkish border provinces (Urfa, Diyarbakir and Siirt), which for reasons of national security are normally out-of-bounds to foreign visitors. It seemed to us that if the area was to be reconnoitered, a joint Turkish-American venture was in order. In late 1962 the Oriental Institute joined forces with the department of prehistory of Istanbul University to establish a joint Prehistoric Project, and the authors of this article were made its codirectors. The project received the support of the National Science Foundation and the Wenner-Gren Foundation for Anthropological Research.

We proposed that a surface survey of the three provinces be made in the fall of 1963 and that exploratory digging be undertaken in the spring of 1964. We presently received the necessary approvals, which in this border region meant not only the cooperation of the Directorate of Antiquities of the Turkish Republic but also the active support of the Prime Minister, of many high civil and military authorities and of the governors of the three provinces and their staffs.

Thanks to the interest of all concerned, we were able to begin our sur-

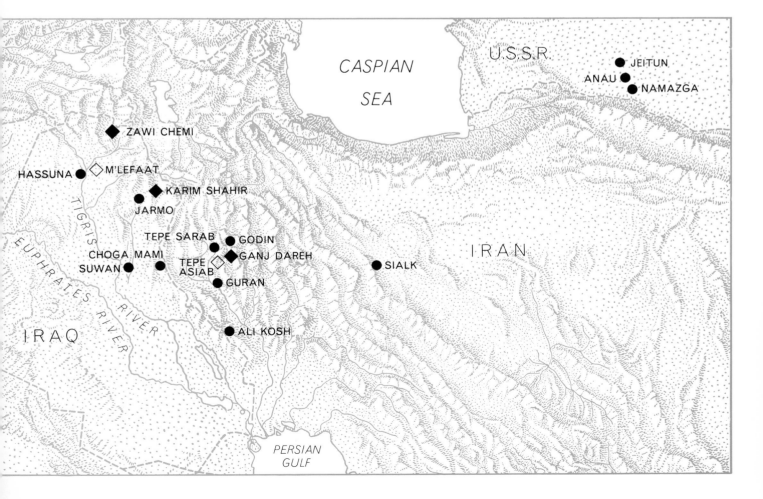

face survey in the province of Siirt early in October of 1963. We moved on to Diyarbakir in mid-November and ended the season with a five-day survey in Urfa in mid-December. Since the three provinces cover a total of more than 46,000 square kilometers, the reconnaissance could scarcely be an intensive one. The most detailed work was done in two valley regions: the plains of Kurtalan in Siirt and the Ergani plain in Diyarbakir. We found a total of 134 archaeological sites, plotted their location and roughly classified the materials we could collect on the surface at the main sites.

Our survey showed that this part of Turkey had been continuously occupied by men at least from the time (between 100,000 and 200,000 years ago) when stone tools of the Acheulean type were commonplace. So far as our particular interests were concerned, sites that looked as though they might be the remains of early farming villages were located in both the Kurtalan and the Ergani valleys. Still other sites in these val-

leys evidently represented more fully evolved village-farming communities. Some of the sites belonged to the developed village-farming phase termed Halafian (after Tell Halaf in northern Syria).

So far as settlements that might have belonged to the initial level of incipient food production are concerned, the most we can say at the moment is that our survey turned up no artifacts that, even in general terms, could be called representative of either the Natufian or the Karim Shahirian assemblages. Although it is probable that an unrelated third cultural tradition at the general level of incipient food production existed in this part of Turkey, we have yet to identify its traces.

In late April of 1964 we returned to the area of our survey prepared to undertake a number of test excavations. Bruce Howe of Harvard University, who had joined the project with the support of the American Schools of Oriental Re-

search, tackled two small open sites in the area northwest of the provincial capital of Urfa. Named Biris Mezarligi and Söğüt Tarlasi, the sites contained numerous specialized stone tools produced from blades of flint. The inventory seems to represent some end phase of the Paleolithic period in the region. The sites did not yield samples adequate for carbon-14 dating, so that the age of this blade industry is a matter of conjecture; our guess is that the tools were made around 10000 B.C. or perhaps a little later. At Söğüt Tarlasi, but not at Biris Mezarligi, the blade-tool horizon was overlain by material of a time somewhat before 3000 B.C., contemporary with the Uruk phase of Sumerian culture in neighboring Mesopotamia.

While Howe worked in Urfa, the majority of the workers on the project moved on to Diyarbakir in order to investigate a promising mound some five kilometers southwest of the town of Ergani. Known as Çayönü Tepesi, the mound is about 200 meters in diameter;

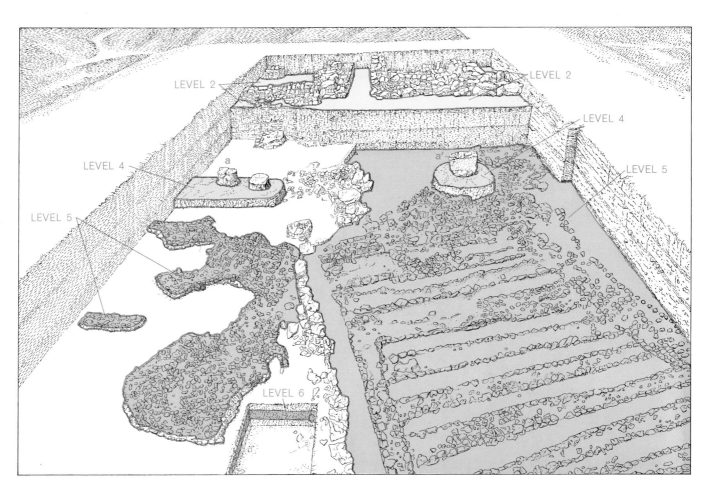

SUCCESSIVE LEVELS exposed during excavation on the crest of the mound are shown in a drawing based on composite photographs. At the rear of the dig, only a little below the mound surface, are the stone foundations of mud-brick structures that had been built at Level 2. In the middle distance (*a, a'*), still surrounded by unremoved earth, are the bases of the two stone monoliths found at Level 4. Sections of the cobble pavement found at Level 5 are in the foreground at left. In the foreground at right is the grill-like stone foundation of the elaborate structure exposed at Level 5. The two-by-two-meter pit, foreground, descends beyond Level 6.

it stands on the north bank of a minor tributary of the Tigris. At some time in the past part of the mound's south side was washed away. At the foot of the talus slope on the river side we found fragments of crude and easily crumbled pottery that had been made by hand, rather than with the potter's wheel. Some additional potsherds were present on the northeast slope of the mound and in the top 10 or 15 centimeters of soil in our test excavations (about the depth to which the soil had been disturbed by modern plowing). Below that our 1964 excavations revealed no pottery. The presence in these lower levels of figurines made of clay shows that clay was known and used in the early days of Çayönü Tepesi. Like the people of Jarmo and some other early village-farming communities, however, the inhabitants of Çayönü Tepesi evidently got along without the clay bowls, jars and other containers that are commonplace in the villages of later farmers.

We worked at Çayönü Tepesi for two seasons—in 1964 and again in 1968—and we expect to work there again this year. Our main evidence concerning the early occupation of the site comes from a 10-by-15-meter area we excavated on the crest of the mound and a five-by-eight-meter trench we cut into the mound on the river side; both excavations were undertaken during the 1964 season [see illustrations on page 204]. Those who explore village sites in southwestern Asia come to expect that each new excavation will exhibit an exuberant characteristic that is distinctively its own. Çayönü Tepesi was no exception: its special characteristic is its architecture. Among the buildings we uncovered, several must have been quite imposing. The trench we cut back from the river revealed part of what could have been a building interior or perhaps an open court. The area was floored with a broad pavement of smooth flagstones, around which the stone bases of thick walls rose to a height of a meter or more. Spaced along the main axis of the paved area were the broken bases of a pair of large stone slabs that had once stood upright. From one of the stone walls buttresses projected at the points nearest the broken slabs. Another partly intact slab marked the area's short axis. Unfortunately erosion had eaten away the southern portions of this elaborate structure, so that its full plan is beyond recovery.

At the crest of the mound we dug down to a depth of more than three meters, encountering traces of at least six

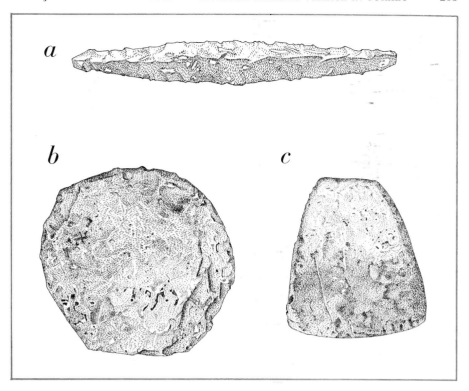

THREE STONE IMPLEMENTS from Çayönü Tepesi are a flint projectile point (a), found during the 1968 season, a scraper of flint (b) and a polished stone celt, the bit of a compound cutting tool (c), unearthed in 1964. The artifacts are shown at their actual size.

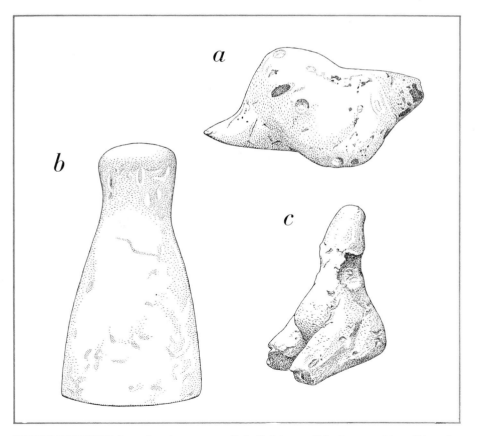

THREE ODDITIES from the site are a snail shell (a), a polished stone object (b) and a crude clay figurine (c). The shell, imported from the Mediterranean, has been smoothed and drilled with holes, presumably for decorative inserts. The stone, about three inches high, is one of 22 found in a cache during the 1968 season; their function is unknown. The figure seems to represent a pregnant woman; it may be a portrayal of the familiar "fertility deity."

AIR VIEW of Çayönü Tepesi, on the bank of a tributary of the Tigris River in southeastern Turkey, shows the work done by the
authors in 1964. Near the river (*right*) digging uncovered stone
walls and a floor of flagstones. On the crest of the village mound
(*left*) six successive levels of occupation have been exposed;
the next-to-lowest level contained objects made from copper.

GROUND VIEW of Çayönü Tepesi, from a rise on the south side of
the river, shows a stretch of the broad Ergani plain beyond the site.
On the northern horizon are the first ranges of the Taurus Mountains, here distinctively marked by light-colored bands of rock.

successive levels of occupation. At the fourth level the bases of two more upright slabs rose from a broad pavement of fist-sized limestone cobbles; the broken upper portion of one slab lay beside its base. The fifth level, also paved with cobbles, contained the stone foundations of still another substantial structure. What we could perceive of the foundation plan showed a curious grill-like pattern [see illustration on page 202]. Our work in 1968 exposed another of these grill-like foundations. A similar foundation, although it is smaller and built of sun-dried mud walling rather than stone, was unearthed at Jarmo. We are still puzzled as to the function of such foundations.

The purpose of the upright slabs at Çayönü Tepesi is equally puzzling. We are of two minds about whether they could have been supports for roof beams. Our first notion was that the slabs might have been ceremonial stones set up within unroofed courts, but the actual function of the structures containing them is not yet clear. We are much impressed by the substantial proportions of the buildings and by the relative sophistication of their construction, but we are still loath to press any suggestion that they served a public or a sacred purpose.

In addition to its impressive architecture, Çayönü Tepesi yielded tools chipped from flint and obsidian or fashioned from stone by grinding, ornaments made of polished stone, the clay figurines mentioned above and one shell ornament. The last object indicates contact, direct or indirect, with the Mediterranean coast. If one adds to this inventory evidence what seems to be a primitive form of wheat and the remains of domesticated dogs, pigs, sheep and probably goats, one gains some sense of the quality of life here and in similar communities across southwestern Asia as the arts of farming and animal husbandry became established during the eighth millennium B.C. If that were all Çayönü Tepesi had to tell us, it would be enough. A combination of geological propinquity and archaeological good fortune, however, has made the site even more significant. We have found here what is so far the earliest evidence of man's intentional use of metal.

Turkey is rich in minerals; one of its major mining centers today—a deposit of native copper, copper ores and related minerals such as malachite—is less than 20 kilometers from Çayönü Tepesi. In our excavation at the crest of the mound we noticed, from just below the surface downward, dozens of fragments of a bright green substance that we took to be malachite. Below the fourth occupation level we began to find actual artifacts made of malachite: drilled beads, a carefully smoothed but undrilled ellipsoid and a small tablet. Next we found part of a tool—one end of a reamer with a square cross section—that had been hammered into shape out of a lump of native copper. Finally we uncovered three tiny objects of copper that are perhaps analogous to the ordinary modern straight pin. In two of these pins, which do not appear to be complete, the metal had been abraded to form a point at one end; the third pin was pointed at both ends and was sharply bent [see illustration on page 199].

Metallurgy, of course, involves the hot-working of metals, including such arts as smelting, alloying, casting and forging. We are making no assertion that any kind of metallurgy, however primitive, existed at Çayönü Tepesi; there is not even any unanimity of opinion among the experts about whether the reamer, the only article that had certainly been hammered, was worked cold or hot. The fact remains that sometime just before 7000 B.C. the people of Çayönü Tepesi not only were acquainted with metal but also were shaping artifacts out of native copper by abrading and hammering.

What we suggest is that the Çayönü Tepesi copper reveals the moment in man's material progress when he may first have begun to sense the properties of metal as metal, rather than as some peculiar kind of stone. Looking back from the full daylight of our own age of metals, these first faint streaks of dawn are exciting to behold.

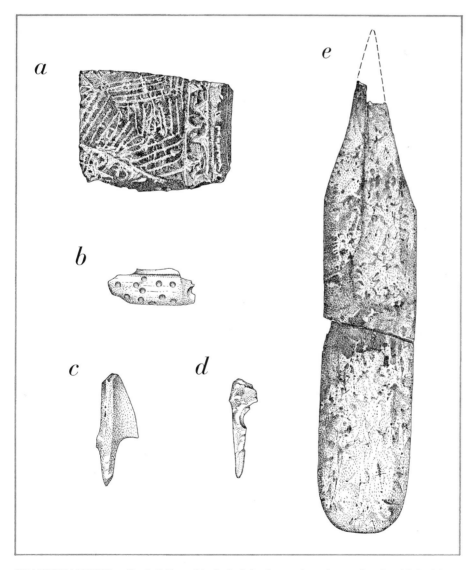

CRAFTSMANSHIP at Çayönü Tepesi included the decoration of stone bowls with incisions (a) and bone objects with drilled patterns (b). Drills flaked from flint (c, d) were used to work the bone. Bone awls (e) were probably used to produce wooden and leather items.

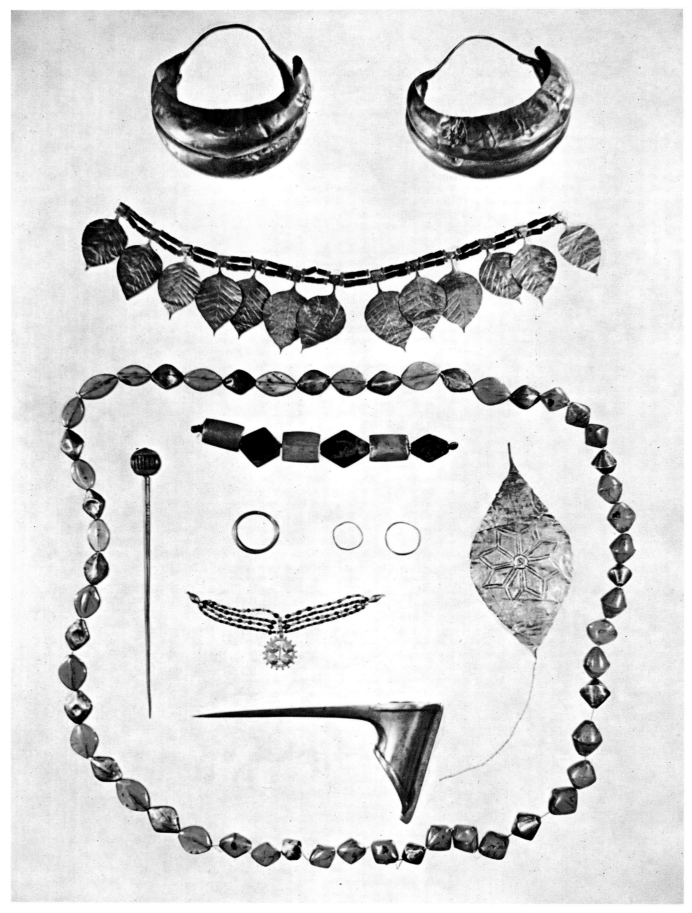

ROYAL GRAVE OFFERINGS from later tombs at Ur indicate the concentration of wealth that accompanied the emergence of a kingly class. Dated at about 2500 B.C., the objects include large gold earrings (*top*); a headdress with gold leaves; beads of gold, lapis and carnelian; gold rings; a gold leaf; a hairpin of gold and lapis; an ornament with a gold pendant; an adz head of electrum.

21

THE ORIGIN OF CITIES

ROBERT M. ADAMS
September 1960

The agricultural revolution ultimately made it possible for men to congregate in large communities, and to take up specialized tasks. The first cities almost certainly arose in Mesopotamia

The rise of cities, the second great "revolution" in human culture, was pre-eminently a social process, an expression more of changes in man's interaction with his fellows than in his interaction with his environment. For this reason it marks not only a turning but also a branching point in the history of the human species.

Earlier steps are closely identified with an increasing breadth or intensity in the exploitation of the environment. Their distinguishing features are new tools and techniques and the discovery of new and more dependable resources for subsistence. Even in so advanced an achievement as the invention of agriculture, much of the variation from region to region was simply a reflection of local differences in subsistence potential.

In contrast the urban revolution was

MAP OF NIPPUR on a clay tablet dates from about 1500 B.C. Two lines at far left trace the course of Euphrates River; adjacent lines show one wall of the city. Square structures at far right are temples; the two vertical lines at right center represent a canal.

EARLY GRAVE OFFERINGS from Mesopotamian tombs of about 3900 B.C. consist mainly of painted pottery such as two vessels at left. Vessels of diorite (*center and right center*) and alabaster (*far right*), found in tombs of about 3500 B.C. and later, reflect growth of trade with other regions and increasing specialization of crafts. These vessels and objects on opposite page are in the University Museum of the University of Pennsylvania.

a decisive cultural and social change that was less directly linked to changes in the exploitation of the environment. To be sure, it rested ultimately on food surpluses obtained by agricultural producers above their own requirements and somehow made available to city dwellers engaged in other activities. But its essential element was a whole series of new institutions and the vastly greater size and complexity of the social unit, rather than basic innovations in subsistence. In short, the different forms that early urban societies assumed are essentially the products of differently interacting political and economic—human —forces. And the interpretive skills required to understand them are correspondingly rooted more in the social sciences and humanities than in the natural sciences.

Even the term urban needs qualification. Many of the qualities we think of as civilized have been attained by societies that failed to organize cities. At least some Egyptologists believe that civilization advanced for almost 2,000 years under the Pharaohs before true cities appeared in Egypt. The period was marked by the development of monumental public works, a formal state superstructure, written records and the beginnings of exact science. In the New World, too, scholars are still searching the jungles around Maya temple centers in Guatemala and Yucatán for recognizably urban agglomerations of dwellings. For all its temple architecture and high art, and the intellectual achievement represented by its hieroglyphic writing and accurate long-count calendar, classic Maya civilization apparently was not based on the city.

These facts do not detract from the fundamental importance of the urban revolution, but underline its complex character. Every high civilization other than possibly the Mayan did ultimately produce cities. And in most civilizations urbanization began early.

There is little doubt that this was the case for the oldest civilization and the earliest cities: those of ancient Mesopotamia. The story of their development, which we will sketch here, is still a very tentative one. In large part the uncertainties are due to the state of the archeological record, which is as yet both scanty and unrepresentative. The archeologist's preoccupation with early temple-furnishings and architecture, for example, has probably exaggerated their importance, and has certainly given us little information about contemporary secular life in neighboring precincts of the same towns.

Eventually written records help overcome these deficiencies. However, 500 or more years elapsed between the onset of the first trends toward urbanism and the earliest known examples of cuneiform script. And then for the succeeding 700 or 800 years the available texts are laconic, few in number and poorly understood. To a degree, they can be supplemented by cautious inferences drawn from later documents. But the earliest chapters rest primarily on archeological data.

Let us pick up the narrative where Robert J. Braidwood left it in the preceding article, with the emergence of a fully agricultural people, many of them grouped together in villages of perhaps 200 to 500 individuals. Until almost the end of our own story, dating finds little corroboration in written records. Moreover, few dates based on the decay of radioactive carbon are yet available in Mesopotamia for this crucial period. But by 5500 B.C., or even earlier, it appears that the village-farming community had fully matured in southwestern Asia. As a way of life it then stabilized internally for 1,500 years or more, although it con-

tinued to spread downward from the hills and piedmont where it had first crystallized in the great river valleys.

Then came a sharp increase in tempo. In the next 1,000 years some of the small agricultural communities on the alluvial plain between the Tigris and Euphrates rivers not only increased greatly in size, but changed decisively in structure. They culminated in the Sumerian city-state with tens of thousands of inhabitants, elaborate religious, political and military establishments, stratified social classes, advanced technology and widely extended trading contacts [see "The Sumerians," by Samuel Noah Kramer; SCIENTIFIC AMERICAN, October, 1957]. The river-valley agriculture on which the early Mesopotamian cities were established differed considerably from that of the uplands where domestication had begun. Wheat and barley remained the staple crops, but they were supplemented by dates. The date palm yielded not only prodigious and dependable supplies of fruit but also wood. Marshes and estuaries teemed with fish, and their reeds provided another building material. There was almost no stone, however; before the establishment of trade with surrounding areas, hard-fired clay served for such necessary agricultural tools as sickles.

The domestic animals—sheep, goats, donkeys, cattle and pigs by the time of the first textual evidence—may have differed little from those known earlier in the foothills and northern plains. But they were harder to keep, particularly the cattle and the donkeys which were needed as draft animals for plowing. During the hot summers all vegetation withered except for narrow strips along the watercourses. Fodder had to be cultivated and distributed, and pastureland was at a premium. These problems of management may help explain why the herds rapidly became a responsibility of people associated with the temples. And control of the herds in turn may have provided the stimulus that led temple officials frequently to assume broader control over the economy and agriculture.

Most important, agriculture in the alluvium depended on irrigation, which had not been necessary in the uplands. For a long time the farmers made do with small-scale systems, involving breaches in the natural embankments of the streams and uncontrolled local flooding. The beginnings of large-scale canal networks seem clearly later than the advent of fully established cities.

In short, the immediately pre-urban society of southern Mesopotamia consisted of small communities scattered along natural watercourses. Flocks had to forage widely, but cultivation was confined to narrow enclaves of irrigated plots along swamp margins and stream banks. In general the swamps and rivers provided an important part of the raw materials and diet.

Where in this pattern were the inducements, perhaps even preconditions, for urbanization that explain the precocity of the Mesopotamian achievement? First, there was the productivity of irrigation agriculture. In spite of chronic water-shortage during the earlier part of the growing season and periodic floods around the time of the harvest, in spite of a debilitating summer climate and the ever present danger of salinity in flooded or over-irrigated fields, farming yielded a clear and dependable surplus of food.

Second, the very practice of irrigation must have helped induce the growth of cities. It is sometimes maintained that the inducement lay in a need for centralized control over the building and maintaining of elaborate irrigation systems, but this does not seem to have been the case. As we have seen, such systems came after the cities themselves. However, by engendering inequalities in access to productive land, irrigation contributed to the formation of a stratified society. And by furnishing a reason for border disputes between neighboring communities, it surely promoted a warlike atmosphere that drew people together in offensive and defensive concentrations.

Finally, the complexity of subsistence pursuits on the flood plains may have indirectly aided the movement toward cities. Institutions were needed to medi-

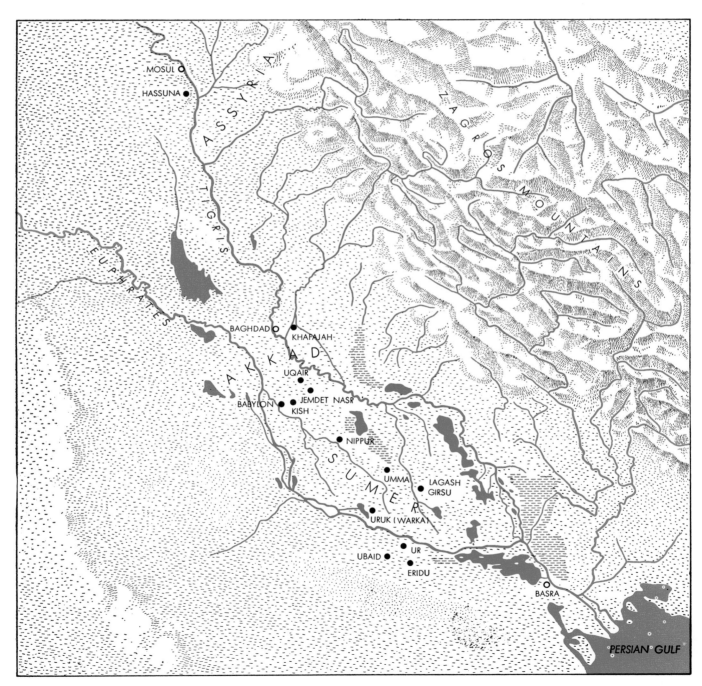

ANCIENT CITIES of Mesopotamia (*black dots*) were located mainly along Tigris and Euphrates rivers and their tributaries. In ancient times these rivers followed different courses from those shown on this modern map. Modern cities are shown as open dots.

CITY OF ERBIL in northern Iraq is built on the site of ancient city of Arbela. This aerial view suggests the character and appearance of Mesopotamian cities of thousands of years ago, with streets and houses closely packed around central public buildings.

ate between herdsman and cultivator; between fisherman and sailor; between plowmaker and plowman. Whether through a system of rationing, palace largesse or a market that would be recognizable to us, the city provided a logical and necessary setting for storage, exchange and redistribution. Not surprisingly, one of the recurrent themes in early myths is a rather didactic demonstration that the welfare of the city goddess is founded upon the harmonious interdependence of the shepherd and the farmer.

In any case the gathering forces for urbanization first become evident around 4000 B.C. Which of them furnished the

initial impetus is impossible to say, if indeed any single factor was responsible. We do not even know as yet whether the onset of the process was signaled by a growth in the size of settlements. And of course mere increase in size would not necessarily imply technological or economic advance beyond the level of the village-farming community. In our own time we have seen primitive agricultural peoples, such as the Yoruba of western Nigeria, who maintained sizable cities that were in fact little more than overgrown village-farming settlements. They were largely self-sustaining because most of the productive inhabitants were full-time farmers.

The evidence suggests that at the beginning the same was true of Mesopotamian urbanization: immediate economic change was not its central characteristic. As we shall see shortly, the first clear-cut trend to appear in the archeological record is the rise of temples. Conceivably new patterns of thought and social organization crystallizing within the temples served as the primary force in bringing people together and setting the process in motion.

Whatever the initial stimulus to growth and reorganization, the process itself clearly involved the interaction of many different factors. Certainly the institutions of the city evolved in different

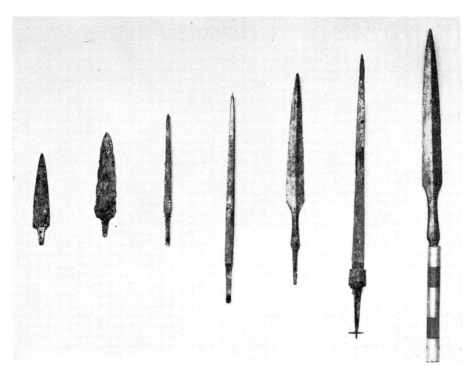

SPEARHEADS of copper and bronze from the royal cemetery at Ur date back to the third millenium B.C. The workmanship of these weapons matches that of the jewelry on page 206.

and adopted architectural features that afterward permanently characterized Mesopotamian temples. The development continued into the Early Dynastic period, when we see a complex of workshops and storehouses surrounding a greatly enlarged but rigidly traditional arrangement of cult chambers. No known contemporary structures were remotely comparable in size or complexity to these establishments until almost the end of the Protoliterate period.

At some point specialized priests appeared, probably the first persons released from direct subsistence labor. Their ritual activities are depicted in Protoliterate seals and stone carvings. If not immediately, then quite early, the priests also assumed the role of economic administrators, as attested by ration or wage lists found in temple premises among the earliest known examples of writing. The priestly hierarchies continued to supervise a multitude of economic as well as ritual activities into (and beyond) the Early Dynastic period, although by then more explicitly political forms of organization had perhaps become dominant. For a long time, however, temples seem to have been the largest and most complex institutions that existed in the communities growing up around them.

The beginnings of dynastic political regimes are much harder to trace. Monumental palaces, rivaling the temples in size, appear in the Early Dynastic period, but not earlier. The term for "king" has not yet been found in Protoliterate texts. Even so-called royal tombs apparently began only in the Early Dynastic period.

Lacking contemporary historical or archeological evidence, we must seek the origins of dynastic institutions primarily in later written versions of traditional myths. Thorkild Jacobsen of the University of Chicago has argued persuasively that Sumerian myths describing the world of the gods reflect political institutions as they existed in human society just prior to the rise of dynastic authority. If so, they show that political authority in the Protoliterate period rested in an assembly of the adult male members of the community. Convoked only to meet sporadic external threat, the assembly's task was merely to select a short-term war leader.

Eventually, as the myths themselves suggest, successful war leaders were retained even in times of peace. Herein lies the apparent origin of kingship. At times springing up outside the priestly corporations, at times coming from them,

directions and at different rates, rather than as a smoothly emerging totality. Considering the present fragmentary state of knowledge, it is more reasonable here to follow some of these trends individually rather than to speculate from the shreds (or, rather, sherds!) and patches of data about how the complete organizational pattern developed.

Four archeological periods can be distinguished in the tentative chronology of the rise of the Mesopotamian city-state. The earliest is the Ubaid, named for the first site where remains of this period were uncovered [see map on page 209]. At little more than a guess, it may have lasted for a century or two past

4000 B.C., giving way to the relatively brief Warka period. Following this the first written records appeared during the Protoliterate period, which spanned the remainder of the fourth millennium. The final part of our story is the Early Dynastic period, which saw the full flowering of independent city-states between about 3000 and 2500 B.C.

Of all the currents that run through the whole interval, we know most about religious institutions. Small shrines existed in the early villages of the northern plains and were included in the cultural inventory of the earliest known agriculturalists in the alluvium. Before the end of the Ubaid period the free-standing shrine had lost its original fluidity of plan

ROYAL WAR-CHARIOT carved on limestone plaque from city of Ur reflects increasing concern of Mesopotamian cities about methods of warfare in middle of third millennium B.C.

new leaders emerged who were preoccupied with, and committed to, both defensive and offensive warfare against neighboring city-states.

The traditional concerns of the temples were not immediately affected by the new political leadership. Palace officials acquired great landed estates of their own, but the palace itself was occupied chiefly with such novel activities as raising and supplying its army, maintaining a large retinue of servants and entertainers and constructing a defensive wall around the city.

These undertakings took a heavy toll of the resources of the young city-states, perhaps too heavy to exact by the old "democratic" processes. Hence it is not surprising that as permanent, hereditary royal authority became established, the position of the assembly declined. In the famous epic of Gilgamesh, an Early Dynastic king of Uruk, the story opens with the protests of the citizenry over their forced labor on the city walls. Another episode shows Gilgamesh manipulating the assembly, obviously no longer depending on its approval for his power. Rooted in war, the institution of kingship intensified a pattern of predatory expansionism and shifting military rivalries. The early Mesopotamian king could trace his origin to the need for military leadership. But the increasingly militaristic flavor of the Early Dynastic period also can be traced at least in part to the interests and activities of kings and their retinues as they proceeded to consolidate their power.

As society shifted its central focus from temple to palace it also separated into classes. Archeologically, the process can best be followed through the increasing differentiation in grave offerings in successively later cemeteries. Graves of the Ubaid period, at the time when monumental temples were first appearing, hold little more than a variable number of pottery vessels. Those in the cemetery at Ur, dating from the latter part of the Early Dynastic period, show a great disparity in the wealth they contain. A small proportion, the royal tombs (not all of whose principal occupants may have belonged to royal families), are richly furnished with beautifully wrought weapons, ornaments and utensils of gold and lapis lazuli. A larger number contain a few copper vessels or an occasional bead of precious metal, but the majority have only pottery vessels or even nothing at all. Both texts and archeological evidence indicate that copper and bronze agricultural tools were beyond the reach of the ordinary

RELIGIONS of ancient Mesopotamia were dominated by the idea that man was fashioned to serve the gods. Here a worshipper followed by figure with pail brings a goat as an offering to goddess seated at right. A divine attendant kneels before her. This impression and the one below were made from stone cylinder-seals of Akkadian period (about 2400 B.C.).

peasant until after the Early Dynastic period, while graves of the well-to-do show "conspicuous consumption" of copper in the form of superfluous stands for pottery vessels even from the beginning of the period.

Early Dynastic texts likewise record social and economic stratification. Records from the main archive of the Baba Temple in Girsu, for example, show substantial differences in the allotments from that temple's lands to its parishioners. Other texts describe the sale of houseplots or fields, often to form great estates held by palace officials and worked by communities of dependent clients who may originally have owned the land. Still others record the sale of slaves, and the rations allotted to slaves producing textiles under the supervision of temple officials. As a group, however, slaves constituted only a small minority of the population until long after the Early Dynastic period.

Turning to the development of technology, we find a major creative burst in early Protoliterate times, involving very rapid stylistic and technical advance in the manufacture of seals, statuary and ornate vessels of carved stone, cast copper or precious metals. But the number of craft specialists apparently was very small, and the bulk of their products seems to have been intended only for cult purposes. In contrast the Early Dynastic period saw a great increase in production of nonagricultural commodities, and almost certainly a corresponding increase in the proportion of the population that was freed from the tasks of primary subsistence to pursue their craft on a full-time basis. Both stylistically and technologically, however, this expansion was rooted in the accomplishments of the previous period and produced few innovations of its own.

Production was largely stimulated by three new classes of demand. First, the burgeoning military establishment of the palace required armaments, including not only metal weapons and armor but also more elaborate equipment such as chariots. Second, a considerable vol-

GILGAMESH, early Mesopotamian king and hero of legend, may be figure attacking water buffalo (right center). Figure stabbing lion may be his companion, the bull-man Enkidu.

ume of luxury goods was commissioned for the palace retinue. And third, a moderate private demand for these goods seems to have developed also. The mass production of pottery, the prevalence of such articles as cylinder seals and metal utensils, the existence of a few vendors' stalls and the hoards of objects in some of the more substantial houses all imply at least a small middle class. Most of these commodities, it is clear, were fabricated in the major Mesopotamian towns from raw materials brought from considerable distance. Copper, for example, came from Oman and the Anatolian plateau, more than 1,000 miles from the Sumerian cities. The need for imports stimulated the manufacture of such articles as textiles, which could be offered in exchange, and also motivated the expansion of territorial control by conquest.

Some authorities have considered that technological advance, which they usually equate with the development of metallurgy, was a major stimulant or even a precondition of urban growth. Yet, in southern Mesopotamia at least, the major quantitative expansion of metallurgy, and of specialized crafts in general, came only after dynastic city-states were well advanced. While the spread of technology probably contributed further to the development of militarism and social stratification, it was less a cause than a consequence of city growth. The same situation is found in New World civilizations. Particularly in aboriginal Middle America the technological level remained very nearly static before and after the urban period.

Finally we come to the general forms of the developing cities, perhaps the most obscure aspect of the whole process of urbanization. Unhappily even Early Dynastic accounts do not oblige us with extensive descriptions of the towns where they were written, nor even with useful estimates of population. Contemporary maps also are unknown; if they were made, they still elude us. References to towns in the myths and epics are at best vague and allegorical. Ultimately archeological studies can supply most of these deficiencies, but at present we have little to go on.

The farming villages of the pre-urban era covered at most a few acres. Whether the villages scattered over the alluvial plain in Ubaid times were much different from the earlier ones in the north is unclear; certainly most were no larger, but the superficial appearance of one largely unexcavated site indicates that they may have been more densely built up and more formally laid out along a regular grid of streets or lanes. By the end of the Ubaid period the temples had begun to expand; a continuation of this trend is about all that the remains of Warka and early Protoliterate periods can tell us thus far. Substantial growth seems to have begun toward the end of the Protoliterate period and to have continued through several centuries of the Early Dynastic. During this time the first battlemented ring-walls were built around at least the larger towns.

A few Early Dynastic sites have been excavated sufficiently to give a fairly full picture of their general layout. Radiating out from the massive public buildings of these cities, toward the outer gates, were streets, unpaved and dusty, but straight and wide enough for the passage of solid-wheeled carts or chariots. Along the streets lay the residences of the well-to-do citizenry, usually arranged around spacious courts and sometimes provided with latrines draining into sewage conduits below the streets. The houses of the city's poorer inhabitants were located behind or between the large multiroomed dwellings. They were approached by tortuous, narrow alleys, were more haphazard in plan, were less well built and very much smaller. Mercantile activities were probably concentrated along the quays of the adjoining river or at the city gates. The marketplace or bazaar devoted to private commerce had not yet appeared.

Around every important urban center rose the massive fortifications that guarded the city against nomadic raids and the usually more formidable campaigns of neighboring rulers. Outside the walls clustered sheepfolds and irrigated tracts, interspersed with subsidiary villages and ultimately disappearing into the desert. And in the desert dwelt only the nomad, an object of mixed fear and scorn to the sophisticated court poet. By the latter part of the Early Dynastic period several of the important capitals of lower Mesopotamia included more than 250 acres within their fortifications. The city of Uruk extended over 1,100 acres and contained possibly 50,000 people.

For these later cities there are written records from which the make-up of the population can be estimated. The overwhelming majority of the able-bodied adults still were engaged in primary agricultural production on their own holdings, on allotments of land received from the temples or as dependent retainers on large estates. But many who were engaged in subsistence agriculture also had other roles. One temple archive, for example, records that 90 herdsmen, 80 soldier-laborers, 100 fishermen, 125 sailors, pilots and oarsmen, 25 scribes, 20 or 25 craftsmen (carpenters, smiths, potters, leather-workers, stonecutters, and mat- or basket-weavers) and probably 250 to 300 slaves were numbered among its parish of around 1,200 persons. In addition to providing for its own subsistence and engaging in a variety of specialized pursuits, most of this group was expected to serve in the army in time of crisis.

Earlier figures can only be guessed at from such data as the size of temple establishments and the quantity of craft-produced articles. Toward the end of the Protoliterate period probably less than a fifth of the labor force was substantially occupied with economic activities outside of subsistence pursuits; in Ubaid times a likely figure is 5 per cent.

It is not easy to say at what stage in the whole progression the word "city" becomes applicable. By any standard Uruk and its contemporaries were cities. Yet they still lacked some of the urban characteristics of later eras. In particular, the development of municipal politics, of a self-conscious corporate body with at least partially autonomous, secular institutions for its own administration, was not consummated until classical times.

Many of the currents we have traced must have flowed repeatedly in urban civilizations. But not necessarily all of them. The growth of the Mesopotamian city was closely related to the rising tempo of warfare. For their own protection people must have tended to congregate under powerful rulers and behind strong fortifications; moreover, they may have been consciously and forcibly drawn together by the elite in the towns in order to centralize political and economic controls. On the other hand, both in aboriginal Central America and in the Indus Valley (in what is now Pakistan) great population centers grew up without comprehensive systems of fortification, and with relatively little emphasis on weapons or on warlike motifs in art.

There is not one origin of cities, but as many as there are independent cultural traditions with an urban way of life. Southern Mesopotamia merely provides the earliest example of a process that, with refinements introduced by the industrial revolution and the rise of national states, is still going on today.

22

AN EARLY CITY IN IRAN

C. C. AND MARTHA LAMBERG-KARLOVSKY
June 1971

Tepe Yahyā, midway between Mesopotamia and India, was a busy center of trade 5,500 years ago. An outpost of Mesopotamian urban culture, it played a key role in the spread of civilization from west to east

The kingdom of Elam and its somewhat better-known neighbor, Sumer, were the two earliest urban states to arise in the Mesopotamian area during the fourth millennium B.C. Archaeological findings now show that the Elamite realm also included territory at least 500 miles to the east. For more than 10 centuries, starting about 3400 B.C., the hill country of southeastern Iran some 60 miles from the Arabian Sea was the site of a second center of Elamite urban culture.

Today all that is left of the city that stood halfway between the Euphrates and the Indus is a great mound of earth located some 4,500 feet above sea level in the Soghun Valley, 150 miles south of the city of Kerman in the province of the same name. Known locally as Tepe Yahyā, the mound is 60 feet high and 600 feet in diameter. Its record of occupation begins with a 6,500-year-old Neolithic village and ends with a citadel of the Sassanian dynasty that ruled Persia early in the Christian Era. Intermediate levels in the mound testify to the connections between this eastern Elamite city and the traditional centers of the kingdom in the west.

Such a long archaeological sequence has much value for the study of man's cultural development from farmer to city dweller, but three unexpected elements make Tepe Yahyā a site of even greater significance. First, writing tablets made of clay, recovered from one of the lower levels in the mound, have been shown by carbon-14 analysis of associated organic material to date back to 3560 B.C. (±110 years). The tablets are inscribed with writing of the kind known as proto-Elamite. Proto-Elamite inscriptions and early Sumerian ones are the earliest known Mesopotamian writings, which are the oldest known anywhere. The Tepe Yahyā tablets are unique in that they are the first of their kind that can be assigned an absolute date. It comes as a surprise to find these examples of writing—as early as the earliest known—in a place that is so far away from Mesopotamia.

The second surprise is evidence that Elamite trade with neighboring Sumer in an unusual commodity—steatite, the easily worked rock also known as soapstone—formed a major part of the commerce at Tepe Yahyā. Unlike Sumer, which was surrounded by the featureless floodplains of lower Mesopotamia, Elam was a hill kingdom rich in natural resources. Elamite trade supplied the Sumerians with silver, copper, tin and lead, with precious gems and horses, and with commoner materials such as timber, obsidian, alabaster, diorite and soapstone. To find that the soapstone trade reached as far east as Tepe Yahyā adds a new dimension to our knowledge of fourth-millennium commerce.

Third, the discovery of Tepe Yahyā has greatly enlarged the known extent of ancient Elam, which was hazily perceived at best. Susa, the most famous Elamite city, lies not far from such famous Sumerian centers as Ur and Eridu. As for other Elamite cities named in inscriptions (Awan, for example, or Madaktu), their location remains a mystery. To discover a prosperous Elamite city as far east of Mesopotamia as Tepe Yahyā is both a surprise and something of a revelation. It suggests how urban civilization, which arose in lower Mesopotamia, made its way east to the valley of the Indus (in what is now West Pakistan).

The British explorer-archaeologist Sir Aurel Stein was the first to recognize that southeastern Iran is a region with important prehistoric remains. Two sites that Stein probed briefly in the 1930's—Tal-i-Iblis near Kerman and Bampur in Persian Baluchistan—have recently been excavated, the first by Joseph R. Caldwell of the University of Georgia and the second by Beatrice de Cardi of the Council for British Archaeology. Although it is the largest mound in southeastern Iran, Tepe Yahyā remained unknown until the summer of 1967, when our reconnaissance group from the Peabody Museum at Harvard University discovered it during an archaeological survey of the region.

We have now completed three seasons of excavation at Tepe Yahyā in coopera-

LARGE EARTH MOUND, over a third of a mile in circumference, was raised to a

tion with the Iran Archaeological Service and have established a sequence of six principal occupation periods. The site was inhabited almost continuously from the middle of the fifth millennium B.C. until about A.D. 400. Following the end of the Elamite period at Tepe Yahyā, about 2200 B.C., there is a 1,000-year gap in the record that is still unexplained but finds parallels at major sites elsewhere in Iran. Tepe Yahyā remained uninhabited until 1000 B.C., when the site was resettled by people of an Iron Age culture.

Our main work at Tepe Yahyā began in the summer of 1968 with the digging of a series of excavations, each 30 feet square, from the top of the mound to the bottom [see illustration below]. Small test trenches were then made within the series of level squares. During our second and third season the excavations were extended by means of further horizontal exposures on the top of the mound and to the west of the main explorations. In addition we opened a stepped trench 12 feet wide on the opposite face of the mound as a check on the sequences we had already exposed.

The earliest remains of human occupation at Tepe Yahyā, which rest on virgin soil in a number of places, consist of five superimposed levels of mud-brick construction. We have assigned them to a single cultural interval—Period VI—that is shown by carbon-14 analysis to lie in the middle of the fifth millennium B.C. The structures of Period VI seem to be a series of square storage areas that measure about five feet on a side. Most of them have no doorways; they were probably entered through a hole in the roof. The walls are built either of sun-dried mud bricks that were formed by hand or of hand-daubed mud [see top illustration on page 219]. Fragments of reed matting and timber found on the floors of the rooms are traces of fallen roofs.

The tools of Period VI include implements made of bone and flint. Many of the flints are very small; they include little blades that were set in a bone handle to make a sickle. The most common kind of pottery is a coarse, hand-shaped ware; the clay was "tempered" by the addition of chaff. The pots are made in the form of bowls and large storage jars and are decorated with a red wash or painted with red meanders. Toward the end of Period VI a few pieces of finer pottery appear: a buff ware with a smooth, slip-finished surface and a red ware with decorations painted in black.

Human burials, all of infants, were found under the floor in a few of the structures. The limbs of the bodies had been tightly gathered to the trunk before burial, and accompanying the bodies are unbroken coarse-ware bowls. In one room a small human figurine was found face down on the floor, resting on a collection of flint and bone tools. The sculpture is 11 inches long and was carved out of dark green soapstone [see illustration on next page]. The carving clearly delineates a female figure. Its elongated form and the presence of a hole at the top of the head, however, suggest a dual symbol that combines male and female characteristics.

The Neolithic culture of Period VI evidently included the practice of agriculture and animal husbandry. Identifiable animal bones include those of wild gazelles and of cattle, sheep and goats. Camel bones are also present, but it is not clear whether or not they indicate that the animal had been domesticated at this early date. The domesticated plants include a variety of cereal grains. In the Tepe Yahyā area today raising crops involves irrigation; whether or not this was the case in Neolithic times is also unclear. At any rate the Neolithic occupation of the mound continued until about 3800 B.C.

The transition from Period VI to the Early Bronze Age culture that followed

height of 60 feet over a 5,000-year period as new settlements were built on the rubble of earlier ones. Located in southeastern Iran and known locally as Tepe Yahyā, the site was first occupied by a Neolithic community in the middle of the fifth millennium B.C.

NEOLITHIC FIGURINE was found in one of the storerooms in the earliest structure at Tepe Yahyā, associated with tools made of flint and bone. The sculpture was apparently intended to be a dual representation: a female figure imposed on a stylized phallic shape.

occurred without any break in continuity. The structures of Period V contain coarse-ware pottery of the earlier type. The finer, painted pottery becomes commoner and includes some new varieties. One of these, with a surface finish of red slip, has a decorative geometric pattern of repeated chevrons painted in black. We have named this distinctive black-on-red pottery Yahyā ware, and we call the material culture of Period V the Yahyā culture.

The commonest examples of Yahyā ware are beakers. These frequently have a potter's mark on the base, and we have so far identified nine individual marks. Evidence that outside contact and trade formed part of the fabric of Early Bronze Age life at Tepe Yahyā comes from the discovery at Tal-i-Iblis, a site nearly 100 miles closer to Kerman, of almost identical painted pottery bearing similar potter's marks. There is other evidence of regional contacts. Yahyā ware shows a general similarity to the painted pottery at sites elsewhere in southeastern Iran, and a black-on-buff ware at Tepe Yahyā closely resembles pottery from sites well to the west, such as Bakun. Moreover, the Period V levels at Tepe Yahyā abound in imported materials. There are tools made of obsidian, beads made of ivory, carnelian and turquoise, and various objects made of alabaster, marble and mother-of-pearl. One particularly handsome figure is a stylized representation of a ram, seven inches long, carved out of alabaster [see top illustration on page 222]. No local sources are known for any of these materials.

Although the architecture of Period V demonstrates a continuity with the preceding Neolithic period, the individual structures are larger than before. Several of them measure eight by 11½ feet in area and are clearly residential in character. Some rooms include a hearth and chimney. In the early levels the walls are still built of hand-formed mud bricks. Bricks formed in molds appear in the middle of Period V, which carbon-14 analyses show to have been around 3660 B.C. (±140 years).

The bronze implements of Period V, like much of the earliest bronze in the world, were produced not by alloying but by utilizing copper ores that contained "impurities." This was the case in early Sumer, where the ore, imported from Oman on the Arabian peninsula, contained a high natural percentage of nickel. Early bronzesmiths elsewhere smelted copper ores that were naturally rich in arsenic. Chisels, awls, pins and spatulas at Tepe Yahyā are made of such an arsenical bronze.

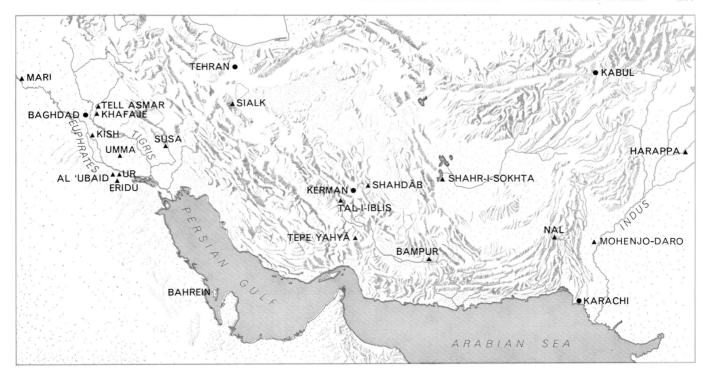

FIRST CITIES arose in the kingdom of Sumer in lower Mesopotamia (*left*). The earliest known forms of writing appeared in Sumer and in nearby Elam at cities such as Susa and Sialk. The discovery of proto-Elamite writing at Tepe Yahyā (*center*), which is 500 miles to the east, suggests that trade between the region and the early cities of Mesopotamia led to the rise of cities in this part of ancient Persia in the fourth millennium B.C. and to the later development of the urban Harappan civilization in the Indus region.

Six artifacts from the site have been analyzed by R. F. Tylecote and H. Mc-Kerrell of the University of Newcastle upon Tyne. They found that the bronze had been produced by smelting, which shows that the metalworkers of Period V were able to obtain the high temperatures needed to smelt copper ores into molten metal. The final shapes were not made by casting, however, but by hot and cold forging, a more primitive technique. One of the articles, a chisel, proved to contain 3.7 percent arsenic, which leads us to believe that the metalworkers consciously selected for smelting ores with a high arsenic content. This finding is further testimony in support of trade at Tepe Yahyā; none of the copper deposits native to the region could have been used to make arsenical bronze.

With the beginning of Period IV, around 3500 B.C., the appearance of writing at Tepe Yahyā allows the city to be identified as a proto-Elamite settlement. Much of the pottery representative of the first two phases of this period, IV-C and IV-B, is typical of the preceding Yahyā culture in both shape and decoration. Although there is plentiful evidence of external contact, the transition to Period IV at Tepe Yahyā, like the one that preceded it, occurred without any break in continuity. There is no need at Tepe Yahyā to conjure up that hackneyed instrument of cultural change: a new people arriving with luggage labeled "Proto-Elamite."

Architecture, however, was considerably transformed. The site ceased to be a residential area and became an administrative one. A large structure we have unearthed at the IV-C level of the mound is carefully oriented so that its walls run north-south and east-west. The walls consist of three courses of mold-formed brick in a new size. The earlier mold-formed bricks had been six by six by 12 inches; the new ones were 9½ by 9½ by 4¾ inches—a third wider and less than half as thick. So far we have identified five of an undetermined number of rooms within the large structure, although we have fully cleared only part of one room. Both the structure and the partially excavated room continue toward the center of the mound; the size of each remains to be determined.

The part of the room that has been cleared measures about 10 by 20 feet. Its contents strongly suggest a commercial function. Among the objects in the room are bowls with beveled rims made of a coarse ware. The vessels have counterparts at numerous sites in Mesopotamia. They are believed to have served as standard measures. Three large storage jars, which proved to be empty, were also found in the room; near them were some 24 "sealings": jar stoppers made of clay and marked with a seal impression. The seals used to mark the sealings were cylindrical; the designs resemble those on cylinder seals found at Susa, the Elamite capital in the Mesopotamian area. The finding creates the possibility that goods from Susa were reaching Tepe Yahyā early in Period IV.

Lying on the floor of the room were 84 blank clay tablets and six others that bore inscriptions. The tablets are all the same shape; they are made of unbaked dark brown clay, are convex in profile and measure 1⅛ by two inches. The six inscribed tablets bear a total of 17 lines of proto-Elamite writing. The inscriptions were impressed in the soft clay with a stylus; they read from right to left along the main axis of the tablet and from top to bottom. When an inscription continues from one side of a tablet to the other, the writer rotated the tablet on its main axis so that the bottom line of the obverse inscription and the top line of the reverse inscription lie opposite each other.

The Tepe Yahyā inscriptions are being deciphered now. Preliminary examination indicates that they are records or receipts dealing with goods. The fact that inscribed and otherwise identical blank tablets were found in the same room is strong evidence that the writing was done on the spot. Therefore the goods they describe must have been either entering or leaving the administrative area.

Until the discovery at Tepe Yahyā the only other proto-Elamite tablets known were from Susa or from Sialk in northwestern Iran. Susa yielded nearly 1,500 such tablets, Sialk only 19. Proto-Elamite writing has been found recently at Shahdāb, a site north of Kerman that is being excavated by the Iran Archaeological Service. The writing there is not on tablets but consists of brief inscriptions, with a maximum of seven signs, incised on pottery.

A second change in architectural style is evident in the single IV-B structure examined so far. It is a building, nine by 24 feet in area, that is oriented without reference to north-south and east-west. It is built of bricks of a still newer size and shape. They are oblong rather than square, and are either 14 or 17 inches long; the other two dimensions remained the same. The structure is subdivided into two main rooms and a few smaller rooms that contain large storage bins built of unbaked clay. Its walls are only one brick thick, and their inside surfaces are covered with plaster.

Storage vessels in one of the main

rooms still held several pounds of grain. The grain was charred, which together with the fact that the matting on the floor and the bricks in the wall were burned indicates that the building was destroyed by fire. Amid the debris on the floors were cylinder seals and, for the first time at Tepe Yahyā, stamp seals as well.

Some bronze tools of the IV-B period have also been discovered. Needles and chisels, unearthed in association with soapstone artifacts, were probably used to work the soapstone. A bronze dagger some seven inches long was found by Tylecote and McKerrell to have been made by forging smelted metal, as were the bronze tools of Period V. Analysis showed that the dagger, unlike the earlier artifacts of arsenical bronze, was an alloy comprising 3 percent tin. Tin is not found in this part of Iran, which means that either the dagger itself, the tin contained in it or an ingot of tin-alloyed bronze must have been imported to Tepe Yahyā.

The proof that writing was known at Tepe Yahyā as early as it was known anywhere is a discovery of major importance to prehistory. Perhaps next in

importance, however, is the abundant evidence suggesting a unique economic role for the city beginning late in the fourth millennium B.C. The IV-B phase at Tepe Yahyā is known from carbon-14 analyses to have extended from near the end of the fourth millennium through the first two centuries of the third millennium. During that time the city was a major supplier of soapstone artifacts.

Objects made of soapstone, ranging from simple beads to ornate bowls and all very much alike in appearance, are found in Bronze Age sites as far apart as Mohenjo-Daro, the famous center of Harappan culture on the Indus, and Mari on the upper Euphrates 1,500 miles away. Mesopotamia, however, was a region poor in natural resources, soapstone included. The Harappans of the Indus also seem to have lacked local supplies of several desired materials. How were the exotic substances to be obtained? Sumerian and Akkadian texts locate the sources of certain luxury imports in terms of place-names that are without meaning today: Dilmun, Maluhha and Magan.

Investigations by Danish workers on the island of Bahrein in the Persian Gulf have essentially confirmed the belief that the island is ancient Dilmun. There is also a degree of agreement that the area or place known as Maluhha lay somewhere in the valley of the Indus. Even before we began our work at Tepe Yahyā it had been suggested that the area known as Magan was somewhere in southeastern Iran. Our excavations have considerably strengthened this hypothesis. A fragmentary Sumerian text reads: "May the land Magan [bring] you mighty copper, the strength of . . . diorite, 'u-' stone, 'shumash' stone." Could either of the untranslated names of stones stand for soapstone? Were Tepe Yahyā and its hinterland a center of the trade? Let us examine the evidence from the site.

More soapstone has been found at Tepe Yahyā than at any other single site in the Middle East. The total is more than 1,000 fragments, unfinished pieces and intact objects; the majority of them belong to Period IV-B. Among the intact pieces are beads, buttons, cylinder seals, figurines and bowls. Unworked blocks of soapstone, vessels that are partially hollowed out and unfinished seals and beads are proof that Tepe Yahyā was a manufacturing site and not merely a transshipment point.

Some of the soapstone bowls are plain, but others are elaborately decorated with carvings. The decorations include geometric and curvilinear designs, animals and human figures. Among the decora-

TWO CYLINDER SEALS from the level at Tepe Yahyā overlying the first proto-Elamite settlement appear at left in these photographs next to the impressions they produce. The seal designs, which show pairs of human figures with supernatural attributes, are generally similar to the designs on seals of Mesopotamian origin but appear to be of local workmanship.

EARLIEST STRUCTURE at Tepe Yahyā is a storage area consisting of small units measuring five feet on a side. Few of the units have doorways; apparently they were entered through a hole in the roof. The walls were built either of sun-dried mud bricks, formed by hand rather than in molds, or simply of hand-daubed mud. White circle (*left*) shows where female figurine was found.

TWO ELAMITE BUILDINGS at Tepe Yahyā left the traces seen in this photograph. The walls of the earlier building (*left*) were built sometime around 3500 B.C. of mold-formed mud bricks 9½ inches on a side. The walls run from north to south and from east to west. The walls of the later structure (*right*) are not oriented in these directions. It was built sometime after 3000 B.C. of oblong mold-formed mud bricks of two lengths. Both structures seem to have been administrative rather than residential. The earlier one contained storage pots and measuring bowls. Near one angle of its walls a pile of 84 unused writing tablets is visible.

tions are examples of every major motif represented on the numerous soapstone bowls unearthed at Bronze Age sites in Mesopotamia and the Indus valley. Moreover, motifs found on pottery unearthed at sites such as Bampur, to the east of Tepe Yahyā, and Umm-an-Nai on the Persian Gulf are repeated on soapstone bowls from IV-B levels.

During our 1970 season we located what was probably one of the sources of Tepe Yahyā soapstone. An outcrop of the rock in the Ashin Mountains some 20 miles from the mound shows evidence of strip-mining in the past. This is unlikely to have been the only source. Soapstone deposits are often associated with deposits of asbestos and chromite. There is a chromite mine only 10 miles from Tepe Yahyā, and we have noted veins of asbestos in stones unearthed during our excavation of the mound. Reconnaissance in the mountains to the north might locate additional soapstone exposures.

Taking into consideration the large quantities of soapstone found at the site, the evidence that many of the soapstone

articles were manufactured locally, the availability of raw material nearby and the presence in both Mesopotamia and Harappan territory of soapstone bowls that repeat motifs found at Tepe Yahyā, it is hard to avoid the conclusion that the city was a major producer of soapstone and a center of trade in the material. Before turning to the broader significance of such commercial activity in this geographically remote area, we shall briefly describe the remaining occupation periods at Tepe Yahyā.

At present there is little to report concerning the final phase of Period IV, which drew to a close about 2200 B.C. It is then that the break occurs in the continuity at Tepe Yahyā. The Iron Age reoccupation of the site, which lasted roughly from 1000 to 500 B.C., comprises Period III. It is evidenced by a series of living floors and by pottery that shows strong parallels to wares and shapes produced during the same period in northwestern Iran. We have not yet uncovered a major structure belonging to Period III; both the nature of the culture and Tepe Yahyā's relations with

its Iron Age neighbors remain unclarified.

Period II at Tepe Yahyā, which consists of more than 200 years of Achaemenian occupation, was a time of large-scale construction. The building material remained mud brick, but we have yet to uncover a complete structure. The appearance of the two large rooms excavated thus far suggests, however, that the site had once more become at least partly residential.

A subsequent 600 years or so of Parthian and Sassanian occupation, representing Period I, is the final period of urban civilization at Tepe Yahyā. We have uncovered suggestions of large-scale architecture, including courtyards and part of a massive mud-brick platform made by laying four courses of brick one on the other. By Sassanian times (early in the third century) the accumulated debris of thousands of years had raised the mound to an imposing height; the structure that has been partly exposed probably was a citadel standing on the summit.

Most of the Sassanian pottery consists

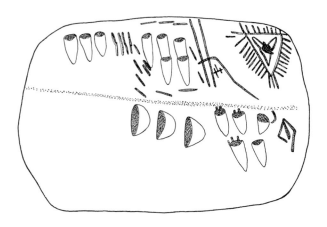

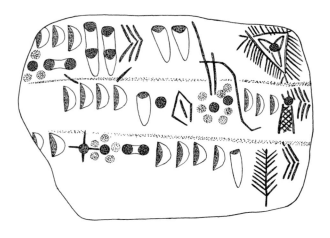

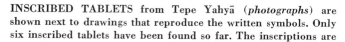

INSCRIBED TABLETS from Tepe Yahyā (*photographs*) are shown next to drawings that reproduce the written symbols. Only six inscribed tablets have been found so far. The inscriptions are in proto-Elamite, written from right to left across the length of the tablet by pressing the blunt or sharp end of a stylus into the soft clay. Similar written tablets have been unearthed at Susa and Sialk.

of coarse, thick-walled storage jars. An abundance of beads and several small glass and pottery bottles, perhaps containers for perfume, suggest a degree of prosperity during Period I. The presence of iron and bronze swords, axes and arrowheads adds a military flavor. A single work of art, a small clay figurine, represents a warrior with a distinctive headdress [see bottom illustration on next page]. Thereafter, from sometime in the fifth century on, Tepe Yahyā was occupied only by occasional squatters or transient nomads. The few scattered surface finds are of early Islamic age; none of the visitors lingered or built anything of substance.

What role did Elamite Tepe Yahyā play in the transmission of the urban tradition from west to east? The city's position suggests that Elamite culture, which is now revealed as being far more widespread than was realized previously, was instrumental in the contact between the first urban civilization in Mesopotamia and the civilization that subsequently arose in the Indus valley. It appears that the Elamites of eastern Persia may have accomplished much more than that. To assess this possibility it is necessary to examine the evidence for direct contact, as distinct from trade through middlemen, between Mesopotamia and the Indus valley.

A small number of artifacts that are possibly or certainly of Harappan origin have been found at sites in Mesopotamia. Because much of the archaeological work there was done as long as a century ago, it is not surprising that both the age and the original location of many of these artifacts can only be roughly estimated. Nonetheless, Mesopotamia has yielded six stamp seals, one cylinder seal and a single clay sealing, all of the Harappan type, that are evidence of some kind of contact between the two civilizations. Certain seals are engraved with Harappan writing. On others the writing is combined with animal figures that are indisputably Harappan in style: a "unicorn," an elephant, a rhinoceros. Evidence of contact, yes. But was the contact direct or indirect?

The single Indus sealing found in Mesopotamia was discovered by the French archaeologist G. Contenau at Umma in southern Iraq during the 1920's. It suggests the arrival there of freight from Harappan territory that had been identified with the sender's personal mark before shipment. The seven seals, however, are evidence of a more equivocal kind. Mesopotamian contact with the Indus evidently did not resemble the later trade

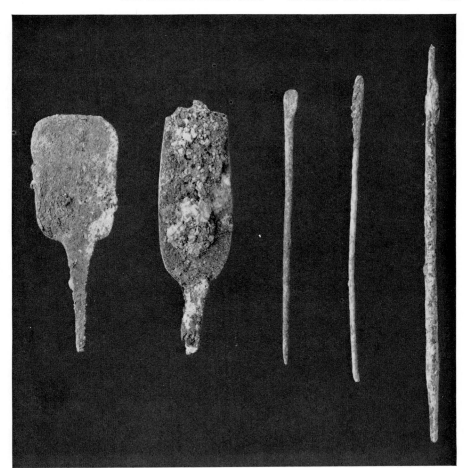

BRONZE OBJECTS contemporaneous with peak of work and trade in soapstone at Tepe Yahyā include two chisels (*left*) and three needle-like forms; the longest object measures 6½ inches. The bronze was not produced by alloying but by utilizing copper that naturally included significant amounts of arsenic. The enriched ores were obtained through trade.

SOAPSTONE BOWLS, many of them elaborately decorated, were among the numerous objects made at Tepe Yahyā and traded eastward and westward during the first half of the third millennium B.C. Fragments of bowls with decorations like the ones on these bowl fragments from Tepe Yahyā have been found from Mesopotamia to the Indus valley.

FIGURINE OF A RAM carved out of alabaster is one of the numerous articles made from imported materials that are found at Tepe Yahyā at the time of its first urban settlement about 3800 B.C. Evidences of trade between the city and outlying areas include, in addition to alabaster, mother-of-pearl from the Persian Gulf, marble, turquoise and carnelian.

FIGURINE OF A WARRIOR modeled in clay is from the final period of occupation at Tepe Yahyā, when a Sassanian military outpost stood on the top of the mound from sometime in the third century B.C. to about A.D. 400. Thereafter only nomads visited the dead city.

between Mesopotamia and, say, the Hittite realm to the west. In that instance Assyrian trading colonies were housed within special quarters of such Hittite strongholds as Kültepe and Hattusha [see "An Assyrian Trading Outpost," by Tahsin Özgüç; SCIENTIFIC AMERICAN, February, 1963]. There is simply no good evidence that Mesopotamians ever visited the Indus to set up residence and trade, or that Harappans did the reverse.

What, then, were the seals of Harappan traders doing in Mesopotamia? What was the function of the three unearthed at Ur, the two at Kish and the two at Tell Asmar? So far there is no persuasive answer to these questions. It is tempting to look on these seals not as credentials but as souvenirs of indirect trade contact; all of them are handsome objects. At the same time another equally puzzling question presents itself. Some objects of Indus origin have been found in Mesopotamia. Why has nothing of any kind from Mesopotamia been found at any Indus site?

Evidence of direct trade contact between the two civilizations thus remains almost entirely absent. Other kinds of trade, however, are equally well known. One of the oldest and most widespread is simple exchange, which can interpose any number of witting or unwitting intermediaries between two principals. Exchange is notable for presenting the archaeologist with difficulties of interpretation; intangibles such as style and function are likely to travel along with the goods.

A system of exchange that involves a single intermediary seems to provide the theoretical model that best approximates the situation at Tepe Yahyā. Such a system is known as "central place" trade; we suggest that Tepe Yahyā was just such a central place in southeastern Persia during Elamite times.

A central place can lie outside the sphere of influence of either principal and at the same time produce goods or control natural resources desired by both. In addition to (or even instead of) exporting its own products, a central place can transship goods produced by either principal. Bahrein—ancient Dilmun—provides a good example of a central place whose prosperity was based on the transshipment of goods bound for Mesopotamia. Whether or not transshipment was important at Tepe Yahyā, the city's basic central-place role in Elamite times was clearly that of a producer manufacturing and exporting articles made of soapstone.

The names of the Mesopotamian sites that contain soapstone bowls identical in shape and decorative motif with those we unearthed at Tepe Yahyā read like an archaeologist's checklist: Adab, Mari, Tell Asmar, Tell Aqrab, Khafaje, Nippur, Telloh, Kish, Al 'Ubaid and Ur. Bowls of Tepe Yahyā style have also been found at Mohenjo-Daro on the Indus and at Kulli-Damb in Pakistani Baluchistan. In addition to bevel-rim bowls of the Uruk type at Tepe Yahyā as evidence of contact with the west, the mound has yielded Nal ware, a kind of Indus painted pottery that predates the rise of Harappan civilization, as evidence of contact with the east.

Tepe Yahyā was not, however, the only central place in eastern Persia. It seems rather to have been one of several that comprised a local loose Elamite federation astride the middle ground between the two civilizations. Shahr-i-Sokhta, a site 250 miles northeast of Tepe Yahyā, appears to have been another central place, exporting local alabaster and transshipping lapis lazuli from Afghanistan. The links between Tepe Yahyā and other possible central places in the region such as Tal-i-Iblis, Shahdāb and Bampur—mainly demonstrated by similarities in pottery—have already been mentioned.

How did this remote Elamite domain, which in the case of Tepe Yahyā predates the appearance of Harappan civilization by at least three centuries, influence developments in the Indus valley? In spite of exciting new evidence that trade networks existed as long ago as the early Neolithic, a strong tendency exists to view trade exclusively as an ex post facto by-product of urbanism. Trade, however, has certainly also been one of the major stimuli leading to urban civilization. This, it seems to us, was exactly the situation in ancient Kerman and Persian Baluchistan.

We suggest that trade between resource-poor Mesopotamia and the population of this distant part of Persia provided the economic base necessary for the urban development of centers such as Tepe Yahyā during the fourth millennium B.C. It can further be suggested that, once an urban Elamite domain was established there, its trade with the region farther to the east provided much of the stimulus that culminated during the third millennium B.C. with the rise of Harappan civilization. Sir Mortimer Wheeler has declared that "the idea of civilization" crossed from Mesopotamia to the Indus. It seems to us that the Elamite central places midway between the two river basins deserve the credit for the crossing.

23

CARBON 14 AND THE PREHISTORY OF EUROPE

COLIN RENFREW
October 1971

Tree-ring measurements have shown that early carbon-14 dates are off by as much as 700 years. As a result the view that cultural advances diffused into Europe from the east is no longer tenable

Our knowledge of European prehistory is currently being revolutionized. The immediate cause of the revolution is a recently discovered discrepancy between the actual ages of many archaeological sites and the ages that have been attributed to them on the basis of carbon-14 analysis. Some sites are as much as seven centuries older than they had been thought to be. This revelation has destroyed the intricate system of interlocking chronologies that provided the foundation for a major edifice of archaeological scholarship: the theory of cultural diffusion.

For more than a century a basic assumption of prehistorians has been that most of the major cultural advances in ancient Europe came about as the result of influences from the great early civilizations of Egypt and Mesopotamia. For example, megalithic tombs in western Europe feature single slabs that weigh several tons. The prevailing view of their origin was that the technical skills and religious motivation needed for their construction had come from the eastern Mediterranean, first reaching Spain and Portugal and then France, Britain and Scandinavia. To take another example, it was generally supposed that the knowledge of copper metallurgy had been transmitted by Mediterranean intermediaries to the Iberian peninsula and to the Balkans from its place of origin in the Near East. The revolution in chronology shows, however, that the megalithic tombs of western Europe and the copper metallurgy of the Balkans are actually older than their supposed Mediterranean prototypes.

When the scholars of a century ago wanted to date the monuments and objects of prehistoric Europe, they had little to help them. C. J. Thomsen, a Danish student of antiquities, had established a "three ages" frame of reference in 1836; structures and objects were roughly classified as Stone Age (at first there was no distinction between Paleolithic and Neolithic), Bronze Age or Iron Age. To assign such things an age in years was a matter of little more than guesswork.

Prehistoric finds are of course by their nature unaccompanied by written records. The only possible recourse was to work from the known to the unknown: to try to move outward toward the unlettered periphery from the historical civilizations of Egypt and Mesopotamia, where written records were available. For example, the historical chronology of Egypt, based on ancient written records, can be extended with considerable confidence back to 1900 B.C. because

MEGALITHIC MONUMENT near Essé in Brittany is typical of the massive stone structures that were raised in France as long ago as the fifth millennium B.C. Called "Fairies' Rock," it is made of 42 large slabs of schist, some weighing more than 40 tons. Because of the great effort that must have been required to raise such monuments, scholars traditionally refused to credit the barbarian cultures of prehistoric Europe with their construction and instead attributed them to influences from civilized eastern Mediterranean.

the records noted astronomical events. The Egyptian "king lists" can then be used, although with far less confidence, to build up a chronology that goes back another 11 centuries to 3000 B.C.

The need to establish a link with Egypt in order to date the prehistoric cultures of Europe went naturally with the widespread assumption that, among prehistoric sites in general, the more sophisticated ones were of Near Eastern origin anyway. In 1887, when the brothers Henri and Louis Siret published the results of their excavations in the cemeteries and settlements of "Copper Age" (late Neolithic) Spain, they reported finding stone tombs, some roofed with handsome corbeled stonework and others of massive megalithic construction. In the tombs there were sometimes human figurines carved in stone, and daggers and simple tools made of copper. That these structures and objects had evolved locally did not seem likely; an origin in the eastern Mediterranean—in Egypt or the Aegean—was claimed for all their more exotic features.

In the first years of this century this method of building up relationships and using contacts with the early civilized world to establish a relative chronology was put on a systematic basis by the Swedish archaeologist Oskar Montelius. In 1903 Montelius published an account of his "typological method," where the development of particular types of tools or weapons within a given area was reconstructed and the sequence was then compared with those of neighboring areas. Adjacent regions could thus be linked in a systematic manner, until a chain of links was built up stretching from the Atlantic across Europe to Egypt and Mesopotamia. It was still assumed that most of the innovations had come from the Near East, and that the farther from the "hearthlands" of civilization they were found, the longer it would have taken them to diffuse there.

Some diffusionist scholars went to extremes. In the 1920's Sir Grafton Smith argued the view that nearly all the innovations in the civilizations around the world could be traced back to Egypt. In this hyperdiffusionist theory the high cultures of the Far East and even the early civilizations of Central America and South America had supposedly stemmed from Egypt. Today very few continue to suppose that the essential ingredients of civilization were disseminated from Egypt to the rest of the world, perhaps in papyrus boats. There were, of course, scholars whose views lay at the other extreme, such as the German ultranationalist Gustaf Kossinna, whose chauvinist writings fell into a predictable pattern. For these men the truly great advances and fundamental discoveries always seem to have been made in the land of their birth. The *Herrenvolk* fantasies of Aryan supremacy in the Nazi era were rooted in Kossinna's theory of Nordic primacy.

Appalled by both of these extremes, the British prehistorian V. Gordon Childe tried to steer a middle course. In *The Dawn of European Civilisation*, published in 1925, Childe rejected Smith's fantasy that the ancient Egyptians were responsible for all the significant advances in prehistoric Europe. Working in the same framework as Montelius but with a detailed and sympathetic consideration of the prehistoric cultures of each region, he built up a picture in terms of what one colleague, Glyn E. Daniel, has termed "modified diffusionism."

Childe saw two main paths whereby a chronological link could be established between Europe and the Near East. First there were the Spanish "Copper Age" finds. Earlier writers had likened the megalithic tombs of Spain, particularly those with corbeled vaults, to the great tholos tombs of Mycenae, which were built around 1500 B.C. Childe saw that the Mycenaean tombs were too recent to have served as a model, and he suggested instead a link between the Spanish tombs and the round tombs of Bronze Age Crete, which had been built

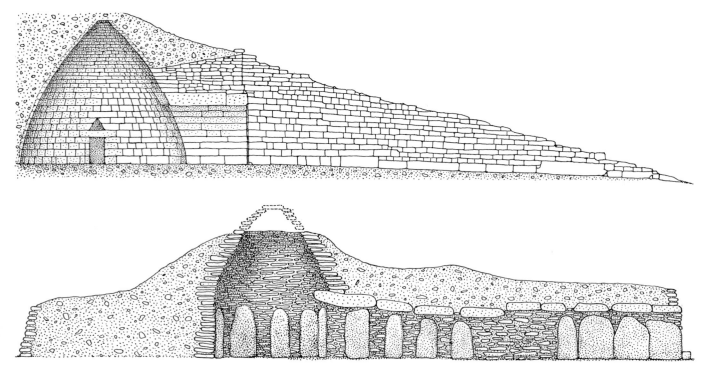

TWO SIMILAR STRUCTURES with corbeled domes are the famous "Treasury of Atreus," a Mycenaean tomb built around 1500 B.C. (*top*), and a megalithic passage grave, Île Longue in Brittany, which is probably some 6,000 years old (*bottom*). Unaware of the true age of the French passage graves, the prehistorian V. Gordon Childe nonetheless dismissed the notion that they were inspired by a civilization as recent as Mycenae. He suggested that they were probably modeled on earlier Minoan tombs built around 2500 B.C.

about 2500 B.C. As subsequent work provided more detail, it was even suggested that colonists from the Aegean had set up settlements in Spain and Portugal. With them they would have brought their knowledge of architecture, their custom of collective burial, their belief in a "mother goddess" and their skill in metallurgy. The fortifications at one or two of these early Iberian sites resemble those at the settlement of Chalandriani on the Aegean island of Syros [*see bottom illustration at right*].

It was on this basis that the earliest megalithic tombs of the Iberian peninsula were assigned an age of around 2500 B.C. The similar French and British tombs, some of which also have stone vaults, were assigned to times a little later in the third millennium.

Similar logic was used in assigning dates to the striking stone temples of Malta. Sculptured slabs in some of the island's temples are handsomely decorated with spirals. These spirals resemble decorations from Crete and Greece of the period from 1800 to 1600 B.C. The Maltese temples were therefore assumed to date from that time or a little later.

Childe's second path for chronological links between western Europe and the Near East was the Danube. Artifacts of the late Neolithic period found at Vinča in Yugoslavia were compared by him to material from the early Bronze Age "cities" at Troy. The Trojan finds can be dated to within a few centuries of 2700 B.C. It was concluded that metallurgy had arisen in the Balkans as a result of contacts with Troy. This view was strengthened by certain similarities between the clay sculptures found at Vinča and various artistic products of the early Bronze Age Aegean.

These twin foundations for the prehistoric chronology of Europe have been accepted by most archaeologists since Childe's day. The appearance of metallurgy and of other striking cultural and artistic abilities in the Balkans, and of monumental architecture on the Iberian peninsula, were explained as the result of contacts with the Aegean. Such skills make their appearance in the Aegean around 2500 B.C., a point in time that is established by finds of datable Egyptian imports in Crete and of somewhat later Cretan exports in datable contexts in Egypt. The chronology of Crete and the southern Aegean is soundly based on the chronology of Egypt and has not been affected by the current revolution.

It should be noted that, as Childe himself pointed out, these conclusions rested on two basic assumptions. First, it

TWO SIMILAR SPIRALS are the decorations on a stele from a Mycenaean shaft grave (*top*) and decorations at temple of Tarxien in Malta (*bottom*). Mycenaean spirals were carved about 1650 B.C. Maltese ones were held on grounds of resemblance to be same age.

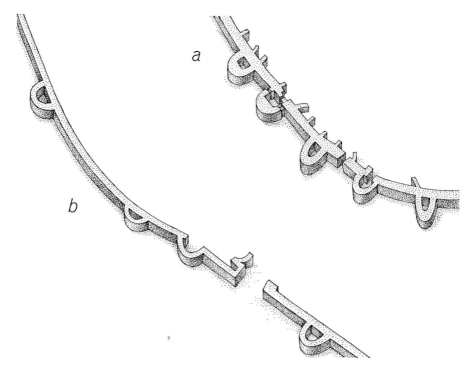

TWO SIMILAR FORTIFICATIONS are the bastioned walls at Chalandriani (*a*), a site on the Aegean island of Syros, and the walls of Los Millares (*b*), a "Copper Age" site near Málaga in Spain. The likeness was once attributed to the work of Aegean colonists in Spain.

was assumed that "parallel" developments in different regions—the appearance of metallurgy or the beginning of monumental tomb architecture—were not entirely independent innovations. Second, it was assumed that if the developments had indeed diffused from one region to another, the ancient civilizations of the Near East were the innovators and the barbarians of Europe were the beneficiaries. Childe realized that these assumptions could be questioned, but in the absence of any independent dating method the only way prehistoric Europe could be dated at all was to relate it to the dated civilizations of the Near East. In practice this meant full acceptance of the assumptions. As Childe remarked of his work, "the sole unifying theme was the irradiation of European barbarism by Oriental civilization."

The discovery of carbon-14 dating in 1949 offered, in principle at least, the possibility of establishing a sound absolute chronology without the need for the assumptions that Childe had had to make. Even without carbon-14 dating, however, some of the arguments of the modified diffusionist school were susceptible to criticism. For example, there are no megalithic tombs in the Aegean, so that some special pleading is needed to argue a Near Eastern origin for those of western Europe. Again, detailed studies in the Aegean area show that the resemblances between the pottery and figurines of the Iberian peninsula and those of Greece, the supposed homeland of the "colonists," are not as close as had been supposed. Nor are the Balkan Neolithic finds really very closely related to the Aegean ones from which they were supposedly derived. There was certainly room for doubt about some of the details in the attractive and coherent picture that diffusionist theory had built up.

Although the introduction of carbon-14 dating did not disrupt the diffusionist picture or the chronology based on it, the dates did produce a few anomalies. A decade ago there were already hints that something was wrong. The carbon-14 method, originated by Willard F. Libby, ingeniously exploits the production of atoms of this heavy isotope of carbon in the upper atmosphere. The carbon-14 atoms are produced by the absorption of neutrons by atoms of nitrogen 14. The neutrons in turn are produced by the impact of cosmic ray particles on various atoms in the atmosphere. Carbon 14 is radioactive, and like all radioactive elements it decays in a regular way. Its half-life was originally estimated by Libby to be some 5,568 years.

The manufacture of the radioactive isotope by cosmic radiation and its diminution through decay sets up a balance so that the proportion of carbon 14 to carbon 12, the much more abundant nonradioactive isotope, is approximately constant. The atoms of the radioactive isotope in the atmosphere, like the atoms of normal carbon, combine with oxygen to form carbon dioxide. This substance is taken up by plants through photosynthesis and by animals feeding on the plants, and in that way all living things come to have the two kinds of carbon in the same proportion in their tissues while they are alive. At death, however, the cycle is broken: the organisms no longer take up any fresh carbon and the proportion of the two isotopes steadily changes as the radioactive isotope decays. Assuming that the proportion of the two isotopes in the atmosphere has always been constant, one can measure how much carbon 14 is left in plant or animal remains (in charcoal, say, or bone) and, knowing the half-life of the radioactive isotope, can calculate how long the decay process has been going on and therefore how old the sample is.

This, put rather simply, is the principle of the dating method. In practice it is complicated by the very small number of carbon-14 atoms in the atmosphere and in living things compared with the number of carbon-12 atoms: approximately one per million million. The proportion is of course further reduced in dead organic material as the rare isotope decays, making accurate measurement a delicate task. Nonetheless, samples from archaeological sites began to yield coherent and consistent dates soon after 1949. In general the carbon-14 dates in Europe tallied fairly well with those built up by the "typological method"

CONVENTIONAL CARBON-14 DATES IN CARBON-14 YEARS

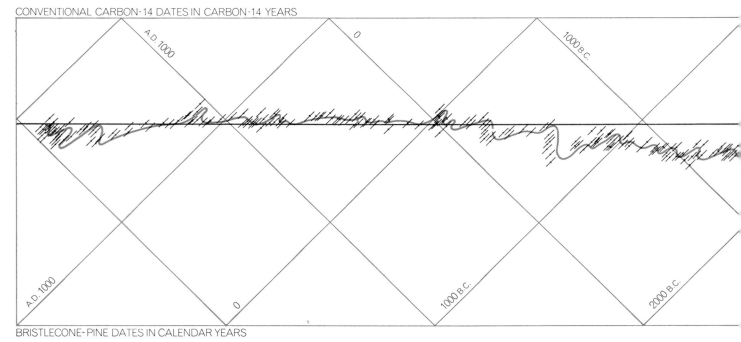

BRISTLECONE-PINE DATES IN CALENDAR YEARS

BRISTLECONE-PINE CALIBRATION worked out by Hans E. Suess of the University of California at San Diego makes it possible to correct carbon-14 dates. The dates running across the top and the lines on which they rest refer to carbon-14 dates in carbon-14 years; the dates running across the bottom and the lines on which they rest refer to bristlecone-pine dates in calendar years. The col-

back to about 2500 B.C. The great surprise was how early the Neolithic period, defined by the appearance of farming villages, began everywhere. Instead of yielding the expected dates of around 4000 or 4500 B.C., the earliest villages in the Near East proved to date back to as early as 8000 B.C.

These dates for the early Neolithic period were most important. Indeed, their impact on prehistoric archaeology can be regarded as the first carbon-14 revolution. The sharp increases in age did not, however, actually disrupt the diffusionist picture. Farming developments in the Near East remained in general earlier than those in Europe. The pattern did not change nor did the Near East lose its primacy; it was just that all the dates were earlier than had been expected. Everyone had always been aware that, for the period before 3000 B.C., which is when the Egyptian chronology begins, all dates were guesswork. What the first carbon-14 dates demonstrated was that the guesses had not been bold enough.

Thus the first carbon-14 revolution did not seriously challenge the relationships that had previously been established in terms of relative chronology between the different areas of Europe and the Near East. Even with respect to the crucial period after 3000 B.C., for which the Egyptian historical chronology provided a framework of absolute rather than relative dating, the new dates seemed to harmonize fairly well with the traditional ones. Just three troublesome problems hinted that all was not yet well. First, whereas many of the early carbon-14 dates for the megalithic tombs in western Europe fell around 2500 B.C., which fitted in with Childe's traditional chronology, the dates in France were somewhat earlier. In Brittany, for example, the dates of several corbeled tombs were earlier than 3000 B.C. This did not agree with the established picture of megalithic tombs diffusing from Spain to France sometime after 2500 B.C. Most scholars simply assumed that the French laboratories producing these dates were no better than they ought to be, and that the anomaly would probably disappear when more dates were available.

Second, the dates for the Balkan Neolithic were far too early. Sites related to the Vinča culture gave carbon-14 readings as early as 4000 B.C. This implied that not only copper metallurgy but also the attractive little sculptures of the Balkans were more than a millennium older than their supposed Aegean prototypes. Clearly something was wrong. Some archaeologists, led by Vladimir Milojčić, argued that the entire carbon-14 method was in error. Others felt that some special factor was making the Balkan dates too early, since the dates in other regions, with the exception of Brittany, seemed to be in harmony with the historical dates for the third millennium B.C.

Third, the dates for Egypt were too late. In retrospect this now seems highly significant. Egyptian objects historically dated to the period between 3000 and 2000 B.C. consistently yielded carbon-14 dates that placed them several centuries later. With the early inaccuracies and uncertainties of the carbon-14 method these divergences could at first be dismissed as random errors, but as more dates accumulated such an excuse was no longer possible. The archaeologists kept on using their historical dates and did not bother too much about the problems raised by the new method.

The physicists were more concerned, but they supposed, to use Libby's words, "that the Egyptian historical dates beyond 4000 years ago may be somewhat too old, perhaps five centuries too old at 5000 years ago, with decrease in error to [zero] at 4000 years ago.... It is noteworthy that the earliest astronomical fix is at 4000 years ago, that all older dates have errors and that these errors are more or less cumulative with time before 4000 years ago." For once, however, the archaeologists were right. The discrepancy was to be set at the door of the physicist rather than the Egyptologist. The consequences were dramatic.

Remote as it may seem from European archaeology, it was the venerable pine trees in the White Mountains of

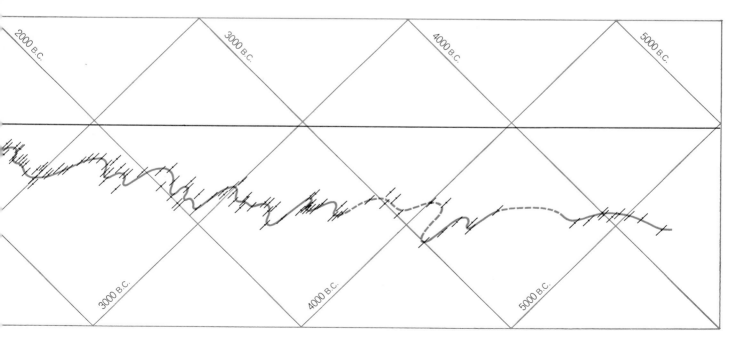

ored curve, which follows many individual measurements, shows how the carbon-14 dates go off with time. To calibrate a carbon-14 date, say 2000 B.C., one follows the line for that date until it meets the colored curve. At that point a diagonal is drawn parallel to the bristlecone-pine lines and the date is read off on the bristlecone-pine scale. The corrected date would be about 2500 B.C.

YEARS B.C.	EGYPT	AEGEAN	BALKANS	ITALY	MALTA
1500	DYNASTY XVIII	MYCENAE			TARXIEN CEMETERY
		MIDDLE BRONZE AGE	FÜZESABONY	POLADA	
2000		EARLY BRONZE AGE	NAGYREV		
2500	PYRAMIDS	LERNA III			TARXIEN
3000	DYNASTY I	TROY I		REMEDELLO	
		EARLY HELLADIC I			GGANTIJA
3500	GERZEAN	FINAL NEOLITHIC	LATE GUMELNITSA	LAGOZZA	ZEBBUG
4000		LATE NEOLITHIC		CHIOZZA	
4500	AMRATIAN		LATE VINČA		RED SKORBA
			EARLY VINČA		

REVISED CHRONOLOGY, taking the Suess calibration into account, destroys the basis for the diffusionist theory of European prehistory. Colored area at left marks the portion of Egyptian and Aegean chronology that is related to historical records. Colored

California that brought about the revolution in Old World prehistory. These trees have provided a reliable check of the carbon-14 method and have produced significant modifications. By 1960 one major assumption of the method was already coming into question. This was that the rate of production of carbon 14 in the atmosphere, and hence its proportion in all living things, had been constant over the past 40,000 years. The assumption was first really checked when Eric H. Willis, Henrik Tauber and Karl Otto Münnich analyzed samples of wood from the stump of a giant sequoia that could be dated exactly by counting its annual growth rings. Although the carbon-14 dates and the tree-ring dates agreed to within 100 years all the way back to A.D. 650, some minor but real fluctuations were observed. This suggested that there had been definite small changes in the rate of carbon-14 production in the past.

It was obviously desirable to check back to even earlier periods. Fortunately the fantastically long life of the California bristlecone pine (*Pinus aristata*) was known to the late Edmund Schulman of the Laboratory of Tree-Ring Research at the University of Arizona. Bristlecone pines as old as 4,600 years had been authenticated. Since Schulman's death the study of the trees has been energetically pursued by Charles Wesley Ferguson of the same laboratory. With ring sequences from many bristlecones, Ferguson has succeeded in building up a continuous absolute chronology

reaching back nearly 8,200 years. The compilation of such a chronology, with due provision for multiple growth rings and missing rings, is a formidable task. Ferguson and his colleagues have developed computer programs for the comparison and matching of the ring sequence of different trees. This admirably systematic work has been the indispensable foundation of the second carbon-14 revolution.

Ferguson supplied wood samples whose absolute age had been determined by ring-counting to three independent carbon-14 laboratories: one at the University of Arizona, one at the University of Pennsylvania and one at the University of California at San Diego. The carbon-14 determinations, which in general agree fairly well with one another, reveal major discrepancies between previously accepted carbon-14 dates and actual dates. At San Diego, Hans E. Suess has analyzed more than 300 such samples and has built up an impressively clear and coherent picture of these discrepancies.

The divergence between the carbon-14 and tree-ring dates is not serious after 1500 B.C. Before that time the difference becomes progressively larger and amounts to as much as 700 years by 2500 B.C. The carbon-14 dates are all too young, but Suess's analysis can be used to correct them [see illustration on preceding two pages].

One problem that has emerged is that, in addition to a large first-order divergence, Suess's calibration curve shows

smaller second-order fluctuations or "kinks." Sometimes the rate of carbon-14 production has fluctuated so rapidly that samples of different ages show an identical concentration of carbon 14 in spite of the fact that the older sample allowed more time for radioactive decay. This means that a given carbon-14 date can very well correspond to several different calendar dates.

The reasons for the fluctuations are not yet known with certainty, but the Czechoslovakian geophysicist V. Bucha has shown that there is a striking correlation between the divergence in dates and past changes in the strength of the earth's magnetic field. The first-order variation is probably due to the fact that as the strength of the earth's field changed it deflected more or fewer cosmic rays before they could enter the atmosphere. There are strong indications that the second-order fluctuations are correlated with the level of solar activity. Both the low-energy particles of the "solar wind" and the high-energy particles that are the solar component of the cosmic radiation may affect the cosmic ray flux in the vicinity of the earth. Climatic changes may also have influenced the concentration of carbon 14 in the atmosphere.

To the archaeologist, however, the reliability of the tree-ring calibration is more important than its physical basis. Libby's principle of simultaneity, which states that the atmospheric level of carbon 14 at a given time is uniform all

IBERIA	FRANCE	BRITISH ISLES	NORTH EUROPE
EL ARGAR		MIDDLE BRONZE AGE	BRONZE HORIZON III
	EARLY BRONZE AGE	STONEHENGE III	HORIZON II
			HORIZON I
BEAKER			
	BEAKER		
	SEINE-OISE-MARNE CULTURE	STONEHENGE I	MIDDLE NEOLITHIC (PASSAGE GRAVES)
LOS MILLARES			
		NEW GRANGE	
ALMERIAN	LATE PASSAGE GRAVE	NEOLITHIC	TRICHTERBECKER "A"
EARLY ALMERIAN			
			ERTEBØLLE
	EARLY CHASSEY	EARLY NEOLITHIC	

area at right indicates periods when megalithic monuments were built in the European areas named. Lines and names in color show "connections" now proved to be impossible.

over the world, has been in large measure substantiated. Tests of nuclear weapons have shown that atmospheric mixing is rapid and that irregularities in composition are smoothed out after a few years. The California calibration should therefore hold for Europe. There is no need to assume that tree growth or tree rings are similar on the two continents, only that the atmospheric level of carbon 14 is the same at a given time.

There remains the question of whether some special factor in the bristlecone pine itself might be causing the discrepancies. For example, the diffusion of recent sap across the old tree rings and its retention in them might affect the reading if the sap were not removed by laboratory cleaning procedures. Studies are now in progress to determine if this is a significant factor; present indications are that it is not. Even if it is, it would be difficult to see why the discrepancy between carbon-14 dates and calendar dates should be large only before 1500 B.C.

The general opinion, as reflected in the discussions at the Twelfth Nobel Symposium at Uppsala in 1969, is that the discrepancy is real. Suess's calibration curve is the best now available, although corrections and modifications can be expected. It is particularly satisfying that when the carbon-14 dates for Egypt are calibrated, they agree far better with the Egyptian historical calendar. Further work is now in progress at the University of California at Los Angeles and at the British Museum on

Egyptian samples specially collected for the project, so that a further check of the extent to which the calibrated carbon-14 dates and the historical chronology are in harmony will soon be available.

The revision of carbon-14 dates for prehistoric Europe has a disastrous effect on the traditional diffusionist chronology. The significant point is not so much that the European dates in the third millennium are all several centuries earlier than was supposed but that the dates for Egypt do not change. Prehistorians have always used the historical dates for Egypt because they seemed more accurate than the carbon-14 dates. They have been proved correct; the calibrated carbon-14 dates for Egypt agree far better with the historical chronology than the uncalibrated ones did. Hence the Egyptian historical calendar, and with it the conventional Egyptian chronology, remains unchanged. The same is true for the Near East in general and for Crete and the southern Aegean. The carbon-14 dates for the Aegean formerly seemed too young; they too agree better after calibration.

For the rest of Europe this is not true. Over the past decade prehistorians in Europe have increasingly been using carbon-14 dates to build up a chronology of the third millennium B.C. Except in Brittany and the Balkans, this chronology had seemed to work fairly well. The dates had still allowed the megalithic tombs of Spain to have been built around 2500 B.C. There was no direct contradiction between the diffusionist

picture and the uncalibrated carbon-14 chronology.

All that is now changed. A carbon-14 date of about 2350 B.C. for the walls and tombs at Los Millares in Spain must now be set around 2900 B.C. This makes the structures older than their supposed prototypes in the Aegean. Whereas the carbon-14 inconsistency in western Europe was formerly limited to Brittany, it now applies to the entire area. In almost every region where megalithic tombs are found the calibrated carbon-14 dates substantially predate 2500 B.C. The view of megalithic culture as an import from the Near East no longer works.

The same thing seems to be happening in Malta, although there are still too few carbon-14 dates to be certain. A date of 1930 B.C. for the period *after* the temples now becomes about 2200 B.C. Clearly the spirals in the temples cannot be the result of Aegean influence around 1800 B.C.

The Balkans are affected too. The figurines of the Vinča culture now have dates earlier than 4500 B.C.; to associate them with the Aegean of the third millennium becomes ludicrous. The revision of dates also shows that in the Balkans there was a flourishing tradition of copper metallurgy, including such useful artifacts as tools with shaft holes, before metal production was well under way in the Aegean.

Similar changes are seen all over Europe. Stonehenge was until recently considered by many to be the work of skilled craftsmen or architects who had come to Britain from Mycenaean Greece around 1500 B.C. The monument is now seen to be several centuries older, and Mycenaean influence is clearly out of the question.

All is not confusion, however. As we have seen, the chronology of Egypt, the Near East, Crete and the Aegean is not materially changed in the third millennium B.C. Although the actual dates are altered in the rest of Europe, when we compare areas dated solely by carbon 14 the relationships between them are not changed. The great hiatus comes when we compare areas that have calibrated carbon-14 dates with areas that are dated by historical means. The hiatus may be likened to a geological fault; the chronological "fault line" extends across the Mediterranean and southern Europe.

On each side of the fault line the relationships and the successions of cultures remain unaltered. The two sides have shifted, however, *en bloc* in relation to each other, as the geological stra-

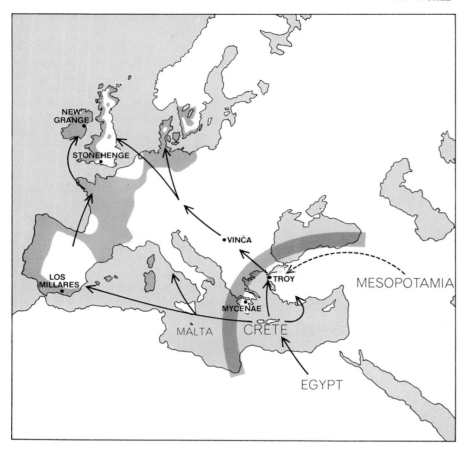

CHRONOLOGICAL "FAULT LINE" (*curved bar*) divides all Europe except the Aegean from the Near East. Arrows above the fault line are supposed chronological links now discredited. Areas of Europe that contain megalithic chamber tombs are in color at left.

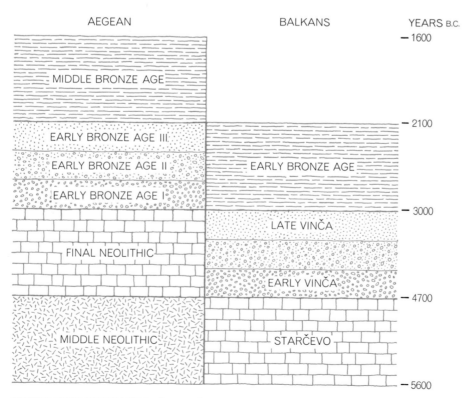

FAULT-LINE SLIPPAGE is shown schematically as it affects the chronological connection between the barbarian Balkans and the civilized Aegean. Strata with the same markings were once thought to be contemporary. Estimated Balkan dates, however, were too recent.

ta on two sides of a fault might. As a result much of what Montelius and Childe wrote about relationships and relative chronologies within continental Europe still stands. It is only the absolute chronology in calendar years and certain key links—between Spain and the Aegean and between the Balkans and the Aegean—that are ruptured. The dates for Europe as a whole have moved back in time, and the old diffusionist view of links connecting Europe and the Near East is no longer tenable.

The really important effect of tree-ring calibration is not that it changes the dates for prehistoric Europe by a few centuries. What matters is that it transforms our picture of what happened in prehistoric Europe and of how Europe developed. No longer can the essential theme of European prehistory be Childe's "irradiation of European barbarism by Oriental civilization." Indeed, the very early dates for some of the achievements of the prehistoric inhabitants of Europe make the term barbarism quite inappropriate.

Now it is clear that megalithic chamber tombs were being built in Brittany earlier than 4000 B.C., a millennium before monumental funerary architecture first appears in the eastern Mediterranean and 1,500 years before the raising of the pyramids. The origins of these European burial customs and monuments have to be sought not in the Near East but in Europe itself. The temples of Malta must likewise be viewed as remarkable, indeed unique, local creations: the oldest freestanding stone monuments in the world.

Even metallurgy may have been independently invented in the Balkans, and possibly in Spain as well. Certainly it was flourishing in the Balkans earlier than it was in Greece. The possibility remains, however, that the art of metalworking was learned from the Near East, where it was known even earlier than in the Balkans.

The central moral is inescapable. In the past we have completely undervalued the originality and the creativity of the inhabitants of prehistoric Europe. It was a mistake, as we now can see, always to seek in the Near East an explanation for the changes taking place in Europe. Diffusion has been overplayed. Of course, contact between prehistoric cultures often allowed ideas and innovations to pass between them. Furthermore, evidence might easily emerge for occasional contacts between western or southern Europe and the Near East in very early times. This, however, is not an adequate model for the explanation of culture change. Nor is there any case for turning the tables on the old diffusionists by suggesting that the early monuments and innovations in Europe inspired the pyramids of Egypt or other achievements in the Near East. That would merely be to reverse the arrows on the diffusionist map, and to miss the real lesson of the new dating.

The initial impact of the carbon-14 revolution will be to lead archaeologists to revise their dates for prehistoric Europe. This is the basic factual contribution that the tree-ring calibration has to make, although inevitably it will be some years before we can develop a definitive and reliable calibrated chronology for the entire area. The more profound impact, however, will be on the kind of explanation that prehistorians will accept in elucidating cultural change. A greater reluctance to swallow "influences" or "contacts" as sufficient explanations in themselves, without a much more detailed analysis of the actual mechanisms involved, is to be expected. This is in keeping with much current archaeological thinking. Today social and economic processes are increasingly seen as more important subjects for study than the similarities among artifacts.

When the textbooks are rewritten, as they will have to be, it is not only the European dates that will be altered. A shift in the basic nature of archaeological reasoning is necessary. Indeed, it is already taking place in Europe and in other parts of the world. This is the key change that tree-ring calibration, however uncertain some of its details remain, has helped to bring about.

ANCIENT PINE, its trunk scarred and its branches twisted, is one of the many trees of the bristlecone species (*Pinus aristata*) that grow in the White Mountains of California. An analysis of this tree's growth rings proves it to be more than 4,500 years old. Using this and other specimens, Charles Wesley Ferguson and his co-workers at the University of Arizona have built up a continuous tree-ring chronology with a span of more than 8,000 years.

The Rise of Civilization
in the New World

THE RISE OF
CIVILIZATION IN
THE NEW WORLD

In the first prehistory section we addressed ourselves to Old World hunters and gatherers and learned that late Paleolithic hunters migrated as far as Australia in quest of game. Specialized hunters of the Pleistocene made their way to the New World as well, and debate continues as to whether these specialized hunters were the first human inhabitants of the New World.

In "Elephant-hunting in North America," C. Vance Haynes argues that the earliest firm evidence of occupation of the New World occurs about 12,000 years ago (10,000 B.C.), at which time specialized hunters of the giant Pleistocene elephants, using fluted spear-points of a type found first at Clovis, New Mexico and probably travelling in bands, pursued their quarry from Alaska, in an ice-free corridor through what is now Canada, down into what are now the United States and Mexico. By making demographic calculations and estimating the production rate of Clovis points, Haynes suggests that these bands of hunters grew and segmented rapidly and that if the hunters had no competitors they easily could have travelled from their northernmost site to their southernmost site, in Mexico—filling in the North American continent from west to east—in 500 years, perhaps killing enough of the *Mammuthus* elephants to lead toward the extinction of the genus.

Richard S. MacNeish's first contribution to this volume, "Early Man in the Andes," suggests that hunters were established in the highlands of South America at least 20,000 years ago (18,000 B.C.), or 8000 years before the first Clovis point elephant hunters made their way to Mexico. MacNeish also makes the case for human occupations in North America that antedated the Clovis hunters, and suggests that these earlier tool making traditions might have had their origins in the Old World. Inasmuch as the majority of the archaeological sites in North America alleged to be older than 10,000 B.C. are open to serious doubt about their antiquity for reasons Haynes outlined in the preceding essay as well as for others, MacNeish's analyses of tool design will certainly help establish credible antiquity for otherwise dubious sites. MacNeish maintains that the most significant implications of his excavations at Ayachuco are that three of the four oldest cultural traditions in the New World can be derived from specific Old World predecessors. But even if, in the next decade, archaeologists come to agree that human populations entered the New World from Asia more than 25,000 years ago, the distance between Asia and South America, the technologic state of late Paleolithic man, who travelled on foot, and the obstacles he encountered en route, all make it seem improbable that direct links to the 20,000-year-old tool complexes of the Andes would be found at Asian sites.

MacNeish's second contribution to this volume, "The Origins of New World Civilization," lays out the masterful sleuth-work conducted by himself and Paul Mangelsdorf in Tamaulipas and Tehuacán to discover the major loci of crop domestication in Mexico, and the relationship of this agricultural revolution to the rise of civilization in the New World. We learn that though crops were domesticated in the New World almost as early as crops were domesticated in the Old World, the major New World crops—corn, beans, and squash—are not the same plants that were domesticated in the Old World. Although Old World cultures domesticated more animals and fewer plants, MacNeish shows how inhabitants of Tehuacán Valley domesticated a wide variety of plants and few animals, only, however, after hunters and gatherers had occupied that valley for millennia. After they became predominantly gatherers of food plants about 6700 B.C., several centuries passed before these inhabitants domesticated just two plants, squashes and avocados. And after corn, amaranth, beans, and chili peppers were domesticated as crops around 5000 B.C., the valley dwellers continued to rely for much of their subsistence on hunting and gathering. It was not until 3400 B.C. that sedentary village life began to develop; during the next 3000 years progress toward city life and civilization was rapid.

Rene Millon's essay, "Teotihuacán," describes Mexico's magnificent Teotihuacanos city, building of which was begun in the first century B.C. in accordance with a precise grid plan, in the style of earlier ceremonial center prototypes. Teotihuacán lasted until about 750 A.D., at which time perhaps through a combination of environmental and social factors it deteriorated and its central district was looted and burned. Millon speculates about the imposing temples and the role of the priesthood in integrating and directing the life of the city, in which coordinated urban renewal programs were undertaken that reduced Teotihuacán's size as the population density increased. At one time Teotihuacán housed between 50,000 and 100,000 inhabitants, serving clearly as a major political, religious, economic, and social center in the Valley of Mexico. Other cities later supplanted Teotihuacán's influence in the valley, one of the most beautiful and spectacular of them being nearby Tenochtitlan, the city of the Aztecs described vividly by the Spanish conquerors. But before its decline Teotihuacán, larger in 500 A.D. than imperial Rome, was the center of influence extending to the Mayan highlands and lowlands of what is now Guatemala.

24

ELEPHANT-HUNTING IN NORTH AMERICA

C. VANCE HAYNES, JR.
June 1966

Bones of elephants that vanished from the continent 10,000 years ago are found together with the projectile points early men used to kill them. Indeed, the hunters may have caused the elephants' extinction

Elephant-hunting today is a specialized activity confined to a handful of professionals in parts of Africa and Asia; 11,000 years or so ago it provided a living for one of the earliest groups of humans to inhabit the New World. At that time hunting bands whose craftsmen made a particular kind of stone projectile point by the thousands ranged across North America from the east coast to the west coast, as far north as Alaska and as far south as central Mexico. Two generations ago such a statement would have been hard to support. Since 1932, however, the excavation of no fewer than six stratified ancient sites of mammoth-hunting activity in the western U.S. and the discovery of scores of significant, if less firmly documented, sites elsewhere in North America have proved its validity beyond the possibility of challenge. It is the purpose of this article to present what we know of the lives of these mammoth-hunters and to suggest when they arrived in the New World.

The first evidence that man had been present in the New World much before 2000 B.C. touches only indirectly on the history of the mammoth-hunters. This was a discovery made near Folsom, N.M., by an expedition from the Denver Museum of Natural History in 1926. Careful excavation that year and during the next two seasons uncovered 19 flint projectile points of unusual shape and workmanship lying 10 feet below the surface among the bones of 23 bison. The bison were of a species that paleontologists had thought had been extinct for at least 10,000 years. The Denver Museum excavation at Folsom thus made it plain that as long ago as 8000 B.C. hunters armed with a distinctive type of flint point had inhabited what is now the western U.S. The association of the projectile points with the bison bones made it almost certain that the bison were the hunters' prey; any doubts on this score were settled when Frank H. H. Roberts of the Smithsonian Institution, digging at the Lindenmeyer site in Colorado, found a Folsom point firmly lodged in a bison vertebra.

In 1932 a cloudburst near Dent, Colo., hastened the erosion of a gully near the South Platte River and exposed a large concentration of mammoth bones. Investigators from the Denver Museum went to work at the site; the bones proved to represent 11 immature female mammoths and one adult male. Along with the animal remains they found three flint projectile points and a number of boulders that were evidently not native to the surrounding accumulation of silt. In the 1930's the carbon-14 technique of dating had not yet been invented, but the geologists in the party estimated that the Dent site was at least as old as the Folsom site and perhaps older. Certainly the projectile points found at Dent, although they bore a general resemblance to those found at Folsom, were cruder in work-

AMERICAN ELEPHANTS were all of the genus *Mammuthus*. They included the woolly mammoth, which also ranged the Old World, and the imperial, confined to North America. This skeleton of one imperial variety, the Columbian, is 12 feet at the shoulder.

manship. In any case, the excavation at Dent made it evident that early hunters in western North America had preyed not only on extinct bison but also on the mammoth.

Beginning in 1934 John L. Cotter of the Academy of Natural Sciences in Philadelphia excavated a site known as Blackwater Draw near Clovis, N.M., which proved to contain the answer to the relative antiquity of the Folsom and Dent finds. In the Clovis sediments projectile points like those from Folsom were found in the upper strata associated with bison bones. Below these strata, associated with the remains of two mammoths, were four of the cruder, Dent-style projectile points and several flint tools of a kind that could have been used for butchering. Also found at Clovis was an entirely new kind of artifact—a projectile point fashioned out of bone. At the completion of nearly two decades of work at the site by investigators from the Philadelphia Academy and other institutions, students of New World prehistory were generally agreed that two separate groups of hunters had once inhabited western North America. The earlier group, using flint projectile points of the type found in the lower Clovis strata, had been primarily mammoth-hunters; the later group, using Folsom points, had been primarily bison-hunters.

The most obvious characteristic that Clovis and Folsom points have in common is that they are "fluted." After the flint-knapper had roughed out the point's general shape he beveled its base; then, with a deft blow against the beveled base, he detached a long flake, leaving a channel that extended a third or more of the point's length [see illustration at right.] The fluting, on one or both sides of the point, gave the point a hollow-ground appearance. It has been suggested that the flute channels facilitated the bleeding of the prey, as do the blood-gutters of a modern hunting knife. A more plausible explanation is that the fluting made the point easier to fit into the split end of a wooden shaft. The assumption that the points were hafted in this manner is strengthened by the fact that their edges are generally dulled or ground smooth for a distance from the base about equal to the length of the flute channel. If a sinew lashing was used to mount the point in a split shaft, it would be mandatory to have dull edges where the lashing was wrapped; otherwise the flint would cut through the taut sinew.

To judge from the ease with which

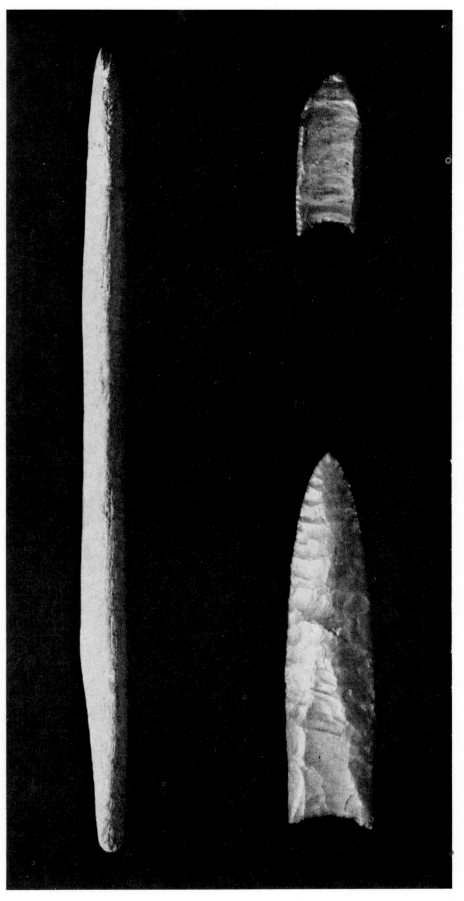

PROJECTILE POINTS used by early hunting groups in North America include one of bone (*left*) and one of flint (*lower right*) found near Clovis, N.M., in the mid-1930's. These artifacts were used to kill mammoths. The smaller flint point (*upper right*) was made by a later group that hunted bison. The first of these were found near Folsom, N.M., in 1926.

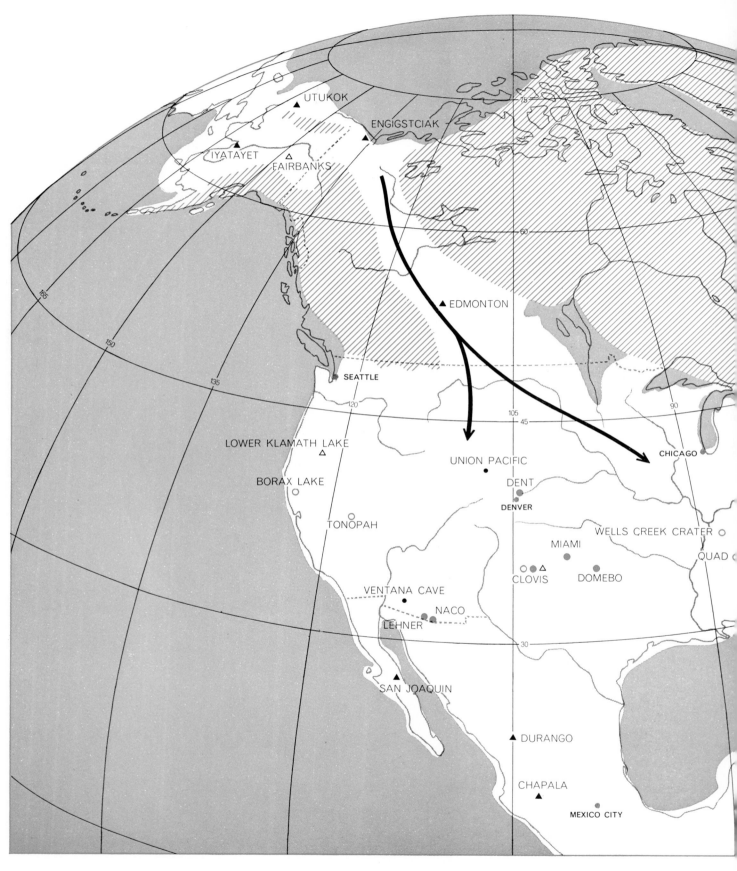

CLOVIS KILL SITE   ○   CAMP SITE   △   ISOLATED FINDS OF CYLINDRICAL BONE POINTS

ICE-FREE CORRIDOR in western Canada may have opened some 12,000 years ago. The author suggests that the mammoth-hunters who made both the characteristically fluted flint projectile points and the needle-like bone ones left the Bering Strait area earlier than that and reached the unglaciated part of North America some 11,500 years ago. Symbols by the names distinguish among campsites, kill

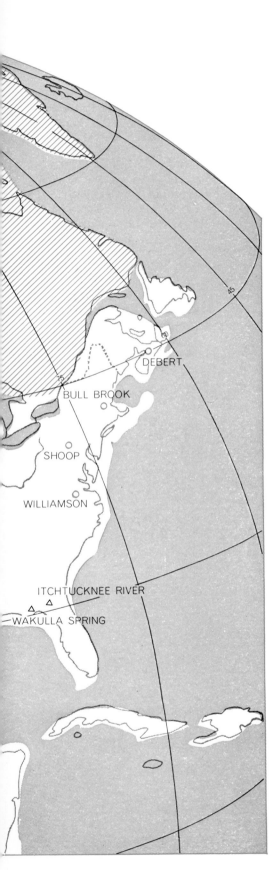

sites and significant isolated finds. In the northeast Debert and Bull Brook probably include non-Clovis Paleo-Indian material.

a few self-taught flint-knappers today can turn out a classic Clovis or Folsom point in a matter of minutes by striking raw flint with a "baton" of deer antler or hardwood, it is reasonable to believe that the early hunters also used this technique of baton percussion, at least in roughing out their points. There are even indications that such roughed-out blanks were produced at various flint quarries and then carried back to campsites for the finishing touches. Detaching the channel flake or flakes was obviously the crucial step; once successfully fluted, the point was finished by sharpening the tip, trimming the edges either by rasping or by pressure-flaking, and dulling the lower edges where the lashing would be wrapped around. If the tip of a point broke off, the point might be sharpened again [see top illustration on page 243].

Although the points from any one site exhibit a considerable range in size and appearance, it is usually not difficult to distinguish between Folsom and Clovis points. The fluting of a Folsom point is typically a single channel that extends all the way to the tip of the point or nearly so, and the edges of the point are delicately chipped. A Clovis point is typically larger, with coarsely chipped edges; usually more than one flake has been removed to produce the flute channel and these have "broken out" less than halfway to the tip in what is called a "hinge" fracture. In some cases the hinge fracture broke inward rather than outward, snapping the unfinished point in half. If early man used profane language, such an incident must surely have inspired an epithet or two.

Carbon-14 dating has now established the antiquity of four of the six sites in which mammoth bones are associated with Clovis points. Two of the sites are Clovis itself and Dent; the others are Domebo Canyon in Oklahoma, where a single mammoth was found together with three Clovis points and an assembly of flint butchering tools, and Lehner Ranch Arroyo in New Mexico, where among the bones of nine immature mammoths Emil Haury of the Arizona State Museum uncovered 13 Clovis points and eight butchering tools in 1955 and 1956. It was charcoal from a campfire hearth at the Lehner site that in 1959 yielded the first Clovis carbon-14 dates to be determined; they averaged 11,260 ± 360 years before the present, or a little earlier than 9000 B.C. The carbon-14 dates from Dent, Clovis and Domebo fall in this same time in-

terval, as do the dates of two other early sites in the western U.S. that may or may not have Clovis connections. These are Union Pacific, Wyo., where mammoth bones and flint tools are found, and Ventana Cave in Arizona, which has no mammoth remains. The other two stratified Clovis sites that contain mammoth bones—Miami in the Texas Panhandle and Naco, Ariz., where Haury and his associates uncovered the bones of a single mammoth in 1951 with five out of eight Clovis points concentrated in its chest area—have not been dated by the carbon-14 method.

These and other carbon-14 determinations, together with geological analyses, have established a general framework for North American prehistory in the Rocky Mountains, the Great Plains and the Southwest. The earliest period ends about 10,000 B.C.; its fossil fauna include the mammoth and extinct species of camel, horse and bison, but there are no artifacts associated with their remains that positively indicate man's presence. There follows a gap of about 500 years for which information is lacking. In the next period, between 9500 and 9000 B.C., the early fauna is still present and Clovis projectile points are frequently found in association with mammoth remains. In the following period, between 9000 and 8000 B.C., mammoth, camel and horse have all disappeared; only the extinct bison species remains, and the artifacts found among the bison bones include Folsom projectile points rather than Clovis. The next cultural complexes overlap Folsom somewhat and are dated between 8500 and 7000 B.C. Several sites in this span of time are assigned to the Agate Basin complex. Finally, between 7000 and 6000 B.C., the Agate Basin complex is replaced by the Cody complex. These later "Paleo-Indian" cultures do not concern us. What is interesting is that, in spite of their wide geographical distribution, all the dated Clovis sites apparently belong to the same relatively narrow span of time.

Although the Clovis sites mentioned thus far are all in the western U.S., it would be a mistake to think that the mammoth-hunters were confined to that part of North America. Clovis points have been found in every one of the mainland states of the U.S. and there are more Clovis points at any one of three eastern sites than at all the stratified western sites combined. The trouble is that, with a very few exceptions, the eastern Clovis artifacts are found on the surface or only inches below the surface; it is impossible to assign dates to them with any degree of reliability. An example of the complexity of the problem is provided by the Williamson site near Dinwiddie, Va., where Clovis points and Civil War bullets are found side by side in the same plowed field.

In spite of the problem of dating the eastern discoveries, no grasp of the vigor and extent of the mammoth-hunters' culture is possible without consideration of its maximum range. In addition to the sites in the western U.S. already mentioned, Clovis points—flaked from obsidian rather than flint—have been unearthed at Borax Lake, a site north of San Francisco. Here, unfortunately, the stratigraphy is disturbed and artifacts of various ages are mixed

together. Another western Clovis site is near Tonopah, Nev., where fluted points were found on the surface around a dry lake, together with flint scrapers, gravers and perforators. Neither the site nor the artifacts have been described in detail, however, and the Tonopah material is not available for study. (It is in a private collection.)

Projectile points made of bone and ivory, nearly identical with the ones found at Clovis, have also been found elsewhere in the West. Two come from deposits of muck in central Alaska that contain mammoth bones. Unfortunately the Alaskan muck is notorious for its mixed stratigraphy, and the relative ages of artifacts and animal remains in it are not easily determined. The other

bone points have been found at Klamath Lake in California, in deposits as yet undated. These deposits also contain mammoth bones, but the artifacts and animal remains are not in direct association.

In the eastern U.S. large numbers of similar bone points have been found underwater at two locations in Florida: the Itchtucknee River and Wakula Spring. The latter site has also yielded mammoth remains. Something of the difficulty facing investigators who wish to assign dates to such underwater discoveries as the 600 bone points from Wakula Spring can be appreciated when one considers that the same six-foot stretch of sandy bottom may yield a bone point, a mammoth tooth and a

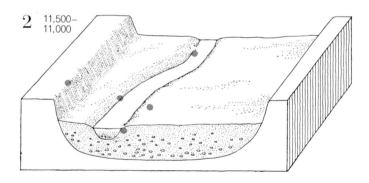

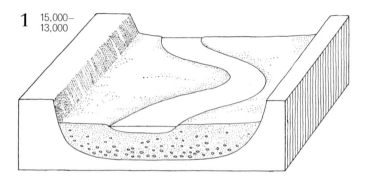

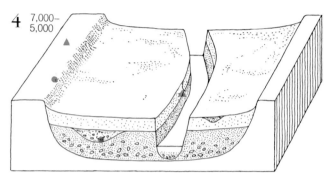

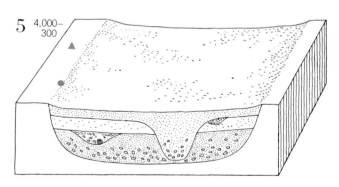

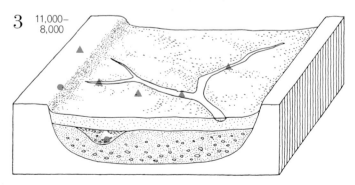

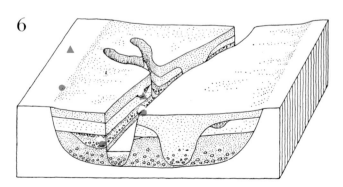

SEQUENCE OF DEPOSITS at a hypothetical valley site shows how a sediment-filled river valley (*1*) was inhabited by the Clovis mammoth-hunters (*2*). Dates are given in number of years before the present. Next (*3*) the Clovis valley sites are covered by fresh sediments on which the later Folsom bison-hunters camped. Both the Clovis and the Folsom campsites on the terrace above the valley escape burial; surface sites of this kind are difficult to date. Later cycles of erosion and deposit (*4 and 5*) leave the Clovis and Folsom valley sites deeply buried. Finally (*6*), today's situation is shown; erosion has now bared two superposed kill sites (*center*).

soft-drink bottle. The prospect of dating the abundant Clovis finds elsewhere in the East is in most instances not much brighter. Nevertheless, thanks to amateur archaeologists who have taken pains to report the exact location of their surface discoveries, it is now apparent that the greatest concentration of fluted projectile points is centered on Ohio, Kentucky and Tennessee. When the places in which Clovis points have been discovered are plotted on a map, the distribution of the points corresponds closely to that of mammoth fossils and those of the other New World proboscid, the mastodon.

The curious fact remains that, with one possible exception, no Clovis point in the eastern U.S. has ever been found in association with animal bones. The possible exception is a Clovis point found in 1898 at Big Bone Lick in Kentucky, where mammoth bones have also been uncovered. At the time, of course, the point was not recognized for what it was, and there is no evidence that the point was found in association with the mammoth bones.

The major surface discoveries of Clovis artifacts in eastern North America have been made at the Williamson site in Virginia, at the Shoop site near Harrisburg, Pa., at the Quad site in northern Alabama and at Wells Creek Crater in Tennessee [*see illustration on pages 240 and 241*]. To judge from the hundreds of Clovis points and thousands of other flint tools that have been picked up at these locations, each must represent a large campsite.

The same is probably true of Bull Brook near Ipswich, Mass.; hundreds of fluted points from this site have been analyzed by Douglas S. Byers of the R. S. Peabody Foundation in Andover, Mass. Unfortunately the stratigraphy at Bull Brook is disturbed. No campfire hearths or clear-cut levels of human habitation are known; four charcoal samples that may or may not be associated with the flint points yield carbon-14 dates that range from 4990 ± 800 B.C. to 7350 ± 400 B.C. It is evident that the Bull Brook deposits cover a considerable span of time.

The only other significant stratified site in eastern North America that has yielded carbon-14 dates is near Debert in the Canadian province of Nova Scotia. Debert is being studied by investigators from the R. S. Peabody Foundation and the National Museum of Canada. Here fluted projectile points have been found that are neither Clovis nor Folsom in style. The average of

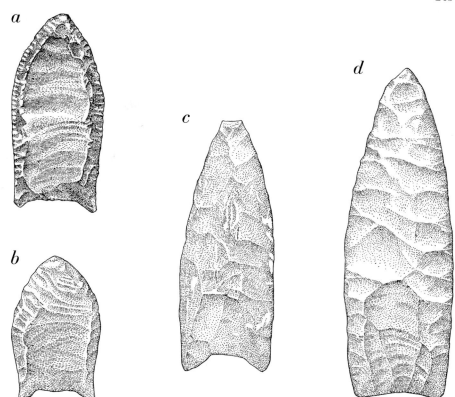

CHARACTERISTIC DIFFERENCES between Folsom (*"a" and "b"*) and Clovis (*"c" and "d"*) projectile points include the Folsom point's long neat flute scar, produced by the detachment of a single flake, and the delicate chipping of its cutting edges. Clovis points tend to be coarser and larger; flute scars are short and often show the detachment of more than one flake. The shorter of the Folsom points may have been repointed after its tip broke off.

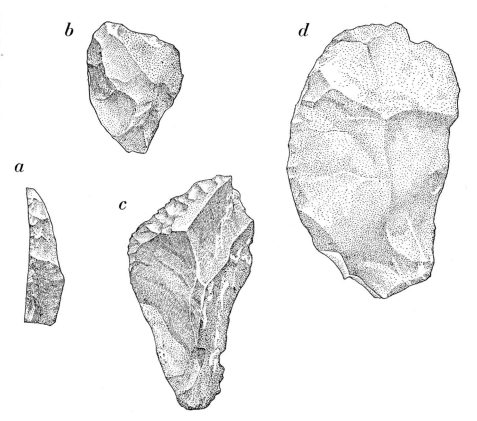

STONE TOOLS found at the Lehner site in New Mexico include keeled scrapers (*a*) and a variety of sidescrapers (*"b," "c" and "d"*). The latter were made from large flakes of flint knapped on one side. Choppers suitable for butchering were also found at this Clovis site.

carbon-14 dates at Debert is 8633 ± 470 B.C., or roughly 1,000 years later than the Clovis sites in the western U.S.

East or west, buried or exposed, most Clovis discoveries can be classified either as campsites or sites where animals were killed. A campsite is characterized by the presence of a wide variety of flint implements in addition to fluted points. A kill site is characterized by the presence of animal bones together with fluted points and a few flint butchering tools or no other tools at all. Recent excavations at Clovis itself indicate that the area around an extinct lake that attracted game to the site was used by the mammoth-hunters for both killing and camping. Not only butchering tools but also flint scrapers, gravers and knives have been discovered in the lower strata of the Clovis site. Apart from Clovis, however, the only other campsites in the western U.S. appear to be Tonopah, with its mixture of points and other artifacts, and Borax Lake.

Fortunately the major Clovis sites in the eastern U.S. provide abundant evidence of camp life. Some contain literally thousands of flint implements in addition to the characteristic fluted points; these include choppers, gravers, perforators, scrapers and knives made out of flint flakes. The locations of these sites show the kind of place the mammoth-hunters preferred as a camp. Shoop, Williamson, Quad and Wells Creek Crater are all on high ground, such as a stream-cut terrace or a ridge, overlooking the floodplain of a river or creek.

Analysis of the kill sites, in turn, reveals something about the Clovis people's hunting techniques, although many questions remain unanswered. The number of points found with each kill, for example, is inconsistent. At the Dent site only three Clovis points were found among the remains of a dozen mammoths. At Naco the skeleton of a single mammoth was associated with eight points. One interpretation of this seeming contradiction is that the Naco mammoth may have been one that got away, escaping its hunters to die alone some time after it was attacked. The 12 mammoths at Dent, according to the same interpretation, were butchered on the spot and the hunters recovered most of their weapons. One piece of negative evidence in support of this interpretation is that no butchering tools were found at Naco. Such tools, however, are also absent from Dent.

The Dent site affords a reasonably clear picture of one hunt. The mammoth bones were concentrated at the mouth of a small gully where an intermittent stream emerges from a sandstone bluff to join the South Platte River. It seems plausible that here the Clovis hunters had stampeded a mammoth herd over the edge of the bluff. Some of the animals may have been killed by the fall; others may have es-

STAMPEDED MAMMOTHS were unearthed near Dent, Colo., in 1932 by workers from the Denver Museum of Natural History. Among the bones of 11 immature female elephants and one adult male elephant they found several boulders and three typical Clovis projectile points. Photographed at the site were (*left to right*) Rev. Conrad Bilgery, S.J., an unidentified Regis College student, two Denver Museum trustees (W. C. Mead and C. H. Hanington) and Frederick Howarter of the museum's paleontology department.

caped. Those that were too badly hurt to fight free of the narrow gully may then have been stunned with boulders—an assumption that helps to explain the presence of these misplaced stones among the mammoth bones—and finally dispatched with spear thrusts. The bag of 11 cows and one bull would have constituted a highly successful day's work, but it may also have been the result of several hunts.

All six mammoths found at Clovis could also have been taken by stampeding a herd, in this case into shallow water where the footing was treacherous. Whether this actually happened, or whether the animals were simply surprised while watering, is impossible to determine. Clovis nonetheless affords a tantalizing glimpse into another of the mammoth-hunters' thought processes. One of the springs that fed the lake contains hundreds of flint flakes and a number of intact flint tools, including three Clovis points. Did the ancient hunters deliberately toss waste chips and usable artifacts into the spring? If not, how did these objects accumulate?

The concept of cutting a herd—separating the young and less dangerous animals from the more formidable adults—may be what is demonstrated by the remains at the Lehner site, where all nine mammoths were immature or even nurslings. At Lehner, as at Domebo (where only a single adult was killed), the animals apparently had been attacked while watering along a spring-fed stream.

Although the way in which the hunters' fluted projectile points were mounted seems clear, the kind of haft on which they were mounted remains unknown. That the points were used as arrowheads seems unlikely; the bow reached the New World or was independently invented there at a much later date. The Clovis points must therefore have been mounted on spears or darts. Whether launched from the hand or propelled by a spear-thrower, neither may have been a weapon of much effectiveness against an infuriated mammoth. It seems possible that, when the prey showed fight, most of the hunters devoted their efforts to keeping the mammoth at bay while a daring individual or two rushed in to drive a spear home to its heart from behind the foreleg.

The analysis of kill sites provides one further fact about the Clovis hunters. Although they were evidently specialists in the pursuit of mammoths, they were not unwilling to take other kinds

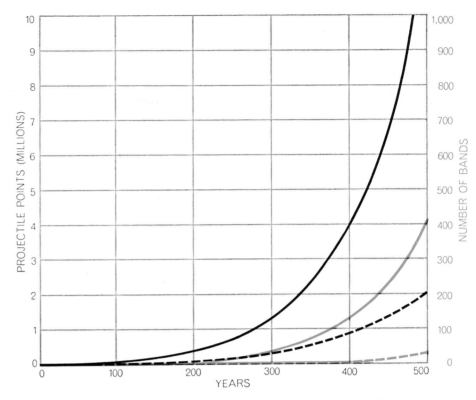

POPULATION INCREASE among the mammoth-hunters in the course of 500 years is calculated on the assumption that an original 30-member hunting band multiplied by a factor of 1.2 or 1.4 each 28-year generation (*color*). Black curves show the total number of Clovis points produced during 500 years, assuming that one person in four made five each month.

of quarry. At two of the sites—Clovis and Lehner—bison bones are also found.

The fluted projectile point is a highly specialized artifact that must have passed through a considerable period of development, yet no precursors are known in the New World or elsewhere. Obviously the archaeological record is incomplete, and perhaps it will remain so. For the time being, however, this absence of evident precursors suggests that the Clovis people arrived in the New World, already equipped with their specialized tool kit, between 12,000 and 13,000 years ago. Carbon-14 dates obtained during the past 15 years have built up a reasonably consistent picture of the way in which the New World was peopled during the final stages of the Pleistocene ice age. When the most recent glacial period was at its peak, 14,000 to 20,000 years ago, a large portion of the earth's water supply was stored in the Northern Hemisphere's ice sheets. The so-called land bridge between Alaska and Siberia in the area of the Bering Strait, exposed by the low level of the earth's oceans at that time, was no narrow isthmus but a broad land mass joining Asia and North America in a single continent.

The Bering land mass, however, was not a thoroughfare from the Old World

to the whole of the New. The Cordilleran ice cap covered the Canadian Rockies from Vancouver to eastern Alaska, and the Laurentide ice cap covered most of the rest of Canada and much of the northern U.S. These two glacial formations merged at the foot of the Canadian Rockies, leaving central Alaska, the Bering land mass and eastern Siberia unglaciated but cut off from the more southerly Americas by an ice barrier.

A little more than 12,000 years ago there occurred a marked period of glacial retreat known as the Two Creeks interval. Carbon-14 dates indicate that the warm interval came to an end scarcely more than a century or two later, or about 9900 B.C.; another glacial advance began soon thereafter. As we have seen, Clovis points make their first appearance in western North America in 9500 B.C., or roughly half a millennium after the Two Creeks interval. A tenable hypothesis connecting the two events is that the Two Creeks glacial retreat opened a trans-Canadian corridor between the Cordilleran and the Laurentide ice caps. The progenitors of the Clovis people, confined until then to central Alaska but already specialists in big-game hunting, could thus make their way down an ice-free corridor into a world where big game abounded and

CLOVIS BONE POINT, partly cleared of surrounding matrix at lower right, lies in direct association with the bones of a mammoth foreleg. Unearthed at Clovis, this evidence of early man's hunting ability is displayed at the Philadelphia Academy of Natural Sciences.

had scarcely been hunted until that time.

This, of course, is no more than a hypothesis, but it is a useful one on two counts. First, it provides a logical explanation for the abrupt appearance of Clovis points in North America at about 9500 B.C. Second, it is easily tested. All that is needed to destroy the Two Creeks hypothesis, for example, is the discovery of a Clovis site more than 12,000 years old located south of the ice sheet. Thus far no such Clovis site has been found. Meanwhile the Two Creeks hypothesis can also be tested indirectly in demographic terms.

Assuming that the first Clovis people passed through northwestern Canada some 12,000 years ago, they would have had to travel at the rate of four miles a year to reach the most southerly of their western U.S. sites, 2,000 miles away, within 500 years. Is such a rate of human diffusion realistic? Edward S. Deevey, Jr., of Yale University has noted that, under conditions of maximal increase in an environment empty of competitors, mankind's best efforts produce a population increase by a factor of 1.4 in each 28-year generation [see "The Human Population," by Edward S. Deevey, Jr.; SCIENTIFIC AMERICAN Offprint 608]. James Fitting of the University of Michigan has recently investigated a prehistoric hunting camp in Michigan; he suggests that Paleo-Indian family hunting bands numbered between 30 and 60 individuals.

Making conservative use of these findings, I have assumed that the first and only Clovis band to pass down the corridor opened by the Two Creeks interval numbered about 30, say five families averaging six persons each: two grandparents, two parents and two offspring. I have assumed further that one in four knew how to knap flint and produced Clovis points at the rate of five a month. In case Deevey's growth factor of 1.4 is too high, I have also made my calculation with a smaller factor—1.2—on the grounds that a plausible extrapolation probably lies somewhere between the two.

Applying these production rates, I find that in 500 years an original band of 30 mammoth-hunters evolves into a population numbering between 800 and 12,500, comprised of 26 to 425 hunting bands. In the same 500 years the bands' flint-knappers will have made—and left scattered across the land—between two million and 14 million Clovis points. Assuming that the demographic model is a reasonable one, the Clovis hunters could easily have spread across North America from coast to coast in the brief span of time allotted to them. Indeed, if the higher figure is in any way realistic, the rapid increase in the number of mammoth-hunters could easily be one of the main reasons why these animals became extinct in North America sometime around 9000 B.C., leaving the succeeding Folsom hunters with no larger prey than bison.

25

EARLY MAN IN THE ANDES

RICHARD S. MACNEISH
April 1971

Stone tools in highland Peru indicate that men lived there 22,000 years ago, almost twice the old estimate. They also imply that the first cultural traditions of the New World had their roots in Asia

Recent archaeological discoveries in the highlands of Peru have extended the prehistory of the New World in two significant respects. First, the finds themselves indicate that we must push back the date of man's earliest known appearance in South America from the currently accepted estimate of around 12,000 B.C. to perhaps as much as 20,000 B.C. Second and even more important is the implication, in the nature of the very early Andean hunting cultures now brought to light, that these cultures reflect Old World origins of even greater antiquity. If this is so, man may have first arrived in the Western Hemisphere between 40,000 and 100,000 years ago. The discoveries and the conclusions they suggest seem important enough to warrant this preliminary report in spite of the hazard that it may prove to be premature.

The new findings were made in 1969 and 1970 near Ayacucho, a town in the Peruvian province of the same name. All the sites lie within a mountain-ringed valley, most of it 6,500 feet above sea level, located some 200 miles southeast of Lima [*see top illustration on page 249*]. The valley is rich in prehistoric remains (we noted some 500 sites during our preliminary survey) and archaeological investigations have been conducted there since the 1930's. For me and my associates in the Ayacucho Archaeological-Botanical Project, however, the valley was interesting for other reasons as well.

A number of us had already been involved in a joint archaeological-botanical investigation at Tehuacán in the highlands of Mexico under the sponsorship of the Robert S. Peabody Foundation for Archaeology. Our prime target was early botanical evidence of the origin and development of agriculture in the area. This we sought by archaeological methods, while simultaneously recording the relation between agricultural advances and the material evidence of developing village life (and ultimately urban life) in Mexico before the Spanish conquest. By the time our fieldwork at Tehuacán had been completed in the mid-1960's we had gained some understanding of the changes that had come about in highland Mesoamerica between its initial occupation by preagricultural hunters and gatherers around 10,000 B.C. and the rise of pre-Columbian civilization [see the article "The Origins of New World Civilization," by Richard S. MacNeish, beginning on page 259].

There was, however, at least one other major New World center that had been the site of a similar development from hunting bands to farmers and city folk. This is western South America. Its inhabitants had cultivated some plants that were unknown to the farmers of Mesoamerica, and they had domesticated animals that were similarly unique to the region. Mesoamerica certainly interacted with South America, but the earliest stages of this second regional development apparently took place in isolation. It seemed logical that the record of these isolated advances might provide the foundation for functional comparisons with the Tehuacán results and perhaps lead us to some generalizations about the rise of civilization in the New World.

This was the objective that brought several veterans of the Tehuacán investigation, myself included, to Peru. The work was again sponsored by the Peabody Foundation, where I now serve as director. Reconnaissance of a number of highland areas led us to select the Ayacucho valley as the scene of our investigations. Our decision was based primarily on ecological grounds: within a radius of 15 miles the varied highland environment includes areas of subtropical desert, thorn-forest grassland, dry thorn forest, humid scrub forest and subarctic tundra [*see bottom illustration on page 249*]. It is the consensus among botanists who have studied the question that many of the plants first domesticated in western South America were indigenous to the highlands and that their domestication had probably taken place in Peru. The Peruvian ecologist J. A. Tosi had concluded that the most probable locale for the event would be a highland valley that included a wide range of environments. An additional consideration was that the area where we worked should contain caves that could have served as shelters in the past and thus might prove to be the repositories of animal and plant remains. The Ayacucho valley met both requirements.

Two caves in the valley have in fact turned out to be particularly rich repositories. One of them, located about eight miles north of the town of Ayacucho, is known locally as Pikimachay, or Flea Cave. It lies some 9,000 feet above sea level on the eastern slope of a hill composed of volcanic rock; the mouth of the cave is 40 feet high in places and 175 feet wide, and the distance from the

front of the cave to the deepest point inside it is 80 feet. Rocks that have fallen from the roof occupy the northern third of the interior of the cave and form a pile that reaches a height of 20 feet. In 1969 Flea Cave yielded the single most dramatic discovery of the season. During our last week of excavation a test trench, dug to a depth of six feet near the south end of the cave, revealed stone tools in association with bones of an extinct ground sloth of the same family as the fossil North American sloth *Megatherium*. One of the bones, a humerus, has been shown by carbon-14 analysis to be 14,150 (±180) years old.

The other notable cave site, some 11 miles east of the town of Ayacucho, is known locally as Jayamachay, or Pepper Cave. Although Pepper Cave is as high and nearly as wide as Flea Cave, it is only 15 feet deep. Excavations were made at Pepper Cave with rewarding results in both the 1969 and the 1970 seasons. Because the significance of the findings at this site arises largely from a comparison of the material from both caves, I shall first describe the strata at Flea Cave.

What has been revealed in general by our work at all the cave and open-air sites in the Ayacucho valley (a total of 12 excavations) is a series of remains representative of successive cultures in an unbroken sequence that spans the millenniums from 20,000 B.C. to A.D. 1500. The archaeological sequence documents man's progression from an early hunter to an incipient agriculturist to a village farmer and finally to the role of a subject of imperial rule. The material of the most significance to the present discussion, however, is contained in the strata representing the earliest phases of this long prehistoric record. These strata have yielded a succession of stone-tool types that began some 20,000 years ago and continued until about 10,500 years ago. The earliest part of the record is found in the lowest levels at Flea Cave.

The oldest stratified deposit in the cave lies in a basin-like hollow in the lava flow that forms the cave floor. The stratum lies just above the bedrock of the basin. Labeled Zone k, the stratum consists of soils, transported into the cave by natural means, that are mixed with disintegrated volcanic tuffs from the rocks of the cave itself. Zone k is eight inches deep. Just before the deposition of the stratum ended, some animal vertebrae and a rib bone (possibly from an extinct ground sloth) were deposited in it. So were four crude tools fashioned from

AYACUCHO VALLEY, between Lima and Cuzco, is undergoing joint botanical and archaeological investigation that will allow comparisons with a study of Tehuacán, in Mexico. The Robert S. Peabody Foundation for Archaeology is the sponsor of both studies.

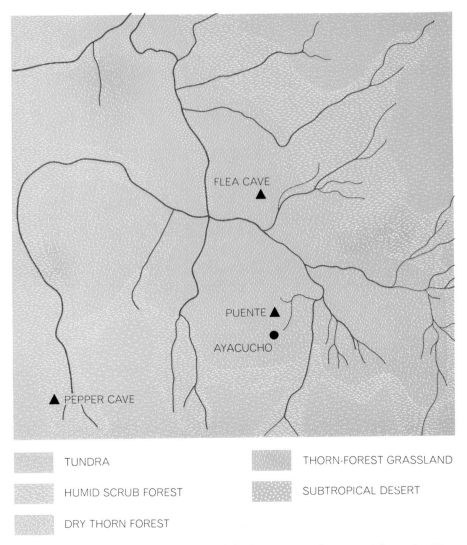

TUNDRA

HUMID SCRUB FOREST

DRY THORN FOREST

THORN-FOREST GRASSLAND

SUBTROPICAL DESERT

MAJOR SITES in the Ayacucho valley include Puente, near the town of Ayacucho, Flea Cave, a few miles north of Puente, and Pepper Cave, a few miles southwest. The existence of five distinct zones of vegetation in the valley (key) was a factor in its selection for study.

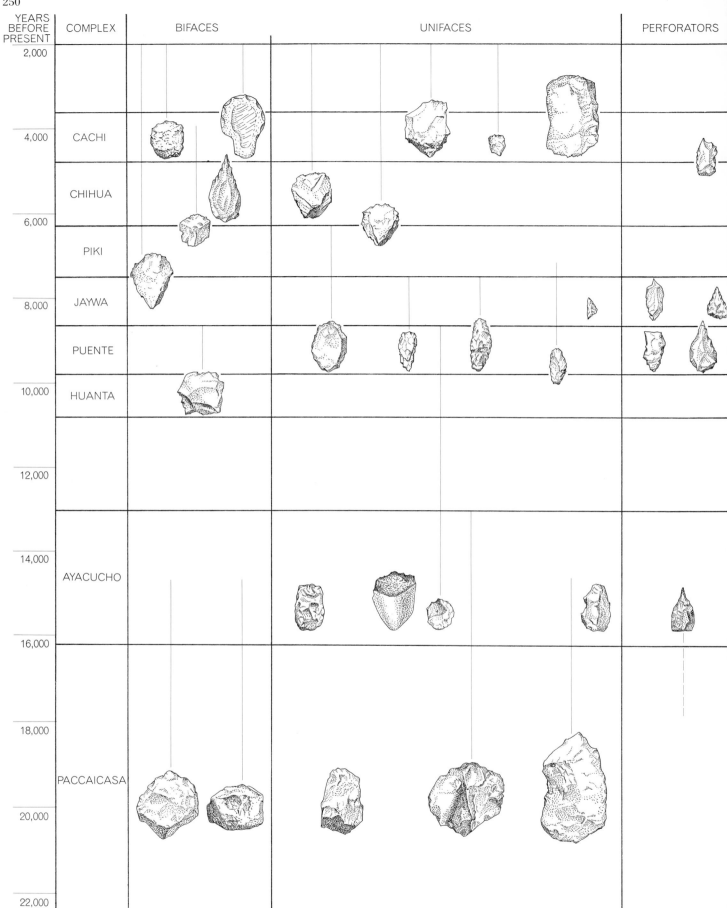

KINDS OF TOOLS discovered at 12 excavations in the Ayacucho valley appear in this chart in association with the complex (*names at left*) that first includes them. No complex more recent than the Puente, some 9,000 years old, is relevant to man's earliest arrival

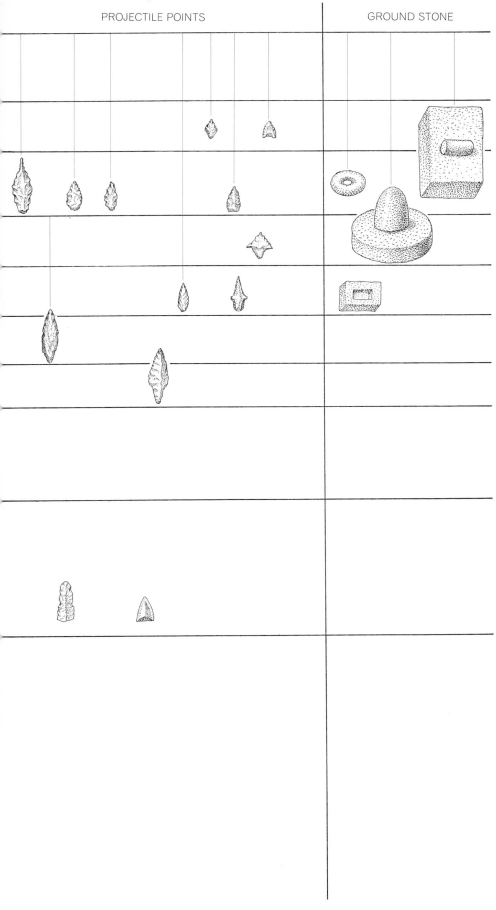

PROJECTILE POINTS   GROUND STONE

in Peru. The first crude tools (*bottom*) are reminiscent of chopping tools found in Asia.
In the next complex projectile points first appear; some were made out of bone (*far right*).

volcanic tuff and a few flakes that had
been struck from tools. One of the flakes
is of a green stone that could only have
come from outside the cave.

The soils in Zone k are neutral in terms
of acidity, which suggests that the vegetation outside the cave when the soils
were formed was of the grassland variety, in contrast to the dry thorn-forest
vegetation found today. The period of
deposition that formed Zone k may have
begun more than 23,000 years ago. It
remains to be seen whether the climate
at that time, as indicated by the neutral
acidity of the soil, can be exactly correlated with any of the several known
glacial fluctuations in the neighboring
Andes.

Three later strata, all containing the
bones of extinct animals and additional
stone implements, overlie Zone k. They
are labeled, in ascending order, zones j,
i1 and i. Zone j is a brown soil deposit
12 inches thick. In various parts of this
stratum we unearthed three vertebrae
and two rib fragments of an extinct
ground sloth and the leg bone of a smaller mammal, perhaps an ancestral species
of horse or camel. Zone j yielded 14 stone
tools; like those in Zone k, they are
crudely made from volcanic tuff. There
are in addition some 40 stone flakes, evidently the waste from toolmaking. Car-
bon-14 analysis of one of the ground-
sloth vertebrae shows it to be 19,600
($\pm$3,000) years old.

Zone i1, above Zone j, is a deposit of
a more orange-colored soil; it is 15 inches
thick, and it contains tools and both fossilized and burned animal bone. Carbon-
14 analysis of one of the bones, a fragment of sloth scapula, indicates that it is
16,050 ($\pm$1,200) years old. The soils of
zones j and i1 are both quite acid, suggesting that they were formed when the
climate was less arid and the vegetation
outside Flea Cave included forest cover.

The uppermost of the four strata, Zone
i, consists of 18 inches of a slightly
browner soil. The soil approaches that of
Zone k in neutral acidity, suggesting a
return to drier climatic conditions. Distributed through the deposit are crude
stone artifacts, waste flakes and the
bones of sloth and horse. Carbon-14
analysis of one of the bones shows it to
be 14,700 ($\pm$1,400) years old.

The stone tools from all four of the
lowest Flea Cave strata are much alike.
There are 50 of them in all, uniformly
large and crude in workmanship. The
tool types include sidescrapers, choppers, cleavers, "spokeshaves" and denticulate (sawtoothed) forms. Most of

FLEA CAVE, the site that contains the oldest evidence of man's presence thus far unearthed in South America, lies at an altitude of 9,000 feet in an area of intermingled thorn forest and grassland. The mouth of the cave (*center*) is 175 feet wide and 40 feet high.

PEPPER CAVE, the other major cave site in the Ayacucho area, lies at an altitude of 11,000 feet on a hill where humid scrub forest gives way to upland tundra vegetation. The lowest strata excavated at Pepper Cave are evidently the product of local glacial outwashes.

them were made from volcanic tuff, which does not flake well, and it takes a skilled eye to distinguish many of them from unworked tuff detached from the cave walls by natural processes. A few of the tools, however, were made from other materials, such as rounded pebbles and pieces of basalt, that were collected outside the cave and carried back to be fashioned into implements. The tools in these four levels represent the earliest assemblage of tools, or tool complex, unearthed so far at a stratified site anywhere in South America. We call it the Paccaicasa complex, after a nearby village. The men who fashioned its distinctive tools occupied the Ayacucho valley from as much as 22,000 years ago to about 13,000 years ago.

The strata at Flea Cave that contain the Paccaicasa complex were excavated during the 1970 season. The previous year we thought we had already reached bedrock when we reached the top of the stratum just above Zone i: it was a very hard, yellowish layer of soil that included numerous small flakes of volcanic tuff. With the season nearly at an end we proceeded no farther. The yellow layer, now known as Zone h1, actually turned out to lie just above bedrock over an area of some 150 square yards of cave floor except for the natural basin near the south end of the cave. Digging into this stratum with some difficulty at the start of the 1970 season, we found that its 20-inch depth contained not only the bones of sloth, horse and possibly saber-toothed tiger but also numerous flakes of waste stone and some 70 tools, most of them quite different from the crude tuff artifacts of the strata below. A few tools of the older kind were present in Zone h1, but the majority are made from such materials as basalt, chalcedony, chert and pebbles of quartzite.

The use of new tool materials is also characteristic of Zone h, a 12-inch stratum of softer, light orange soil that overlies Zone h1. Here, however, the animal remains include many not found in the older strata. A kind of ancestral camel appears to be represented in addition to the sloth and the horse. There are also the remains of the puma, the hog-nosed skunk, an extinct species of deer and several unidentified species, possibly including the mastodon. This larger faunal assemblage suggests a return of the countryside around Flea Cave to forest cover. Indeed, the soil of Zone h is strongly acid, unlike the neutral soils of Zone i and Zone h1.

The tools in Zone h are abundant; in addition to more than 1,000 fragments of waste stone there are some 250 fin-

YEARS BEFORE PRESENT (ESTIMATED)	ASSOCIATED C-14 DATES (YEARS BEFORE PRESENT)		TOOL COMPLEX	CLIMATE AND VEGETATION	POSSIBLE GLACIATION STAGE
	FLEA CAVE	PEPPER CAVE			
8,000	f1	C 8,250 (±125)	JAYWA	MODERN CLIMATE AND VEGETATION	ICE IN HIGH ANDES ONLY
		D 8,360 (±135)			
	8,860 (±125)	E			
	f2	F	PUENTE		
		G			
		H 8,980 (±140)			
		I			
	ROCKFALL	J	HUANTA	COOL	FINAL ICE RETREAT
		J1 9,460 (±145)			
		J2			
		J3			
		K			
		L			
		M			
12,000	g	N	BLADE, BURIN, LEAF-POINT?	COLD	FINAL ICE ADVANCE
		GRAVEL			
	h (underlined)				
	h		AYA-CUCHO	WARM FOREST	INTERSTADIAL
	14,150 (±180)				
	h1			COLD	ICE
16,000				GRASSLAND	ADVANCE
	i				
	14,700 (±1,400)		PACCAI-CASA		
	i1			WARM FOREST	INTERSTADIAL?
	16,050 (±1,200)				
	j				
	19,600 (±3,000)				
20,000					
	k			COLD GRASSLAND	EARLY ICE ADVANCE?
	ROCK FLOOR				

SEQUENCE OF STRATA at the major Ayacucho cave sites is correlated in this chart with the five earliest tool complexes that have been identified thus far. Carbon-14 determinations of the age of certain strata are shown in relation to estimates of the overall temporal sequence. The climate and vegetation are linked to probable stages of glaciation.

LIMB BONE of an extinct ground sloth (*center*) was found at Flea Cave in a stratum that also contained stone and bone tools representative of the Ayacucho complex. Carbon-14 analysis of the bone shows that the stratum was deposited at least 14,000 years ago.

ished artifacts. Some of these artifacts are in the "core" tradition of tool manufacture: they were made by removing flakes from a stone to produce the desired shape. Among them are both the choppers and spokeshaves typical of the lower strata and new varieties of tool such as split-pebble scrapers and fluted wedges. The core tools are outnumbered, however, by tools consisting of flakes: burins, gravers, sidescrapers, flake spokeshaves, denticulate flakes and unifacial projectile points (points flaked only on one side). The unifacial points are the oldest projectile points found at Ayacucho.

At this stage the inhabitants of Flea Cave were also fashioning tools out of bone: triangular projectile points, polishers, punches made out of antler and "fleshers" formed out of rib bones. There is even one polished animal toe bone that may have been an ornament.

Zone h is the rich stratum that yielded the 14,000-year-old sloth humerus in 1969. The change in tool materials apparent in Zone h1 and the proliferation of new tool types in Zone h suggest that at Flea Cave a second tool complex had taken the place of the earlier Paccaicasa complex. We have named the distinctive assemblage from these two strata the Ayacucho complex.

The stratum immediately overlying Zone h is found in only a few parts of the excavation. It consists of a fine, powdery yellow soil that is neutral in acidity. This sparse formation, labeled Zone h, has so far yielded only three stone artifacts: a blade, a sidescraper and a large denticulate scraper. The lack of soil acidity suggests that the interval represented by Zone h was characterized by dry grassland vegetation. Further investigation may yield enough artifacts to indicate whether or not the stratum contains a distinctive tool complex suited to the changed environment. For the time being we know too little about Zone h to come to any conclusions.

For the purposes of this discussion the Flea Cave story ends here. Above Zone h at the time our work began was a three-foot layer of fallen rock, including some individual stones that weighed more than three tons. This rock was apparently associated with the much heavier fall in the northern half of the cave. A small stratum above the rock debris, labeled Zone f1, contained charcoal, the bones of modern deer and llamas, and a few well-made bifacial tools (stone tools flaked on both sides). These tools closely resemble tools of known age at Puente, an open-air site near Ayacucho where only the remains of modern animals have been found. On this basis one can conclude that the time of the rockfall at Flea Cave was no later than 10,000 years ago. It is worth mentioning that before any of the strata below the rock layer could be excavated, the rocks had to be broken up by pickax and carried out of the cave. The three-foot rock stratum was labeled Zone g.

The strata that tell the rest of our story are in a deep deposit in the southeast corner of Pepper Cave. Situated at an altitude of nearly 11,000 feet, this cave is surrounded today by humid scrub forest. It is adjacent to a tributary of the Cachi River, whose bed lies 150 feet below the level of the cave. The bottom stratum of the deep deposit at Pepper Cave consists of stratified sands and gravels close to the top of a high water-built terrace. This fluvial deposit is labeled Zone N. It is overlain by a three-foot layer of rocks that have fallen from the roof of the cave, mixed with stratified sands that indicate a continuation of fluvial terrace building. The mixed stratum comprises zones M and L. Preliminary geological studies suggest that the terrace was formed by outwash from the final advance of the Andean glaciers. There is no evidence of human activity in the three lowest strata at Pepper Cave.

Overlying these sterile layers is a 28-inch stratum of windblown sand and disintegrated volcanic tuff that has been labeled Zone K. Artifacts were found in the upper four inches of the deposit, and a few were also unearthed in one reddish area near the bottom of it. The artifacts represent a new complex of tools that was also found in the next three strata:

floors of human habitation that are labeled in ascending order zones J3, J2 and J1. No animal remains have been recovered from Zone K, but the three J zones contain the bones of horses, of extinct species of deer and possibly of llamas.

The characteristic artifacts of the new tool complex, which we have named Huanta after another town in the valley, include bifacially flaked projectile points with a "fishtail" base, gravers, burins, blades, half-moon-shaped sidescrapers and teardrop-shaped end scrapers. A carbon-14 analysis of one of the animal bones from the uppermost stratum, Zone J1, indicates that the Huanta complex flourished until about 9,500 years ago.

The five strata overlying the Huanta complex at Pepper Cave, like the single layer above the rockfall at Flea Cave, hold remains typical of the Puente complex. These strata have been designated zones J through F. One stratum near the middle, Zone H, is shown by a carbon-14 analysis of charcoal to have been laid down about 9,000 years ago. This date is in good agreement with the known age of material excavated at the Puente site. The contents of the strata above the Puente complex zones at Pepper Cave (zones E through A), like the contents of zones f1 through a at Flea Cave, will not concern us here.

Having reviewed the facts revealed at Ayacucho, let us consider their broader implications. What follows is not only interpretive but also somewhat speculative; it goes well beyond the direct evidence now at our disposal. Stating the implications straightforwardly, however, may serve two useful purposes. First, in doing so we are in effect putting forward hypotheses to be proved or disproved by future findings. Second, in being explicit we help to define the problems that remain to be solved.

Let us first consider the implications of our evidence concerning changes in vegetation and climate. Remains of the Puente complex overlie the sequences of earlier strata at both caves: they are on top of the material of uncertain character at Flea Cave and on top of the Huanta complex at Pepper Cave. To judge from carbon-14 measurements, the earliest appearance of the Puente complex, with its advanced tools and remains of modern animal species, may have been around 9,700 years ago. At about that time, then, the association of early man and extinct animals in this highland area evidently came to an end.

We have not yet completed the soil studies and the analyses of pollens in the soil that will add many details to the record of climate and vegetation. For the time being, however, I tentatively propose that the last of the pre-Puente strata at Flea Cave (Zone h) and the sterile zones N through L at Pepper Cave coincide with the last Andean glacial advance. Zone h at Flea Cave, with its acid soil and remains of forest animals, appears to represent an earlier "interstadial" period in the glacial record—a breathing spell rather than a full-scale retreat. Zones h1 and i, below Zone h, are characterized by the remains of different animals and by soil of neutral acidity, suggesting a colder climate and a glacial advance. Evidence from the still earlier zones i1 and j suggests a second interstadial period of relative warmth. Zone k, the lowest in the Flea Cave excavation, apparently represents another period of advancing ice. If the Ayacucho evidence holds true for Andean glacial activity in general, the South American glacial advances and retreats do not coincide with those of the Wisconsin glaciation in North America [*see illustration on this page*]. This apparent lack of correlation presents interesting problems. If glaciation is caused by worldwide climatic change, why are the South American oscillations so unlike the North American ones? If, on the other hand, widespread climatic change is not the cause of glaciation, what is? The precise sequence of Andean glacial advances and retreats obviously calls for further study.

What are the implications of the Ayacucho findings with respect to early man, not only in South America but also elsewhere in the New World? The results of local studies of the earliest phases of prehistory in South America are all too seldom published, so that the comments that follow are particularly speculative. Having warned the reader, let me suggest that the Paccaicasa complex in the Peruvian central highlands may well represent the earliest stage of man's appearance in South America.

To generalize from Ayacucho material, this earliest stage seems to be characterized by a tool assemblage consisting of large corelike choppers, large sidescrapers and spokeshaves and heavy denticulate implements. This I shall call the Core Tool Tradition; it is certainly represented by the Paccaicasa assemblage in South America and may just possibly be represented in North America by the controversial finds at the Calico site in the Mojave Desert north of Barstow, Calif. In South America the Core Tool Tradition appears to have flourished from about 25,000 years ago to 15,000 years ago.

Man's next stage in South America I call the Flake and Bone Tool Tradition. The only adequate definition of this tradition so far is found in the Ayacucho tool complex. That complex is characterized by a reduction in the proportion of core tools and a sudden abundance of tools made out of flakes: projectile points, knives, sidescrapers, gravers, burins, spokeshaves and denticulate tools.

YEARS BEFORE PRESENT	AYACUCHO VALLEY	NORTH AMERICA
9,000	FINAL RETREAT	VALDERS ADVANCE
11,000	FINAL ADVANCE	TWO CREEKS INTERVAL
13,000	INTERSTADIAL	CARY ADVANCE / MANKATO ADVANCE
15,000	SECOND ADVANCE	INTERSTADIAL
17,000	INTERSTADIAL	TAZEWELL ADVANCE / WISCONSIN MAXIMUM
MORE THAN 23,000	FIRST ADVANCE	PORT TALBOT INTERVAL

PHASE REVERSAL with respect to the glacial advances and retreats in the Northern Hemisphere during the final period of Pleistocene glaciation appears to characterize the record of fluctuations preserved at Ayacucho. The graph compares estimated Andean advances, retreats and interstadial phases with the phases of the Wisconsin glaciation.

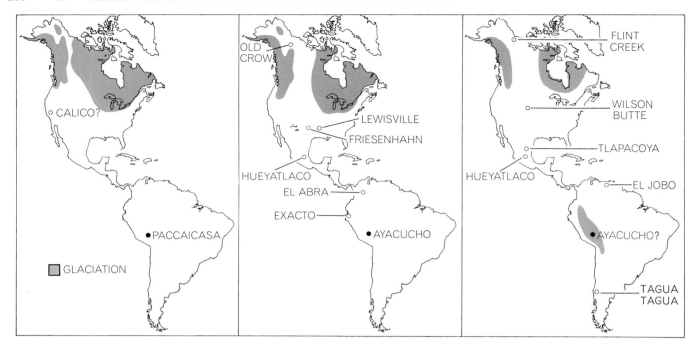

THREE TRADITIONS in New World prehistory are the Core Tool Tradition (*left*), the Flake and Bone Tool Tradition (*center*) and the Blade, Burin and Leaf-Point Tradition (*right*). The age of each tradition in North America, in cases where the age of a representative site is known, is substantially greater than it is in South America, suggesting that they stem from earlier Old World roots.

An important element in the tradition is the presence of bone implements, including projectile points, awls and scrapers. The Flake and Bone Tool Tradition apparently flourished from about 15,000 years ago to 13,000 or 12,000 years ago. Elsewhere in South America, although the evidence is scanty, the tradition may be reflected in surface finds attributed to the Exacto complex of coastal Ecuador and in flake tools from the El Abra cave site in highland Colombia; the El Abra material is estimated to be 12,500 years old. Some of the rare worked flakes from the Chivateros "red zone" of coastal central Peru may also represent this tradition [see "Early Man in South America," by Edward P. Lanning and Thomas C. Patterson; SCIENTIFIC AMERICAN, November, 1967]. Not all the North American sites that may be representative of the tradition are adequately dated. Where dates are available, however, they are from 10,000 to more than 20,000 years earlier than their South American counterparts.

The third South American stage I call the Blade, Burin and Leaf-Point Tradition. At present it is very poorly represented at our highland sites, consisting only of the three artifacts from Zone *h* at Flea Cave. The tradition is far better defined, however, in the El Jobo phase of Venezuela, where double-ended points, blades, burins and corelike scrapers have been unearthed in association with the bones of extinct animals. The

El Jobo phase is not adequately dated, but estimates suggest that its tool industry flourished roughly between 10,000 and 14,000 years ago. A small amount of material found at Laguna de Tagua Tagua in central Chile may also belong to this third tradition; carbon-14 analysis indicates that the Chilean material is about 11,300 years old. The precise duration of the Blade, Burin and Leaf-Point Tradition is not yet known. My guess is that it flourished from 13,000 or 12,000 years ago until 11,000 or 10,000 years ago. Like the preceding tradition, it is represented at sites in North America that, where age estimates exist, appear to be somewhat older.

Seen from the perspective of the Ayacucho valley, early man's final stage in South America, which I call the Specialized Bifacial Point Tradition, appears to have flourished from 11,000 or 10,000 years ago to 9,000 or 8,000 years ago. At Ayacucho the tradition is defined in the Huanta complex at Pepper Cave and in the later Puente complex there and elsewhere in the valley. It is characterized by bifacially flaked projectile points that evidently represent a specialization for big-game hunting. The tradition's other characteristic implements include specialized end scrapers and knives suited to skinning and butchering. Elsewhere in South America the tradition is represented at Fell's Cave in southern Chile, where a number of carbon-14 determinations suggest ages clustering

around 11,000 years ago. Other artifacts probably in this tradition are those from a stratum overlying the red zone at Chivateros (which are evidently some 10,-000 years old), from Toquepala Cave in southernmost Peru (which are about 9,500 years old) and from a number of other South American sites. Sites representative of the Specialized Bifacial Point Tradition in North America are almost too numerous to mention.

What might these four postulated traditions signify concerning man's arrival in the New World from Asia? Considering first the latest tradition—the Specialized Bifacial Point Tradition—we find a bewildering variety of complexes throughout North America at about the time when the late Paleo-Indian stage ends and the Archaic Indian stage begins. Nearly all the complexes have something in common, however: a specialization in bifacially flaked projectile points of extraordinary workmanship. I suggest that these specialized point industries all belong to a single tradition, that for the most part they represent local New World developments and that there is little use in trying to trace them to some ancestral assemblage on the far side of the Bering Strait. Carbon-14 analysis of charcoal from Fort Rock Cave in Oregon indicates that the earliest known specialized projectile points in the New World are some 13,200 years old. On the basis of this finding I propose that the Specialized Bifacial Point Tradition originated in the New World, beginning about 14,000 years ago in North America, and reached South America 3,000 to 4,000 years later.

North American artifacts related to the preceding tradition—the Blade, Burin and Leaf-Point Tradition—in South America include material from Tlapacoya and Hueyatlaco in Mexico, respectively some 23,000 and 22,000 years old, and material at least 15,000 years old from the lower levels of Wilson Butte Cave in Idaho. Some artifacts of the Cordilleran tradition in Canada and Alaska may also be related to the South American tradition. Again there apparently is a lag in cultural transmission from north to south that at its longest approaches 10,000 years. If there was a similar lag in transmission from Asia to North America, it is possible that the Blade, Burin and Leaf-Point Tradition originated with the Malt'a and Buret tool industries of the Lake Baikal region in eastern Siberia, which are between 15,000 and 30,000 years old.

As for the still older Flake and Bone Tool Tradition, adequately dated North American parallels are more difficult to find. Artifacts from Friesenhahn Cave in central Texas and some of the oldest material at Hueyatlaco show similarities to tools in the Ayacucho complex, but in spite of hints that these North American sites are very old the finds cannot be exactly dated. There are bone tools from a site near Old Crow in the Canadian Yukon that carbon-14 analysis shows to be from 23,000 to 28,000 years old. It is my guess that the Yukon artifacts belong to the Flake and Bone Tool Tradition, but many more arctic finds of the same kind are needed to change this guess into a strong presumption. A few flake tools from the site at Lewisville, Tex., may also be representative of the Ayacucho complex. Their estimated age of 38,000 years is appropriate. Figuring backward from the time the tradition appears to have arrived in South America, it would have flourished in North America between 25,000 and 40,000 years ago. Is it not possible that the Flake and Bone Tool Tradition is also an import from Asia? Perhaps it came from some Old World source such as the Shuitungkuo complex of northern China, reportedly between 40,000 and 60,000 years old.

We now come to the most difficult question, which concerns the oldest of the four traditions: the Core Tool Tradition. I wonder if any of my more conservative colleagues would care to venture the flat statement that no Core Tool

Tradition parallel to the one in the Paccaicasa strata at Flea Cave will ever be unearthed in North America? If it is found, is it not likely that it will be from 40,000 to as much as 100,000 years old? To me it seems entirely possible that such a core-tool tradition in the New World, although one can only guess at it today, could be derived from the chopper and chopping-tool tradition of Asia, which is well over 50,000 years old. (An example of such a tradition is the Fenho industry of China.) I find there is much reason to believe that three of the four oldest cultural traditions in the New World can be derived from specific Old World predecessors. That seems to be the most significant implication of our findings at Ayacucho. However much this conclusion may be modified by future work, one thing is certain: our knowledge of early man in the New World is in its infancy. An almost untouched province of archaeology awaits exploration.

YEARS BEFORE PRESENT	SOUTH AMERICA	MEXICO CENTRAL AMERICA	U.S. AND CANADA	EASTERN ASIA	
9,000	PUENTE HUANTA	IZTAPAN LERMA			SPECIALIZED POINT TRADITION
10,000	FELL'S CAVE (11,000)	AJUREADO			
11,000	EL JOBO		PLAINVIEW FOLSOM CLOVIS		
12,000	TAGUA TAGUA (11,300)		FORT ROCK CAVE (13,200)		
13,000	AYACUCHO				
	EL ABRA (12,500)				
14,000	AYACUCHO (14,150)		WILSON, BUTTE (15,000)		
15,000					
16,000	PACCAICASA (19,600)	HUEYATLACO (21,850)			BLADE, BURIN, LEAF-POINT TRADITION
20,000		TLAPACOYA (23,150)		MALT'A-BURET U.S.S.R.	
25,000		HUEYATLACO	FRIESENHAHN CAVE		
			OLD CROW (23,000-28,000)		
30,000			LEWISVILLE (38,000)		FLAKE BONE TOOL TRADITION
40,000				SHUITUNG-KUO, CHINA	
50,000			CALICO (?)		
60,000				FENHO, CHINA	CORE TOOL TRADITION
75,000					

OLD WORLD SOURCES of the three earliest prehistoric traditions in the New World are suggested in this chart. A fourth and more recent tradition, marked by the presence of finely made projectile points for big-game hunting, seems to have been indigenous rather than an Old World import. Although much work will be required to establish the validity of all three proposed relationships, the foremost weakness in the hypothesis at present is a lack in the Northern Hemisphere of well-dated examples of the core-tool tradition.

26

THE ORIGINS OF NEW WORLD CIVILIZATION

RICHARD S. MACNEISH
November 1964

*In the Mexican valley of Tehuacán bands of hunters
became urban craftsman in the course of 12,000
years. Their achievement raises some new questions
about the evolution of high cultures in general.*

Perhaps the most significant single occurrence in human history was the development of agriculture and animal husbandry. It has been assumed that this transition from food-gathering to food production took place between 10,000 and 16,000 years ago at a number of places in the highlands of the Middle East. In point of fact the archaeological evidence for the transition, particularly the evidence for domesticated plants, is extremely meager. It is nonetheless widely accepted that the transition represented a "Neolithic Revolution," in which abundant food, a sedentary way of life and an expanding population provided the foundations on which today's high civilizations are built.

The shift from food-gathering to food production did not, however, happen only once. Until comparatively recent times the Old World was for the most part isolated from the New World. Significant contact was confined to a largely one-way migration of culturally primitive Asiatic hunting bands across the Bering Strait. In spite of this almost total absence of traffic between the hemispheres the European adventurers who reached the New World in the 16th century encountered a series of cultures almost as advanced (except in metallurgy and pyrotechnics) and quite as barbarous as their own. Indeed, some of the civilizations from Mexico to Peru possessed a larger variety of domesticated plants than did their European

conquerors and had made agricultural advances far beyond those of the Old World.

At some time, then, the transition from food-gathering to food production occurred in the New World as it had in the Old. In recent years one of the major problems for New World prehistorians has been to test the hypothesis of a Neolithic Revolution against native archaeological evidence and at the same time to document the American stage of man's initial domestication of plants (which remains almost unknown in both hemispheres).

The differences between the ways in which Old World and New World men achieved independence from the nomadic life of the hunter and gatherer are more striking than the similarities. The principal difference lies in the fact that the peoples of the Old World domesticated many animals and comparatively few plants, whereas in the New World the opposite was the case. The abundant and various herds that gave the peoples of Europe, Africa and Asia meat, milk, wool and beasts of burden were matched in the pre-Columbian New World only by a half-domesticated group of Andean cameloids: the llama, the alpaca and the vicuña. The Andean guinea pig can be considered an inferior equivalent of the Old World's domesticated rabbits and hares; elsewhere in the Americas the turkey was an equally inferior counterpart of the Eastern Hemisphere's many

varieties of barnyard fowl. In both the Old World and the New, dogs presumably predated all other domestic animals; in both beekeepers harvested honey and wax. Beyond this the New World list of domestic animals dwindles to nothing. All the cultures of the Americas, high and low alike, depended on their hunters' skill for most of their animal produce: meat and hides, furs and feathers, teeth and claws.

In contrast, the American Indian domesticated a remarkable number of plants. Except for cotton, the "water bottle" gourd, the yam and possibly the coconut (which may have been domesticated independently in each hemisphere), the kinds of crops grown in the Old World and the New were quite different. Both the white and the sweet potato, cultivated in a number of varieties, were unique to the New World. For seasoning, in place of the pepper and mustard of the Old World, the peoples of the New World raised vanilla and at least two kinds of chili. For edible seeds they grew amaranth, chive, panic grass, sunflower, quinoa, apazote, chocolate, the peanut, the common bean and four other kinds of beans: lima, summer, tepary and jack.

In addition to potatoes the Indians cultivated other root crops, including manioc, oca and more than a dozen other South American plants. In place of the Old World melons, the related plants brought to domestication in the New World were the pumpkin, the

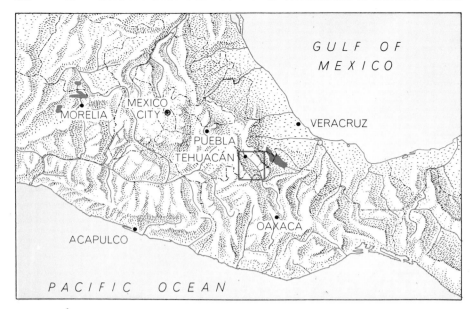

TEHUACÁN VALLEY is a narrow desert zone in the mountains on the boundary between the states of Puebla and Oaxaca. It is one of the three areas in southern Mexico selected during the search for early corn on the grounds of dryness (which helps to preserve ancient plant materials) and highland location (corn originally having been a wild highland grass).

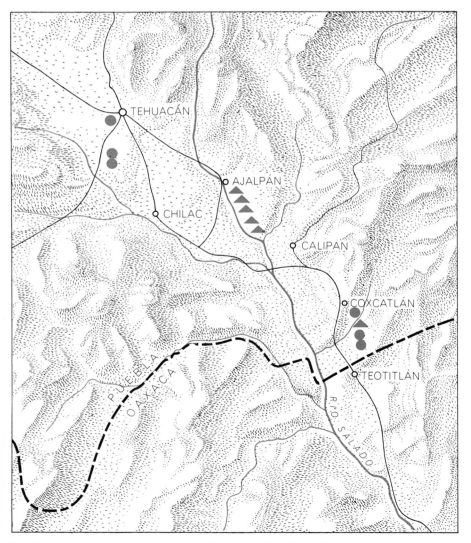

SIX CAVES (*dots*) and six open-air sites (*triangles*) have been investigated in detail by the author and his colleagues. Coxcatlán cave (*top dot at right*), where early corn was found in 1960, has the longest habitation record: from well before 7000 B.C. until A.D. 1500.

gourd, the chayote and three or four distinct species of what we call squash. Fruits brought under cultivation in the Americas included the tomato, avocado, pineapple, guava, elderberry and papaya. The pioneering use of tobacco—smoked in pipes, in the form of cigars and even in the form of cane cigarettes, some of which had one end stuffed with fibers to serve as a filter—must also be credited to the Indians.

Above all of these stood Indian corn, *Zea mays*, the only important wild grass in the New World to be transformed into a food grain as the peoples of the Old World had transformed their native grasses into wheat, barley, rye, oats and millet. From Chile to the valley of the St. Lawrence in Canada, one or another of 150 varieties of Indian corn was the staple diet of the pre-Columbian peoples. As a food grain or as fodder, corn remains the most important single crop in the Americas today (and the third largest in the world). Because of its dominant position in New World agriculture, prehistorians have long been confident that if they could find out when and where corn was first domesticated, they might also uncover the origins of New World civilization.

Until little more than a generation ago investigators of this question were beset by twin difficulties. First, research in both Central America and South America had failed to show that any New World high culture significantly predated the Christian era. Second, botanical studies of the varieties of corn and its wild relatives had led more to conflict than to clarity in regard to the domesticated plant's most probable wild predecessor [see "The Mystery of Corn," by Paul C. Mangelsdorf; SCIENTIFIC AMERICAN Offprint 26]. Today, thanks to close cooperation between botanists and archaeologists, both difficulties have almost vanished. At least one starting point for New World agricultural activity has been securely established as being between 5,000 and 9,000 years ago. At the same time botanical analysis of fossil corn ears, grains and pollen, together with plain dirt archaeology, have solved a number of the mysteries concerning the wild origin and domestic evolution of corn. What follows is a review of the recent developments that have done so much to increase our understanding of this key period in New World prehistory.

The interest of botanists in the history of corn is largely practical: they study the genetics of corn in order to produce improved hybrids. After the wild ancestors of corn had been sought for nearly a century the search had narrowed to two tassel-bearing New World grasses—teosinte and *Tripsacum*—that had features resembling the domesticated plant. On the basis of crossbreeding experiments and other genetic studies, however, Paul C. Mangelsdorf of Harvard University and other investigators concluded in the 1940's that neither of these plants could be the original ancestor of corn. Instead teosinte appeared to be the product of the accidental crossbreeding of true corn and *Tripsacum*. Mangelsdorf advanced the hypothesis that the wild progenitor of corn was none other than corn itself—probably a popcorn with its kernels encased in pods.

Between 1948 and 1960 a number of discoveries proved Mangelsdorf's contention to be correct. I shall present these discoveries not in their strict chronological order but rather in their order of importance. First in importance, then, were analyses of pollen found in "cores" obtained in 1953 by drilling into the lake beds on which Mexico City is built. At levels that were estimated to be about 80,000 years old—perhaps 50,000 years older than the earliest known human remains in the New World—were found grains of corn

pollen. There could be no doubt that the pollen was from wild corn, and thus two aspects of the ancestry of corn were clarified. First, a form of wild corn has been in existence for 80,000 years, so that corn can indeed be descended from itself. Second, wild corn had flourished in the highlands of Mexico. As related archaeological discoveries will make plain, this geographical fact helped to narrow the potential range—from the southwestern U.S. to Peru—within which corn was probably first domesticated.

The rest of the key discoveries, involving the close cooperation of archaeologist and botanist, all belong to the realm of paleobotany. In the summer of 1948, for example, Herbert Dick, a graduate student in anthropology who had been working with Mangelsdorf, explored a dry rock-shelter in New Mexico called Bat Cave. Digging down through six feet of accumulated deposits, he and his colleagues found numerous remains of ancient corn, culminating in some tiny corncobs at the lowest level. Carbon-14 dating indicated that these cobs were between 4,000 and 5,000 years old. A few months later, exploring the La Perra cave in the state of Tamaulipas far to the north of Mexico City, I found similar corncobs that proved to be about 4,500 years old. The oldest cobs at both sites came close

to fitting the description Mangelsdorf had given of a hypothetical ancestor of the pod-popcorn type. The cobs, however, were clearly those of domesticated corn.

These two finds provided the basis for intensified archaeological efforts to find sites where the first evidences of corn would be even older. The logic was simple: A site old enough should have a level of wild corn remains older than the most ancient domesticated cobs. I continued my explorations near the La Perra cave and excavated a number of other sites in northeastern Mexico. In them I found more samples of ancient corn, but they were no older than those that had already been discovered. Robert Lister, another of Mangelsdorf's co-workers, also found primitive corn in a cave called Swallow's Nest in the Mexican state of Chihuahua, northwest of where I was working, but his finds were no older than mine.

If nothing older than domesticated corn of about 3000 B.C. could be found to the north of Mexico City, it seemed logical to try to the south. In 1958 I went off to look for dry caves and early corn in Guatemala and Honduras. The 1958 diggings produced nothing useful, so in 1959 I moved northward into Chiapas, Mexico's southernmost state. There were no corncobs to be found,

EXCAVATION of Coxcatlán cave required the removal of one-meter squares of cave floor over an area 25 meters long by six meters wide until bedrock was reached at a depth of almost five meters. In this way 28 occupation levels, attributable to seven distinctive culture phases, were discovered. Inhabitants of the three lowest levels lived by hunting and by collecting wild-plant foods.

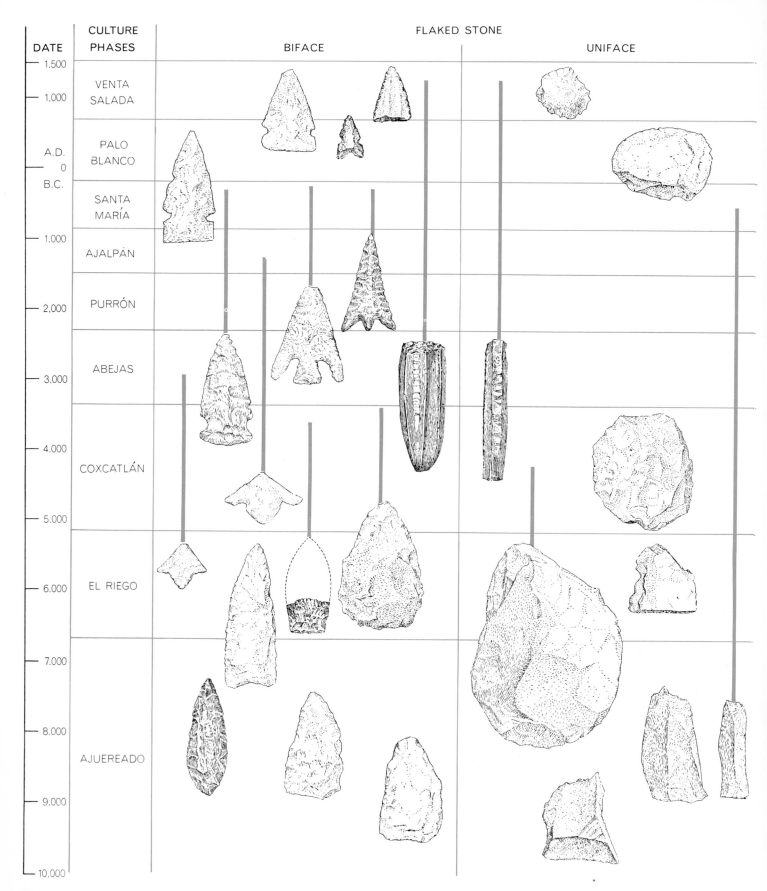

STONE ARTIFACTS from various Tehuacán sites are arrayed in two major categories: those shaped by chipping and flaking (*left*) and those shaped by grinding and pecking (*right*). Implements that have been chipped on one face only are separated from those that show bifacial workmanship; both groups are reproduced at half their natural size. The ground stone objects are not drawn to a common scale. The horizontal lines define the nine culture phases thus far distinguished in the valley. Vertical lines (*color*) indicate the extent to which the related artifact is known in cultures other than the one in which it is placed. At Tehuacán the evolution of civilization failed to follow the classic pattern established by the Neolithic Revolution in the Old World. For instance, the mortars,

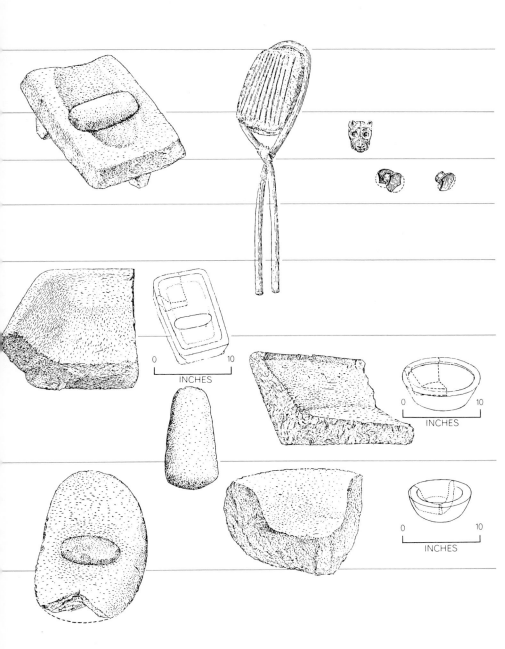

INCHES

INCHES

INCHES

pestles and other ground stone implements that first appear in the El Riego culture phase antedate the first domestication of corn by 1,500 years or more. Not until the Abejas phase, nearly 2,000 years later (marked by sizable obsidian cores and blades and by grinding implements that closely resemble the modern mano and metate), do the earliest village sites appear. More than 1,000 years later, in the Ajalpán phase, earplugs for personal adornment occur. The grooved, withe-bound stone near the top is a pounder for making bark cloth.

but one cave yielded corn pollen that also dated only to about 3000 B.C. The clues provided by paleobotany now appeared plain. Both to the north of Mexico City and in Mexico City itself (as indicated by the pollen of domesticated corn in the upper levels of the drill cores) the oldest evidence of domesticated corn was no more ancient than about 3000 B.C. Well to the south of Mexico City the oldest date was the same. The area that called for further search should therefore lie south of Mexico City but north of Chiapas.

Two additional considerations enabled me to narrow the area of search even more. First, experience had shown that dry locations offered the best chance of finding preserved specimens of corn. Second, the genetic studies of Mangelsdorf and other investigators indicated that wild corn was originally a highland grass, very possibly able to survive the rigorous climate of highland desert areas. Poring over the map of southern Mexico, I singled out three large highland desert areas: one in the southern part of the state of Oaxaca, one in Guerrero and one in southern Puebla.

Oaxaca yielded nothing of interest, so I moved on to Puebla to explore a dry highland valley known as Tehuacán. My local guides and I scrambled in and out of 38 caves and finally struck pay dirt in the 39th. This was a small rock-shelter near the village of Coxcatlán in the southern part of the valley of Tehuacán. On February 21, 1960, we dug up six corncobs, three of which looked more primitive and older than any I had seen before. Analysis in the carbon-14 laboratory at the University of Michigan confirmed my guess by dating these cobs as 5,600 years old—a good 500 years older than any yet found in the New World.

With this find the time seemed ripe for a large-scale, systematic search. If we had indeed arrived at a place where corn had been domesticated and New World civilization had first stirred, the closing stages of the search would require the special knowledge of many experts. Our primary need was to obtain the sponsorship of an institution interested and experienced in such research, and we were fortunate enough to enlist exactly the right sponsor: the Robert S. Peabody Foundation for Archaeology of Andover, Mass. Funds for the project were supplied by the National Science Foundation and by the agricultural branch of the Rockefeller

EVOLUTION OF CORN at Tehuacán starts (*far left*) with a fragmentary cob of wild corn of 5000 B.C. date. Next (*left to right*) are an early domesticated cob of 4000 B.C., an early hybrid variety of 3000 B.C. and an early variety of modern corn of 1000 B.C. Last (*far right*) is an entirely modern cob of the time of Christ. All are shown four-fifths of natural size.

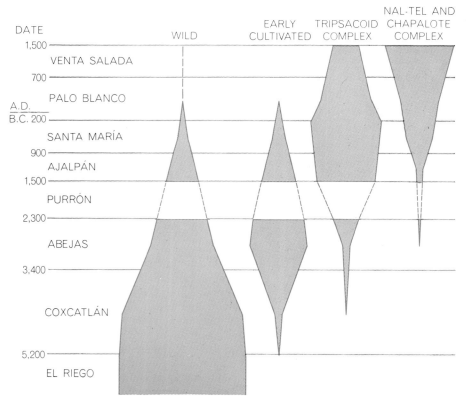

MAIN VARIETIES OF CORN changed in their relative abundance at Tehuacán between the time of initial cultivation during the Coxcatlán culture phase and the arrival of the conquistadors. Abundant at first, wild corn had become virtually extinct by the start of the Christian era, as had the early cultivated (but not hybridized) varieties. Thereafter the hybrids of the tripsacoid complex (produced by interbreeding wild corn with introduced varieties of corn-*Tripsacum* or corn-teosinte hybrids) were steadily replaced by two still extant types of corn, Nal-Tel and Chapalote. Minor varieties of late corn are not shown.

Foundation in Mexico, which is particularly interested in the origins of corn. The project eventually engaged nearly 50 experts in many specialties, not only archaeology and botany (including experts on many plants other than corn) but also zoology, geography, geology, ecology, genetics, ethnology and other disciplines.

The Coxcatlán cave, where the intensive new hunt had begun, turned out to be our richest dig. Working downward, we found that the cave had 28 separate occupation levels, the earliest of which may date to about 10,000 B.C. This remarkably long sequence has one major interruption: the period between 2300 B.C. and 900 B.C. The time from 900 B.C. to A.D. 1500, however, is represented by seven occupation levels. In combination with our findings in the Purrón cave, which contains 25 floors that date from about 7000 B.C. to 500 B.C., we have an almost continuous record (the longest interruption is less than 500 years) of nearly 12,000 years of prehistory. This is by far the longest record for any New World area.

All together we undertook major excavations at 12 sites in the valley of Tehuacán [*see bottom illustration on page 260*]. Of these only five caves—Coxcatlán, Purrón, San Marcos, Tecorral and El Riego East—contained remains of ancient corn. But these and the other stratified sites gave us a wealth of additional information about the people who inhabited the valley over a span of 12,000 years. In four seasons of digging, from 1961 through 1964, we reaped a vast archaeological harvest. This includes nearly a million individual remains of human activity, more than 1,000 animal bones (including those of extinct antelopes and horses), 80,000 individual wild-plant remains and some 25,000 specimens of corn. The artifacts arrange themselves into significant sequences of stone tools, textiles and pottery. They provide an almost continuous picture of the rise of civilization in the valley of Tehuacán. From the valley's geology, from the shells of its land snails, from the pollen and other remains of its plants and from a variety of other relics our group of specialists has traced the changes in climate, physical environment and plant and animal life that took place during the 12,000 years. They have even been able to tell (from the kinds of plant remains in various occupation levels) at what seasons of the year many of the floors in the caves were occupied.

Outstanding among our many finds was a collection of minuscule corncobs that we tenderly extracted from the lowest of five occupation levels at the San Marcos cave. They were only about 20 millimeters long, no bigger than the filter tip of a cigarette [*see top illustration on opposite page*], but under a magnifying lens one could see that they were indeed miniature ears of corn, with sockets that had once contained kernels enclosed in pods. These cobs proved to be some 7,000 years old. Mangelsdorf is convinced that this must be wild corn—the original parent from which modern corn is descended.

Cultivated corn, of course, cannot survive without man's intervention; the dozens of seeds on each cob are enveloped by a tough, thick husk that prevents them from scattering. Mangelsdorf has concluded that corn's wild progenitor probably consisted of a single seed spike on the stalk, with a few pod-covered ovules arrayed on the spike and a pollen-bearing tassel attached to the spike's end [*see bottom illustration at right*]. The most primitive cobs we unearthed in the valley of Tehuacán fulfilled these specifications. Each had the stump of a tassel at the end, each had borne kernels of the pod-popcorn type and each had been covered with only a light husk consisting of two leaves. These characteristics would have allowed the plant to disperse its seeds at maturity; the pods would then have protected the seeds until conditions were appropriate for germination.

The people of the valley of Tehuacán lived for thousands of years as collectors of wild vegetable and animal foods before they made their first timid efforts as agriculturists. It would therefore be foolhardy to suggest that the inhabitants of this arid highland pocket of Mexico were the first or the only people in the Western Hemisphere to bring wild corn under cultivation. On the contrary, the New World's invention of agriculture will probably prove to be geographically fragmented. What can be said for the people of Tehuacán is that they are the first whose evolution from primitive food collectors to civilized agriculturists has been traced in detail. As yet we have no such complete story either for the Old World or for other parts of the New World. This story is as follows.

From a hazy beginning some 12,000 years ago until about 7000 B.C. the people of Tehuacán were few in number. They wandered the valley from season to season in search of jackrabbits, rats, birds, turtles and other small animals, as well as such plant foods as be-

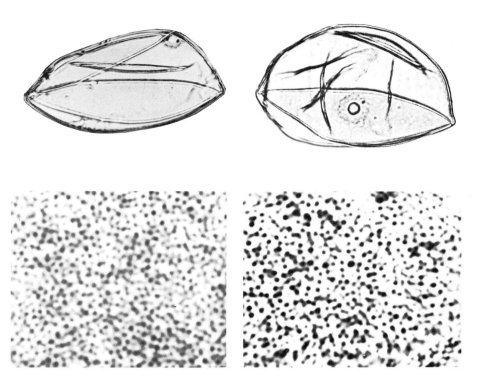

ANTIQUITY OF CORN in the New World was conclusively demonstrated when grains of pollen were found in drilling cores taken from Mexico City lake-bottom strata estimated to be 80,000 years old. Top two photographs (*magnification 435 diameters*) compare the ancient corn pollen (*left*) with modern pollen (*right*). Lower photographs (*magnification 4,500 diameters*) reveal similar ancient (*left*) and modern (*right*) pollen surface markings. The analysis and photographs are the work of Elso S. Barghoorn of Harvard University.

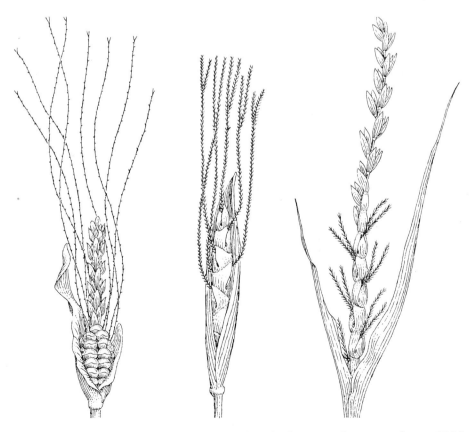

THREE NEW WORLD GRASSES are involved in the history of domesticated corn. Wild corn (*reconstruction at left*) was a pod-pop variety in which the male efflorescence grew from the end of the cob. Teosinte (*center*) and *Tripsacum* (*right*) are corn relatives that readily hybridized with wild and cultivated corn. Modern corn came from such crosses.

came available at different times of the year. Only occasionally did they manage to kill one of the now extinct species of horses and antelopes whose bones mark the lowest cave strata. These people used only a few simple implements of flaked stone: leaf-shaped projectile points, scrapers and engraving tools. We have named this earliest culture period the Ajuereado phase [*see illustration on pages 262 and 263*].

Around 6700 B.C. this simple pattern changed and a new phase—which we have named the El Riego culture from the cave where its first evidences appear—came into being. From then until about 5000 B.C. the people shifted from being predominantly trappers and hunters to being predominantly collectors of plant foods. Most of the plants they collected were wild, but they had domesticated squashes (starting with the species *Cucurbita mixta*) and avocados, and they also ate wild varieties of beans, amaranth and chili peppers. Among the flaked-stone implements, choppers appear. Entirely new kinds of stone tools—grinders, mortars, pestles and pounders of polished stone—are found in large numbers. During the growing season some families evidently gathered in temporary settlements, but these groups broke up into one-family bands during the leaner periods of the year. A number of burials dating from this culture phase hint at the possibility of part-time priests or witch doctors who directed the ceremonies involving the dead. The El Riego culture, however, had no corn.

By about 5000 B.C. a new phase, which we call the Coxcatlán culture,

had evolved. In this period only 10 percent of the valley's foodstuffs came from domestication rather than from collecting, hunting or trapping, but the list of domesticated plants is long. It includes corn, the water-bottle gourd, two species of squash, the amaranth, black and white zapotes, the tepary bean (*Phaseolus acutifolius*), the jack bean (*Canavalia ensiformis*), probably the common bean (*Phaseolus vulgaris*) and chili peppers.

Coxcatlán projectile points tend to be smaller than their predecessors; scrapers and choppers, however, remain much the same. The polished stone implements include forerunners of the classic New World roller-and-stone device for grinding grain: the mano and metate. There was evidently enough surplus energy among the people to allow the laborious hollowing out of stone water jugs and bowls.

It was in the phase following the Coxcatlán that the people of Tehuacán made the fundamental shift. By about 3400 B.C. the food provided by agriculture rose to about 30 percent of the total, domesticated animals (starting with the dog) made their appearance, and the people formed their first fixed settlements—small pit-house villages. By this stage (which we call the Abejas culture) they lived at a subsistence level that can be regarded as a foundation for the beginning of civilization. In about 2300 B.C. this gave way to the Purrón culture, marked by the cultivation of more hybridized types of corn and the manufacture of pottery.

Thereafter the pace of civilization in

the valley speeded up greatly. The descendants of the Purrón people developed a culture (called Ajalpán) that from about 1500 B.C. on involved a more complex village life, refinements of pottery and more elaborate ceremonialism, including the development of a figurine cult, perhaps representing family gods. This culture led in turn to an even more sophisticated one (which we call Santa María) that started about 850 B.C. Taking advantage of the valley's streams, the Santa María peoples of Tehuacán began to grow their hybrid corn in irrigated fields. Our surveys indicate a sharp rise in population. Temple mounds were built, and artifacts show signs of numerous contacts with cultures outside the valley. The Tehuacán culture in this period seems to have been strongly influenced by that of the Olmec people who lived to the southeast along the coast of Veracruz.

By about 200 B.C. the outside influence on Tehuacán affairs shifted from that of the Olmec of the east coast to that of Monte Alban to the south and west. The valley now had large irrigation projects and substantial hilltop ceremonial centers surrounded by villages. In this Palo Blanco phase some of the population proceeded to full-time specialization in various occupations, including the development of a salt industry. New domesticated food products appeared—the turkey, the tomato, the peanut and the guava. In the next period—Venta Salada, starting about A.D. 700—Monte Alban influences gave way to the influence of the Mixtecs. This period saw the rise of true

COXCATLÁN CAVE BURIAL, dating to about A.D. 100, contained the extended body of an adolescent American Indian, wrapped in a pair of cotton blankets with brightly colored stripes. This bundle in turn rested on sticks and the whole was wrapped in bark cloth.

cities in the valley, of an agricultural system that provided some 85 percent of the total food supply, of trade and commerce, a standing army, large-scale irrigation projects and a complex religion. Finally, just before the Spanish Conquest, the Aztecs took over from the Mixtecs.

Our archaeological study of the valley of Tehuacán, carried forward in collaboration with workers in so many other disciplines, has been gratifyingly productive. Not only have we documented one example of the origin of domesticated corn but also comparative studies of other domesticated plants have indicated that there were multiple centers of plant domestication in the Americas. At least for the moment we have at Tehuacán not only evidence of the earliest village life in the New World but also the first (and worst) pottery in Mexico and a fairly large sample of skeletons of some of the earliest Indians yet known.

Even more important is the fact that we at last have one New World example of the development of a culture from savagery to civilization. Preliminary analysis of the Tehuacán materials indicate that the traditional hypothesis about the evolution of high cultures may have to be reexamined and modified. In southern Mexico many of the characteristic elements of the Old World's Neolithic Revolution fail to appear suddenly in the form of a new culture complex or a revolutionized way of life. For example, tools of ground (rather than chipped) stone first occur at Tehuacán about 6700 B.C., and plant domestication begins at least by 5000 B.C. The other classic elements of the Old World Neolithic, however, are slow to appear. Villages are not found until around 3000 B.C., nor pottery until around 2300 B.C., and a sudden increase in population is delayed until 500 B.C. Reviewing this record, I think more in terms of Neolithic "evolution" than "revolution."

Our preliminary researches at Tehuacán suggest rich fields for further exploration. There is need not only for detailed investigations of the domestication and development of other New World food plants but also for attempts to obtain similar data for the Old World. Then—perhaps most challenging of all—there is the need for comparative studies of the similarities and differences between evolving cultures in the Old World and the New to determine the hows and whys of the rise of civilization itself.

SOPHISTICATED FIGURINE of painted pottery is one example of the artistic capacity of Tehuacán village craftsmen. This specimen, 2,900 years old, shows Olmec influences.

27

TEOTIHUACÁN

RENÉ MILLON
June 1967

*The first and largest city of the pre-Columbian New World
arose in the Valley of Mexico during the first millenium
A.D. At its height the metropolis covered a larger area
than imperial Rome*

When the Spaniards conquered Mexico, they described Montezuma's capital Tenochtitlán in such vivid terms that for centuries it seemed that the Aztec stronghold must have been the greatest city of pre-Columbian America. Yet only 25 miles to the north of Tenochtitlán was the site of a city that had once been even more impressive. Known as Teotihuacán, it had risen, flourished and fallen hundreds of years before the conquistadors entered Mexico. At the height of its power, around A.D. 500, Teotihuacán was larger than imperial Rome. For more than half a millennium it was to Middle America what Rome, Benares or Mecca have been to the Old World: at once a religious and cultural capital and a major economic and political center.

Unlike many of the Maya settlements to the south, in both Mexico and Guatemala, Teotihuacán was never a "lost" city. The Aztecs were still worshiping at its sacred monuments at the time of the Spanish Conquest, and scholarly studies of its ruins have been made since the middle of the 19th century. Over the past five years, however, a concerted program of investigation has yielded much new information about this early American urban center.

In the Old World the first civilizations were associated with the first cities, but both in Middle America and in Peru the rise of civilization does not seem to have occurred in an urban setting. As far as we can tell today, the foundation for the earliest civilization in Middle America was laid in the first millennium B.C. by a people we know as the Olmecs. None of the major Olmec centers discovered so far is a city. Instead these centers—the most important of which are located in the forested lowlands along the Gulf of Mexico on the narrow Isthmus of Tehuantepec—were of a ceremonial character, with small permanent populations probably consisting of priests and their attendants.

The Olmecs and those who followed them left to many other peoples of Middle America, among them the builders of Teotihuacán, a heritage of religious beliefs, artistic symbolism and other cultural traditions. Only the Teotihuacanos, however, created an urban civilization of such vigor that it significantly influenced the subsequent development of most other Middle American civilizations—urban and nonurban—down to the time of the Aztecs. It is hard to say exactly why this happened, but at least some of the contributing factors are evident. The archaeological record suggests the following sequence of events.

A settlement of moderate size existed at Teotihuacán fairly early in the first century B.C. At about the same time a number of neighboring religious centers were flourishing. One was Cuicuilco, to the southwest of Teotihuacán in the Valley of Mexico; another was Cholula, to the east in the Valley of Puebla. The most important influences shaping the "Teotihuacán way" probably stemmed from centers such as these. Around the time of Christ, Teotihuacán began to grow rapidly, and between A.D. 100 and 200 its largest religious monument was raised on the site of an earlier shrine. Known today as the Pyramid of the Sun, it was as large at the base as the great pyramid of Cheops in Egypt [*see bottom illustration on page 274*].

The powerful attraction of a famous holy place is not enough, of course, to explain Teotihuacán's early growth or later importance. The city's strategic location was one of a number of material factors that contributed to its rise. Teotihuacán lies astride the narrow waist of a valley that is the best route between the Valley of Mexico and the Valley of Puebla. The Valley of Puebla, in turn, is the gateway to the lowlands along the Gulf of Mexico.

The lower part of Teotihuacán's valley is a rich alluvial plain, watered by permanent springs and thus independent of the uncertainties of highland rainfall.

CEREMONIAL HEART of Teotihuacán is seen in an aerial photograph looking southeast toward Cerro Patlachique, one of a pair of mountains that flank the narrow valley dominated by the city. The large pyramid in

The inhabitants of the valley seem early to have dug channels to create an irrigation system and to provide their growing city with water. Even today a formerly swampy section at the edge of the ancient city is carved by channels into "chinampas": small artificial islands that are intensively farmed. Indeed, it is possible that this form of agriculture, which is much better known as it was practiced in Aztec times near Tenochtitlán, was invented centuries earlier by the people of Teotihuacán.

The valley had major deposits of obsidian, the volcanic glass used all over ancient Middle America to make cutting and scraping tools and projectile points. Obsidian mining in the valley was apparently most intensive during the city's early years. Later the Teotihuacanos appear to have gained control of deposits of obsidian north of the Valley of Mexico that were better suited than the local material to the mass production of blade implements. Trade in raw obsidian and obsidian implements became increasing-ly important to the economy of Teotihuacán, reaching a peak toward the middle of the first millennium A.D.

The recent investigation of Teotihuacán has been carried forward by specialists working on three independent but related projects. One project was a monumental program of excavation and reconstruction undertaken by Mexico's National Institute of Anthropology, headed by Eusebio Dávalos. From 1962 to 1964 archaeologists under the direction of Ignacio Bernal, director of the National Museum of Anthropology, unearthed and rebuilt a number of the structures that lie along the city's principal avenue ("the Street of the Dead"); they have also restored Teotihuacán's second main pyramid ("the Pyramid of the Moon"), which lies at the avenue's northern end. Two of the city's four largest structures, the Pyramid of the Sun and the Citadel, within which stands the Temple of Quetzalcoatl, had been cleared and restored in the 1900's and the 1920's respectively. Among other notable achievements, the National Institute's work brought to light some of the city's finest mural paintings.

As the Mexican archaeologists were at work a group under the direction of William T. Sanders of Pennsylvania State University conducted an intensive study of the ecology and the rural-settlement patterns of the valley. Another group, from the University of Rochester, initiated a mapping project under my direction. This last effort, which is still under way, involves preparing a detailed topographic map on which all the city's several thousand structures will be located. The necessary information is being secured by the examination of surface remains, supplemented by small-scale excavations. One result of our work has been to demonstrate how radically different Teotihuacán was from all other settlements of its time in Middle America. It was here that the New World's urban revolution exploded into being.

It had long been clear that the center

the foreground is the Pyramid of the Moon. The larger one beyond it is the Pyramid of the Sun. Many of the more than 100 smaller religious structures that line the city's central avenue, the Street of the Dead, are visible in the photograph. South of the Pyramid of the Sun and east of the central avenue is the large enclosure known as the Citadel. It and the Great Compound, a matching structure not visible in the photograph, formed the city's center. More than 4,000 additional buildings, most no longer visible, spread for miles beyond the center. At the peak of Teotihuacán's power, around A.D. 500, the population of the city was more than 50,000.

of Teotihuacán was planned, but it soon became apparent to us that the extent and magnitude of the planning went far beyond the center. Our mapping revealed that the city's streets and the large majority of its buildings had been laid out along the lines of a precise grid aligned with the city center. The grid was established in Teotihuacán's formative days, but it may have been more intensively exploited later, perhaps in relation to "urban renewal" projects undertaken when the city had become rich and powerful.

The prime direction of the **grid is** slightly east of north (15.5 degrees). **The** basic modular unit of the plan is close to 57 meters. A number of residential structures are squares of this size. The plan of many of the streets seems to repeat various multiples of the 57-meter

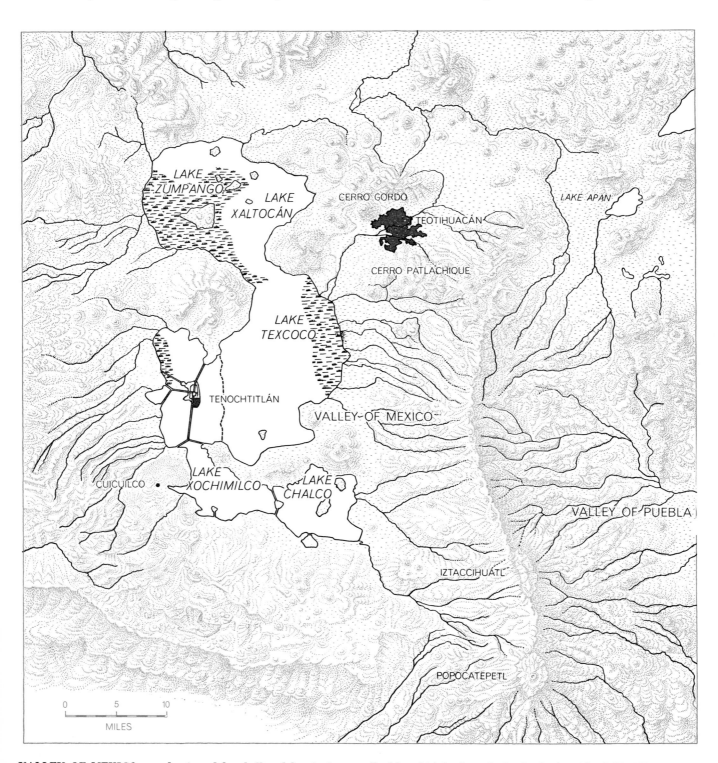

VALLEY OF MEXICO was dominated by shallow lakes in late pre-Hispanic times; in the rainy season they coalesced into a single body of water. Teotihuacán was strategically located; it commanded a narrow valley a few miles northeast of the lakes that provided the best route between the Valley of Mexico and the Valley of Puebla, which leads to the lowlands along the Gulf of Mexico (*see map at top of opposite page*). It was an important center of trade and worship from 100 B.C. until about A.D. 750. Centuries after its fall the Aztec capital of Tenochtitlán grew up in the western shallows of Lake Texcoco, 25 miles from the earlier metropolis.

unit. The city's major avenues, which run parallel to the north-south axis, are spaced at regular intervals. Even the river running through the center of the city was canalized to conform to the grid. Miles from the city center the remains of buildings are oriented to the grid, even when they were built on slopes that ran counter to it. A small design composed of concentric circles divided into quadrants may have served as a standard surveyor's mark; it is sometimes pecked into the floors of buildings and sometimes into bare bedrock. One such pair of marks two miles apart forms a line exactly perpendicular to the city's north-south axis. The achievement of this kind of order obviously calls for an initial vision that is both audacious and self-confident.

A city planner's description of Teotihuacán would begin not with the monumental Pyramid of the Sun but with the two complexes of structures that form the city center. These are the Citadel and the Great Compound, lying respectively to the east and west of the city's main north-south avenue, the Street of the Dead. The names given the various structures and features of Teotihuacán are not, incidentally, the names by which the Teotihuacanos knew them. Some come from Spanish translations of Aztec names; others were bestowed by earlier archaeologists or by our mappers and are often the place names used by the local people.

The Street of the Dead forms the main axis of the city. At its northern end it stops at the Pyramid of the Moon, and we have found that to the south it extends for two miles beyond the Citadel-Compound complex. The existence of a subordinate axis running east and west had not been suspected until our mappers discovered one broad avenue running more than two miles to the east of the Citadel and a matching avenue extending the same distance westward from the Compound.

To make it easier to locate buildings over so large an area we imposed our own 500-meter grid on the city, orienting it to the Street of the Dead and using the center of the city as the zero point of the system [see bottom illustration at right]. The heavy line defining the limits of the city was determined by walking around the perimeter of the city and examining evidence on the surface to establish where its outermost remains end. The line traces a zone free of such remains that is at least 300 meters wide and that sharply separates the city from

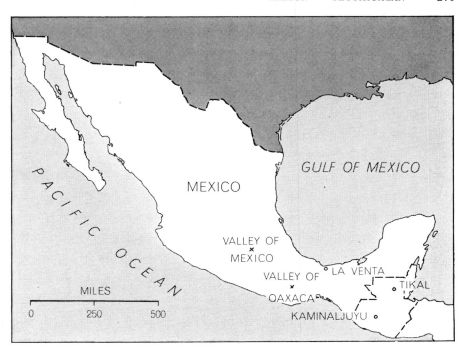

EARLY CIVILIZATION in Middle America appeared first in the lowlands along the Gulf of Mexico at such major centers of Olmec culture as La Venta. Soon thereafter a number of ceremonial centers appeared in the highlands, particularly in the valleys of Oaxaca, Puebla and Mexico. Kaminaljuyu and Tikal, Maya centers respectively in highlands and lowlands of what is now Guatemala, came under Teotihuacán's influence at the height of its power.

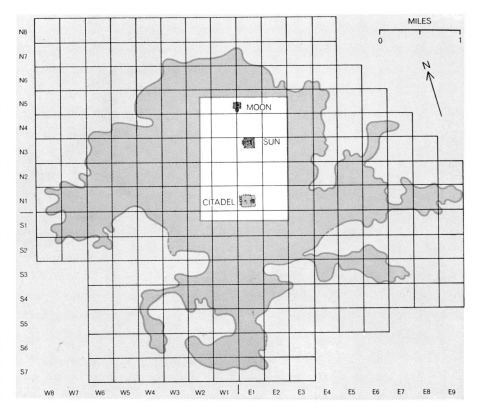

IRREGULAR BOUNDARY of Teotihuacán is shown as a solid line that approaches the edges of a grid, composed of 500-meter squares, surveyed by the author's team. The grid parallels the north-south direction of the Street of the Dead, the city's main avenue. One extension of the city in its early period, which is only partly known, has been omitted. A map of Teotihuacán's north-central zone (light color) is reproduced on the next page.

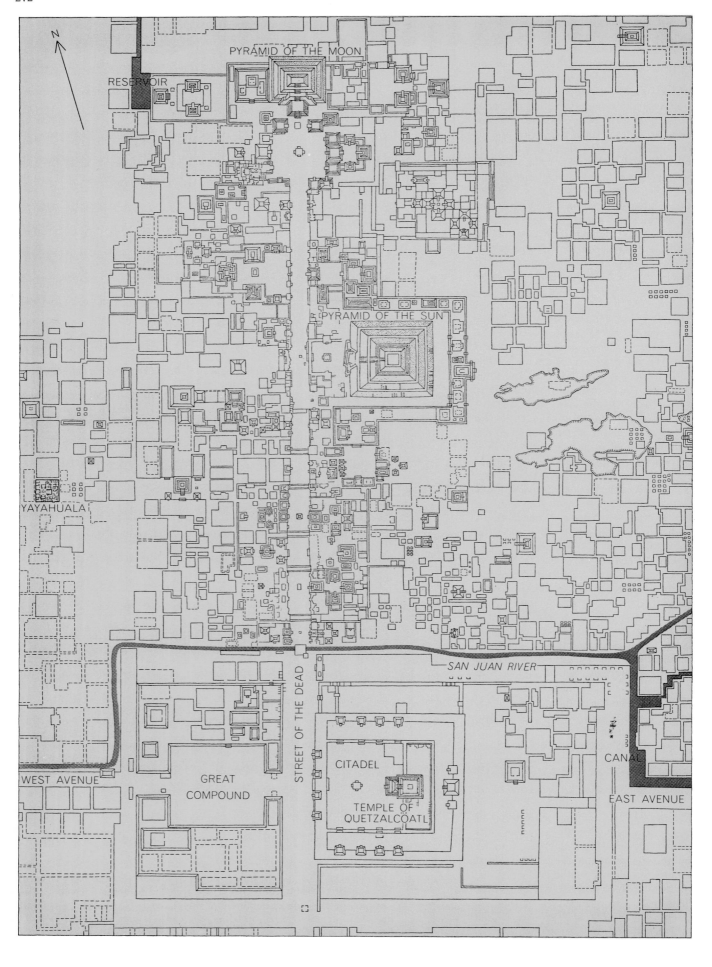

N

RESERVOIR

PYRAMID OF THE MOON

PYRAMID OF THE SUN

YAYAHUALA

SAN JUAN RIVER

STREET OF THE DEAD

CANAL

WEST AVENUE

GREAT
COMPOUND

CITADEL

TEMPLE OF
QUETZALCOATL

EAST AVENUE

the countryside. The Street of the Dead, East Avenue and West Avenue divide Teotihuacán into quadrants centered on the Citadel-Compound complex. We do not know if these were formally recognized as administrative quarters of the city, as they were in Tenochtitlán. It is nonetheless possible that they may have been, since there are a number of other similarities between the two cities.

Indeed, during the past 25 years Mexican scholars have argued for a high degree of continuity in customs and beliefs from the Aztecs back to the Teotihuacanos, based partly on an assumed continuity in language. This hypothetical continuity, which extends through the intervening Toltec times, provides valuable clues in interpreting archaeological evidence. For example, the unity of religion and politics that archaeologists postulate at Teotihuacán is reinforced by what is known of Aztec society.

The public entrance of the Citadel is a monumental staircase on the Street of the Dead. Inside the Citadel a plaza opens onto the Temple of Quetzalcoatl, the principal sacred building in this area. The temple's facade represents the most successful integration of architecture and sculpture so far discovered at Teotihuacán [see bottom illustration on page 276].

The Great Compound, across the street from the Citadel, had gone unrecognized as a major structure until our survey. We found that it differs from all other known structures at Teotihuacán and that in area it is the city's largest. Its main components are two great raised platforms. These form a north and a south wing and are separated by broad entrances at the level of the street on the east and west. The two wings thus flank a plaza somewhat larger than the one within the Citadel. Few of the structures on the platforms seem to have been temples or other religious buildings. Most of them face away from the Street of the Dead, whereas almost all the other known structures along the avenue face toward it.

CITY CENTER is composed of two sets of structures, the Great Compound and the Citadel (bottom of illustration on opposite page). They stand on either side of the Street of the Dead, the main north-south axis of the city. A pair of avenues approaching the center of the city from east and west form the secondary axis. The city's largest religious monuments were the Pyramid of the Sun, the Pyramid of the Moon and the Temple of Quetzalcoatl, which lies inside the Citadel. Yayahuala (left of center) was one of many residential compounds. Its architecture is shown in detail on page 277.

One therefore has the impression that the Compound was not devoted to religious affairs. In the Citadel there are clusters of rooms to the north and south of the Temple of Quetzalcoatl, but the overall effect conveyed by the temples and the other buildings that surround the Citadel's plaza is one of a political center in a sacred setting. Perhaps some of its rooms housed the high priests of Teotihuacán.

The plaza of the Compound is a strategically located open space that could have been the city's largest marketplace. The buildings that overlook this plaza could have been at least partly devoted to the administration of the economic affairs of the city. Whatever their functions were, the Citadel and the Compound are the heart of the city. Together they form a majestic spatial unit, a central island surrounded by more open ground than is found in any other part of Teotihuacán.

The total area of the city was eight square miles. Not counting ritual structures, more than 4,000 buildings, most of them apartment houses, were built to shelter the population. At the height of Teotihuacán's power, in the middle of the first millennium A.D., the population certainly exceeded 50,000 and was probably closer to 100,000. This is not a particularly high figure compared with Old World religious-political centers; today the population of Mecca is some 130,000 and that of Benares more than 250,000 (to which is added an annual influx of a million pilgrims). One reason Teotihuacán did not have a larger population was that its gleaming lime-plastered residential structures were only one story high. Although most of the inhabitants lived in apartments, the buildings were "ranch-style" rather than "high-rise."

The architects of Teotihuacán designed apartments to offer a maximum of privacy within the crowded city, using a concept similar to the Old World's classical atrium house [see illustration on page 277]. The rooms of each apartment surrounded a central patio; each building consisted of a series of rooms, patios, porticoes and passageways, all secluded from the street. This pattern was also characteristic of the city's palaces. The residential areas of Teotihuacán must have presented a somewhat forbidding aspect from the outside: high windowless walls facing on narrow streets. Within the buildings, however, the occupants were assured of privacy. Each patio had its own drainage system; each admitted light and air to the surrounding apartments; each made it possible for the in-

habitants to be out of doors yet alone. It may be that this architectural style contributed to Teotihuacán's permanence as a focus of urban life for more than 500 years.

The basic building materials of Teotihuacán were of local origin. Outcrops of porous volcanic rock in the valley were quarried and the stone was crushed and mixed with lime and earth to provide a kind of moisture-resistant concrete that was used as the foundation for floors and walls. The same material was used for roofing; wooden posts spaced at intervals bore much of the weight of the roof. Walls were made of stone and mortar or of sunbaked adobe brick. Floors and wall surfaces were then usually finished with highly polished plaster.

What kinds of people lived in Teotihuacán? Religious potentates, priestly bureaucrats and military leaders presumably occupied the top strata of the city's society, but their number could not have been large. Many of the inhabitants tilled lands outside the city and many others must have been artisans: potters, workers in obsidian and stone and craftsmen dealing with more perishable materials such as cloth, leather, feathers and wood (traces of which are occasionally preserved). Well-defined concentrations of surface remains suggest that craft groups such as potters and workers in stone and obsidian tended to live together in their own neighborhoods. This lends weight to the hypothesis that each apartment building was solely occupied by a "corporate" group, its families related on the basis of occupation, kinship or both. An arrangement of this kind, linking the apartment dwellers to one another by webs of joint interest and activity, would have promoted social stability.

If groups with joint interests lived not only in the same apartment building but also in the same general neighborhood, the problem of governing the city would have been substantially simplified. Such organization of neighborhood groups could have provided an intermediate level between the individual and the state. Ties of cooperation, competition or even conflict between people in different neighborhoods could have created the kind of social network that is favorable to cohesion.

The marketplace would similarly have made an important contribution to the integration of Teotihuacán society. If the greater part of the exchange of goods and services in the city took place in one or more major markets (such as the one that may have occupied the plaza

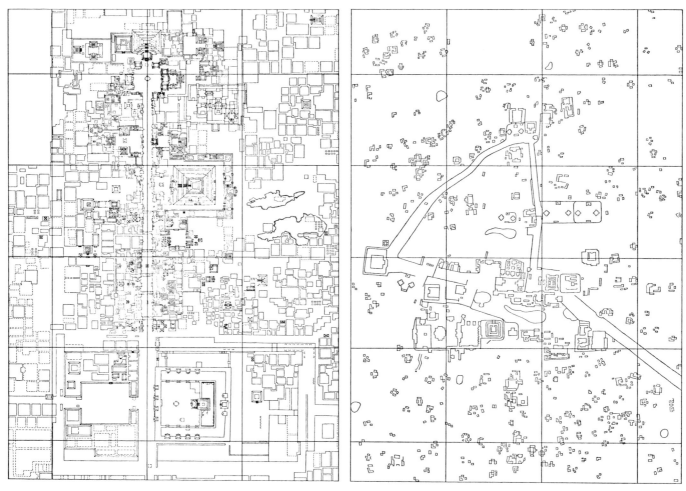

DENSITY OF SETTLEMENT at Teotihuacán is compared with that at Tikal, largest of the lowland Maya ceremonial centers in Middle America. The maps show the central area of each settlement at the same scale. The data for Teotihuacán (*left*) are from surveys by the author and the Mexican government. Those for Tikal (*right*) are from a survey by the University of Pennsylvania. Even though its center included many public structures, Teotihuacán's concentrated residential pattern shows its urban character.

PYRAMID OF THE SUN is as broad at the base as the great pyramid of Cheops in Egypt, although it is only half as high. It was built over the site of an earlier shrine during Teotihuacán's first major period of growth, in the early centuries of the Christian era.

of the Great Compound), then not only the Teotihuacanos but also the outsiders who used the markets would have felt a vested interest in maintaining "the peace of the market." Moreover, the religion of Teotihuacán would have imbued the city's economic institutions with a sacred quality.

The various social groups in the city left some evidence of their identity. For example, we located a walled area, associated with the west side of the Pyramid of the Moon, where large quantities of waste obsidian suggest that obsidian workers may have formed part of a larger temple community. We also found what looks like a foreign neighborhood. Occupied by people who apparently came to Teotihuacán from the Valley of Oaxaca, the area lies in the western part of the city. It is currently under study by John Paddock of the University of the Americas, a specialist in the prehistory of Oaxaca. Near the eastern edge of the city quantities of potsherds have been found that are characteristic of Maya areas and the Veracruz region along the Gulf of Mexico. These fragments suggest that the neighborhood was inhabited either by people from those areas or by local merchants who specialized in such wares.

We have found evidence that as the centuries passed two of the city's important crafts—the making of pottery and obsidian tools—became increasingly specialized. From the third century A.D. on some obsidian workshops contain a high proportion of tools made by striking blades from a "core" of obsidian; others have a high proportion of tools made by chipping a piece of obsidian until the desired shape was obtained. Similar evidence of specialization among potters is found in the southwestern part of the city. There during Teotihuacán's period of greatest expansion one group of potters concentrated on the mass production of the most common type of cooking ware.

The crafts of Teotihuacán must have helped to enrich the city. So also, no doubt, did the pilgrim traffic. In addition to the three major religious structures more than 100 other temples and shrines line the Street of the Dead. Those who visited the city's sacred buildings must have included not only peasants and townspeople from the entire Valley of Mexico but also pilgrims from as far away as Guatemala. When one adds to these worshipers the visiting merchants, traders and peddlers attracted by the markets of Teotihuacán, it seems likely

HUMAN FIGURE, wearing a feather headdress, face paint and sandals, decorates the side of a vase dating from the sixth century A.D. Similar figures often appear in the city's murals.

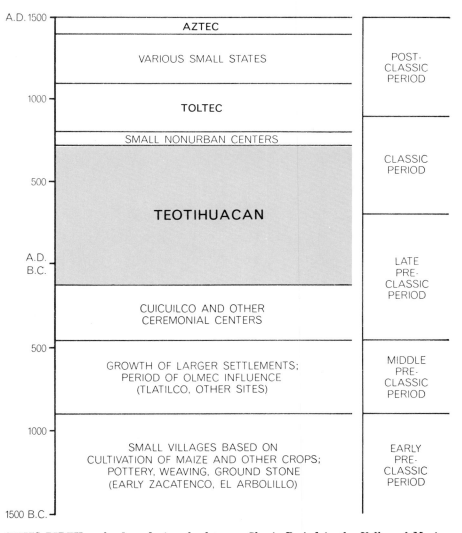

CITY'S BIRTH took place during the late pre-Classic Period in the Valley of Mexico, about a century before the beginning of the Christian era. Other highland ceremonial centers such as Cuicuilco in the Valley of Mexico and Cholula in the Valley of Puebla were influential at that time. Although Teotihuacán fell in about A.D. 750, near the end of the Classic Period, its religious monuments were deemed sacred by the Aztecs until Hispanic times.

PYRAMID OF THE MOON, excavated in the early 1960's by a Mexican government group under the direction of Ignacio Bernal, stands at the northern end of the Street of the Dead. The façade presented to the avenue (*above*) consists of several interlocking, truncated pyramids thrusting toward the sky. The structure, 150 feet high and 490 feet wide at the base, is smaller than the Pyramid of the Sun but is architecturally more sophisticated.

TEMPLE OF QUETZALCOATL is the major religious structure within the Citadel, the eastern half of Teotihuacán's city center. The building is believed to represent the most successful integration of sculpture and architecture to be achieved throughout the city's long history. A covering layer of later construction protected the ornate facade from damage.

that many people would have been occupied catering to the needs of those who were merely visiting the city.

Radical social transformations took place during the growth of the city. As Teotihuacán increased in size there was first a relative and then an absolute decline in the surrounding rural population. This is indicated by both our data from the city and Sanders' from the countryside. Apparently many rural populations left their villages and were concentrated in the city. The process seems to have accelerated around A.D. 500, when the population of the city approached its peak. Yet the marked increase in density within the city was accompanied by a reduction in the city's size. It was at this time, during the sixth century, that urban renewal programs may have been undertaken in areas where density was on the rise.

Such movements of rural and urban populations must have conflicted with local interests. That they were carried out successfully demonstrates the prestige and power of the hierarchy in Teotihuacán. Traditional loyalties to the religion of Teotihuacán were doubtless invoked. Nevertheless, one wonders if the power of the military would not have been increasingly involved. There is evidence both in Teotihuacán and beyond its borders that its soldiers became more and more important from the fifth century on. It may well be that at the peak of its power and influence Teotihuacán itself was becoming an increasingly oppressive place in which to live.

The best evidence of the power and influence that the leaders of Teotihuacán exercised elsewhere in Middle America comes from Maya areas. One ancient religious center in the Maya highlands—Kaminaljuyu, the site of modern Guatemala City—appears to have been occupied at one time by priests and soldiers from Teotihuacán. Highland Guatemala received a massive infusion of Teotihuacán cultural influences, with Teotihuacán temple architecture replacing older styles. This has been recognized for some time, but only recently has it become clear that Teotihuacán also influenced the Maya lowlands. The people of Tikal in Guatemala, largest of the lowland Maya centers, are now known to have been under strong influence from Teotihuacán. The people of Tikal adopted some of Teotihuacán's artistic traditions and erected a massive stone monument to Teotihuacán's rain god. William R. Coe of the University of Pennsylvania and his colleagues, who are working at

Tikal, are in the midst of evaluating the nature and significance of this influence.

Tikal provides an instructive measure of the difference in the density of construction in Maya population centers and those in central Mexico. It was estimated recently that Tikal supported a population of about 10,000. As the illustration at the top of page 274 shows, the density of Teotihuacán's central area is strikingly different from that of Tikal's. Not only was Teotihuacán's population at least five times larger than Tikal's but also it was far less dispersed. In such a crowded urban center problems of integration, cohesion and social control must have been of a totally different order of magnitude than those of a less populous and less compact ceremonial center such as Tikal.

What were the circumstances of Teo-

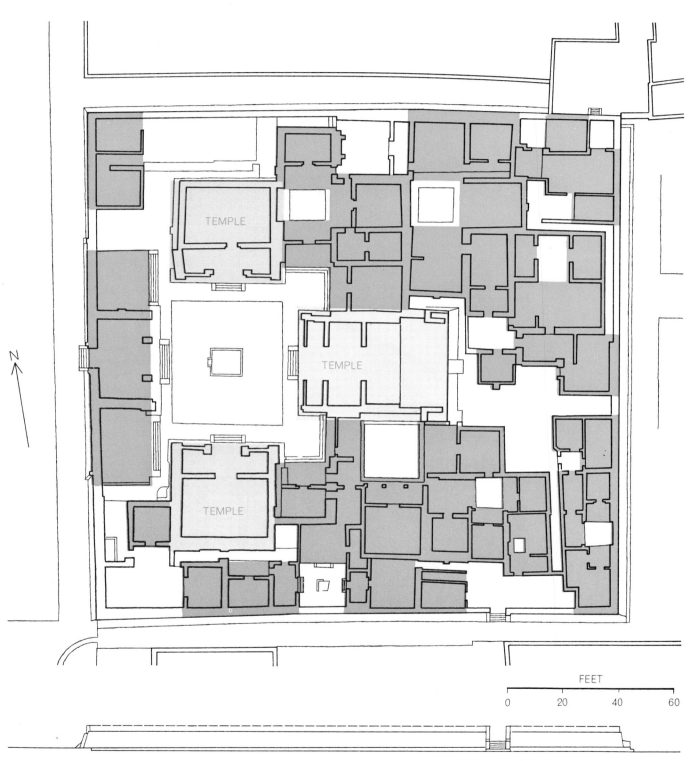

SOUTH ELEVATION

APARTMENT HOUSE typical of the city's many multiroomed dwellings was excavated in 1961 by Laurette Séjourné. The outer walls of the compound conform with the 57-meter module favored by the city's planners. Within its forbidding exterior (*see south façade at bottom of illustration*) individual apartments comprised several rooms grouped around unroofed patios (*smaller white areas*).

FEATHERED SERPENT, from one of the earlier murals found at Teotihuacán, has a free, flowing appearance. The animal below the serpent is a jaguar; the entire mural, which is not shown, was probably painted around A.D. 400. It may portray a cyclical myth of creation and destruction. The city's principal gods were often represented in the form of animals.

LATER SERPENT GOD, with a rattlesnake tail, is from a mural probably painted less than a century before the fall of Teotihuacán. The figure is rendered in a highly formal manner. A trend toward formalism is apparent in the paintings produced during the city's final years.

tihuacán's decline and fall? Almost certainly both environmental and social factors were involved. The climate of the region is semiarid today, and there is evidence that a long-term decline in annual rainfall brought the city to a similar condition in the latter half of the first millennium A.D. Even before then deforestation of the surrounding hills may have begun a process of erosion that caused a decrease in the soil moisture available for crops. Although persistent drought would have presented increasingly serious problems for those who fed the city, this might have been the lesser of its consequences. More ominous would have been the effect of increasing aridity on the cultivators of marginal lands and the semisedentary tribesmen in the highlands north of the Valley of Mexico. As worsening conditions forced these peoples to move, the Teotihuacanos might have found themselves not only short of food but also under military pressure along their northern frontier.

Whether or not climatic change was a factor, some signs of decline—such as the lowering of standards of construction and pottery-making—are evident during the last century of Teotihuacán's existence. Both a reduction in population and a tendency toward dispersion suggest that the fabric of society was suffering from strains and weaknesses. Once such a process of deterioration passed a critical point the city would have become vulnerable to attack.

No evidence has been found that Teotihuacán as a whole had formal defenses. Nonetheless, the valley's drainage pattern provides some natural barriers, large parts of the city were surrounded by walls or massive platforms and its buildings were formidable ready-made fortresses. Perhaps the metropolis was comparatively unprotected because it had for so long had an unchallenged supremacy.

In any case, archaeological evidence indicates that around A.D. 750 much of central Teotihuacán was looted and burned, possibly with the help of the city's own people. The repercussions of Teotihuacán's fall seem to have been felt throughout civilized Middle America. The subsequent fall of Monte Alban, the capital of the Oaxaca region, and of many Maya ceremonial centers in Guatemala and the surrounding area may reasonably be associated with dislocations set in motion by the fall of Teotihuacán. Indeed, the appropriate epitaph for the New World's first major metropolis may be that it was as influential in its collapse as in its long and brilliant flowering.

III

CULTURAL ANTHROPOLOGY

Whereas cultural anthropologists have concerned themselves traditionally with the subjects of kinship organization, primitive economics and law, magic and folklore, and arts, crafts, and other subjects of material culture, many of them are now turning their attention to the discrepancies between the nature and quality of the lives of the powerful and the powerless, the dominant and the dominated. The following essays are arranged in such a way that the reader can trace the elaboration of main trends in cultural anthropology that has taken place in the past decade and a half.

Traditional Concerns:
Kinship, Polity, Economy, Society

TRADITIONAL CONCERNS: KINSHIP, POLITY, ECONOMY, SOCIETY

The first essay, "Primitive Kinship" by Meyer Fortes, deals with the topic most fitting for a beginning. Perhaps no ethnological subject has drawn more analysis and debate over the past century than kinship organization. Fortes compares the kinship organization of the Ashanti and Tallensi tribes in Ghana, West Africa. His discussion makes it clear why kinship is of interest and importance to anthropologists by distinguishing "citizen" societies, in which family members are subject to significant influence from beyond the family, from "kinsmen" societies, in which a family member's primary loyalties are to kinsmen. The family organization among the societies in which economy, polity, and even religion are embedded in kinship relations and obligations is most often consanguineal, centering on a patrilineal or matrilineal descent, but the family organization among modern Western nations is re-formed with each new marriage and is most often bilateral, an individual being considered as closely related to the relatives of the father as to the relatives of the mother. Fortes thus lays the ground work for further study of why and in what ways kinship societies change their kinship relations when they are influenced by industrialized citizen societies, and we will see how other researchers have pursued this topic in the last section of the book.

Max Gluckman draws our attention to political competition for scarce resources and the emergence of wars of conquest among tribes in southeastern Africa in "The Rise of a Zulu Empire." Gluckman focuses on the Zulu tribe of what is now Durban, and he shows how in 1816 one leader, Shaka, succeeded in waging wars that explicitly destroyed earlier kinship and tribal organizations, which resulted in the conquest of a territory of some 80,000 square miles and the disruption of peoples through a third of Africa. Shaka's predecessor, Dingiswayo, had conquered thirty tribes, including the Zulu, sixteen years earlier, but his battles were fought in traditional ways with minimum slaughter. Gluckman points out that tribes before Dingiswayo's time had warred only when scarcity of resources necessitated it, and Dingiswayo's conquests were attempted as a way of subduing that warfare. Dingiswayo was a temperate victor, retaining the tribal organization of the groups he conquered, but Shaka was an innovative, ruthless warrior who sought to shatter the chiefly families after his victory over them. Although Shaka was a more successful conqueror than Dingiswayo, the scale of Shaka's realm made it necessary for him to disperse power, which enabled Zulu tribal traditions to reassert themselves; Shaka's violent personality lead to mutiny and to his own assassination.

The BaMbuti Pygmies of the Ituri Forest of the Congo have been made famous by Colin Turnbull's sympathetic treatments of their life style. In his essay here, "The Lesson of the Pygmies," Turnbull describes how these forest people have persisted in maintaining their hunting- and gathering-based culture even though, through periodic visits, they are in regular contact with village tribes, for whom they provide meat and occasional labor. Some observers have, in the past, concluded that the presence of BaMbuti tribes in the villages was an indication that the BaMbuti life style was undergoing a transition from forest adaptation to village adaptation. But their village contact is not evidence that the BaMbuti and the villagers have developed a symbiotic relationship. For although the BaMbuti Pygmies adapt to village ways to aid in trading, they are not dependent upon any of the goods they receive through their trade, and although the villagers try to establish domination over the BaMbuti through village rites and the appointment of BaMbuti leaders, the BaMbuti do not consider themselves bound by these social controls when they return to the forest. Nevertheless, when camping near villages, the BaMbuti do undergo profound changes, dividing bands into families and transforming hunters into traders, and exchanging goods and services with the same villager on each visit. But these changes are only temporary. Turnbull emphasizes that because anthropologists have seen Pygmies only near or in non-Pygmy villages, they have mistakenly thought them to be vassals of the taller village dwellers and have tried to persuade the BaMbuti to establish independent villages, always unsuccessfully, however, for the BaMbuti are determined to continue their dependence on the forest, where the hunting and gathering are best.

Edward P. Dozier, author of "The Hopi and the Tewa," was a Tewa man himself who died recently and suddenly, having written many important works on Pueblo culture. His paper on the Hopi and the Hopi-Tewa Pueblo Indians of New Mexico may be wishful and optimistic about some points, especially in its explanations of how the smaller Tewa population came to provide role models for the Hopi, and how the more numerous Hopi then desired to become wage workers in enterprises owned and operated by white people. Nevertheless, he also describes how the enormous disruptions caused by whites at one point in time—the Spanish in New Mexico in the late seventeenth century—had deleterious effects on Pueblo life. We also learn that white American disruptions two centuries later helped to solve some old, persistent inter-Pueblo problems caused by the first massive disruption, creating a cultural climate in which the coexistence of the Indian groups became attractive. This example of contact between nonwhite cultures, and the preceding examples from Africa of the Zulu and the BaMbuti, have all made reference to conditions shaped, not always wittingly, by white culture. Each example is so different from the others, however, that all are of significance for anthropologists. The Zulu conquered territory; the villagers obtain meat from BaMbuti Pygmies who engage in non-necessary exchanges; and the Hopi and the Hopi-Tewa merely endured one another at the least inconvenience to the Hopis.

The final paper in this section is addressed to the intricacies of subsistence economy and peasant marketing operations. Sidney W. Mintz, in "Peasant Markets," explains that Haitian peasants diversify the crops on their small parcels of land, exploiting roots, tubers, vines, grains, and trees together in the same garden, in order to maintain an adequate supply of food to eat and a dependable supply of products to sell. Mintz analyzes the network of rural markets in which goods are transported, processed, priced, bought, and sold, as well as the sundry participants in these networks. Although the amazing complexity of the marketing traditions is constantly threatened by the attempts of urban capitalists and government officials to increase revenue, and by the opposing desires of rural tradesmen to control peasant exchanges, the Haitian peasants have achieved a balanced order in their domestic markets that will not yield to these threats — if their cautious trading behavior is an accurate indication — without a considerable battle of wits and strategies.

28

PRIMITIVE KINSHIP

MEYER FORTES
June 1959

In most primitive societies the family is an organization far more complex than the family of Western civilization. This organization reflects the larger role played by the family in primitive cultures

Ministers, political orators and editorial writers are apt to tell us that the family is the keystone of society. From the biological point of view it would indeed seem to be the ultimate social institution. The conjugal family—husband and wife and their children—gives social expression to the function of human reproduction. Early travelers from our civilization were sometimes shocked because they could find no obvious counterpart of our family among primitive peoples. When they found large communal households, inhabited by men, women and children having the most bizarre and sometimes downright indecent relationships to one another (in the terminology of our family), they took this as conclusive evidence that these cultures were barbaric.

We have come to know primitive peoples at closer range in recent years. What they have taught us has radically altered our judgment of their family organizations and given us an humbler understanding of our own. Primitive family types vary in their constitution, but they are always precisely structured institutions, embracing the primary loyalty and life activity of their large memberships and enduring from generation to generation. The exact prescription of relationships among members gives each individual a significantly defined connection to a wide circle of his kin. To the individual member, the family's property is the source of livelihood, its ancestors are his gods, its elders his government and its young men his defense and his support in old age. In simpler cultures (*e.g.*, the Australian aborigines) family and society are actually coterminous: all men are either kinsmen or potential enemies.

We, in contrast, are primarily citizens, not kinsmen. The family is organized anew with each marriage. It must share our allegiance with the many competing claims of our society: the loyalties we owe to the institutions that employ us, to our professional organizations, to political parties, to community and nation. A family of such reduced status and scope is, as a matter of fact, distinctly out of the ordinary as families go. The Hebrew families of the Bible and the Roman *gens* more closely resemble the extended family systems of contemporary primitive cultures than they do our own. Of all the primitive societies I know, the one that most closely resembles ours in isolating the conjugal family as the basic social unit is the Iban, a tribe of head-hunters in North Borneo. The vocabulary we employ to

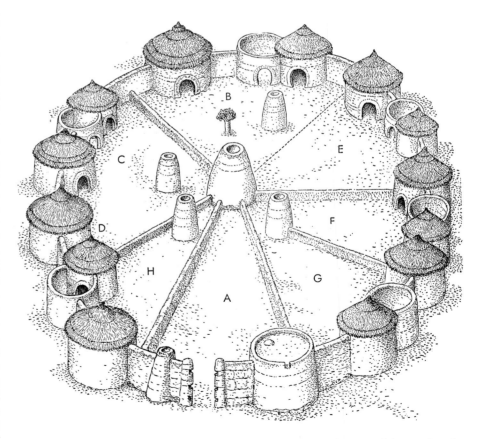

TALLENSI DWELLING depicted in this schematic drawing is far more elaborate than the one shown in greater detail on page 287. It includes the patriarch's cattle yard (A); his senior wife's bedroom, pantry and kitchen (B); a similar unit for his second wife (C), including a hut (D) for her adult child, his second son; a unit for his third wife (E); his eldest son's domain, including units for the latter's first wife (F) and second wife (G); a unit for the third son (H). The basic Tallensi house plan can be expanded to any size. Large joint families of this kind are typical of primitive societies that are not nomadic.

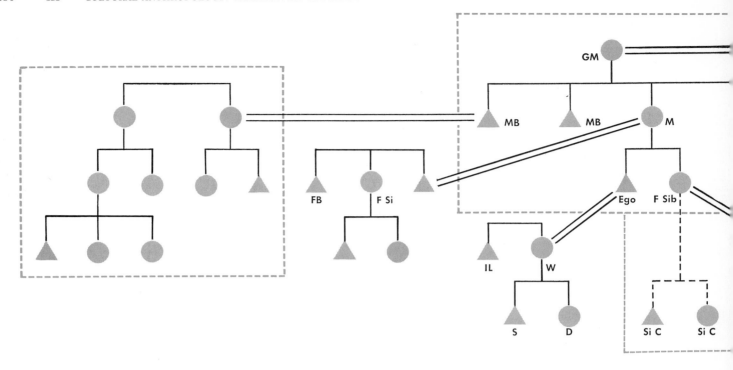

ASHANTI MATRILINEAL FAMILY is depicted in this family tree. The symbols are explained in the first key at right. The letters, which indicate the relations of each family member to the individual labeled "ego," are explained in the second key. Note that, according to the "classificatory" type of kinship terminology used by the Ashanti, "ego's" aunt as well as his own female parent is called "mother"; his aunt's children as well as his own brothers and sisters are called "siblings." "Ego's" own domestic household is shown in the broken colored rectangle at the center of the chart. Below this rectangle is a smaller one, representing a possible fourth

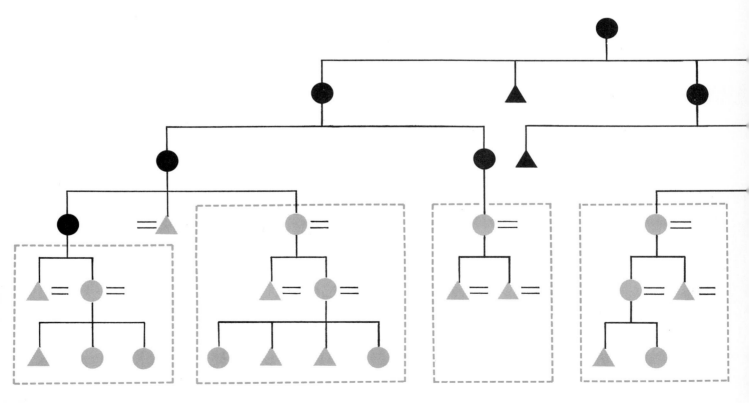

LIVING FEMALE
DECEASED FEMALE
LIVING MALE
DECEASED MALE
MARRIED MEMBERS

ASHANTI LINEAGE shown in this chart represents the common ancestry of six domestic families, traced through the female line (mothers and grandmothers, not fathers and grandfathers) to a single ancestress

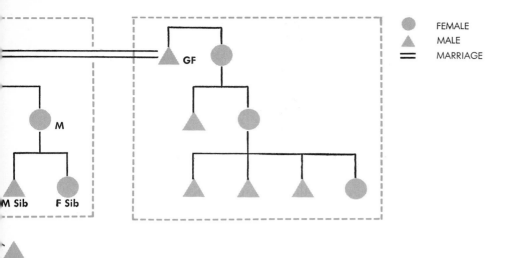

●	FEMALE
▲	MALE
=	MARRIAGE

D	DAUGHTER
Ego	SPEAKER
F	FATHER
FB	FATHER'S BROTHER
F Si	FATHER'S SISTER
F Sib	FEMALE SIBLING
GF	GRANDFATHER
GM	GRANDMOTHER
IL	IN-LAW (AFFINE)
M	MOTHER
MB	MOTHER'S BROTHER
M Sib	MALE SIBLING
S	SON
Si C	SISTER'S CHILD
W	WIFE

generation in "ego's" family. The fourth generation, comprising his sister's children, will be his heirs. His own wife lives apart from him in another matrilineal household elsewhere in the village. His children are heirs not of himself but of his male affinal relations ("in-laws"), who share his wife's household. Also shown in this chart, in whole or part, are four households in which dwell spouses of other members of "ego's" family.

describe our kin—our uncles, aunts and cousins—beyond the immediate conjugal family fails to suggest the compelling ties that bind the kinship of peoples other than those of modern European and American civilization. Students of primitive kinship systems have found that they employ a terminology wholly unlike our own: the "classificatory" system, which groups relatives by status rather than sorting out their genetic interrelationships. It appears that all kinship systems obey certain universal principles governing the separation, inner unity and orderly sequence of generations. Viewed from the vantage point of such understanding, our family appears to be the much-curtailed form of a once far more elaborate and comprehensive organization.

Two "facts of life" necessarily provide the basis of every family: the fact of sexual intercourse is institutionalized in marriage; the fact of parturition is institutionalized in parenthood. Societies differ greatly, however, in which of these institutions they select as the more important. Our society selects marriage: the result is the conjugal family, centered upon a single marital relationship and the children it produces. Most human societies, however, rate parenthood above marriage. This results in the consanguineal family, centered upon a single line of descent.

Biologically our lineal inheritance derives equally from both sides of the family according to Mendelian law. Societies that prize lineage, however, restrict social inheritance either to the maternal or the paternal line. The social heritage—that is, property, citizenship, office, rank—passes either through the father or through the mother. "Patrilineal" descent (father to son) was the rule in ancient Rome, China and Israel, and occurs in many primitive societies. "Matrilineal" descent (mother's brother

(top). This "matrilineal" descent does not mean that Ashanti property and authority pass from mother to daughter; rather they descend from a woman's brother to her son.

to sister's son) is common in Asia, Africa, Oceania and aboriginal America.

One matrilineal society that flourishes today is the ancient, wealthy and artistic kingdom of Ashanti in Ghana, West Africa. While European mores have made some inroads among the Ashanti, back-country Ashanti villages still keep to their strictly matrilineal ways. Let us consider how such a society works.

First of all, let us note that a matrilineal society is not a matriarchal society: it is not ruled by women. So far as I know there is not, nor has there ever been, such a thing as a genuine matriarchal government. In every preliterate society men, not women, hold the political, legal and economic power; the women usually remain legal minors all their lives, subject to the authority of their menfolk. Primitive peoples usually understand quite well why men, not women, must be the rulers. The women, they say, are incapacitated for warfare

and the affairs of state by the necessity of bearing and rearing children. Many peoples, including the Ashanti, believe that women are magically dangerous to men during menstruation and after childbirth.

In describing the Ashanti kinship system I am going to use common English terms (like "aunt" and "cousin") rather than attempt to translate the native terminology. The typical Ashanti household consists of an old woman, her daughters, their children and one or two of her sons. The old woman, the daughters and the sons are all married, but where are their spouses? We can suppose that all of these people are on good terms with their husbands and wives; nevertheless they do not form part of the same household with them, because they do not belong to the same clan. The spouses all live nearby, in households belonging to their own clans. The legal head of the household is one of the old woman's sons; he inherited his role from his mother's brother, not his father; he will pass it on to his sister's son, not his own [see illustration at bottom of preceding two pages].

Among the Ashanti marriage is governed by strict moral, legal and religious rules. Yet it is clear that the Ashanti find the fact of descent much more important than the fact of marriage. That is why the households are formed by mothers and children rather than by husbands and wives. The lineage group to which the old woman and her children belong is united by the bond of common descent from an ancestress of perhaps the 10th

generation before that of the youngest members. Through this ancestress the group traces its descent from an even more remote mythological ancestress: the progenitor of their clan, one of the eight clans into which the Ashanti people is divided.

It is considered a sin and a crime for members of the same Ashanti lineage to have sexual relations; by this token they must look for spouses of independent descent, that is, of a different clan. Since husband and wife commonly reside in separate households, they must live near each other if they are to have a normal marital relationship. More than 80 per cent of all marriages occur within the village community. Usually, therefore, one or two lineages of each of the eight clans is found in a village of average size.

The Ashanti rule of matrilineal descent has implications that reach far beyond the domestic household. Every Ashanti is by birth a citizen of the chiefdom to which his maternal lineage belongs. A man or woman can build a house freely on any vacant site in this chiefdom, and can farm any piece of unclaimed soil in the lands that it owns. An individual has no such rights in any other chiefdom. By the rule of matrilineal descent, a man can will property to his own children; they belong to another household and another clan: his wife's. A man's heirs and successors are his sisters' sons. On his death his property and any position of hereditary rank he may hold pass automatically to his

B	BROTHER
BL	BROTHER-IN-LAW
D	DAUGHTER
Ego	SPEAKER
F	FATHER
M	MOTHER
MB	MOTHER'S BROTHER
M Si	MOTHER'S SISTER
S	SON
Si	SISTER
Si L	SISTER-IN-LAW
W	WIFE

⬤ FEMALE

▲ MALE

= MARRIAGE

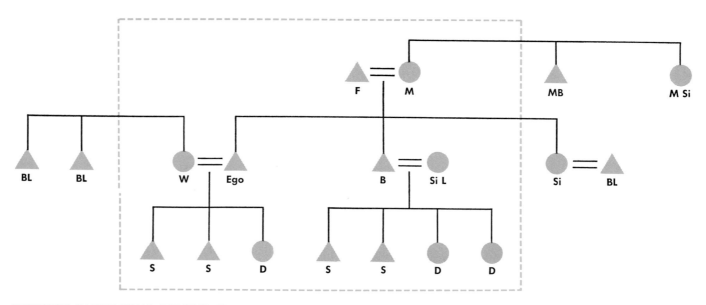

TALLENSI PATRILINEAL FAMILY differs from the Ashanti family (see chart at bottom of preceding two pages) in that it is a community of fathers, sons and their wives, not one of mothers, their brothers and their children, all living apart from their husbands and wives. It resembles the Ashanti family, however, in its use of classificatory terminology; e.g., "ego" addresses his brother's children, as well as his own, as "son" or "daughter," a common practice with peoples who live in large joint households.

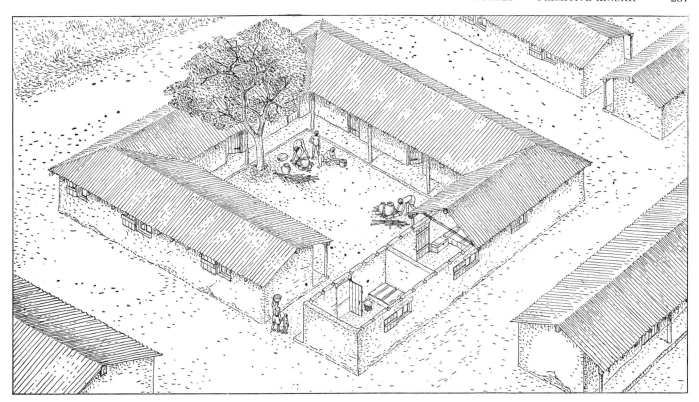

MATRILINEAL HOUSEHOLD is characteristic of the Ashanti tribe in Ghana, West Africa. A typical Ashanti household includes a grandmother, her sons and daughters and their children. Each adult occupies one room. Their spouses live apart from them in their own matrilineal households nearby. In this drawing part of the tin roof is removed, showing the interior of the adobe rooms.

PATRILINEAL HOUSEHOLD typifies the Tallensi tribe, also of Ghana. While more primitive than the Ashanti, they have more highly structured households. Outside the gate, by the sacred tree and conical ancestor shrine, is a social area for the men of the house. Inside the gate the patriarch of the household stands in the cattle yard, his special domain. To the right is the flat-roofed cattle shed where his ancestral spirits dwell. Behind him, at the hub of the homestead, is its granary, from which only he may dispense grain. Clockwise around the homestead, starting to the left of the gate, are a room for adolescent boys; the bedroom, pantry and unroofed dry-season kitchen of the patriarch's mother; and the bedroom, kitchen and pantry of his wife, himself and his children.

oldest nephew. If he wishes his own sons and daughters to benefit from his property, he must be content to make them gifts during his lifetime. They can accept his gifts only with the consent of his matrilineal heirs and of the elders in his lineage group. In the Ashanti tradition the individual comes under the authority of the mother's brother, not the father. It is the mother's brother whose consent is legally essential for a girl or boy to marry; he is also responsible for any costs that arise from divorce or other suits against them.

How do marriage and parenthood work out in such a system of kinship rules? It is undeniable that the Ashanti have delicate problems of marital adjustment. Both husband and wife must reach a compromise between their primary loyalties to matrilineal kin and their attachment to each other and to their children. When a man marries, he acquires legal rights to his wife's marital fidelity and to domestic services such as the regular provision of his meals. If a wife commits adultery, her husband can claim damages from the other man and apologies and a gift of placation from the wife, even if, as often happens, he does not divorce her. He can and will insist on divorce if his wife neglects her household duties or refuses to sleep with him. The husband is in turn obliged to provide food, clothing and general care for his wife and children. If he fails in these duties, his wife can divorce him. In fact, divorce is very common among the Ashanti. Usually it is free of acrimony, for it does not involve the splitting of a household.

What an Ashanti man does not acquire by marriage is rights over his wife's reproductive powers, that is, over the children she bears him. These belong to her lineage, as opposed to his. An Ashanti man cannot demand help from his sons, for example in farming or in the payment of a debt, as he can from his sisters' sons. He can punish his nephew, but not his sons. He can order his nieces to marry a man of his choice, but not his daughter.

At the opposite extreme from the Ashanti are the Tallensi, who live nearby in Ghana's remote northern uplands. The Tallensi kinship and marriage sys-

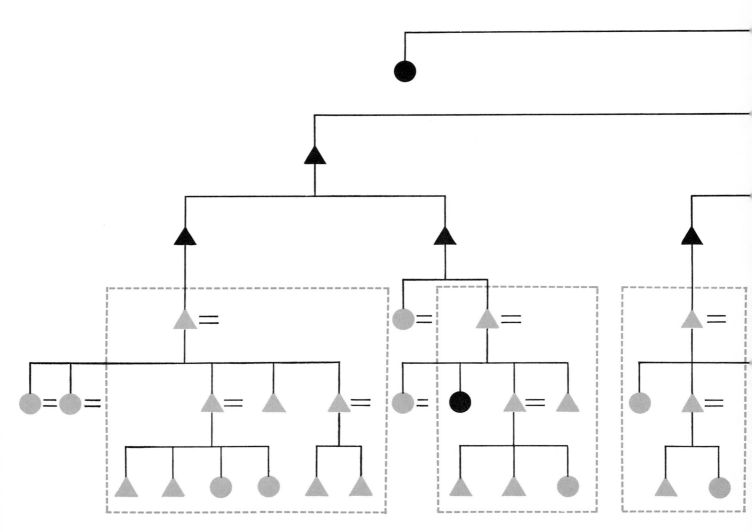

LIVING FEMALE
DECEASED FEMALE
LIVING MALE
DECEASED MALE
MARRIED MEMBERS

TALLENSI LINEAGE depicted here is shared in common by six domestic families. Unlike the Ashanti, the Tallensi lineage is traced in the male line: from father to son. This family tree includes six genera-

tem is the mirror image of that of the Ashanti. The Tallensi household is not matrilineal but patrilineal; it consists of a group of men, usually a man and his sons and grandsons, together with their wives and unmarried daughters. The men of this household and others in the immediate neighborhood all share the same patrilineal descent, which they can trace back in the male line to a single male ancestor [*see illustration on these two pages*]. Tallensi men share their land, are equally eligible for family offices and join in the worship of ancestral spirits. Like the Ashanti, the Tallensi are "exogamous"; their children must marry members of clans other than their own. Among the Tallensi, however, a woman joins her husband's household

on marriage, because he has rights not only to her domestic services and marital fidelity, but also to her children. This is the crucial distinction between matrilineal and patrilineal systems.

Our Western way of reckoning kinship is neither matrilineal nor patrilineal. Rather, it is "bilateral" [*see illustration at bottom of next two pages*]. That is, we consider our mothers' kin to be as closely related to us as our fathers'. Nowadays we follow the same etiquette with both maternal and paternal relatives. Our terminology distinctly reflects the equality of our conjugal family system. Since we rate the conjugal (husband-wife) over the lineal (parent-child) bond, the paternal or maternal orienta-

tion of the lineage becomes a matter of indifference. In naming our spouses' relatives we assimilate them to our own: a mother-in-law is a kind of mother, a brother-in-law is a kind of brother, and we treat them accordingly.

Our kinship terminology, like that of the Eskimos and a few other peoples, follows the so-called descriptive system. We have separate labels for each category of our kin, according to their generation, their sex and their linkage to us by descent or marriage. We distinguish our parents ("father" and "mother") from their male siblings ("uncles") and their female siblings ("aunts"). We have different appellations for our own siblings ("brother," "sister") and for our aunts' and uncles' children ("cousins").

Most primitive peoples use the entirely different labels of the classificatory system. This system often strikes Westerners as odd, although it is widespread among the peoples of mankind. Its principle is that in each generation all relatives of the same sex are addressed in the same way, no matter how remote the relationship. A sister and a female first- or second-cousin are all called "sister"; a father, an uncle and more distant male collaterals of their generation are called "father." A woman addresses her nieces and nephews, as well as her own offspring, as "my children." The nieces and nephews, as well as her own children, call her "mother." The Tallensi, the Swazi of South Africa and many other societies even use words for "father" with a feminine suffix added, to designate the sisters of all the men they address as "father." A Swazi calls his mother's brother a "male mother."

This terminology was recognized for the first time nearly a century ago by a great U. S. anthropologist, Lewis H. Morgan. His *Systems of Consanguinity and Affinity of the Human Family*, published in 1871, founded the modern study of kinship systems. Morgan and his followers believed that classificatory terminology had survived from an extremely primitive stage of social organization, in which a group of sisters would mate promiscuously with a group of brothers and would rear the offspring in common.

By now Morgan's theory of "group marriage" has been completely discredited. Modern anthropology has discovered far more cogent reasons for the existence of classificatory terminology. If a man calls all the male relatives of his generation "brother," it is not because at some remote period the promiscuity of the elder generation made it impossible to tell one's brother from

tions, all derived from a single male. In each generation the women marry into other households and their children do not continue their lineage but that of their husbands.

SEPARATION OF GENERATIONS from one another, a universal feature of kinship systems which serves to maintain the authority of seniors over juniors, is represented in this series of photographs.

The photograph at left depicts the Tallensi custom of avoidance between a father (*center of photograph*) and his eldest son, who may not share his father's plate, although a younger son is shown

one's cousin. The reason is that such generalized terminology expresses the deep sense of corporate unity in the extended family. A child in such a family knows very well which of the women of the household is his physiological mother. Like children anywhere in the world, he will love his real mother as he loves none of her sisters or female cousins. Yet in the joint family those sisters and cousins share his mother's duties to him, and he must observe the same code of politeness with each of them. If his real mother should die, another of the women he calls "mother" will replace her. The classificatory terminology binds together groups that share status and responsibilities. To people like the Ashanti and Tallensi the word "mother" has a social rather than a biological significance: it defines one rank in a complex family system.

The need to define relationships is crucial in every society, and all kinship systems have evolved in response to this need. We are indebted to A. R. Radcliffe-Brown, the distinguished British anthropologist, for the most satisfactory statement of the underlying principles. The first of these establishes a clear demarcation between successive generations. The elders are not only physiological progenitors of their young; they also protect and nurture them throughout childhood and provide their first training in the crafts, customs and morals of the tribe. This all-important relationship requires not only love on the part of the parents but also respect on the part of the children. Parental authority is incompatible with complete intimacy.

Most societies banish everything sexual from the parent-and-child relationship; the universal taboo on incest between parent and child epitomizes the cleavage between elder and younger generations. Many societies enforce certain "avoidances" that help to maintain social distance between generations. The Tallensi, for example, forbid an eldest son to eat from his father's dish [*see illustration at top of these two pages*]. Some central African tribes carry avoidance to extremes. One tribe, the Nyakyusa, requires fathers and children to

A	AUNT
B	BROTHER
BL	BROTHER-IN-LAW
C	COUSIN
D	DAUGHTER
Ego	SPEAKER
F	FATHER
GF	GRANDFATHER
GM	GRANDMOTHER
M	MOTHER
Ne	NEPHEW
Ni	NIECE
S	SON
Si	SISTER
Si L	SISTER-IN-LAW
U	UNCLE
W	WIFE

⬤ FEMALE

▲ MALE

═ MARRIAGE

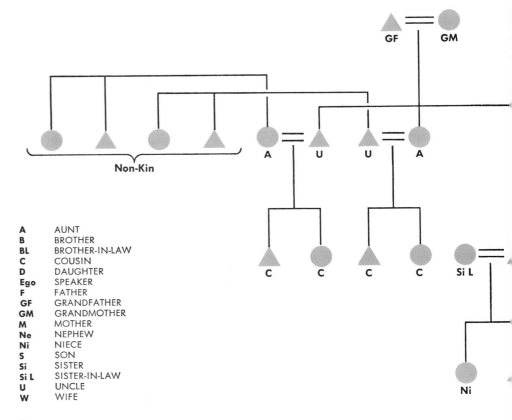

MODERN EUROPEAN FAMILY is neither matrilineal nor patrilineal, but bilateral. The modern Western family (*broken rec-*

doing so. The photographs at center and on the page at right show a Tallensi custom that illustrates the succession of juniors to the authority of their seniors. An eldest son whose father has died wears his father's tunic turned inside out. While his eldest sister clutches the garment, he marches around the homestead, then enters his father's cattle shed, thus canceling the avoidance taboo.

live in separate villages. In the matrilineal Ashanti society, on the other hand, it is the uncle to whom children show respect (or at least resentful submission). Ashanti fathers are not figures of authority to their children and need not keep aloof from them. Indeed, the father's lack of authority over his children is compensated for by warm bonds of trust and affection.

Radcliffe-Brown's second principle is the so-called sibling rule of unity and loyalty among the members of a single generation. The unity among siblings (meaning cousins as well as brothers and sisters) is the converse of the first principle of separation between each generation of siblings and the next. Internally, of course, each generation is differentiated by sex and order of birth. Yet the rule generally prevails that siblings

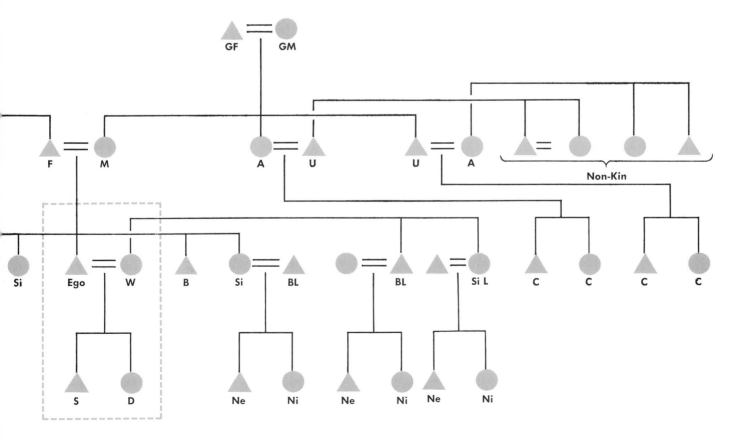

tangle) is smaller than the Ashanti or Tallensi and centered upon marriage, not lineage. Since neither maternal nor paternal lineage has exclusive importance, we acknowledge relatives on both sides and give them similar names (e.g., "mother," "mother-in-law").

share all things on equal terms. Frequently the sibling principle is generalized to include all tribesmen of the same generation. In East and West Africa this is institutionalized in the so-called age-grade system. The pastoral Masai, for example, initiate youths into their lowest "grade" of junior warriors every seven years, two successive grades forming a "generation set." Members of a set are classificatory brothers to each other and are classificatory fathers to the next set. Cattle-keeping and warfare are the tasks of the junior sets, while government is the prerogative of the senior sets.

The third principle of kinship, according to Radcliffe-Brown's scheme, accounts for the orderly succession of the distinct sibling groups in time: this is the rule of "filiation." Most societies, as we have seen, stress this rule more strongly than we do. Filiation is usually traced on strictly matrilineal or patrilineal lines. Occasionally the two modes are combined. In some African tribes the individual inherits land and political offices from his father, and livestock and religious-cult memberships from his mother. The bond of common filiation forms social groups that reach beyond the single household in time as well as space. These groups are often called clans. Frequently they are exogamous; as among the Ashanti and Tallensi, their members may not marry one another but must seek mates from other clans. This establishes "affinal" (in-law) relationships between clans and binds them into a still larger unit: the tribe.

What happens to kinship-based societies when industry, a money economy and Western education impinge on them? Recent investigation shows an increasing breakdown of both patrilineal and matrilineal family systems under such conditions. In their place bilateral systems similar to our own become established. The reasons are obvious. Industry and commerce require the individual to earn wages and to enter legal contracts not as a member of a family but on his own. Western law and education emphasize the responsibilities of individual citizenship and parenthood, as opposed to group citizenship and collective responsibility of kinfolk to children. In his legal and economic roles the individual separates from his kin group. The family constituted by marriage becomes his primary concern. In Africa and elsewhere, as people become industrialized, we are witnessing processes of social evolution analogous to those that shaped the much more limited institution that we call the family.

29

THE RISE OF A ZULU EMPIRE

MAX GLUCKMAN
April 1960

In 1816 Shaka, chief of the Zulus, began a series of conquests that eventually disrupted a third of Africa. The story of his brief and bloody reign is a case history in the sociology of war

Thou that art great as the sky!
Thou that art great as the earth!
Thou that art great as the mountains!
Thou that art black!
Thou that art vast as the sea!
Thou who growest while others are distracted!

This is a translation of the chant of the Zulus in praise of Shaka, their warrior king. In 1824 a small party of English traders, seeking an audience with Shaka, splashed ashore with their horses and supplies at Port Natal (now Durban) on the east coast of Africa. After his agents had reported them to be friendly, Shaka sent gifts of cattle and ivory and an ambassador to guide them to his capital. They traveled for two days, crossing rivers, acacia-covered grasslands and densely forested hills to reach the royal Bulawayo kraal, a ring of beehive-shaped dwellings built around a central cattle enclosure two miles across [*see illustration below*].

Here is how one of the traders, Henry Fynn, described their reception at Bulawayo: "On entering the great cattle kraal we found drawn up within about 80,000 natives in their war attire." After an exchange of speeches and gifts "Shaka then raised the stick in his hand and after striking with it right and left and springing out from amidst the chiefs, the whole mass broke from their position and formed up into regiments. Portions of these rushed to the river and the surrounding hills, while the remainder, forming themselves into a circle, commenced dancing with Shaka in their midst. It was a most exciting scene, surprising to us, who could not have im-

THE ZULU CAPITAL was the royal kraal, a ring of beehive-shaped thatched huts built around two central enclosures. This 19th-century engraving depicts the kraal of Dingane, Shaka's successor, which was built when the Zulu empire was at its zenith. The chief's hut is at upper left; the smaller huts belong to his many wives. Three kraals belonging to the chief's ministers are in the distance.

agined that a nation termed 'savages' could be so well disciplined. Regiments of girls, headed by officers of their own sex, then entered the center of the arena to the number of 8,000 to 10,000, each holding a slight staff in her hand. They joined in the dance, which continued for about two hours. Shaka now came toward us, evidently seeking our applause."

Fynn and his companions were told that Shaka had built this disciplined nation and army in less than 10 years after he became chief of a small tribe of about 2,000 people. The kingdom he established in Natal became so powerful that long after his death it engaged the British in a major war (the Anglo-Zulu war of 1879). Shaka's armies and the tribes fleeing them cut swaths of devastation through south and south-central Africa, and many of the fugitives were themselves destroyed in their slaughtering flight.

When Shaka defeated his major rival, the Ndwandwe chief Zwide, some of the vanquished Ndwandwes fled to the north and west. One of these tribes established its rule in what is now Mozambique and extorted tribute from the Portuguese trading stations on the Zambezi River. Others went farther inland, conquering and absorbing tribes along the way, and later split into the several Ngoni kingdoms of central Africa. A group of Basuto tribes sought refuge 1,500 miles away along the upper reaches of the Zambezi, where they conquered Barotseland and ruled it for 30 years. Moshesh, chief of another Basuto tribe, gathered broken tribes around him in the mountainous region now known as Basutoland; in this stronghold they formed the powerful Basuto nation, which has recently taken an important step toward self-government. To the north the example set by the Zulus led the Swazis to unite into a kingdom of their own that still survives. Swaziland, like Basutoland, is now a British protectorate, although the Union of South Africa is currently demanding their annexation.

What sort of man was this Shaka, whose conquest disturbed a third of a continent? How was he able to weld hundreds of quarrelsome and fiercely independent small tribes into a mighty nation? A contemporary of Bonaparte, he has been called "the Black Napoleon" and "the African Attila." Even in scholarly works Shaka's exploits have been accounted for in terms of his genius as an organizer and military leader, his ruthless energy and his vision of empire.

That is no doubt part of the story. But his rise to power was probably also the result of tides that had been running in the life of the African peoples for two centuries: the rising population in the interior of Africa, the emigration from the interior that was crowding the pasture lands of Natal, and the increasing contacts with European settlers and traders. Shaka's abrupt, brief and bloody appearance in history thus provides significant insights into the all too little-known history of the "Dark Continent."

The evidence from which it is possible to reconstruct his career and its historical setting comes from two sources. The first is native folklore, as recorded by the Englishmen who knew Shaka, and later by other whites. These stories can be cross-checked with those handed down in the folklore of peoples that fled from Natal and first came in contact with whites many decades later. When the traditions of several geographically separated tribes agree, they are likely to be a faithful record of the facts. The other source of information is the journals of seamen shipwrecked on the coast of Natal from 1552 onward; their accounts shed light on the social and historical background of the tribes and provide a further check on the native folklore.

Most historians agree that the Natal region remained relatively untouched throughout the millennium in which commerce with Asia brought flourishing cities into existence on the African coast farther to the north. From the fifth century onward, at ports like Kilwa, Mombasa and Sofala [see map on page 296], merchants and traders from Arabia, Persia, India and even China exchanged porcelain, crockery, beads and colored cloth for slaves, gold, silver, nickel, ivory and rhinoceros horns, brought from the interior. This trade fostered the growth of the advanced inland civilizations that built the medieval stone cities of Zimbabwe and Inyanga in Southern Rhodesia. European settlers, reluctant to believe that native Africans could have created these cities, often insist that the great ruins at Zimbabwe are the site of King Solomon's mines. The inhabitants of the region are known to have mined ores to depths of more than 100 feet, and worked iron in large quantities. They irrigated vast hillside terraces and built walls and palaces of granite. In the 16th century their civilizations had already fallen into decline, and the end came when the European powers—principally Portugal—raided the coastal cities and severed the old trade routes across the Indian Ocean.

But the Arab traders who had visited the coastal ports had never ventured farther south than Sofala for fear of contrary winds and currents. Natal was untouched by the outside world until Vasco da Gama opened the sea route to India around the Cape of Good Hope in 1497. Later many European ships were wrecked on the coast of Natal, and the journals of some of the survivors relate their experiences with the local tribes.

The survivors of the Dutch vessel *Stavenisse*, wrecked in 1686 about 60 miles south of the present city of Durban, gave this account of their experiences: "Being now destitute of everything, and the boat being broken in pieces, we consulted how we could best support ourselves, and by what means we could secure ourselves from starvation. The natives, indeed, offered us bread and cattle for sale, but we had nothing wherewith to purchase the one or the other. Nothing is esteemed there but beads and copper rings for the neck or the arms. For nails, bolts, and other ironwork of the wreck, we, indeed, got some bread and corn, but as the natives set to work themselves, and by chopping and burning fully supplied themselves with iron, we not being at first aware that it was so much regarded, nor daring to prevent them for fear of provoking them, as they had sometimes fully a thousand armed men, they had everything in abundance, while we suffered from want." Portuguese castaways used to burn their wrecks to prevent the natives from obtaining a free supply of iron, which was one of the principal items of trade.

The castaways, like many modern students of African history, were inclined to regard the natives as "savages" who would attack and rob strangers unless frightened away. This was surely not the case; the tribes were well-organized societies with elaborate codes of law and ethics. A careful survey of the records has convinced me that the natives did not slaughter and steal only when they felt they were stronger than the shipwrecked party, and trade and parley only when they were afraid; the situation was much more complicated. The natives had a great need for iron, copper and other metals: many of their javelins were made of wood hardened by fire, and in some tribes women cultivated with sticks rather than with iron hoes. They were therefore very eager to get metal, and were ready to trade for it by generous offers of cattle and milk and grain—if they had cattle and milk and grain. If they did not, they attacked

ZULULAND TODAY looks much as it did in Shaka's time. The subsistence farming and pasturing practiced by the Zulus keep their homesteads widely scattered. Each homestead is relatively self-sufficient, and each is the residence of a single family or clan.

WARRIORS DANCE in praise of the Zulu king, who is visiting the kraal of their chief. In Shaka's time warriors on the eve of battle pantomimed in dance the heroic deeds that they intended to perform in combat. They were expected to live up to their boasts.

the castaways and stole their goods. Seven fairly complete journals kept by castaways show that the parties were attacked either in years of widespread drought or after the invasion of locusts, when food was short among the natives; or when they were wrecked just before the harvest and the natives were in want as they waited for the new crops. In good seasons and after the harvest the people came dancing to meet the Portuguese, and freely offered food for the scarce metals.

This analysis is confirmed by the fact that the castaways were attacked even in good years when they encountered individual tribes suffering from want and conversely were welcomed in bad years when they came to isolated tribes enjoying better fortune. Even in bad years, however, castaways who dropped out of the march from weakness were often succored by the very people who had been harassing them. Men from later shipwrecks occasionally met these castaways; often they had been given cattle, wives and land, and had assumed important places among their saviors. The early Natal tribes thus had, like all societies, some rules of compassion and human sympathy. Yet the people were starved for metal and ready to fight for it if necessary.

The journals and the native traditions make it clear that Natal was occupied by a great number of small independent tribes organized around kinship groups. Castaways who traded metal and remnants of cargo for cattle reported that they were able to drive their herds across each chief's territory in a few days. A chief visiting the castaways was escorted by only 50 warriors or so; the force of attackers on less happy oc-

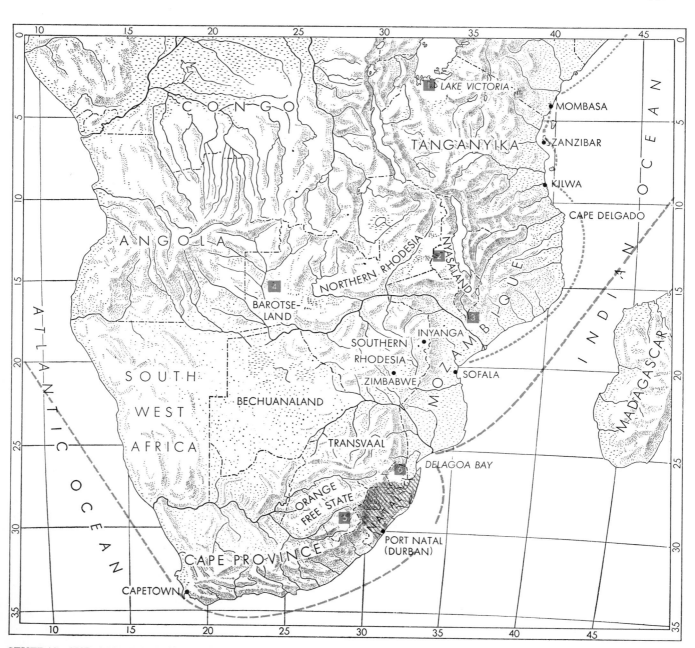

CENTRAL AND SOUTH AFRICA were devastated by Shaka's armies and the terrorized tribes fleeing them. When Shaka defeated the Ndwandwe to become master of Natal (*hatched area*) some of the Ndwandwe tribes fled as far north as Lake Victoria (1); others settled in Nyasaland (2) and still others in Mozambique (3). A fleeing group of Basutos conquered Barotseland (4) and another founded a powerful nation in what is now Basutoland (5). Shaka's example prompted the Swazis to unite into a nation that still survives in Swaziland (6). The heavy broken line indicates Portuguese trade routes; the light broken line, those of the medieval Arabs.

casions was never more than 300. Native folklore indicates that the tribes had come into the region from the north and west in the general population movement attending the expansion of the Bantu peoples that had begun hundreds of years before. Some of the tribes were in flight from Bantu conquerors and some, including the Zulu tribes, were offshoots of the Bantu stock. Together they displaced the indigenous pastoral Bushmen.

As the tribes moved, they often split. A chief had several wives of varying status, and he placed important ones in different parts of his territory and attached followers to them. When the eldest son of an important wife grew up, he thus had an army to support him if he tried to seize the throne after his father's death. According to custom the rightful heir was a son born to a wife married after his father became chief—a son "born in the purple." If a man became chief when he was nearing middle age, this meant that the rightful heir might be a child when his father died, while there were grown-up sons already able to rule. One or more of them might attempt to seize the throne. Sometimes an uncle was appointed regent; when his ward grew up, the regent (as in Europe) might resist giving up power. Often a section of the tribe, ruled by a prince not likely to succeed, moved off to seek independence. A common outcome of a dynastic dispute was thus the splitting of a tribe, and such splitting operated to keep each tribe fairly small.

Without doubt economic forces were at work along with personal ambition in this process of political fission. The tribes obtained their food by farming and by pasturing cattle on the range, so their habitations were necessarily widely dispersed. The success of this way of life is reflected in the growth of the Bantu population, but their rising numbers placed a steadily increasing pressure on the resources of each tribe's territory. Sections of the tribes accordingly moved away to better lands and to independence. The dynastic struggles of the period doubtless arose in part from this competition for dwindling resources. In addition, given the existing techniques of control and administration, it is possible that a chief could not hold a tribe together once its population exceeded a certain size. Sections of the tribe would hive off to take up independent existence in an organization that was in all important respects identical with that from which they had broken away. The tribes did not attempt to subdue one another

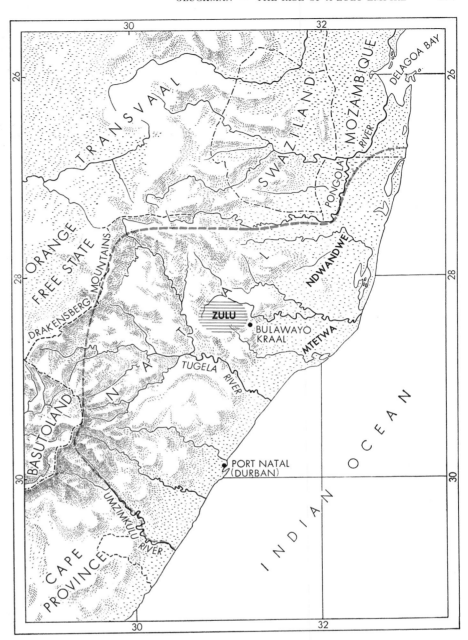

SHAKA'S EMPIRE (*broken line*) occupied an area of 80,000 square miles. Shaka built it after becoming chief of the Zulu tribe, which originally occupied the small hatched area at center. The locations of Bulawayo, and the Mtetwa and Ndwandwe tribes are also indicated.

by force and extend their domain: tribal wars were brief and occasional, aimed at cattle and ransom. In this restless political equilibrium the tribes existed from at least 1500 until nearly 1800. They must have waxed and waned in size, around some optimum related to their technology, economy and polity.

The situation changed radically just after 1800. Then in northern Natal there emerged a chief of the Mtetwa tribe called Dingiswayo. He had fled from his home under the charge of plotting to kill his father, the Mtetwa chief, and there is a legend (which is probably

false) that he lived for a time among the whites in the Cape Colony. It does seem true that he was befriended by a white traveler, and that when this man was killed, Dingiswayo took his horse and gun and turned again toward his homeland. He arrived to find his father dead and his brother on the throne. Dingiswayo promptly killed his brother and seized the Mtetwa chieftainship. According to stories told some 16 years later to the English traders who visited Shaka, Dingiswayo declared that the constant fighting among the tribes was against the wish of the Creator, and that he intended to conquer them all and make them live in peace. He proceeded to subdue some 30 tribes. He organized the larger forces that came under his command into regiments and acquired military power unexampled in the previous history of these peoples. But Dingiswayo was temperate in victory. After subduing a tribe with as little slaughter as possible, he left it under its own chiefly family, perhaps choosing from it a favorite of his own to rule, though the young men of the tribe had to serve in his army.

Among the tribes conquered by Dingiswayo was the Zulu, to which Shaka belonged. Shaka was the illegitimate son of the Zulu chief—illegitimate in two senses. He was conceived out of wedlock, and his father and mother were related distantly, but sufficiently closely, to make it unlawful for them to marry. Shaka's mother was hurried into a disgraced marriage with her lover. After Shaka's birth she bore a daughter, but she and her children were ill-treated and not accepted by the tribe, and her husband finally drove her away. She and her children wandered until they found refuge in the land of the Mtetwa, where Shaka became one of Dingiswayo's

bravest warriors. He rose to regimental commander and then, still at a youthful age, to commander of the entire Mtetwa army.

It was then that he began to show his martial genius. He decided that it was stupid to use javelins: Why hurl your weapon away and then wait unarmed until you could pick up one of the enemy's? He contrived instead a heavy, short-hafted, broad-bladed, stabbing spear [*see bottom illustration on page 299*]. He trained his men to fight at close quarters and to use their big shields to hook away the shield of the enemy, exposing him to a stab at the heart. Shaka also changed military tactics. In the traditional, somewhat chivalric warfare tribes fought by arranging their champions in broad ranks that stood about 50 yards apart; the warriors threw javelins at each other until one rank yielded. Shaka arranged his warriors in a close-order, shield-to-shield formation with two "horns" designed to encircle the enemy or to feint at his flanks, the main body of troops at the center and the reserves in the rear ready to exploit the opportunities of battle [*see illustration on page 300*]. These innovations revo-

lutionized African warfare, changing it from a skirmish with few deaths to a destructive slaughter.

In 1816, when Shaka's father died, Dingiswayo helped him become chief of the Zulus. With 500 warriors trained to fight with his new weapons and tactics, he surprised and overwhelmed his opponents, who expected to fight the old type of fairly bloodless war. Shaka drafted the survivors into his army, marching them off into Zulu territory and sending Zulu tribesmen to colonize their lands.

Meanwhile Dingiswayo's example had inspired Zwide, chief of the neighboring Ndwandwe tribe, to undertake a career as a conqueror. In 1818 Zwide captured and killed Dingiswayo. Shaka seized the rule of the disintegrating Mtetwa kingdom, and was attacked by Zwide. Skillfully drawing Zwide's more powerful armies after him into territory he had stripped of food, he defeated them, thus clearing the way to establishing his rule over all the region. By 1822 he had made himself master over 80,000 square miles, an area approximately that of the state of Nebraska and a vast ter-

CLOSE-UP OF KRAAL depicts the construction and arrangement of a Zulu hut. To build it, saplings are sharpened and driven into the ground in a 12- to 15-foot circle. A second circle of saplings is placed across the first row at a sharp angle. They are then bent to join at the top, lashed together and covered with thatch. A small hearth is built directly inside the door, which is low and small. Near the back is the most important part of the hut, the *umsamo,* the dwelling place of spirits, where pots and utensils are kept.

ZULU REGIMENT is halted by its commander during ceremonies in honor of a visit by the Zulu king. The modern Zulus in this photograph are armed with clubs instead of spears, and many of them carry shields smaller than those used by Shaka's troops.

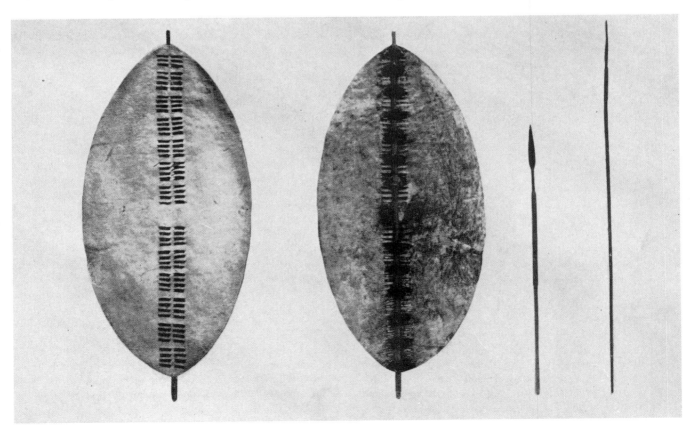

ZULU WEAPONS used by Shaka's troops consisted of a rawhide shield (*shown in front view at left and back view at center*) and a short, broad-bladed stabbing spear (*second from right*) for close combat. Shaka changed war from skirmishing to slaughter by sub-stituting the stabbing spear for the light javelin (*far right*), which was usually hurled at the enemy from a distance of about 50 yards. At this range the javelins could not penetrate the tough five-foot-tall shields, which were hardened by dipping them in water.

ritory to have mastered only with foot-soldiers armed with spears. His army had grown from 500 men to some tens of thousands.

The slaughter and terror wrought by this army depopulated a vast region surrounding Shaka's kingdom. From 1824 onward his troops had to march across miles of barren lands to seize cattle and to teach distant tribes to fear the name of Shaka.

From the beginning Shaka ruled as a tyrant. He impaled and killed those of his kin who had treated his mother and himself badly in his early years. After each battle troops who had retreated and other alleged cowards were executed. The English traders who visited him described how he would arbitrarily indicate men for death; almost every day men were seized and killed at his whim. His disposition fluctuated from extreme generosity to barbarous cruelty. When his mother died, some 7,000 people were killed in an orgy of mourning. Fynn, who was present when Shaka was told of his mother's death, stated that Shaka stood motionless for about 20 minutes with his head bowed upon his shield. After shedding a few tears, Shaka broke the silence with frantic yells. The tribe took the signal and likewise burst into shouts and wailings that continued through the night and into the next day. Shaka ordered a general massacre of those not displaying sufficient grief. He also ordered that for the next year, upon penalty of death, husbands and wives should abstain from sexual intercourse, that cows should not be milked and that crops should not be planted. Giving his army no rest, he sent it on one distant campaign after another.

The interference with the food supply and the reckless brutality of the year of mourning finally evoked the spirit of mutiny among his subjects. When he sent the army to raid the Portuguese settlement at Delagoa Bay in 1828, two of his brothers, Dingane and Mhlangane, seized the opportunity to assassinate him; Dingane then had Mhlangane killed, and the returning army, reduced by hunger, fatigue and malaria, acclaimed him king.

So ended the reign of the conqueror and tyrant who six years after his accession to a small chieftainship built a nation with a powerful army. He ruled it for only six years more. Yet the Zulu kingdom he had created survived his death and continued under the rule of his family. A half-century later its army was there to fight the British. In 1879 the Zulu army was at last crushed by the British and the nation brought under British sway. Yet despite the weight of

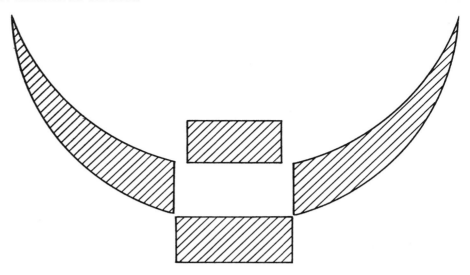

ZULU BATTLE-FORMATION (*hatched areas*) employed by Shaka consisted of four groups of warriors lined up shield-to-shield. The two "horns" were designed to encircle the enemy or to feint at his flanks. Several regiments of seasoned veterans (*center*) did the bulk of the fighting, while the reserves waited in the rear with their backs to the battle.

white overlordship the Zulu nation and the people's adulation of the Zulu royal family still survive.

From this brief chronicle of his life it becomes clear that Shaka was a genius of a kind. But his extraordinary personality does not by itself account for his martial and political triumphs. His life must be seen in the context of the time in which he lived. By the time Shaka reached manhood, Dingiswayo had already upset the pattern of Zulu warfare by waging wars of conquest, and Zwide had followed this example. There is no reason why men so intelligent and energetic as these should not have been born into the tribes during the previous three centuries. Many Portuguese, Dutch and English seamen were adopted by the tribes; any one of them could have inspired a native chieftain to imperial visions on the European scale. In fact it seems odd that none of these castaways attempted to seize and extend power themselves. A possible explanation is that in earlier years there was no point to building up power. The tribal economy was simple and undifferentiated; even in a good year the available technology did not allow a man to produce much beyond his own needs. There was little trade and no luxury, so even a conqueror could not make himself more comfortable than he had been before. One cannot build a palace with grass and mud, and if the only foods are grains, milk and meat, and the only clothes are hides, one cannot live much above the standard of ordinary men.

I believe that the main cause of imperial developments was the shortage of land. The productivity of native African agriculture is low; by the end of the 18th century the population increase had produced a land crisis. The old process of recurrent tribal splitting could no longer solve the problem. Some historians also suggest that increasing traffic with white men may have helped to start the epoch of conquest. It is known that early in his reign Dingiswayo had opened up a trade in ivory and hides with the settlement at Delagoa Bay.

Dingiswayo's attempt at large-scale conquest surely helped to create the social climate that gave Shaka his chance. But why did Shaka succeed where Dingiswayo failed? Undoubtedly here his military genius was decisive, but his personality was also important. Dingiswayo had fought his wars according to the old pattern, with as little slaughter as possible; when he conquered a people, he did not alter their tribal organization. Three times he captured and spared his rival Zwide because Zwide was his brother-in-law; then Zwide captured and killed him. On the other hand, Shaka stated quite clearly that to build a nation he had to destroy the tribal organization. Perhaps he hated that organization because he was doubly illegitimate by its laws and had suffered under it. Shaka explicitly set out to break up the tribes, to mix their peoples and to shatter the chiefly families, which he saw as rivals to his rule.

Yet in this objective not even he could succeed. Because his subjects were widely scattered, he could administer them only by organizing them into counties. He built his kingdom so rapidly that he had to leave untouched those chiefs who surrendered to him voluntarily. He also had to reward his close supporters, and his only means of doing so was to give them land and followers. They became county chiefs, each with his own army, and the old tribal system thus reasserted itself. When one of the county chiefs died, his son succeeded him. Shaka was aware that his subjects' loyalty to his chieftains was a danger to his own rule and the stability of his empire. In short, without a change in the farming and pasturing methods of his people, without new means of communication, and without an extensive trade to integrate the territorial segments of his kingdom, Shaka was forced to disperse power to people who became the tribal chiefs he had feared. Even in death he was mocked by the tribal rules of the past: When he was killed, no chief opposed the claim of his brothers to the throne. His conquests had validated the title of his family to the throne, according to the Zulu custom.

Shaka himself had had no children. He said that a son would kill him for the throne. He had many concubines but no wives, and any concubine who became pregnant was killed. I believe that this, and other data on his sexual life, show that Shaka was at least a latent homosexual and possibly psychotic. Very likely this motivated another of his military innovations: He forbade his men to marry or have sexual relations with women until he gave them permission to do so in middle age, and he quartered all his men in great barracks, as in any modern army. It is significant that his regimental barracks system was not retained by his successors and imitators, though they used his other inventions.

Shaka became a conqueror because he was born into a system where changes in the ratio of population to land, and perhaps increased trade with Europeans through intermediary lands, were producing a drive toward the emergence of an overlord of the region. Some tribe was bound to achieve that overlordship. Chance, luck and his own energy and genius made Shaka the conqueror. But his emotional outlook, which led him to try to destroy the tribal system and to establish his regiments of highly trained bachelors fighting for the right to marry, was also extremely important.

The Zulu social heritage that he attempted to change reasserted itself in new forms. His story not only shows how a devastating individual can revolutionize his society; it also demonstrates that even a tyrant's power is ultimately restricted by the past he has inherited.

30

THE LESSON OF THE PYGMIES

COLIN M. TURNBULL
January 1963

It has long been assumed that these inhabitants of the African rain forest had adapted to a kind of serfdom in villages. The discovery that they have not has implications for the problems of Africa today

In the welter of change and crisis confronting the lives of the peoples of Africa it would seem difficult to work up concern for the fate of the 40,000 Pygmies who inhabit the rain forests in the northeastern corner of the Congo. The very word "pygmy" is a term of derogation. According to early explorers and contemporary anthropologists, the Pygmies have no culture of their own—not even a language. They became submerged, it is said, in the village customs and beliefs of the Bantu and Sudanic herdsmen—cultivators who occupied the periphery of the forest and reduced them to a kind of serfdom some centuries ago. By the testimony of colonial administrators and tourists they are a scurvy lot: thievish, dirty and shrouded with an aura of impish deviltry. Such reports reflect in part the sentiments of the village tribes; in many villages the Pygmies are regarded as not quite people.

To argue that the Pygmies are people —even to show that they maintain to this day the integrity of an ancient culture—will not avert or temper the fate that is in prospect for them. The opening of the rain forests of Central Africa to exploitation threatens to extinguish them as a people. The Pygmies are, in truth, *bamiki nde ndura:* children of the forest. Away from the villages they are hunters and food gatherers. The forest provides them with everything they need, generally in abundance, and enables them to lead an egalitarian, co-operative and leisured existence to

which evil, in the sense of interpersonal malevolence, is so foreign that they have no word for it. After centuries of contact with the "more advanced" cultures of the villages and in spite of all appearances, their acculturation to any other mode of life remains almost nil. They have fooled the anthropologists as they have fooled the villagers. For this reason if for no other, the Pygmies deserve the concerned attention of the world outside. Their success should make us pause to reconsider the depth of acculturation that we have taken for granted as existing elsewhere, as industrial civilization has made its inexorable conquest of the earth.

The reason for the prevailing erroneous picture of the Pygmies is now clear. It has hitherto been generally impossible to have access to them except through the offices of the village headman, who would call the local Pygmies in from the forest to be interviewed. To all appearances they lived in some sort of symbiosis, if not serfdom, with the village people, subject to both the secular and the religious authority of the village. The fact that Pygmy boys undergo the village ritual of initiation in a relation of subservience to village boys was cited as evidence of ritual dependence, and it has been held that the Pygmies are economically dependent on the villages for metal and for plantation foods, presumably needed to supplement the meat they hunt in the forest. The few investigators who got away from the

villages did not manage to do so without an escort of villagers, acting as porters or guides. Even in the forest the presence of a single villager transforms the context as far as the Pygmies are concerned; therefore all such observations were still basically of Pygmies in the village, not in their natural habitat.

My own initial impression was just as erroneous. By good fortune my contact with the Pygmies circumvented the village and was established from the outset on a basis that identified me with the world of the forest. Seeing them almost exclusively in the context of the forest, I saw a picture diametrically opposed to the one generally drawn. Instead of dependence, I saw at first independence of the village, a complete lack of acculturation—in fact, little contact of any kind. It was only after two additional stays in the Ituri Forest, the home ground of the Congo Pygmies, that I was able to put the two contradictory pictures of their life together and to see the whole. It turned out that neither is wrong; each is right in its particular context. The relation of the Pygmies to the villagers is a stroke of adaptation that has served their survival and even their convenience without apparent compromise of the integrity of their forest-nurtured culture.

The BaMbuti, as the Pygmies of the Ituri Forest are known to themselves and to their neighbors, may be the original inhabitants of the great stretch of rain forest that reaches from the Atlantic

PYGMY WOMEN and children rest in the shade of the forest while the men collect honey from nearby trees. The women often accompany the men on honey-gathering and hunting expeditions, but they do not take part in the final stages of these activities.

PYGMY MEN remove from one of their vine nets a small forest antelope they have caught and killed. One edge of the net, which the men and older boys set up, can be seen at lower left center. The women served as beaters to drive the animal into the net.

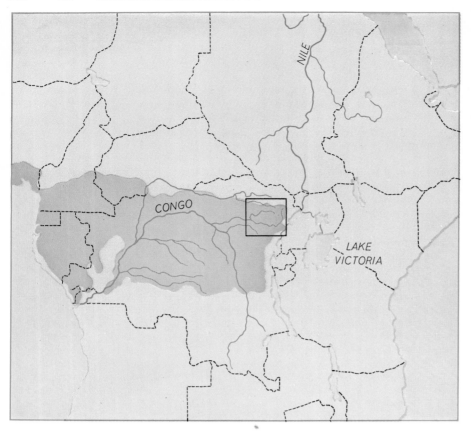

ITURI FOREST inhabited by the Pygmies occupies an area of roughly 50,000 square miles in the northeastern corner of the tropical rain forest of the Congo, in Central Africa.

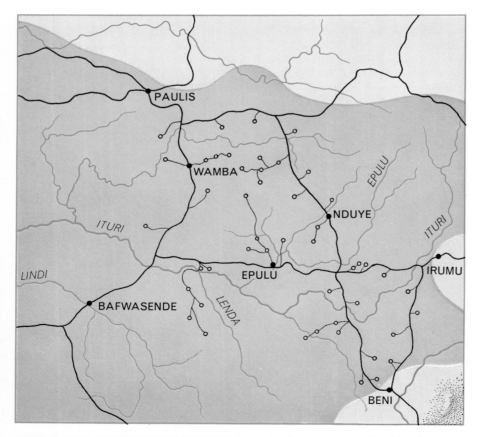

DETAIL MAP OF THE ITURI FOREST shows the Pygmy camps visited by the author (*small open circles*), villages (*black dots*) and various rivers (*blue lines*). The camps are connected by forest paths (*thin black lines*), the villages by roads (*heavy black lines*).

coast right across Central Africa to the open grassland country on the far side of the chain of great lakes that divides the Congo from East Africa. Their origin, along with that of Negrito peoples elsewhere in the world, is lost in the prehistoric past. Most Pygmies have unmistakable features other than height (they average less than four and a half feet) that distinguish them from Negroes. They are well muscled, usually sway-backed and have legs that are short in proportion to their torsos. Their faces, with wide-set eyes and flat, broad noses, have a characteristically alert expression, direct and unafraid, as keen as the attitude of the body, which is always poised to move with speed and agility at a moment's notice. They do not envy their neighbors, who jeer at them for their puny stature; in the enclosure of the forest, where life may depend on the ability to move swiftly and silently, the taller Negroes are as clumsy as elephants. For his part the Pygmy hunter wins his spurs by killing an elephant, which he does by running underneath the animal and piercing its bladder with a succession of quick jabs from a short-shafted spear.

A BaMbuti hunting band may consist of as many as 30 families, more than 100 men, women and children in all. On the move from one encampment to another they fill the surrounding forest with the sound of shouted chatter, laughter and song. Along with the venting of high spirits, this ensures that lurking leopards and buffaloes will be flushed into the forest well ahead of the band and not be accidentally cornered on the trail. The women, carrying or herding the infants, dart from the trail to gather food, and the men scout the forests for game on the flanks and in the van of the ragged procession. Arriving at the campsite in no particular order, all join in the task of building huts. The men usually cut the saplings to make the frames and sometimes also the giant Phrynium leaves to cover them; the women take charge of the actual building. The saplings are driven securely into the ground around a 10-foot circle, then deftly bent and intertwined to form a lattice dome; on this structure the leaves are hung like shingles, in overlapping tiers. Before nightfall, with the first arrivals helping the stragglers to complete their tasks, the camp is built and the smoke of cooking fires rises into the canopy of the forest. The entire enterprise serves to demonstrate a salient feature of BaMbuti life: everything gets done with no direction and with no apparent organization.

A morning is usually all that is needed to secure the supply of food. The women know just where to look for the wild fruits that grow in abundance in the forest, although they are hidden to outsiders. The women recognize the undistinguished *itaba* vine, which leads to a cache of nutritious, sweet-tasting roots; the kind of weather that brings mushrooms springing to the surface; the exact moment when termites swarm and must be harvested to provide an important delicacy. The men hunt with bows and poison-tipped arrows, with spears for larger game and with nets. The last involves the Pygmy genius for co-operation. Each family makes and maintains its own net, four feet high and many yards long. Together they string the nets across a strategically chosen stretch of ground. The hunters, often joined by the women and older children, beat the forest, driving the game into the nets.

By afternoon they have brought enough food into camp and sometimes a surplus that will enable them to stay in camp the next day. Time is then spent repairing the nets, making new bows and arrows, baskets and other gear and performing various other chores. This still leaves a fair amount of free time, which is spent, apart from eating and sleeping, either in playing with the children and teaching them adult activities or in gathering in impromptu groups for song and dance.

The BaMbuti have developed little talent in the graphic arts beyond the occasional daubing of a bark cloth with red or blue dye, smeared on with a finger or a twig. They do, however, have an intricate musical culture. Their music is essentially vocal and noninstrumental. It displays a relatively complex harmonic sense and a high degree of rhythmic virtuosity. With the harmony anchored in the dominant and therefore all in one chord, the singing is often in canon form, with as many parts as there are singers and with improvisations and elaborations contributed freely by each. A song may have some general meaning, but it may also be totally devoid of words and consist simply of a succession of vowel sounds. The real meaning of the song, its importance and power, is in the sound. In the crisis festival of the *molimo,* the closest approximation to a ritual in the unformalized life of the BaMbuti, the men of the band will sing, night after night, through the night until dawn. The function of the sound now is to "awaken the forest" so that it will learn the plight of its children or hear of their joy in its bounty.

The spirit of co-operation, seen in every activity from hunting to singing, takes the place of formal social organization in the BaMbuti hunting band. There is no headman, and individual authority and individual responsibility are shunned by all. Each member of the band can expect and demand the co-operation of others and must also give it. In essence the bonds that make two brothers hunt together and share their food are not much greater than those that obtain between a member of a band

HUT IN FOREST CAMP is larger than such huts usually are because a section has been added to accommodate a visiting relative. The average hut is the size of the section with an entrance. Camps are built in clearings like this one, found throughout the forest.

PYGMIES AND VILLAGERS dance together during the initial two-week period of the initiation rite described in the text. Of the 10 men in the immediate foreground, from left to right including the one with a white shirt at center, all are Pygmies except the fourth from left and the third from right. The villagers' legs are longer in proportion to their bodies.

VILLAGE CAMP on the outskirts of Epulu, formerly known as Camp Putnam, includes a village-style house built by a Pygmy, to the author's knowledge the only successful such attempt by a Pygmy in this section of the forest. Usually the villagers provide a house or the Pygmies construct leaf huts. Some of the village houses appear in the background.

and a visiting Pygmy, even if he is totally unrelated. Any adult male is a father to any child; any woman, a mother. They expect the same help and respect from all children and they owe the same responsibilities toward them.

When the Pygmies encamp for a while near a village, the character of the band and its activities undergo profound and complete transformation. This happens even when a lone villager pays a visit to a Pygmy camp. Not only do such activities as singing and dancing and even hunting change, but so also does the complex of interpersonal relations. The Pygmies then behave toward each other as they would if they were in a village. They are no longer a single, united hunting band, co-operating closely, but an aggregate of individual families, within which there may even be disunity. On periodic visits to the village with which their hunting band is associated, the Pygmies occupy their own semipermanent campsite between the village and the forest. Each family usually has a particular village family with which it maintains a loose and generally friendly exchange relation. At such times the Pygmies not only supply meat, they may also supply some labor. Their main function, as the villagers see it, is to provide such forest products as meat, honey and the leaves and saplings needed for the construction of village houses. The villagers do not like the forest and go into it as seldom as possible.

It is on these occasions that travelers have seen the Pygmies and decided that they are vassals to the villagers, with no cultural identity of their own. It is true that this is how the BaMbuti appear while they are in the villages, because in this foreign world their own code of behavior does not apply. In the village they behave with a shrewd sense of expediency. It in no way hurts them to foster the villagers' illusion of domination; it even helps to promote favorable economic relations. As far as the BaMbuti are concerned, people who are not of the forest are not people. The mixture of respect, friendship and cunning with which they treat their village neighbors corresponds to the way they treat the animals of the forest: they use them as a source of food and other goods, respecting them as such and treating them with tolerant affection when they are not needed. The Pygmies have a saying that echoes the proverb of the goose and the golden egg, to the effect that they never completely and absolutely eat the villagers, they just eat them.

In the mistaken interpretations of

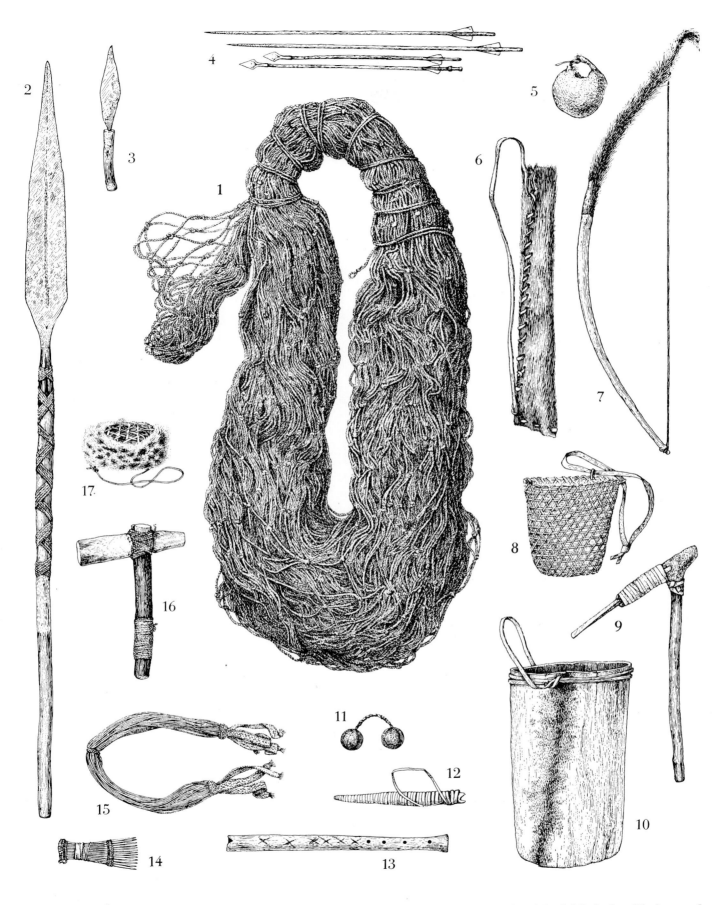

PYGMY ARTIFACTS are depicted at about a seventh of actual size: hunting net (1), metal-tipped spear (2), paring knife (3), pair of poison arrows and pair of metal-tipped nonpoisonous arrows (4), wrist guard made of monkey skin (5) for use with the bow (7), quiver made of antelope skin (6), child's basket (8), honey adz (9), bark pail for gathering honey (10), castanets (11), honey whistle (12), flute (13), comb (14), belt (15), hammer with a head of elephant tusk used in making bark cloth (16) and a hat (17).

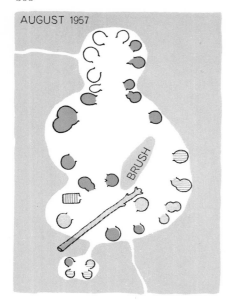

AUGUST 1957

BRUSH

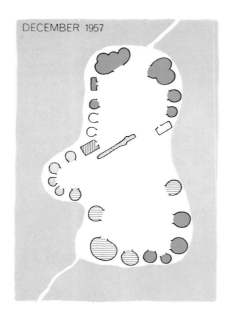

DECEMBER 1957

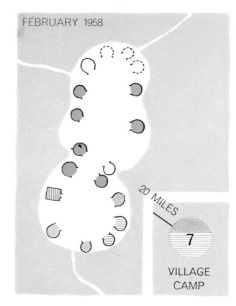

FEBRUARY 1958

20 MILES

7

VILLAGE CAMP

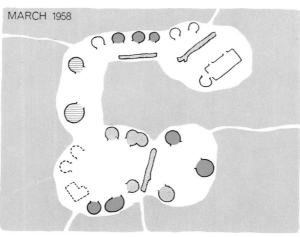

MARCH 1958

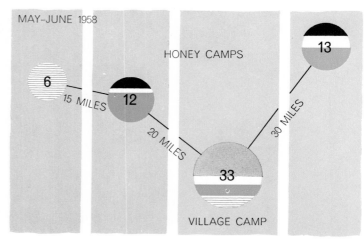

MAY–JUNE 1958

HONEY CAMPS

13

6

15 MILES

12

20 MILES

30 MILES

33

VILLAGE CAMP

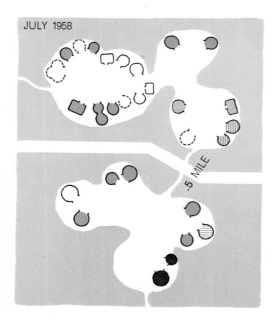

JULY 1958

.5 MILE

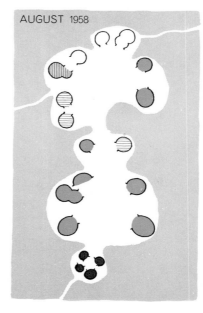

AUGUST 1958

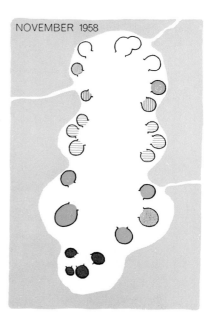

NOVEMBER 1958

FOREST CAMPS change structure and constitution in cyclical fashion as Pygmies move from one campsite to another; they become increasingly fragmented at the approach of the honey season (May through June), break up during the season (*figures show number of families*) and re-form afterward. The disposition of huts, directions in which they face and their shapes are as shown; some were later abandoned (*broken lines*). Of the clans constituting the group with which the author stayed during this period, the main one was the Bapuemi (*solid-colored areas*). A quarrel resulted in a split camp (*lower left*), which gradually re-formed.

this peculiar relation the fact that the Pygmies seem to have lost their original language is often cited as evidence of their acculturation to the village. Linguists, on the other hand, see nothing surprising in this fact. Small, isolated hunting bands, caught up in the intertribal competition that must have attended the Bantu invasion that began half a millennium ago, could well have lost their own language in a couple of generations. It is by no means certain, however, that the Pygmy language is extinct. Certain words and usages appear to be unique to the Pygmies and do not occur in the languages and dialects of any of the numerous neighboring tribes. What is more, the Pygmies' intonation is so distinctive, no matter which of the languages they are speaking, as to render their speech almost unintelligible to the villager whose language it is supposed to be.

Some authorities maintain that the Pygmies rely on the villagers for food and metal. As for food, my own experience has shown that the BaMbuti hunting bands are perfectly capable of supporting themselves in the forest without any help from outside. The farther away from the villages they are, in fact, the better they find the hunting and gathering. If anything, it is the villagers who depend on the Pygmies, particularly for meat to supplement their protein-deficient diet.

It is more difficult to determine to what extent the BaMbuti are dependent on village metal. A few old men speak of hardening the points of their wooden spears in fire, and children's spears are still made in this way. Except for elephant hunting the spear is mostly a defensive weapon, and the loss of metal spear blades would not be serious. Knife and ax blades are more important; the word *machetti*—for the long, heavy-bladed brush-slashing knife—is well established in the Pygmy vocabulary. There are thorny vines, however, that can serve adequately as scrapers and others that when split give a sharp if temporary cutting edge, like that of split bamboo. When I have pressed the question, it has been stated to me that, in the absence of metal blades, "we would use stones." On the other hand, I have never succeeded in persuading a Pygmy to show me how. The answer to such a request was invariably: "Why should I go to all that trouble when it is so easy to get metal tools from the villagers?"

This is in fact the core of the Pygmies' economic relation with the villagers, and it renders the term "symbiosis" inapplicable. There is nothing they need badly enough to make them dependent on the villagers, although they use many artifacts acquired from them. Metal cooking utensils are a good example: the Pygmies can get along without these comfortably. They use them only for the cooking of village foods that require boiling, such as rice; forest foods call for no such utensils. The BaMbuti will exchange goods with the villagers and even work for them, but only as long as it suits their convenience and no longer. No amount of persuasion will hold them. If a villager attempts coercion, the Pygmy simply packs up and goes back to the forest, secure in the knowledge that he will not be followed. On the next occasion he will offer his goods in another village. Tribal records are full of disputes in which one villager has accused another of stealing "his" Pygmies.

In the absence of effective economic control the villagers attempt to assert political and religious authority. The villagers themselves are the source of the myth that they "own" the Pygmies in a form of hereditary serfdom. They appoint Pygmy headmen, each responsible for his band to the appropriate village headman. Because the bands not only shift territorially but also change as to their inner composition, however, a village headman can no more be sure which Pygmy families comprise "his" band than he can tell at any time where the band has wandered. In his appointed Pygmy headman he has a scapegoat he can blame for failure of the band to fulfill its side of some exchange transaction. But the Pygmy has no wealth with which to pay fines and can rarely be caught for the purpose of enforcing any other restitution.

The villagers nonetheless believe themselves to be the masters. They admit it is a hard battle and point out that the Pygmies are in league with the powerful and tricky spirits of the forest. The fear the villagers have of the forest goes beyond a fear of the animals; it is also a respect based on the knowledge that they are newcomers, if of several hundred years' standing. This respect is even extended to the Pygmies. Some villages make offering to the Pygmies of the first fruit, acknowledging that the Pygmies were there before them and so have certain rights over the land. This offering is also expected to placate the forest spirits. Ultimately, however, the villagers hope to subject the Pygmies to the village spirits and thereby to assume total domination.

In carrying the contest into the realm of the supernatural, the villagers invoke the full armory of witchcraft and sorcery. To the villagers these methods of social control are just as scientific and real as, say, political control through armed force. Moreover, although witchcraft and sorcery generally get their results by psychological pressure, they can sometimes be implemented by physiological poisons. There are strange tales of illness and of death due to sorcery, and no Pygmy wants to be cursed by a villager. On receiving threats of this kind the hunting band takes to the forest, secure in the belief that village magic is no more capable of following them into the forest than are the villagers themselves.

More subtly, the villagers engage the Pygmies in the various important rituals of the village culture. A Pygmy birth, marriage or death, occurring when the hunting band is bivouacked near a village, sets in motion the full village ceremonial appropriate to the occasion. The "owner" of the Pygmy in each case assumes the obligation of providing the child-protecting amulet, of negotiating the exchange of bride wealth or of paying the cost of the obsequies. Such intervention in a Pygmy marriage not only ensures that the union is regularized according to village ritual; it also gives the owners in question indissoluble rights, natural and supernatural, over the new family. The Pygmies willingly submit to the ritual because it means a three-day festival during which they will be fed by the villagers and at the end of which, with luck, they will be able to make off with a portion of the bride wealth. On returning to the forest the couple may decide that it was just a flirtation and separate, leaving the villagers to litigate the expense of the transaction and the wedding feast. Although they are economically the losers, the villagers nonetheless believe that by forcing or cajoling the Pygmies through the ritual they have subjected them, at least to some extent, to the control of the village supernatural.

The same considerations on both sides apply to a funeral. The ritual places certain obligations on the family of the deceased and lays supernatural sanctions on them; death also involves, almost invariably, allegations of witchcraft or sorcery. Once again, therefore, the villagers are eager to do what is necessary to bring the Pygmies within the thrall of the local spirit world. And once again the Pygmies are willing to co-operate, knowing that the village funerary ritual prescribes a funerary feast. Even though their custom calls

COLLECTING HONEY takes place during a season that lasts approximately two months. The Pygmy reaching into the tree with his left hand holds a honey adz in his right. This instrument is used whenever it becomes necessary to open the tree in order to get at the hive. The honey is usually found much higher up in a tree. All the photographs that appear in this article were made by the author.

for quick and unceremonious disposal of the dead, they are glad to let the villagers do the disposing and even to submit to head-shaving and ritual baths in return for a banquet.

By far the most elaborate ritual by which the villagers hope to bring the Pygmies under control is the initiation of the Pygmy boys into manhood through the ordeal of circumcision, called *nkumbi.* All village boys between the ages of nine and 12 are subject to this practice, which takes place every three years. Pygmy boys of the appropriate age who happen to be in the vicinity are put through the same ceremony with the village boys. A Pygmy boy is sent first "to clean the knife," as the villagers put it, and then he is followed by a village boy. These two boys are thereafter joined by the blood they shed together in the unbreakable bond of *kare,* or blood brotherhood. Any default, particularly on the part of the Pygmy, will invoke the wrath of the ancestors and bring all manner of curses on the offender. So once more the Pygmies are placed under the control of the village spirits and the putative bonds between the serfs and their owners are reinforced. Some villagers also see this practice as a means of securing for them-

selves an assured complement of Pygmy serfs to serve them in the afterworld.

As in all the other ritual relations, the BaMbuti have their own independent motivation and rationalization for submitting their sons to the pain and humiliation of *nkumbi.* For one thing, the Pygmy boys acquire the same secular adult status in the village world as their village blood brothers. The Pygmies, moreover, have the advantage of knowing that the bonds they do not consider unbreakable nonetheless tie their newly acquired village brothers; they made use of this knowledge by imposing on their *kare.* Finally, for the adult male relatives of the Pygmy initiates the ceremony means three months or so of continuous feasting at the expense of the villagers.

Once the *nkumbi* is over and the Pygmies have returned to the forest, it becomes clear that the ritual has no relevance to the inner life of the family and the hunting band. The boys who have gone to such trouble to become adults in the village sit on the laps of their mothers, signifying that they know they are really still children. In Pygmy society they will not become adults until they have proved themselves as hunters. Back in the forest the Pygmies once again become forest people. Their coun-

ter to the villagers' efforts to bring them under domination is to keep the two worlds apart. This strategy finds formal expression in the festival of the *molimo.* The *molimo* songs are never sung when a band is making a visitation to a village or is encamped near it. Out in the forest, during the course of each night's singing, the trail leading off from the camp in the direction of the village is ceremonially blocked with branches and leaves, shutting out the profane world beyond.

The relation between the Pygmy and the village cultures thus resolves itself in a standoff. Motivated as it is by economics, the relation is inherently an adversary one. The villagers seek to win the contest by domination; the Pygmies seek to perpetuate it by a kind of indigenous apartheid. Because the relation is one of mutual convenience rather than necessity, it works with reasonable success in the economic realm. The villagers ascribe the success, however, to their spiritual domination; any breakdown they cannot correct they are content to leave to rectification by the supernatural, a formula that works within their own society. The Pygmies hold, on the other hand, that the forest looks after its own, a belief that is borne out by their

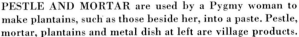

PESTLE AND MORTAR are used by a Pygmy woman to make plantains, such as those beside her, into a paste. Pestle, mortar, plantains and metal dish at left are village products.

DRYING MEAT OVER A FIRE preserves it against the time when it will be taken to the villages to be traded. Otherwise the meat would rot quickly. The Pygmies never store or preserve food for their own use.

daily experience. In the nature of the situation, each group is able to think it has succeeded, as indeed in its own eyes it has. The very separateness of the two worlds makes this dual solution possible. But it is a solution that can work only in the present context.

A breakdown began when the Belgians insisted that the villagers plant cotton and produce a food surplus. The villagers then needed the Pygmies even more as a source of manpower. At the same time, with roads being cut through the forest, the movement of game became restricted. If the process had continued, the Pygmies would have found it increasingly difficult to follow their hunting and food-gathering way of life and would indeed have become the economic dependents of the villagers. The present political turmoil in the Congo has given the Pygmies a temporary reprieve.

In some areas, however, the Belgians had decided to pre-empt the untapped Pygmy labor force for themselves and had already set about "liberating" the Pygmies from the mythical yoke of the villagers, persuading them to set up plantations of their own. The result was disastrous. Used to the constant shade of the forest, to the purity of forest wa-

ter and to the absence of germ-carrying flies and mosquitoes, the Pygmies quickly succumbed to sunstroke and to various illnesses against which the villagers have some immunity. Worse yet, with the abandoning of hunting and food gathering the entire Pygmy social structure collapsed. Forest values were necessarily left behind in the forest, and there was nothing to take their place but a pathetic and unsuccessful imitation of the new world around them, the world of villagers and of Europeans.

This whole problem was much discussed among the Pygmies just prior to the independence of the Congo. In almost every case they reached the determination that as long as the forest existed they would try to go on living as they had always lived. More than once I was told, with no little insight, that "when the forest dies, we die." So for the Pygmies, in a sense, there is no problem. They have seen enough of the outside world to feel able to make their choice, and their choice is to preserve the sanctity of their own world up to the very end. Being what they are, they will doubtless continue to play a masterful game of hide-and-seek, but they will not easily sacrifice their integrity.

It is for future administrations of the Congo that the problem will be a real one, both moral and practical. Can the vast forest area justifiably be set aside as a reservation for some 40,000 Pygmies? And if the forest is to be exploited, what can one do with its inhabitants, who are physically, temperamentally and socially so unfitted for any other form of life? If the former assessment of the Pygmy-villager relation had been correct and the Pygmies had really been as acculturated as it seemed, the problem would have resolved itself into physiological terms only, serious enough but not insuperable. As it is, seeing that the Pygmies have for several hundred years successfully rejected almost every basic element of the foreign cultures surrounding them, the prospects of adaptation are fraught with hazards.

Traditional values die hard, it would seem, and continue to thrive even when they are considered long since dead and buried. In dealing with any African peoples, I suspect, we are in grave danger if we assume too readily that they are the creatures we like to think we have made them. If the Pygmies are any indication, and if we realize it in time, it may be as well for us and for Africa that they are not.

FIRST MESA in Arizona, the site of the coexistence of the Hopi and the Tewa Pueblo Indians, is shown in this aerial photograph. In the foreground is Tewa Village. At the center and far tip of the mesa, respectively, are the Hopi villages of Sichomovi and Walpi.

31

THE HOPI AND THE TEWA

EDWARD P. DOZIER
June 1957

A tale of two adjacent villages which maintained distinct cultures for two centuries. Then a change in social environment brought them together, demonstrating one way in which minorities are assimilated

The problem of the relations between a dominant population and a minority—Negroes, Jews or an immigrant group—is one of the most interesting, as well as one of the most important, in the realm of social science. Sociologists and anthropologists have carried out many and varied studies in efforts to understand the factors that make for assimilation, on the one hand, or separation, on the other [see "The Jewish Community of Rome," by Leslie C. and Stephen P. Dunn; SCIENTIFIC AMERICAN, March]. This article will report a case study of an altogether unique situation. It concerns two groups of Pueblo Indians living side by side in the mesa country of Arizona. Ethnically and in many other ways they are very alike. Yet for more than 200 years they remained aliens in practically the same village. Then, through what might be considered a historical accident, the two groups were rapidly brought together, barriers fell and they began to live in happy harmony.

The groups are the Hopi and a small colony of families descended from Tewa Indians of the Santa Fe area. In 1949-50, as a graduate student in anthropology, I spent a year living with these people, and since then I have been able to revisit them several times, following up the study on foundation grants. To learn anything about their history and culture it was necessary to establish trustful relations with them and assure them that information was sought only to advance scientific knowledge. Unfortunately the sacred and colorful ceremonies of the Pueblo Indians have in the past been made to appear ludicrous in sensational magazine articles; the Indians now prohibit photographs of these events and have closed many of them to white observers.

Our story begins with the Spanish occupation of the Southwest in the 16th century. The coming of the Spaniards fell as a catastrophe upon the peaceful Pueblo Indians in the Santa Fe area. The white man's diseases and fanatical attempts to Christianize and "civilize" the Indians took a great toll of the Pueblos' lives. Finally in 1680 the Indians rebelled and drove the Spaniards from Santa Fe.

Among the leaders of the rebellion were a Tewa group who lived in five "pueblos" (towns of mud-walled

POLACCA VILLAGE at the foot of First Mesa is named for its Tewa founder, Tom Polacca. Modeled on the pattern of the whites' villages, it helped gain Hopi respect for the Tewa.

houses) south and east of. Santa Fe. They had numbered some 4,000; now they were reduced to less than 1,000. When the Spaniards were driven out, these people moved into Santa Fe. But 13 years later Don Diego de Vargas returned with a well-armed Spanish force and quickly subdued them. Most of the Tewa in the town were taken as slaves; a few hundred resettled in a village north of Santa Fe. Three years later these Tewa, still rebellious and suffering repeated Spanish punitive expeditions, made a final raid on the city, killed their Catholic missionary and fled 400 miles west to the mesa country of the Hopi Indians.

The 200 men, women and children who made the journey did not find the bounteous welcome they had expected. According to a legend which their de-

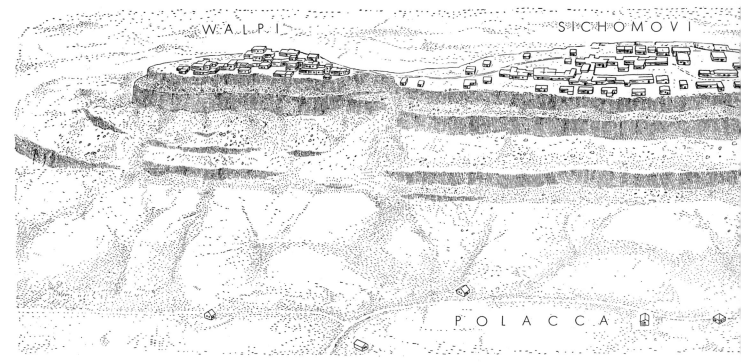

FIRST MESA COMMUNITIES are represented here as they are seen from the east. Though Sichomovi and Tewa Village are architecturally identical, and to all appearances are joined on the mesa, the unmarked border between the villages was well established in

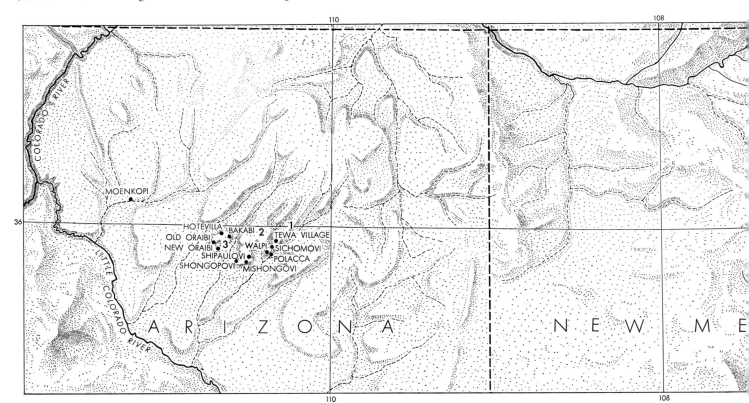

LAND OF THE PUEBLO INDIANS is shown in this map. South of Santa Fe (*right*) is the original home of the Tewa who migrated to Hopi territory (*left*). These people are now called the Southern Tewa. The area north of Santa Fe is still inhabited by a Tewa

scendants have kept alive from generation to generation, Hopi chiefs had repeatedly invited the Tewa to come, promising them land, food, sexual privileges with the Hopi women and assistance in settling in a permanent home. These inducements were offered be-

the minds of the two Indian groups during the 200-year period of mutual hostility.

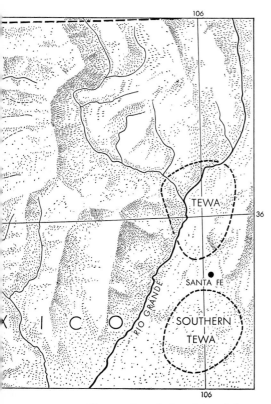

group. The numbers 1, 2 and 3 at left represent the First, Second and Third mesas.

cause the Hopi needed the doughty Tewa as warriors to drive off their enemies. But after the Tewa had performed this service, says the legend, the Hopi failed to make good their promises, and the Tewa received only a meager village site at the end of a mesa (a flat-topped finger of land bordered by ravines). The Tewa responded by putting a "curse" upon the Hopi. They dug a pit between their village and the neighboring Hopi one, made the Hopi spit into the pit, then spat upon the spittle of the Hopi and filled the pit with earth. This action was intended to seal the Tewa culture forever from appropriation by the Hopi.

Whether or not this legend is literally true, it has been effective in keeping the two peoples separate for hundreds of years. It has reinforced basic psychological and social factors which operated against assimilation.

First, and perhaps most important, the Tewa were a small but proud minority—only about 200 against several thousand Hopi. They refused to be assimilated; the passive Hopi, on the other hand, made no effort to impose their language or customs on the handful of militarily useful newcomers.

Secondly, while the two peoples were alike in many respects—both of them Pueblo Indian tribes of farmers at about the same technological level and with much the same ceremonial forms—they were temperamentally very different. The Tewa had come from a border region where they had constantly had to defend themselves against the Plains Indians and later against the Spaniards. They had lived in a country of rivers—the Rio Grande and its tributaries—in which it was possible to work with nature to irrigate their crops. They had been exposed to a century of Spanish example in asserting control over the environment. As a result the Tewa had developed a high measure of active self-reliance.

The Hopi, in contrast, lived in a region where men easily persuaded themselves that there was little they could do about the environment. In the mesa country there were no streams, and agriculture was at the mercy of the weather. They planted maize, beans and melons in the flat washes below their mesas—a series of finger-like projections at the southern end of the great Black Mesa which runs north almost into Utah. When too little rain fell, their plants withered and died in the hot sun; when it poured, raging floods uprooted the plants and washed them away. Thus weather was the most important concern

of the Hopi, and it shaped their attitude toward nature and human existence.

The contrasting attitudes of the Tewa and the Hopi are expressed in their religious beliefs and practices. The Tewa religion has its share of magical concepts, but they fortify their appeals to magic with practical steps. Their medicine men not only perform magical rites but also administer medicinal herbs, massage and treatments for the injured: they are expert in setting broken bones. Their songs and dances exalt warrior prowess. When enemies threatened in the past, they formed war parties to meet them. In any crisis the Tewa offer prayers and then take action.

In the Hopi religion the dominant theme is reliance on the mystical forces which are believed to control the weather and natural environment. Elaborate ceremonies have been developed to coax these powers to favor the petitioners with bountiful harvests. The Hopi believe that if their rites and ceremonies are properly and regularly performed with a "good heart," there will always be enough to eat and everyone will be healthy. They depend upon the magical powers not only to provide rain for their crops but also to thwart sickness and ward off their enemies; rather than take up arms against attackers they appeal to the deities to deflect or immobilize the enemy. The deities believed to control the destinies of men are a group of vaguely conceived ancestral gods called the *katcina*. In the Hopi ceremonies men dressed in elaborate masked costumes represent these gods. The Hopi also carve dolls in the likeness of the deities and give them to young girls as fertility symbols. At regular intervals during the year the members of secret fraternal organizations go into retreats and emerge to perform rites to propitiate the gods. One of these ceremonies is the annual Snake Dance performed by the Hopi Snake Society.

The religious differences between the Tewa and the Hopi clearly illustrate the nature of the two peoples—the one aggressive and self-reliant, the other passive and mystical. From the start their incompatibility of outlook, together with the Tewa's resentment as an unhonored minority, made them hostile neighbors. The Hopi feared and disliked their protectors; the Tewa responded with aloofness and contempt.

The Tewa took up residence on what is known as the First Mesa. Their village, which the Tewa call Tewa and the Hopi call Hano, adjoins a Hopi vil-

TEWA WOMAN clad in traditional garments stands before a *kiva*, the meeting place of secret religious societies, in Tewa Village. Such clothes are worn only on festive occasions.

thority and by reminders of the curse.

The Tewa have maintained an important difference in social organization from their neighbors. A Hopi village is a loose aggregation of clans. The maternal clans are virtually autonomous units. Once a year the clan heads meet to discuss the welfare of the village, but by and large ceremonial and political activities are controlled by the individual clans. The Tewa village, on the other hand, has a centralized organization. It is divided into two general units. The members of one group are called "winter people," of the other, "summer people." Every child is initiated into one of the two groups between the ages of six and 10. Each group has its own *kiva* (ceremonial house) and its own chief. The two chiefs cooperate in conducting the village's ceremonial and governmental activities, and each has certain special responsibilities for one half of the year. The general form of this organization is characteristic of all Tewa pueblos in New Mexico, and the Tewa who came to live on the First Mesa in Arizona have retained its major outlines.

For two centuries the Tewa and Hopi villages, despite their physical proximity, remained separate social islands. Intermarriage was discouraged or forbidden. The Tewa population continued to be a small minority: it still numbered only 200. The Hopi tolerated this independent group as mercenaries who performed useful functions as protectors and go-betweens in their relations with outsiders. They turned over to the Tewa the handling of all their relations with other Indian tribes and with the white authorities, but the Hopi looked down upon these functions as work suitable only for inferiors.

This state of arm's-length separation might have continued indefinitely if whites had not begun to move into the mesa country of the Hopis toward the end of the last century. The new white settlers had no intention of introducing social changes among the Indians; indeed, they were probably unaware of the differences between the Hopi and the Tewa. But their coming brought a change in cultural climate which had a subtle and powerful effect upon the Indian community.

The Tewa suddenly found themselves in a situation in which their qualities were highly valued. The white scheme of values favored the practical and aggressive spirit over the mystical. The practical Tewa readily and enthusiastically took to stock-raising, wagework and the white man's schools. Their chil-

lage named Sichomovi. Thus the Tewa live literally next door to the Hopi. Their houses are indistinguishable; Tewa Village has all the appearances of a typical Hopi town. But for more than 250 years both groups have been keenly aware of a sharp boundary separating the two villages.

The sharpest division is in language. With constant invocation of the curse against transmission of their culture and secrets to the Hopi, the Tewa have restricted their language to their own group. Even when a Hopi marries a Tewa, the Hopi spouse does not learn the Tewa language. The Tewa, on the other hand, do speak Hopi: to maintain necessary communication they have become bilingual. Yet they have succeeded in defending their own language so well that only a single Hopi term has crept into the Tewa language in two and a half centuries. And this word has gained only a partial entry. It is the expression for "thank you": the Tewa men now use the Hopi term for "thank you," but the Tewa women still use the Tewa term.

The Tewa have borrowed a major so-cial institution from the Hopi; it is, however, an institution which serves to preserve their exclusiveness. This acquisition is the Hopi system of maternal descent. In the Tewa village, as among the Hopi, women are the important members of the family. They own the land and houses, dispense the food and make the important decisions. The men perform religious rites, exercise disciplinary powers, support the family and teach the children how to "make a living," but they have little authority in the home. Residence and the family allegiance belong strictly to the mother. When a man marries, he goes to live in his wife's house, but he frequently visits his mother's house and considers that his home.

It is clear that this system supports the Tewa determination to maintain their own culture. A Tewa household is impervious to Hopi influence, even in cases of intermarriage. The Hopi husband would find it extremely difficult to impose Hopi values and customs on his children, even if he were disposed to do so. Any attempt at such subversion would be countered by the mother's au-

dren, already trained in two languages, learned English more quickly than the Hopi's. Moreover, their higher ardor as a minority spurred them to excel in the classroom. They became models for the Hopi children.

The Hopi began to develop a new respect for the Tewa. The Tewa's role as emissaries and interpreters to the white people grew in importance and prestige. Their value orientation, remarkably like that of the new white residents, no longer had to take a back seat. The Hopi saw that "it paid to be like the whites." They were greatly impressed by the achievements of some of the Tewa in this new climate. One of these was Tom Polacca, an interpreter who spoke five languages (Tewa, Hopi, Navaho, Spanish and English) and had been a leader in contacts with the U. S. Indian Service and other outsiders. He became a prosperous livestock raiser, built a large house below the First Mesa and started a new community which is now named Polacca Village. Equally impressive were the accomplishments of a Tewa woman named Nampeyo. She revived the art of pottery-making, copying old designs exacavated from Indian ruins in the area, and this quickly became an important industry, not only among the Tewa but also among the Hopi villagers.

With remarkable speed the antagonism and distinctions between the Hopi and Tewa began to disappear. The Tewa were accepted as "equals" and shed their onus as a minority. Their population grew: it has doubled in the past half-century. Intermarriage became common. The Hopi and Tewa worked together in pottery manufacture, in cattle cooperatives and even in religious rituals and ceremonies. The ancient legend that had divided the groups faded in influence, and social differences began to disappear. Curiously the Tewa have remained clannish about their language, but since they are equally fluent in Hopi, there are no barriers to communication.

Today hostility between the two groups has virtually disappeared. Only the old men try to keep alive the ancient Hopi "injustices," but the young people tend to laugh off their admonitions and bury the memory of the "curse."

The history of this little episode in human relations may hold some useful lessons. Social scientists differ on the possibility of manipulating human societies to desired ends, but one may hope that case studies such as this one will help mankind to find cures for groups in conflict and trouble.

32

PEASANT MARKETS

SIDNEY W. MINTZ
August 1960

In a primarily agricultural country such as Haiti the market is the central economic institution. Chaotic though they may seem, these gatherings possess an elaborate underlying order

On market days in Haiti the towns and the country market-places gather thousands of peasants for hours of busy and noisy activity. The people come for gossip, courtship and the playing-out of personal rivalries, to visit a clinic or to register a birth; but above all they come for business—to sell the tiny surpluses of their little farms and to buy necessities. They press together in the ragged lanes among the stalls and the heaps of produce spread on the ground, inspecting and handling the displays of textiles, hardware, spices, soap and cooking oils, buying, selling and chaffering. Children push by hawking trays of sweets; farmers pull produce-laden animals through the crowds, calling loudly for the right of way. Trucks back up and turn around, their drivers honking horns, apparently oblivious of the people and the great piles of goods. There are vigorous arguments, sometimes ending in blows and arrests. In the very intensity of color, sound and smell the outsider is overwhelmed with an impression of confusion and disorder.

But for all its apparent anarchy the market place is characterized by an elaborate underlying order. Wherever they exist, peasant markets reveal a great deal about the societies they serve. They are a central economic institution in many countries where large numbers of small-scale farmers work their own land. To follow the movement of marketers and stock through the system is an ideal way to begin to study the economy and to trace the distribution of economic and political power in the society.

In the simpler economies, wherein producers merely exchange local commodities, the market place may do little more than facilitate barter. In societies that use money but have fixed or traditional prices, the market place reflects

that isolation from the world market; its transactions neither affect nor respond to economic events in the world at large. Where trade crosses national boundaries, links diverse regions and supports specialist traders, the market place takes on a new significance, joining local activities to the world outside.

As the underdeveloped areas of the world—for example, Jamaica, Haiti, Ghana, Nigeria, India, Burma, Indonesia —move more fully into the orbit of world trade, their market systems have been passing from the earliest of these stages to the next. The transition disrupts traditional relationships and creates new alignments and rivalries in the society, and these are nowhere more dramatically revealed than in the market place. It is here that the peasant trades his surplus for the necessities he cannot produce from his own holding, and it is the market place that determines, directly or indirectly, the prices at which the exporter will purchase the peasant's produce for delivery to the world market. In certain countries the connection that the market establishes between the peasant producer and the world market is the keystone of national development. Those who hold political power may use the peasant market-system to try to educate, persuade, coerce and manipulate the peasantry, particularly with the aim of maintaining or increasing export production. The market places are primarily loci of trade, but they are also the arena where the diverse interests of the peasantry, traders and officials are pitted and exposed.

The study of the tangle of interests that animates the peasant market thus brings into the open numerous connections between regions, classes and interest groups. Traditional anthropologi-

cal studies, which focus on small, local groups, cannot yield comparable insights into such large, differentiated societies as those of India and Nigeria or even Haiti. Courts and legislatures provide good settings for observation of the competing elements in a society. But the market place reveals far more because it allows these elements so much greater freedom to express themselves.

Though man has probably been a trader since the beginnings of society, his trading activities have not invariably produced market places. When the Spanish conquerors came to the New World, for example, they were stunned by the size and grandeur of such Aztec market places as Tlatelolco, where 50,-000 traders assembled on market day. A wealthy merchant group, the *pochteca,* controlled trade and wielded considerable power, and also served as efficient spies for the military. But in the great contemporary Andean empire of the Incas the conquistadors found neither market places nor merchants. Instead of trade they found royal monopolies in gold, silver, coca and fine textiles. Thus while market places are not found everywhere, their very absence tells us something about a society. The presence of markets does not necessarily imply a particular course of social development. Yet there are striking similarities among the peasant markets of the world, especially those of the new nations of Africa, Asia and tropical America.

Haiti is an older nation, with a history of political independence. But at its present stage of economic evolution this Caribbean republic is representative of the new nations that are emerging in the colonial regions of the world. Before the revolution of 1791-1804, Haitian slaves grew their food on plantation waste-lands, selling surpluses in supervised

BUSTLING ACTIVITY OF MARKET DAY animates a clearing in rural Haiti. Tradeswomen are grouped by commodity they sell. In this photograph woman in left foreground inspects wares of grain seller. At left in middle distance is lean-to of tuber sellers.

HAITIAN FARMS CLING TO TERRACED HILLSIDES near rural village of Kenskoff. Characteristically cluttered, the Haitian farm grows small but widely diversified crops.

ROAD TO MARKET PLACE is crowded with peasants. Whole families often walk all night, carrying their crop surpluses, in order to arrive at the market in time for early trading.

market places. In the 1790's the French observer Moreau de Saint Méry described such a market place, where 15,000 slaves traded on market day. The revolution destroyed the plantations that had made the island of Saint-Domingue one of the richest colonies in history, and substantially eliminated the French planters. Gradually Haiti became a peasant country where small-scale landholders cultivated their subsistence crops for local sale and a few items for export. The cash they received paid for the soap, cloth, oil, metal tools and flour they needed and could not produce. The national government sustained itself almost entirely by taxes on imports and exports; the local government, by levies on dealings in the market place.

Today, 150 years later, nearly 90 per cent of the people live in the country-side, and 80 per cent of them work their own land. Haitian peasants still cultivate much of their own food and produce a small surplus destined for export or for consumption in the domestic economy through sale in the peasant market. By aiming at these three different production goals they try to minimize risk and to secure a reasonably stable subsistence. They further hedge their investment of time and capital by diversifying the cultivation of their land, and this accounts for the curiously cluttered look of their little plots. Like other Caribbean farmers, the Haitian peasant makes thorough use of his land: he grows root crops underground, vines and creepers on the surface, grains above ground and trees and climbing vines in the air. Though technologically backward, the method provides a constant trickle of varied produce for the household where storage is difficult or impractical, a supply of craft and medicinal materials as required and a small quantity of items for sale at various times. It is upon this foundation that the Haitian market-system rests.

The peasant's wife most often handles the market transactions of the family, selling what the land has produced for sale and using the cash received to buy household necessities. Many peasant women become professional traders in this way. This further distributes the family's economic risks, since the men do the farming and the women do the trading partly as separate ventures.

Most of the trade in Haiti goes on in the nearly 300 officially controlled market places. In each region one or more central market-places services other, smaller centers. The larger centers are established in the towns; the satellite country market-places spring up over-

WOMEN DOMINATE TRADE in perishables in Haiti. In photograph at left, purchaser holds a measuring-can while bean seller fills it. They may fill and empty the can again before agreeing that it is properly filled. At right is section of the tuber market.

SUCCESSFUL TRADESWOMAN operates between markets. Her annual volume of business may amount to thousands of dollars.

SALT VENDOR'S CHILD arranges stock of coarse, unrefined salt for sale. Salt is among the few commodities shipped in bulk.

night as little towns that last only through the day to gather in and to absorb the peasant buying-power. Market days are staggered, enabling itinerant buyers and sellers to move from one market to another. Most of the important market places are on well-traveled truck routes. Thus the markets form a network, and the produce bought in one is put up for resale—after bulking, processing and transport—in another. For example, pork purchased in one market is cut up, salted and shipped to the next, while rice, millet and maize are husked or ground between purchase and resale to increase their value. The whole system of market places constantly adjusts and readjusts to seasonal changes, to the success or failure of harvests, to the growth and contraction of production areas, to the expansion of roads and trucking.

Trade begins beyond the fringes of the market, where licensed tradesmen from the towns, called *spéculateurs,* maintain outposts at which they buy commodities for export. Peasant women on their way to market stop to sell their coffee, beeswax and sisal to the *spéculateurs,* and then proceed to market with the cash they have received. Because competition is heavy and supplies uncertain, *spéculateurs* do not always wait for the peasants to come to them. They often send illegal buyers called "zombies" or "submarines" to make purchases directly at the farms.

But it is in the tumult of the market place that most trading activity goes on. Only after many days of observing and classifying the actors and their activities does the underlying order become apparent. Sellers of the necessities that peasants come to buy are present each day in a given market place. Perishable foods come and go seasonally, but grains are nearly always available. Prices for different products fluctuate differently, perishables showing the greatest eccentricity, cloth and hardware changing very little from week to week, though perceptibly from season to season. Watching the market place each market day, one sees women dealing in the same goods always clustered together; grain sellers, corn-meal retailers and sellers of spice and sundries arrange themselves in rows. For the seller this permits a quicker check on the day's trade, on one's favored customers, and of course on prices. When sellers of the same stocks are together, the speed with which price is established, and with which it changes during the trading, is increased. Buyers of particular goods come regularly where the sellers are clustered.

PEASANT MEN WORK AS ARTISANS in the market, rarely as tradesmen. At left is a cobbler who rebuilds discarded shoes and sells them. At right a blacksmith hammers sheet metal into hoes. Artisans usually tend their farms on other than market days.

Behind the facade of apparently uniform and competitive prices, however, there exists a relationship called *pratique*, in which the retailer gives her favored customers certain concessions in price or quantity or in the terms of credit in return for assurances of the customer's patronage when the market is glutted and prices are low. The retailer also makes *pratique* with her suppliers, thus assuring herself of a stock when certain commodities are scarce. Since *pratique* is a clandestine relationship, it can only be understood by carefully noting the details of many transactions.

Even the casual observer soon notices that the important heavy trade in perishables and the small-scale retailing of imports are carried on entirely by women. Men rarely trade; both sexes believe women are commercially shrewd-

er than men. There are, to be sure, male traders, but with the exception of the peasant who has come to market to sell livestock or craft articles they are almost always townsmen. The peasant woman makes her entrance into the market as a trader on the most modest terms, first as her household's representative in the market, then perhaps with a small stake borrowed from relatives or other traders. In a country where a handful of grain makes a meal and a bit of land a farmer, a few pennies constitute operating capital for the middleman, and what one can carry in one's hands is enough stock to begin trading. If the woman is resourceful she may parlay her small stake in a series of small trading transactions to a sum sufficient to secure her status as a *revendeuse* (literally reseller).

Thousands of these women move from market place to market place, each deal-

ing in small amounts, but together buying and selling vast quantities of stock. They live by connecting centers of supply and demand; their potential profit rests in the price differentials between regions and in their ability to contribute to the value of products by carrying, processing, storing, bulking and breaking bulk. They often render services at incredibly low cost. Thus salt retailers in one market place interpose themselves between truckers and consumers, breaking bulk and retailing salt for earnings that sometimes fall below five cents a day. If these services were not provided, consumers would have to buy in uneconomically large quantities, or truckers would have to sell in uneconomically small ones. The fact that consumers buy from them even though they sit only a few feet from the trucks that bring the salt is proof that the service they sell is

TRUCKING AND TINKERING are other male occupations. Trucks carry resellers and their stock between markets. They serve a vital function because regular bulk shipments are unknown. Tinker (*right*) does brisk business because new pots are expensive.

MARKETING OF FISH is characteristic of way trade is conducted in Haiti. Resellers wade out to fishing boats to buy fish (*photograph at top*); return to shore to sell them to waiting consumers (*photograph at bottom*). Fishermen will not deal directly with consumers.

worth buying. In their intermediary activities, the *revendeuses* scour remote countrysides. They buy basic commodities at their sources, where they are cheap, because the economic integration of the back country with the national economy is incomplete. Thus, by servicing buyers and sellers both, they help unite the peasant plot and the local market place with national currents of exchange, stabilizing general price levels and contributing to economic growth. The path to success is uncertain, but some few reach the top. The volume of a *revendeuse's* business may approach that of the famous "market mammies" of Nigeria, whose transactions amount to thousands of dollars a year. Though all apparently aspire to become city retailers, women with rural family-attachments incline to remain in the countryside and usually identify themselves with the peasantry.

For transportation from market place to market place the *revendeuses* depend upon the truckers. Demand is not sufficiently firm and centralized to give the truckers bulk cargoes to haul. It is not surprising, therefore, to discover that they are essentially passenger carriers, whose business it is to transport the *revendeuses* and their modest stocks. Trucking is a risky enterprise in a country where roads are few, maintenance facilities are poor and high taxes are levied against fuel and passengers. The trucker is a relatively new figure in the economy. His economic interests are at present firmly identified with those of the *revendeuses* and opposed to the *rentiers,* merchants and officials of the towns and cities. With the *revendeuses* he is against any forces aimed at the restriction and centralization of trade in Haiti. On the other hand, if the growth and evolution of the economy should make it possible for the trucker to profit by bulk transport, this general accord might well vanish.

In such an eventuality the truckers might find themselves allied with the townsmen. The *spéculateurs,* coffee processors, wholesalers and merchants, separately and in combination, all aim to encompass as much of the peasants' economic activity as possible. For although each peasant may be poor, the wealth that changes hands when thousands of peasants shop in the market place is considerable. Successful market places outside the towns constantly tempt the town merchants, particularly cloth- and shoe-sellers, who carry large stocks from their town shops into the country on market day. The townsmen would of course prefer that all peasant trading took place in towns, where markets could be centralized, and the small reseller subjected to more control. To that end they have inspired repeated attempts at restrictive legislation. In this they are joined by the *rentiers*, the value of whose property would appreciate with increase in town trade. The importers and exporters among the city merchants would prefer to see export production rise, even at the cost of subsistence crops.

Officials of the national government are often similarly disposed. Unlike the local governments, which are largely supported by taxes on market-place transactions, the national government derives its revenues chiefly from taxes on imports and exports. Hence the state officials want to see peasant agriculture producing more exportable goods. One could say that their aim is to maximize the peasantry's taxable income.

In the market place one sees the whole structure of official power: police, military, judicial, executive. All market places in Haiti are under some supervision by state officials, who carry on two major and familiar functions: maintaining order and collecting taxes and license fees. At the top this structure is tied to the ministries in the capital; at the bottom it embraces notaries, justices of the peace, soldiery and local political leaders. It is within the market place, in the regulation of concrete economic transactions, that the penetration of political control is seen at its most complete as well as its most trivial. State officials supervise the workers who clean and maintain the market place; they catch and imprison thieves; they stop fights. They are supported by the lowest ranks of political officials, the *chefs de section*, who come from the rural areas to the market place to oversee peasants from their neighborhoods. The peasantry's name for any official, no matter how lowly, is always *l'état*.

Traders are taxed or licensed for taking livestock to market, for butchering, for selling animals, for selling meat, for selling foods of any kind, for selling alcoholic beverages and tobacco, for dealing as intermediaries in all other agricultural products, for tethering beasts of burden and for the stands and sheds they use to display meat and other products for sale. This revenue goes largely to governments of the *arrondissements*, though part is drained off by the national government. Tax revenues are used for the operation of local governments, and to pay for tax collectors' salaries and the administration of the tax system.

Just as the political and commercial elements of the towns seek to centralize and control the markets, so the rural tradesmen seek to maintain the status quo. Their interests dictate a diffuse and open market in which ingenuity and intelligence enable them to compensate for lack of capital, and where they may hope to make the transition from perishable-produce dealers to hard-goods wholesalers or credit merchants.

The contention of these various groups, however, is ultimately intelligible only in terms of the behavior and power of the peasant, whose best interests do not lie decisively in either camp. In determining how he may maximize his cash income by transactions in the market place, he weighs the demand and prices of the domestic market against the opportunities offered by the export market. In striking a balance between the two alternatives he may incline toward the production of export goods to supplement his cash, but he is wary of export-market fluctuations which can deeply affect him and which he cannot control. His choices are not entirely free, for the various factions of the nation, especially those that favor increased production for export, exert considerable pressure upon him. As the source of his cash income, the market places are the peasantry's first line of defense against greater dependence upon the world market and a greater involvement with the officialdom of the state.

Apparently the alignments of interest that may be discerned in the peasant markets today have characterized Haitian society for many years. During the 19th century Haiti's seacoast towns sought to maintain economic hegemony over the inland towns. In the struggles of town merchants against the peasantry, and of the seacoast against the interior, climaxed by the capital's economic dominion over the nation, there are startling parallels with conflicts waged during the growth of capitalism in the nations of Western Europe. In both cases groups with vested economic interests sought to restrict the spread of competitive trading activity.

Thus study of an internal market-system may provide a lively vision of relationships among key economic and political groups in a society. Eventually it may be possible to compare internal market-systems in different societies as total systems, thereby revealing similarities and differences among the societies themselves that might otherwise be difficult to discover.

A Variation on Traditional Concerns:
The Neofunctional Ecology of Hunters,
Farmers, and Pastoralists

A VARIATION ON
TRADITIONAL
CONCERNS:
THE NEOFUNCTIONAL
ECOLOGY OF HUNTERS,
FARMERS,
AND PASTORALISTS

All of the papers in this section deal with the relationships between societies and their natural environments. Two of the three papers signal a revival of functionalist anthropology. This mode of inquiry and explanation prevailed in British anthropology for the first half of the twentieth century (and was adopted by a few American anthropologists), but subsided somewhat because of persistent criticisms about the tautological nature of functionalist explanations and, after the publication in 1949 of *Les Structures Élémentaires de la Parente* by Claude Lévi-Strauss, because of the increasing influence of the works of French and European structuralism on British anthropology. Structuralists have sought to explain observable cultural phenomena, such as marriage patterns, through rules or structures that are themselves manifestations of deeper, unobservable structures.

Considered generally, functionalism attempts to analyze cultural and social phenomena by posing the question: What parts do the phenomena play in the operation of a given system? Adherents to functionalism assume that systems of related parts exist, and further, that in much the same way an organism functions, each part contributes to the maintenance of the system, individual needs being fulfilled when the system is maintained. Functionalists do not presuppose that the subjects of a study recognize a cause-and-effect relationship between their actions and their goals, but rather, that social systems are nonrational and explainable in nonagentive, physical terms. Indeed, they assume general laws that explain the functions they analyze. Although no explicit inductive or deductive methods have been devised, functionalists have sought to discover the relations among parts that are truly essential for maintaining the society. However, key terms such as "essential" have never been defined and measured, and consequently, have not been tested, because a proposition must be definable or measurable before it can be put to a test. An untestable proposition cannot be falsified; therefore functional analysis—the assumption that systems exist and that each part in the system has a function to perform that is truly essential to the system—remains limited to unfalsifiable discoveries about systems: to wit, no matter what "function" the functionalist observes, that function seems essential to the system by definition. In logical terms, functionalism makes the fallacy of affirming phenomena that arise as a consequence of premise.*

By defining cultural or social systems in terms of parts that adjust (rather than "function") to protect the system when it is challenged or threatened, neofunctionalists attempt to avoid this fallacy. Ideally, a society can then be assessed by the degree to which the parts have

---

*See Robert Brown, *Explanations in Social Science*; Chicago: Aldine Publishing Company, pages 109–132, 1963. See also Carl G. Hempel, "The Logic of Functional Analysis," in *Symposium on Sociological Theory*, Llewellyn Gross, ed.; New York: Harper and Row, pages 271–307, 1959.

changed, and the change is alleged to be the adjustment or adaptation of the nonrational system. The parts, which often include conditions in the environment beyond the society, are often definable and measurable, even though no explicit methodology—inductive or otherwise—is used to test for the relations among parts. But neofunctionalism is also prey to logical and methodological attack, and if it is to develop into a rigorous form of analysis, diachronic multivariate analysis or other formal techniques will have to be devised that can test assertions about adjustments and adaptations of systems, and "systems" will have to be formally defined so that we will know precisely what is a system and what isn't a system.

The neofunctionalism exemplified in the readings of this section retains the philosophy of the earlier concept of functionalism, describing nonrational systems composed of parts, each part playing a role in maintaining the system. But in asserting that the systems are maintained through self-regulation and are regulated through negative feedback mechanisms, the neofunctionalists borrow some terms from automatic machine theory. The general functionalist approach, however, was given its functionalist label by Bronislaw Malinowski.*
The major innovation of neofunctionalism is the consideration of environmental variables as parts in a system and the study of how these variables relate to each other and to social systems and human biology (for the purposes of our readings we could add, especially nutrition).

William B. Kemp's essay, "The Flow of Energy in a Hunting Society," does not fit the functionalist mold, old or new, although Kemp's careful accounting of the sources and uses of energy from food, heat, and power suggests an approach toward neofunctionalist concerns. Kemp analyzes the energy flow in an Eskimo village in the eastern Canadian Arctic, pointing out first that a significant factor in contemporary Eskimo life is the introduction of Canada's cash economy into their subsistence economy. Because money has become important to the Eskimos, new adaptive strategies have been necessary to enable them to continue participating in the fragile ecosystem. Their contemporary hunting economy makes use of ammunition, gasoline, outboard engines and snowmobiles, and imported food, and is integrated with the greater capitalist political economy of North America through the trade of skins for these goods. Kemp ably describes the fluctuation in the availability of subsistence goods throughout the year, the mechanism of visiting (and consequently, sharing), the cooperation by which food is distributed among everyone when resources are scarce, and the village feasts at which meat is shared when a large animal is caught. These community activities, according to Kemp, "divert a successful hunter's calorie acquisi-

---

*See, for example, Bronislaw Malinowski, *Magic, Science and Religion*; Garden City, New York: Doubleday Anchor Books, 1954.

tions for the benefit of a group larger than his own household." Kemp sees three kinds of groups forming within the Eskimo society. One consists of wage earners in the larger communities. Another is an externally oriented group that regulates the input from the outside world. The third is the vastly dispersed group of hunters. The fluctuating resource base and the fragility of the ecosystem, Kemp believes, have set rather tight boundaries within which the Eskimo hunting economy can be maintained, as long as the outward-oriented Eskimos provide stability to the three-group system, tempering the relation of the current technology to the traditional hide and fur industry.

The neofunctionalist variables assessed by Roy A. Rappaport in "The Flow of Energy in an Agricultural Society" are the relationships among the Tsembaga people in New Guinea, "swidden" agriculture (in which forest land is cleared by burning), pig raising, and a tropical rainforest environment inducive of rapid plant growth. The Tsembaga employ a gardening strategy that is very similar to the strategy employed by Haitian peasants, and peasants elsewhere generally, intermingling plants of several crops together in small plots. Tsembaga staples are taro and sweet potato, although Tsembagans name more than 260 varieties of some 36 species of plants as edible and plant most of the main crops—root, vine, and tree together—in most of the gardens. These crops include yams, cassavas, bananas, beans, peas, maize, sugarcane, leafy greens, edible flowers, cucumber, and pumpkin. Furthermore, there is no single harvest season. The Tsembaga dig and pick their products from the various strata of the gardens throughout the year. One difference between the Haitian peasants and Tsembaga farmers is that Haitian strategy is motivated in part by the vagaries of the market locally, nationally, and even internationally, whereas the Tsembaga farmer's strategy is dependent on daily food needs. The Tsembaga also raise pigs, which they use for ritual slaughter. Rappaport suggests that the growing time of pigs, which eat the output raised on fully a third of the land, may be instrumental in "regulating" intergroup relations: ceremonies preceding tribal wars can be held when there are sufficient mature pigs for slaughter; not only does the foraging of pigs in abandoned gardens increase the speed at which these lands are returned to forest, pigs also mature to provide high quality protein to Tsembagan individuals at the time it will be most likely needed. Malinowski has said that social needs derive from human needs, and that both needs are satisfied when the "system" is in proper working order. The system Rappaport describes is a nonrational one in which individual nutrition, the tropical forest ecosystem, and agriculture technique must also be considered as variables in a working system. Rappaport's details about environment and his calorie data surpass the work done by Malinowski.

In an article on African pastoralists, "Subsistence Herding in Uganda," Rada and Neville Dyson-Hudson describe what appears to be another nonrational system, that of Uganda's Karimojong tribe, who herd cattle even though they seldom eat meat and have not developed marketable dairy or meat products. The Dyson-Hudsons explain this phenomenon as an example of functional ecology. The populations studied in the previous two essays occupy environments in which the resources are unstable and exhaustible or in which there is competition for resources by neighboring peoples. Now we learn that the Karimojong live in an environment in which both problems exist. As a consequence, the Karimojong do some farming and gathering, but move their livestock regularly, using what food and water they encounter as they go (other tribes will use the same resources if they don't) and not conserving the natural fodder. On the other hand, they do conserve their herds, milking cattle and tapping cattle blood, but slaughtering cattle only for religious ceremonies during which the meat is shared expansively. According to the Dyson-Hudsons, who attempt to account for the maintenance of large herds by showing the interrelations of cultural practices and natural environment, the Karimojong maximize the use of the total environment. Indeed, the Dyson-Hudsons are so impressed with the interrelations they describe that they incline toward the opinion that modern agribusiness ranching or dairying developments in the area would not surpass Karimojong strategies. But if we reject the concept of nonrational systems for a moment, and if we can imagine the growth of cities in Uganda, Kenya, and elsewhere in East Africa, we can certainly envisage the creation of an enormous cattle and dairy industry based on feeder lots on Karimojong territory to help supply these potential urban markets. Such a system would be rational, of course, not nonrational, nor would it be part of a self-regulating system. The following papers suggest that urbanization will continue in Africa and elsewhere, and if East African city-dwellers are to eat meat and dairy products, the cattle industry will have to be rationalized through marketing or socialist distribution.

33

THE FLOW OF ENERGY IN A HUNTING SOCIETY

WILLIAM B. KEMP
September 1971

Early man obtained food and fuel from the wild plants and animals of his environment. How the energy from such sources is channeled is investigated in a community of modern Eskimos on Baffin Island

The investment of energy in hunting and gathering has provided man's livelihood for more than 99 percent of human history. Over the past 10,000 years the investment of energy in agriculture, with its higher yield per unit of input, has transformed most hunting peoples into farmers. Among the most viable of the remaining hunters are the Eskimos of Alaska, Canada and Greenland. What are the characteristic patterns of energy flow in a hunting group? How is the available energy channeled among the various activities of the group in order for the group to survive? In 1967 and 1968 I undertook to study such energy flows in an isolated Eskimo village in the eastern Canadian Arctic.

I observed two village households in particular. When I lived in the village, one of the two households was characterized by its "modern" ways; the other was more "traditional." I was able to measure the energy inputs and energy yields of both households in considerable detail. (The quantitative data presented here are based on observations made during a 54-week period from February 14, 1967, to March 1, 1968.) The different patterns of energy use exhibited by the two households help to illuminate the process of adaptation to nonhunting systems of livelihood and social behavior that faces all contemporary hunting societies.

For the Eskimos the most significant factor in the realignment of economic and social activity has been the introduction of a cash economy. The maintenance of a hunting way of life within the framework of such an economy calls for a new set of adaptive strategies. Money, or its immediate equivalent, is now an important component in the relation between the Eskimo hunter and the natural environment.

The village where I worked is one of the few remaining all-Eskimo settlements along the southern coast of Baffin Island on the northern side of Hudson Strait [*see illustrations on next page*]. In this village hunting still dominates the general pattern of daily activity. The economic adaptation is supported by the household routine of the women and is reflected in the play of the children. Villages of this type were once the characteristic feature of the settlement pattern of southern Baffin Island. Within recent years, however, many Eskimos have abandoned the solitary life in favor of larger and more acculturated settlements.

The community I studied is in an area of indented coastline that runs in a northwesterly direction extending from about 63 to 65 degrees north latitude. The land rises sharply from the shore to an interior plateau that is deeply incised by valleys, many containing streams and lakes that serve as the only routes for overland travel. At these latitudes summer activities can proceed during some 22 hours of daylight; the longest winter night lasts 18 hours. Perhaps the most noticeable feature of the Hudson Strait environment is tides of as much as 45 feet. Such tides create a large littoral environment; bays become empty valleys, islands appear and disappear and strong ocean currents prevail. In winter the tides build rough barriers of broken sea ice, and at low tide the steeper shorelines are edged with sheer ice walls. In summer coastal navigation and the selection of safe harbors are difficult, and in winter crossing from the sea ice to the land tries the temper of men and the strength of dogs and machines.

The varying length of the day, the seasonal changes of temperature, the tides and to some extent the timing of the annual freeze-up and breakup are predictable events, easily built into the round of economic activity. Superimposed on these events is the variability and irregularity of temperature, moisture and wind, which affect the pattern of energy flow for the community on a day-to-day basis. In winter the temperatures reach −50 degrees Fahrenheit, with a mean around −30. In summer the temperature may climb above 80 degrees, although temperatures in the low 50's are more typical. Throughout the year there may be large temperature changes from one day to the next. Midwinter temperatures have gone from −30 degrees to above freezing in a single night, bringing a thaw and sometimes even rain.

The heaviest precipitation is in the spring and fall, and strong winds can arise any day throughout the year. Winds of more than 40 miles per hour are common; on four occasions I measured steady winds in excess of 70 m.p.h. Speaking generally, the weather is most stable in March and April and least stable from late September into November.

Within this setting the Eskimos harvest at least 20 species of game. All the marine and terrestrial food chains are exploited in the quest for food, and all habitats—from the expanses of sea ice and open water to the microhabitats of

BLEAK TERRAIN of the Canadian Arctic is seen in the aerial photograph on the opposite page. The steep shore and treeless hinterland are part of an islet in Hudson Strait off the coast of southern Baffin Island. By hunting sea mammals the Eskimos of the region can obtain enough food and valuable by-products to keep them well above the level of survival.

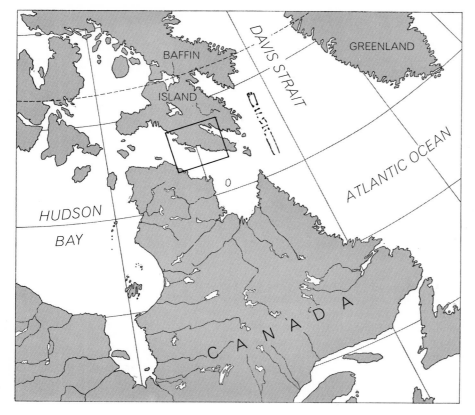

BAFFIN ISLAND extends for nearly 1,000 miles in the area between the mouth of Hudson Bay and the Greenland coast. The villagers' hunting ranges lie within the black rectangle.

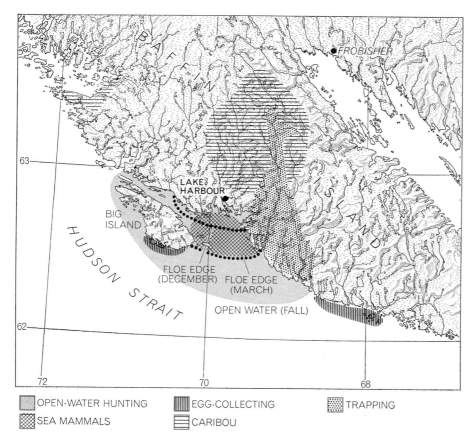

OPEN-WATER HUNTING   EGG-COLLECTING   TRAPPING

SEA MAMMALS   CARIBOU

HUNTING RANGES of one Eskimo village in southern Baffin Island change with the season. The most productive months of the year are spent hunting in coastal waters. Trapping and caribou hunting, generally winter activities, carry the hunters into different areas.

tidal flats, leeward waters and protected valleys—are utilized. Traditionally the Eskimos of southern Baffin Island are mainly hunters of sea mammals: the small common (or ring) seal, the much larger bearded seal and on occasion the beluga whale and the walrus.

Survival in such a harsh environment has two primary requirements. The first is an adequate caloric intake in terms of food and the second is maintenance of a suitable microclimate in terms of shelter and clothing. In the village where I worked the Eskimos met these requirements by hunting and trapping and by buying imported foods and materials. They also bought ammunition for their guns and gasoline for two marine engines and two snowmobiles, transportation aids that increased their hunting efficiency. The money for such purchases was obtained by the sale of skins and furs (products of the hunt) and of stone and ivory carvings (products of artistic skill and of the Eskimos' recognition of consumer preferences). Because government "social assistance" and some work for wages were available, certain individuals had an occasional source of additional cash.

The daily maintenance of life in the village called for an initial input of human energy in the pursuit of game, in the mining of soapstone and in the manufacture of handicrafts. The expenditures of human energy for the 54-week period were 12.8 million kilocalories. They were augmented by expenditures of imported energy: 10,900 rounds of ammunition and 885 gallons of gasoline. The result was the acquisition of 12.8 million kilocalories of edible food from the land and seven million kilocalories of viscera that were used as dog food. To this was added 7.5 million kilocalories of purchased food. By eating the game and the purchased food the hunters and their dependents were able to achieve a potential caloric input of 3,000 kilocalories per day, which was enough to sustain a level of activity well above the maintenance level. The general pattern of energy flow into, through and out of the village is shown in the illustration on pages 336 and 337.

During my stay the population of the village varied between 26 and 29. The people lived in four separate dwellings. One, a wood house, had been built from prefabricated materials supplied by the government. The other three were the traditional *quagmaq:* a low wood-frame tent some 20 feet long, 15 feet wide and seven feet high. These structures were covered with canvas, old

BEARDED SEAL (*left*) is a relatively uncommon and welcome kill. It weighs more than 400 pounds, compared with the common seal's 80 pounds, and its skin is a favorite material. Flat-bottomed rowboat (*rear*) is used to retrieve seals killed at the floe-ice edge.

mailbags and animal skins and were insulated with a 10-inch layer of dry shrubs. Inside they were lined with pages from mail-order catalogues and decorated with a fantastic array of trinkets and other objects. The rear eight feet of each *quagmaq* was occupied by a large sleeping platform, leaving some 180 square feet for household activities during waking hours. The wood house (Household II) was occupied by six people comprising a single family unit. One *quagmaq* (Household I) was occupied by nine people: a widower, his son, three daughters, a son-in-law and three grandchildren.

The *quagmaq* was heated in the traditional manner with stone lamps that burned seal oil. The occupants of the wood house heated it with a kerosene stove. In a period when the highest outdoor temperature during the day was −30 degrees, I measured the consumption of fuel and recorded the indoor temperatures of the wood house and the *quagmaq*. The *quagmaq* was heated by three stone lamps, two at each side of the sleeping platform and one near the entrance. In a 24-hour period the three lamps burned some 250 ounces (slightly less than two imperial gallons) of seal oil. The fat from a 100-pound seal shot in midwinter yields approximately 640 ounces of oil, which is about a 60-hour supply at this rate of consumption. The

interior temperature of the *quagmaq* never rose above 68 degrees. The average was around 56 degrees, with troughs in the low 30's because the lamps were not tended through the night.

In the wood house the kerosene stove burned a little less than three imperial gallons every 24 hours. This represented a daily expenditure of about $1 for fuel oil during the winter months. (Since 1969 this cost has been fully subsidized by the government.) The interior temperature of the house sometimes reached 80 degrees, and the nightly lows were seldom below 70. One result of the difference between the indoor and outdoor temperature—frequently more than 100 degrees—was that the members of Household II complained that they were uncomfortably warm, particularly when they were carving or doing some other kind of moderately strenuous work.

Before the Eskimos of southern Baffin Island had acquired outboard motors, snowmobiles and a reliable supply of fuel they shifted their settlements with the seasons. Fall campsites were the most stable element in the settlement pattern and were the location for the *quagmaq* shelters. During the rest of the year the size and location of the camps depended on which of the food resources were being exploited.

The movements of settlements to resources served to minimize the distance

a hunter needed to travel in a day. Thus little energy was wasted traversing unproductive terrain, and good hunting weather could be exploited immediately. This is no longer the practice. Long trips by the hunters are common, but seasonal movements involving an entire household are rare. Therefore the location of the village never shifts. The four dwellings of the village I studied are more or less occupied throughout the year. Tents are still used in summer, but they are set up within sight of the winter houses. There is a major move each August, when the villagers set up camp at the trading post, a day's journey from the village. There they await the coming of the annual medical and supply ships and also take advantage of any wage labor that may be available.

The hunters' ability to get to the right place at the right time is ensured by a large whaleboat with a small inboard engine, a 22-foot freight canoe driven by a 20-horsepower outboard motor, and the two snowmobiles. In addition the villagers have several large sledges and keep 34 sled dogs. The impact of motorized transport (particularly of the marine engines) on the stability of year-round residence and on the increase in hunting productivity is evident in the remark of an older man: "As my son gets motors for the boats, we are always living here. As my son always gets animals we are no longer hungry. Do you know what I mean?"

The threat of hunger is a frequent theme in village conversation, but the oral tradition that serves as history gives little evidence of constant privation for the population of southern Baffin Island. Although older men and women tell stories of hard times, the fear of starvation did not generate the kind of social response known elsewhere. In the more hostile parts of the Arctic female infanticide was common well into the first quarter of this century. The existence of the practice is supported by statistical data compiled by Edward M. Weyer, Jr., in 1932. For example, among the Netsilik Eskimos the ratio of females to males in the population younger than 19 was 48 per 100; in the Barren Grounds area the ratio was 46 per 100.

Census data from Baffin Island in 1912 indicate that female infanticide was not common along the southern coast. In that year a missionary recorded the population for the region; the total was some 400 Eskimos. Among those younger than 19 there were 89 females per 100 males. Among those 19 or older the ratio was 127 females per 100 males; hunters often had short lives. The vital statistics that have been kept since 1927 by the Royal Canadian Mounted Police support the impression that death by starvation was a rare occurrence on southern Baffin Island. On the other hand, hunting accidents were the cause of 15 percent of the deaths. The causes of trouble or death most usually cited by the villagers were peculiarities of the weather, ice conditions and mishaps of the hunt. Starvation was commonplace in the dog population, but for human groups disasters were local. A 75-year-old resident of the southern coast was able to recall only one year when severe hunger affected a large segment of the population.

A major factor in reducing the possibility of hunger is the Eskimos' increasing access to imported goods. Although store foods are obviously of prime importance in this respect, energy in the form of gasoline for fuel is also significant. The snowmobiles in the village are owned by an individual in each household, but all the hunters help to buy the gasoline needed to run these machines and the marine engines. The two snowmobiles consumed about twice as much fuel as the two boat motors. A snowmobile pulling a loaded sled can run for about 35 minutes on a gallon of gasoline. A trip from the village to the

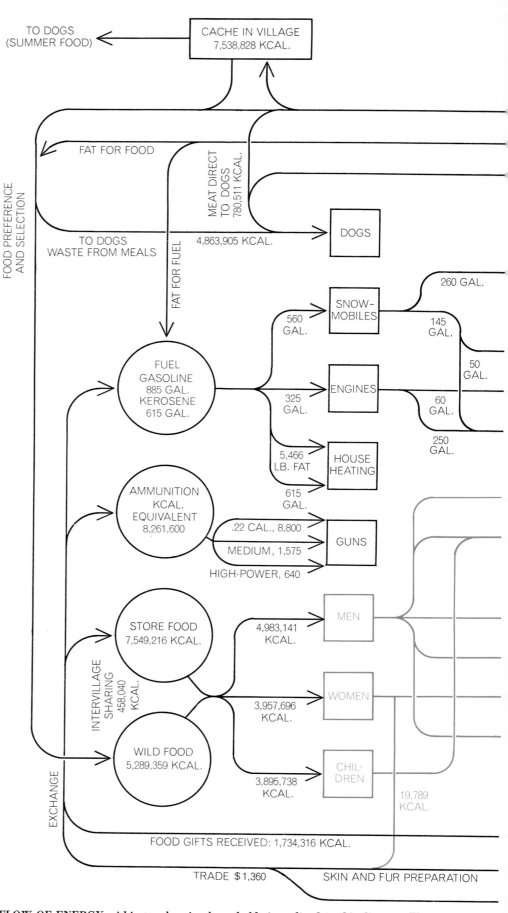

FLOW OF ENERGY within two hunting households is outlined in this diagram. The inputs and yields were recorded by the author in kilocalories and other units during his 13-month residence in an Eskimo hunting village. The input of imported energy in the form of fuel and ammunition, along with the input of native game and imported foodstuffs (*far*

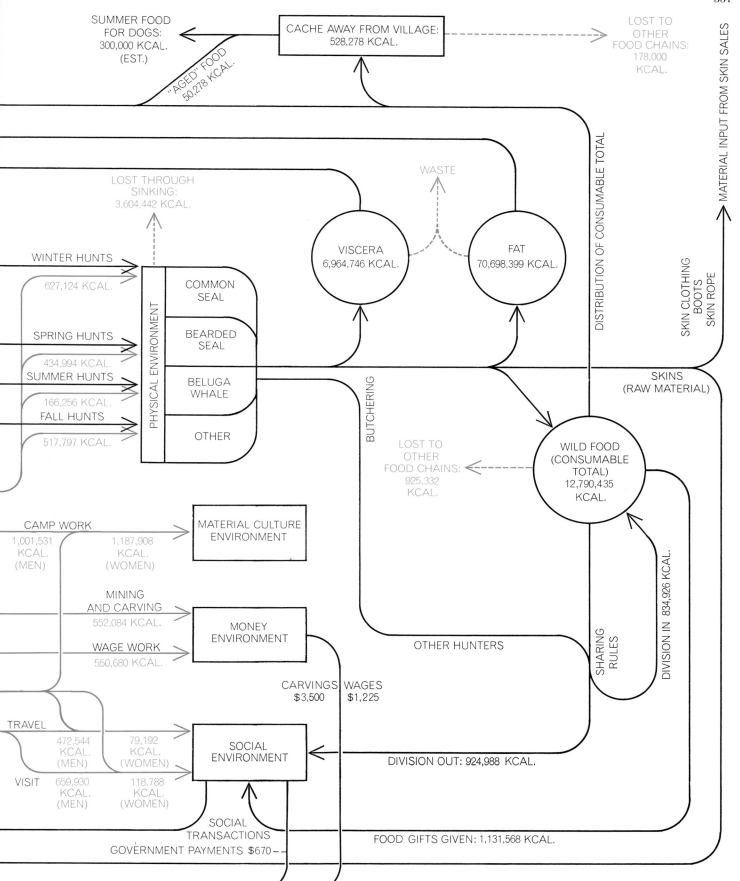

SUMMER FOOD
FOR DOGS:
300,000 KCAL.
(EST.)

CACHE AWAY FROM VILLAGE:
528,278 KCAL.

LOST TO
OTHER
FOOD CHAINS:
178,000
KCAL.

MATERIAL INPUT FROM SKIN SALES

"AGED" FOOD
50,278 KCAL.

LOST THROUGH
SINKING:
3,604,442 KCAL.

WASTE

VISCERA
6,964,746 KCAL.

FAT
70,698,399 KCAL.

DISTRIBUTION OF CONSUMABLE TOTAL

SKIN CLOTHING
BOOTS
SKIN ROPE

WINTER HUNTS

627,124 KCAL.

PHYSICAL ENVIRONMENT

COMMON
SEAL

BEARDED
SEAL

SPRING HUNTS

434,994 KCAL.

SUMMER HUNTS

166,256 KCAL.

BELUGA
WHALE

FALL HUNTS

517,797 KCAL.

OTHER

BUTCHERING

SKINS
(RAW MATERIAL)

LOST TO
OTHER
FOOD CHAINS:
925,332
KCAL.

WILD FOOD
(CONSUMABLE
TOTAL)
12,790,435
KCAL.

CAMP WORK

1,001,531
KCAL.
(MEN)

1,187,908
KCAL.
(WOMEN)

MATERIAL CULTURE
ENVIRONMENT

DIVISION IN 834,926 KCAL.

MINING
AND CARVING
552,084 KCAL.

MONEY
ENVIRONMENT

WAGE WORK
550,680 KCAL.

OTHER HUNTERS

SHARING
RULES

CARVINGS WAGES
$3,500 $1,225

TRAVEL

472,544
KCAL.
(MEN)

79,192
KCAL.
(WOMEN)

SOCIAL
ENVIRONMENT

VISIT

659,930
KCAL.
(MEN)

118,788
KCAL.
(WOMEN)

DIVISION OUT: 924,988 KCAL.

SOCIAL
TRANSACTIONS

GOVERNMENT PAYMENTS $670

FOOD GIFTS GIVEN: 1,131,568 KCAL.

left), enabled the four hunters and their kin (*left, color*) to heat
their dwellings and power their machines (*left, black*), and also
to join in many seasonal activities (*colored arrows*) that utilized
various parts of the environment in the manner indicated (*right*).

The end results of these combined inputs of energy are shown as a
series of yields and losses from waste and other causes (*far right*).
The net yields then feed back through various channels (*lines at
borders of diagram*) to reach the starting point again as inputs.

edge of the floe ice 10 miles away took 55 minutes in each direction and cost nearly $3.

Variations in fuel purchases are not necessarily correlated with variations in hunting yield or cash income. Debt can be used to overcome fluctuations in income, and the desire to visit distant relatives may be as important a consideration as the need to hunt. The largest monthly gasoline purchase was made in September, 1967. Wages paid for construction work were used to buy a combined total of 170 gallons of gasoline. This fuel was utilized for the intensive hunting of sea mammals in order to make up for a summer when the Eskimos had been earning wages instead of hunting.

Hunting was a year-long village occupation in spite of considerable seasonal variation in the kind and amount of game available. An analysis of the species represented in the Eskimos' annual kill confirms the predominance of sea mammals. The common seal (with an average weight of 80 pounds) provided nearly two-thirds of the villagers' game calories. When one adds bearded seals (with an average weight of more than 400 pounds) and occasional beluga whales, the sea mammals' contribution was more than 83 percent of the annual total. Caribou accounted for a little more than 4 percent of the total, and all the other land mammals together came to less than 1 percent. Indeed, the contribution of eider ducks and duck eggs to the villagers' diet (some 7 percent) was larger than that of all land mammals

combined. The harvest of birds, fish, clams and small land mammals may not contribute significantly to the total number of calories, but it does provide diversity in hunting activities and in diet.

The common seal is hunted throughout the year and is the basic source of food for both the Eskimos and their dogs. From January through March sea mammals are hunted first at breathing holes in the sea ice and then at the boundary between open water and the landfast ice. The intensity of sea-mammal hunting during the winter months varies according to the amount of food left over from the fall hunt and the alternative prospects for trapping foxes and hunting caribou.

In winter some variety in the food supply is provided by the hunting of sea birds and small land mammals, but for the most part seal meat remains the basic item in the diet. In April hunting along the edge of the floe ice is intensified, and the canoe is hauled to the open water beyond the floe ice for hunting the bearded seals. In May and June hunting along the edge of the floe ice (on foot or by canoe) continues; the quarry is the seal and the beluga whale. In late spring seals are also stalked as they bask on top of the ice. By the middle of July open-water hunting is the most common activity, although much of the potential harvest is lost because the animals sink when they are shot. In 1967 and 1968 the villagers lost five whales, five bearded seals and 47 common seals.

The sinking of marine mammals serves to illustrate the interplay of physi-

cal, biological and technological factors the hunter must contend with. In late spring the seal begins to fast and therefore loses fat. At the same time the melting of snow and sea ice reduces the salinity of the surface waters. These interacting factors reduce the buoyancy of the seal, and a killed seal is likely to sink unless it is immediately secured with a hand-thrown harpoon. The high-powered rifle separates the hunter from his prey; it may increase the frequency of kill but it does not increase the frequency of harvest. In 30 hours of continuous hunting on July 20 and 21 only five out of the 13 seals killed were actually harvested.

From May through July the hunts are usually successful, even with sinkage losses as high as 60 percent. It is at this time of the year that a large amount of meat goes into dog food for the summer and early fall. Meat is also cached in areas the Eskimos expect to visit when they are trapping the following winter. The caches are deliberately only partly secured with rocks; their purpose is to bait areas of potential trapping. In May the variety of foods begins to increase. Seabirds, ptarmigans, geese, fish, clams and duck eggs are taken in large numbers and become the most important component of the food input. Only an occasional seal or the edible skin of a beluga whale is carried home to eat. The great variety of small game is consumed within a few days. With the exception of duck eggs, about half of which are cached until after Christmas, none of these foods is stored.

In September the sea mammals again become the primary objective. Open-water hunting continues until early November, when the sea begins to freeze. Just before freeze-up the beluga whales pass close to the village and are hunted from the shore with the aid of rifles and harpoons. The success of the fall whale-hunting is the key to the villagers' evaluation of the adequacy of their winter provisions.

As the sea ice thickens and extends, hunting seals at their breathing holes in the bays becomes the most common activity. The unfavorable interaction of physical, biological and technological factors that affects open-water seal-hunting in spring and summer is reversed where breathing-hole hunting is concerned. As the sea begins to freeze, some seals migrate away from the land in order to stay in open water. Others remain closer to the shore, using their claws and teeth to maintain a cone-shaped hole through the ice. The seal's breathing is

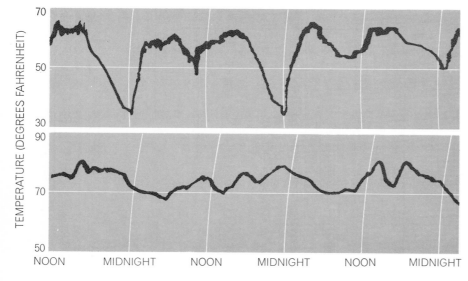

CONTRASTING METHODS of heating maintained different house microclimates with the consumption of different amounts of fuel. In Household I (*top*), the more traditional one, the use of three lamps that burned seal oil produced an average temperature of 58 degrees F. A kerosene stove (*bottom*) in the more modern Household II kept the average closer to 75 degrees. As a result Household II used three gallons a day to the other's two.

now confined to specific points the hunter can easily find on the surface of the ice. The hunting technique calls for locating the breathing holes and distributing the available men to maximize the chance of a kill. The hunting skill calls for the patience to wait motionless for periods of as much as two hours and to depend on hearing rather than sight. By mid-December the new ice is covered by a deep layer of drifting snow, and the breathing holes become harder to locate. The Eskimos then move out to the edge of the floe ice and the seasonal cycle begins anew.

The analysis of hunting success on a month-to-month basis shows great variability in the total caloric input and in each member's contribution to the total [see illustration on next page]. The peak hunting months for the two households were June (some 2.5 million kilocalories), October (more than three million) and November (2.9 million). Stockpiling provides the motivation for the big October and November kills. Game taken in these months will remain frozen and unspoiled through the winter and will help to feed the hunters and their dependents in February, March and April.

In the fall days grow short and winds often restrict the choice of hunting areas. Daylight hours are utilized to the full, and the evening darkness is filled with the sound of the hunters struggling to get their catch across the difficult terrain of the tidal flats. In this period almost all the food is brought back to the village; it is stored in a small meat house, on elevated platforms, under the hulls of old boats and on top of the wood house. A few of the seals shot in early fall are cached on the land in order for the meat to "age." These carcasses are retrieved in the spring, and the meat is considered one of the more flavorsome food inputs.

The large kill in June results from the fact that the daylight hours are at a maximum and that there is a much greater choice of resources. If weather conditions hamper open-water hunting, basking seals can be pursued. Under conditions of severe wind or poor ice, spearfishing for arctic char is possible and duck eggs can be collected. Summer hunts last for three or four days; the hunters sleep during the few hours of least light or during brief pauses in the hunt. Game killed in June will thaw in the summer months, so that almost all the two million kilocalories of sea mammals harvested that month is destined for the dogs.

Compared with the high caloric inputs of the spring and fall, winter hunting is much less productive in terms of

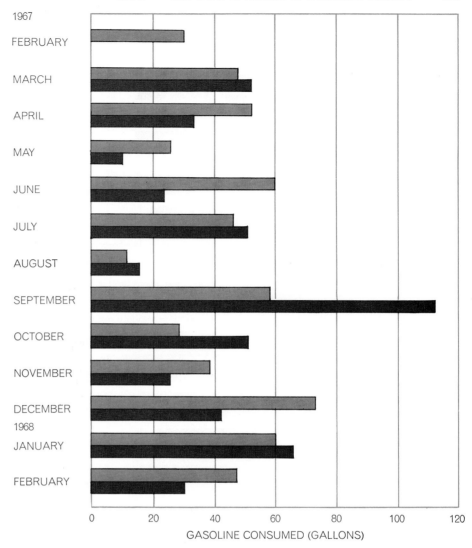

GASOLINE CONSUMPTION by two Eskimo households is shown over a 12-month period. The fuel was used to power the two snowmobiles and the marine engines that greatly increased the villagers' hunting efficiency. Purchases by the three hunters of Household I are shown in black and those by the single hunter of Household II are in gray. Gasoline is second only to imported food among the exotic energy inputs to the Eskimo hunting society.

total harvest. For example, February, 1967, was only a fair hunting month for Household I and a very bad month for Household II. The combined kill (more than 70 percent common seals) provided only 166,500 kilocalories of food; more than 90 percent of the total was taken by Household I. A month of low food input does not, however, mean hardship. Such a February is an example of the important role storage plays in the villagers' management of energy resources. The fall hunt had provided enough food for the winter, and as a result in February the villagers did more visiting than hunting. Visiting is therefore one mechanism that takes hunters out of the productive sector of the economy and creates a better balance between energy availability and energy need. The same pattern holds true throughout the winter months, so that the 500,000 calories that was harvested from February through April was as much a caloric expression of leisure as it was of poorer hunting conditions. The differential hunting success of individuals or of households in the month of February did not greatly influence energy distribution within the social unit. Although one hunter may have more skins to trade, food is stored in bulk and is generally available to all.

The records show that although caribou are hunted only occasionally, the animals are then present in substantial numbers. In the lean February of 1967 caribou made up some 7 percent of the kill, providing about 11,000 kilocalories of food. The following month caribou comprised more than 37 percent of the kill, amounting to a total of 90,000 kilo-

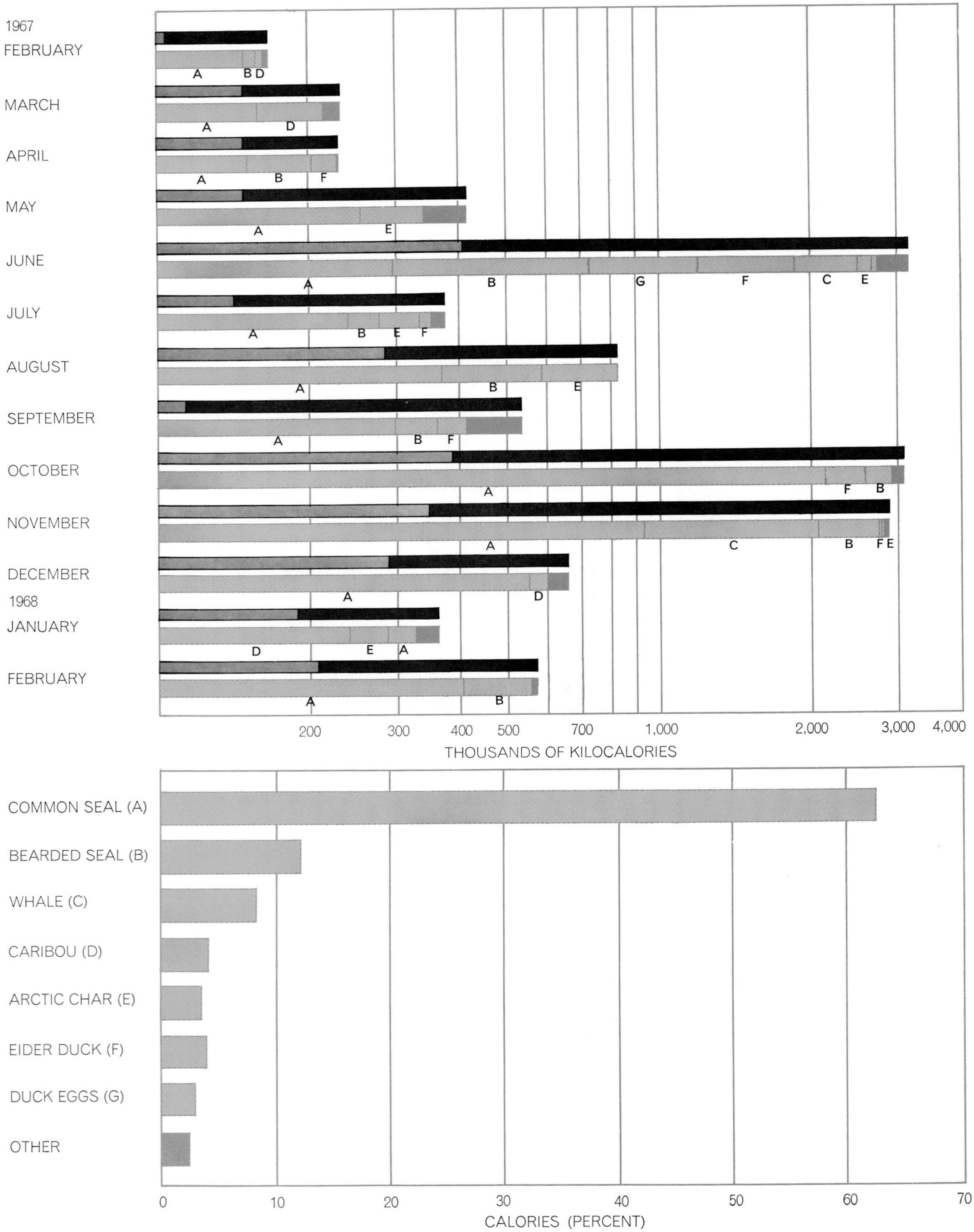

HUNTERS' BAG varies considerably from month to month as a result of chance and preference and also because of seasonal fluctuations. The top graph shows the wild foods acquired by Household I (*black*) and Household II (*gray*) in the course of 13 months. A fish known as arctic char, birds such as murres, geese and ducks, duck eggs and even berries add variety to the Eskimo diet from April through October, while caribou contribute to the smaller game bag of winter months. The 13-month totals, however, show that sea mammals (the common seal in particular) provide most of the Eskimo households' consumable kilocalories (*bottom graph*).

calories. After that caribou were almost absent from the villagers' diet until January, 1968, when they furnished nearly 70 percent of the kill for a yield of 245,-000 kilocalories.

Today no Eskimo community depends exclusively on hunting for its food. Each day the adults of the village consumed an average of half a pound of imported wheat flour in the form of a bread called bannock, a pan-baked mixture of flour, lard, salt and water. Bannock has long been an Eskimo staple; it is eaten in the largest quantities where hunting has fallen off the most.

In addition to this basic breadstuff the villagers consumed imported sugar, biscuits, candy and soft drinks, and they fed nonnursing infants and young children a kind of reconstituted milk. A daily ration consisted of 48 ounces of water containing 1.2 ounces of dry whole milk and 1.7 ounces of sugar.

I kept a 13-month record of the kind and amount of imported foods bought by the two households. During this period the more traditional household bought store foods totaling almost 3.3 million kilocalories and the more modern household store foods totaling 3.75 million kilocalories. The purchases provided 531,000 kilocalories of store food per adult in Household I and 477,300 per adult in Household II. The larger number of adults in Household I is reflected in the size of its flour purchase, which made up 53 percent of the total, compared with 40 percent in Household II. The larger purchase of lard by Household II (23 percent compared with 10 percent) is a measure of preference, not consumption. Household I prefers to use the fat from whales for bannock; hence its smaller purchase [see illustration on next page]. The consumption of the third imported staple—sugar—was about the same in both households.

The quantities of store food that were bought from month to month showed substantial variations. In March, 1967, the store purchases of the two households rose above one million kilocalories because both households received a social-assistance payment. In February, 1968, social assistance was again given each household, and as before the money was used to buy more than the average amount of food. The rather high caloric input from store food in September, 1967, is attributable to money available from wage labor.

Store foods, unlike food from the land, are not stockpiled and they are not often shared. Except for the staples and tea, tobacco and candy, there is no strong desire for non-Eskimo foods.

When vegetables are bought, it is usually by mistake. Canned meats, although occasionally eaten, are not recognized as "real" food. The villagers like fruit, but it is never bought in large quantity. Jam, peanut butter, honey, molasses, oatmeal and crackers all find their way into the two households. They are consumed almost immediately.

The data on food input support the general findings from other areas that show the Eskimo diet to be high in protein. At least in this Eskimo group, even though imported carbohydrates were readily available and there was money enough to buy imports almost ad libitum, the balance was in favor of protein.

Over the 13-month period the villagers acquired 44 percent of their calories in the form of protein, 33 percent in the form of carbohydrate and 23 percent in fat. Almost all the protein (93 percent) came from game; 96 percent of the carbohydrate was store food. The figures suggest how nutritional problems can arise when hunting declines. As store-food calories take the place of calories from the hunt, the change frequently involves increased flour consumption and consequently a greater intake of carbohydrate. This was the case in Household II during September, 1967, a period when the family worked for wages. The caloric input remained at 2,700 kilocalories per person per day, but 62 percent of the calories were carbohydrate and only 9 percent were protein.

A framework of social controls surrounds all the activities of the village, directing and mediating the flow of energy in the community. For example, even though all the inhabitants are ostensibly related (either by real kinship or by assigned ties), the community is actually divided into two social groups, each operating with a high degree of economic and social independence. Food is constantly shared within each social group, and the boundary between groups is ignored when a large animal is killed.

Village-wide meals serve to divert a successful hunter's caloric acquisitions for the benefit of a group larger than his own household. The meal that follows the arrival of hunters with a freshly killed seal is the most frequent and the most important of these events. It is called alopaya, a term that refers to using one's hands to scoop fresh blood from the open seal carcass. The invitation to participate is shouted by one of the children, and all the villagers gather, the men in one group and the women in another, to eat until they are full. The parts of the seal are apportioned accord-

ing to the eater's sex. The men start by eating a piece of the liver and the women a piece of the heart. The meat from the front flippers and the first third of the vertebrae and the ribs goes to the women. The men eat from the remaining parts of the seal. This meal, like almost all other Eskimo meals, does not come at any specific time of the day. People eat when they are hungry or, in the case of village-wide meals, when the hunters return. If anything remains at the end of an alopaya meal, the leftovers are divided equally among all the families and can be eaten by either sex.

Whaleboats and freight canoes began to replace the kayak for water transportation in southern Baffin Island some 30 years ago; by the end of the 1950's outboard motors had been substituted for oars and paddles. The latter change, which made possible more efficient open-water hunting, coincided with a high market price for sealskins. In the early 1960's a single skin might bring as much as $30, and the value of the annual village catch was between $3,000 and $4,000. The good sealskin market enabled the villagers to buy their first snowmobile in the fall of 1963. A decline in skin prices that began in 1964 has since been offset to some extent by the growth of handicraft sales and by the availability of work for wages.

As a result of these new economic inputs a new kind of material flow is now observable. It consists of the movement of secondhand non-Eskimo goods. The flow is channeled through a network of kinship ties between individuals with an income higher than average and those with an income lower. By 1971 anyone who wanted a snowmobile or some other item of factory-made equipment could utilize this network and get what he wanted through a combination of salvage, gift and purchase.

For the individual the exploitation of economic alternatives and the pattern of activity vary according to taste and lifestyle. Although life-style is in large degree dictated by age, the effect within the village is integrative rather than disruptive. A son's snowmobile gives the father the advantage of a quick ride to the edge of the floe ice, and the son can rely on the father's dogs to tow a broken machine or to help pull heavy loads over rough terrain. The integration extends to areas beyond the hunt. At home it is not unusual to find the father making sealskin rope or repairing a sledge while the son carves soapstone. Neither considers the other's work either radical or impossibly old-fashioned.

Social controls also affect the expendi-

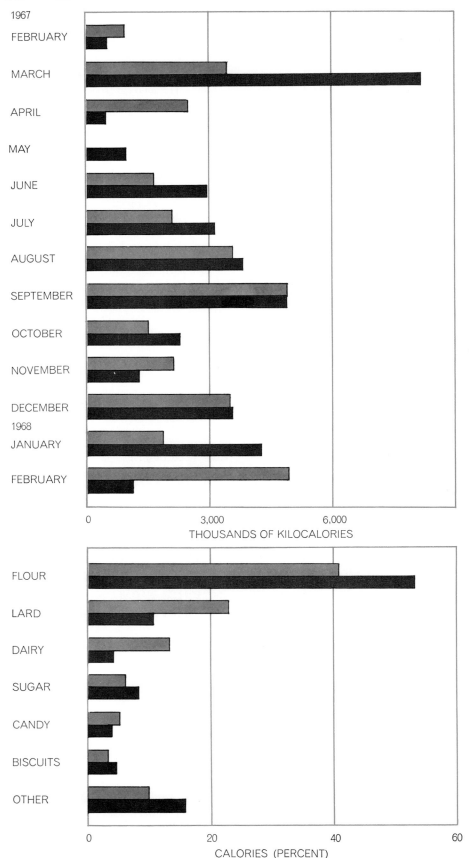

PURCHASES OF IMPORTED FOOD also show large monthly variations. The top graph shows the kilocalorie values of staples such as flour, lard and sugar and of lesser items such as powdered milk, biscuits, soft drinks and candy acquired over 13 months by Household I (*black*) and Household II (*gray*). Most of the flour and lard went to make a kind of bread called bannock. The 13-month totals (*bottom graph*) show how the two households differed in the percentage of all store-food purchases that each allotted to flour and to lard.

ture of personal energy within the household. The losers are the teen-age girls. Among the men of the village there is little emphasis on authority structure or leadership; decision-making is left to the individual. Choices for the most part converge, so that joint efforts are a matter of course. Among the women, however, authority structure is emphasized. A girl is subordinate not only to the older women but also to her male relatives. One can make the general statement that those who because of sex, age and kinship ties are most subject to the demands of others expend a disproportionate amount of energy in household and village chores.

One series of social controls has been radically altered by the introduction of non-Eskimo technology, energy and world view. These controls are the beliefs and rituals relating the world of nature to the world of thought. In the traditional Eskimo society the two worlds were closely related. All living organisms, for example, were believed to have a soul. In his ritual the Eskimo recognized the fragility of the Arctic ecosystem and sought to foster friendly relations with the same animals he hunted for food. Obviously the friendship could not be a worldly one, but it did exist in the realm of the spirit. A measure of the strength of this belief was the great care taken by the Eskimo never to invite unnecessary hardship by offending the soul of the animal he killed.

Today ritual control of the forces of nature and of the food supply has almost disappeared; technology is considered the mainspring of well-being. Prayers may still be said for good hunting and good traveling conditions, and the Sunday service may include an analysis of a hunting success and even a request for guidance in the hunts to follow. Hunting decisions may also be affected by dreams. None of these activities, however, has the regulatory powers of the intricate symbols and beliefs of earlier times. The hunters complain of a change in the seals' behavior. Nowadays, they say, only the young animals are curious and can be coaxed to come closer to the boat or the edge of the floe ice. The mutual trust between man and his food supply has evidently been lost in the report of the high-powered rifle and the rumble of the outboard motor.

What conclusions can we draw from the analysis of energy flows in a hunting society? The Eskimos do not differ from other hunters in that the processes surrounding the quest for food involve much more than a simple interplay of environment and technology. There are many times when a technological advance is fatal to an ecological balance; this was particularly evident in the near-extermination of the caribou herds west of Hudson Bay with the introduction of the rifle and the relaxation of traditional beliefs. In southern Baffin Island, however, there is not yet any evidence of a trend toward "overkill." At the same time that motorized transport has enhanced the ability to kill game, other social and economic factors have acted to reduce the amount of time available for hunting and have kept the kill within bounds. Snowmobiles give quick access to the edge of the floe ice; they also make it easy to visit distant kinsmen. A regular day of rest on Sunday has a religious function; it also contributes to the management of energy resources.

Do hunting societies have a long-term future? In the case of the Eskimo one can reply with a conditional yes. The universal pressure on resources makes continued exploitation of the Arctic a certainty, and Eskimos should be able to profit from these future ventures. Already it is possible to see three distinct groups emerging within Eskimo culture. One of them consists of the wage earners in the larger communities. Another, which is just beginning to make its appearance, is an externally oriented group that seems destined to regulate and control the inputs from the outside world: the non-Eskimo energy flows and material flows that, as we have seen, now play a vital part in the hunters' lives.

Finally, there is a third group, small in numbers but vast in terms of territory, made up of the hunters who will continue the traditional Eskimo participation in the fragile, far-flung Arctic ecosystem. There will be linkages—exchanges of materials and probably of people—between the wage earner and the hunter. Those who choose to live off the land may appear to be the more traditional of the three groups, but their lives will be dynamic enough because the variables that define the hunting way of life are constantly changing. If a snowmobile is perceived to have greater utility than a dog sled, then the ownership of a snowmobile will become one of the criteria defining the traditional Eskimo hunter. With the outward-oriented Eskimos providing stability for the three-group system through their control of exotic inputs, the northern communities should be able to evolve further without developing disastrous strains. But the fundamental linkage—the relation between the hunter and the Arctic ecosystem—will remain the same.

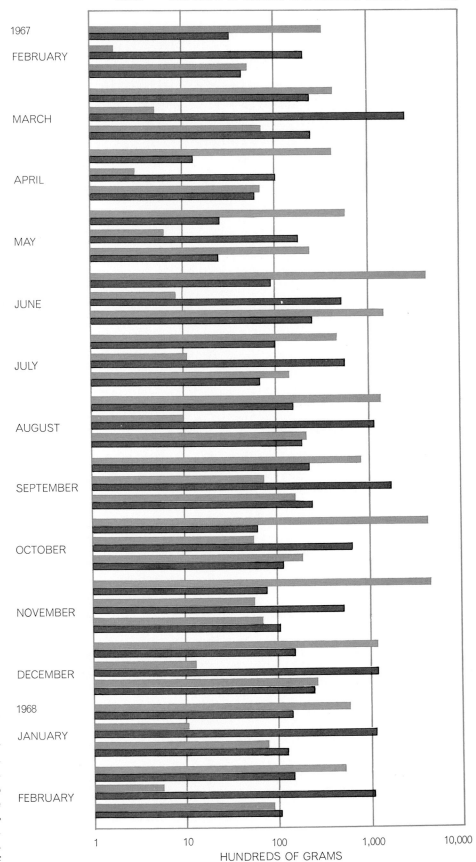

HUNDREDS OF GRAMS

COMPOSITION OF DIET is presented for a 13-month period in terms of monthly acquisitions of protein (*top pair of bars*), carbohydrate (*middle pair of bars*) and fat (*bottom pair of bars*), measured in hundreds of grams. The colored bar of each pair indicates the number of grams acquired by hunting and gathering and the black bar indicates the number acquired in the form of store food. Protein outranked the others in total acquisitions: 2.1 million grams, compared with 1.1 million grams of carbohydrate and .7 million grams of fat.

34

THE FLOW OF ENERGY IN AN AGRICULTURAL SOCIETY

ROY A. RAPPAPORT
September 1971

*The invention of agriculture gave mankind a more
abundant source of solar energy. The energetics of
a primitive agricultural system are examined in
New Guinea, with a moral for modern agriculturists*

Raising crops and husbanding animals are man's most important means of exploiting the energy that is continuously stored in primary plant production. Man's manipulation through the practice of agriculture of this energy store and of the food chains it supports has enabled him to progress beyond the bare subsistence provided by hunting and gathering, and long ago placed human culture on the road leading to the complex social systems of today. Here we shall examine the flow of energy in an agricultural society that practices a mode of gardening known for millenniums, a mode likely to have been the first to enable pioneer farmers to exploit an almost unpopulated part of the world: the humid Tropics.

An examination of this type of gardening is particularly appropriate to the theme of this issue because the flow of energy within it is easy to trace; its practitioners have no power sources other than fire and their own muscle and have only the simplest tools. At the same time their kind of gardening and swine husbandry makes relatively light demands on the farmers in terms of energy inputs, provides for almost all their dietary needs and, if properly practiced, alters ecosystems less than other modes of agriculture of comparable productivity do. We shall compare this kind of farming with the ecologically more disruptive methods of modern agriculture, and we shall examine how the flow of energy and materials in agricultural systems affects the diversity and stability of ecosystems in general. We shall also consider the re-

lation between social evolution, with its ever increasing demand for expenditures of energy, and ecological degradation.

The system of gardening is called "swiddening," and the place where I observed it is the tropical rain forest of New Guinea. The term comes from the Old Norse word for "singe." The method has often been applied in forest environments outside the Tropics, including the forests of medieval England where it got its name. It has many variants, but basic aspects of the procedure are much the same everywhere in temperate or tropical forests. A clearing is cut in the forest, the cuttings are usually burned (sometimes they are removed by hand or allowed to rot), a garden is planted and harvested and the clearing is then abandoned to the returning forest. On occasion the clearing is planted two or three times before it is abandoned, but a single planting is more typical.

The mature tropical rain forest is probably the most intricate, productive, efficient and stable ecosystem that has ever evolved. Men are able to use directly for food only a tiny fraction of the forest's biomass: its total store of living matter. The unmodified rain forest can support perhaps one human being per square mile. From the human viewpoint such an environment is seriously deficient, and swiddening provides a sophisticated and even elegant means of overcoming its deficiencies. With swiddening population densities comparable to those of industrialized countries are

maintained with considerably less degradation of the environment resulting.

The swiddening farmers with whom we are specifically concerned are the Tsembaga, one of several local groups speaking the Maring language that live in the central highlands of the Australian Trust Territory of New Guinea some five degrees south of the Equator [*see top illustration on page 347*]. The Tsembaga occupy a territory on the southern side of the Simbai River valley in the Bismarck Range. From its lowest point along the riverbank, about 2,200 feet above sea level, their land rises in less than three miles to the mountain ridge at an altitude of 7,200 feet. In 1962 and 1963, when I was visiting the Tsembaga, their territory was 3.2 square miles and their population totaled 204.

Not all of the Tsembaga land is arable. The part that lies above 6,000 feet is usually blanketed by clouds and its vegetation consists of a moss forest unaltered by man. The next zone, between 6,000 and 5,000 feet, is cultivable on a marginal basis, but most of it has been left as unaltered mature rain forest. Below this zone, between 5,000 and 2,200 feet, is the main area of agricultural activity, although portions of the land are too rocky or too steep for gardening. Just over 1,000 acres here were occupied either by gardens or by fallow secondary-forest vegetation in 1962.

Forty-six acres—about .2 acre per person—had been newly planted that year. Since some gardens yield a harvest for two years or more, this practice means that as many as 90 to 100 acres of Tsembaga land are often in cultivation simultaneously. Conversely, at any one time at least 90 percent (and sometimes more) is lying fallow. If one adds to these 900-odd acres the 340 acres or so of marginally arable land in the zone between 5,000 and 6,000 feet that have never

GARDEN PLOTS that exemplify a very ancient method of farming lie scattered through the swath of second-growth forest in the aerial photograph on the opposite page. The agricultural area lies on the east bank of the Simbai River in the central highlands of New Guinea. Most gardens are located in the lower third of the area (*see detailed map on next page*). In any year 90 percent of the land lies fallow, slowly returning once again to forest.

been cultivated, the percentage of potentially arable land actually under cultivation becomes even smaller.

In terms of their entire territory the Tsembaga in 1962–1963 were maintaining a population density of 64 per square mile. In terms of all potentially arable land the density was 97 per square mile, and in terms of land that was then or ever had been under cultivation the density was 124 per square mile. Even this figure is below the carrying capacity of the Tsembaga territory; without altering the horticultural regime of keeping 90 percent of the land fallow the Tsembaga's 1,000 best acres might have supported a population of 200 or more per square mile.

Horticulture provides 99 percent of the everyday Tsembaga diet, but the unaltered forest beyond the gardens and the secondary forest that covers the fallow land also play an economic role. For example, the Tsembaga husbandry of pigs depends on feral boars that roam the forests. The Tsembaga castrate their own boars because they believe it makes for larger and more docile animals; the sows (which wander free during the day, returning home at dusk) must thus be impregnated by chance contact with feral boars. Feral pigs are also a source of some protein for the Tsembaga, as are the marsupials, snakes, lizards, birds and woodgrubs also found in the forest. Some forest animals and hundreds of species of forest plants provide the raw materials for tools, house construction, clothing, dyestuffs, cosmetics, medicines, ornaments, wealth objects and the supplies and paraphernalia of ritual. The greatest contribution of the forest, however, is providing a favorable setting for the Tsembaga gardens.

In 1963 I kept detailed records of the activities involved in transforming an 11,000-square-foot area of secondary forest into a garden. (These observations were supplemented by a wide range of measurements of similar activities of the same people and others at different sites.) Situated at an altitude of 4,200 feet, the land had been fallow for 20 to 25 years. On it, in addition to underbrush, were 117 trees with a trunk six inches or more in circumference, including a number that measured at least two feet. The canopy of leaves met some 30 feet overhead and had become dense enough to kill a good deal of the underbrush by its shade. In order to make estimates of energy input during various stages of the clearing work, I conducted time and motion studies in the field. These studies, in conjunction with the findings of E. H. Hipsley and Nancy Kirk of the Commonwealth of Australia Department of Health, provided a basis for my calculations. Hipsley and Miss Kirk, working with other New Guinea highlanders, the Chimbu, measured individual metabolic rates during the performance of everyday tasks. My estimates of crop yields are based on a daily weighing of the harvests from some 25 Tsembaga gardens over a period of almost a year. I have used various standard sources in calculating the energetic values of the produce.

In making a garden the Tsembaga prefer to clear secondary forest rather than primary forest because secondary growth is easier to cut and burn. Even in the secondary forest, clearing the underbrush is hard work, although it was made easier when machetes were introduced to the area in the 1950's. I found that the performance of men and women in clearing the brush was surprisingly uniform. Although in an hour some women clear little more than 200 square feet and some of the more robust men clear nearly 300 square feet, the larger

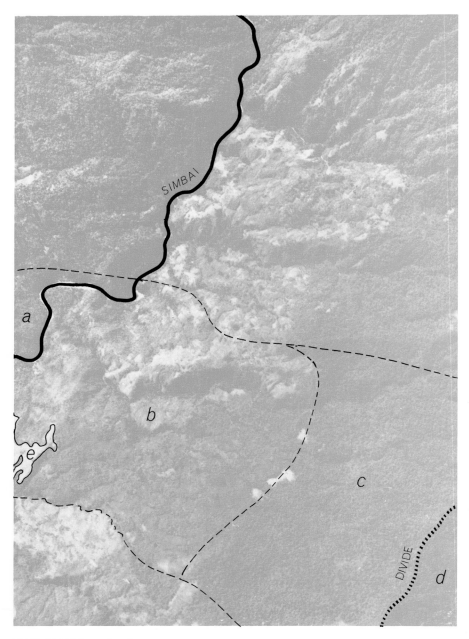

AREA OF STUDY has four major divisions. One forested zone (s) just west of the Simbai River is land as yet little used for gardens. The major agricultural zone is uphill from the river to the south (b); it rises from about 2,300 feet above sea level at the river to about 5,200 feet at its boundary with a zone of largely virgin forest (c) farther uphill. The highest land, which is not farmed, lies in this zone and the adjacent one (d) on both sides of a mountain ridge some 7,200 feet above sea level. The light patch (e) is a stand of kunai grass that has sprung up in a cleared area and is resistant to the process of reforestation.

men expend more energy per minute than the women. The energy input of each sex is approximately equal: some .65 kilocalorie per square foot, or 28,314 kilocalories per acre.

Once the underbrush is cut about two weeks are allowed to pass before the next step: clearing the trees. This is exclusively men's work. On this occasion most of the 117 trees in the garden were felled. Their branches were then lopped off and scattered over the piles of drying underbrush. Trees whose thick trunks would have been hard to burn and a nuisance to drag away were left standing, but most or all of their limbs were removed. The process of tree-clearing is far less strenuous than clearing underbrush: the energy investment is about .26 kilocalorie per square foot, or 11,325 kilocalories per acre.

The next step is to make a fence to keep out pigs, both feral and domestic. The trunks of the felled trees are cut into lengths of from eight to 10 feet and dragged to the edge of the clearing. The thicker logs are split into rails, and the logs and the rails are lashed together with vines to form the fence. Fence-building is heavy work, even without taking into consideration frequent trips to higher altitudes for the gathering of the strong vines needed for lashing. I estimate that the construction effort alone involved an input of something over 46 kilocalories per running foot of fence. Assuming a need for 370 feet of fence per acre of garden and making allowance for the energy expended in gathering vines, I have calculated that the total input for fencing is 17,082 kilocalories per acre. It is little wonder that the Tsembaga tend to cluster their gardens; clustering reduces the length of fence required per unit of area.

After fences are built, and between one month and four months after clearing begins (depending on how steadily the gardener works and on the weather), the felled litter on the site is burned. This is a step of considerable importance in the swiddening regime. Burning not only disposes of the litter but also liberates the mineral nutrients in the cut vegetation and makes them available to the future crop. Since the layer of fertile soil under tropical forests is remarkably thin (seldom more than two inches in Tsembaga territory) and is easily depleted, the nutrients freed from the fallen trees by burning are beneficial, if not crucial, to the growth of garden plants.

Not much energy is expended in the burning process, although one burning is never enough to finish the job. More-

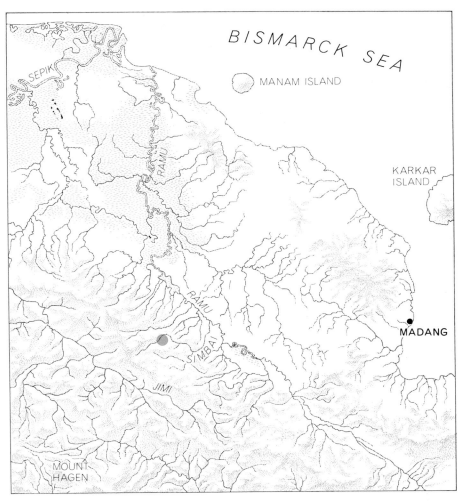

CENTRAL HIGHLANDS of the Australian Trust Territory of New Guinea are drained by the Sepik and Ramu rivers; the Simbai River is a tributary of the Ramu. The colored dot marks the territory of the Tsembaga, the group whose farming practices the author analyzed.

over, since considerable time usually elapses between the clearing of the underbrush and the burning, it is necessary to weed the garden area before the burning. I estimate that two burnings and a weeding involve an energy input of 9,484 kilocalories per acre.

While the women gather the litter into piles for the second burning, the men put aside some of the lighter unburned logs. Some are laid across the grade of the slope to retain the soil. The rest are used to mark individual garden plots. This task is also light work; I estimate

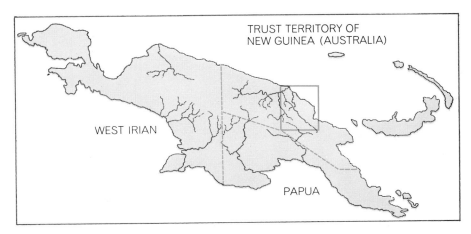

TRUST TERRITORY of New Guinea is one of the island's three political divisions. West Irian (left) is a part of the Republic of Indonesia and Papua is an Australian territory.

LITTER IS BURNED in the clearing where a Tsembaga family is preparing to plant a garden. Tree trunks that are not consumed may be used as soil-retainers or plot-markers. Burning releases nutrients in the cut vegetation that are utilized by the garden plants.

that the total energy input is 7,238 kilo-calories per acre.

Burning completed and plot-markers and soil-retainers laid, gardens are ready to be planted. For planting stock the Tsembaga depend primarily on cuttings, although they raise a few crops from seed. The gathering and planting of the cuttings, which are set into holes punched in the untilled soil with a heavy stick, is relatively demanding work. I

estimate that the men and women who do the planting expend .38 kilocalorie per square foot, or 16,553 kilocalories per acre.

It is appropriate here to list the plants the Tsembaga grow and also to describe the appearance of a growing garden. The Tsembaga can name at least 264 varieties of edible plants, representing some 36 species. The staples are taro and sweet potato. Other starchy vege-

tables such as yams, cassavas and bananas are of lesser importance. Sweet potatoes and cassavas are used as pig feed as well as for human consumption. Beans, peas, maize and sugarcane are also grown, along with a number of leafy greens, including hibiscus. Hibiscus leaves are in fact the most important plant source of protein in the Tsembaga diet. An asparagus-like plant, *Setaria palmaefolia*, and a relative of sugarcane

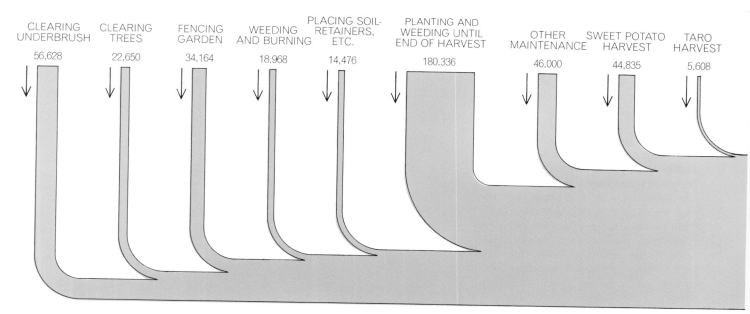

CLEARING UNDERBRUSH	CLEARING TREES	FENCING GARDEN	WEEDING AND BURNING	PLACING SOIL-RETAINERS, ETC.	PLANTING AND WEEDING UNTIL END OF HARVEST	OTHER MAINTENANCE	SWEET POTATO HARVEST	TARO HARVEST
56,628	22,650	34,164	18,968	14,476	180,336	46,000	44,835	5,608

TWELVE MAJOR INPUTS of energy are required in gardening. The flow diagram shows the inputs in terms of the kilocalories per acre required to prepare and harvest a pair of gardens (*see illustration on page 350*). Weeding, a continual process after the garden

NEW CLEARING in second-growth forest contains many stumps of trees that have been cut high for use as props for growing plants. Some, although stripped of their leaves, will survive; along with invading tree seedlings they will slowly reforest the garden site.

known as *pitpit* are valued for their edible flowering parts. So is the *Marita* pandanus, one of the screw pines; its fruit is the source of a thick, fat-rich red fluid that the Tsembaga use as a sauce on greens. Minor garden crops include cucumber, pumpkin, watercress and breadfruit.

Most of the principal crops are to be found in most of the gardens and each is often represented by several varieties

of the same species. As Clifford Geertz of the University of Chicago has remarked, there is a structural similarity between a swidden garden and a tropical rain forest. In the garden, as in the forest, species are not segregated by rows or sections but are intricately intermingled, so that as they mature the garden becomes stratified and the plants make maximum use of surface area and of variations in vertical dimensions. For

example, taro and sweet potato tubers mature just below the surface; the cassava root lies deeper and yams are the deepest of all. A mat of sweet potato leaves covers the soil at ground level. The taro leaves project above this mat; the hibiscus, sugarcane and *pitpit* stand higher still, and the fronds of the banana spread out above the rest. This intermingling does more than make the best use of a fixed volume. It also dis-

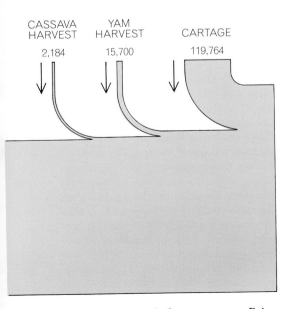

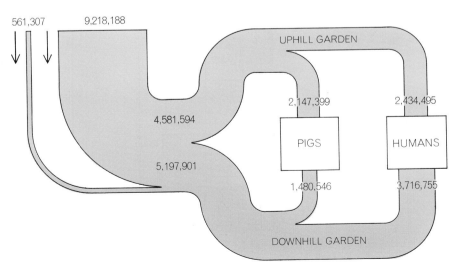

is planted, demands the most energy. Bringing in the garden harvest (*right*) ranks next.

BIOMASS OF CROP YIELD, also measured in kilocalories, gives more than a 16-to-one return on the human energy investment. The Tsembaga use much of the harvest as pig feed.

PLANT

YIELD PER ACRE (KILOCALORIES)

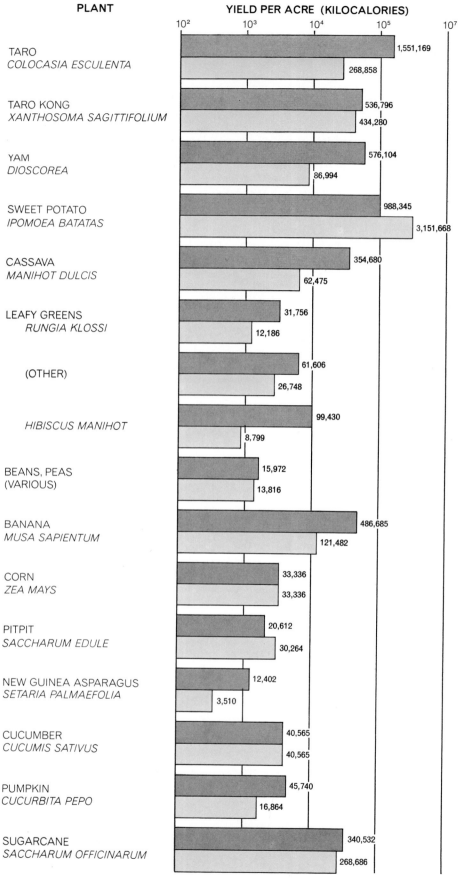

TARO *COLOCASIA ESCULENTA*	1,551,169 / 268,858
TARO KONG *XANTHOSOMA SAGITTIFOLIUM*	536,796 / 434,280
YAM *DIOSCOREA*	576,104 / 86,994
SWEET POTATO *IPOMOEA BATATAS*	988,345 / 3,151,668
CASSAVA *MANIHOT DULCIS*	354,680 / 62,475
LEAFY GREENS *RUNGIA KLOSSI*	31,756 / 12,186
(OTHER)	61,606 / 26,748
HIBISCUS MANIHOT	99,430 / 8,799
BEANS, PEAS (VARIOUS)	15,972 / 13,816
BANANA *MUSA SAPIENTUM*	486,685 / 121,482
CORN *ZEA MAYS*	33,336 / 33,336
PITPIT *SACCHARUM EDULE*	20,612 / 30,264
NEW GUINEA ASPARAGUS *SETARIA PALMAEFOLIA*	12,402 / 3,510
CUCUMBER *CUCUMIS SATIVUS*	40,565 / 40,565
PUMPKIN *CUCURBITA PEPO*	45,740 / 16,864
SUGARCANE *SACCHARUM OFFICINARUM*	340,532 / 268,686

TWO KINDS OF GARDEN are planted by Tsembaga families, whose pigs are too numerous for one garden to feed. Usually one garden is downhill from the other. The downhill garden (*gray*) is planted with more of the family staples: taro and yam. The uphill garden (*color*) is planted with more sweet potato, which is a staple food for pigs. The graph shows the 16 principal Tsembaga garden crops and the comparative yields from two gardens.

courages plant-specific insect pests, it allows advantage to be taken of slight variations in garden habitats, it is protective of the thin tropical soil and it achieves a high photosynthetic efficiency.

If a Tsembaga man and his wife have only one or two pigs, they usually plant one major garden in the middle altitudes, generally between 4,000 and 4,500 feet. But pigs are given a ration from the gardens, and when their numbers increase, their owners are likely to plant two gardens, one above 4,500 feet and the other between 3,000 and 4,000 feet. These gardens differ in the proportions of the major crops with which they are planted. The lower-altitude gardens include more taros and yams and the higher-altitude gardens more sweet potatoes, this last crop forming the largest part of the pigs' ration.

After planting is completed the most laborious of the gardening tasks, weeding, still lies ahead. The Tsembaga recognize and name several successive weedings, but after the first weeding is done (five to seven weeks after planting) the chore becomes virtually continuous. I estimate the total energy input for this task to be about 2.07 kilocalories per square foot, or 90,168 kilocalories per acre. Other miscellaneous tasks performed at the same time (for example tying sugarcane to stumps or other supports) require an additional 14,500 kilocalories per acre. It is noteworthy that weeding aims at uprooting any herbaceous competitors invading the garden but that tree seedlings are spared and even protected. Indeed, a Tsembaga gardener is almost as irritated when a visitor damages a tree seedling as when he heedlessly tramples on a taro plant.

The Tsembaga recognize the importance of the regenerating trees; they call them collectively *duk mi,* or "mother of gardens." Allowing tree seedlings to remain and grow avoids a definite grassy stage in the succession following the abandonment of the garden and for one thing ensures a more rapid redevelopment of the forest canopy. For another, during the cropping period itself the young trees provide a web of roots that penetrate deeper into the ground than the roots of any of the crops and are able to recover nutrients that might otherwise be lost through leaching. Above the ground the developing leaves and branches not only provide additional protection for the thin forest soil against tropical downpours but also immobilize nutrients recovered from the soil for release to future gardens. They also make it increasingly difficult for gardeners to harvest and weed. As a result the people are induced to abandon their gardens before they have seriously depleted the soil, even before the crops are completely harvested. The developing trees, whose growth they themselves have encouraged, make harvesting more laborious at the same time that it is becoming less rewarding. It is interesting to note here that both Ramón Margalef of the University of Barcelona and Howard T. Odum of the University of Florida have argued that in complex ecosystems successful species are not those that merely capture energy more efficiently than their competitors but those that sustain the species supporting them. It is clear that the Tsembaga support not only the garden species that provide them with food but also the species on which they ultimately depend: the species of the forest, which sustain their gardens.

Technological limitations and the nature of crops prevent the Tsembaga from storing most of the food they grow. As a result there is no special harvest period. From the time the crops begin to mature a little harvesting is done every day or two. The strategy is to do as little damage as possible to the plant that yields the crop. For example, hibiscus shrubs are not stripped of all their leaves at one time. Instead every few days a few leaves are plucked from each of several shrubs. This method increases the total yield by allowing the plants to recover in the interval between successive harvestings.

Harvesting continues almost daily from the time crops mature until those in a garden planted in the succeeding year are ready. With the advent of a new garden, harvesting becomes less frequent in the old garden, finally ceasing altogether somewhere between 14 and 28 months after planting. Gardens at lower altitudes are usually shorter-lived than those higher on the mountainside because secondary forest regenerates more quickly on them.

Energy expenditure for harvesting differs slightly between the two types of garden. I estimate that 40,966 kilocalories per acre are expended in harvesting taro-yam gardens and 44,168 kilocalories per acre in sweet potato gardens. Food is consumed at home, homes are at some distance from the gardens and produce therefore must be carried from gardens to houses. An estimated 48,360 kilocalories are expended in transporting produce from sweet potato gardens, which are at approximately the same altitude as the houses. I estimate that 71,404 kilocalories per acre

FENCE-BUILDING is one of the more energy-consuming tasks in preparing a garden. Fences must be pig-proof to keep out both domestic swine and feral swine from the forest.

are needed to bring home produce from the taro-yam gardens, which are usually 1,000 to 2,000 feet lower on the mountainside.

Combining all the inputs and comparing input with yield, I found that the Tsembaga received a reasonable short-term return on their investment. The ratio of yield to input was about 16.5 to one for the taro-yam gardens and about 15.9 to one for the sweet potato gardens. Moreover, in 1963, when these observations were made, the distances between the gardens and the residences of the Tsembaga were greater than usual. It was a festival year and the dwellings, instead of being dispersed among the gardens as is customary, were all clustered around a dance ground. If the normal residential pattern had been in effect, garden-to-house distances might have been reduced by as much as 80 percent, and the yield ratios would have risen respectively to 20.1 to one and 18.4 to one.

I have indicated that swine husbandry is intimately related to gardening among the Tsembaga because they devote a substantial proportion of their principal crops to feeding their pigs. Each adult pig receives a daily ration that equals an adult man's ration in weight, although it differs from the human ration in composition. Around the world most pigs are raised to be eaten. This is the ultimate fate that befalls a Tsembaga pig, but such consumption involves social and political relations and religious beliefs and practices, not simply a desire for meat.

The Tsembaga and other groups that speak the Maring language are prevented by strong religious prohibitions from initiating warfare until they have completed a year-long festival that culminates in large-scale sacrifices of pigs to their ancestors, rewarding them for their presumed support in the last round of warfare. The festival itself is the climax of a prolonged ritual cycle that begins years earlier with the sacrifices terminating warfare, sacrifices in which all adult and many juvenile pigs are killed. The Tsembaga held such a festival during my visit in 1962–1963.

When the festival began, the Tsembaga pigs numbered 169 animals with an average per capita weight of from 120 to 150 pounds. This sizable herd was eating 54 percent of all the sweet potatoes and 82 percent of all the cassavas growing in the Tsembaga gardens: some 36 percent of all the tubers of any kind that the Tsembaga grew. The operation called for the commitment of about a third of all garden land to the production of pig feed (not even taking into account household garbage, which the pigs also consumed). At the end of the festival the Tsembaga herd had been reduced to some 60 juvenile pigs, each weighing an average of from 60 to 70 pounds. Thus in terms of live weight the slaughter had decreased the herd sixfold. In anticipation of this decrease the Tsembaga had earlier in 1963 set the area of new land being put into gardens at what amounted to 36.1 percent below the level of the previous year.

For the Tsembaga swine husbandry is obviously an expensive business. The input in human energy, both in growing pig food and in managing the animals, I estimate to be about 45,000 kilocalories per pig per year. Because 10 years or so are needed to bring the herd up from a minimum following the sacrifices terminating warfare to a size large enough for a festival, the ratio of energy yield to energy input in Tsembaga pig husbandry is certainly no better than two to one and is probably worse than one to one. It is evident that keeping pigs cannot be justified or even interpreted in terms of energetics alone. Other possible benefits must also be considered.

First, Maring pig husbandry is part of the means for regulating relations between autonomous local groups such as the Tsembaga. It has already been indicated that the frequency of warfare is regulated by a ritual cycle, but the timing of the cycle is itself a function of the speed of growth in the pig population. Since it usually takes a decade or more to accumulate enough pigs to hold the festival terminating a cycle, the initiation of warfare is held to once per decade or less.

Second, the animals form a link in the detritus food chain by consuming both garbage and the unassimilated vegetable content of human feces, materials that would otherwise be wasted. Moreover, the pigs are regularly penned in abandoned gardens, where they root up unharvested tubers and where, by eliminating herbaceous growth that competes with tree seedlings, they may hasten the return of the forest.

Third, it must be remembered that a diet must provide more than mere energy to a consumer, and it is as converters of carbohydrates of vegetable origin into high-quality protein that pigs are most important in the Tsembaga diet. The importance of their protein contribution is magnified by the circumstances surrounding their consumption. Except for the once-a-decade festival

and for certain rites associated with warfare that are equally infrequent, it is rare for the Tsembaga to kill and eat a pig. The ritual occasions that do call for this unusual behavior are associated with sickness, injury or death. I have argued elsewhere that the sick, the injured, the dying and their kin and associates in Tsembaga society all suffer physiological stress, with an associated net loss of nitrogen (meaning protein) from their body tissues. Now, since the regular protein intake of the Tsembaga is marginal, their antibody production is likely to be low and their rate of recovery from injury or illness slow. In such circumstances nitrogen loss can be a serious matter. The condition of a nitrogen-depleted organism, however, improves rather quickly with the intake of high-quality protein. The nutritional significance of the Tsembaga pigs thus outweighs their high cost in energy input. They provide a source of high-quality protein when it is needed most.

In summary, swiddening and swine husbandry provide the Tsembaga with on the one hand an adequate daily energy ration and on the other an emergency source of protein. The average adult Tsembaga male is four feet 10½ inches tall and weighs 103 pounds; the average adult female is four feet 6½ inches tall and weighs 85 pounds. The garden produce provides the men with some 2,600 kilocalories per day and the women with some 2,200 kilocalories. At the same time the Tsembaga's treatment of the ecosystem in which they live is sufficiently gentle to ensure the continuing regeneration of secondary forest and a continuing supply of fertile garden sites.

We may reflect here on the general strategy of swiddening. It is to establish temporary associations of plants directly useful to man on sites from which forest is removed and to encourage the return of forests to those sites after the useful plants have been harvested. The return of the forest makes it possible, or at least much easier, to establish again an association of cultivated plants sometime in the future. Moreover, the gardens are composed of many varieties of many plant species. If one or another kind of plant succumbs to pests or blight, other plants are available as substitutes. This multiplicity of plants enhances the stability of the Tsembaga subsistence base in exactly the same way that the complexity of the tropical rain forest ensures its stability.

How does such an agricultural pattern compare with farming methods that

LAYERS OF GROWTH characterize the Tsembaga garden. Root crops develop at different depths and their leaves reach different heights. Bananas (*foreground*) are the tallest plants.

remove the natural flora over extensive regions and put in their place varieties of one or a few plant species? Before we take up this question let us consider ecosystems in general and the interactions among the participants in ecosystems in particular. All ecosystems are basically similar. Solar energy is photosynthetically fixed by plants—the primary producers—and then passes along food chains that are chiefly made up of animal populations with various feeding habits: herbivores, one or more levels of carnivores and eventually decomposers (which reduce organic wastes into inorganic constituents that can again be taken up by the plants).

Examined in terms of the flow of matter the ecosystem pattern is roughly circular; the same substances are cycled again and again. The flow of energy in ecosystems is linear. It is not recycled but is eventually lost to the local system.

The energy supply is steadily degraded into heat with each successive step along the food chain. For example, of the organic material synthesized by a plant from 80 to 90 percent is available under ordinary circumstances to the herbivore that consumes the plant. The herbivore expends energy, however, not only in feeding and in other activities but also in metabolic processes. When the amount of energy captured by one organism in a food chain is compared with the amount of energy the organism yields to the organism that preys on it, the figure is usually of the order of 10 to one, which means an energy loss of 90 percent.

Just as there are general similarities among ecosystems, so there are differences in the numbers and the kinds of species that participate in each system and in the relations among them. These differences are the result of evolutionary processes. Associations of species adapt to their habitat, and with the passage of time they pass through more or less distinct stages known as successions. As the work of Margalef and of Eugene P. Odum of the University of Georgia has demonstrated, these successions also show certain general similarities.

One similarity is that in any ecosystem the total biomass increases as time passes. There is a corresponding but not linearly related increase in primary productivity—that is, photosynthesis—whether it is expressed as the total amount of energy fixed or as the total quantity of organic material synthesized. What allows the increase in primary productivity is a parallel increase in the number of plant species that have become specialized and are thus able to

GARDEN MAINTENANCE includes light tasks such as tying up sugarcane. Here the stalks of cane (*left*) have been lashed to a tree stump by a gardener with a length of vine.

conduct photosynthesis under a greater variety of circumstances in a wider range of microhabitats. The increase in plant biomass and plant productivity may allow some increase in animal biomass too. It certainly encourages an increase in the diversity of animal species, since the increase in the diversity of plants favors specialization among herbivores.

Not only are there more species in the maturer stages of a succession but also the species are likely to be of a different kind. Species typical of immature succession stages—"pioneer" species—are characteristically able to disperse themselves over considerable distances, to re-

produce prodigally, to compete strongly for dominance and to survive under unstable and even violently fluctuating conditions. They also tend to be short-lived, that is, their populations are quickly replaced. Therefore in immature ecosystems the ratio of productivity to biomass is high.

In contrast, the species characteristic of more mature stages of succession often cannot disperse themselves easily over long distances, produce few offspring and are relatively long-lived. Their increasing specialization militates against overt competition among them; instead the relations among species are often characterized by an increased mutual reliance. In effect, as the ecosystem becomes maturer it becomes more complex for the number of species, and their interdependence increases. As its complexity increases so does its stability, since there are increasing numbers of alternative paths through which energy and materials can flow. Therefore if one or another species is decimated, the entire system is not necessarily endangered.

The maturing ecosystem also becomes more efficient. In the immature stage productivity per unit of biomass is high and total biomass is likely to be low. As stage follows stage both productivity and biomass increase, but there is a decrease in the ratio of productivity to biomass. For example, it takes less energy to support a pound of biomass in a mature tropical rain forest than it does in the grassy or scrubby forest stages that precede maturity.

It is not really surprising that increased stability and increased efficiency should be characteristic of mature ecosystems. Some of the implications of this trend, however, are not altogether obvious. I have alluded to the arguments of Margalef and Howard Odum suggesting that in mature ecosystems selection is not merely a matter of competition between individuals or species occupying the same level in the food chain. Rather, it favors those species that contribute positively to the stability and efficiency of the entire ecosystem. Organisms with positions well up along the food chain can "reward" the organisms they depend on by returning to these lower organisms materials they require or by performing services that are beneficial to them. An exploitive population—one that consumes at a rate greater than the productivity of the species it depends on or does not reward that species—will eventually perish.

Margalef and others have pointed out that human intervention tends to reduce the maturity of ecosystems. Both in terms of the small number of species present and of the lack of ecological complexity a farm or a plantation more closely resembles an immature stage of succession than it does a mature stage. Furthermore, in ecosystems dominated by man the chosen species are usually quick to ripen—that is, they are short-lived—and the productivity per unit of biomass is likely to be high. Yet there is a crucial difference between natural pioneer associations and those dominated by man.

Pioneers in an immature ecosystem are characterized by their ability to survive under unstable conditions. Man's favored cultigens, however, are seldom if ever notable for hardiness and self-sufficiency. Some are ill-adapted to their surroundings, some cannot even propagate themselves without assistance and some are able to survive only if they are constantly protected from the competition of the natural pioneers that promptly invade the simplified ecosystems man has constructed. Indeed, in man's quest for higher plant yields he has devised some of the most delicate and unstable ecosystems ever to have appeared on the face of the earth. The ultimate in human-dominated associations are fields planted in one high-yielding variety of a single species. It is apparent that in the ecosystems dominated by man the trend of what can be called successive anthropocentric stages is exactly the reverse of the trend in natural ecosystems. The anthropocentric trend is in the direction of simplicity rather than complexity, of fragility rather than stability.

We return to our question of how the pattern of Tsembaga agriculture compares with the pattern of agriculture based on one crop. The question really concerns the interaction of man's expanding social, political and economic organization on the one hand and local natural ecosystems on the other. The trend of anthropocentric succession can best be understood as one aspect of the evolution of human society.

We can place the Tsembaga and other "primitive" horticulturists early in such successions. The Tsembaga are politically and economically autonomous. They neither import nor export foodstuffs, and it is necessary for them to maintain as wide a range of crops in their gardens as they wish to enjoy. Economic self-sufficiency obviously encourages a generalized horticulture, but economic self-sufficiency and production for use protect ecological integrity in more

FERAL PIG (*foreground*) has been roasted and is being dismembered. Feral animals are eaten whenever they are killed, but domestic swine are killed only on ceremonial occasions.

important ways. For one thing, the management of cultivation is only slightly concerned, if at all, with events in the outside world. On the contrary, it attends almost exclusively to the needs of the cultivators and the species sustaining them. Moreover, in the absence of exotic energy sources the ability of humans to abuse the species on which they depend is limited by those species, because it is only from them that energy for work can be derived. In such systems, however, abuses seldom need to be repaid by declining yields because they are quickly signaled to those responsible by subtler signs of environmental degradation. Information feedback from the environment is sensitive and rapid in small autonomous ecological systems, and such systems are likely to be rapidly self-correcting.

The fact remains that autonomous local ecological systems such as the Tsembaga system have virtually disappeared. All but a few have been absorbed into an increasingly differentiated and complex social and economic organization of worldwide scope. The increasing size and complexity of human organization is related to man's increasing ability to harness energy. The relationship is not simple; rather it is one of mutual causation. As an example, increases in the available energy allow increases in the size and differentiation of human societies. Increased numbers and increasingly complex organizations require still more energy to sustain them and at the same time facilitate the development of new techniques for capturing more energy, and so on. The system is characterized by positive feedback.

Leslie A. White of the University of Michigan suggested that cultural evolution can be measured in terms of the increasing amount of energy harnessed per capita per annum. This is a yardstick that seems generally to agree with the historical experience of mankind. The development of energy sources that are independent of immediate biological processes has been the factor of greatest importance. Industrialized societies harness many times more energy per capita per annum than nonindustrial ones, and the energy-rich have enjoyed a great advantage in their relations with the energy-poor. In areas where the two have competed the nonindustrial societies have inevitably been displaced, absorbed or destroyed.

Agriculture is not exempt from the increasing specialization that characterizes social evolution generally. Not only individual farms but also regions

COSTUMED FOR DANCING, a group of Tsembaga men stands ready near the dance ground. During this ceremony in 1963 the Tsembaga butchered and distributed 109 pigs.

and even nations have been turned into man-made immature ecosystems such as cotton plantations or cane fields. It is important to note that the transformation would be virtually impossible without sources of energy other than local biological processes. Fossil fuels come into play. When such energy sources are available, the pressures that can be brought to bear on specific ecosystems are no longer limited to the energy that the ecosystem itself can generate, and alterations become feasible that were formerly out of reach. A farmer may even expend more energy in the gasoline consumed by his farm machinery than is returned by the crop he raises. The same nonbiological power sources make it possible to provide the world agricultural community with the large quantities of pesticides, fertilizers and other kinds of assistance that many man-made immature ecosystems require in order to remain productive. Moreover, the entire infrastructure of commercial agriculture—high-speed transportation and communications, large-scale storage facilities and elaborate economic institutions—depends on these same sources of nonbiological energy.

As man forces the ecosystems he dominates to be increasingly simple, however, their already limited autonomy is further diminished. They are subject not only to local environmental stress but also to extraneous economic and political vicissitudes. They come to rely more and more on imported materials; the men who manipulate them become more and more subject to distant events, interests and processes that they may not even grasp and certainly do not control. National and international concerns replace local considerations, and with the

regulation of the local ecosystems coming from outside, the system's normal self-corrective capacity is diminished and eventually destroyed.

Margalef has observed that in exchanges among systems differing in complexity of organization the flow of material, information and energy is usually from the less highly organized to the more highly organized. This principle may find expression not only in the relations between predator and prey but also in the relations between "developed" and "underdeveloped" nations. André Gunder Frank has argued that in the course of the development of underdeveloped agrarian societies by industrialized societies the flow of wealth is usually from the former to the latter. Be this as it may, economic development surely accelerates ecological simplification; it inevitably encourages a shift from more diverse subsistence agriculture to the cultivation of a few crops for sale in a world market.

It may not be improper to characterize as ecological imperialism the elaboration of a world organization that is centered in industrial societies and degrades the ecosystems of the agrarian societies it absorbs. Ecological imperialism is in some ways similar to economic imperialism. In both there is a flow of energy and material from the less organized system to the more organized one, and both may simply be different aspects of the same relations. Both may also be masked by the same euphemisms, among which "progress" and "development" are prominent.

The anthropocentric trend I have described may have ethical implications, but the issue is ultimately not a matter of morality or even of *Realpolitik*. It is

one of biological viability. The increasing scope of world organization and the increasing industrialization and energy consumption on which it depends have been taken by Western man virtually to define social evolution and progress. It must be remembered that man is an animal, that he survives biologically or not at all, and that his biological survival, like that of all animals, requires the survival of the other species on which he depends. The general ecological perspective outlined here suggests that some aspects of what we have called progress or social evolution may be maladaptive. We may ask if a worldwide human organization can persist and elaborate itself indefinitely at the expense of decreasing the stability of its own ecological foundations. We cannot and would not want to return to a world of autonomous ecosystems such as the Tsembaga's; in such systems all men and women are and must be farmers. We may ask, however, if the chances for human survival might not be enhanced by reversing the modern trend of successions in order to increase the diversity and stability of local, regional and national ecosystems, even, if need be, at the expense of the complexity and interdependence of worldwide economic organization. It seems to me that the trend toward decreasing ecosystemic complexity and stability, rather than threats of pollution, overpopulation or even energy famine, is the ultimate ecological problem immediately confronting man. It also may be the most difficult to solve, since the solution cannot easily be reconciled with the values, goals, interests and political and economic institutions prevailing in industrialized and industrializing nations.

35

SUBSISTENCE HERDING IN UGANDA

RADA AND NEVILLE DYSON-HUDSON
February 1969

*The Karimojong drink the milk and blood of their cattle but
rarely eat meat. Why do they not adopt the successful
dairying and ranching practice of advanced nations?
The answer is rooted in human ecology*

Wide areas of Africa are savanna grassland. It is a habitat most suited to grazing animals, and where it is exploited by man it is most often used for raising livestock. As a result livestock are a major natural resource in many African nations; in some countries (such as Mauritania and Chad) they may be the only significant economic resource in sight. Yet in Africa livestock have proved to be an exceedingly difficult resource to exploit economically on a national scale.

The reason for the difficulty is a simple one. Traditional African systems of livestock exploitation, in spite of their many variations across the continent, have one thing in common: the people who operate them survive not by ranching or by dairy farming but by subsistence herding. The common aim of ranchers and dairy farmers is the conversion of herbage (either naturally available or grown for the purpose) into marketable produce, and their objective is achieved by associating small numbers of people with large herds of livestock. In subsistence herding large numbers of livestock are associated with large numbers of people, and the aim, within the limits of the available technology, is the production not of a marketable surplus but of a regular daily supply of food. In short, in market-oriented livestock systems the herds support the minimum population needed for livestock care; in a subsistence-oriented livestock system the herds support the maximum population that can be regularly fed from their produce. Indeed, in subsistence systems continuity of food supply is so emphasized that live-animal products (milk, milk fats and often blood tapped from live animals) are the ones most utilized, with terminal products (meat and the blood of recently slaughtered animals)

used only to mark special occasions, to make the best of accidental livestock death or to stave off famine.

The contrast between the market orientation of the rancher or dairy farmer and the continuous-feeding orientation of the subsistence herder is so pronounced that it has frustrated many well-intentioned advisers to African nations. The obvious inefficiency, in market terms, of traditional livestock systems has even prompted the argument that the African savannas can best be exploited by wild-game cropping rather than by domestic animal husbandry. The absence of market rationality in traditional herding systems is beyond dispute: herd structure, husbandry practices and the explicit comments of the herders themselves all confirm it. Too often, however, the absence of market rationality in traditional herding systems is taken to be the absence of rationality of any kind. Tribal herders are given no credit for intent and design in their livestock operations. Quite commonly innate cultural backwardness or mere ecological ignorance is invoked to explain the nature (and remarkable persistence) of traditional herding systems. It is a commonplace among conservation-minded world travelers that the tropical herdsman is thoughtlessly bent on ruining his environment. Such misinterpretations are possible only because of a shortage of hard data on the actual day-to-day operation of traditional herding systems. In the present age of the economic planner's dominance in developing nations these misinterpretations may bring hardship to many of Africa's tribal groups.

Let us take as an example a single East African tribe: the Karimojong, who live in the southern part of the Karamoja District in Uganda. The Karimojong, to be sure, are only a tiny fraction of Afri-

ca's population—about 60,000 persons. They occupy an infinitesimal part of its land—about 4,000 square miles of semi-arid plain in northeastern Uganda. Nonetheless, in their emotional and economic commitment to herding as the best means of survival in an uncertain environment they represent a significant part of the African continent and its peoples. Moreover, in their livestock practices they clearly represent the skills and rationality of traditional African livestock production, which have too often been misunderstood (or simply overlooked) by observers raised in a different tradition and oriented toward other goals.

To be rigorous, in fact, we must begin with a much smaller example than even a single tribe, because the Karimojong will not give outsiders information about their livestock any more than an American businessman would open his financial records to a stranger. The minimum example from which we start is the herd of one Karimojong man named Loput, whose herding movements were tracked, whose herd structure was tallied and whose livestock yields were regularly sampled over a 13-month period. For purposes of comparison less complete yield measurements were obtained from two other herds, and the herding movements were tracked over a two-year period for seven homesteads that together formed a residential community of some 250 people. Beyond this the assessment of the representative nature of the herd data for the tribe as a whole depended on direct questioning and independent observation during close but casual interaction with many tribesmen. Corroboration in some respects, and a wider frame of reference, were provided by detailed records for native cattle kept as a dairy herd at Karamoja District

CATTLE CAMP in the western highlands of the Karimojong tribal area in northeastern Uganda has thornbush corrals for the animals and rough huts of straw for the herdsmen. Grazing is abundant in season here, and a camp like this may be occupied for many weeks.

HOME SETTLEMENT of a Karimojong herd owner is a large stockade with a separate compound for each wife. A corral for cattle is at upper right, a circular pen for goats and sheep at center. The structures on stilts outside the stockade are bins for grain storage.

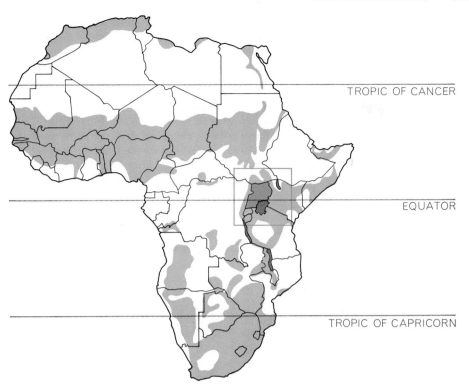

DISTRIBUTION OF CATTLE in Africa (*light color*) includes stock in areas north of the Sahara and in the far south. Extensive rangelands occupy a region from south of the Sahara to and below the Equator. Uganda, where the authors' study was conducted, is in dark color.

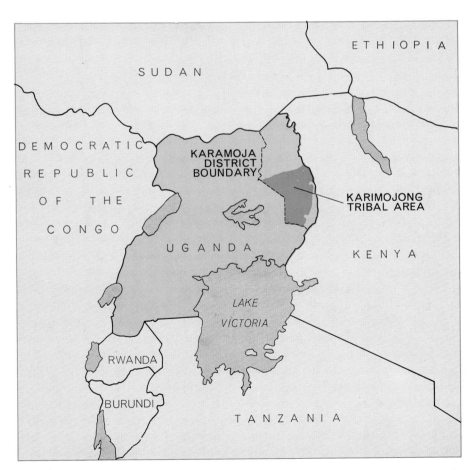

KARIMOJONG TRIBAL AREA lies near the border between Uganda and Kenya in northeastern Uganda, occupying half of the Karamoja District. Although its year can be divided into a wet and a dry season, rainfall is erratic and grazing and water are highly variable.

headquarters and by livestock censuses conducted by the Uganda Veterinary Department. The statistical shortcomings of such an investigation are obvious, but the detail provided by intensive investigation compensates by yielding many insights that cannot be derived from superficial extensive investigations. It is perhaps worth noting that even the minimum example from which we start was the result of almost three years of field study, including more than two years of close daily association with Loput, who was moved to adopt us into his own family group.

Understanding Karimojong herding operations means understanding that, to the Karimojong, cattle mean many things. Cattle are property, and accordingly they represent variable degrees of wealth, of social status and of community influence. They are a man's legacy to his sons. They can be exchanged to symbolize formal contracts of friendship and mutual assistance. The transfer of cattle from the groom's family to the bride's is needed to validate a marriage. The sacrifice of cattle is a vital feature of religious observances. The focus of Karimojong aspirations is the acquisition of cattle, and disputed cattle ownership is at the root of most Karimojong quarrels. Cattle are considered proper objects of man's affection, and this conviction is an integral part of each man's life cycle. As a boy he is given a specially named male calf to identify himself with, to care for and to decorate, to commemorate in song at dances and beer parties, and to incorporate into the style of his most formal name as an adult. Interesting and important as all these elements are, they are cultural elaborations of one central fact: cattle are the major source of subsistence for the Karimojong. First, last and always the role of cattle in Karimojong life is to transform the energy stored in the grasses, herbs and shrubs of the tribal area into a form easily available to the people.

The Karimojong do practice subsistence agriculture in addition to livestock husbandry; they also collect wild fruits and berries and occasionally hunt wild game. Because of the uncertainties of the environment this method of exploitation helps to ensure a continuity of food supply that a single food source could not. The most reliable food source is nonetheless livestock, herded by men who may build their rough camps anywhere on the Karimojong tribal land. In most years there are localized rainstorms in some part of the tribal land, and the livestock can be moved to where grass and water are available. Occasionally, however, there are major droughts of four months or more over all the tribal land, and the shortage of grazing and water reduces to a very low level the yield of those livestock that do survive. There are also epidemics of livestock disease that can decimate the herds, and the neighboring tribes, particularly the Suk and the Turkana, are in a perpetual state of war with the Karimojong, so that a man's entire herd may be stolen. For the Karimojong to live entirely on their herds would be risky.

Subsistence agriculture is practiced primarily by the women, who live in the relatively comfortable permanent settlements in the center of the Karimojong tribal land. Agriculture too is perilous; a short local drought of three or four weeks during the growing season (a frequent occurrence) severely damages the crops, and they cannot be moved to areas of better rainfall. Nonetheless, excellent crops can be harvested all over the tribal land in certain years, and in certain areas in most years. Sorghum, the major crop, is used to supplement the blood and milk from the livestock. Wild game and bush foods, although they enabled the few Karimojong surviving after the major livestock and human epidemics of the 1890's to reestablish themselves as a major tribe, are not now sufficiently abundant to be more than an occasional supplement to the basic Karimojong diet of livestock and agricultural products.

The relative importance of herd products, agricultural products and bush foods varies from year to year and from individual to individual. Married women and their daughters normally live in the permanent settlements and mainly eat cereal food, supplemented by milk when the cattle herds are nearby, but in years of crop failure all the people may move to the camps and subsist on milk and cattle blood until a new crop is harvested. Many young men and boys live almost exclusively on milk and cattle blood, but if a man is poor in cattle, the whole family may have to depend almost entirely on agricultural products and food gathered in the bush. Here we shall examine in detail only the husbandry practices of the Karimojong, to demonstrate how they are a response to the exigencies of both the biological and the social environment.

Karimojong husbandry involves total use of the environment: immediate utilization of resources, leaving none for a later time. Three reasons can be suggested for this basic principle of the Karimojong herdsman. First, in the past tropical cattle-keepers have migrated over large areas, simply moving from pasture to pasture as the forage was exhausted and driving out other people if they were in the way. The entire political history of East Africa is that of grazing areas changing hands from tribe to tribe, so that to maintain good grazing not only is dubious economically—who knows who will be taking advantage of

it in the future?—but also invites outside competition into the area.

Second, in the past cattle and human epidemics have periodically led to a great reduction in the human and stock populations, giving the vegetation a chance to recover. The last population crash was late in the 19th century, and until very recently (certainly until the 1930's) Karimojong tribal land has almost certainly been underpopulated and undergrazed. Third, grazing in Karamoja is a tribal right, so that what one man saves only leaves something for another man to use.

For these reasons the Karimojong have no notion of the necessity—or even the desirability—to conserve grazing and to limit the number of cattle. The aim of the Karimojong herdsmen is to conserve their herds. They exploit their livestock largely by consuming the products of living animals: milk and blood.

All lactating cows are milked twice daily—morning and evening. First the calf is allowed to feed, in order to bring down the milk, then the cow is milked, and finally the calf is allowed to finish nursing. In addition, some four to eight pints of blood are taken at three- to five-month intervals from any animal except a bull or a cow that is pregnant or giving milk. The blood is tapped by tightening a thong around the neck of the animal enough to make the jugular vein stand out but not enough to choke the animal. Then an arrow with its tip wrapped in string (so that only about an inch can

KARIMOJONG HERDS stand at midday near a watering place in the western plains of the tribal area. The cattle show the humps and dewlaps characteristic of zebu stock. Here, at the end of the dry season, their humps are sagging (*note ox in right foreground*).

CATTLE BLOOD, a vital part of the Karimojong diet, is taken from an animal by piercing the jugular vein with an arrow wrapped in string. A thong is tied around the animal's neck, causing the vein to swell. Cattle are bled only once every three to five months.

penetrate) is shot into the vein. The blood flows freely, but when enough has been taken and the thong is released, the flow stops immediately.

The primary reason for exploiting the products of living cattle is the difficulty of storing herd produce in an area with an undeveloped technology located two degrees north of the Equator. The only animal product normally stored is ghee: butter that is churned from fresh milk curdled with cow's urine and then boiled and put in gourds. Otherwise the milk and blood products can be kept for only a few hours.

Meat can be dried and stored for long periods. If a Karimojong man has 400 pounds of meat from an ox slaughtered within his own settlement, however, his family will certainly receive less than a quarter of it; the rest must be shared with relatives, neighbors and friends. A man cannot refuse the begging of others, because reciprocal begging among the Karimojong is their method of social insurance. He never knows when his herd may be decimated, or when his wife's crops may fail. Thus a herd owner's family is better off taking milk and blood from an animal and keeping the animal until it dies. It is only the meat that the family need share with the neighbors.

The herding environment of the Karimojong is characterized by many uncer-

tainties, the greatest of which is rainfall. It is impossible in the Karimojong tribal land to predict when the rain will fall, where it will fall and how much will fall. For example, in Moroto, the best-documented rainfall station, one can predict within 80 percent certainty that in the second week of March the rainfall will amount to anywhere from zero to 4.8 inches. Clearly the Karimojong cannot predict when the rain will fall. Neither can they predict where the rain will fall. In one year (1955) a station on the plains at Kangole recorded a rainfall of 20.01 inches, and a station only eight miles away at Lotome recorded 42.13 inches. Yet this is not a predictable pattern, since often Kangole has more rain than Lotome. Finally, the Karimojong cannot predict with any certainty how much rain will fall. The longest record of a rainfall station (Moroto) shows an annual rainfall of between 18 inches and 58 inches over a 34-year period.

Indeed, in the semiarid country of the Karimojong only two facts about rainfall seem beyond dispute. The first is that in general more rain will fall between September and March than between March and September (which enables the Karimojong to distinguish a wet season and a dry one). The second is that in general more rain will fall on the highlands than on the plains (which usually enables the

Karimojong to find dry-season grazing for their cattle somewhere in the highlands). There is no month of the year without some probability of rainfall, and during the dry season anything from one inch to five inches may fall somewhere; it is also possible for areas to be without rain for four months of the dry season. Such extreme variability, affecting as it does the growth of herbage available to the livestock, has marked effects on Karimojong herding operations. The only two indubitable facts provide too narrow a base for anything but contingent strategies of livestock husbandry.

Topographically the setting for Karimojong herding is about 4,000 square miles of high plains (3,600 to 4,500 feet above sea level). The corners of the Karimojong tribal land are roughly marked by the mountain masses of four long extinct volcanoes, and the tribal land's eastern flank is a rocky ridge forming the watershed between the Nile and the Red Sea. Topographic and rainfall variability, together with variations in soil composition, water supply and vegetational cover, present the herdsman with a variety of habitats in which to operate.

The extreme eastern and western flanks of the country are both highland areas that we shall call Zone I. The shallow rocky or sandy soils are covered by

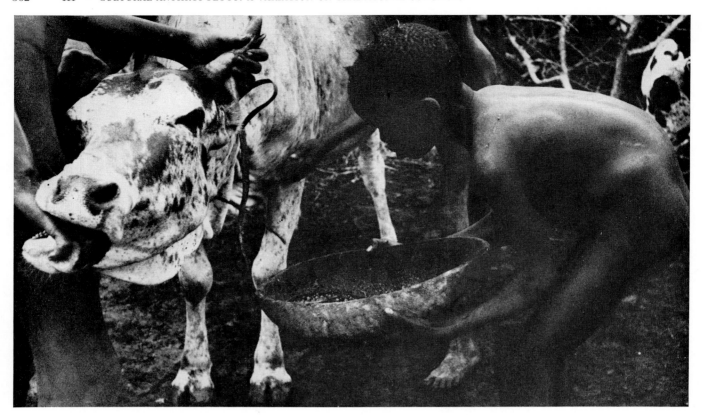

BLOOD IS CAUGHT in a bowl held by a herdboy. From four to eight pints will be taken and bleeding stops when the thong is loosened. A mixture of blood and milk is the standard food of the cattle camps, so that the herders literally live off their animals.

open deciduous woodland with a ground cover of perennial grasses. Rainfall is usually sufficient to keep water in at least some of the springs, rock pools and the stony upper courses of rivers.

The central region (Zone II), which is crossed by several wide rivers, has sandy and clay loams and rich alluvial soil. Subsurface water is always available at known areas in the sandy riverbeds and can be tapped by digging wells. This is the region of most intensive land use. The Karimojong permanent settlements are located near the areas of alluvial soil, which are used for the cultivation of crops. Cattle are grazed near the settlements during the rainy season, and flocks of goats and sheep stay in the area all year. As a result the original vegetation has been destroyed and there is a secondary growth of scattered *Lannea* and acacia bushes or dense thickets of acacia and *Sansevieria*. The ground cover is mainly annual grasses and herbs. The rainfall varies markedly from year to year and from place to place.

The western plains (Zone III) are an area of red sandy loam ridges alternating with depressions of poorly drained heavy dark clay. It has a good growth of perennial grasses. The red ridges are treeless; the clay valleys are marked by a growth of scattered spindly *Acacia drepanolobium.* In this zone the rivers disappear underground, but their courses are marked by open woodlands of water-loving trees, particularly *Acacia seyal* and *Acacia gerrardii.* Sparse muddy ponds provide permanent or semipermanent water sources, and clay pans hold water for some three weeks after dry-season rainstorms.

It is clear that the Karimojong herdsman must evaluate many variables in planning his herding program. Very few permanent sources of water are available on the western clay plains and in the eastern highlands (although the eastern highlands, with their higher rainfall, rarely lack water somewhere). The central area has relatively abundant permanent water, but its grazing, although nutritionally rich, is sparse during the rains and nonexistent during the dry season. The western plains and eastern highlands have abundant perennial grasses and extensive grazing areas, but their grasses, when dry, are nutritionally deficient. Dry-season rainstorms are needed to make the nutritionally rich green sprouts grow from the perennial roots, and particularly on the western plains such storms are infrequent. The waterlogged, sticky clay soils of the western plains are hazardous for cattle and herdsmen in the wet season, as are the tall grasses, which shelter predators dangerous to both livestock and herder. In the eastern highlands there is East Coast fever, a tick-borne disease usually fatal to cattle, and north on the watershed there are the Suk, who regularly raid Karimojong cattle and kill the herders.

The Karimojong respond to these stern conditions by manipulating the environment itself, by manipulating the internal structure of the herd and by manipulating the herd in relation to the environment. They are, however, far from being able to engage in each kind of manipulation to the same degree or with the same degree of success. The Karimojong manipulation of the environment to increase productivity is limited; its most important element is controlled burning. Karimojong herdsmen burn the dry grass on parts of the peripheral grazing area each year in the hope that the dry-season rains will come and the livestock can subsist on the remaining dry grass, supplemented by the fresh green shoots (*anomot*) that grow from the roots of the perennial grasses after burning. Even if the "grass rains" fail, the cattle can survive on the dry grass. The cattle, however, cannot maintain good condition without the nutritious *anomot*.

The Karimojong recognize and name various diseases, and they try to control the movement of men and animals to avoid the spread of disease. Moreover, they dig and maintain *atapars:* ponds to

MILKING at a home settlement is done by a mother-and-daughter team. The daughter stands, holding the cow's calf (*right*), which has been allowed to suckle briefly. The mother crouches with a vessel between her knees and draws milk while the cow grooms its calf. After some milk has been taken for settlement use the calf will be allowed to suckle again.

BUTTER FOR HOMESTEAD USE is made by a girl during a visit to an outlying cattle camp. She shakes a thong-wrapped gourd filled with curdled milk. When the butter forms, she will boil it to make ghee, which she will carry back to the homestead. Because the Karimojong have no means of refrigeration, ghee is the only milk product they can preserve.

catch and hold water through at least part of the dry season. The custom is falling into disuse since the government started to dig wells and build dams. This is the extent to which the Karimojong manipulate their environment.

Manipulation within the Karimojong herd is also limited. The Karimojong select certain male animals to be herd bulls. Apparently bulls of light hide colors are preferred, and also bulls with a pendulous penis; the Karimojong believe this indicates an animal's female progeny will be good milkers. They do not castrate their bulls young, since calf mortality is high (up to 17 percent, even in a year without an epidemic) and they might end up with no bulls if they castrated the male stock before three months, as is common in the U.S. Castration is delayed until the male animal is more than a year old and the herd owner can be reasonably certain it will survive to maturity.

The Karimojong value their female animals highly and do not trade or kill them. Oxen (and an occasional barren cow) are slaughtered at religious ceremonies. The meat is then distributed to the people at the ceremony, with the largest quantity usually going to the old men. Since religious ceremonies are held most frequently in times of poor rainfall or after a crop failure, this is a way to reduce the herds slightly and to distribute meat to the human population when other foods are in short supply.

The Karimojong do not, however, employ slaughter or sale to systematically eliminate from their herds male stock, or female stock of low fertility or low milk yield. There is no obvious advantage to a herdsman's family in slaughtering culls from the herd. The government cattle buyer purchases only large oxen and cows, animals with which the Karimojong herdsmen do not readily part, and he pays little. With the money received for an 800-pound ox (which would yield some 400 pounds of dressed meat) a Karimojong could buy less than 300 pounds of cornmeal, the only food sold in relatively large quantities by the local shops. Furthermore, there are advantages for the Karimojong in keeping animals of low productivity. They are a source of blood, and they provide most of the livestock that is given away in bridewealth exchange and formal friendship contracts.

Bridewealth exchange and formal friendship are the means whereby a Karimojong herd owner can extend his circle of supporters. Administration and police protection provided by the government are minimal at the local level. The main concern of the administration is to prevent intertribal raiding and cattle theft (which is considered by the Karimojong to be a valid means of enhancing their livelihood, not a crime). Murder would almost certainly be dealt with by the government, but the Karimojong have to depend on their friends and relatives, or on help from a magico-religious practitioner, to recover stolen property or prevent a man's rights from being denied by another Karimojong. The giving of livestock is the only way a man can extend his supporters beyond those relatives he was born with. He can marry a woman with many relatives and give each some livestock at the marriage ceremony. He can also contribute to the bridewealth of another man and thus ac-

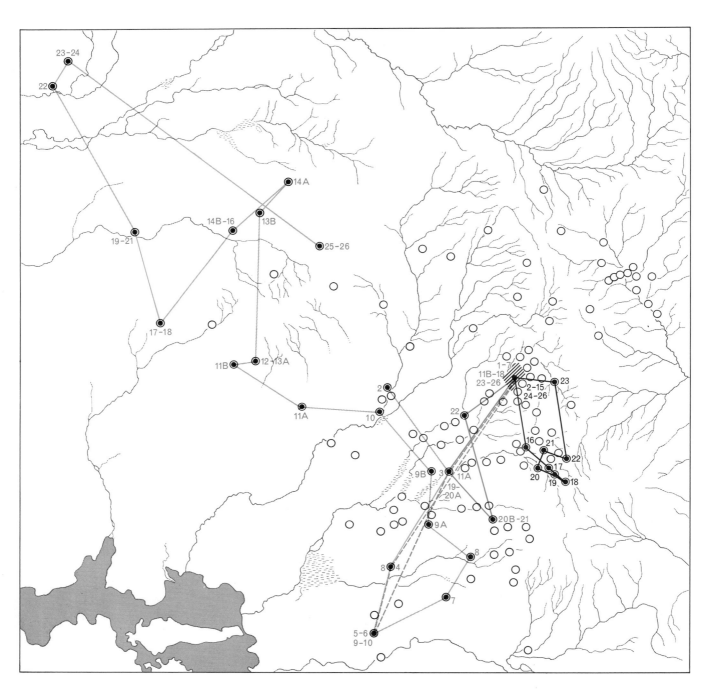

SEARCH FOR GRAZING sends Karimojong herdsmen far afield. The open circles locate cattle camps used by one or another of seven homesteads in the Emoruangaberru area over a 25-month period. The agricultural activities of the homesteads were confined to a small nuclear area (black hatching). The effect of family size on herding practices is evident in the contrast between the movements of Pulukol's and Apalokosem's herds. With five senior herdsmen and four herdboys, Pulukol divided his cattle into two herds. One, a far-ranging camp herd, traveled up to 55 miles from home and never camped twice in the same place (light colored line). Numbers by each campsite indicate the months spent there; an accompanying letter indicates a stay of less than a month. Pulukol's second herd stayed at his homestead during the rainy seasons and made two circuits nearby during the two dry seasons (colored solid and broken lines). Apalokosem, an elderly man with only one grown son, could not divide his herd or move it far. For 15 months, a period of exceptionally good rainfall, his herd stayed at his homestead. Its maximum journey, some 12 miles, was made during the following dry season (black line). The authors could not determine the location of two of the herds during the first month of the period.

among the families. The category accounting for the greatest expenditure in each family was furniture. Although all families possessed five essential articles of furniture—a bed, a mattress, a table, a shelf for use as an altar and a shelf for dishes—not all owned a chair or a wardrobe, nor did all the families own a radio, though all considered these articles essential. Belongings that could be easily pawned or were quickly worn out had the shortest life in the family, but religious objects and tools were retained the longest. Families owning basic tools, such as a sewing machine, were better off than those without tools, saving money that otherwise would be spent for manufactured products and sometimes earning income from manufacturing in the home.

"Squatter Settlements" by William Mangin is a study of the shantytowns (called *barriadas* or *callampas*) that have sprung up on the outskirts of Lima, Peru since the mid-1940's. Originally these *barriadas* were products of trial occupations of, and forcible evictions from, undeveloped public land. But subsequently the building of *barriadas* became the product of well organized, articulate, politicized groups of families fleeing city slums and rural regions in the hope of establishing permanent settlements in the unoccupied areas around cities. By mobilizing widespread popular sympathy, *barriada* organizers have forced the city and national governments to tolerate them. Governed by their own membership associations, *barriadas* exemplify, in the words of Mangin, "a really remarkable capacity for initiative, self-help and community organization." Houses in these rent-free communities are at first made of straw mats that can be erected within hours, but through time these are replaced with bricks and other permanent materials. Whereas the squatter settlers are generally poor people with little access to permanent jobs and resources, their educational level is higher than that of the general population in Peru, and *barriada* families are relatively stable compared with families in city slums, so *barriada* dwellers display an *esprit de corps* in organizing and managing a settlement that gives them hope. Yet there is also a persistent cynicism because of bickering over jobs, political decisions, and the economic advantages taken by some over others within the *barriada*.

36

THE URBANIZATION OF THE HUMAN POPULATION

KINGSLEY DAVIS
September 1965

*As the population of the world increases, the proportion
of people in cities increases at a higher rate. More than
half of the world's people will probably be living in
cities of 100,000 or more by 1990*

Urbanized societies, in which a majority of the people live crowded together in towns and cities, represent a new and fundamental step in man's social evolution. Although cities themselves first appeared some 5,500 years ago, they were small and surrounded by an overwhelming majority of rural people; moreover, they relapsed easily to village or small-town status. The urbanized societies of today, in contrast, not only have urban agglomerations of a size never before attained but also have a high proportion of their population concentrated in such agglomerations. In 1960, for example, nearly 52 million Americans lived in only 16 urbanized areas. Together these areas covered less land than one of the smaller counties (Cochise) of Arizona. According to one definition used by the U.S. Bureau of the Census, 96 million people—53 percent of the nation's population—were concentrated in 213 urbanized areas that together occupied only .7 percent of the nation's land. Another definition used by the bureau puts the urban population at about 70 percent. The large and dense agglomerations comprising the urban population involve a degree of human contact and of social complexity never before known. They exceed in size the communities of any other large animal; they suggest the behavior of communal insects rather than of mammals.

Neither the recency nor the speed of this evolutionary development is widely appreciated. Before 1850 no society could be described as predominantly urbanized, and by 1900 only one—Great Britain—could be so regarded. Today, only 65 years later, all industrial nations are highly urbanized, and in the world as a whole the process of urbanization is accelerating rapidly.

Some years ago my associates and I at Columbia University undertook to document the progress of urbanization by compiling data on the world's cities and the proportion of human beings living in them; in recent years the work has been continued in our center—International Population and Urban Research—at the University of California at Berkeley. The data obtained in these investigations are reflected in the illustration on the next two pages, which shows the historical trend in terms of one index of urbanization: the proportion of the population living in cities of 100,000 or larger. Statistics of this kind are only approximations of reality, but they are accurate enough to demonstrate how urbanization has accelerated. Between 1850 and 1950 the index changed at a much higher rate than from 1800 to 1850, but the rate of change from 1950 to 1960 was twice that of the preceding 50 years! If the pace of increase that obtained between 1950 and 1960 were to remain the same, by 1990 the fraction of the world's people living in cities of 100,-000 or larger would be more than half. Using another index of urbanization— the proportion of the world's population living in urban places of all sizes— we found that by 1960 the figure had already reached 33 percent.

Clearly the world as a whole is not fully urbanized, but it soon will be. This change in human life is so recent that even the most urbanized countries still exhibit the rural origins of their institutions. Its full implications for man's organic and social evolution can only be surmised.

In discussing the trend—and its implications insofar as they can be perceived—I shall use the term "urbanization" in a particular way. It refers here to the proportion of the total population concentrated in urban settlements, or else to a rise in this proportion. A common mistake is to think of urbanization as simply the growth of cities. Since the total population is composed of both the urban population and the rural, however, the "proportion urban" is a function of both of them. Accordingly cities can grow without any urbanization, provided that the rural population grows at an equal or a greater rate.

Historically urbanization and the growth of cities have occurred together, which accounts for the confusion. As the reader will soon see, it is necessary to distinguish the two trends. In the most advanced countries today, for example, urban populations are still growing, but their proportion of the total population is tending to remain stable or to diminish. In other words, the process of urbanization—the switch from a spread-out pattern of human settlement to one of concentration in urban centers—is a change that has a beginning and an end, but the growth of cities has no inherent limit. Such growth could continue even after everyone was living in cities, through sheer excess of births over deaths.

The difference between a rural village and an urban community is of course one of degree; a precise operational distinction is somewhat arbitrary, and it varies from one nation to another. Since data are available for communities of various sizes, a dividing line can be chosen at will. One convenient index of urbanization, for example, is the proportion of people living in places of 100,000 or more. In the following analysis I shall depend on two indexes: the one just mentioned and the proportion of population classed as "urban" in the official statistics of each country. In practice the two indexes are highly correlated; therefore either one can be used as an index of urbanization.

Actually the hardest problem is not that of determining the "floor" of the urban category but of ascertaining the boundary of places that are clearly urban by any definition. How far east is the boundary of Los Angeles? Where along the Hooghly River does Calcutta leave off and the countryside begin? In the past the population of cities and towns has usually been given as the number of people living within the political boundaries. Thus the population of New York is frequently given as around eight million, this being the population of the city proper. The error in such a figure was not large before World War I, but since then, particularly in the advanced countries, urban populations have been spilling over the narrow political boundaries at a tremendous rate. In 1960 the New York–Northeastern New Jersey urbanized area, as delineated by the Bureau of the Census, had more than 14 million people. That delineation showed it to be the largest city in the world and nearly twice as large as New York City proper.

As a result of the outward spread of urbanites, counts made on the basis of political boundaries alone underestimate the city populations and exaggerate the rural. For this reason our office delineated the metropolitan areas of as many countries as possible for dates around 1950. These areas included the central, or political, cities and the zones around them that are receiving the spillover.

This reassessment raised the estimated proportion of the world's population in cities of 100,000 or larger from 15.1 percent to 16.7 percent. As of 1960 we have used wherever possible the "urban agglomeration" data now furnished to the United Nations by many countries. The U.S., for example, provides data for "urbanized areas," meaning cities of 50,000 or larger and the built-up agglomerations around them.

It is curious that thousands of years elapsed between the first appearance of small cities and the emergence of urbanized societies in the 19th century. It is also curious that the region where urbanized societies arose—northwestern Europe—was not the one that had given rise to the major cities of the past; on the contrary, it was a region where urbanization had been at an extremely low ebb. Indeed, the societies of northwestern Europe in medieval

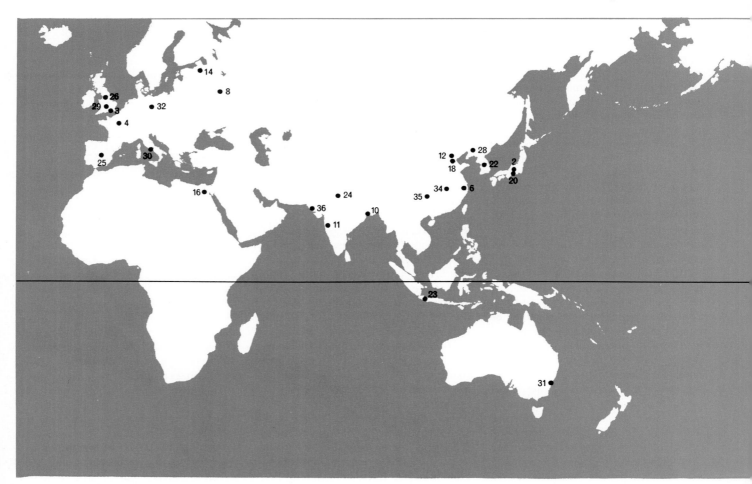

MAJOR CITIES OF THE WORLD are depicted as they rank in size according to data on "urban agglomeration" furnished to the United Nations by several countries. The data are intended to take into account not only the population within the political bounda-

times were so rural that it is hard for modern minds to comprehend them. Perhaps it was the nonurban character of these societies that erased the parasitic nature of towns and eventually provided a new basis for a revolutionary degree of urbanization.

At any rate, two seemingly adverse conditions may have presaged the age to come: one the low productivity of medieval agriculture in both per-acre and per-man terms, the other the feudal social system. The first meant that towns could not prosper on the basis of local agriculture alone but had to trade and to manufacture something to trade. The second meant that they could not gain political dominance over their hinterlands and thus become warring city-states. Hence they specialized in commerce and manufacture and evolved local institutions suited to this role. Craftsmen were housed in the towns, because there the merchants could regulate quality and cost. Competition among towns stimulated specialization and technological innovation. The need for literacy, accounting skills and geographical knowledge caused the towns to invest in secular education.

Although the medieval towns remained small and never embraced more than a minor fraction of each region's population, the close connection between industry and commerce that they fostered, together with their emphasis on technique, set the stage for the ultimate breakthrough in urbanization. This breakthrough came only with the enormous growth in productivity caused by the use of inanimate energy and machinery. How difficult it was to achieve the transition is agonizingly apparent from statistics showing that even with the conquest of the New World the growth of urbanization during three postmedieval centuries in Europe was barely perceptible. I have assembled population estimates at two or more dates for 33 towns and cities in the 16th century, 46 in the 17th and 61 in the 18th. The average rate of growth during the three centuries was less than .6 percent per year. Estimates of the growth of Europe's population as a whole between 1650 and 1800 work out to slightly more than .4 percent. The advantage of the towns was evidently very slight. Taking only the cities of 100,000 or more inhabitants, one finds that in 1600

their combined population was 1.6 percent of the estimated population of Europe; in 1700, 1.9 percent, and in 1800, 2.2 percent. On the eve of the industrial revolution Europe was still an overwhelmingly agrarian region.

With industrialization, however, the transformation was striking. By 1801 nearly a tenth of the people of England and Wales were living in cities of 100,000 or larger. This proportion doubled in 40 years and doubled again in another 60 years. By 1900 Britain was an urbanized society. In general, the later each country became industrialized, the faster was its urbanization. The change from a population with 10 percent of its members in cities of 100,000 or larger to one in which 30 percent lived in such cities took about 79 years in England and Wales, 66 in the U.S., 48 in Germany, 36 in Japan and 26 in Australia. The close association between economic development and urbanization has persisted; as the bottom illustration on page 378 shows, in 199 countries around 1960 the proportion of the population living in cities varied sharply with per capita income.

Clearly modern urbanization is best understood in terms of its connection with economic growth, and its implications are best perceived in its latest manifestations in advanced countries. What becomes apparent as one examines the trend in these countries is that urbanization is a finite process, a cycle through which nations go in their transition from agrarian to industrial society. The intensive urbanization of most of the advanced countries began within the past 100 years; in the underdeveloped countries it got under way more recently. In some of the advanced countries its end is now in sight. The fact that it will end, however, does not mean that either economic development or the growth of cities will necessarily end.

The typical cycle of urbanization can be represented by a curve in the shape of an attenuated S [see illustrations on page 379]. Starting from the bottom of the S, the first bend tends to come early and to be followed by a long attenuation. In the United Kingdom, for instance, the swiftest rise in the proportion of people living in cities of 100,000 or larger occurred from 1811 to 1851. In the U.S. it occurred from 1820 to 1890, in Greece from 1879 to 1921. As the proportion climbs above 50 percent the curve begins to flatten out; it falters, or even declines, when the proportion urban has reached about 75 percent. In

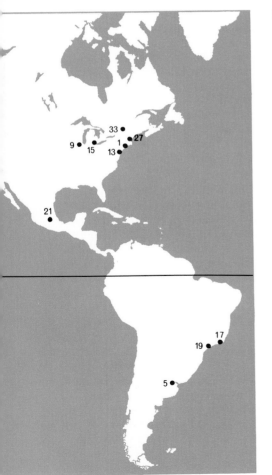

RANK	NAME	POPULATION
1	NEW YORK	14,114,927
2	TOKYO	10,177,000
3	LONDON	8,176,810
4	PARIS	7,369,387
5	BUENOS AIRES	7,000,000
6	SHANGHAI	6,900,000
7	LOS ANGELES	6,488,791
8	MOSCOW	6,354,000
9	CHICAGO	5,959,213
10	CALCUTTA	4,518,655
11	BOMBAY	4,422,165
12	PEKING	4,010,000
13	PHILADELPHIA	3,635,228
14	LENINGRAD	3,552,000
15	DETROIT	3,537,309
16	CAIRO	3,418,400
17	RIO DE JANEIRO	3,223,408
18	TIENTSIN	3,220,000
19	SÃO PAULO	3,164,804
20	OSAKA	3,151,000
21	MEXICO CITY	3,050,723
22	SEOUL	2,983,324
23	DJAKARTA	2,906,533
24	DELHI	2,549,162
25	MADRID	2,443,152
26	MANCHESTER	2,442,090
27	BOSTON	2,413,236
28	SHENYANG (MUKDEN)	2,411,000
29	BIRMINGHAM	2,377,230
30	ROME	2,278,882
31	SYDNEY	2,215,970
32	WEST BERLIN	2,176,612
33	MONTREAL	2,156,000
34	WUHAN	2,146,000
35	CHUNGKING	2,121,000
36	KARACHI	2,060,000

ries of a city but also that in the city's metropolitan area. The UN defines an urban agglomeration as the city proper and the "thickly settled territory . . . adjacent" to the city.

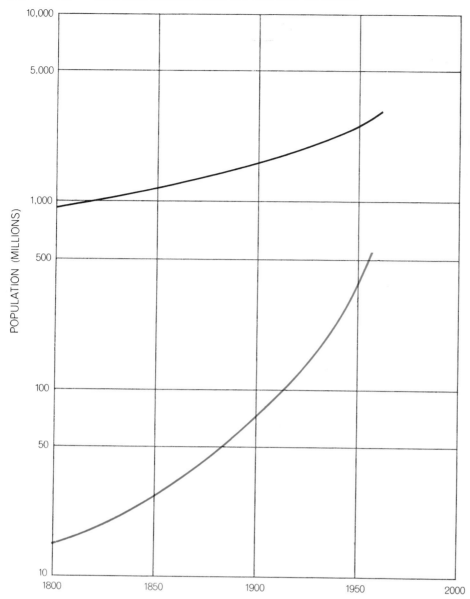

POPULATION (MILLIONS)

RAPID URBANIZATION of the world's population is evident in this comparison of total population (*black curve*) with the population in cities of more than 100,000 inhabitants (*colored curve*) over more than a century and a half. The use of cities of 100,000 or larger to define an urban population shows a close correlation with other definitions of urbanism.

ently never been the case. Indeed, a chief obstacle to the growth of cities in the past has been their excessive mortality. London's water in the middle of the 19th century came mainly from wells and rivers that drained cesspools, graveyards and tidal areas. The city was regularly ravaged by cholera. Tables for 1841 show an expectation of life of about 36 years for London and 26 for Liverpool and Manchester, as compared to 41 for England and Wales as a whole. After 1850, mainly as a result of sanitary measures and some improvement in nutrition and housing, city health improved, but as late as the period 1901–1910 the death rate of the urban counties in England and Wales, as modified to make the age structure comparable, was 33 percent higher than the death rate of the rural counties. As Bernard Benjamin, a chief statistician of the British General Register Office, has remarked: "Living in the town involved not only a higher risk of epidemic and crowd diseases...but also a higher risk of degenerative disease—the harder wear and tear of factory employment and urban discomfort." By 1950, however, virtually the entire differential had been wiped out.

As for birth rates, during rapid urbanization in the past they were notably lower in cities than in rural areas. In fact, the gap tended to widen somewhat as urbanization proceeded in the latter half of the 19th century and the first quarter of the 20th. In 1800 urban women in the U.S. had 36 percent fewer children than rural women did; in 1840, 38 percent and in 1930, 41 percent. Thereafter the difference diminished.

With mortality in the cities higher and birth rates lower, and with reclassification a minor factor, the only real source for the growth in the proportion of people in urban areas during the industrial transition was rural-urban migration. This source had to be plentiful enough not only to overcome the substantial disadvantage of the cities in natural increase but also, above that, to furnish a big margin of growth in their populations. If, for example, the cities had a death rate a third higher and a birth rate a third lower than the rural rates (as was typical in the latter half of the 19th century), they would require each year perhaps 40 to 45 migrants from elsewhere per 1,000 of their population to maintain a growth rate of 3 percent per year. Such a rate of migration could easily be maintained as long as the rural portion of the population was large, but when this condition

the United Kingdom, one of the world's most urban countries, the proportion was slightly higher in 1926 (78.7 percent) than in 1961 (78.3 percent).

At the end of the curve some ambiguity appears. As a society becomes advanced enough to be highly urbanized it can also afford considerable suburbanization and fringe development. In a sense the slowing down of urbanization is thus more apparent than real: an increasing proportion of urbanites simply live in the country and are classified as rural. Many countries now try to compensate for this ambiguity by enlarging the boundaries of urban places; they did so in numerous censuses taken around 1960. Whether in these cases the old classification of

urban or the new one is erroneous depends on how one looks at it; at a very advanced stage the entire concept of urbanization becomes ambiguous.

The end of urbanization cannot be unraveled without going into the ways in which economic development governs urbanization. Here the first question is: Where do the urbanites come from? The possible answers are few: The proportion of people in cities can rise because rural settlements grow larger and are reclassified as towns or cities; because the excess of births over deaths is greater in the city than in the country, or because people move from the country to the city.

The first factor has usually had only slight influence. The second has appar-

New Concerns: "Haves" and "Have-Nots"

NEW CONCERNS: "HAVES" AND "HAVE-NOTS"

In this, the final section of the book, we see several examples of the most current trends in anthropological analysis. For most of the last century anthropologists have addressed themselves to study of the simple forms of economy, polity, and society that exist beyond, but not beyond the influence of, the industrialized Western nations. In the past decade they have not been able, nor has it been rewarding, to confine research to these topics. Many societies in which there are potential subjects of anthropological research—particularly the tribal peoples around the world who lead lives that, by traditional Western standards, are underdeveloped, a Third World—are protesting the nature and very assumptions of some anthropological research. Inasmuch as the protest has come to be shared by many contemporary anthropologists, research is sometimes difficult to conduct among Third World peoples.

Wittingly or unwittingly, some anthropologists have aligned themselves with the political goals of the major Western nations and allowed use of observations made ostensibly as disinterested research in other than the best interests of the people they study. Whether they know it or not, anthropologists have supplied information and tendered advice to various nations attempting to develop, gain the confidence of, or even to pacify or control native populations in Third World nations. Recognition of this has come about in large nations that fund anthropological teams and in small underdeveloped nations in which many anthropologists work. As a consequence of this, access to major Third World countries for purposes of anthropological research is becoming more difficult. The most notable instances of such restrictions have occurred in Chile, Thailand, and India.*

There is another reason why nonindustrialized societies are cautious about cultural studies conducted by Western anthropologists. Many Third World nations today are aware that development benefits only a few other nations and that they are contributing to that development without receiving the benefits from it. Indeed, it is clear that development and underdevelopment go hand in hand. Increased development is gained at the cost of deepening underdevelopment, Third World nations becoming progressively underdeveloped while the large, industrial nations grow at their expense. One measure of this underdevelopment is the poverty observable in Third World nations, nations that were undeveloped but not underdeveloped before colonialism and imperialism.

---

*See the following accounts for further details about politics and anthropology. Joseph G. Jorgensen, "On Ethics and Anthropology," *Current Anthropology*, Vol. 12, No. 3, pages 321–361; June 1971. Eric R. Wolf and Joseph G. Jorgensen, "Anthropology on the Warpath in Thailand," *New York Review of Books*, Vol. 15, No. 9, pages 26–35; November 19, 1970. Gerald R. Berreman, "Academic Colonialism: Not So Innocent Abroad," *The Nation*, pages 505–508; November 10, 1969. Irving L. Horowitz, *The Rise and Fall of Project Camelot*; Cambridge, Mass.: M.I.T. Press, 1967.

Poverty is not restricted to Third World nations, however. It is massive and increasing around the world. In the most developed nations there are ruling or upper classes of people who own and control resources, lower or working classes who produce goods, and bourgeoisie or middle classes who manage, exchange, and distribute products, but there are also ever-growing underclasses or lumpenproletariat classes of rural and urban poor, people often set apart by racial characteristics, for whom there is no participation in any of these activities in the giant, powerful, industrial nations.

Anthropologists are now turning their attention toward the problem of people in poverty, assessing how they got there and how they have coped with it. We will see some of the products of this work in the final readings.

The paper by Kingsley Davis, "The Urbanization of the Human Population," and that of Earl Cook, "The Flow of Energy in an Industrial Society," provide essential background information. Davis shows how populations everywhere, in both developed and underdeveloped nations, are becoming increasingly urban, which is not to say that more and more people are becoming *urbane*, enjoying the amenities of middle class consumerism in cities, but that population density, through natural increase and some artificial effects of modern medicine, is causing overcrowding in rural areas. In underdeveloped nations, overcrowding among agricultural peoples who depend on subsistence farming is caused by high man-to-land ratios. It is caused by the growth of production and the marked change of labor-time requirements in the developed nations where, as farm technology becomes more complex, food production becomes more expensive and small-scale farmers are forced out of business by large corporations, higher tax rates, or both. Many of those who leave farms migrate to cities. Today the rural areas of a developed nation are relatively less populated than the rural areas of the underdeveloped nations. It is probable, however, that internationally centralized agribusinesses will begin displacing the rural populations in the Third World nations if this can be profitably done. The portent of huge, underfed, underconsuming urban populations with little or no access to strategic resources and the locus of power is a sobering thought.

Cook shows the discrepancy between the powerful, industrial nations and their powerless counterparts. We learn that 30 percent of the world's people consume 80 percent of the world's energy. Furthermore, the United States, with but 6 percent of the world's population, consumes 35 percent of the energy. As United States corporations expropriate oil and other raw resources from around the world, most people in the nations from which these resources are drawn receive nothing for the loss of resources. Therefore, as the Third World populations grow, their resources shrink and they have few prospects of gaining ownership or control over the resources that remain. For the developed nations—those that control the world's capital—the problems that stem from increased energy expenditure are those of managing physical resources and finding still more sources of fuel energy. It should be added that another of the resources that will have to be managed is international wealth, and another source of "energy" may have to be the distribution of international wealth owned and controlled by multinational corporations to the have-nots in those nations where the wealth is generated. In the United States and Canada redistribution to the underclasses is predominantly conducted through welfare schemes.

David Simpson's paper, "The Dimensions of World Poverty," written in 1968, is perhaps overly optimistic, because in it Simpson anticipates that poverty livelihoods—life at the margin of subsistence—will be the lot of *most* of the people of the world *for only twenty years longer*. Simpson uses per capita income as an average measure of comparative wealth in the world, acknowledging the faults of the measure first, and then discussing the problems of poverty in the two-thirds of the world in which per capita income is less than $300. The most critical problem among the world's poor is hunger, rather than the relative deprivation experienced, say, by someone who wants a transistor radio, has a reasonable expectation of the radio, but does not control the cash to buy it. Simpson remarks that some societies with low levels of material production are not seriously deprived of basic necessities. But in societies that are deprived of food, disease is a critical factor in poverty. So are poor housing, inadequate sanitation, and crowded living space, leaving very little hope. Indeed, lack of hope may be a factor in poverty. Simpson closes his article by suggesting that in areas of serious poverty people are literally too weak to protest for alleviation of their condition.

The final three papers depart from the first three. Whereas Davis, Simpson, and Cook have provided broad generalizations about world poverty, Oscar Lewis and William Mangin show us the insides of poverty—the anthropology of poor people. In "The Culture of Poverty" Lewis focuses on poverty within capitalist nations, and he describes the features of the syndrome that typifies a poverty culture as a "subculture of western society with its own structure and rationale." By comparing the lives of a group of slum residents in San Juan, Puerto Rico, with the lives of their relatives in New York City, Lewis strips away stereotyped images of poverty to show that it is not restricted to the Third World, or a fortuity, or the product of lazy, shiftless people in a free and open society in which success (as an alternative to poverty) could arbitrarily be achieved by all.

In "The Possessions of the Poor" Lewis makes a fascinating analysis of the possessions of members of fourteen families in Mexico City who see plenitude but have few belongings. From household to household, Lewis observed marked differences within each of thirteen categories of belongings, the value of religious objects in the poorest households far outstripping, for example, the value of such objects in the best off. But Lewis also found interesting similarities

ceased to obtain, the maintenance of the same urban rate meant an increasing drain on the countryside.

Why did the rural-urban migration occur? The reason was that the rise in technological enhancement of human productivity, together with certain constant factors, rewarded urban concentration. One of the constant factors was that agriculture uses land as its prime instrument of production and hence spreads out people who are engaged in it, whereas manufacturing, commerce and services use land only as a site. Moreover, the demand for agricultural products is less elastic than the demand for services and manufactures. As productivity grows, services and manufac-

tures can absorb more manpower by paying higher wages. Since nonagricultural activities can use land simply as a site, they can locate near one another (in towns and cities) and thus minimize the friction of space inevitably involved in the division of labor. At the same time, as agricultural technology is improved, capital costs in farming rise and manpower becomes not only less needed but also economically more burdensome. A substantial portion of the agricultural population is therefore sufficiently disadvantaged, in relative terms, to be attracted by higher wages in other sectors.

In this light one sees why a large flow of people from farms to cities was

generated in every country that passed through the industrial revolution. One also sees why, with an even higher proportion of people already in cities and with the inability of city people to replace themselves by reproduction, the drain eventually became so heavy that in many nations the rural population began to decline in absolute as well as relative terms. In Sweden it declined after 1920, in England and Wales after 1861, in Belgium after 1910.

Realizing that urbanization is transitional and finite, one comes on another fact—a fact that throws light on the circumstances in which urbanization comes to an end. A basic feature of

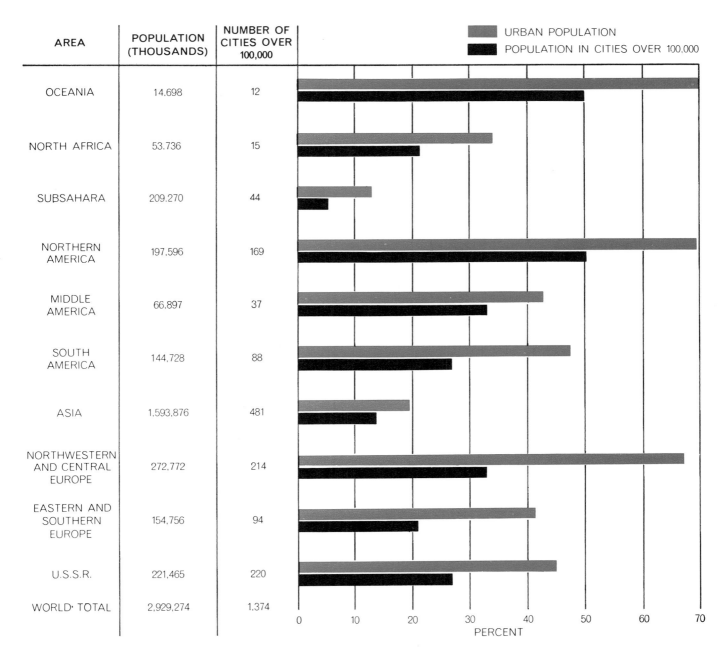

AREA	POPULATION (THOUSANDS)	NUMBER OF CITIES OVER 100,000
OCEANIA	14,698	12
NORTH AFRICA	53,736	15
SUBSAHARA	209,270	44
NORTHERN AMERICA	197,596	169
MIDDLE AMERICA	66,897	37
SOUTH AMERICA	144,728	88
ASIA	1,593,876	481
NORTHWESTERN AND CENTRAL EUROPE	272,772	214
EASTERN AND SOUTHERN EUROPE	154,756	94
U.S.S.R.	221,465	220
WORLD· TOTAL	2,929,274	1,374

■ URBAN POPULATION
■ POPULATION IN CITIES OVER 100,000

DEGREE OF URBANIZATION in the major regions of the world is indicated according to two different methods of classification. One uses the "urban" population as defined by each country of a region. The other uses the population in cities of 100,000 or more.

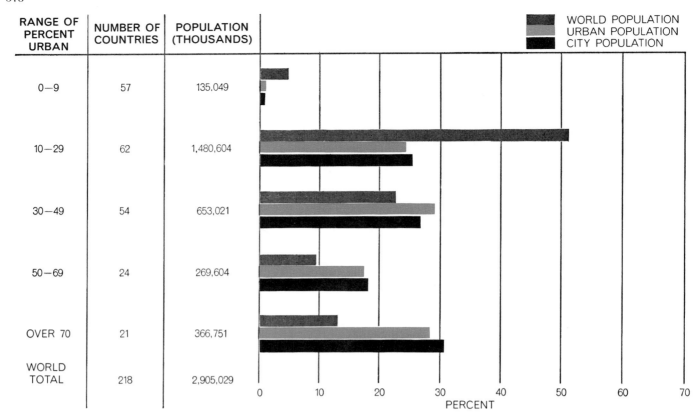

RANGE OF PERCENT URBAN	NUMBER OF COUNTRIES	POPULATION (THOUSANDS)
0—9	57	135,049
10—29	62	1,480,604
30—49	54	653,021
50—69	24	269,604
OVER 70	21	366,751
WORLD TOTAL	218	2,905,029

WORLD POPULATION
URBAN POPULATION
CITY POPULATION

PERCENT

GROUPING OF NATIONS according to degree of urbanization shows that more than half are less than 30 percent urbanized and that 45 are more than 50 percent urbanized. The chart can also be read cumulatively from the bottom to show, for example, that 22 percent of the world's population live in countries that are more than 50 percent urbanized and that those countries have 45 percent of the world's urban people and 48 percent of its city people. The approximate date of the population statistics used is 1960.

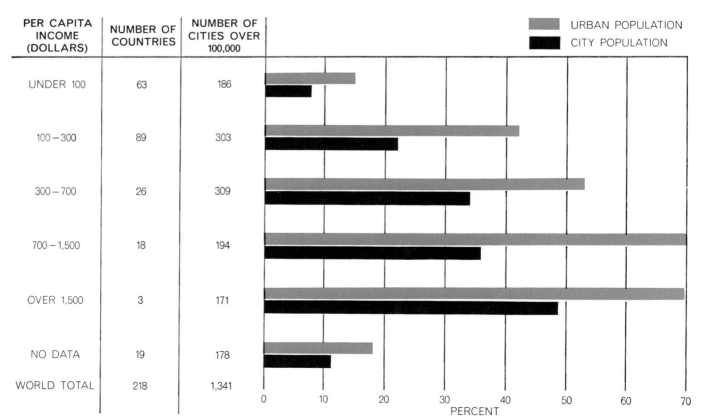

PER CAPITA INCOME (DOLLARS)	NUMBER OF COUNTRIES	NUMBER OF CITIES OVER 100,000
UNDER 100	63	186
100—300	89	303
300—700	26	309
700—1,500	18	194
OVER 1,500	3	171
NO DATA	19	178
WORLD TOTAL	218	1,341

URBAN POPULATION
CITY POPULATION

PERCENT

URBANIZATION AND INCOME are compared. It is apparent that a linear correlation exists between per capita income and degree of urbanization. Thus the three countries with a per capita income of $1,500 or more a year have the highest degree of urban-ization—and the 63 countries with per capita income under $100 a year have the lowest degree—by either of two classifications of urbanization: the urban population as defined by each country or the population living in cities of 100,000 or more inhabitants.

the transition is the profound switch from agricultural to nonagricultural employment. This change is associated with urbanization but not identical with it. The difference emerges particularly in the later stages. Then the availability of automobiles, radios, motion pictures and electricity, as well as the reduction of the workweek and the workday, mitigate the disadvantages of living in the country. Concurrently the expanding size of cities makes them more difficult to live in. The population classed as "rural" is accordingly enlarged, both from cities and from true farms.

For these reasons the "rural" population in some industrial countries never did fall in absolute size. In all the industrial countries, however, the population dependent on agriculture—which the reader will recognize as a more functional definition of the nonurban population than mere rural residence—decreased in absolute as well as relative terms. In the U.S., for example, the net migration from farms totaled more than 27 million between 1920 and 1959 and thus averaged approximately 700,000 a year. As a result the farm population declined from 32.5 million in 1916 to 20.5 million in 1960, in spite of the large excess of births in farm families. In 1964, by a stricter American definition classifying as "farm families" only those families actually earning their living from agriculture, the farm population was down to 12.9 million. This number represented 6.8 percent of the nation's population; the comparable figure for 1880 was 44 percent. In Great Britain the number of males occupied in agriculture was at its peak, 1.8 million, in 1851; by 1961 it had fallen to .5 million.

In the later stages of the cycle, then, urbanization in the industrial countries tends to cease. Hence the connection between economic development and the growth of cities also ceases. The change is explained by two circumstances. First, there is no longer enough farm population to furnish a significant migration to the cities. (What can 12.9 million American farmers contribute to the growth of the 100 million people already in urbanized areas?) Second, the rural nonfarm population, nourished by refugees from the expanding cities, begins to increase as fast as the city population. The effort of census bureaus to count fringe residents as urban simply pushes the definition of "urban" away from the notion of dense settlement and in the direction of the term "nonfarm." As the urban population becomes more "rural," which is to say less densely set-

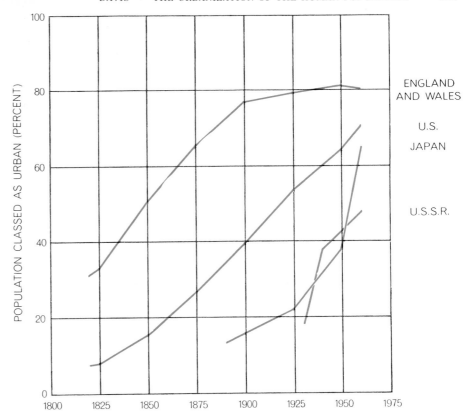

INDUSTRIALIZED NATIONS underwent a process of urbanization that is typified by the curves shown here for four countries. It was closely related to economic development. The figures for 1950 and 1960 are based on a classification that counts as urban the fringe residents of urbanized areas; that classification was not used for the earlier years shown.

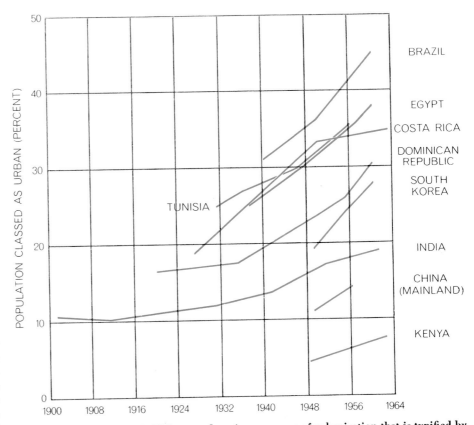

NONINDUSTRIAL NATIONS are undergoing a process of urbanization that is typified by these curves. The process started much later than in the industrialized nations, as can be seen by comparing this chart with the one at the top of the page, and is attributable more to the rapid rise of total population in these countries than to economic development.

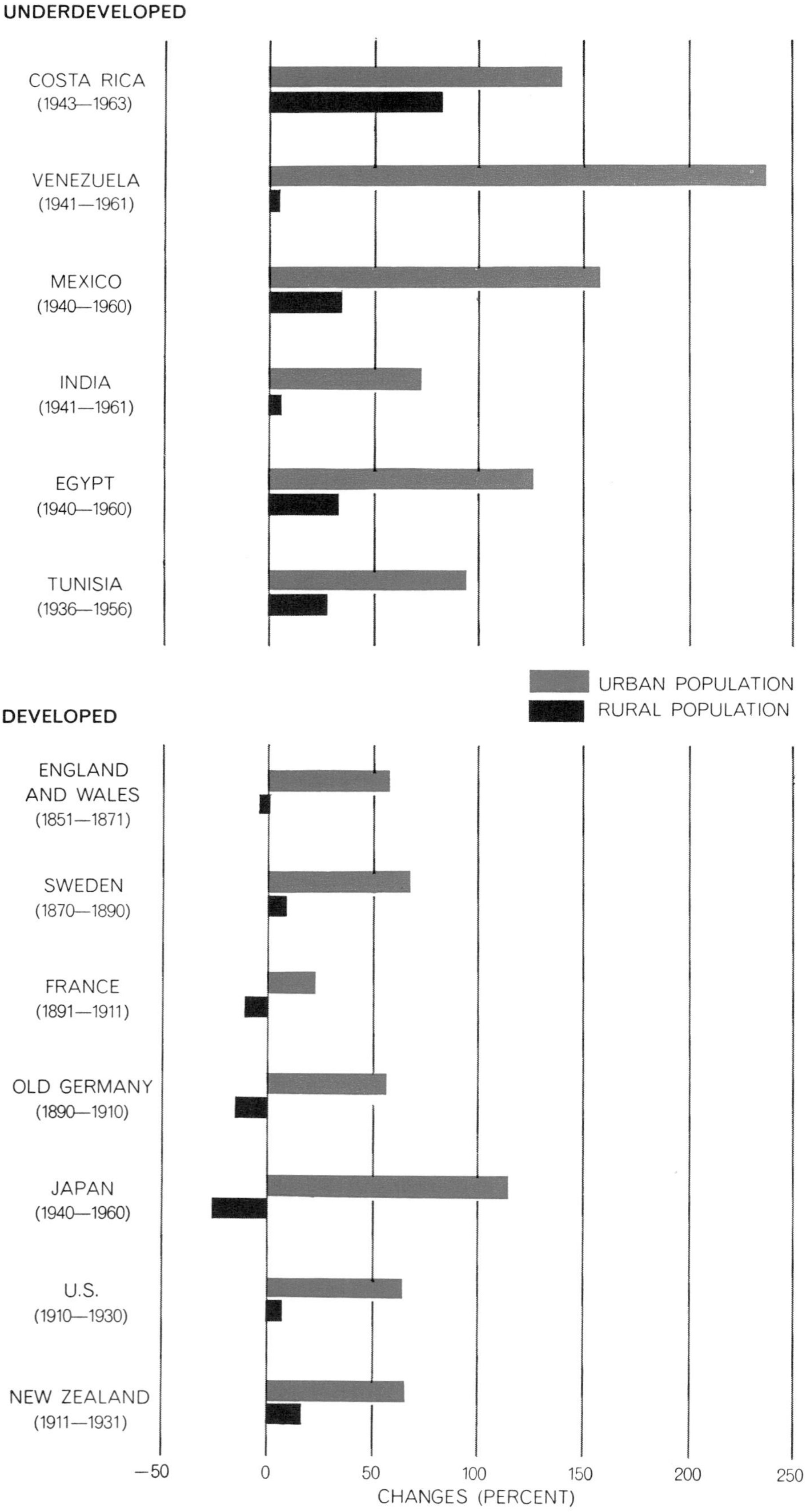

UNDERDEVELOPED

COSTA RICA
(1943—1963)

VENEZUELA
(1941—1961)

MEXICO
(1940—1960)

INDIA
(1941—1961)

EGYPT
(1940—1960)

TUNISIA
(1936—1956)

URBAN POPULATION
RURAL POPULATION

DEVELOPED

ENGLAND
AND WALES
(1851—1871)

SWEDEN
(1870—1890)

FRANCE
(1891—1911)

OLD GERMANY
(1890—1910)

JAPAN
(1940—1960)

U.S.
(1910—1930)

NEW ZEALAND
(1911—1931)

−50   0   50   100   150   200   250
CHANGES (PERCENT)

RURAL AND URBAN POPULATIONS of several underdeveloped countries are compared
with those in the currently developed countries at a time when they were undergoing rapid
urbanization. It is evident that in the underdeveloped countries the rural population is
rising in spite of urbanization, whereas in the earlier period it rose slightly or dropped.

tled, the advanced industrial peoples
are for a time able to enjoy the amenities of urban life without the excessive
crowding of the past.

Here, however, one again encounters
the fact that a cessation of urbanization
does not necessarily mean a cessation
of city growth. An example is provided
by New Zealand. Between 1945 and
1961 the proportion of New Zealand's
population classed as urban—that is, the
ratio between urban and rural residents
—changed hardly at all (from 61.3 percent to 63.6 percent) but the urban population increased by 50 percent. In
Japan between 1940 and 1950 urbanization actually decreased slightly, but
the urban population increased by 13
percent.

The point to be kept in mind is that
once urbanization ceases, city growth
becomes a function of general population growth. Enough farm-to-city migration may still occur to redress the
difference in natural increase. The reproductive rate of urbanites tends,
however, to increase when they live at
lower densities, and the reproductive
rate of "urbanized" farmers tends to decrease; hence little migration is required
to make the urban increase equal the
national increase.

I now turn to the currently underdeveloped countries. With the advanced
nations having slackened their rate of
urbanization, it is the others—representing three-fourths of humanity—that are
mainly responsible for the rapid urbanization now characterizing the world as
a whole. In fact, between 1950 and
1960 the proportion of the population
in cities of 100,000 or more rose about
a third faster in the underdeveloped
regions than in the developed ones.
Among the underdeveloped regions the
pace was slow in eastern and southern
Europe, but in the rest of the underdeveloped world the proportion in cities
rose twice as fast as it did in the industrialized countries, even though the latter countries in many cases broadened
their definitions of urban places to include more suburban and fringe residents.

Because of the characteristic pattern
of urbanization, the current rates of
urbanization in underdeveloped countries could be expected to exceed those
now existing in countries far advanced
in the cycle. On discovering that this is
the case one is tempted to say that the
underdeveloped regions are now in the
typical stage of urbanization associated
with early economic development. This
notion, however, is erroneous. In their

urbanization the underdeveloped countries are definitely not repeating past history. Indeed, the best grasp of their present situation comes from analyzing how their course differs from the previous pattern of development.

The first thing to note is that today's underdeveloped countries are urbanizing not only more rapidly than the industrial nations are now but also more rapidly than the industrial nations did in the heyday of their urban growth. The difference, however, is not large. In 40 underdeveloped countries for which we have data in recent decades, the average gain in the proportion of the population urban was 20 percent per decade; in 16 industrial countries, during the decades of their most rapid urbanization (mainly in the 19th century), the average gain per decade was 15 percent.

This finding that urbanization is proceeding only a little faster in underdeveloped countries than it did historically in the advanced nations may be questioned by the reader. It seemingly belies the widespread impression that cities throughout the nonindustrial parts of the world are bursting with people. There is, however, no contradiction. One must recall the basic distinction between a change in the proportion of the population urban, which is a ratio, and the absolute growth of cities. The popular impression is correct: the cities in underdeveloped areas are growing at a disconcerting rate. They are far outstripping the city boom of the industrializing era in the 19th century. If they continue their recent rate of growth, they will double their population every 15 years.

In 34 underdeveloped countries for which we have data relating to the 1940's and 1950's, the average annual gain in the urban population was 4.5 percent. The figure is remarkably similar for the various regions: 4.7 percent in seven countries of Africa, 4.7 percent in 15 countries of Asia and 4.3 percent in 12 countries of Latin America. In contrast, in nine European countries during their period of fastest urban population growth (mostly in the latter half of the 19th century) the average gain per year was 2.1 percent. Even the frontier industrial countries—the U.S., Australia–New Zealand, Canada and Argentina—which received huge numbers of immigrants, had a smaller population growth in towns and cities: 4.2 percent per year. In Japan and the U.S.S.R. the rate was respectively 5.4 and 4.3 percent per year, but their economic growth began only recently.

How is it possible that the contrast in growth between today's underdeveloped countries and yesterday's industrializing countries is sharper with respect to the absolute urban population than with respect to the urban share of the total population? The answer lies in another profound difference between the two sets of countries—a difference in total population growth, rural as well as urban. Contemporary underdeveloped populations have been growing since 1940 more than twice as fast as industrialized populations, and their increase far exceeds the growth of the latter at the peak of their expansion. The only rivals in an earlier day were the frontier nations, which had the help of great streams of immigrants. Today the underdeveloped nations—already densely settled, tragically impoverished and with gloomy economic prospects—are multiplying their people by sheer biological increase at a rate that is unprecedented. It is this population boom that is overwhelmingly responsible for the rapid inflation of city populations in such countries. Contrary

DENSE URBANIZATION of northeastern U.S. is portrayed in a mosaic of aerial photographs beginning on this page and continued on the next four pages. At left center is the lower part of Manhattan Island. In this and succeeding photographs southwest is to right.

to popular opinion both inside and outside those countries, the main factor is not rural-urban migration.

This point can be demonstrated easily by a calculation that has the effect of eliminating the influence of general population growth on urban growth. The calculation involves assuming that the total population of a given country remained constant over a period of time but that the percentage urban changed as it did historically. In this manner one obtains the growth of the absolute urban population that would have occurred if rural-urban migration were the only factor affecting it. As an example, Costa Rica had in 1927 a total population of 471,500, of which 88,600, or 18.8 percent, was urban. By 1963 the country's total population was 1,325,200 and the urban population was 456,600, or 34.5 percent. If the total population had remained at 471,500 but the percentage urban had still risen from 18.8 to 34.5, the absolute urban population in 1963 would have been only 162,700. That is the growth that would have occurred in the urban population if rural-urban migration had been the only factor. In actuality the urban population rose to 456,600. In other words, only

20 percent of the rapid growth of Costa Rica's towns and cities was attributable to urbanization per se; 44 percent was attributable solely to the country's general population increase, the remainder to the joint operation of both factors. Similarly, in Mexico between 1940 and 1960, 50 percent of the urban population increase was attributable to national multiplication alone and only 22 percent to urbanization alone.

The past performance of the advanced countries presents a sharp contrast. In Switzerland between 1850 and 1888, when the proportion urban resembled that in Costa Rica recently, general population growth alone accounted for only 19 percent of the increase of town and city people, and rural-urban migration alone accounted for 69 percent. In France between 1846 and 1911 only 21 percent of the growth in the absolute urban population was due to general growth alone.

The conclusion to which this contrast points is that one anxiety of governments in the underdeveloped nations is misplaced. Impressed by the mushrooming in their cities of shantytowns filled with ragged peasants, they attribute the fantastically fast city growth to rural-

urban migration. Actually this migration now does little more than make up for the small difference in the birth rate between city and countryside. In the history of the industrial nations, as we have seen, the sizable difference between urban and rural birth rates and death rates required that cities, if they were to grow, had to have an enormous influx of people from farms and villages. Today in the underdeveloped countries the towns and cities have only a slight disadvantage in fertility, and their old disadvantage in mortality not only has been wiped out but also in many cases has been reversed. During the 19th century the urbanizing nations were learning how to keep crowded populations in cities from dying like flies. Now the lesson has been learned, and it is being applied to cities even in countries just emerging from tribalism. In fact, a disproportionate share of public health funds goes into cities. As a result throughout the nonindustrial world people in cities are multiplying as never before, and rural-urban migration is playing a much lesser role.

The trends just described have an important implication for the rural population. Given the explosive overall

MOSAIC CONTINUED shows more of the heavily populated area, often called a megalopolis, between New York and Washington.   At left above, about an inch below right-angle bend of Delaware River, is Trenton; at right, where river bends upward, is Phila-

population growth in underdeveloped countries, it follows that if the rural population is not to pile up on the land and reach an economically absurd density, a high rate of rural-urban migration must be maintained. Indeed, the exodus from rural areas should be higher than in the past. But this high rate of internal movement is not taking place, and there is some doubt that it could conceivably do so.

To elaborate I shall return to my earlier point that in the evolution of industrialized countries the rural citizenry often declined in absolute as well as relative terms. The rural population of France—26.8 million in 1846—was down to 20.8 million by 1926 and 17.2 million by 1962, notwithstanding a gain in the nation's total population during this period. Sweden's rural population dropped from 4.3 million in 1910 to 3.5 million in 1960. Since the category "rural" includes an increasing portion of urbanites living in fringe areas, the historical drop was more drastic and consistent specifically in the farm population. In the U.S., although the "rural" population never quite ceased to grow, the farm contingent began its long descent shortly after the turn of the century; today it is less than two-fifths of

what it was in 1910.

This transformation is not occurring in contemporary underdeveloped countries. In spite of the enormous growth of their cities, their rural populations—and their more narrowly defined agricultural populations—are growing at a rate that in many cases exceeds the rise of even the urban population during the evolution of the now advanced countries. The poor countries thus confront a grave dilemma. If they do not substantially step up the exodus from rural areas, these areas will be swamped with underemployed farmers. If they do step up the exodus, the cities will grow at a disastrous rate.

The rapid growth of cities in the advanced countries, painful though it was, had the effect of solving a problem—the problem of the rural population. The growth of cities enabled agricultural holdings to be consolidated, allowed increased capitalization and in general resulted in greater efficiency. Now, however, the underdeveloped countries are experiencing an even more rapid urban growth—and are suffering from urban problems—but urbanization is not solving their rural ills.

A case in point is Venezuela. Its capital, Caracas, jumped from a popula-

tion of 359,000 in 1941 to 1,507,000 in 1963; other Venezuelan towns and cities equaled or exceeded this growth. Is this rapid rise denuding the countryside of people? No, the Venezuelan farm population increased in the decade 1951–1961 by 11 percent. The only thing that declined was the amount of cultivated land. As a result the agricultural population density became worse. In 1950 there were some 64 males engaged in agriculture per square mile of cultivated land; in 1961 there were 78. (Compare this with 4.8 males occupied in agriculture per square mile of cultivated land in Canada, 6.8 in the U.S. and 15.6 in Argentina.) With each male occupied in agriculture there are of course dependents. Approximately 225 persons in Venezuela are trying to live from each square mile of cultivated land. Most of the growth of cities in Venezuela is attributable to overall population growth. If the general population had not grown at all, and internal migration had been large enough to produce the actual shift in the proportion in cities, the increase in urban population would have been only 28 percent of what it was and the rural population would have been reduced by 57 percent.

The story of Venezuela is being re-

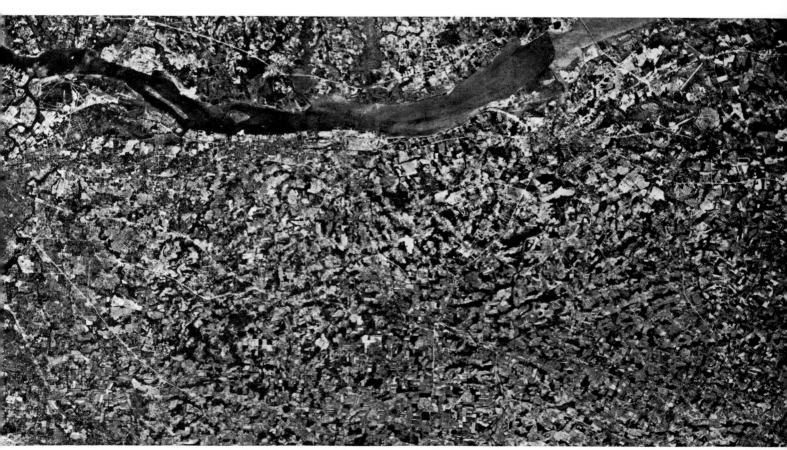

delphia. Near top left on this page the Schuylkill River joins the Delaware; five inches to the right is Wilmington, Del. Photographs were taken from an altitude of 34,000 feet; scale is about 4.5 miles per inch. The dominant checkerboard pattern is made by farms.

peated virtually everywhere in the underdeveloped world. It is not only Caracas that has thousands of squatters living in self-constructed junk houses on land that does not belong to them. By whatever name they are called, the squatters are to be found in all major cities in the poorer countries. They live in broad gullies beneath the main plain in San Salvador and on the hillsides of Rio de Janeiro and Bogotá. They tend to occupy with implacable determination parks, school grounds and vacant lots. Amman, the capital of Jordan, grew from 12,000 in 1958 to 247,000 in 1961. A good part of it is slums, and urban amenities are lacking most of the time for most of the people. Greater Baghdad now has an estimated 850,000 people; its slums, like those in many other underdeveloped countries, are in two zones—the central part of the city and the outlying areas. Here are the *sarifa* areas, characterized by self-built reed huts; these areas account for about 45 percent of the housing in the entire city and are devoid of amenities, including even latrines. In addition to such urban problems, all the countries struggling for higher living levels find their rural population growing too and piling up on already crowded land.

I have characterized urbanization as a transformation that, unlike economic development, is finally accomplished and comes to an end. At the 1950–1960 rate the term "urbanized world" will be applicable well before the end of the century. One should scarcely expect, however, that mankind will complete its urbanization without major complications. One sign of trouble ahead turns on the distinction I made at the start between urbanization and city growth per se. Around the globe today city growth is disproportionate to urbanization. The discrepancy is paradoxical in the industrial nations and worse than paradoxical in the nonindustrial.

It is in this respect that the nonindustrial nations, which still make up the great majority of nations, are far from repeating past history. In the 19th and early 20th centuries the growth of cities arose from and contributed to economic advancement. Cities took surplus manpower from the countryside and put it to work producing goods and services that in turn helped to modernize agriculture. But today in underdeveloped countries, as in present-day advanced nations, city growth has become increasingly unhinged from economic de-

velopment and hence from rural-urban migration. It derives in greater degree from overall population growth, and this growth in nonindustrial lands has become unprecedented because of modern health techniques combined with high birth rates.

The speed of world population growth is twice what it was before 1940, and the swiftest increase has shifted from the advanced to the backward nations. In the latter countries, consequently, it is virtually impossible to create city services fast enough to take care of the huge, never ending cohorts of babies and peasants swelling the urban masses. It is even harder to expand agricultural land and capital fast enough to accommodate the enormous natural increase on farms. The problem is not urbanization, not rural-urban migration, but human multiplication. It is a problem that is new in both its scale and its setting, and runaway city growth is only one of its painful expressions.

As long as the human population expands, cities will expand too, regardless of whether urbanization increases or declines. This means that some individual cities will reach a size that will make 19th-century metropolises look

MOSAIC COMPLETED begins (*left*) about 30 miles north of Baltimore, which is at right center below an arm of Chesapeake Bay. At right center on opposite page is Washington; the light spot three-quarters of an inch in from the right edge of the photograph, on a

like small towns. If the New York urbanized area should continue to grow only as fast as the nation's population (according to medium projections of the latter by the Bureau of the Census), it would reach 21 million by 1985 and 30 million by 2010. I have calculated that if India's population should grow as the UN projections indicate it will, the largest city in India in the year 2000 will have between 36 and 66 million inhabitants.

What is the implication of such giant agglomerations for human density? In 1950 the New York–Northeastern New Jersey urbanized area had an average density of 9,810 persons per square mile. With 30 million people in the year 2010, the density would be 24,000 per square mile. Although this level is exceeded now in parts of New York City (which averages about 25,000 per square mile) and many other cities, it is a high density to be spread over such a big area; it would cover, remember, the suburban areas to which people moved to escape high density. Actually, however, the density of the New York urbanized region is dropping, not increasing, as the population grows. The reason is that the territory covered by the urban agglomeration is growing faster than the population: it grew by 51 percent from 1950 to 1960, whereas the population rose by 15 percent.

If, then, one projects the rise in population and the rise in territory for the New York urbanized region, one finds the density problem solved. It is not solved for long, though, because New York is not the only city in the region that is expanding. So are Philadelphia, Trenton, Hartford, New Haven and so on. By 1960 a huge stretch of territory about 600 miles long and 30 to 100 miles wide along the Eastern seaboard contained some 37 million people. Since the whole area is becoming one big poly-nucleated city, its population cannot long expand without a rise in density. Thus persistent human multiplication promises to frustrate the ceaseless search for space —for ample residential lots, wide-open suburban school grounds, sprawling shopping centers, one-floor factories, broad freeways.

How people feel about giant agglomerations is best indicated by their headlong effort to escape them. The bigger the city, the higher the cost of space; yet, the more the level of living rises, the more people are willing to pay for low-density living. Nevertheless, as ur-banized areas expand and collide, it seems probable that life in low-density surroundings will become too dear for the great majority.

One can of course imagine that cities may cease to grow and may even shrink in size while the population in general continues to multiply. Even this dream, however, would not permanently solve the problem of space. It would eventually obliterate the distinction between urban and rural, but at the expense of the rural.

It seems plain that the only way to stop urban crowding and to solve most of the urban problems besetting both the developed and the underdeveloped nations is to reduce the overall rate of population growth. Policies designed to do this have as yet little intelligence and power behind them. Urban planners continue to treat population growth as something to be planned for, not something to be itself planned. Any talk about applying brakes to city growth is therefore purely speculative, overshadowed as it is by the reality of uncontrolled population increase.

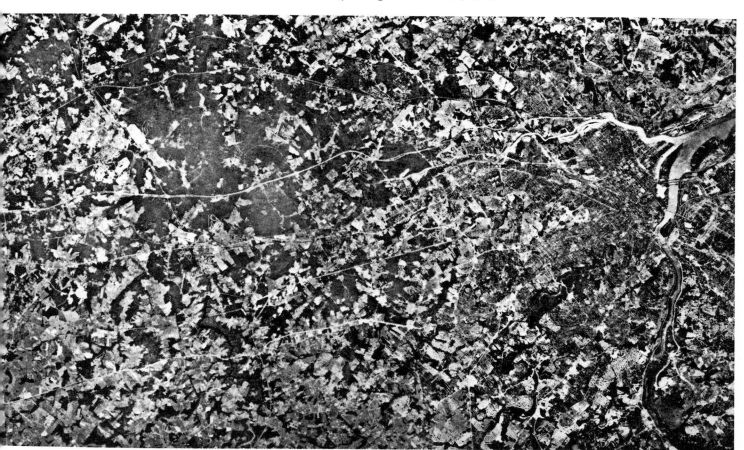

dark point of land adjoining the Potomac River, is the Tidal Basin, with the White House visible in dark spot an eighth of an inch to left of basin. Some 27 million people—more than 14 percent of the U.S. population—live in area between New York and Washington.

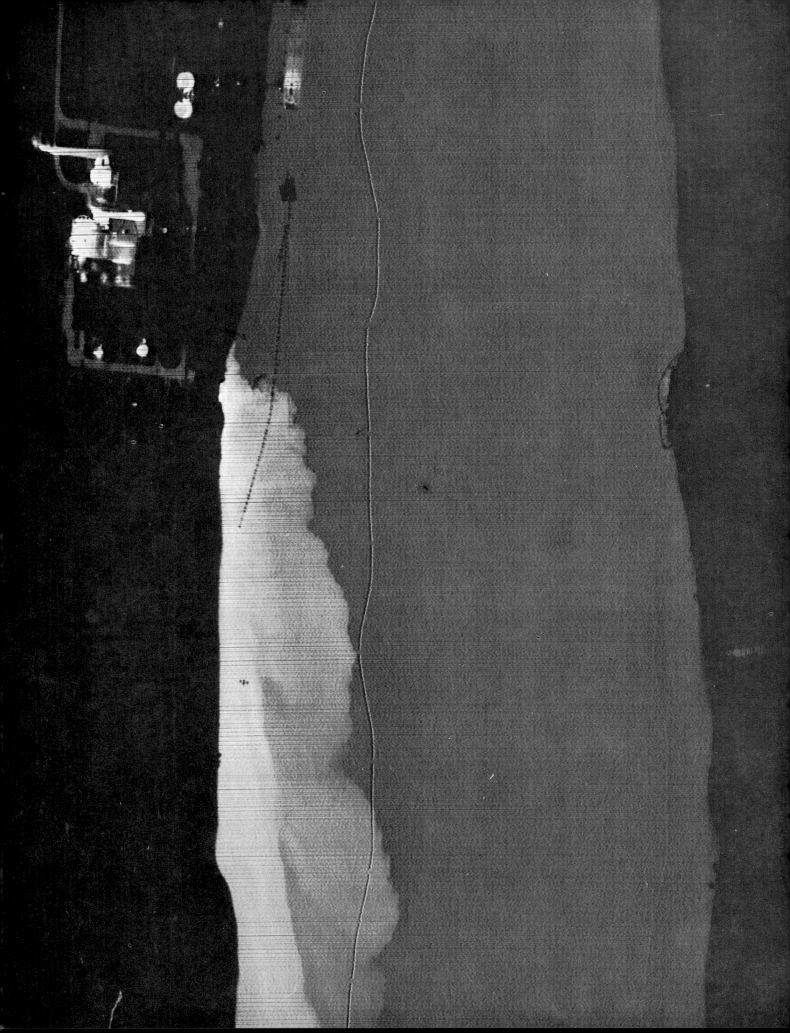

37

THE FLOW OF ENERGY IN AN INDUSTRIAL SOCIETY

EARL COOK

September 1971

*The U.S., with 6 percent of the world's population, uses
35 percent of the world's energy. In the long run the
limiting factor in high levels of energy consumption
will be the disposal of the waste heat*

This article will describe the flow of energy through an industrial society: the U.S. Industrial societies are based on the use of power: the rate at which useful work is done. Power depends on energy, which is the ability to do work. A power-rich society consumes—more accurately, degrades—energy in large amounts. The success of an industrial society, the growth of its economy, the quality of the life of its people and its impact on other societies and on the total environment are determined in large part by the quantities and the kinds of energy resources it exploits and by the efficiency of its systems for converting potential energy into work and heat.

Whether by hunting, by farming or by burning fuel, man introduces himself into the natural energy cycle, converting energy from less desired forms to more desired ones: from grass to beef, from wood to heat, from coal to electricity. What characterizes the industrial societies is their enormous consumption of energy and the fact that this consumption is primarily at the expense of "capital" rather than of "income," that is, at the expense of solar energy stored in coal, oil and natural gas rather than of solar radiation, water, wind and muscle power. The advanced industrial societies, the U.S. in particular, are further characterized by their increasing dependence on electricity, a trend that has direct effects on gross energy consumption and indirect effects on environmental quality.

The familiar exponential curve of increasing energy consumption can be considered in terms of various stages of human development [*see illustration on next page*]. As long as man's energy consumption depended on the food he could eat, the rate of consumption was some 2,000 kilocalories per day; the domestication of fire may have raised it to 4,000 kilocalories. In a primitive agricultural society with some domestic animals the rate rose to perhaps 12,000 kilocalories; more advanced farming societies may have doubled that consumption. At the height of the low-technology industrial revolution, say between 1850 and 1870, per capita daily consumption reached 70,000 kilocalories in England, Germany and the U.S. The succeeding high-technology revolution was brought about by the central electric-power station and the automobile, which enable the average person to apply power in his home and on the road. Beginning shortly before 1900, per capita energy consumption in the U.S. rose at an increasing rate to the 1970 figure: about 230,000 kilocalories per day, or about 65×10^{15} British thermal units (B.t.u.) per year for the country as a whole. Today the industrial regions, with 30 percent of the world's people, consume 80 percent of the world's energy. The U.S., with 6 percent of the people, consumes 35 percent of the energy.

In the early stages of its development in western Europe industrial society based its power technology on income sources of energy, but the explosive growth of the past century and a half has been fed by the fossil fuels, which are not renewable on any time scale meaningful to man. Modern industrial society is totally dependent on high rates of consumption of natural gas, petroleum and coal. These nonrenewable fossil-fuel resources currently provide 96 percent of the gross energy input into the U.S. economy [*see top illustration on page 389*]. Nuclear power, which in 1970 accounted for only .3 percent of the total energy input, is also (with present reactor technology) based on a capital source of energy: uranium 235. The energy of falling water, converted to hydropower, is the only income source of energy that now makes any significant contribution to the U.S. economy, and its proportional role seems to be declining from a peak reached in 1950.

Since 1945 coal's share of the U.S. energy input has declined sharply, while both natural gas and petroleum have increased their share. The shift is reflected in import figures. Net imports of petroleum and petroleum products doubled between 1960 and 1970 and now constitute almost 30 percent of gross consumption. In 1960 there were no imports of natural gas; last year natural-gas imports (by pipeline from Canada and as liquefied gas carried in cryogenic tankers) accounted for almost 4 percent of gross consumption and were increasing.

The reasons for the shift to oil and gas are not hard to find. The conversion of railroads to diesel engines represented a large substitution of petroleum for coal. The rapid growth, beginning during World War II, of the national

HEAT DISCHARGE from a power plant on the Connecticut River at Middletown, Conn., is shown in this infrared scanning radiograph. The power plant is at upper left, its structures outlined by their heat radiation. The luminous cloud running along the left bank of the river is warm water discharged from the cooling system of the plant. The vertical oblong object at top left center is an oil tanker. The luminous spot astern is the infrared glow of its engine room. The dark streak between the tanker and the warm-water region is a breakwater. The irregular line running down the middle of the picture is an artifact of the infrared scanning system. The picture was made by HRB-Singer, Inc., for U.S. Geological Survey.

network of high-pressure gas-transmission lines greatly extended the availability of natural gas. The explosion of the U.S. automobile population, which grew twice as fast as the human population in the decade 1960–1970, and the expansion of the nation's fleet of jet aircraft account for much of the increase in petroleum consumption. In recent years the demand for cleaner air has led to the substitution of natural gas or low-sulfur residual fuel oil for high-sulfur coal in many central power plants.

An examination of energy inputs by sector of the U.S. economy rather than by source reveals that much of the recent increase has been going into household, commercial and transportation applications rather than industrial ones [see bottom illustration on opposite page]. What is most striking is the growth of the electricity sector. In 1970 almost 10 percent of the country's useful work was done by electricity. That is not the whole story. When the flow of energy from resources to end uses is

charted for 1970 [see illustration on pages 390 and 391], it is seen that producing that much electricity accounted for 26 percent of the gross consumption of energy, because of inefficiencies in generation and transmission. If electricity's portion of end-use consumption rises to about 25 percent by the year 2000, as is expected, then its generation will account for between 43 and 53 percent of the country's gross energy consumption. At that point an amount of energy equal to about half of the useful work done in the U.S. will be in the form of waste heat from power stations!

All energy conversions are more or less inefficient, of course, as the flow diagram makes clear. In the case of electricity there are losses at the power plant, in transmission and at the point of application of power; in the case of fuels consumed in end uses the loss comes at the point of use. The 1970 U.S. gross consumption of 64.6×10^{15} B.t.u. of energy (or 16.3×10^{15} kilocalories, or 19×10^{12} kilowatt-hours) ends up as

32.8×10^{15} B.t.u. of useful work and 31.8×10^{15} B.t.u. of waste heat, amounting to an overall efficiency of about 51 percent.

The flow diagram shows the pathways of the energy that drives machines, provides heat for manufacturing processes and heats, cools and lights the country. It does not represent the total energy budget because it includes neither food nor vegetable fiber, both of which bring solar energy into the economy through photosynthesis. Nor does it include environmental space heating by solar radiation, which makes life on the earth possible and would be by far the largest component of a total energy budget for any area and any society.

The minute fraction of the solar flux that is trapped and stored in plants provides each American with some 10,000 kilocalories per day of gross food production and about the same amount in the form of nonfood vegetable fiber. The fiber currently contributes little to the energy supply. The food, however, fu-

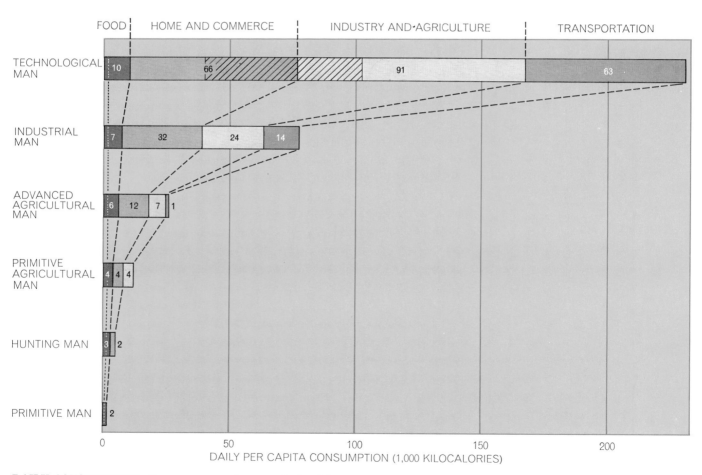

DAILY CONSUMPTION of energy per capita was calculated by the author for six stages in human development (and with an accuracy that decreases with antiquity). Primitive man (East Africa about 1,000,000 years ago) without the use of fire had only the energy of the food he ate. Hunting man (Europe about 100,000 years ago) had more food and also burned wood for heat and cooking. Primitive agricultural man (Fertile Crescent in 5000 B.C.) was grow-

ing crops and had gained animal energy. Advanced agricultural man (northwestern Europe in A.D. 1400) had some coal for heating, some water power and wind power and animal transport. Industrial man (in England in 1875) had the steam engine. In 1970 technological man (in the U.S.) consumed 230,000 kilocalories per day, much of it in form of electricity (hatched area). Food is divided into plant foods (far left) and animal foods (or foods fed to animals).

els man. Gross food-plant consumption might therefore be considered another component of gross energy consumption; it would add about 3×10^{15} B.t.u. to the input side of the energy-flow scheme. Of the 10,000 kilocalories per capita per day of gross production, handling and processing waste 15 percent. Of the remaining 8,500 kilocalories, some 6,300 go to feed animals that produce about 900 kilocalories of meat and 2,200 go into the human diet as plant materials, for a final food supply of about 3,100 kilocalories per person. Thus from field to table the efficiency of the food-energy system is 31 percent, close to the efficiency of a central power station. The similarity is not fortuitous; in both systems there is a large and unavoidable loss in the conversion of energy from a less desired form to a more desired one.

Let us consider recent changes in U.S. energy flow in more detail by seeing how the rates of increase in various sectors compare. Not only has energy consumption for electric-power generation been growing faster than the other sectors but also its growth rate has been increasing: from 7 percent per year in 1961–1965 to 8.6 percent per year in 1965–1969 to 9.25 percent last year [see top illustration on page 392]. The energy consumed in industry and commerce and in homes has increased at a fairly steady rate for a decade, but the energy demand of transportation has risen more sharply since 1966. All in all, energy consumption has been increasing lately at a rate of 5 percent per year, or four times faster than the increase in the U.S. population. Meanwhile the growth of the gross national product has tended to fall off, paralleling the rise in energy sectors other than fast-growing transportation and electricity. The result is a change in the ratio of total energy consumption to G.N.P. [see bottom illustration on page 392]. The ratio had been in a long general decline since 1920 (with brief reversals) but since 1967 it has risen more steeply each year. In 1970 the U.S. consumed more energy for each dollar of goods and services than at any time since 1951.

Electricity accounts for much of this decrease in economic efficiency, for several reasons. For one thing, we are substituting electricity, with a thermal efficiency of perhaps 32 percent, for many direct fuel uses with efficiencies ranging from 60 to 90 percent. Moreover, the fastest-growing segment of end-use consumption has been electric air conditioning. From 1967 to 1970 consumption for

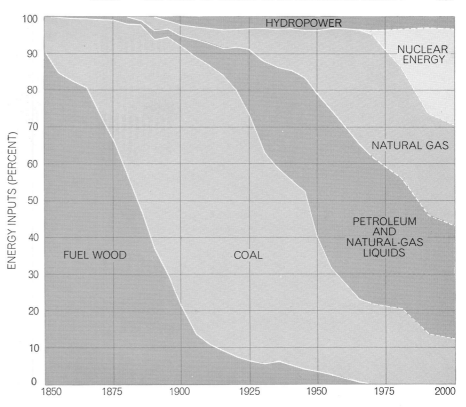

FOSSIL FUELS now account for nearly all the energy input into the U.S. economy. Coal's contribution has decreased since World War II; that of natural gas has increased most in that period. Nuclear energy should contribute a substantial percent within the next 20 years.

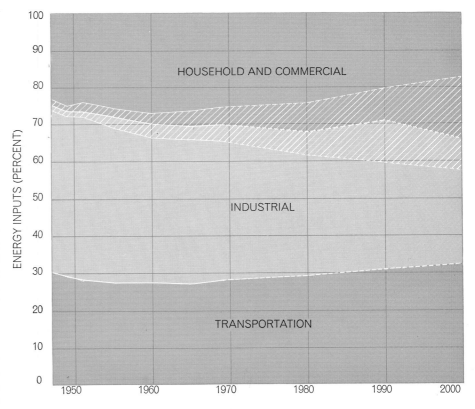

USEFUL WORK is distributed among the various end-use sectors of the U.S. economy as shown. The trend has been for industry's share to decrease, with household and commercial uses (including air conditioning) and transportation growing. Electricity accounts for an ever larger share of the work (hatched area). U.S. Bureau of Mines figures in this chart include nonenergy uses of fossil fuels, which constitute about 7 percent of total energy inputs.

air conditioning grew at the remarkable rate of 20 percent per year; it accounted for almost 16 percent of the total increase in electric-power generation from 1969 to 1970, with little or no multiplier effect on the G.N.P.

Let us take a look at this matter of efficiency in still another way: in terms of useful work done as a percentage of gross energy input. The "useful-work equivalent," or overall technical efficiency, is seen to be the product of the con-version efficiency (if there is an intermediate conversion step) and the application efficiency of the machine or device that does the work [*see bottom illustration on page 393*]. Clearly there is a wide range of technical efficiencies in energy systems, depending on the conversion devices. It is often said that electrical resistance heating is 100 percent efficient, and indeed it is in terms, say, of converting electrical energy to thermal energy at the domestic hot-water heater. In terms of the energy content of the natural gas or coal that fired the boiler that made the steam that drove the turbine that turned the generator that produced the electricity that heated the wires that warmed the water, however, it is not so efficient.

The technical efficiency of the total U.S. energy system, from potential energy at points of initial conversion to work at points of application, is about 50 percent. The economic efficiency of

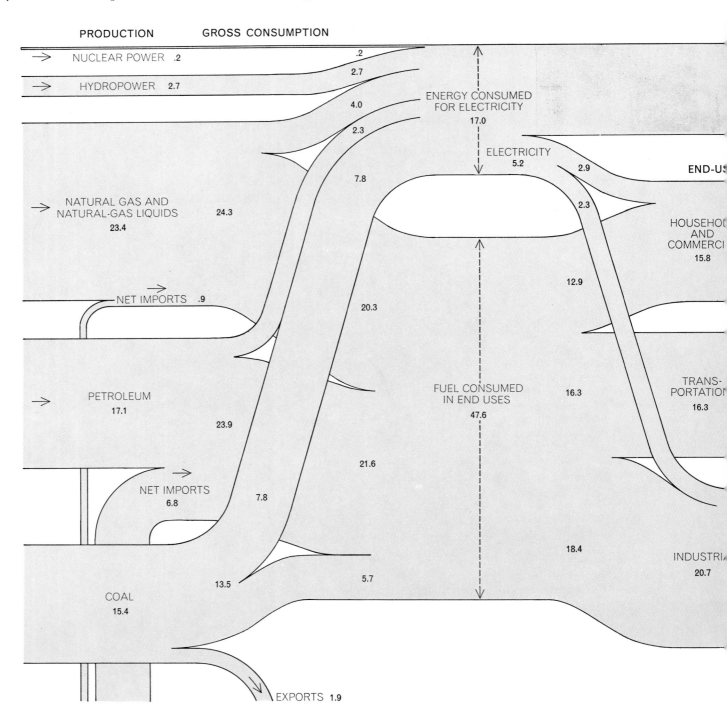

FLOW OF ENERGY through the U.S. system in 1970 is traced from production of energy commodities (*left*) to the ultimate conversion of energy into work for various industrial end products and waste heat (*right*). Total consumption of energy in 1970 was 64.6 × 10¹⁵ British thermal units. (Adding nonenergy uses of fossil fuels, primarily for petrochemicals, would raise the total to 68.8 × 10¹⁵ B.t.u.) The overall efficiency of the system was about 51 percent. Some of the fossil-fuel energy is consumed directly and

the system is considerably less. That is because work is expended in extracting, refining and transporting fuels, in the construction and operation of conversion facilities, power equipment and electricity-distribution networks, and in handling waste products and protecting the environment.

An industrial society requires not only a large supply of energy but also a high use of energy per capita, and the

society's economy and standard of living are shaped by interrelations among resources, population, the efficiency of conversion processes and the particular applications of power. The effect of these interrelations is illustrated by a comparison of per capita energy consumption and per capita output for a number of countries [see illustration on page 394]. As one might expect, there is a strong general correlation between the two measures, but it is far from be-

ing a one-to-one correlation. Some countries (the U.S.S.R. and the Republic of South Africa, for example) have a high energy consumption with respect to G.N.P.; other countries (such as Sweden and New Zealand) have a high output with relatively less energy consumption. Such differences reflect contrasting combinations of energy-intensive heavy industry and light consumer-oriented and service industries (characteristic of different stages of economic development) as well as differences in the efficiency of energy use. For example, countries that still rely on coal for a large part of their energy requirement have higher energy inputs per unit of production than those that use mainly petroleum and natural gas.

A look at trends from the U.S. past is also instructive. Between 1800 and 1880 total energy consumption in the U.S. lagged behind the population increase, which means that per capita energy consumption actually declined somewhat. On the other hand, the American standard of living increased during this period because the energy supply in 1880 (largely in the form of coal) was being used much more efficiently than the energy supply in 1800 (largely in the form of wood). From 1900 to 1920 there was a tremendous surge in the use of energy by Americans but not a parallel increase in the standard of living. The ratio of energy consumption to G.N.P. increased 50 percent during these two decades because electric power, inherently less efficient, began being substituted for the direct use of fuels; because the automobile, at best 25 percent efficient, proliferated (from 8,000 in 1900 to 8,132,000 in 1920), and because mining and manufacturing, which are energy-intensive, grew at very high rates during this period.

Then there began a long period during which increases in the efficiency of energy conversion and utilization fulfilled about two-thirds of the total increase in demand, so that the ratio of energy consumption to G.N.P. fell to about 60 percent of its 1920 peak although per capita energy consumption continued to increase. During this period (1920–1965) the efficiency of electric-power generation and transmission almost trebled, mining and manufacturing grew at much lower rates and the services sector of the economy, which is not energy-intensive, increased in importance.

"Power corrupts" was written of man's control over other men but it applies also to his control of energy re-

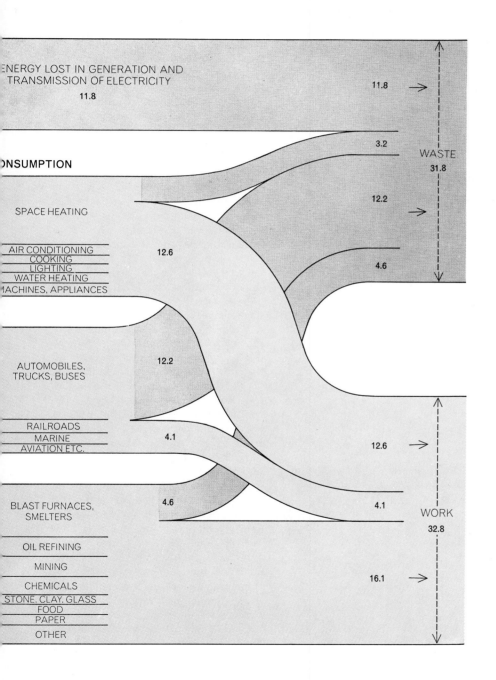

some is converted to generate electricity. The efficiency of electrical generation and transmission is taken to be about 31 percent, based on the ratio of utility electricity purchased in 1970 to the gross energy input for generation in that year. Efficiency of direct fuel use in transportation is taken as 25 percent, of fuel use in other applications as 75 percent.

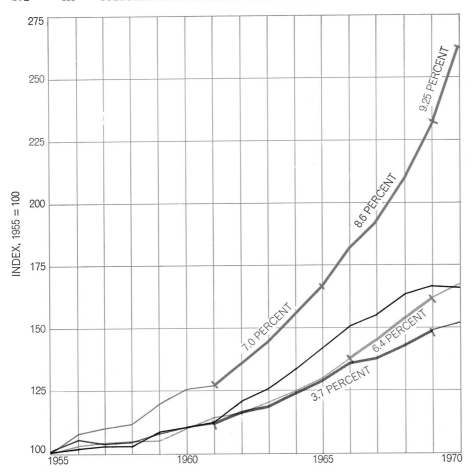

INCREASE IN CONSUMPTION of energy for electricity generation (*dark color*), transportation (*light color*) and other applications (*gray*) and of the gross national product (*black*) are compared. Annual growth rates for certain periods are shown beside heavy segments of curves. Consumption of electricity has a high growth rate and is increasing.

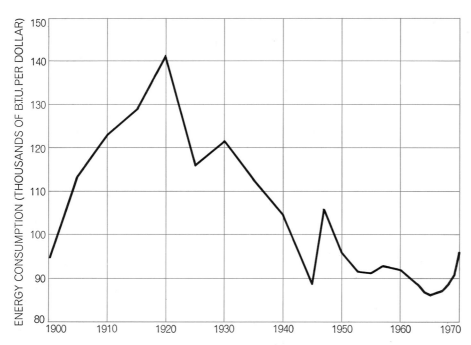

RATIO OF ENERGY CONSUMPTION to gross national product has varied over the years. It tends to be low when the G.N.P. is large and energy is being used efficiently, as was the case during World War II. The ratio has been rising steadily since 1965. Reasons include the increase in the use of air conditioning and the lack of advance in generating efficiency.

sources. The more power an industrial society disposes of, the more it wants. The more power we use, the more we shape our cities and mold our economic and social institutions to be dependent on the application of power and the consumption of energy. We could not now make any major move toward a lower per capita energy consumption without severe economic dislocation, and certainly the struggle of people in less developed regions toward somewhat similar energy-consumption levels cannot be thwarted without prolonging mass human suffering. Yet there is going to have to be some leveling off in the energy demands of industrial societies. Countries such as the U.S. have already come up against constraints dictated by the availability of resources and by damage to the environment. Another article in this issue considers the question of resource availability [see "The Energy Resources of the Earth," by M. King Hubbert; SCIENTIFIC AMERICAN Offprint 663]. Here I shall simply point out some of the decisions the U.S. faces in coping with diminishing supplies, and specifically with our increasing reliance on foreign sources of petroleum and petroleum products. In the short run the advantages of reasonable self-sufficiency must be weighed against the economic and environmental costs of developing oil reserves in Alaska and off the coast of California and the Gulf states. Later on such self-sufficiency may be attainable only through the production of oil from oil shale and from coal. In the long run the danger of dependence on dwindling fossil fuels—whatever they may be—must be balanced against the research and development costs of a major effort to shape a new energy system that is neither dependent on limited resources nor hard on the environment.

The environmental constraint may be more insistent than the constraint of resource availability. The present flow of energy through U.S. society leaves waste rock and acid water at coal mines; spilled oil from offshore wells and tankers; waste gases and particles from power plants, furnaces and automobiles; radioactive wastes of various kinds from nuclear-fuel processing plants and reactors. All along the line waste heat is developed, particularly at the power plants.

Yet for at least the next 50 years we shall be making use of dirty fuels: coal and petroleum. We can improve coal-combustion technology, we can build power plants at the mine mouth (so that the air of Appalachia is polluted instead of the air of New York City), we can make clean oil and gas from coal and oil

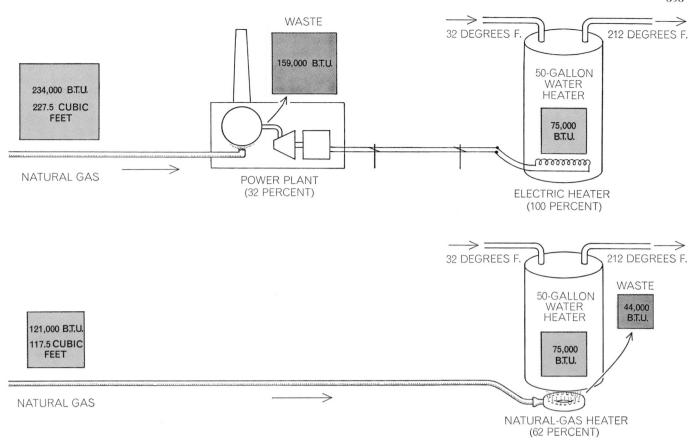

EFFICIENCIES OF HEATING WATER with natural gas indirectly by generating electricity for use in resistance heating (*top*) and directly (*bottom*) are contrasted. In each case the end result is enough heat to warm 50 gallons of water from 32 degrees Fahrenheit to 212 degrees. Electrical method requires substantially more gas even though efficiency at electric heater is nearly 100 percent.

from shale, and sow grass on the mountains of waste. As nuclear power plants proliferate we can put them underground, or far from the cities they serve if we are willing to pay the cost in transmission losses. With adequate foresight, caution and research we may even be able to handle the radioactive-waste problem without "undue" risk.

There are, however, definite limits to such improvements. The automobile engine and its present fuel simply cannot be cleaned up sufficiently to make it an acceptable urban citizen. It seems clear that the internal-combustion engine will be banned from the central city by the year 2000; it should probably be banned right now. Because our cities are shaped for automobiles, not for mass transit, we shall have to develop battery-powered or flywheel-powered cars and taxis for inner-city transport. The 1970 census for the first time showed more metropolitan citizens living in suburbs than in the central city; it also showed a record high in automobiles per capita, with the greatest concentration in the suburbs. It seems reasonable to visualize the suburban two-car garage of the future with one car a recharger for "downtown" and

	PRIMARY ENERGY INPUT (UNITS)	SECONDARY ENERGY OUTPUT (UNITS)	APPLICATION EFFICIENCY (PERCENT)	TECHNICAL EFFICIENCY (PERCENT)
AUTOMOBILE				
INTERNAL-COMBUSTION ENGINE	100		25	25
FLYWHEEL DRIVE CHARGED BY ELECTRICITY	100	32	100	32
SPACE HEATING				
BY DIRECT FUEL USE	100		75	75
BY ELECTRICAL RESISTANCE	100	32	100	32
SMELTING OF STEEL				
WITH COKE	100	94	94	70
WITH ELECTRICITY	100	32	32	32

TECHNICAL EFFICIENCY is the product of conversion efficiency at an intermediate step (if there is one) and application efficiency at the device that does the work. Losses due to friction and heat are ignored in the flywheel-drive automobile data. Coke retains only about 66 percent of the energy of coal, but the energy recovered from the by-products raises the energy conservation to 94 percent.

the other, still gasoline-powered, for suburban and cross-country driving.

Of course, some of the improvement in urban air quality bought by excluding the internal-combustion engine must be paid for by increased pollution from the power plant that supplies the electricity for the nightly recharging of the downtown vehicles. It need not, however, be paid for by an increased draft on the primary energy source; this is one substitution in which electricity need not decrease the technical efficiency of the system. The introduction of heat pumps for space heating and cooling would be

another. In fact, the overall efficiency should be somewhat improved and the environmental impact, given adequate attention to the siting, design and operation of the substituting power plant, should be greatly alleviated.

If technology can extend resource availability and keep environmental deterioration within acceptable limits in most respects, the specific environmental problem of waste heat may become the overriding one of the energy system by the turn of the century.

The cooling water required by power

plants already constitutes 10 percent of the total U.S. streamflow. The figure will increase sharply as more nuclear plants start up, since present designs of nuclear plants require 50 percent more cooling water than fossil-fueled plants of equal size do. The water is heated 15 degrees Fahrenheit or more as it flows through the plant. For ecological reasons such an increase in water released to a river, lake or ocean bay is unacceptable, at least for large quantities of effluent, and most large plants are now being built with cooling ponds or towers from which much of the heat of the water is dissi-

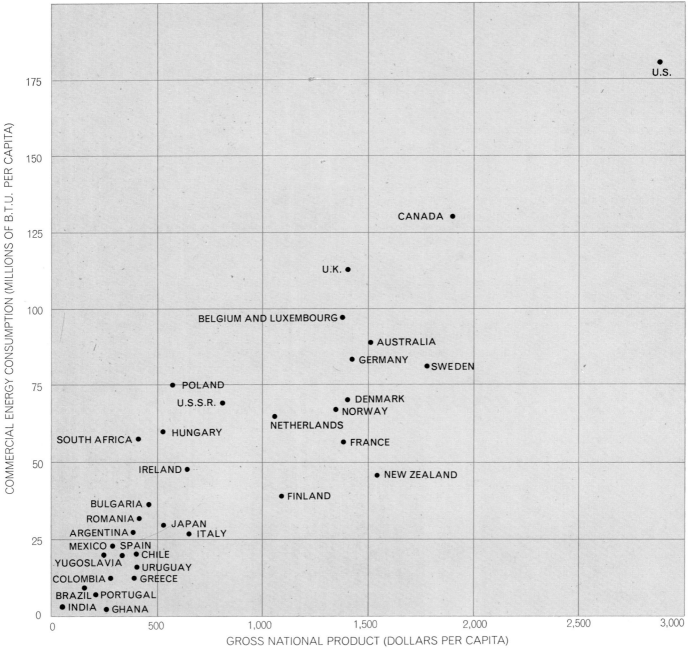

ROUGH CORRELATION between per capita consumption of energy and gross national product is seen when the two are plotted together; in general, high per capita energy consumption is a prerequisite for high output of goods and services. If the position plotted for the U.S. is considered to establish an arbitrary "line," some countries fall above or below that line. This appears to be related to a country's economic level, its emphasis on heavy industry or on services and its efficiency in converting energy into work.

pated to the atmosphere before the water is discharged or recycled through the plant. Although the atmosphere is a more capacious sink for waste heat than any body of water, even this disposal mechanism obviously has its environmental limits.

Many suggestions have been made for putting the waste heat from power plants to work: for irrigation or aquaculture, to provide ice-free shipping lanes or for space heating. (The waste heat from power generation today would be more than enough to heat every home in the U.S.!) Unfortunately the quantities of water involved, the relatively low temperature of the coolant water and the distances between power plants and areas of potential use are serious deterrents to the utilization of waste heat. Plants can be designed, however, for both power production and space heating. Such a plant has been in operation in Berlin for a number of years and has proved to be more efficient than a combination of separate systems for power production and space heating. The Berlin plant is not simply a conserver of waste heat but an exercise in fuel economy; its power capacity was reduced in order to raise the temperature of the heated water above that of normal cooling water.

With present and foreseeable technology there is not much hope of decreasing the amount of heat rejected to streams or the atmosphere (or both) from central steam-generating power plants. Two systems of producing power without steam generation offer some long-range hope of alleviating the waste-heat problem. One is the fuel cell; the other is the fusion reactor combined with a system for converting the energy released directly into electricity [see "The Con-

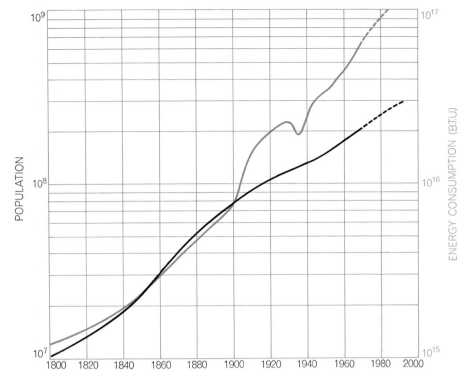

U.S. ENERGY-CONSUMPTION GROWTH (*curve in color*) has outpaced the growth in population (*black*) since 1900, except during the energy cutback of the depression years.

version of Energy," by Claude M. Summers; SCIENTIFIC AMERICAN Offprint 668]. In the fuel cell the energy contained in hydrocarbons or hydrogen is released by a controlled oxidation process that produces electricity directly with an efficiency of about 60 percent. A practical fusion reactor with a direct-conversion system is not likely to appear in this century.

Major changes in power technology will be required to reduce pollution and manage wastes, to improve the efficiency of the system and to remove the resource-availability constraint. Making

the changes will call for hard political decisions. Energy needs will have to be weighed against environmental and social costs; a decision to set a pollution standard or to ban the internal-combustion engine or to finance nuclear-power development can have major economic and political effects. Democratic societies are not noted for their ability to take the long view in making decisions. Yet indefinite growth in energy consumption, as in human population, is simply not possible.

38

THE DIMENSIONS OF WORLD POVERTY

DAVID SIMPSON
November 1968

Two-thirds of the people in the world live in countries whose annual income per capita is less than $300. The pressing problem is hunger, and under present plans it will remain critical for at least 20 years

The economic gulf that has divided the poorer countries of the world from the richer countries is rapidly widening. Whereas the affluent nations continue to become richer, the impoverished nations continue to increase in population without raising their food production fast enough to reach a state of self-sustaining growth. Even though there have been recent gains in their agricultural production, and even if one makes the most optimistic assumptions about the programs instituted to limit the growth of populations, the prospect remains bleak. It is highly probable that for at least the next 20 years most of the people in the world will continue to exist at the margin of subsistence.

Where is poverty the most serious? How many people are critically deprived of food and the other necessities of life? In this review of the available evidence concerning world poverty I shall attempt to answer these questions, concluding with some proposals as to what can be done about the groups that are critically underfed.

There is no single statistical indicator by which one can distinguish people who are seriously deprived from those who are merely poor. One can make only rough estimates based on a number of indicators, all of them crude. The justification for using such necessarily uncertain statistics is that, in Gunnar Myrdal's words, "it is better to paint with a wide brush of unknown thickness than to leave the canvas blank."

The measure of a country's material progress that has been most widely adopted is per capita national income, which is to say the net value of goods and services produced by a nation within one year per head of population. As a comparative measure of the standard of living or of the degree of well-being, it nonetheless has at least three weaknesses. The first is the difficulty of measurement: A comparison between the national incomes of two countries essentially involves valuing two bundles of goods. Inasmuch as similar goods have different prices depending on the country, two answers are possible according to which set of prices is used in the valuation. The second weakness is more fundamental: The satisfactions that people in different societies gain from similar goods are not comparable. It is argued that even if a Burmese peasant and an American housewife consumed similar goods at the same prices, and the American consumed 40 times as much as the Burmese, it would not follow that the American was 40 times better off. Finally, per capita income is an average measure; it cannot reflect the distribution of income within a country.

In spite of these shortcomings per capita income can be defended as an indicator of the level of output of goods and services within a country, and indeed it is widely used as such. Even when the estimate of income can only be crude, it nevertheless reveals differences in the order of magnitude of the incomes of the rich and the poor regions of the world. Thus on the basis of figures for 1965 (or the most recent year available) the average per capita income of the poorest region of Latin America is more than twice that of the poorer regions of Asia and Africa. The countries of Europe have average incomes that are 10 times greater than those of the poorer regions of Asia and Africa; in Oceania national incomes are larger by a factor of 14 and in North America they are larger by a factor of 28. It should be mentioned, however, that the way these estimates are prepared tends to overstate the differences between the richest and the poorest regions of the world.

It is clear that within continents there is considerable variation between regions and countries. South Asia and Indonesia have much lower incomes than East Asia or West Asia. The average income of the North African region is more than twice that of eastern and southern Africa. On both continents there are rich countries such as Japan, Singapore, Israel, Cyprus, Libya and the Republic of South Africa, whose average incomes approach European levels or even surpass them.

If we regard per capita income as a first approximation to the identification of the poorest regions of the world, it indicates that these regions include eastern, northeastern, southern, western and central Africa together with South and Southeast Asia and Indonesia. This impression is confirmed when one ranks the countries of the world whose average incomes are less than $300 per head according to relative wealth, dividing them into four classes.

First of all are countries with the lowest average incomes, namely a range from $30 to $79 per head. Of the 22 countries, 17 are African and account for more than half of the continent's population, or about 167 million people. In this class there are only five Asian countries: Afghanistan, Burma, Laos, Nepal and Yemen, with a population totaling less than 60 million.

The next income class ($80 to $99) is important because it includes India, Indonesia and Pakistan, the three major

countries of South Asia, whose population amounts to almost 700 million.

In the third class ($100 to $199) fall China, most of the Arab countries and four countries of Latin America (Bolivia, Ecuador, Honduras and Paraguay). The estimate of the per capita income of China is extremely uncertain, but I feel reasonably confident in placing China within this range.

The fourth and relatively highest income range ($200 to $299) includes Iran, Turkey, the Philippines and Brazil but only two African countries, Ghana and Rhodesia. The countries in this range could be described as being on the threshold of economic development: all the countries in the range below them

($100 to $199) are clearly not developed, whereas Cuba, Costa Rica, Portugal and Yugoslavia, whose incomes fall in the range above them ($300 to $399), clearly are.

It would be unwise to propose any single value of per capita income above which a country can be judged to have passed out of the stage of economic backwardness or underdevelopment, both because of the uncertainty of the estimates and the variation in circumstances among countries. If a line must nevertheless be drawn for practical purposes, then $300 would appear to be a reasonable level at which to draw it. Whereas there are many countries clustered below $300, there are relatively few spread

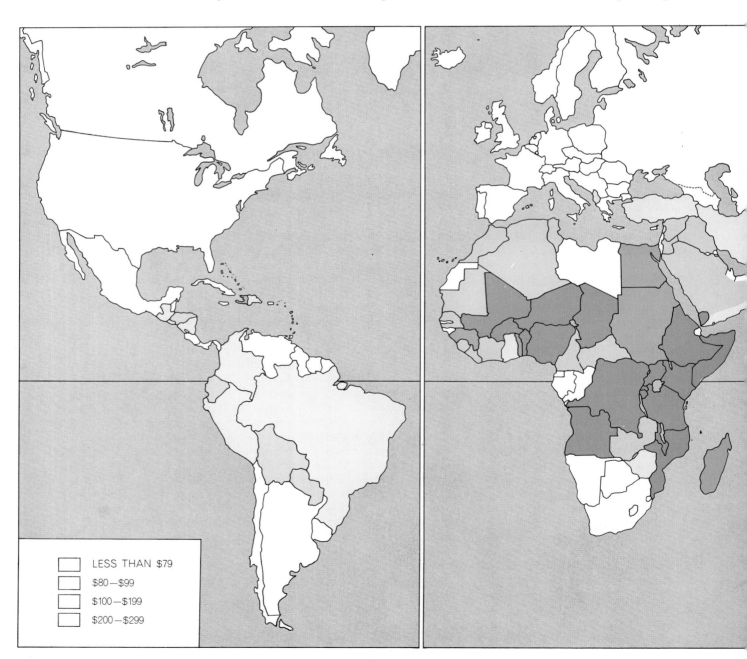

IMPOVERISHED COUNTRIES are grouped according to their average per capita income for 1965 (or the most recent year available). Estimates have not been made for some of the smaller countries. The income and population of the larger countries

over the wide range of incomes between $300 and $700. About 2.1 billion people, or 64 percent of the world's population, live in countries whose average income is less than $300, and almost 1.9 billion of these people live in countries whose average income falls below $200. A world poverty line at $300 is of course far below the level at which the poverty line would be drawn in the richer regions of the world. Taking four people as the average number in an American family, the simple U.S. poverty line works out at $750 per head.

An interesting characteristic of the countries with incomes less than $300, which we shall now call the low-income countries, is that their distribution in

terms of population is extremely skewed. About 67 percent of the people in this group live in only four countries: China, India, Indonesia and Pakistan. At the other end of the scale, 50 small countries of Africa, Asia and Latin America account for less than .6 percent of the people in the group. These facts alone suggest that there are no simple universal prescriptions for economic development.

As an index of the economic progress of the low-income countries, the level of per capita income is of course less important than the rate of its growth. Estimates of the annual growth rates of per capita income are available for only a few of these countries. Statisticians at

the United Nations have, however, estimated the average growth rate of per capita income (at constant prices) of developing, or poorer, countries as a group. During the 1950's their growth rate was 2.3 percent, and it dropped slightly to 2.2 percent during the period from 1960 to 1964. The corresponding figures for the developed countries were 2.7 percent and 3.7 percent, thus the widening gap between rich and poor. Naturally these averages conceal a wide variety of experience in different countries. Per capita income actually dropped in Morocco, Haiti and Syria in the 1950's and in Guyana and Uruguay from 1960 to 1965. On the other hand, the annual rate of growth of per capita income was 4.3 percent in Burma in the 1950's and 3.5 percent in Iran between 1960 and 1965. Over the same two periods the incomes of India and Nigeria grew modestly but steadily, whereas Pakistan moved from an annual growth rate of .6 percent in the 1950's to a rate of 3.2 percent in the 1960's.

It should be remembered that a growing per capita income is quite compatible with a simultaneous increase in the absolute number of people in the country who are subsisting at the lowest income level. The statistics used in the calculation of the level and rate of growth of income are national averages. For an appreciation of the extent of poverty within a country a knowledge of the distribution of income is essential. Unfortunately the available statistics of income distribution in the low-income countries are seriously limited in both quantity and quality. The most thorough analyst of these data, Simon Kuznets of Harvard University, draws the conclusion that the upper-income groups in the countries below the $300 line receive a larger share of total income than their counterparts in the rich countries do; below the top-income groups there is a greater equality in the distribution.

If we interpret poverty to mean sustained deprivation, then per capita income is not necessarily the best measure, and it is certainly not the only measure, of such poverty. It is possible, for example, to envision a society that has a very low per capita income as a result of a low level of material production but at the same time is not seriously deprived of the basic necessities of life: food, shelter, clothing and reasonable conditions of health. What precisely constitutes sustained deprivation or serious poverty is a matter that could be discussed at length. Fortunately such a discussion is unnecessary, because the number of statistical indicators that are relevant to any rea-

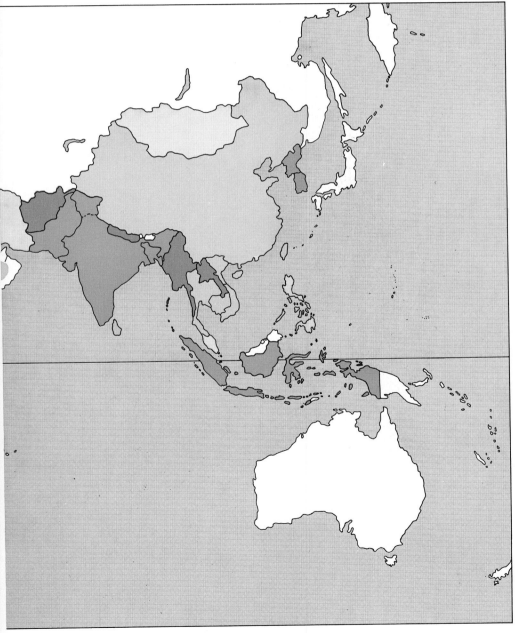

are listed on the next two pages. The data used here and in subsequent illustrations in this article are based on statistics of United Nations agencies and estimates of the author.

sonable definition of serious poverty and also are actually available is quite limited. It is therefore simpler to consider these indicators in turn and to allow the impression of poverty to be formed by them.

As far as the lack of shelter is concerned, the available quantitative evidence does not allow us to draw any conclusions that are relevant to our purpose. We know the average number of inhabitants per room for some segments of the population, but we do not know the number of inhabitants per square foot. A country with a high proportion of dwellings without electricity or without a piped-in water supply can be considered poor, but this does not necessarily represent serious hardship. Dwellings are not easily comparable from country to country, and needs vary. Similar considerations apply to the availability of clothing as a measure of poverty.

In the cities of the poorer countries there is of course dramatic and visible evidence of the qualitative inadequacy of housing. The population of such cities as Nairobi, Calcutta, Caracas, Bogotá and São Paulo is growing faster than the rate at which even rudimentary housing facilities can be provided. A recent account of housing conditions in Calcutta illustrates the magnitude of the problem there. The 1966 development plan of the Calcutta Metropolitan Planning Organisation states that adequate housing is "not within the bounds of feasible achievement over a 25-year period." The

COUNTRY	INCOME PER CAPITA (U.S. DOLLARS)	POPULATION (MILLIONS)
LAOS	59	2.6
LEBANON	204	2.4
LIBERIA	148	1.0
LIBYA	636	1.6
MADAGASCAR	83	6.4
MALAWI	38	3.9
MALAYA	257	8.0
MALI	57	4.6
MAURITANIA	106	1.1
MEXICO	412	42.7
MONGOLIA	250	1.1
MOROCCO	174	13.3
MOZAMBIQUE	40	7.0
NEPAL	66	10.1
NETHERLANDS	1,265	12.3
NEW ZEALAND	1,706	2.6
NICARAGUA	298	1.7
NIGER	78	3.3
NIGERIA	63	57.5
NORWAY	1,453	3.7
PAKISTAN	89	102.9
PANAMA	425	1.2
PARAGUAY	186	2.0
PERU	218	11.7
PHILIPPINES	219	32.3
POLAND	904	31.5
PORTUGAL	351	9.2
PUERTO RICO	959	2.6
RHODESIA	206	4.3
ROMANIA	691	19.0

COUNTRY	INCOME PER CAPITA (U.S. DOLLARS)	POPULATION (MILLIONS)
AFGHANISTAN	47	15.7
ALBANIA	239	1.9
ALGERIA	195	11.9
ANGOLA	56	5.2
ARGENTINA	740	22.4
AUSTRALIA	1,620	11.4
AUSTRIA	970	7.3
BELGIUM	1,406	9.5
BOLIVIA	144	3.7
BRAZIL	217	82.2
BRUNEI	1,395	.1
BULGARIA	691	8.2
BURMA	56	24.7
BURUNDI	38	3.2
CAMBODIA	112	6.1
CAMEROON	104	5.2
CANADA	1,825	19.6
CENTRAL AFRICAN REPUBLIC	123	1.4
CEYLON	130	11.2
CHAD	60	3.3
CHILE	515	8.6
CHINA	147	700.0
COLOMBIA	237	18.1
CONGO (KINSHASA)	66	15.6
COSTA RICA	353	1.4
CUBA	319	7.6
CYPRUS	623	0.6
CZECHOSLOVAKIA	1,482	14.2
DAHOMEY	55	2.4

WEALTH OF NATIONS is expressed in annual income per head of population. The impoverished countries, those with per capita income less than $300 (*color*), are seen to be predominant. Countries with a population under one million are omitted from this dimensions of the problem are so enormous that the plan does not anticipate the provision of houses but rather the construction of open-sided sheds to serve as shelters. One estimate suggests that 77 percent of the families in Calcutta at present have less than 40 square feet (an area a little more than six feet square) of living space per person. Nevertheless, the problem of housing in the cities may be not so much a problem of shelter as a problem of sanitation, and therefore of disease. In cities such as Calcutta the lack of housing means that the spread of disease in the slum areas is literally uncontrollable.

The problem of disease in the poorer countries is inextricably linked to other social conditions: lack of sanitation, lack of food and lack of medical facilities. It would therefore seem that the incidence of particular diseases would be a useful indicator of levels of poverty. Although diseases such as hookworm, trachoma and malaria, respiratory diseases (tuberculosis, whooping cough), intestinal diseases (typhoid, dysentery, gastroenteritis) and deficiencies arising from malnutrition (kwashiorkor, anemia, goiter, beriberi, rickets) are known to be prevalent in some of the poorer countries, there is no reliable evidence of their incidence. The reason is that the countries require notification of only a limited number of illnesses and the reporting of these is incomplete. It is of interest, however, that the global incidence of malaria, a disease that is prevalent in tropical Africa, East Asia and South America, has been esti-

RWANDA	3.1	38
SAUDI ARABIA	6.8	125
SENEGAL	3.5	149
SIERRA LEONE	2.4	123
SINGAPORE	1.9	508
SOMALIA	2.5	48
SOUTH AFRICA	20.3	509
SPAIN	31.6	594
SUDAN	13.5	90
SWEDEN	7.7	2,046
SWITZERLAND	5.9	1,928
SYRIA	5.3	156
TAIWAN	12.4	185
TANZANIA	10.8	64
THAILAND	30.6	105
TOGO	1.6	82
TUNISIA	4.4	179
TURKEY	31.2	244
UGANDA	7.6	77
U.S.S.R.	231.0	1,195
UNITED ARAB REPUBLIC	29.6	96
UNITED KINGDOM	54.6	1,451
U.S.	194.6	2,893
UPPER VOLTA	4.9	35
URUGUAY	2.7	537
VENEZUELA	87	745
VIETNAM, NORTH	19.0	113
VIETNAM, SOUTH	16.1	113
YEMEN	5.0	36
YEMEN, SOUTH	1.1	246
YUGOSLAVIA	19.5	319
ZAMBIA	3.7	174

DENMARK	4.8	1,652
DOMINICAN REPUBLIC	3.6	212
ECUADOR	5.2	183
EL SALVADOR	2.9	236
ETHIOPIA	22.6	42
FINLAND	4.6	1,399
FRANCE	48.9	1,436
GERMANY, EAST	17.1	1,458
GERMANY, WEST	59.0	1,447
GHANA	7.7	245
GREECE	8.6	566
GUATEMALA	4.4	281
GUINEA	3.5	83
HAITI	4.4	80
HONDURAS	2.3	194
HONG KONG	3.7	291
HUNGARY	10.1	1,031
INDIA	486.8	86
INDONESIA	104.5	85
IRAN	24.8	211
IRAQ	8.2	193
IRELAND	2.9	783
ISRAEL	2.6	1,067
ITALY	51.6	883
IVORY COAST	3.8	188
JAMAICA	1.8	407
JAPAN	98.0	696
JORDAN	2.0	179
KENYA	9.3	77
KOREA, NORTH	12.1	88
KOREA, SOUTH	28.4	88
KUWAIT	0.5	3,184

chart and subsequent ones; exceptions here are Brunei, Cyprus and Kuwait, whose high incomes in relation to nearby countries illustrate the variation in wealth within geographic regions. There are fewer poor countries in Latin America than in Africa and Asia.

mated to be about 140 million cases per year, from which result just under a million deaths per year.

Perhaps the most useful single index of the health conditions prevailing in a community is the infant death rate. Deaths, unlike illnesses, are usually reported, at least in towns, and the death of children under the age of one year reflects a multitude of diseases and the entire spectrum of social and economic conditions. Currently the highest infant mortality rate is that of Cameroon, which has 137.2 infant deaths per 1,000 live births; for comparison the average rate in North America and western Europe is fewer than 25 deaths per 1,000 live births. These figures are national averages, and one would expect the rates in particular localities to be much higher. For example, in a recent year the infant mortality rate in the state of Alagoas in northeastern Brazil was 266.9. On the whole, infant mortality is higher in African countries than it is in most Asian countries. What may be surprising is that the rate in many Latin-American countries is higher than it is in Asian countries; Chile, Ecuador, Peru and Guatemala, all with rates close to 100, are the outstanding examples.

Another indication of the extent of poverty in a country is the number of inhabitants per physician. Whereas Indonesia and all the African countries except those in the north have more than 30,000 inhabitants per physician, South, East and West Asia have 6,000 people or fewer for each physician. The differences between individual countries are great: in thousands of population per physician Upper Volta has 63, Niger 65, Ethiopia 69 and Rwanda 97; yet countries with only slightly higher levels of per capita income, such as Burma, Pakistan, India and South Korea, have figures of 11.7, 6.2, 5.8 and 2.7 respectively. With the exception of Haiti all the Latin-American countries have rates lower than 5.2, and the rates of most of them are less than 3.0, as are those of North America and Europe. This indicator thus underlines the impression created by the others, namely that the impoverished countries of Africa are worse off than their Asian counterparts, and that the impoverished Latin-American countries are in general much better off than their Asian counterparts.

Let us now consider one other measure of poverty: nutrition. If there is one form of deprivation in the interdependent pattern of poverty that could be described as fundamental, it is the deprivation of food. Hunger weakens an individual's resistance to disease, lowering his ability to perform work, and therefore his ability to provide himself and his family with food for the future. The most widespread nutritional diseases arise from the lack of calories and the lack of protein. Whereas calorie deficiency (undernutrition) is due to an insufficient quantity of food, protein deficiency (a form of malnutrition) reflects the inadequate quality of a diet. Since proteins are one source of calories (the others are fats and cereals), a diet that contains enough proteins is also likely to provide enough calories. The reverse is not true. Calorie deficiency, then, is much less common than protein deficiency but much more serious.

Since calorie deficiency is precisely measurable, at least in principle, and also the mark of sustained deprivation of food, it is potentially a good indicator of the existence of serious poverty. A deficiency of calories, however, means a shortage of supply in relation to requirement, and in the measurement of both supply and requirement there are ambiguities. During the several stages between the production of food in the poorer countries and its consumption by an individual there is wastage varying from 20 to 50 percent of the calorie content. The estimate of calorie supply therefore depends on the stage at which the estimate has been made, and on the allowance that has been made for losses at later stages. On the other hand, the definition of the number of calories required varies according to the weight, sex, age and other characteristics of the individual, including the intensity of his activity and the climate in which he is working. Even the standard requirement for a reference individual, worked out by the Food and Agriculture Organization (FAO), has been revised (downward) over the years (inspiring the remark that physiology is "even more inexact a science than economics").

In spite of these recognized difficulties, the FAO has estimated calorie supplies by country and calorie requirements by region, and these data upset the hierarchy of poverty established by the previous indicators. They show the lowest-calorie regions to be not in Africa but in Asia and in parts of Latin America. Almost 1.8 billion people live in the calorie-deficient regions and 1.6 billion of these people are in Asia. As we shall see, this does not mean that so large a number of people are suffering from undernutrition, nor does it mean that we can ignore the possibility of undernutrition in the calorie-surplus regions. In order to reach an estimate of the number of people who are suffering from calorie deficiency, one must first know something about the distribution of calories within countries.

The problem of the distribution of food within a country has a space dimension and a time dimension. The movement of food from the food-surplus regions of a country to the food-deficit regions may be restricted by lack of

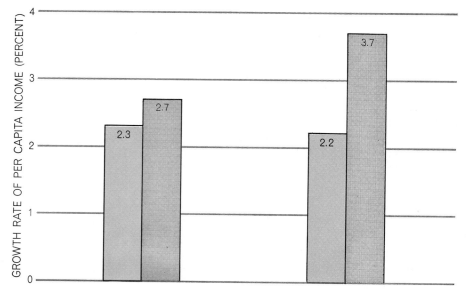

DIFFERENTIAL INCOME GROWTH indicates a widening economic gap between the poorer countries of the world (*color*) and the richer countries (*gray*). The average per capita income of the poorer nations actually grew somewhat more rapidly during the 1950's (*left*) than from 1960 to 1964 (*right*). Constant prices were used in estimating income growth.

transportation facilities, by political difficulties or both. Within regions the distribution of food is obviously limited by the distribution of purchasing power; even if a distribution to households in proportion to each household's needs were somehow ensured, there is no guarantee of an appropriate distribution within the household. Indeed, in many impoverished societies custom dictates that those who require the most calories (women of childbearing age, children aged one to four and adolescents) receive less than their requirement and the adult male receives more than his requirement.

An unequal distribution of calories over a period of time arises from inadequate methods of storage, so that the "hungry months" before harvest are a familiar feature of poor societies. Again, a harvest may fail in one year, or a succession of years, leading to a temporary drop in the food supply below the level of requirements. The availability of food grains in India is estimated to have fallen from 19 ounces per head per day in 1965 to 16.5 in 1966.

Putting together the results of household-diet surveys of India, Pakistan, Ceylon and Burma, and certain hypothetical distributions of calorie requirements for these countries, P. V. Sukhatme made a pioneering estimate of the numbers of people in the world who suffer from calorie deficiency. He put the total figure at between 300 and 500 million. It is important to emphasize that these figures refer only to the numbers suffering from undernutrition as distinct from protein deficiency. Sukhatme estimates the number of the latter to be between a third and half of the world's population.

Where are the 300 million or more people in the world who are undernourished? For the reasons given above, their number and location vary from year to year as circumstances change. Nonetheless, one can use such indicators as child mortality (age one to four years), not to be confused with infant mortality (from birth to one year), and crop yields

INFANT DEATH RATES (birth to one year) reflect social and economic conditions and thus are an index of poverty. The average rate in North America and western Europe is fewer than 25 deaths per 1,000 live births. Rates for Algeria, Brazil, Burma and Nigeria refer only to towns. The death rate of Bantu infants in South Africa is not known.

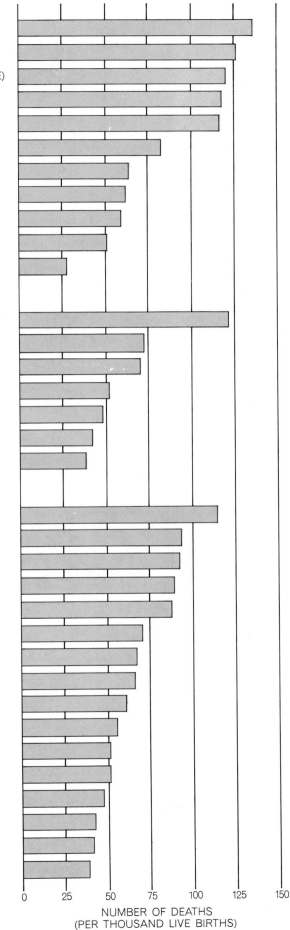

AFRICA
CAMEROON
TOGO
SOUTH AFRICA (ASIATIC-WHITE)
ALGERIA
UNITED ARAB REPUBLIC
MOZAMBIQUE
GUINEA
NIGERIA
SOUTH AFRICA (ASIATIC)
MADAGASCAR
SOUTH AFRICA (WHITE)

ASIA
BURMA
INDIA
PHILIPPINES
CEYLON
MALAYA
JORDAN
THAILAND

LATIN AMERICA
CHILE
ECUADOR
PERU
GUATEMALA
COLOMBIA
BRAZIL
DOMINICAN REPUBLIC
COSTA RICA
MEXICO
ARGENTINA
NICARAGUA
PUERTO RICO
VENEZUELA
PANAMA
JAMAICA
CUBA

0   25   50   75   100   125   150
NUMBER OF DEATHS
(PER THOUSAND LIVE BIRTHS)

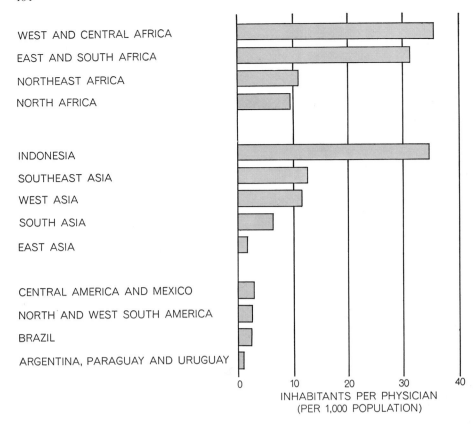

WEST AND CENTRAL AFRICA

EAST AND SOUTH AFRICA

NORTHEAST AFRICA

NORTH AFRICA

INDONESIA

SOUTHEAST ASIA

WEST ASIA

SOUTH ASIA

EAST ASIA

CENTRAL AMERICA AND MEXICO

NORTH AND WEST SOUTH AMERICA

BRAZIL

ARGENTINA, PARAGUAY AND URUGUAY

INHABITANTS PER PHYSICIAN
(PER 1,000 POPULATION)

PROPORTION OF PHYSICIANS in a population also indicates the level of poverty. In this breakdown rich countries are omitted, as are China, Ghana, North Korea, North Vietnam, Somalia, South Yemen, Yemen and part of Rhodesia. There are fewer than 1,000 people per physician in Australia, Europe, New Zealand, North America and the U.S.S.R.

per acre to identify some of the more critical areas. Child-mortality rates are particularly sensitive to protein and calorie deficiency.

Any estimate of the total number and distribution of the underfed in the world must lean heavily on the assumptions that are made about China, a country for which little reliable information has been available for the past 10 years. Sukhatme estimated that 20 percent of the population of China (some 140 million people) were undernourished, but this fraction appears rather high if one considers food production in China in 1965. The total cereal production per head of population appears to have been almost 50 percent higher in China than in India in that year, and one also expects there to be a more equal distribution of food in China. For these reasons it would seem unrealistic to suggest that more than 100 million people are undernourished in China, and the true figure might be nearer 50 million.

There is no reason to doubt Sukhatme's estimate that 25 percent of the population of India and Pakistan is underfed. A careful nutrition survey of East Pakistan recently carried out by the Office of International Research of the U.S. National Institutes of Health discovered that "46 percent of the households studied had an inadequate calorie intake." Hence India and Pakistan together could account for between 100 to 150 million of the undernourished of the world. Indonesia, where Java is a critical area, might provide about 20 million more people, and the rest of Asia—East, Southeast and West—perhaps another 20 million. In Africa there may be about 40 million underfed people. West Africa and Ethiopia are the most serious areas, although the high child-mortality rate in West Africa may reflect a deficiency of protein rather than of calories. In Latin America the hungriest areas would appear to be in Guatemala, Honduras, Bolivia and Ecuador and in northeastern Brazil. Taken together, these areas could account for the remaining 20 million people.

The evidence we have reviewed suggests that hunger is primarily an Asian problem, and that more than two-thirds of the people in the world who are undernourished are to be found in four countries: India, Pakistan, China and Indonesia. On the other hand, material poverty and health conditions appear to be worse in African countries. As we have seen, 17 countries, representing more than half the population of Africa, are in the very lowest income range. All the indicators suggest that, with the exception of one or two countries or areas within countries, Latin America is much better off than either of the other two continents.

It would be inappropriate to conclude this review of world poverty without commenting on the prospects for its alleviation. What can be done?

If we take hunger as the most urgent form of poverty, then the prospects of achieving a solution range from the euphoric to the cataclysmic. The difference between the two extreme views— that there is a world food surplus and that famine is just around the corner— turns on the question of distribution. The world's calorie supply slightly exceeds the world's calorie requirement. Given the continuation of present trends in food production, a worldwide food shortage is improbable. In this sense it is true to say that there is a world food surplus. This fact, however, is of little comfort to the low-calorie countries if their rate of food production cannot keep pace with their food requirements, and if balance-of-payment considerations place a limit on the amount of food they can import from the high-calorie countries. Similarly, a country's total food production may be growing fast enough to meet total requirements, but maldistribution may mean that grave food shortages can be expected in certain regions. In many respects the food problem is really a distribution problem rather than a production problem. Nonetheless, it may be easier to achieve increases in production than improvements in distribution.

It would be fair to say of the national and international plans designed to increase food production in the low-calorie countries that they have concentrated on long-run solutions. This is so because it is recognized that a significant increase in agricultural production presupposes changes in habits and attitudes, which can seldom be altered rapidly. The production of food in these countries is not expected to match their nutritional requirements for 15 to 25 years. The programs to control the growth of populations must also be classed as long-run solutions. It has been estimated that even if current birth-control programs are extremely successful, the overall food requirements of the low-calorie countries in 1985 will be at most 11 percent lower.

Nor do official plans usually provide for any change in the present distribution pattern of food supplies. Yet in the absence of any deliberate policy of redistribution it is clear that still larger total supplies would be necessary to ensure nutritionally adequate diets to major sections of the population. V. M. Dandekar goes so far as to suggest that in India the average daily intake of calories would have to be 3,000 or more if "the usual inequalities in the distribution of essential food supplies among individuals are to be allowed for." For most of the low-calorie countries the achievement of such an average level of calorie intake is much more than 20 years away.

Thus according to current development plans there appears to be no prospect of a solution to the problem of hunger for 20 years at the very least. Given the resources that are at the disposal of the rich countries, it seems quite unreasonable to condemn at least 300 million people to wait 20 years for their hunger to be satisfied. What is required to complement the long-run development strategy is a short-term program to alleviate the most extreme cases of hunger and other forms of poverty. Such a program might include three features: first, surveys of the health and nutritional status of the populations in the poorest areas of the world to establish priorities and requirements; second, food given to women and children either at schools or clinics (or both) in exchange for their attendance at instruction on elementary points of nutrition and hygiene; third, food given to men in exchange for work on projects yielding some immediate and visible return, such as improving the supply and distribution of water.

Such a program could not be more than a holding operation, but it would have two clear advantages. By feeding those who normally have the least food in relation to their needs (women and children), it would reduce the long-run food production requirement, because fewer calories would be needed to lift the lower end of the population distribution free from the level of undernutrition. Furthermore, a program of this kind would be less likely to encounter the current political resistance to transfer of resources from the rich countries to the poor ones. From the point of view of the donor country each unit of aid would have visible and immediate results; from the recipient country's point of view there would be no interference in its long-run development strategy.

There are of course many organizations, both official and voluntary, that already carry out functions such as those I have proposed. These activities are, however, only a drop in an ocean of need. The major objection to giving these proposals a systematic basis is the problem of administration: one recoils instinctively at the prospect of still another international-aid bureaucracy, yet some administration is essential to organize the transport and distribution of food and medicine. One possible solution might be to use the most effective organization already existing in each country; in many countries this might be the armed forces.

A further objection is that such a scheme would never work because of its low political priority: in the areas of serious poverty people are literally too weak to protest. Unless some such scheme is put into effect, however, there seems to be little prospect of making any reduction in the number of people suffering from serious poverty in the world during the next 20 years.

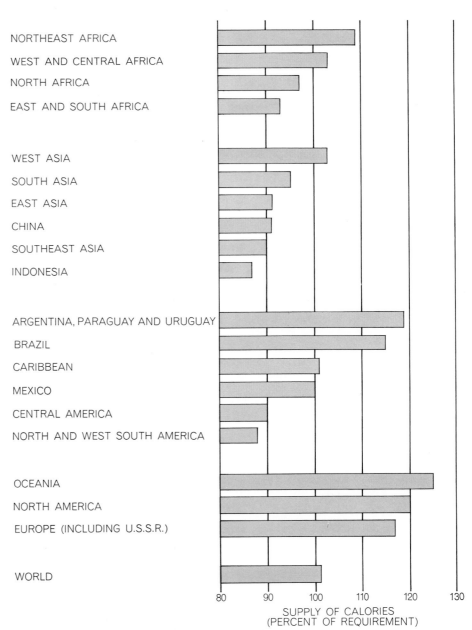

CALORIE PROVISIONS, in proportion to need, are another rough indicator of poverty (but one that does not tell how calories are distributed within a population). Almost 1.8 billion people live in calorie-deficient countries, 1.6 billion of these people in Asia. Oceania is chiefly Australia and New Zealand. Regions of Africa and Asia do not include rich countries.

SAN JUAN SLUM AREA in the Santurce district sprawls along the edge of the tidal inlet (*top*) that connects the city's harbor with San José Lake. Rickety buildings have been erected on stilts be- yond the high-water line and narrow alleyways crisscross the dis- trict. Compared to this area, many of New York's worst slum areas, such as the ones that appear below, are nearly middle-class.

EL BARRIO, the original nuclear Latin-American slum area of Manhattan, occupies the greater part of this aerial photograph. Lying roughly between Central Park and the East River north of 99th Street and south of 125th Street in Manhattan, this is the area that received the pioneer Puerto Rican immigrants to New York in the early years of this century. Photograph was made in 1961.

39

THE CULTURE OF POVERTY

OSCAR LEWIS
October 1966

Does membership in a group that has been poor for generations constitute belonging to a separate culture? A study of Puerto Ricans in both Puerto Rico and New York indicates that it does

Poverty and the so-called war against it provide a principal theme for the domestic program of the present Administration. In the midst of a population that enjoys unexampled material well-being—with the average annual family income exceeding $7,000—it is officially acknowledged that some 18 million families, numbering more than 50 million individuals, live below the $3,000 "poverty line." Toward the improvement of the lot of these people some $1,600 million of Federal funds are directly allocated through the Office of Economic Opportunity, and many hundreds of millions of additional dollars flow indirectly through expanded Federal expenditures in the fields of health, education, welfare and urban affairs.

Along with the increase in activity on behalf of the poor indicated by these figures there has come a parallel expansion of publication in the social sciences on the subject of poverty. The new writings advance the same two opposed evaluations of the poor that are to be found in literature, in proverbs and in popular sayings throughout recorded history. Just as the poor have been pronounced blessed, virtuous, upright, serene, independent, honest, kind and happy, so contemporary students stress their great and neglected capacity for self-help, leadership and community organization. Conversely, as the poor have been characterized as shiftless, mean, sordid, violent, evil and criminal, so other students point to the irreversibly destructive effects of poverty on individual character and emphasize the corresponding need to keep guidance and control of poverty projects in the hands of duly constituted authorities. This clash of viewpoints reflects in part the infighting for political control of the program between Federal and local officials. The confusion results also from the tendency to focus study and attention on the personality of the individual victim of poverty rather than on the slum community and family and from the consequent failure to distinguish between poverty and what I have called the culture of poverty.

The phrase is a catchy one and is used and misused with some frequency in the current literature. In my writings it is the label for a specific conceptual model that describes in positive terms a subculture of Western society with its own structure and rationale, a way of life handed on from generation to generation along family lines. The culture of poverty is not just a matter of deprivation or disorganization, a term signifying the absence of something. It is a culture in the traditional anthropological sense in that it provides human beings with a design for living, with a ready-made set of solutions for human problems, and so serves a significant adaptive function. This style of life transcends national boundaries and regional and rural-urban differences within nations. Wherever it occurs, its practitioners exhibit remarkable similarity in the structure of their families, in interpersonal relations, in spending habits, in their value systems and in their orientation in time.

Not nearly enough is known about this important complex of human behavior. My own concept of it has evolved as my work has progressed and remains subject to amendment by my own further work and that of others. The scarcity of literature on the culture of poverty is a measure of the gap in communication that exists between the very poor and the middle-class personnel—social scientists, social workers, teachers, physicians, priests and others—who bear the major responsibility for carrying out the antipoverty programs. Much of the behavior accepted in the culture of poverty goes counter to cherished ideals of the larger society. In writing about "multiproblem" families social scientists thus often stress their instability, their lack of order, direction and organization. Yet, as I have observed them, their behavior seems clearly patterned and reasonably predictable. I am more often struck by the inexorable repetitiousness and the iron entrenchment of their lifeways.

The concept of the culture of poverty may help to correct misapprehensions that have ascribed some behavior patterns of ethnic, national or regional groups as distinctive characteristics. For example, a high incidence of common-law marriage and of households headed by women has been thought to be distinctive of Negro family life in this country and has been attributed to the Negro's historical experience of slavery. In actuality it turns out that such households express essential traits of the culture of poverty and are found among diverse peoples in many parts of the world and among peoples that have had no history of slavery. Although it is now possible to assert such generalizations, there is still much to be learned about this difficult and affecting subject. The absence of intensive anthropological studies of poor families in a wide variety of national contexts—particularly the lack of such studies in socialist countries—remains a serious handicap to the formulation of dependable cross-cultural constants of the culture of poverty.

My studies of poverty and family life have centered largely in Mexico. On occasion some of my Mexican friends have suggested delicately that I turn to a study of poverty in my own country. As a first step in this direction I am currently engaged in a study of Puerto Rican families. Over the past three years my staff and I have been assembling data on 100 representative families in four slums of Greater San Juan and some 50 families of their relatives in New York City.

Our methods combine the traditional techniques of sociology, anthropology and psychology. This includes a battery of 19 questionnaires, the administration of which requires 12 hours per informant. They cover the residence and employment history of each adult; family relations; income and expenditure; complete inventory of household and personal possessions; friendship patterns, particularly the *compadrazgo*, or godparent, relationship that serves as a kind of informal social security for the children of these families and establishes special obligations among the adults; recreational patterns; health and medical history; politics; religion; world view and "cosmopolitanism." Open-end interviews and psychological tests (such as the thematic apperception test, the Rorschach test and the sentence-completion test) are administered to a sampling of this population.

All this work serves to establish the context for close-range study of a selected few families. Because the family is a small social system, it lends itself to

WATERFRONT SHACKS of a Puerto Rican slum provide a sharp contrast to the modern construction that characterizes the prosperous parts of San Juan's Santurce district (*rear*). The author has found that residents in clearly delineated slum neighborhoods such as this one often have a community sense similar to that characteristic of villagers in rural areas. Such *esprit de corps* is

the holistic approach of anthropology. Whole-family studies bridge the gap between the conceptual extremes of the culture at one pole and of the individual at the other, making possible observation of both culture and personality as they are interrelated in real life. In a large metropolis such as San Juan or New York the family is the natural unit of study.

Ideally our objective is the naturalistic observation of the life of "our" families, with a minimum of intervention. Such intensive study, however, necessarily involves the establishment of deep personal ties. My assistants include two Mexicans whose families I had studied; their "Mexican's-eye view" of the Puerto Rican slum has helped to point up the similarities and differences between the Mexican and Puerto

uncommon among participants in the culture of poverty; although gregarious, they seldom manage to become well organized.

Rican subcultures. We have spent many hours attending family parties, wakes and baptisms, responding to emergency calls, taking people to the hospital, getting them out of jail, filling out applications for them, hunting apartments with them, helping them to get jobs or to get on relief. With each member of these families we conduct tape-recorded interviews, taking down their life stories and their answers to questions on a wide variety of topics. For the ordering of our material we undertake to reconstruct, by close interrogation, the history of a week or more of consecutive days in the lives of each family, and we observe and record complete days as they unfold. The first volume to issue from this study is to be published next month under the title of *La Vida, a Puerto Rican Family in the Culture of Poverty—San Juan and New York* (Random House).

There are many poor people in the world. Indeed, the poverty of the two-thirds of the world's population who live in the underdeveloped countries has been rightly called "the problem of problems." But not all of them by any means live in the culture of poverty. For this way of life to come into being and flourish it seems clear that certain preconditions must be met.

The setting is a cash economy, with wage labor and production for profit and with a persistently high rate of unemployment and underemployment, at low wages, for unskilled labor. The society fails to provide social, political and economic organization, on either a voluntary basis or by government imposition, for the low-income population. There is a bilateral kinship system centered on the nuclear progenitive family, as distinguished from the unilateral extended kinship system of lineage and clan. The dominant class asserts a set of values that prizes thrift and the accumulation of wealth and property, stresses the possibility of upward mobility and explains low economic status as the result of individual personal inadequacy and inferiority.

Where these conditions prevail the way of life that develops among some of the poor is the culture of poverty. That is why I have described it as a subculture of the Western social order. It is both an adaptation and a reaction of the poor to their marginal position in a class-stratified, highly individuated, capitalistic society. It represents an effort to cope with feelings of hopelessness and despair that arise from the

realization by the members of the marginal communities in these societies of the improbability of their achieving success in terms of the prevailing values and goals. Many of the traits of the culture of poverty can be viewed as local, spontaneous attempts to meet needs not served in the case of the poor by the institutions and agencies of the larger society because the poor are not eligible for such service, cannot afford it or are ignorant and suspicious.

Once the culture of poverty has come into existence it tends to perpetuate itself. By the time slum children are six or seven they have usually absorbed the basic attitudes and values of their subculture. Thereafter they are psychologically unready to take full advantage of changing conditions or improving opportunities that may develop in their lifetime.

My studies have identified some 70 traits that characterize the culture of poverty. The principal ones may be described in four dimensions of the system: the relationship between the subculture and the larger society; the nature of the slum community; the nature of the family, and the attitudes, values and character structure of the individual.

The disengagement, the nonintegration, of the poor with respect to the major institutions of society is a crucial element in the culture of poverty. It reflects the combined effect of a variety of factors including poverty, to begin with, but also segregation and discrimination, fear, suspicion and apathy and the development of alternative institutions and procedures in the slum community. The people do not belong to labor unions or political parties and make little use of banks, hospitals, department stores or museums. Such involvement as there is in the institutions of the larger society—in the jails, the army and the public welfare system—does little to suppress the traits of the culture of poverty. A relief system that barely keeps people alive perpetuates rather than eliminates poverty and the pervading sense of hopelessness.

People in a culture of poverty produce little wealth and receive little in return. Chronic unemployment and underemployment, low wages, lack of property, lack of savings, absence of food reserves in the home and chronic shortage of cash imprison the family and the individual in a vicious circle. Thus for lack of cash the slum householder makes frequent purchases of small quantities of food at higher prices. The slum economy turns inward; it shows a high incidence of pawning of personal goods, borrowing at usurious rates of interest, informal credit arrangements among neighbors, use of secondhand clothing and furniture.

There is awareness of middle-class values. People talk about them and even claim some of them as their own. On the whole, however, they do not live by them. They will declare that marriage by law, by the church or by both is the ideal form of marriage, but few will marry. For men who have no steady jobs, no property and no prospect of wealth to pass on to their children, who live in the present without expectations of the future, who want to avoid the expense and legal difficulties involved in marriage and divorce, a free union or consensual marriage makes good sense. The women, for their part, will turn down offers of marriage from men who are likely to be immature, punishing and generally unreliable. They feel that a consensual union gives them some of the freedom and flexibility men have. By not giving the fathers of their children legal status as husbands, the women have a stronger claim on the children. They also maintain exclusive rights to their own property.

Along with disengagement from the larger society, there is a hostility to the basic institutions of what are regarded as the dominant classes. There is hatred of the police, mistrust of government and of those in high positions and a cynicism that extends to the church. The culture of poverty thus holds a certain potential for protest and for entrainment in political movements aimed against the existing order.

With its poor housing and overcrowding, the community of the culture of poverty is high in gregariousness, but it has a minimum of organization beyond the nuclear and extended family. Occasionally slum dwellers come together in temporary informal groupings; neighborhood gangs that cut across slum settlements represent a considerable advance beyond the zero point of the continuum I have in mind. It is the low level of organization that gives the culture of poverty its marginal and anomalous quality in our highly organized society. Most primitive peoples have achieved a higher degree of sociocultural organization than contemporary urban slum dwellers. This is not to say that there may not be a sense of community and *esprit de corps* in a slum neighborhood. In fact, where slums are

isolated from their surroundings by enclosing walls or other physical barriers, where rents are low and residence is stable and where the population constitutes a distinct ethnic, racial or language group, the sense of community may approach that of a village. In Mexico City and San Juan such territoriality is engendered by the scarcity of low-cost housing outside of established slum areas. In South Africa it is actively enforced by the *apartheid* that confines rural migrants to prescribed locations.

The family in the culture of poverty does not cherish childhood as a specially prolonged and protected stage in the life cycle. Initiation into sex comes early. With the instability of consensual marriage the family tends to be mother-centered and tied more closely to the mother's extended family. The female head of the house is given to authoritarian rule. In spite of much verbal emphasis on family solidarity, sibling rivalry for the limited supply of goods and maternal affection is intense. There is little privacy.

The individual who grows up in this culture has a strong feeling of fatalism, helplessness, dependence and inferiority. These traits, so often remarked in the current literature as characteristic of the American Negro, I found equally strong in slum dwellers of Mexico City and San Juan, who are not segregated or discriminated against as a distinct ethnic or racial group. Other traits include a high incidence of weak ego structure, orality and confusion of sexual identification, all reflecting maternal deprivation; a strong present-time orientation with relatively little disposition to defer gratification and plan for the future, and a high tolerance for psychological pathology of all kinds. There is widespread belief in male superiority and among the men a strong preoccupation with *machismo,* their masculinity.

Provincial and local in outlook, with little sense of history, these people know only their own neighborhood and their own way of life. Usually they do not have the knowledge, the vision or the ideology to see the similarities between their troubles and those of their counterparts elsewhere in the world. They are not class-conscious, although they are sensitive indeed to symbols of status.

The distinction between poverty and the culture of poverty is basic to the model described here. There are numerous examples of poor people whose way of life I would not characterize as be-

longing to this subculture. Many primitive and preliterate peoples that have been studied by anthropologists suffer dire poverty attributable to low technology or thin resources or both. Yet even the simplest of these peoples have a high degree of social organization and a relatively integrated, satisfying and self-sufficient culture.

In India the destitute lower-caste peoples—such as the Chamars, the leatherworkers, and the Bhangis, the sweepers—remain integrated in the larger society and have their own panchayat institutions of self-government. Their panchayats and their extended unilateral kinship systems, or clans, cut across village lines, giving them a strong sense of identity and continuity. In my studies of these peoples I found no culture of poverty to go with their poverty.

The Jews of eastern Europe were a poor urban people, often confined to ghettos. Yet they did not have many traits of the culture of poverty. They had a tradition of literacy that placed great value on learning; they formed many voluntary associations and adhered with devotion to the central community organization around the rabbi, and they had a religion that taught them they were the chosen people.

I would cite also a fourth, somewhat speculative example of poverty dissociated from the culture of poverty. On the basis of limited direct observation in one country—Cuba—and from indirect evidence, I am inclined to believe the culture of poverty does not exist in socialist countries. In 1947 I undertook a study of a slum in Havana. Recently I had an opportunity to revisit the same slum and some of the same families. The physical aspect of the place had changed little, except for a beautiful new nursery school. The people were as poor as before, but I was impressed to find much less of the feelings of despair and apathy, so symptomatic of the culture of poverty in the urban slums of the U.S. The slum was now highly organized, with block committees, educational committees, party committees. The people had found a new sense of power and importance in a doctrine that glorified the lower class as the hope of humanity, and they were armed. I was told by one Cuban official that the Castro government had practically eliminated delinquency by giving arms to the delinquents!

Evidently the Castro regime—revising Marx and Engels—did not write off the so-called *lumpenproletariat* as an inherently reactionary and antirevolutionary

PUERTO RICAN BOYS in a Manhattan upper East Side neighborhood use the fenced-off yard of a deserted school as an impromptu playground. The culture of poverty does not cherish childhood as a protected and especially prolonged part of the life cycle. Sexual maturity is early, the male is accepted as a superior and men are strongly preoccupied with *machismo*, or masculinity.

force but rather found in them a revolutionary potential and utilized it. Frantz Fanon, in his book *The Wretched of the Earth,* makes a similar evaluation of their role in the Algerian revolution: "It is within this mass of humanity, this people of the shantytowns, at the core of the *lumpenproletariat,* that the rebellion will find its urban spearhead. For the *lumpenproletariat,* that horde of starving men, uprooted from their tribe and from their clan, constitutes one of the most spontaneous and most radically revolutionary forces of a colonized people."

It is true that I have found little revolutionary spirit or radical ideology among low-income Puerto Ricans. Most of the families I studied were politically conservative, about half of them favoring the Statehood Republican Party, which provides opposition on the right to the Popular Democratic Party that dominates the politics of the commonwealth. It seems to me, therefore, that disposition for protest among people living in the culture of poverty will vary considerably according to the national context and historical circumstances. In contrast to Algeria, the independence movement in Puerto Rico has found little popular support. In Mexico, where the cause of independence carried long ago, there is no longer any such movement to stir the dwellers in the new and old slums of the capital city.

Yet it would seem that any move-ment—be it religious, pacifist or revolutionary—that organizes and gives hope to the poor and effectively promotes a sense of solidarity with larger groups must effectively destroy the psychological and social core of the culture of poverty. In this connection, I suspect that the civil rights movement among American Negroes has of itself done more to improve their self-image and self-respect than such economic gains as it has won although, without doubt, the two kinds of progress are mutually reinforcing. In the culture of poverty of the American Negro the additional disadvantage of racial discrimination has generated a potential for revolutionary protest and organization that is absent in the slums of San Juan and Mexico City and, for that matter, among the poor whites in the South.

If it is true, as I suspect, that the culture of poverty flourishes and is endemic to the free-enterprise, pre-welfare-state stage of capitalism, then it is also endemic in colonial societies. The most likely candidates for the culture of poverty would be the people who come from the lower strata of a rapidly changing society and who are already partially alienated from it. Accordingly the subculture is likely to be found where imperial conquest has smashed the native social and economic structure and held the natives, perhaps for generations, in servile status, or where feu-dalism is yielding to capitalism in the later evolution of a colonial economy. Landless rural workers who migrate to the cities, as in Latin America, can be expected to fall into this way of life more readily than migrants from stable peasant villages with a well-organized traditional culture, as in India. It remains to be seen, however, whether the culture of poverty has not already begun to develop in the slums of Bombay and Calcutta. Compared with Latin America also, the strong corporate nature of many African tribal societies may tend to inhibit or delay the formation of a full-blown culture of poverty in the new towns and cities of that continent. In South Africa the institutionalization of repression and discrimination under *apartheid* may also have begun to promote an immunizing sense of identity and group consciousness among the African Negroes.

One must therefore keep the dynamic aspects of human institutions forward in observing and assessing the evidence for the presence, the waxing or the waning of this subculture. Measured on the dimension of relationship to the larger society, some slum dwellers may have a warmer identification with their national tradition even though they suffer deeper poverty than members of a similar community in another country. In Mexico City a high percentage of our respondents, including those with little or no formal schooling, knew of Cuauhtémoc,

MOTHER AND DAUGHTER stand together by the door of a run-down apartment building on upper Park Avenue. Because common-law marriage offers the female participant in the culture of poverty more protection of her property rights and surer custody of her children than formal marriage does, the mother is usually the head of the household and family ties are to her kin and not the father's.

Hidalgo, Father Morelos, Juárez, Díaz, Zapata, Carranza and Cárdenas. In San Juan the names of Rámon Power, José de Diego, Baldorioty de Castro, Rámon Betances, Nemesio Canales, Lloréns Torres rang no bell; a few could tell about the late Albizu Campos. For the lower-income Puerto Rican, however, history begins with Muñoz Rivera and ends with his son Muñoz Marín.

The national context can make a big difference in the play of the crucial traits of fatalism and hopelessness. Given the advanced technology, the high level of literacy, the all-pervasive reach of the media of mass communications and the relatively high aspirations of all sectors of the population, even the poorest and most marginal communities of the U.S. must aspire to a larger future than the slum dwellers of Ecuador and Peru, where the actual possibilities are more limited and where an authoritarian social order persists in city and country. Among the 50 million U.S. citizens now more or less officially certified as poor, I would guess that about 20 percent live in a culture of poverty. The largest numbers in this group are made up of Negroes, Puerto Ricans, Mexicans, American Indians and Southern poor whites. In these figures there is some reassurance for those concerned, because it is much more difficult to undo the culture of poverty than to cure poverty itself.

Middle-class people—this would cer-tainly include most social scientists—tend to concentrate on the negative aspects of the culture of poverty. They attach a minus sign to such traits as present-time orientation and readiness to indulge impulses. I do not intend to idealize or romanticize the culture of poverty—"it is easier to praise poverty than to live in it." Yet the positive aspects of these traits must not be overlooked. Living in the present may develop a capacity for spontaneity, for the enjoyment of the sensual, which is often blunted in the middle-class, future-oriented man. Indeed, I am often struck by the analogies that can be drawn between the mores of the very rich—of the "jet set" and "café society" —and the culture of the very poor. Yet it is, on the whole, a comparatively superficial culture. There is in it much pathos, suffering and emptiness. It does not provide much support or satisfaction; its pervading mistrust magnifies individual helplessness and isolation. Indeed, poverty of culture is one of the crucial traits of the culture of poverty.

The concept of the culture of poverty provides a generalization that may help to unify and explain a number of phenomena hitherto viewed as peculiar to certain racial, national or regional groups. Problems we think of as being distinctively our own or distinctively Negro (or as typifying any other ethnic group) prove to be endemic in countries where there are no segregated ethnic minority groups. If it follows that the elimination of physical poverty may not by itself eliminate the culture of poverty, then an understanding of the subculture may contribute to the design of measures specific to that purpose.

What is the future of the culture of poverty? In considering this question one must distinguish between those countries in which it represents a relatively small segment of the population and those in which it constitutes a large one. In the U.S. the major solution proposed by social workers dealing with the "hard core" poor has been slowly to raise their level of living and incorporate them in the middle class. Wherever possible psychiatric treatment is prescribed.

In underdeveloped countries where great masses of people live in the culture of poverty, such a social-work solution does not seem feasible. The local psychiatrists have all they can do to care for their own growing middle class. In those countries the people with a culture of poverty may seek a more revolutionary solution. By creating basic structural changes in society, by redistributing wealth, by organizing the poor and giving them a sense of belonging, of power and of leadership, revolutions frequently succeed in abolishing some of the basic characteristics of the culture of poverty even when they do not succeed in curing poverty itself.

40

THE POSSESSIONS OF THE POOR

OSCAR LEWIS
October 1969

The combined value of everything from ashtrays to underwear owned by 14 families in a Mexico City tenement came to an average of $338 per family. What does such material want reveal about poverty in general?

We all recognize poverty when we are confronted with it, but it is not easy to define the condition in objective terms. Income itself is not an entirely adequate measure because it does not tell us how people actually live. We come closer to describing what poverty is when we define it as the inability to satisfy one's material wants or needs. It occurred to me that it might be interesting and useful to study the material possessions of poverty-stricken people as a concrete expression of the lives they lead. In the hope of finding new insights into the nature of poverty, I undertook a systematic examination of the possessions of a group of poor families living in a Mexico City slum tenement.

In many respects such a survey is analogous to an archaeological examination of the material remains of a civilization. From an analysis of material objects the archaeologist can learn much about a people's history, achievements, cultural influences, values and ways of life and can make important generalizations about the society. Similarly, a quantitative analysis of the material possessions of a living society should tell us many things, including information that might escape notice in a direct study of the people themselves. In the case of a living people we have the advantage of being able to supplement the story told by the material objects by questioning the people about their possessions.

The inquiry opens up a mine of interesting questions. What proportions of their income do poor people spend on furniture, on clothing, on religious objects, on luxury items, on medicines? How much of what they buy is new? How much is secondhand? To what extent do they depend on gifts or hand-me-downs? (Welfare contributions did not enter into the picture in my study, as there was no public welfare system in Mexico City.) How do families in poverty finance their purchases? Where do they do their shopping? How wide are their choices? What is the physical condition of their possessions? How long do they manage to hold on to them? I was able to obtain rather detailed information on all these matters.

The scene of my study was a small *vecindad* (tenement), one of the poorest in Mexico City, that housed 14 families totaling 83 people (an average of about six persons per family). The tenement consisted of a row of 14 windowless one-room apartments built of adobe brick and covered with a cement roof that joined them all together. Each apartment had a small entranceway with a makeshift roof of tar paper or metal and a door so low that one had to stoop to enter. These entrances also served as kitchens. A walk of rough stone slabs laid by the tenants to combat the mud ran parallel to the row of apartments and was cluttered with laundry tubs, pails, chamber pots and articles set out to dry in the sun. Firewood, covered with old gunnysacks or pieces of cardboard, was stored on the roof. Some of the tenants, who plied their trade at home, had built flimsy sheds as workshops against the front of their apartment; the sheds were used to store piles of materials and tools. In the yard was a large cement water trough that served all the tenants for washing dishes and laundry and for bathing children. Toward the back of the yard there were two common toilets, dilapidated adobe structures curtained with pieces of torn burlap.

Clotheslines strung on forked poles crisscrossed the yard, and the ground was strewn with rocks and pitted with holes dug by the children. In the day-time the yard was filled with half-naked babies and ragged youngsters playing in the dirt.

The impression of extreme poverty given by the *vecindad* was amply substantiated by my inventory of the possessions of the 14 households. The total value of all their belongings (based on a detailed estimate of the cost or value of each item) was about $4,730 in U.S. dollars, or an average of about $338 per household. There was considerable variation among the households: the amount ranged from $119 for the poorest household to $937 for the "wealthiest." Twelve of the 14 households owned less than $480 worth of goods.

For purposes of analysis I classified the family possessions into 13 categories: furniture and furnishings (including radios and television sets), personal clothing, bedclothes, household equipment, kitchen equipment, household decorations, jewelry and other items of personal adornment, religious objects, toys (including bicycles), medicines, animals, plants, and the tools and materials of those householders who carried on trades at home [*see illustration on next two pages*]. I shall first mention some general findings and then discuss the categories in more detail.

Not surprisingly, my inquiry showed that substantial proportions of the people's possessions had been bought secondhand; this was true, for example, of about 35 percent of all the furniture and 13 percent of the personal clothing owned by the 14 households. Less than 15 percent of all their goods had been purchased in shops; most of their possessions (60 percent) had been bought in open street markets. The tenants' shopping area was narrowly circumscribed: 66 percent of all their purchased possessions had been bought either within the tenement itself or within the neighborhood, and about a fifth of the purchases had been made in markets in nearby neighborhoods. Thus about 85 percent of the purchases were made within a radius of less than a mile from the tenement. Of the remaining purchases 8.9 percent were made in distant neighborhoods of Mexico City and 5.6 percent were made outside the city. Although the tenement was within a few minutes' walk of Mexico City's downtown shopping center, comparatively few of the tenants' possessions had been bought there or in more distant places. (Indeed, apart from occasional religious excursions to pilgrimage centers, most of the families had traveled very little, either within the city or outside it.)

The tenants' principal possession was furniture, accounting for about a third

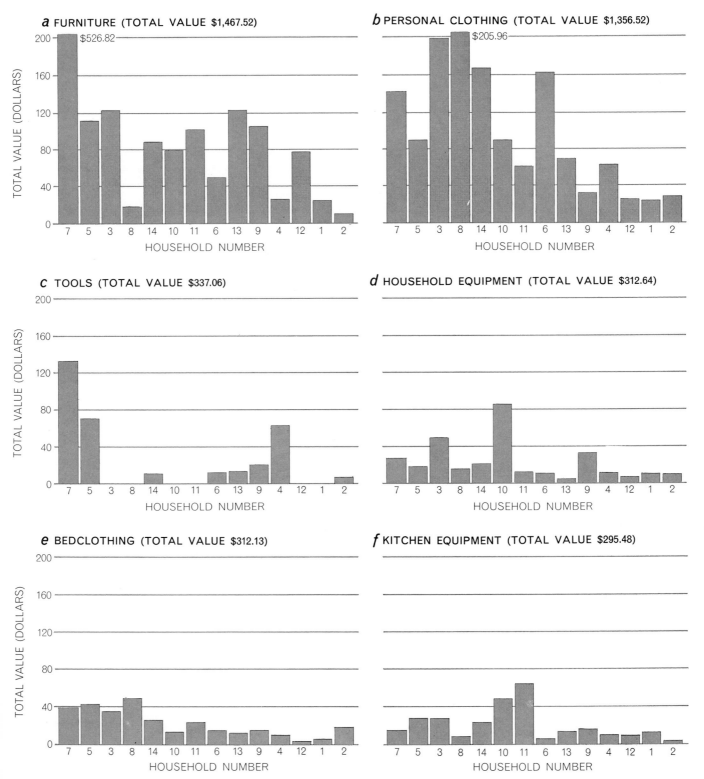

VALUE OF POSSESSIONS in 14 tenement households showed a steady decline from best-off (No. 7) to poorest (No. 2) but varied greatly from family to family. Furniture (a) was the most valuable possession and personal clothing (b) the next. With a total valuation of more than $2,800, the two were worth more than all other possessions combined. More than 90 percent of the best-off family's investment in furniture, however, was in a $480 television set, and nearly half of the value of all the toys (i) owned by the

of all their expenditures on material goods. At the time of my inventory each family had among its furnishings at least one bed, a mattress, a table, a shelf for an altar and a set of shelves for dishes. They considered these items to be the minimal essentials, although most of the families had lived without some or all of them in the past.

The 14 households owned a total of 23 beds for their 83 members, so that in most of the households some members (usually the older sons) had to sleep on straw mats or rags on the floor. Of the 23 beds, seven had been bought new, 13 secondhand and three had been received as gifts. The new beds ranged in price from $4.40 to $12.

The bed or beds usually took up most of the space in the one-room apartment. During the day the bed was used for

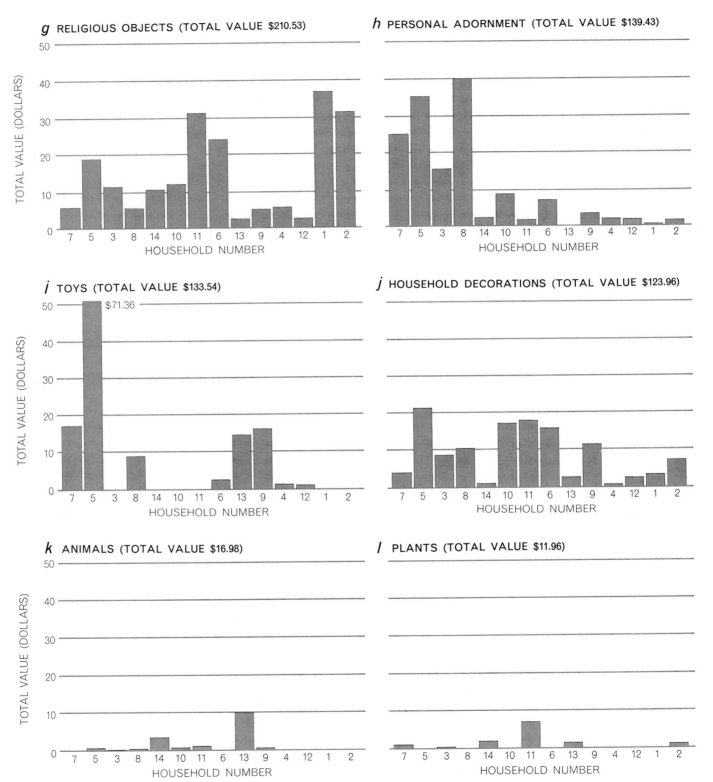

g RELIGIOUS OBJECTS (TOTAL VALUE $210.53)

h PERSONAL ADORNMENT (TOTAL VALUE $139.43)

i TOYS (TOTAL VALUE $133.54)

j HOUSEHOLD DECORATIONS (TOTAL VALUE $123.96)

k ANIMALS (TOTAL VALUE $16.98)

l PLANTS (TOTAL VALUE $11.96)

families that had children was represented by the $64 bicycle in household No. 5. Unevenness in the decline from best-off to poorest in household equipment (*d*) is because households No. 3, No. 10 and No. 9 had sewing machines. Not only clocks but also wrist-watches were found in four of the seven better-off households, but the seven poorer ones had no clocks at all. All, however, had electric light and an electric iron. Only one had no chairs, only two had no wardrobe for clothes and only three had no radio.

416

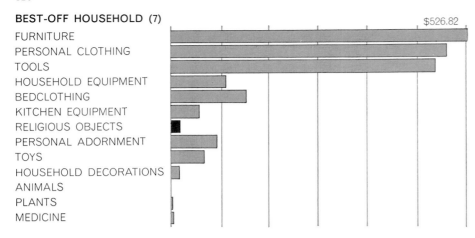

BEST-OFF HOUSEHOLD (7)

- FURNITURE
- PERSONAL CLOTHING
- TOOLS
- HOUSEHOLD EQUIPMENT
- BEDCLOTHING
- KITCHEN EQUIPMENT
- RELIGIOUS OBJECTS
- PERSONAL ADORNMENT
- TOYS
- HOUSEHOLD DECORATIONS
- ANIMALS
- PLANTS
- MEDICINE

$526.82

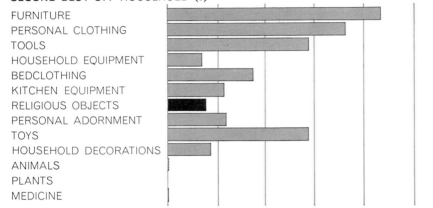

SECOND-BEST-OFF HOUSEHOLD (5)

- FURNITURE
- PERSONAL CLOTHING
- TOOLS
- HOUSEHOLD EQUIPMENT
- BEDCLOTHING
- KITCHEN EQUIPMENT
- RELIGIOUS OBJECTS
- PERSONAL ADORNMENT
- TOYS
- HOUSEHOLD DECORATIONS
- ANIMALS
- PLANTS
- MEDICINE

SECOND-POOREST HOUSEHOLD (1)

- FURNITURE
- PERSONAL CLOTHING
- TOOLS
- HOUSEHOLD EQUIPMENT
- BEDCLOTHING
- KITCHEN EQUIPMENT
- RELIGIOUS OBJECTS
- PERSONAL ADORNMENT
- TOYS
- HOUSEHOLD DECORATIONS
- ANIMALS
- PLANTS
- MEDICINE

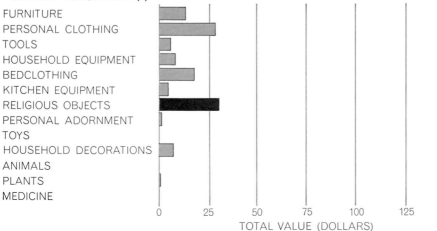

POOREST HOUSEHOLD (2)

- FURNITURE
- PERSONAL CLOTHING
- TOOLS
- HOUSEHOLD EQUIPMENT
- BEDCLOTHING
- KITCHEN EQUIPMENT
- RELIGIOUS OBJECTS
- PERSONAL ADORNMENT
- TOYS
- HOUSEHOLD DECORATIONS
- ANIMALS
- PLANTS
- MEDICINE

0   25   50   75   100   125   150
TOTAL VALUE (DOLLARS)

sitting, for work, for sorting laundry and for many other purposes, including a play area for the children. In families in which a night worker had to sleep during the day, he slept on one side of the bed while the other members of the family sat, worked or played on the other side.

The average length of ownership of a bed among these families was only four years eight months, not because the beds wore out rapidly but because for one reason or another—prolonged illness, family separations, death or economic emergency—the families occasionally had to pawn or sell their furniture to raise money for food and other necessities. The instability of bed ownership was only one instance of the brief and uncertain possession of furniture items among these families. The mean time of possession for all the pieces of furniture in the tenement was only four and a half years, although a majority of the families had lived there for more than 15 years. The brevity of possession was frequently due to the inability of the families to meet the installment payments on furniture bought on credit.

The poverty of the possessions is perhaps most vividly illustrated by the mattresses on which the people slept. Most of the mattresses were of cheap quality and stuffed with lumpy cotton or straw; only four families had invested relatively heavily (from $22 to $44) in better-quality mattresses with springs. The condition of many of the mattresses was incredibly bad because of hard wear and lack of any protective covering. They were almost all stained, torn and infested with bedbugs and fleas. Of the 26 mattresses in the *vecindad,* 14 had been bought new, two were gifts and 10 had been bought secondhand, their poor condition notwithstanding. In spite of the low price of the used mattresses (ranging from 56 cents to $2.40) the total amount invested in mattresses ($178) was higher than the amount invested in

SHARP CONTRAST in value between the possessions of the two best-off and the two poorest households, although it was predictable, had one surprising element. All the possessions in the two poorest households were worth less than half the value of those in No. 5, the second-best-off household, and those in No. 7 were worth nearly twice as much as those in No. 5. The value of holy pictures and other religious objects in either of the poorest households, however, far outstripped the value of such objects in the best-off: combined, they constituted 33 percent of the total value of such objects in all 14 households in the tenement.

PLAZA OF THE *VECINDAD*, or tenement, in Mexico City where the author and his colleagues made their inventory of the material possessions of the inhabitants is an unpaved area that serves as a communal playground, laundry, workshop, barnyard and bath. In the background is the adobe-brick wall of the tenement itself, which consists of 14 one-room apartments in a row. Each apartment is occupied by one family. The population of the tenement at the time of the study was 83, an average of about six per apartment.

WASHING CLOTHES, a tenement housewife combines traditional and modern methods. The cement trough with its pounding stone is a part of the past, as is the decorated pitcher. The tub and buckets of galvanized iron form a part of the residents' inventory of more contemporary equipment. Although dishpans were scarce, the families owned a total of 43 buckets and 21 tubs.

beds ($132). The average duration of mattress ownership was three years eight months.

Each household had at least one shelf for votive candles dedicated to the saints, even if it was only a small board hung with string from nails on the wall. The altar was often loaded with a clutter of nonreligious objects: needles, thread, razors and other things that had to be kept out of reach of children. On holy days it was cleared and decorated with colored tissue paper.

Kitchen shelves were also found in every household, although many of the families had at one time been unable to afford them and had had to keep tableware and food on the floor. The shelves were inexpensive, none costing more than $1.20. The majority of them had been bought secondhand, received as gifts or built by members of the household.

The fifth essential article, a table, was also owned by every family. Some of the better-off families had two or three tables and had managed to paint or varnish them or cover them with oilcloth. The majority of the tables were cheap unpainted wood ones; the most expensive cost $5.20, and three-fourths of them were valued at $1.20 or less. None had been bought in a store; most had been acquired at street markets or from relatives or acquaintances.

In addition to the five indispensable articles of furniture, nearly all the families considered three others to be necessary for a decent standard of living. One of them was a chair. Only one household had no chairs at all; the adults there sat on the bed and the children on the floor. One family had eight chairs; another, seven; most had at least two. The chairs made the single small room of the apartment very crowded indeed. In the tenement as a whole, however, there were only 52 chairs for the 83 residents; at mealtimes many had to sit on the bed, on a low stool or on the floor. Like the other furniture, all the chairs were in-

expensive; none had cost more than $2.

A wardrobe for clothing also was regarded as a necessity, since none of the apartments had a closet. Twelve of the 14 households had a wardrobe; in the other two clothes were hung on nails or kept in boxes. A wardrobe represented a relatively large investment, and the families considered it to be a prestige item. It was often a wedding gift from the husband to the wife.

Most of the wardrobes had been bought new, at an average cost of $16.80, and they were generally the longest-held article of furniture in the apartment. Some had been there for as many as 15 years. In all but a few instances the wardrobe was in poor condition—battered and with the door mirrors either cracked or missing. Only one family had been able to afford to replace its broken mirrors.

Every family considered a radio essential, and at the time of my study 11 of the 14 households had one. One family had two radios. The radio was usually the family's most expensive piece of furniture. More money ($414) had been invested in radios than in any other item except for two television sets. Most of the radios had been bought new on credit, at prices ranging from $20 to $74. Because of the precariousness of the tenants' financial situation, the radio tended to be only a briefly held possession; its ownership averaged less than three years. Frequently the radio had to be given up because the family could not meet installment payments on it or could not afford to have it repaired when it broke down. Many radios were pawned, usually in a clandestine pawnshop that charged 20 percent interest per month on the loan. After losing the radio most families would buy another as soon as circumstances permitted.

Only one of the families was able to buy and hold on to a television set. This family, financially the best-off in the tenement, was managing to keep up the payments on a set costing a little more than $480—an amount greater than the combined value of all the family's other material possessions and greater than the total personal property of 12 of the other tenants. A second family had a television set when I began my study, but it pawned and lost the set before I had completed the investigation. The family bought another set later, committing itself to paying $24 a month for several years; it would be a most extraordinary achievement if the family succeeded in maintaining the payments. Needless to say, everyone in the tenement, particularly the young people, would like to have a television set, but few other families have attempted to buy one.

Some of the families in better economic circumstances had extra items of furniture such as glass-fronted dish cabinets and, in one case, three armchairs. These articles apparently were esteemed by their owners more for prestige value than for utility; in the one-room apartment they were impractical and they crowded the small space to a point of extreme inconvenience. The owner of the armchairs was a young shoemaker who was trying hard to raise his standard of living. He had bought a television set and the first and only gas stove ever used in the *vecindad,* but he had lost both by pawning one and not meeting the time payments on the other.

In nearly all cases furniture items (such as new mattresses, wardrobes and radios) that cost more than a few dollars were bought on credit. The public markets or itinerant salesmen from whom they were bought did not require a down payment, but for the privilege of paying in installments the buyer had to pay twice as much as the cash price of the article. The tenants were aware of this, but their cash resources were so small that they could obtain these articles only by buying them on credit. The weekly installments were usually low, averaging 80 cents, and often extended over more than a year for a single article.

The purchases of secondhand furniture were usually made from relatives or friends, most often within the same tenement. Since 11 of the 14 households were closely related, there was considerable opportunity for intrafamily commerce, usually at bargain prices.

Kitchen equipment in the 14 households was generally restricted to inexpensive items. The largest total in-

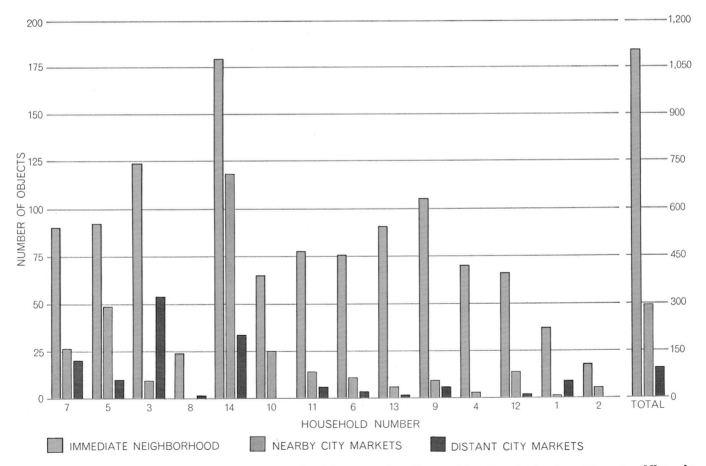

BUYING HABITS of the tenement families were analyzed by finding out where some 1,600 objects had been bought. In every case, buying in the immediate neighborhood and within the tenement itself outweighed purchases at nearby or more distant city markets. In part this reflects buying from itinerant peddlers who visited the tenement regularly. Two households contained more than four objects obtained outside Mexico City; some had come from as far away as Guadalajara, Acapulco and the state of Chiapas.

vestment in this category by any family was $42.63, and the aggregate for the 14 households was $230.36. None of the apartments had a refrigerator. The principal item of kitchen equipment was usually a stove. Eleven apartments had kerosene or petroleum stoves; in the other three cooking was done on a brazier or an earthenware plate over a charcoal hearth on the floor. The cooking vessels were generally inexpensive *ollas* or *cazuelas* (narrow-mouthed or wide-mouthed vessels of clay). Only two families had aluminum pots and only five had copper kettles. Twelve owned frying pans.

Every family had a few spoons that were used for cooking and for eating soup. There were few other eating utensils; only two families owned forks and only seven had table knives. Solid foods were usually eaten with the fingers, often with the aid of a tortilla to wrap or scoop up the food. The eating plates were most commonly "tin" ones (costing from eight to 16 cents); one family had a six-piece place setting of china, which it had owned for 14 years. Because glassware was a favorite gift item in the community, particularly on Mother's Day, the households had more glasses than traditional Mexican clay cups. One family owned 76 glasses. Some families also had serving trays and other "luxury" items that had been received as gifts.

Almost 90 percent of the kitchen equipment had been bought new because it was relatively inexpensive. In spite of the breakable nature of much of it this equipment had a better record of durability (the average was two and a half years) than many of the other articles in our inventories.

Other household equipment, although more meager in quantity than kitchen utensils, was placed in a separate category of study. Household equipment for all the families totaled $294 in value and ranked fourth in the list of categories. Three sewing machines owned by three families accounted for about a third of this total. One of the sewing machines had been pawned three times in three years to pay debts.

All the women in the community sewed; many of them mended and made clothes and bedclothes for the family, much of it from flour sacks. All owned at least one needle and most owned a pair of scissors, although on occasion the scissors might be pawned. Only seven of the households had a thimble, and none of the women owned a sewing basket for storing thread and needles. They usually bought thread in small quantities, sufficient only for the job at

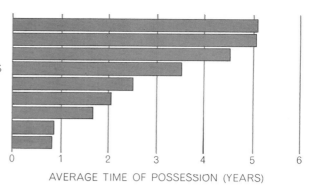

RELIGIOUS OBJECTS
TOOLS
FURNITURE
HOUSEHOLD DECORATIONS
KITCHEN EQUIPMENT
HOUSEHOLD EQUIPMENT
BEDCLOTHING
PERSONAL CLOTHING
PERSONAL ADORNMENT

0   1   2   3   4   5   6
AVERAGE TIME OF POSSESSION (YEARS)

AVERAGE LENGTH OF TIME that objects remained in a tenement household was at its maximum in the case of pictures of saints and other religious items, which were often considered heirlooms. This was also true of tools, which were a source of livelihood for the tenement households that engaged in manufacturing. On the other hand, items that were easily pawned, such as jewelry, or quickly worn out, such as clothing, were soon let go.

hand. Each family had at least one electric iron, in most cases bought secondhand. Two better-off families had ironing boards; in the other households the women ironed on the table.

In the entire tenement there were no wastebaskets and only two ashtrays, although most of the men and many of the women smoked. Nine of the 14 households had no garbage can for the kitchen. Cigarette butts and all other trash were simply thrown on the dirt or cement floor of the room and were eventually swept out. Every family had a broom, generally a crude handmade affair that had to be replaced frequently because of constant use.

Two water taps in the yard were the only source of water for the apartment and every family required several buckets or containers for fetching water. The 14 households had a total of 43 pails. They also owned a total of 21 tubs, some of them quite large, for laundering and for bathing. Fewer than half of the families owned dishpans; only four had a washstand. Toothbrushes were a luxury; in only three families did each person have a toothbrush of his own. Among the more unusual items were three douche bags, a syringe and three eyecups.

Awareness of time and of schedules was increasing among the slum dwellers, and most of the families felt the need of a clock—for feeding babies, giving medicine, getting children off to school on time or listening to favorite radio programs. Still, only half of the families, and only the better-to-do ones, owned a clock. The others kept track of the time either by their radio or by asking their clock-owning neighbors.

All the apartments had electric light. Three households owned gasoline or

kerosene lanterns for use in their workshop at night. One household owned an electric heater; for all the others the only source of heat on cold nights was the cooking stove.

As they did in other respects, the families of the tenement varied considerably in the poverty of their household equipment. The better-to-do families not only owned more items in this category (165 articles for the upper seven families compared with 104 for the lower seven) but also had a wider range of objects. One family (the second-poorest) owned no washtub, no clothespins, no scissors or thimble, no storage receptacles, no dishpan, no floor brush, no clothesbrush, no toothbrush and of course no sewing machine or clock. In the tenement as a whole the length of possession of household equipment was very brief, averaging only two years.

Bedclothes, the fifth most costly material goods in the community, accounted for a value of $279.99, or 6.8 percent of the total. This relatively high figure was due mainly to the expensiveness of blankets and quilts; the number of items was actually quite small. No family had more than 30 articles of bedclothing, including sheets, pillows, pillowcases, blankets and quilts. The best-off family owned a silk bedspread. Much of the bedclothing had been bought new, mainly on credit, but a large proportion was homemade. The women of the *vecindad*, even in the better-off families, usually made their sheets from flour sacks. Four sacks made an average-sized sheet. The length of possession of bedclothing averaged only 1.7 years. This was partly because of wear and partly because even bedclothes sometimes had to be sold to meet more urgent needs.

I shall merely summarize briefly here

the inventory of the other five categories of general household goods: decorative objects, religious objects, animals, plants and medicines. The principal investment in decoration was expended on photographs of family members. There was an average of more than seven photographs per apartment. They were usually framed and often in color and represented a total cost of $82.38. Most of the apartments were also adorned with pictures of saints and with colorful calendars, usually religious ones that had been obtained free. A few households had different types of pictures, painted vases, china figurines of animals and other items.

The investment in religious objects by these impoverished families was remarkably large. A total of 147 pictures of Catholic saints and Biblical scenes, an average of more than 10 pictures per household, hung on the walls of the tenement apartments. There were also flowered vases, candles, small religious figures and a variety of other religious objects displayed on the altars. In the

tenement as a whole the total investment in religious objects was $210.53. About half had been bought by the residents themselves and half had come as gifts.

The emphasis on religious objects was greatest among the poorest families. The family that ranked lowest in total investment in material possessions actually stood highest in the value of its religious objects. This family and the next-poorest had spent almost as much on religious articles as on furniture. If we include the religious gifts they received, their religious possessions represented nearly twice the total value of their furniture. Nearly all the religious objects in the 14 households had been bought new and were kept for an average of 5.07 years, longer than possessions in any other category.

The investment in the other categories of general household belongings—animals, plants and medicines—was so small that it calls for little comment. The tenement residents loved animals; almost every family had a cat or dog (partly as protection against rats and thieves) and

some tenants also kept chickens, pigeons and other birds. Their total cash investment, however, was only $15.94 for animals and $10.20 for plants. The 14 families' entire investment in the medicines on their shelves amounted to $7.76.

In the category of personal possessions, clothing was of course the major item. Clothing ranked second to furniture among the 13 property categories, and it accounted for 27.4 percent of the tenants' total investment in material goods. The 14 families had spent a total of $1,127.36 on the clothing they owned at the time of the inventory. About 87 percent of their purchased clothing had been bought new (usually for cash but a third of it on credit); the rest had been obtained secondhand. A substantial proportion of their total of clothing possessions were gifts and clothing made at home.

The families differed markedly in their expenditures for clothes. The poorest families bought very little, relying mainly on gifts from relatives. One family, for example, had spent only $3.92 for clothing and had received $20.72 worth as gifts. The largest outlay for clothing by any family was $192.64. This family ranked near the bottom in furniture possessions. Generally those families that invested heavily in clothing tended to spend little on furniture.

In every household the women supplemented the clothing purchases and gifts with clothing they made themselves, often out of flour sacks or scraps. Most of this home manufacture was for the women and children. For example, the mother in the family with the largest number of children (eight) had produced 42 articles, including 15 items for her youngest baby, 11 dresses, nine slips and seven shirts.

The clothing of all 14 families was limited to a few basic items. Every woman owned at least a dress and a pair of shoes, usually only one pair, so that much of the time she went barefoot. The adult women had an average of fewer than four dresses apiece; the young girls averaged six apiece. Nearly all the women had a *rebozo*, the traditional Mexican shawl, and most of them also owned a sweater, two or more slips (often homemade), underpants (an average of about three pairs per woman) and brassieres. About half of the women had skirt-and-blouse outfits; none wore slacks. There were only 15 pairs of stockings in the entire community; these belonged mainly to teen-age girls. One woman and five girls had coats, one woman had a bathrobe and one owned

INSTALLMENT-PLAN BICYCLE, undergoing repair in this photograph, was bought as a Christmas present for his son by the head of household No. 5. The $64 that it cost was met by monthly payments of $4.80. To recoup some of the money the father rented it out.

a pocketbook. Handkerchiefs were rare; among the 83 residents in the tenement the only people who had this item were two men and two young girls.

The children and men of the community were better shod than the women. The basic wardrobe of the men consisted of shoes, undershorts (often homemade), a pair of pants, one or more shirts and a jacket or coat against the cold. There were only two suits in the community, belonging to two boys who had worn them at their confirmation. A number of men had no socks or undershirts. No male in the tenement owned a necktie. A few men had working overalls, several had a cap or a straw hat and one owned a bathing suit.

The clothing of this community, generally of poor quality and subjected to frequent wear, had a short lifetime. The average length of possession for all items of clothing was only 9.9 months. Sometimes clothes were sold before they wore out because of a financial crisis. In one instance the man of the household sold much of the family's wardrobe during a prolonged drinking spree, leaving his wife with only a single torn dress.

In the category of personal adornment the list of articles is brief. The entire investment in this category was $126.32, more than half of which was accounted for by five wristwatches owned by comparatively well-off families. Religious medals, finger rings and cheap earrings, also owned mainly by less poor families, constituted the rest of the articles in this category. Women's jewelry was extremely scarce. Not a single woman had a necklace, a bracelet or a brooch. In any case, the possession of such items in this community was ephemeral—averaging only 9.8 months—because of the ready convertibility of jewelry into cash.

Toys were even scarcer than jewelry among these families. Of the total investment of $121.62 in toys, more than half was represented by two bicycles. One had been bought new on installments and was rented out part of the time; the other was a secondhand bicycle without tires. There were also three tricycles in the community, two of them secondhand. Only half of the families in the tenement were able to invest in any toys for their children.

Finally, there were a few households that owned material goods in a special category: tools and materials for manufacturing in the home. In total value this category ranked third, after furniture and personal clothing. Three artisans who worked at home accounted for most of the investment: a shoemaker and two

household heads who made and sold toy water bottles. The shoemaker had a stock of soles, heels, nails and various other things required for shoe repairing. Having little capital, he could maintain only a small supply of materials and had to replenish it every few days. Most of the materials and tools had been bought used. All three artisans had held on to their tools for a comparatively long time (an average of 5.05 years), since the tools constituted the family's means of livelihood and could not be sold or pawned as casually as other household goods.

It is surely significant that two of the three households that had managed to scrape up enough capital to make a substantial investment in income-producing tools and materials were also the most affluent families in the tenement in terms of their total accumulation of material possessions. The best-off family owned $134.38 worth of tools, whereas two of the three poorest families in the tenement had no tools whatever.

What conclusions, if any, can one draw from the inventory of the possessions of these 14 slum families? For one thing, I was struck by the truly remarkable differences within this group of families, all of whom might seem to a casual observer to be living at the same level of poverty. Moreover, the differences in the value of their possessions were greater than differences in their income. If we compare the possessions of the three "wealthiest" families [*Families 7, 5 and 3 in the illustration on pages 414 and 415*] with those of the three poorest families [*Families 12, 1 and 2*], we see that the top three owned a total of $1,754.46 worth of purchased goods, whereas the bottom three owned a total of $250.55—only a seventh as much. The largest differential was in the families' relative investment in furniture and clothing: $1,093.92 for the top three against only $149.49 for the bottom three. There were similar differences in expenditures for luxury items such as jewelry ($71.97 against $2.38) and toys ($86.58 against $13.68).

The only category in which the poorer families had spent more than the better-off was that of religious objects. The difference in amount was small ($23.45 by the poorer families compared with $21.78 by the better-off), but in its proportion to the families' total investment in material goods the contrast was great. Whereas the better-off families had invested only slightly more than 1 percent of their money in religious items, the poorer families had invested nearly 14 percent. Furthermore, religious objects

also predominated in the gifts the poorer families had received; such objects represented nearly half of all gifts received, whereas religious objects accounted for less than 15 percent of the gifts in the better-off families.

The fact that the tenement dwellers had held on to religious objects longer than most of their other possessions attests to the crucial role of religion in the lives of the poor. It appears also that religious objects may be the only things they own long enough to establish a real identification with. Yet even these are held for a fairly brief period, an average of about five years. The brevity of possession, and the singular absence of heirlooms passed down from generation to generation, suggest that the life of the very poor is weak in tradition and is oriented almost exclusively to day-to-day concerns.

It might be supposed that for lack of funds people in poverty are driven to making their own goods such as clothing or furniture. I found, however, that the better-off families in the tenement were the most productive in this sense because only they owned sewing machines or work tools and could afford to buy the materials. These families produced five times as much clothing (in value) as the poorer families did. By the same token they were also able to buy more of their goods new. Whereas about 25 percent of all purchases by the three poorest families were secondhand, only about 7 percent of those by the three best-off families were secondhand. The contrast was greatest in furniture purchases. The poorer families bought three-quarters of their furniture secondhand; the better-off families bought three-quarters of theirs new.

The study of possessions, while confirming some previous findings about the poor, raises questions about others. For instance, there has been reason to believe that the mobility of poor people is highly restricted, that they rarely venture out of their immediate neighborhood. The analysis of the 14 families' possessions, however, showed that the objects came from 43 different markets or localities, some of them at considerable distances from Mexico City. Eight of the families owned objects that came from 14 marketplaces outside the capital. One family had possessions that were bought in 28 marketplaces, 11 of which were in distant cities, one as far away as Chiapas. It therefore appears that at least some of the Mexican urban poor may move about more widely than has been supposed.

41

SQUATTER SETTLEMENTS

WILLIAM MANGIN
October 1967

The shantytowns that have sprung up in developing areas are widely regarded as being sinks of social disorganization. A study of such communities in Peru shows that here, at least, the opposite is true

Since the end of World War II squatter settlements around large cities have become a worldwide phenomenon. In the rapidly urbanizing but not yet industrialized countries millions of families from the impoverished countryside and from the city slums have invaded the outskirts of major cities and there set up enormous shantytowns. These illegal usurpations of living space have everywhere aroused great alarm, particularly among the more affluent city dwellers and government authorities. Police forces have made determined and violent efforts to repel the invasions, but the tide has been too much for them. The squatter settlements give every sign of becoming permanent.

The new shantytowns are without public services, unsanitary and in many respects almost intolerably insecure. Most middle-class and upper-class observers are inclined to regard them as a virulent social disease. Politicians and the police see them as dangerous defiance of law and order. Conservatives are certain that they are seedbeds of revolution and communism. City planners and architects view them as inefficient users of urban real estate and as sores on the landscape. Newspapers treat them as centers of crime and delinquency. Social workers are appalled by the poverty of many of the squatters, by the high incidence of underemployment and low pay, by the lack of medical treatment and sewage facilities and by what they see as a lack of proper, decent, urban, middle-class training for the squatters' children.

The truth is that the shantytowns are not quite as they seem to outside observers. I first became acquainted with some of these settlements in Peru in 1952. Conducting studies in anthropology among villagers in the Peruvian mountains at that time, I occasionally visited some of their friends and relatives living in squatter settlements (they are called *barriadas* in Peru) on the fringes of the city of Lima. I was surprised to find that the squatter communities and the way the people lived differed rather widely from the outside impression of them. Since then I have spent 10 years in more or less continuous study of the *barriadas* of Peru, and it has become quite clear to me that many of the prevalent ideas about the squatter settlements are myths.

The common view is that the squatters populating the Peruvian shantytowns are Indians from the rural mountains who still speak only the Quechuan language, that they are uneducated, unambitious, disorganized, an economic drag on the nation—and also (consistency being no requirement in mythology) that they are a highly organized group of radicals who mean to take over and communize Peru's cities. I found that in reality the people of the *barriadas* around Lima do not fit this description at all.

Most of them had been city dwellers for some time (on the average for nine years) before they moved out and organized the *barriadas*. They speak Spanish (although many are bilingual) and are far removed from the rural Indian culture; indeed, their educational level is higher than that of the general population in Peru. The *barriada* families are relatively stable compared with those in the city slums or the rural provinces. Delinquency and prostitution, which are common in the city slums, are rare in the *barriadas*. The family incomes are low, but most of them are substantially higher than the poorest slum level. My studies, based on direct observation, as well as questionnaires, psychological tests and other measurements, also indicate that the *barriada* dwellers are well organized, politically sophisticated, strongly patriotic and comparatively conservative in their sociopolitical views. Although poor, they do not live the life of squalor and hopelessness characteristic of the "culture of poverty" depicted by Oscar Lewis; although bold and defiant in their seizure of land, they are not a revolutionary "lumpenproletariat."

The squatters around the cities of Peru now number about 700,000, of whom 450,000 live in the *barriadas* of Lima itself. This is a substantial portion of the nation's entire population, which totals about 12 million. Like the squatter settlements in other countries, the *barriadas* of Peru represent the worldwide migration of people from the

country to the city and a revolt of the poor against the miserable, disorganized and expensive life in the city slums. In the shantytowns they find rent-free havens where they feel they can call their homes and the land their own.

The *barriadas* of Lima began some 20 years ago as clusters of families that had spontaneously fled from the city and set up communities of straw shacks on the rocky, barren land outside. The first, small settlements were short-lived, as the police forcibly drove the settlers off, sometimes with fatal beatings of men, women and children, and burned their shacks and household goods. Nevertheless, the squatters kept returning, as many as four times to the same place. They soon learned that there was greater safety in numbers, and the invasions of land and formation of *barriadas* became elaborately planned, secretly organized projects involving large groups.

The enterprise generally took the form of a quasi-military campaign. Its leaders were usually highly intelligent, articulate, courageous and tough, and often a woman was named the "secretary of defense" (a title borrowed from Peruvian labor organizations and provincial clubs). For the projected *barriada* community the leaders recruited married couples under 30 with children; single adults were usually excluded (and still are from most *barriadas*). Lawyers or near-lawyers among the recruited group searched land titles to find a site that was owned, or at least could be said to be owned, by some public agency, preferably the national government. The organizers then visited the place at night and marked out the lots assigned to the members for homes and locations for streets, schools, churches, clinics and other facilities.

After all the plans had been made in the utmost secrecy to avoid alerting the police, the organizers appealed confidentially to some prominent political or religious figure to support the invasion when it took place; they also alerted a friendly newspaper, so that any violent police reaction would be fully reported. On the appointed day the people recruited for the invasion, usually numbering in the hundreds and sometimes more than 1,000, rushed to the *barriada* site in taxis, trucks, buses and even on delivery cycles. On arriving, the families immediately began to put up shelters made of matting on their assigned lots.

More than 100 such invasions to set up *barriadas* have taken place in the Lima area in the past 20 years. The settlers have consistently behaved in a disciplined, courageous, yet nonprovocative manner, even in the face of armed attack by the police. In the end popular sympathy and the fear of the political consequences of too much police violence have compelled the government authorities to allow the squatters to stay. The present liberal regime of President Belaunde tries to prevent squatter invasions, but it does not attack them violently when they occur.

Once a *barriada* has established a foothold, it grows until it has used up its available land. The original settlers are joined by relatives and friends from the provinces and the city. From the relatively flat land where the first houses are built, new shacks gradually creep up the steep, rocky hillsides that overlook the city.

The surface appearance of the *barriadas* is deceptive. At first glance from a distance they appear to be formless collections of primitive straw shacks. Actually the settlements are laid out according to plans, often in consultation with architectural or engineering students. As time goes on most of the shanties are replaced by more permanent structures. As soon as the residents can afford to, they convert their original straw shacks into houses of brick and cement. Indeed, the history of each *barriada* is plainly written in the mosaic of its structures. The new houses clinging to the high hillside are straw shacks; at the foot of the hill the older ones are built of masonry. One of the oldest *barriadas*, known as San Martin, has a paved main street, painted houses and elegant fronts on stores, banks and movie houses.

The squatters improve their houses as they accumulate a little extra money from employment and find spare time. At present the *barriada* communities are far too poor to afford the capital costs of utilities such as water systems and sewers. Water and fuel (mainly kerosene) are transported in bottles or drums by truck, bicycle or on foot. Some houses have electricity supplied by enterprising individuals who have invested in generators and run lines to their clients; a few of these entrepreneurs

SQUATTERS BATTLE POLICE the morning after an "invasion" of unoccupied land near the Engineering School, north of Lima's city limits. The clash occurred in 1963; although police managed to clear the site temporarily, the squatters soon returned to build there.

HILLSIDE SHANTYTOWN in the Rimac district of Lima is seen in the photograph on the opposite page. Many squatter houses, originally straw shacks, are being rebuilt in brick and masonry whenever the earnings of the owners permit. Visible behind an unexcavated pre-Columbian mound (*top*) is one of the few public housing projects in Peru.

have gone so far as to acquire a television set (on time) and charge admission to the show. In some well-established *barriadas* the electric company of Lima has installed lines and service.

The major concern of the *barriada* people, and the greatest source of anxiety, is the problem of finding steady employment. The largest *barriadas* do provide considerable local employment, particularly in construction work. Many families obtain some income by operating stores, bars or shops in their homes; in the *barriada* I have studied most closely about a third of the households offer some kind of goods for sale. By and large, however, the people of the squatter settlements around Lima depend mainly on employment in the city. Most of the men and many of the women commute to jobs in Lima, working in personal services, factories, stores, offices and even in professional occupations. One *barriada* men's club includes among its members a physician, a bank branch manager, a police lieutenant, four lawyers, several businessmen and two Peace Corps volunteers.

The families that colonize a *barriada* are regarded as "owners" of their lots. As time goes on, many rent, trade or sell their lots and houses to others, using beautifully made titles with seals, lawyers' signatures and elaborate property descriptions—but in most cases with no legal standing. (Actually it appears that in Peru even private property is usually clouded by at least two titles, and much of the land is in litigation.) In the *barri-*

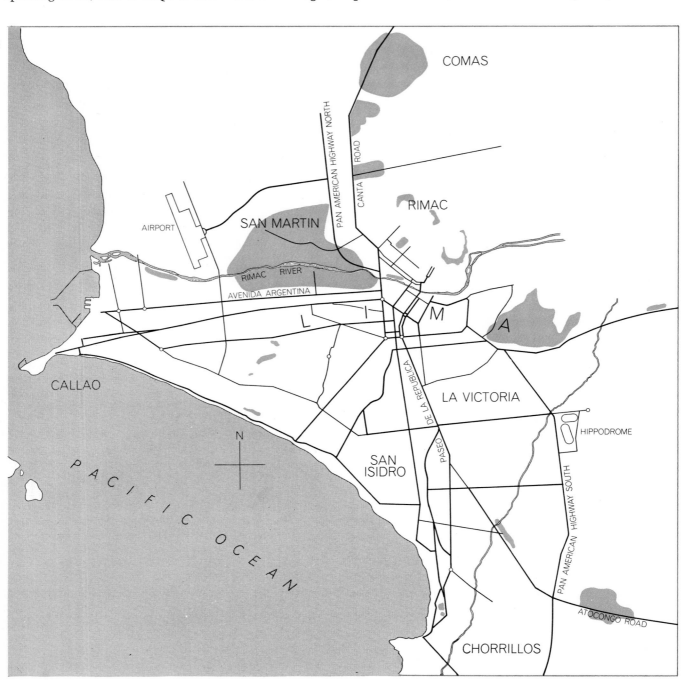

BARRIADAS of the city of Lima and its outskirts (*color*) shelter some 450,000 squatters who began to establish rent-free communities in 1945 on unoccupied hillsides north and south of the Rimac River. Now major *barriadas* also occupy both sides of the river downstream toward the port of Callao; a 20-kilometer stretch of the Pampa de Comas, including some agricultural land, along the road north to Canta, and hillsides bordering the road south to Atocongo, adjacent to the richest residential district in the Peruvian capital.

adas, as elsewhere in the nation, disputes over lot "ownership" arise; the claimants appeal variously to the association that runs the *barriada* or to the National Housing Authority, the Lima city government, the police or the courts. The decisions of these agencies generally have only a provisional character. A law adopted by the Peruvian national legislature in 1957 authorized the granting of land titles to *barriada* dwellers, but for several years it was ignored. In 1962 a group of engineers and architects in the National Housing Authority, taking advantage of the preoccupation of the military junta with other matters, passed out land titles to a few hundred families in two of the oldest *barriadas.* Even these titles, however, were marked "Provisional."

In most matters of public concern the *barriadas* are governed by their own membership associations. They hold elections about once a year—a rarity in Peru, where, except in the *barriadas,* no democratic elections of local officials had been held for more than 60 years before the present national government took office. The *barriada* associations levy taxes (in the form of "dues") on the residents, and they usually manage to collect them from most members. They also screen new applicants, resolve land disputes, try to prevent land speculation and organize cooperative projects. For official papers, such as voting registration and certificates of marriage, birth and death, the *barriada* people must resort to the city hall, and their reception by the town clerks is often so uncordial and whimsical that the quest for an essential document may be a heroic ordeal. (I have seen *barriada* birth certificates stamped "Provisional"!) Lacking authoritative police forces of their own, the *barriada* residents usually take their complaints of crimes and misdemeanors to the city police, but the latter seldom do anything more than register the complaint. For schooling of the children the *barriadas* depend mainly on the city's public and church schools. A few have elementary schools of their own, but generally students must commute to the city in the elementary grades as well as to high school and the university. The *barriada* people also have close connections with the city through their jobs, unions, social clubs, churches and services such as medical care, social security and unemployment insurance.

Many of the *barriada* associations have established working relations with city and national agencies and even

SQUATTER ENTREPRENEURS, residents of a Rimac *barriada,* run a sidewalk cobbler's shop complete with foot-powered stitching machines at the edge of the wholesale market.

AGED BUS is one of the many vehicles, some communally owned, that connect the outlying *barriadas* with downtown Lima. Many squatters commute to steady jobs in the city.

with international organizations such as the Peace Corps and the United Nations. Of the various agencies in a position to assist the *barriadas* perhaps the most important is Peru's National Housing Authority, known as the JNV. The JNV has been beset by power struggles between the national office and local city officials and by other confusions, so that its accomplishments are uneven. In some *barriadas* representatives of the JNV are cheered; in others they are stoned. (In one settlement the agency erected an impressive sign announcing that it was installing a water and sewage-disposal system; after six months had passed with no visible evidence of a start on the project, the residents began to pile fecal matter under the sign, whereupon JNV removed the sign.) Recently, however, the housing agency gave Lima officials authority to adopt and proceed with specific plans, and there is now considerable activity.

WAITING FOR INVASION, a squatter advance party at dawn inspects the previous night's work of blocking out the town plan for a new *barriada*. The rest of the invading squatters, as many as 1,000 in number, will soon arrive in trucks, buses and taxis.

MAT-SHED SETTLEMENT springs up within a few hours after an invasion and a new *barriada* is established. This squatter settlement on the Pampa de Comas is an unusual intrusion on cultivated land; the majority of invasions occupy idle or desert areas.

The *barriada* governments have not lacked the usual trouble of municipal administrations, including charges of corruption and factional splits. Moreover, their prestige and authority have declined as the need for community cohesion and defense against attack from outside has been reduced. There is a compensating trend, however, toward replacement of the original associations by full-fledged, official town governments. The two largest *barriadas* in the Lima area, San Martin and Pampa de Comas, now have elected mayors and town councils.

What, if anything, can be learned from the squatter settlements that will be of value in resolving the monumental problems of today's cities and their desperate people? I should like to present some conclusions from our own 10-year studies. They were carried out on a grant from the U.S. National Institute of Mental Health in cooperation with the Institute of Ethnology of the University of San Marcos and the Department of Mental Hygiene of the Ministry of Public Health in Peru, and with the assistance of a group of psychiatrists, anthropologists and social workers. We concentrated on an intensive study of a particular *barriada*, which I shall call Benavides. It consists of some 600 families. Over the 10-year period I have spent considerable time living in the community (in a rented room), interviewing a large sample of the population and examining their attitudes and feelings as indicated by various questionnaires and inventories, including the Rorschach and thematic apperception tests.

I am bound to say that I have been profoundly impressed by the constructive spirit and achievements of the *barriada* people. They have shown a really remarkable capacity for initiative, self-help and community organization. Visitors to the *barriadas,* many of them trained observers, remark on the accomplishments of the residents in home and community construction, on the small businesses they have created, on the degree of community organization, on how much the people have achieved without government help and on their friendliness. Most of the residents are neither resentful nor alienated; they are understandably cynical yet hopeful. They describe themselves as "humble people," abandoned by society but not without faith that "they" (the powers that be) will respond to people's needs for help to create a life of dignity for

DIGGING A SEWER is typical of squatters' communal ventures in self-improvement. The large brick structure beyond is another communal project, a partly finished church.

YEARLY ELECTIONS are a feature of *barriada* life scarcely known to other citizens of Peru. Until the Belaunde regime took office in 1963, democratic local elections were rare.

SWIFTNESS of a squatter invasion is exemplified by the settled appearance of this quiet lane in a new *barriada* outside Lima. None of these buildings had existed 24 hours earlier.

STREET DOOR of a mat-shed shelter consists of wooden frame and cloth drop that carries the house number. The resident wears conventional city dress. Many in the *barriadas* come to Lima from the country, but most are townfolk fleeing slum rents and slum conditions.

themselves. Recognizing fully that they are living in "infrahuman conditions," the *barriada* dwellers yearn for something better. Given any recognition or encouragement by the government, such as the paving of a street or even the collection of taxes from them, the people respond with a burst of activity in improvement of their homes.

This is not to say that either their spirit or their behavior is in any sense idyllic. There are tensions within the *barriada* and people take economic advantage of one another. They are victims of the same racial prejudice and class inequality that characterize Peruvian society in general. As in the world outside, the *barriada* people identify themselves as city people, country people, coastal people, mountaineers, Indians, Cholos, mestizos, Negroes—and cliques arise. With the passage of time and weakening of the initial *esprit de corps,* bickering within the community becomes more and more common. Charlatans and incompetents sometimes take over leadership of the *barriada.* Moreover, because of the poverty of their resources for financing major projects in community services, the people have a low estimate of their own capabilities and continually look to the government or other outside agencies for solutions to their problems.

Nevertheless, to an outside observer what is most striking is the remarkable progress the *barriada* people have made on their own. They have exhibited a degree of popular initiative that is seldom possible in the tightly controlled community-action programs in the U.S. The *barriadas* of Peru now represent a multimillion-dollar investment in house construction, local small businesses and public services, not to speak of the social and political investment in community organization. Such achievements hold lessons from which more advanced countries may well profit.

Particularly in house construction and land development the *barriada* people have done better than the government, and at much less cost. The failures of governments and private developers everywhere to provide low-cost housing for the poor are notorious. Administrative costs, bureaucratic restrictions and the high cost of materials and construction when government agencies do the contracting generally put the housing rentals beyond the reach of the lowest-income group. Equally disappointing are the failures in the design of this official public housing, which usually disregards the desires and style of life of the people for whom it is intended.

In the Peruvian *barriadas*, by avoiding government control and the requirements of lending institutions, the people have built houses to their own desires and on the basis of first things first. Because they needed shelter immediately, they built walls and a roof and left bathrooms and electricity to be added later. They want flat roofs and strong foundations so that they can add a second story. They want a yard for raising chickens and guinea pigs, and a front room that can serve as a store or a barroom. They have dispensed with the restrictive residential zoning and construction details that middle-class planners and architects consider essential for proper housing.

Like most rural people in Peru, the *barriada* settlers are suspicious of large-scale projects and wary of entering into loan or mortgage arrangements. Indeed, throughout South America there is a general dissatisfaction with large housing projects. Costly mistakes have been made in the construction of "satellite cities" and "superblocks." This has led the national governments and other interested agencies to give more attention to the possibilities in rehabilitating existing housing. In Peru the government is now initiating experiments in offering low-cost loans through credit cooperatives, providing optional technical assistance and other services and letting the prospective housebuilder do his own contracting. As John Turner, an architect with many years' experience in Peru, has pointed out, if people are sold land and allowed to do their own contracting and building with optional help, the costs go down for both the clients and the government.

Our studies of the *barriadas* of Peru show, in brief, that these settlements contain many constructive elements whose significance should not be ignored. The people believe that their present situation is far preferable to what they had in the provinces or the central city slums and that they have an investment in their future and that of their children. What we have learned in Peru is supported by investigations of squatter settlements around the world.

The squatters have produced their own answer to the difficult problems of housing and community organization that governments have been unable to solve. In Peru we may have a chance to study what can happen when a government works with popular initiative rather than fighting it.

TRANSFORMED *BARRIADA* was one of the first in Lima. Today most buildings are brick or stone and many have a second story. Although unsurfaced, its avenue is illuminated.

PROSPEROUS ENTERPRISE, the Restaurant Central, is located in the Pampa de Comas. In 1956 it was a one-story bar in a newly built *barriada* that had no electric power. Now there are streetlights and the restaurant has a second story, a coat of plaster and television.

I BIOLOGICAL ANTHROPOLOGY

HUMAN ORIGINS AND THE HISTORY OF LIFE

1. Crises in the History of Life

BIOTIC ASSOCIATIONS AND EXTINCTION. David Nicol in *Systematic Zoology*, Vol. 10, No. 1, pages 35–41; March, 1961.

EVOLUTION OF LATE PALEOZOIC INVERTEBRATES IN RESPONSE TO MAJOR OSCILLATIONS OF SHALLOW SEAS. Raymond C. Moore in *Bulletin of the Museum of Comparative Zoology at Harvard College*, Vol. 112, No. 3, pages 259–286; October, 1954.

PALEONTOLOGICAL GAPS AND GEOCHRONOLOGY. Norman D. Newell in *Journal of Paleontology*, Vol. 36, No. 3, pages 592–610; May, 1962.

TETRAPOD EXTINCTIONS AT THE END OF THE TRIASSIC PERIOD. Edwin H. Colbert in *Proceedings of the National Academy of Sciences of the U.S.A.*, Vol. 44, No. 9, pages 973–977; September, 1958.

2. The Distribution of Man

HUMAN ANCESTRY FROM A GENETICAL POINT OF VIEW. Reginald Ruggles Gates. Harvard University Press, 1948.

MANKIND IN THE MAKING. William White Howells. Doubleday & Company, Inc., 1959.

RACES: A STUDY OF THE PROBLEMS OF RACE FORMATION IN MAN. Carleton S. Coon, Stanley M. Garn and Joseph B. Birdsell. Charles C Thomas, 1950.

THE STORY OF MAN. Carleton Stevens Coon. Alfred A. Knopf, Inc., 1954.

3. The Earliest Apes

A CRITICAL REAPPRAISAL OF TERTIARY PRIMATES. Elwyn L. Simons in *Genetic and Evolutionary Biology of the Primates: Vol. I*, edited by John Buettner-Janusch. Academic Press Inc., 1963.

NEW FOSSIL APES FROM EGYPT AND THE INITIAL DIFFERENTIATION OF HOMINOIDEA. E. L. Simons in *Nature*, Vol. 205, No. 4967, pages 135–139; January 9, 1965.

ORIGINS OF MAN: PHYSICAL ANTHROPOLOGY. John Buettner-Janusch. John Wiley & Sons, Inc., 1966.

4. Homo Erectus

MANKIND IN THE MAKING. William W. Howells. Doubleday & Company, Inc., revised edition, 1967.

THE NOMENCLATURE OF THE HOMINIDAE. Bernard G. Campbell. Occasional Paper No. 22, Royal Anthropological Institute of Great Britain and Ireland, 1965.

THE TAXONOMIC EVOLUTION OF FOSSIL HOMINIDS. Ernst Mayr in *Classification and Human Evolution*, edited by Sherwood L. Washburn. Viking Fund Publications in Anthropology, No. 37, 1963.

HUMAN GENETICS AND EVOLUTION

5. The Gene

LIFE OF MENDEL. Hugo Iltis. W. W. Norton & Company, Inc., 1932.

ON THE EVOLUTION OF BIOCHEMICAL SYNTHESES. N. H. Horowitz in *Proceedings of the National Academy of Sciences*, Vol. 31, pages 153–157; June, 1945.

WHAT IS LIFE? Erwin Schrödinger. Cambridge University Press, 1948.

6. The Genetic Code: III

THE GENETIC CODE, VOL. XXXI: 1966 COLD SPRING HARBOR SYMPOSIA ON QUANTITATIVE BIOLOGY. Cold Spring Harbor Laboratory of Quantitative Biology, 1967.

MOLECULAR BIOLOGY OF THE GENE. James D. Watson. W. A. Benjamin, Inc., 1965.

RNA CODEWORDS AND PROTEIN SYNTHESIS, VII: ON THE GENERAL NATURE OF THE RNA CODE. M. Nirenberg, P. Leder, M. Bernfield, R. Brimacombe, J. Trupin, F. Rottman and C. O'Neal in *Proceedings of the National Academy of Sciences*, Vol. 53, No. 5, pages 1161–1168; May, 1965.

STUDIES ON POLYNUCLEOTIDES, LVI: FURTHER SYNTHESES, IN VITRO, OF COPOLYPEPTIDES CONTAINING TWO AMINO ACIDS IN ALTERNATING SEQUENCE DEPENDENT UPON DNA-LIKE POLYMERS CONTAINING TWO NUCLEOTIDES IN ALTERNATING SEQUENCE. D. S. Jones, S. Nishimura and H. G. Khorana in *Journal of Molecular Biology*, Vol. 16, No. 2, pages 454–472; April, 1966.

7. Ionizing Radiation and Evolution

THE CAUSES OF EVOLUTION. J. B. S. Haldane. Harper & Brothers, 1932.

THE DARWINIAN AND MODERN CONCEPTIONS OF NATURAL SELECTION. H. J. Muller in *Proceedings of the American Philosophical Society*, Vol. 93, No. 6, pages 459–479; December 29, 1949.

EVOLUTION, GENETICS AND MAN. Theodosius Dobzhansky. John Wiley & Sons, Inc., 1955.

GENETICS, PALEONTOLOGY AND EVOLUTION. Edited by Glenn L. Jepsen, Ernst Mayr and George Gaylord Simpson. Princeton University Press, 1949.

RADIATION AND THE ORIGIN OF THE GENE. Carl Sagan in *Evolution*, Vol. 11, No. 1, pages 40–55; March, 1957.

8. Porphyria and King George III

PORPHYRIA—A ROYAL MALADY: ARTICLES PUBLISHED IN OR COMMISSIONED BY THE BRITISH MEDICAL JOURNAL. British Medical Association, 1968.

DISEASES OF PORPHYRIN METABOLISM. A. Goldberg and C. Rimington. Charles C Thomas, Publisher, 1962.

A CLINICAL REASSESSMENT OF THE "INSANITY" OF GEORGE III AND SOME OF ITS HISTORICAL IMPLICATIONS. Ida Macalpine and Richard Hunter in *Bulletin of the Institute of Historical Research*, Vol. 40, No. 102, pages 166–185; November, 1967.

9. The Present Evolution of Man

EVOLUTION, GENETICS AND MAN. Theodosius Dobzhansky. John Wiley & Sons, Inc., 1955.

MIRROR FOR MAN. Clyde Kluckhohn. McGraw-Hill Book Co., Inc., 1949.

RADIATION, GENES AND MAN. Bruce Wallace and Theodosius Dobzhansky. Henry Holt & Co., Inc., 1959.

EVOLUTION OF ANIMAL BEHAVIOR

10. The Evolution of Behavior

THE STUDY OF INSTINCT. N. Tinbergen. Clarendon Press, 1952.

11. The Evolution of Intelligence

ANIMAL INTELLIGENCE. E. L. Thorndike. The Macmillan Company, 1911.

SOME COMPARATIVE PSYCHOLOGY. M. E. Bitterman, Jerome Wodinsky and Douglas K. Candland in *American Journal of Psychology*, Vol. 71, No. 1, pages 94–110; March, 1958.

TOWARD A COMPARATIVE PSYCHOLOGY OF LEARNING. M. E. Bitterman in *American Psychologist*, Vol. 15, No. 11, pages 704–712; November, 1960.

12. The Social Order of Turkeys

THE GENETICAL EVOLUTION OF SOCIAL BEHAVIOUR: I. W. D. Hamilton in *Journal of Theoretical Biology*, Vol. 7, No. 1, pages 1–16; July, 1964.

THE ADAPTIVE SIGNIFICANCE OF AVIAN SOCIAL ORGANIZATIONS. John Hurrell Crook in *Symposia of the Zoological Society of London, No. 14: Social Organization of Animal Communities*. Zoological Society of London, April, 1965.

ECOLOGICAL ADAPTATIONS FOR BREEDING IN BIRDS. David Lack. Barnes & Noble, 1968.

13. The Social Life of Baboons

BEHAVIOR AND EVOLUTION. Edited by Anne Roe and George Gaylord Simpson. Yale University Press, 1958.

A STUDY OF BEHAVIOUR OF THE CHACMA BABOON, PAPIO URSINUS. Niels Bolwig in *Behaviour*, Vol. 14, No. 1–2, pages 136–163; 1959.

14. Urban Monkeys

BEHAVIOR OF NONHUMAN PRIMATES. Edited by Allan M. Schrier, Harry F. Harlow and Fred Stollnitz. Academic Press, 1965.

EFFECTS OF REARING CONDITIONS UPON THE BEHAVIOR OF RHESUS MONKEYS (MACACA MULATTA). Gene P. Sackett in *Child Development*, Vol. 36, No. 4, pages 855–868; December, 1965.

EFFECT OF HUMAN ENVIRONMENT ON COGNITIVE BEHAVIOR IN THE RHESUS MONKEY. S. D. Singh in *Journal of Comparative & Physiological Psychology*, Vol. 61, No. 2, pages 280–283; April, 1966.

II HUMAN PREHISTORY

TOOLS AND THE DEVELOPMENT OF CULTURE

15. Tools and Human Evolution

CEREBRAL CORTEX OF MAN. Wilder Penfield and Theodore Rasmussen. Macmillan Company, 1950.

THE EVOLUTION OF MAN, edited by Sol Tax. University of Chicago Press, 1960.

THE EVOLUTION OF MAN'S CAPACITY FOR CULTURE. Arranged by J. N. Spuhler. Wayne State University Press, 1959.

HUMAN ECOLOGY DURING THE PLEISTOCENE AND LATER TIMES IN AFRICA SOUTH OF THE SAHARA. J. Desmond Clark in *Current Anthropology*, Vol. I, pages 307–324; 1960.

16. Stone Tools and Human Behavior

LE PALÉOLITHIQUE INFÉRIEUR ET MOYEN DE JABRUD (SYRIE) ET LA QUESTION DU PRÉ-AURIGNACIEN. F. Bordes in *L'Anthropologie*, Vol. 59, Nos. 5–6, pages 486–507; 1955.

THE HUMAN USE OF THE EARTH. Philip L. Wagner. The Free Press of Glencoe, Illinois, 1960.

ME'ARAT SHOVAKH (MUGHARET esSHUBBABIQ). Sally R. Binford in *Israel Exploration Journal*, Vol. 16, No. 1, pages 18–32, No. 2, pages 96–103; 1966.

A PRELIMINARY ANALYSIS OF FUNCTIONAL VARIABILITY IN THE MOUSTERIAN OF LEVALLOIS FACIES. Lewis R. Binford and Sally R. Binford in *American Anthropologist*, Vol. 68, No. 2, Part 2, pages 238–295; April, 1966.

MODERN FACTOR ANALYSIS. Harry H. Harman. The University of Chicago Press, 1967.

17. The Prehistory of the Australian Aborigine

ABORIGINAL MAN IN AUSTRALIA. Edited by Ronald M. Berndt and Catherine H. Berndt. Angus and Robertson, 1965.

AUSTRALIAN ABORIGINAL STUDIES. Edited by H. Sheils. Oxford University Press, 1963.

CULTURE SUCCESSION IN SOUTH EASTERN AUSTRALIA FROM LATE PLEISTOCENE TO THE PRESENT. Norman B. Tindale in *Records of the South Australian Museum*, Vol. 13, No. 1, pages 1–49; April 30, 1957.

THE STONE AGE OF AUSTRALIA. D. J. Mulvaney in *Proceedings of the Prehistoric Society*, New Series, Vol. 27, pages 56–107; December, 1961.

18. Ishango

MISSION J. DE HEINZELIN DE BRAUCOURT. Institut des Parcs Nationaux du Congo (Belge) et du Ruanda-Urundi, 1950.

THE RISE OF CIVILIZATION IN THE OLD WORLD

19. The Agricultural Revolution

ANIMAL DOMESTICATION IN THE PREHISTORIC NEAR EAST. Charles A. Reed in *Science*, Vol. 130, No. 3,389, pages 1,629–1,639; December 11, 1959.

DOMESTICATION OF FOOD PLANTS IN THE OLD WORLD. Hans Helbaek in *Science*, Vol. 130, No. 3,372, pages 365–372; August 14, 1959.

NEAR EASTERN PREHISTORY. Robert J. Braidwood in *Science*, Vol. 127, No. 3,312, pages 1,419–1,430; June 20, 1958.

PREHISTORIC INVESTIGATIONS IN IRAQI KURDISTAN. Robert J. Braidwood and Bruce Howe in *Studies in Ancient Civilization*, No. 31. University of Chicago Press, 1960.

20. An Early Farming Village in Turkey

PREHISTORIC MEN. Robert J. Braidwood. Scott, Foresman and Company, 1967.

NATURAL ENVIRONMENT OF EARLY FOOD PRODUCTION NORTH OF MESOPOTAMIA. H. E. Wright, Jr., in *Science*, Vol. 161, No. 3839, pages 334–339; July 26, 1968.

21. The Origin of Cities

LA CITÉ-TEMPLE SUMÉRIENNE. A. Falkenstein in *Cahiers D'Histoire Mondiale*, Vol. I, No. 4, pages 784–814; April, 1954.

CITY INVINCIBLE: A SYMPOSIUM ON URBANIZATION AND CULTURAL DEVELOPMENT IN THE ANCIENT NEAR EAST. Oriental Institute Special Publication, 1960.

EARLY POLITICAL DEVELOPMENT IN MESOPOTAMIA. Thorkild Jacobsen in *Zeitschrift für Assyriologie und Vorderasiatische Archäologie*, Vol. 52, No. 18, pages 91–140; August, 1957.

THE PREINDUSTRIAL CITY. Gideon Sjoberg in *American Journal of Sociology*, Vol. I, No. 5, pages 438–445; March, 1955.

WHAT HAPPENED IN HISTORY. V. Gordon Childe. Penguin Books, Inc., 1946.

22. An Early City in Iran

THE SUMERIANS: THEIR HISTORY, CULTURE, AND CHARACTER. Samuel Noah Kramer. The University of Chicago Press, 1963.

THE INDUS CIVILIZATION. Sir Mortimer Wheeler. Cambridge University Press, 1968.

EXCAVATIONS AT TEPE YAHYĀ, SOUTHEASTERN IRAN, 1967–1969. C. C. Lamberg-Karlovsky in *Bulletin of the American Journal of Prehistoric Research*, No. 27. Peabody Museum, Harvard University, 1970.

THE PROTO-ELAMITE SETTLEMENT AT TEPE YAHYĀ. C. C. Lamberg-Karlovsky in *Iran*, Vol. 9, 1971.

23. Carbon 14 and the Prehistory of Europe

COLONIALISM AND MEGALITHISMUS. Colin Renfrew in *Antiquity*, Vol. 41, No. 164, pages 276–288; December, 1967.

THE AUTONOMY OF THE SOUTH-EAST EUROPEAN COPPER AGE. Colin Renfrew in *Proceedings of the Prehistoric Society*, Vol. 35, pages 12–47; 1969.

NOBEL SYMPOSIUM 12: RADIOCARBON VARIATIONS AND ABSOLUTE CHRONOLOGY. Edited by Ingrid U. Olsson. John Wiley & Sons, Inc., 1970.

THE TREE-RING CALIBRATION OF RADIO-CARBON: AN ARCHAEOLOGICAL EVALUATION. Colin Renfrew in *Proceedings of the Prehistoric Society*, Vol. 36, pages 280–311; 1970.

THE RISE OF CIVILIZATION IN THE NEW WORLD

24. Elephant-hunting in North America

ANCIENT MAN IN NORTH AMERICA. H. M. Wormington. The Denver Museum of Natural History, 1957.

THE PALEO-INDIAN TRADITION IN EASTERN NORTH AMERICA. Ronald J. Mason in *Current Anthropology*, Vol. 3, No. 3, pages 227–278; June, 1962.

PREHISTORIC MAN IN THE NEW WORLD. Jesse D. Jennings and Edward Norbeck. The University of Chicago Press, 1964.

THE QUATERNARY OF THE UNITED STATES. Edited by H. E. Wright, Jr., and David G. Frey. Princeton University Press, 1965.

25. Early Man in the Andes

ANCIENT MAN IN NORTH AMERICA. H. M. Wormington. The Denver Museum of Natural History, 1957.

EARLY MAN IN THE NEW WORLD. Alex D. Krieger in *Prehistoric Man in the New World*, edited by Jesse D. Jennings and Edward Norbeck. The University of Chicago Press, 1964.

AN INTRODUCTION TO AMERICAN ARCHAEOLOGY, VOL. I: NORTH AND MIDDLE AMERICA. Gordon R. Willey. Prentice-Hall, Inc., 1966.

26. The Origins of New World Civilization

ANCIENT MESOAMERICAN CIVILIZATION. Richard S. MacNeish in *Science*, Vol. 143, No. 3606, pages 531–537; February, 1964.

DOMESTICATION OF CORN. Paul C. Mangelsdorf, Richard S. MacNeish and Walton C. Galinat in *Science*, Vol. 143, No. 3606, pages 538–545; February, 1964.

FIRST ANNUAL REPORT OF THE TEHUACAN ARCHAEOLOGICAL-BOTANICAL PROJECT. Richard Stockton MacNeish. Robert S. Peabody Foundation for Archaeology, 1961.

MEXICO. Michael D. Coe. Frederick A. Praeger, 1962.

SECOND ANNUAL REPORT OF THE TEHUACAN ARCHAEOLOGICAL-BOTANICAL PROJECT. Richard Stockton MacNeish. Robert S. Peabody Foundation for Archaeology, 1962.

27. Teotihuacán

THE CULTURAL ECOLOGY OF THE TEOTIHUACÁN VALLEY. William T. Sanders. Department of Sociology and Anthropology. Pennsylvania State University, 1965.

INDIAN ART OF MEXICO AND CENTRAL AMERICA. Miguel Covarrubias. Alfred A. Knopf, Inc., 1957.

AN INTRODUCTION TO AMERICAN ARCHAEOLOGY, VOL. I: NORTH AND MIDDLE AMERICA. Gordon R. Willey. Prentice-Hall, Inc., 1966.

MESOAMERICA BEFORE THE TOLTECS. Wigberto Jiménez Moreno in *In Ancient Oaxaca*, edited by John Paddock. Stanford University Press, 1966.

MEXICO BEFORE CORTEZ: ART, HISTORY AND LEGEND. Ignacio Bernal. Doubleday & Company, Inc., 1963.

NORTHERN MESOAMERICA. Pedro Armillas in *Prehistoric Man in the New World*, edited by Jesse D. Jennings and Edward Norbeck. The University of Chicago Press, 1964.

III   CULTURAL ANTHROPOLOGY

TRADITIONAL CONCERNS: KINSHIP, POLITY, ECONOMY, SOCIETY

28. Primitive Kinship

AFRICAN SYSTEMS OF KINSHIP AND MARRIAGE. Edited by A. R. Radcliffe-Brown and Daryll Forde. Oxford University Press, 1950.

CUSTOM AND CONFLICT IN AFRICA. Max Gluckman. Basil Blackwell, 1955.

THE FATHER IN PRIMITIVE PSYCHOLOGY. Bronislaw

Malinowski. Kegan Paul, Trench, Trubner & Co. Ltd., 1927.

SOCIAL ORGANIZATION. Robert H. Lowie. Rinehart & Company, 1948.

STRUCTURE AND FUNCTION IN PRIMITIVE SOCIETY. A. R. Radcliffe-Brown. Cohen & West Ltd., 1954.

WE, THE TIKOPIA. Raymond Firth. American Book Company, 1936.

THE WEB OF KINSHIP AMONG THE TALLENSI. Meyer Fortes. Oxford University Press, 1949.

29. The Rise of a Zulu Empire

THE DIARY OF HENRY FRANCIS FYNN. Edited by James Stuart and D. McK. Malcolm. Shuter and Shooter, 1950.

OLDEN TIMES IN ZULULAND AND NATAL. A. T. Bryant. Longmans, Green and Co., 1929.

SHAKA ZULU. E. A. Ritter. G. P. Putnam's Sons, 1957.

THE SOCIAL SYSTEM OF THE ZULUS. Eileen Jensen Krige. Longmans, Green and Co., 1936.

30. The Lesson of the Pygmies

DIE BAMBUTI-PYGMAËN VOM ITURI: ERGEBNISSE ZWEIER FORSCHUNGREISEN ZU DEN ZENTRAL-AFRIKANISCHEN PYGMAËN. Paul Schebesta. Libraire Folk Fils. George von Campenhout, Successeur, 1938.

THE ELIMA: A PREMARITAL FESTIVAL AMONG THE BAMBUTI PYGMIES. Colin Turnbull in Zaïre, Vol. 14, No. 2–3, pages 175–192; 1960.

THE FOREST PEOPLE. Colin Turnbull. Simon and Schuster, Inc., 1961.

LEGENDS OF THE BAMBUTI. Colin Turnbull in The Journal of the Royal Anthropological Institute, Vol. 89, Part 1, pages 45–60; January–June, 1959.

THE MOLIMO: A MAN'S RELIGIOUS ASSOCIATION AMONG THE ITURI BAMBUTI. Colin Turnbull in Zaïre, Vol. 14, No. 4, pages 307–340; 1960.

31. The Hopi and the Tewa

CULTURE IN CRISIS: A STUDY OF THE HOPI INDIANS. Laura Thompson. Harper & Brothers, 1950.

THE HOPI-TEWA OF ARIZONA. Edward P. Dozier. University of California Publications in American Archaeology and Ethnology, Vol. 44, No. 3, pages 259–376. University of California Press, 1954.

RESISTANCE TO ACCULTURATION AND ASSIMILATION IN AN INDIAN PUEBLO. Edward P. Dozier in American Anthropologist, Vol. 53, No. 1, pages 56–66; January-March, 1951.

THE SOCIAL ORGANIZATION OF THE TEWA OF NEW MEXICO. Elsie Clews Parsons. Memoirs of the American Anthropological Association, No. 36. American Anthropological Association, 1929.

32. Peasant Markets

THE ECONOMICS OF MARKETING REFORM. P. T. Bauer and B. S. Yamey in The Journal of Political Economy, Vol. LXII, No. 3, pages 210–235; June, 1954.

INTERNAL MARKET SYSTEMS AS MECHANISMS OF SOCIAL ARTICULATION. Sidney W. Mintz in The Proceedings of the 1959 Annual Spring Meeting of the American Ethnological Society, pages 20–30; 1959.

THE JAMAICAN INTERNAL MARKETING PATTERN: SOME NOTES AND HYPOTHESES. Sidney W. Mintz in Social and Economic Studies, Vol. 4, No. 1, pages 95–103; March, 1955.

TRADE AND MARKET IN THE EARLY EMPIRES. Edited by Karl Polanyi, Conrad M. Arensberg and Harry W. Pearson. The Free Press, 1957.

WEST AFRICAN TRADE. Pèter Tamàs Bauer. Cambridge University Press, 1954.

A VARIATION ON TRADITIONAL CONCERNS: THE NEOFUNCTIONAL ECOLOGY OF HUNTERS, FARMERS, AND PASTORALISTS

33. The Flow of Energy in a Hunting Society

THE NETSILIK ESKIMOS: SOCIAL LIFE AND SPIRITUAL CULTURE. Knud Rasmussen in Report of the Fifth Thule Expedition, 1921–24, No. 8. Copenhagen: Gyldendalake Boghandel, 1931.

THE ESKIMOS: THEIR ENVIRONMENT AND FOLKWAYS. Edward Moffat Weyer, Jr. Yale University Press, 1932.

MAN THE HUNTER. Edited by Richard B. Lee and Irven DeVore. Aldine Publishing Company, 1969.

34. The Flow of Energy in an Agricultural Society

ECOLOGICAL ENERGETICS. John Phillipson. Edward Arnold Publishers, 1966.

PERSPECTIVES IN ECOLOGICAL THEORY. Ramón Margalef. The University of Chicago Press, 1968.

PIGS FOR THE ANCESTORS: RITUAL IN THE ECOLOGY OF A NEW GUINEA PEOPLE. Roy A. Rappaport. Yale University Press, 1968.

ENVIRONMENT, POWER, AND SOCIETY. Howard T. Odum. Wiley-Interscience, 1971.

35. Subsistence Herding in Uganda

THE FAMILY HERDS: A STUDY OF TWO PASTORAL TRIBES IN EAST AFRICA, THE JIE AND TURKANA. P. H. Gulliver. Humanities Press, Inc., 1955.

THE SUBSISTENCE ROLE OF CATTLE AMONG THE PAKOT AND IN EAST AFRICA. Harold K. Schneider in American Anthropologist, Vol. 59, No. 2, pages 278–300; April, 1957.

THE SOCIAL ROLE OF CATTLE. Ian Cunnison in The Sudan Journal of Veterinary Science and Animal Husbandry, Vol. 1, No. 1, pages 8–25; March, 1960.

KARIMOJONG POLITICS. Neville Dyson-Hudson. Oxford University Press, 1966.

NEW CONCERNS: "HAVES" AND
"HAVE-NOTS"

36. The Urbanization of the Human Population

THE GROWTH OF CITIES IN THE NINETEENTH CENTURY: A STUDY IN STATISTICS. Adna Ferrin Weber. Columbia University, 1899.

URBAN RESEARCH METHODS. Edited by Jack P. Gibbs. D. Van Nostrand Company, Inc., 1961.

THE WORLD'S METROPOLITAN AREAS. University of California Press, 1959.

37. The Flow of Energy in an Industrial Society

ENERGY IN THE UNITED STATES: SOURCES, USES, AND POLICY ISSUES. Hans H. Landsberg and Sam H. Schurr. Random House, 1968.

AN ENERGY MODEL FOR THE UNITED STATES, FEATURING ENERGY BALANCES FOR THE YEARS 1947 TO 1965 AND PROJECTIONS AND FORECASTS TO THE YEARS 1980 AND 2000. Warren E. Morrison and Charles L. Readling. U.S. Department of the Interior, Bureau of Mines, No. 8384, 1968.

THE ECONOMY, ENERGY, AND THE ENVIRONMENT: A BACKGROUND STUDY PREPARED FOR THE USE OF THE JOINT ECONOMIC COMMITTEE, CONGRESS OF THE UNITED STATES. Environmental Policy Division, Legislative Reference Service, Library of Congress. U.S. Government Printing Office, 1970.

ENERGY CONSUMPTION AND GROSS NATIONAL PRODUCT IN THE UNITED STATES: AN EXAMINATION OF A RECENT CHANGE IN THE RELATIONSHIP. National Economic Research Associates, Inc., 1971.

38. The Dimensions of World Poverty

THE WORLD'S FOOD SUPPLIES. P. V. Sukhatme in *Journal of the Royal Statistical Society*, Series A, Vol. 129, Part 2, pages 222–241; 1966.

THIRD REPORT ON THE WORLD HEALTH SITUATION 1961–1964. No. 155, Official Records of the World Health Organization, 1967.

WORLD ECONOMIC SURVEY 1967 E4488 ADD. 1–5 E4485. United Nations, Department of Economic and Social Affairs, 1968.

39. The Culture of Poverty

BLUE-COLLAR WORLD: STUDIES OF THE AMERICAN WORKER. Edited by Arthur B. Shostak and William Gomberg. Prentice-Hall, Inc., 1964.

MENTAL HEALTH OF THE POOR: NEW TREATMENT APPROACHES FOR LOW-INCOME PEOPLE. Frank Riessman, Jerome Cohen and Arthur Pearl. The Free Press, 1964.

THE OTHER AMERICA: POVERTY IN THE UNITED STATES. Michael Harrington. The Macmillan Company, 1962.

THE URBAN CONDITION: PEOPLE AND POLICY IN THE METROPOLIS. Edited by Leonard J. Duhl. Basic Books, Inc., Publishers, 1963.

40. The Possessions of the Poor

FIVE FAMILIES: MEXICAN CASE STUDIES IN THE CULTURE OF POVERTY. Oscar Lewis. Basic Books, 1959.

THE CHILDREN OF SÁNCHEZ: AUTOBIOGRAPHY OF A MEXICAN FAMILY. Oscar Lewis. Random House, Inc., 1961.

41. Squatter Settlements

BARRIERS AND CHANNELS FOR HOUSING DEVELOPMENT IN MODERNIZING COUNTRIES. John Turner in *Journal of the American Institute of Planners*, Vol. 33, No. 3, pages 167–181; May, 1967.

CONTEMPORARY CULTURES AND SOCIETIES OF LATIN AMERICA: A READER IN THE SOCIAL ANTHROPOLOGY OF MIDDLE AND SOUTH AMERICA AND THE CARIBBEAN. Edited by Dwight B. Heath and Richard N. Adams. Random House, 1965.

LATIN AMERICAN SQUATTER SETTLEMENTS: A PROBLEM AND A SOLUTION. William Mangin in *Latin American Research Review*, Vol. 2, No. 3, pages 65–98; Summer, 1967.

URBANIZATION IN LATIN AMERICA. Edited by Philip N. Hauser. International Documents Service, Columbia University Press, 1961.

THE USES OF LAND IN CITIES. Charles Abrams in *Scientific American*, Vol. 213, No. 3, pages 150–160; September, 1965.

INDEX